**Chapter in Review Cards** at the back of the Student Edition provide students with portable study tools.

# THE
# SOLUTION

HIST
Are you in?

## ONLINE RESOURCES INCLUDED!

CourseMate   **Engaging. Trackable. Affordable.**

**CourseMate brings course concepts to life with interactive learning, study, and exam preparation tools that support HIST.**

### FOR INSTRUCTORS:
- First Day of Class Instructions
- Custom Options through 4LTR+ Program
- Instructor's Manual
- Test Bank
- PowerPoint® Slides
- Instructor Prep Cards
- Engagement Tracker

### FOR STUDENTS:
- Interactive eBook
- Auto-Graded Quizzes
- Flashcards
- Videos
- Student Review Cards
- Interactive Maps
- Primary Source Exercises

Students sign in at
**www.cengagebrain.com**

## WADSWORTH
### CENGAGE Learning™

**HIST2**
**Kevin M. Schultz**

Senior Publisher: Suzanne Jeans

Senior Sponsoring Editor: Ann West

Development Editor: Margaret Manos

Assistant Editor: Megan Chrisman

Executive Brand Marketing Manager,
    4LTR Press: Robin Lucas

Project Manager, 4LTR Press: Kelli Strieby

Senior Media Editor: Lisa Ciccolo

Senior Marketing Manager: Katherine Bates

Marketing Coordinator: Lorreen Pelletier

Marketing Communications Manager: Caitlin
    Green

Associate Content Project Manager: Anne
    Finley

Senior Art Director: Cate Rickard Barr

Senior Print Buyer: Judy Inouye

Senior Image Rights Acquisition Specialist:
    Jennifer Meyer Dare

Photo Researcher: Katharine S. Cebik

Senior Rights Acquisition Specialist, Text: Katie
    Huha

Production Service: Lachina Publishing Services

Cover Designer: Dutton & Sherman

Cover Images: *St. Louis World Fair*, Hulton
    Archive/Archive Photos/Getty Images.
    *Woman photographing mountains from train,
    rear view,* Andrew Hetherington/The Image
    Bank/Getty Images.

Compositor: Lachina Publishing Services

© 2012, 2010 Wadsworth, Cengage Learning

> For product information and technology assistance, contact us at
> **Cengage Learning Academic Resource Center, 1-800-423-0563.**
> For permission to use material from this text or product,
> submit all requests online at **www.cengage.com/permissions.**
> Further permissions questions can be emailed to
> **permissionrequest@cengage.com.**

Library of Congress Control Number: 2010934032

ISBN-13: 978-0-495-91546-1

ISBN-10: 0-495-91546-7

**Wadsworth**
20 Channel Center Street
Boston, MA 02210
USA

Cengage Learning is a leading provider of customized learning solutions with office locations around the globe, including Singapore, the United Kingdom, Australia, Mexico, Brazil and Japan. Locate your local office at **international.cengage.com/region.**

Cengage Learning products are represented in Canada by Nelson Education, Ltd.

For your course and learning solutions, visit **www.cengage.com.**

Purchase any of our products at your local college store or at our preferred online store **www.cengagebrain.com.**

**Instructors:** Please visit **login.cengage.com** and log in to access instructor-specific resources.

Printed in the United States of America
1  2  3  4  5  6  7  14  13  12  11  10

# HIST2 Brief Contents

## About the Author

Kevin M. Schultz teaches American history at the University of Illinois at Chicago. He has special interests in religion, ethnoracial history, and American intellectual and cultural life, and has written significantly on these subjects. His *Tri-Faith America: How Postwar Catholics and Jews Helped America Realize its Protestant Promise* will be published by Oxford University Press in 2011, and his essays have appeared in *The Journal of American History*, *American Quarterly*, *The Journal of the American Academy of Religion*, *Labor History* and several other venues, popular and academic alike. An award-winning teacher, he received his B.A. from Vanderbilt University and his PhD from UC Berkeley.

# HIST2 Contents

© Mary Evans Picture Library/Alamy

© iStockphoto.com/Ray Roper

© iStockphoto.com/Simon Smith

©iStockphoto.com/Robert Dodge

*Uncle Tom's Cabin Cover © Mary Evans Picture Library / Alamy*

© iStockphoto.com/Lee Pettet

Library of Congress, Prints & Photographs Division, LC-USZ62-1438

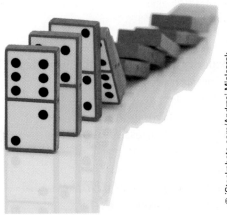

© iStockphoto.com/Andrzej Mielcarek

# CHAPTER 1

# Three Societies on the Verge of Contact

## Learning Outcomes

*After reading this chapter, you should be able to do the following:*

LO**1** Explain current beliefs about how the first peoples settled North America, and discuss the ways in which they became differentiated from one another over time.

LO**2** Describe the African societies that existed at the time the first Africans were brought to the New World as slaves.

LO**3** Describe Europe's experiences during the last centuries before Columbus made his first voyage to the New World in 1492.

# "We will probably never know when the first people set foot on what we now call the United States."

People have been living on the landmass we now know as the United States for at least the past 12,000 years—long before civilizations emerged among the Sumerians in Mesopotamia, the ancient Egyptians, the ancient Greeks, and Jesus Christ, whose esti-

## What do you think?

**Calling North America the "New World" is inaccurate.**

*Strongly Disagree*                                    *Strongly Agree*
1          2          3          4          5          6          7

mated time of arrival, however incorrect, is the measure by which western European time came to be measured. As a political nation, however, the United States is less than 250 years old, encapsulating roughly just nine or ten generations. Although this book is mostly about that relatively recent political nation and the people who lived in it, this chapter deals with the three groups of people—Indians, West Africans, and Europeans—who came together in North America more than five hundred years ago, setting in motion the process by which America would become an independent nation. This chapter begins in the Ice Age and ends as Christopher Columbus sets foot in North America in 1492, becoming, perhaps, the first European to ever do so.

## LO¹ Native America

Early human life in North America can be divided into three periods: (1) the Paleo-Indian, (2) the Archaic, and (3) the Pre-Columbian. Thus we begin by exploring the theories of when the first humans reached North America and describe the progress of these humans up to the point when Columbus discovered the Western Hemisphere.

### The Paleo-Indian Era: The First Settlers (15,000–10,000 years ago)

The first settlers of the Americas seem to have appeared in what we call the Paleo-Indian era. Although we will probably never know when the first people set foot on what we now call the United States, it seems they may have come earlier than was first thought.

### Arrival

For a long time, archaeologists believed that the first people came not for fame, fortune, or freedom (as subsequent immigrants would), but simply because they were hungry. According to this theory, about 12,000 years ago, thousands of young adults and their families left their homes in Asia and crossed a narrow passage of iced-over land called

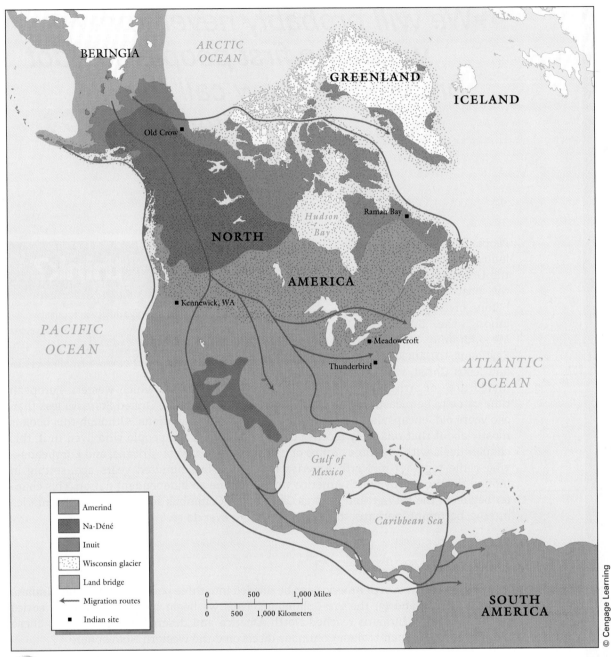

Map 1.1. Settlement of Americas

Beringia, southwest of today's Alaska. These people were supposedly following herds of wooly mammoths, intending to hunt the animals to feed and clothe their families. Many of these hunters followed the herds south along the western coast of present-day Canada and ended up in what is now the United States. Many of their latter-day ancestors continued southward and, after many generations, made it all the way to the southernmost tip of South America, to a place now called Tierra Del Fuego.

Recent evidence casts doubt on this theory. Carbon dating suggests that the first people on the continent were probably here much earlier than 12,000 years ago. This has prompted a reevaluation of the Beringia theory, with some scholars suggesting that the first settlers came on boats, either following whales across the Pacific from Asia, or coming from Europe, along Greenland, in search of fish, or following the Pacific Coast of today's Alaska, British Columbia, and Washington State (see Map 1.1).

In 1996, two men watching hydroplane races in Kennewick, Washington, discovered what turned out to be a 9,000-year-old skeleton. The skeleton, dubbed Kennewick man, baffled scientists, mainly because a physical reconstruction of the skull revealed a man who looked "more like a middle-aged European accountant than he did a Paleo-Indian hunter." People with European features were not thought to have been in North America for another 8,500 years, so Kennewick man presented the possibility that North American settlement happened in different waves from a variety of locations, with older groups dying out and being replaced by yet newer immigrants. Another scientist then suggested that Kennewick man's features resembled those of people living in specific parts of Asia rather than Europe, further complicating the initial origins of humankind in North America. Was he a man with a European face (and genetic origins), an Asian man, or did he resemble one of America's indigenous Indians? Current DNA sampling technology cannot tell us, but a final report written by one of the principal scientists concludes that "methods developed in the near future could be successful in extracting suitable DNA for analysis."

Meanwhile, many of today's Indian tribes resisted the supposed European or Asian appearance of Kennewick man because their beliefs maintain that they are the one, true indigenous group in North America. Regardless of the dispute, and regardless of when or from where Kennewick man came, his age suggests that calling North America the "New World" might be a mistake. England, for instance, was not inhabitable until 12,500 B.C.E., suggesting that the "New World" may actually have a much longer human history than what we now think of as the "Old World." Today we call these initial North American settlers the **Paleo-Indians**.

 Meet Kennewick man.

Although the initial origins and timing are in question, what is known for certain is that the greatest flow of people in this early period came between 20,000 and 10,000 B.C.E.; we also know that sometime between 9500 and 8000 B.C.E. the ocean level rose because of what we would today call global warming. With water covering the Bering Strait that connected Asia to North America, the first major wave of immigration came to an end. That path has remained submerged ever since.

## Expansion and Development

As these migrants moved from region to region across North America, they adapted their lifestyle according to the climate and the land, as people do. The people of the **Paleo-Indian era** (15,000 to 10,000 years ago) thus lived a wide range of lifestyles, developing many languages and belief systems along the way. Some of the most ancient peoples made spears by flaking stones and then chose "kill sites" that large herds traversed. Others hunted herds of animals across great distances. Still others slowly began to cultivate complex systems of sustainable agriculture that allowed them to remain in a single area for years. And still others depended on fishing and the riches of the seas to provide a stable life for their families. Over time, the population of Native North America grew.

 Read more about the Paleo-Indians.

### The Archaic Era: Forging an Agricultural Society (10,000–2,500 years ago)

Between 5,000 and 8,000 years ago, a monumental transition occurred in how people lived their lives. During the **Archaic era**, agriculture gradually became the primary source of sustenance for most of the people of Native North America. This trend was perhaps the most significant development in American prehistory, because settled agriculture permitted the establishment of a **sedentary existence**, without the need to pursue herd animals. Maize, a form of corn, was one key element of this existence. Maize is a highly nutritious cereal, containing more nutrients than wheat, rice, millet, and barley. Its development was a remarkable feat of genetic engineering; some 6,000 years ago, Indians in today's southern Mexico cultivated the crop through the careful selection of desirable seeds, ultimately producing corn.

**Paleo-Indians**
The first people to settle North America, roughly 15,000 to 10,000 years ago

**Paleo-Indian era**
Era beginning about 15,000 years ago and ending about 10,000 years ago, characterized by initial North American settlement

**Archaic era**
Era beginning about 10,000 years ago and lasting until about 2,500 years ago, characterized by increased agricultural development

**sedentary existence**
Life in which settlers can remain in one place cultivating agriculture, instead of pursuing herd animals

© iStockphoto.com/Joe Potato

>> **Stone tools for grinding maize.**

Populations grew larger, not only because food supplies increased, but also because group size was no longer limited by the arduous demands of hunting. Many tribes became semi-sedentary, settling in camps during the agricultural growing season and then breaking camp to follow the herds at other times of year. Others became increasingly urban in their development, building permanent cities, some of monumental proportions.

This was the formative period of the first settled tribes in North America—the immediate ancestors of many of the Indian tribes with which we are most familiar today. The Mesoamerican civilization, founded and developed by the Olmec people, thrived in today's Mexico and served as a precursor to the many maize-based societies that developed throughout North America. Some 5,000 years ago, another successful ancient civilization—the people of Norte Chico in today's Peru—flourished by cultivating cotton, which they used to weave nets and catch the plentiful fish off the Pacific Coast; they then transported the fish to high-altitude cities in the Andes. Although nature has reclaimed much of what these early civilizations created, their developments and accomplishments are testaments to the capacity of humankind to create and develop monumental societies. One historian has argued that the only way to fully grasp the earth-changing significance of these early civilizations is to take a helicopter ride over undeveloped parts of Mexico and Central and South America, realizing that many of the hills and creeks below are actually the buried remains of temples and canals built by those early civilizations.

## The Pre-Columbian Era: Developing Civilizations (500 B.C.E.–1492 C.E.)

Of all the people living in North America before contact with

Europeans, we know the most about the people of the **pre-Columbian era** (500 B.C.E.–1492 C.E.). The great civilizations of the pre-Columbian world (the phrase means "before Columbus") usually based their economy on agriculture and for that reason were able to endure in a single location long enough to create complex, hierarchical societies and to develop long-standing trading networks.

The largest Indian civilization in this period was that of the Incas, who lived on the western coast of South America, from the equator to the southern tip of Chile. The Incas built large cities and fortresses on the steep slopes of the Andes Mountains (and were the beneficiaries of fish deliveries from the people of Norte Chico). Other impressive pre-Columbian societies include the Maya, who, with their step-tiered temples, dominated southern Guatemala and the Yucatan Peninsula (in present-day Mexico) from the fifth to the eighth centuries until an internal civil war weakened the civilization so much that it dissipated. The Teotihuacán society built a city (named Teotihuacán, about an hour's bus ride from Mexico City) that accommodated perhaps as many as 200,000 souls during the fifth century. The Mexica (later labeled "the Aztecs") developed a complex urban society that ruled central Mexico from the ninth to the fifteenth centuries. These were all large, complex societies that, in scientific knowledge, governing capacities, and artistic and architectural development, rivaled any in the world at the time of their particular dominance.

 Learn more about the Aztecs through a simulation, "Colonial Expansion."

### The Anasazi

In the present-day United States, two of the largest pre-Columbian cultures were the Anasazi and the Mississippians. In the American Southwest, the Anasazi founded a vast civilization by combining hunting and gathering with sedentary agriculture in order to sustain a large population in the arid desert of present-day New Mexico.

>> **Olmec head, 1200–900 B.C.E.**

>> The Serpent Mound in Ohio, nearly a quarter of a mile long, is the largest and finest surviving serpentine earthwork.

As a testament to the grandness of their civilization, between 900 and 1150 C.E. the Anasazi built fourteen "great houses" in the Chaco Canyon, each one several stories tall and containing more than two hundred rooms. They were perhaps used as large apartment buildings, as the canyon served as the major trading post for turquoise and other material goods. Several of these great houses still stand today near Albuquerque, New Mexico.

## The Mississippians

A second large, pre-Columbian culture to develop on the land now known as the United States was that of the Mississippians, whose many different tribes lived at about the same time as the Anasazi, from 700 to 1500 C.E., although their civilization peaked about 1100 C.E. The largest Mississippian city was called Cahokia, located 8 miles east of present-day St. Louis. Inhabited by more than 20,000 people (comparable in size to London at that time), Cahokia served as the civilization's crossroads for trade and religion, the land's first metropolis. Webs of roads surrounded the city, connecting rural villagers for hundreds of miles in all directions. The Mississippians developed an accurate cal-

endar and built a pyramid that, at the time, was the third largest structure of any kind in the Western Hemisphere. The Mississippians also left many earthen mounds dotting the landscape.

Some of these early civilizations, like the Anasazi, declined about two hundred years before first contact with Europeans and Africans. Others, such as the Aztecs and some of the Mississippians, were still thriving in 1492. Why did these powerful civilizations decline? There is no single answer to the question. Some scholars say that certain civilizations outgrew their capacity to produce food. Others say that battles with enemy tribes forced them to abandon the principal landmarks of their civilization. Still others cite major droughts.

And indeed, not all of these civilizations did decline by the time of first contact with Europeans. Scholars estimate that in 1491 North and South America had perhaps as many as 100 million inhabitants—making it more populous than Europe at the time. Although these numbers are greatly disputed, the idea that the Americas were barren "virgin" land before first contact with Europeans is clearly wrong. In 1491, American Indians were thriving and transforming the land to suit their needs.

## North America in 1492

By the late 1400s, North America was home to numerous civilizations and tribes, some of which were sizeable, dominating large swaths of land. More than two hundred languages were spoken, among hundreds of different tribes. It was as if each of today's cities spoke its own language and had unique social rituals. Diversity abounded in this land. So did conflict.

### Some Social Similarities of Native North Americans

Despite the wide variety of lifestyles developed by the pre-Columbian peoples, there are some broad general similarities among the tribes in North America during the late

> 66 The Mississippians developed an accurate calendar and built a pyramid that was the third largest structure in the Western Hemisphere. 99

>> Aztec calendar.

**clan system**
Living arrangement in which a tribe was divided into a number of large family groups

**matrilineal**
Family arrangement in which children typically follow the clan of their mother and married men move into the clan of their wives; most often seen in agricultural societies

**polytheistic**
Belief system consisting of belief in many deities

**animistic**
Belief system consisting of belief that supernatural beings, or souls, inhabit all objects and govern their actions

**Iroquois Confederacy**
Group of northeastern tribes that joined to form a political and trading entity and later created an elaborate political system; also known as the Haudenosaunee Confederation

 Learn more about why Chaco Canyon declined.

1400s. Most of the tribes, for instance, were based on a **clan system**, in which a tribe was divided into a number of large family groups. They were also mostly **matrilineal**, meaning that children typically followed the clan of their mother and that a man, when married, moved into the clan of his wife. Matrilineal societies usually develop when agriculture is the primary food source for a society. In these societies women are in charge of farming (Europeans were universally surprised to see women working in the fields). Thus Indian women maintained the tribe's social institutions while men were hunting, fishing, or off to war. This system was by no means universal in Native North America, but it does signify a level of sexual equality absent from Europe at the time. Indeed, women were just as likely as men to wield political power in some of these societies. Many Algonkian tribes, for instance, had a female tribal leader.

Land was customarily held in common as well, although there are some instances in which individual rights are said to have existed and others where clan rights existed. Enslavement (usually of captured enemies) was relatively common, especially in the tribes of the American Southeast, but Indian enslavement varied in severity, and it is unlikely that enslavement was inherited, meaning that the children of slaves were usually not, by accident of birth, born as chattel.

Most Indian religions were **polytheistic** (believing in many deities) and **animistic** (believing that supernatural beings, or souls, inhabit all objects and govern their actions). Indian religions were usually closely related to the physical world, and local terrain was naturally imbued with spiritual meaning.

Placing an emphasis on this world (and not on the next), typical ceremonies featured rain and fertility prayers. Many New England tribes, for example, believed in a ruling deity whom they called Manitou and looked to a dramatic local site (such as Mount Katahdin in Maine) as the source of divine power.

## Regional Variations

These broad similarities aside, the tribes of Native America were rich in regional variety (Map 1.2). Most variations depended on how a tribe adapted to its surrounding terrain, and thus it is possible to make generalizations based on region.

*The Northeast.* Several sizeable societies lived in the northeast corner of the United States, in the area now called New England. These tribes included the Wampanoag, Narragansett, Massachusetts, Mohawk, Oneida, Erie, and Pequot. In general, these groups subsisted on hunting and agriculture, although most of their foodstuffs derived from agriculture. Those that lived along the coast relied on the riches of the ocean. Most of these tribes lived in small villages that were closely surrounded by forests that protected them from attack—something that was always a possibility in the congested northeastern region. Indeed, fear of attack was part of the reason that several of these northeastern tribes came together to create the **Iroquois Confederacy**, a political and trading entity that maintained relations between several tribes. (Iroquois is actually the European name for the Haudenosaunee Confederation.) The local forests provided the raw materials for wooden houses crafted by the tribes of the Haudenosaunee, who called them "longhouses." Most of these tribes remained small, however, only occasionally trading with one another.

Other tribes developed cross-regional alliances. The tribes within the Haudenosaunee Confederacy developed an elaborate political system that incorporated villages into nations, then nations into a large confederation. The confederation's leaders were charged with keeping peace among the tribes under its auspices to ensure continuous trade and peaceful relations. The proximity of one's tribal neighbors in the populous Northeast led many tribes to embrace the politics of the Haudenosaunee. Others, however, viewed the tribes of the Haudenosaunee as their bitter enemies.

> *Women were just as likely as men to wield political power in some of these societies.*

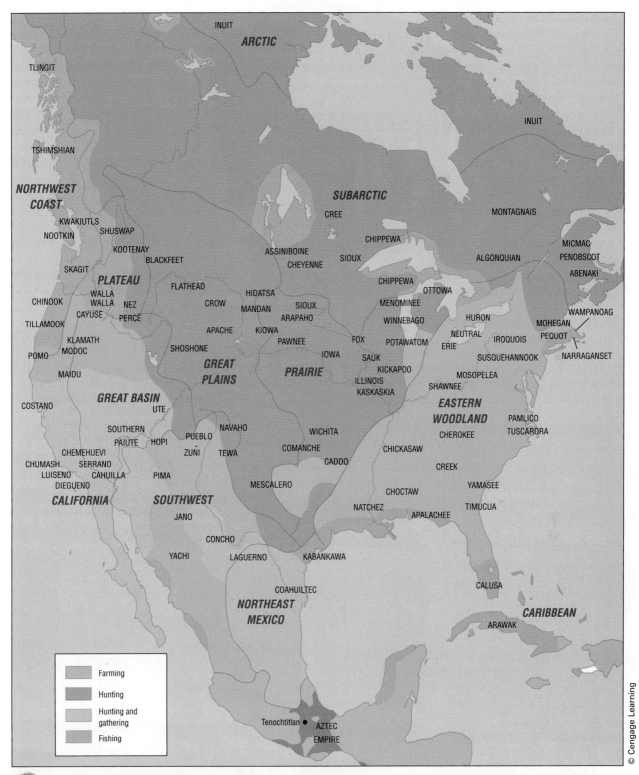

INUIT

ARCTIC

TLINGIT

SUBARCTIC

TSHIMSHIAN

INUIT

NORTHWEST COAST

CREE

MONTAGNAIS

KWAKIUTLS

SHUSWAP

NOOTKIN

CHIPPEWA

MICMAC

KOOTENAY

ASSINIBOINE

SIOUX

ALGONQUIAN

PENOBSCOT

BLACKFEET

CHEYENNE

ABENAKI

SKAGIT

PLATEAU

FLATHEAD

CHIPPEWA

OTTOWA

WALLA WALLA

CHINOOK

CROW

HIDATSA

MENOMINEE

WAMPANOAG

NEZ

MANDAN

SIOUX

WINNEBAGO

HURON

CAYUSE

PERCÉ

ARAPAHO

MOHEGAN

TILLAMOOK

APACHE

KIOWA

NEUTRAL

IROQUOIS

PEQUOT

KLAMATH

PAWNEE

FOX

POTAWATOM

ERIE

NARRAGANSET

POMO

MODOC

SHOSHONE

IOWA

SAUK

SUSQUEHANNOOK

MAIDU

GREAT PLAINS

PRAIRIE

KICKAPOO

MOSOPELEA

ILLINOIS

SHAWNEE

COSTANO

GREAT BASIN

UTE

KASKASKIA

EASTERN WOODLAND

PAMLICO

SOUTHERN PAIUTE

NAVAHO

WICHITA

CHEROKEE

TUSCARORA

CHEMEHUEVI

PUEBLO

HOPI

COMANCHE

CHICKASAW

CHUMASH

SERRANO

ZUNI

TEWA

CADDO

CREEK

LUISENO

CAHUILLA

PIMA

YAMASEE

DIEGUENO

MESCALERO

CHOCTAW

TIMUCUA

CALIFORNIA

SOUTHWEST

NATCHEZ

APALACHEE

JANO

CONCHO

YACHI

LAGUERNO

KABANKAWA

CALUSA

COAHUILTEC

CARIBBEAN

NORTHEAST MEXICO

ARAWAK

Tenochtitlan ● AZTEC EMPIRE

Farming

Hunting

Hunting and gathering

Fishing

© Cengage Learning

Map 1.2. Tribes of North America, 1492

*The Mid-Atlantic.* In the Mid-Atlantic region, where New York, New Jersey, Pennsylvania, Delaware, Maryland, and Virginia are today, lived the Lenni Lenape (Delaware), Susquehannock, and Nanticock, among others. The people in these tribes lived on a mixture of agriculture, shellfish, and game. They lived a semi-sedentary life, occasionally leaving their stable villages to follow herds of roaming animals. They, too, remained mostly local, aware of, but rarely venturing into, the lands of another tribe. Disputes over boundaries routinely led to violence. The Indians who lived in the woodlands of the Northeast or Mid-Atlantic were collectively called "Woodlands Indians."

*The Southeast.* The Southeast—today's Florida, Georgia, North Carolina, South Carolina, Alabama, Mississippi, and Louisiana—was inhabited by the Cherokees (actually named the Tsalagi), Creek, Choctaw, Biloxi, Chicksaw, and Natchez, among others. This was one of the most heavily populated areas of Native America at the time of first contact with the Europeans, a fact that would have profound consequences when the Europeans tried to settle there. These tribes subsisted on agriculture, though those living in Florida and the Gulf Coast relied on fishing as well. They developed strong traditions in ceramics and basket weaving; they traded over long distances; and some, such as the Natchez, developed stable, hierarchical political organizations.

*The prairies.* The prairies, which stretch from today's Dakotas south to Oklahoma, were inhabited by the Omaha, Wichita, Kichai, and Sioux. These tribes usually lived on the edges of the plains, where they lived in semi-sedentary agricultural villages and

>> "Their cabins are in the shape of tunnels [tonnelles] or arbors, and are covered with the bark of trees. They are from twenty-five to thirty fathoms long, more or less, and six wide, having a passage-way through the middle from ten to twelve feet wide, which extends from one end to the other. On the sides there is a kind of bench, four feet high, where they sleep in summer, in order to avoid the annoyance of the fleas, of which there are great numbers. In winter they sleep on the ground on mats near the fire, so as to be warmer than they would be on the platform."
—French explorer Samuel de Champlain, 1616, referring to an Iroquois longhouse

held major hunting parties every year to hunt bison, the chief game animal of the Great Plains. They produced no pottery or basketry, or even much agriculture, as they depended almost entirely on the bison and rivers for their subsistence.

*The High Plains.* The Indians of the High Plains, which extend from today's Montana all the way south to northwestern Texas, included the Blackfeet, Crow, Cheyenne, Arapaho, and Comanche. Like the Native Americans of the prairies, these tribes depended on bison for a large part of their subsistence (especially after contact with European settlers drove them further west), and their only agricultural crop was usually tobacco (again, after contact), which they used for religious purposes and for pleasure.

*The Southwest.* In the Southwest, in today's New Mexico and Arizona (and where the Anasazi had lived), lived the Apache and Navajo tribes, and a large conglomeration of tribes that included the Hopi, Taos, and Zunis, which made up what the Europeans called "the **Pueblo people**." These Indians subsisted almost entirely on agriculture, which is a testament to their ingenuity, considering the slight amount of rain that falls in this region. By about 1200 C.E., several of these tribes had developed villages made up of several multistory buildings built on strategically defensive sites in canyons and river valleys. By the time Columbus had reached the West Indies, some of the Pueblos had developed canals, dams, and hillside terracing to control and channel the limited amount of rainwater. Ceramic pots, which were elaborate and sophisticated during this precontact period, were used to transport water as well. According to one European observer in 1599, the Pueblo people "live very much the same as we do," although he may have said this simply because the Pueblos were one of the few Indian societies to have men, not women, practice agriculture.

*The Northwest.* In the Northwest, in today's Oregon and Washington, lived the Chinook, Tillamook, Yuki, and Squamish, to name just a few. These peoples ate fish and shellfish in addition to fruits, nuts, and berries. They made plank houses of cedar, which they sometimes surrounded with dramatic carved totem poles. Accomplished artists, they placed a priority on the arts of carving and painting and developed the elaborate ornamentation we commonly see on totem poles. Other prized creations were their artistically designed masks. Many of these tribes celebrated annual holidays, maintained social welfare programs, and adhered to a well-developed view of the cosmos.

## Intertribal Harmony and Hostility

Most tribal villages coexisted with their neighbors in a fairly stable balance between peace and warfare, at least until territorial disputes, competition for resources, or traditional rivalries set off battle, which happened often. Indians also went to war to bolster their numbers; male captives taken in war were usually integrated into the victorious tribe's village as slaves, while females and children were commonly integrated as full members. Some societies, such as the Maya and Aztec, developed an entire culture around warfare. The fact that some Indian groups forged defense alliances, such as the Iroquois Confederacy, demonstrates that protective measures were necessary in a sometimes violent Native America.

But the Haudenosaunee (Iroquois) Confederacy demonstrates something else as well: it shows Indians' interest in and ability to promote peaceful and productive interactions. In many parts of the land, neighboring tribes traded fruitfully with each other. A network of dirt and stone roads traversed the continent, and towns became centers for trade and commerce. Although such trade was small in

© iStockphoto.com/ Adam Korzekwa

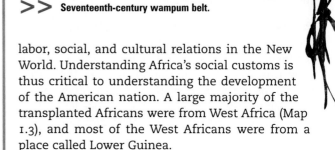

>> **Seventeenth-century wampum belt.**

**wampum**
Beads made of polished shell, used as currency in trading for goods

**roanoke**
Bracelet-like bands made of wampum

**Islam**
Modern religion that flourished throughout the world beginning in the fourteenth and fifteenth centuries; its adherents are called Muslims

**Ghana**
West African kingdom that prospered from the eighth to the thirteenth centuries; famous for its gold deposits

**Mali**
Flourishing Islamic kingdom; it enveloped the kingdom of Ghana by the thirteenth century

**Timbuktu**
Principal city of the kingdom of Mali; cultural capital of Africa in the thirteenth century

scale by European standards, the goods exchanged were vital to each village's way of life: arrowheads, furs, **wampum** (beads made of polished shell), **roanoke** (bracelet-like bands made of wampum), and food. Trade networks could extend over hundreds of miles; for instance, copper goods from the Southwest have been found at Eastern Woodlands sites.

## Economics

This trade made up a part of Indian economic life. Tribes traded foodstuffs like corn and meat, sometimes traveling expansive trading routes; they also traded ornamental items such as jewelry and hunting weapons. Their trading grounds provided an early example of what would come to be called the "middle ground" between the native cultures and European traders, after the Europeans had established settlements in the seventeenth and eighteenth centuries.

Despite their willingness to barter in portable goods, a sizeable majority of the people of Native America did not believe that property could be privately owned. Bequeathed to all, land could be used by anyone so long as they cultivated it properly. In practice, however, tribal leaders granted specific parcels of land to a family for a season or two, and tribes frequently fought bloody battles for control of certain plots of land. When large numbers of Europeans arrived in the 1600s, the tribes of Native America would be forced to reconsider their conception of private property.

# LO² Africa

Of all the immigrants who came to North America between the sixteenth and eighteenth centuries, roughly 250,000 of them came from Africa, as slaves. This was not a huge percentage of all immigrants, but it was a significant one, dramatically influencing labor, social, and cultural relations in the New World. Understanding Africa's social customs is thus critical to understanding the development of the American nation. A large majority of the transplanted Africans were from West Africa (Map 1.3), and most of the West Africans were from a place called Lower Guinea.

## Politics

Africa, the second largest continent on earth (after Asia), is as varied in climate and geography as North America. It follows, then, that there was great range in the way Africans lived their lives. By the time of the first sustained contact with Europeans, in the 1400s and 1500s, some African societies had developed vast civilizations, as trade routes wound through the continent's various regions. Africans had also witnessed the spread of a modern religion, **Islam**, which, in the fourteenth and fifteenth centuries, was probably the most powerful and vibrant religion in the world, expanding rapidly throughout Africa, the Middle East, and Spain. One part of the continent transformed by the rise of Islam was West Africa.

### Ghana

The kingdom of **Ghana** ruled West Africa from the eighth to the thirteenth centuries, beginning a tradition of expansive trade throughout western Africa using horses, camels, and advanced iron weapons to transport goods and ideas. A kingdom as rich in arts and commerce as any in Europe at the time, Ghana was made up of several large cities, where the people produced elaborate works of art and maintained a stable and complex political structure. Ghana was especially famous for its gold. But the kingdom's extensive trade routes caused its eventual demise. In the twelfth century, it lost its trade monopoly, and gold was discovered elsewhere in West Africa. In addition, during the first half of the thirteenth century, North African Muslims used Ghanaian trade routes to invade the kingdom, and by 1235 C.E. they had conquered the ruling parties of Ghana.

### Mali

**Mali**, a flourishing Islamic kingdom, rose in power as Ghana declined. Its principal city, **Timbuktu**, became

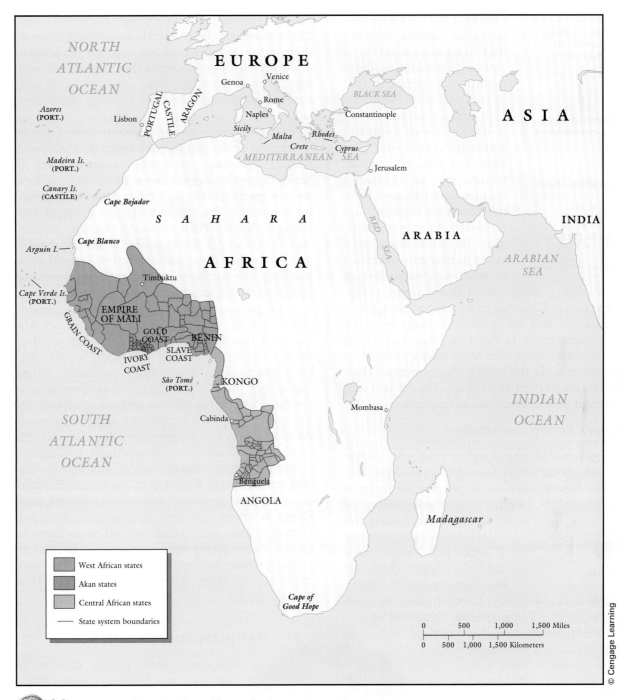

**Map 1.3. Africa in the Fifteenth Century**

**Lower Guinea**
Southernmost part of Mali;
home to the majority of
the Africans who came to
America

**Songhay Empire**
Portion of Mali after that
kingdom collapsed around
1500; this empire controlled
Timbuktu

**Benin**
African empire on the Malian
coast

**Kongo**
African empire on the Malian
coast

Africa's cultural and artistic capital, drawing students from as far away as southern Europe. Timbuktu's cultural wealth was demonstrated in its rich artistic and economic resources, and the recently discovered Timbuktu Manuscripts reveal the depth and beauty of the Mali culture. By the thirteenth century, Mali had enveloped the Ghanaian kingdom and expanded mightily. However, Islam did not permeate all of Mali's territories. In contrast to what was happening in northern Africa, Islam spread slowly in the southernmost part of Mali. This southernmost part, called **Lower Guinea**, was the home of the majority of the Africans who came to America. This meant that many of the Africans who were forced to come to North America via the slave trade maintained their tribal religions rather than Islam. Thus, Islam was not present in North America at this time.

## Songhay, Benin, and Kongo

The kingdom of Mali collapsed around 1500—just as sustained contact with Europeans was beginning. Mali was divided, with the largest portion replaced by the **Songhay Empire**, which took control of

 Learn about the fall of the Mali and Songhay kingdoms.

Timbuktu. Farther along the Malian coast, the empires of **Benin** and **Kongo** were similarly approached by European traders in search of goods and, eventually, slaves. Indeed, by 1500, the ruler of the Kongo people converted to Catholicism, having been impressed by the Portuguese traders he had encountered.

## Society

If political control over the region remained in flux in western Africa during the fifteenth and sixteenth centuries, social customs were slightly more stable. Most of the Africans in Lower Guinea lived in kinship groups and, through them, in villages, which were part of larger kingdoms and woven together by a web of roads. The Africans of Lower Guinea were

mostly farmers, living in settled agricultural areas. The success of their agriculture allowed some in their society to become artists, teachers, tradesmen, and storytellers—professions that earned their society's respect. Above this group of professionals were nobles and priests, who were mostly older men. Below them were farmers and slaves.

As with many North American tribes, family descent in Lower Guinea was typically matrilineal. Gender roles were generally complementary in Lower Guinea, as women frequently worked as local traders, participated in local politics, and played leading roles in the agricultural society. And, as with the agricultural societies of North America, the presence of stable agriculture meant the development of gendered roles. These cultural systems would all be challenged by sustained contact with Europeans and European-based societies.

The Africans of Lower Guinea also possessed slaves—usually captives from wars or debtors who had sold themselves into slavery to pay off their debt. As in most parts of the world, slavery had been practiced in Africa since prehistoric times. But unlike the type of slavery that developed in the New World, the African system of slavery did not enslave captives for life, nor did it necessarily deny them access to education. Significantly, the children of slaves were not routinely predestined to become slaves themselves; African slavery also was not based on a system of racial classification, as would develop in the United States. In fact, most slaves in Africa may have been women, who performed mostly field labor. Not all were laborers, though. Some slaves were servants, others soldiers, and some were artisans. Most slaves in Africa were treated like peasants or tenant farmers rather than human chattel.

## Religion and Thought

Religiously, most of the Africans in Lower Guinea did not embrace Islam; they still believed in their traditional African religions. These religions were as varied as those of Native America, but generally they consisted of belief in a single supreme ruler and several lesser gods. Many of these lesser gods served in worldly capacities—to bring rain and to ensure good harvests, for example.

>> **Ghana was especially famous for its gold.**

Africans honored these gods elaborately, through their art and their celebrations. There was no single transcendent spirit (such as Christ) mediating between this world and the next, but deceased ancestors served as personal mediators between a person and the gods. This emphasis, in turn, nourished a strong tradition of family loyalty.

## Africa on the Eve of Contact

On the eve of European contact, then, West Africa was, in general, an agricultural society divided into villages organized along matrilineal kinship lines. Some of its people were extremely skilled in the arts, and a class of intellectuals existed who were positioned in houses of learning and supported by kings. Politics advanced in large kingdoms that oversaw and protected their citizens and that allowed for expansive lines of trade. On the whole, West Africans participated in sophisticated societies that had highly developed skills for coping with the diverse geographical settings where they lived.

# LO³ Europe

While Africans constituted one large block of immigrants between the sixteenth and eighteenth centuries, the large majority of newcomers to North America came from Europe. These settlers came with a variety of goals and ambitions. Many, but not all, were disappointed in what they found.

## Europe up to 1492

Europeans were the initiators of the clash of cultures that would take place in the New World. But until the twelfth century, most of Europe was an economic and intellectual backwater in comparison to China, the countries of northern Africa, and parts of the Middle East. Intellectual and religious life thrived in Christian Byzantium (encompassing today's Turkey), and the burgeoning Islamic world was spreading episodically through the Middle East, North Africa, and Spain.

A significant factor in Europe's withdrawal from world affairs was feudal lords' domination of large plots of European land called **manors** (see Map 1.4). These men presided over a system of labor that came to be called **feudalism**, in which a lord granted control over a piece of land to an upper-class ally, or vassal. The vassal's grant included authority over all the land's inhabitants. The vassal treated these laborers as servants, guaranteeing them a level of protection in return for a portion of the fruits of their labor. In reality, these servants, called **serfs**, forfeited nearly all of their freedoms to the lord and vassal. With the exception of the Catholic Church, the nobleman was the sole authority on the land, serving as governor, judge, and war leader. The lords' overwhelming authority meant that serfs were not free and could not act autonomously. They could not change their profession or even move without approval from their lord.

Medieval Europe was therefore split into myriad feudal territories, which divided it linguistically and economically. It also suffered from political instability due to Muslim expansion and Viking raids. Trade and learning virtually disappeared as a result of the battles among feudal lords and between feudal lords and various invaders. The Catholic Church was the sole overarching institution, and during parts of the medieval period, the Church was at its most

**manor**
Agricultural estate operated by a lord and worked by peasants in exchange for protection and sustenance

**feudalism**
System of labor in which a lord granted control over a piece of land, and authority over all the land's inhabitants, to an upper-class ally, or vassal

**serf**
Laborer in the feudal system; protected and controlled by the vassal of the estate

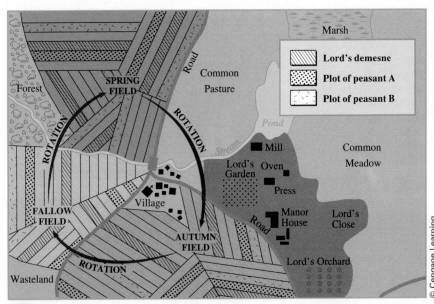

Map 1.4. A Typical Manor

© Cengage Learning

 Learn more about feudalism.

powerful. As long as Europe was composed of hundreds of these feudal fiefdoms and under threat from raiders abroad, there were no entities that could operate like strong nations. The decline of feudalism would propel Europe from its secondary status in world affairs to a dynamic force embarking on far-flung overseas adventures.

## The Decline of Feudalism

By the fifteenth century, the feudal system was rapidly declining in western Europe. In its stead, nations were becoming more powerful. The four causes for this transition were economic, religious, biological, and political (see "The reasons why …"). Together, these changes would lead to the rise of nations, and the competition among these nations would eventu-

# { *The reasons why . . .* }

## There were four causes for the decline of feudalism:

**Expanding trade.** The first inklings of the transition away from feudalism can be seen around 1000 C.E., when Italian coastal traders began to exploit long-distance trade routes. The riches earned at these trading posts gave several city-states the wealth and power to free themselves from feudal lords. Similarly, merchants began to develop a theory of **mercantilism** (although it would not get that name until Adam Smith coined it in the late 1700s), which suggested that a nation or state's prosperity was determined by the total volume of its trade. This was based on the idea that the amount of trade in the world was fixed at a certain level; those who traded favorably simply had a larger piece of the pie. This economic theory gained credence as nations increased in power throughout the sixteenth and seventeenth centuries and as European powers competed to develop colonial empires. It would propel these nations overseas and across continents in search of cheaper or more valuable raw materials.

**The Crusades.** The second reason for the decline of feudalism was religious. The search for riches fused with the power of the Catholic Church to prompt the **Crusades**, a series of campaigns in which Europeans marched to the Middle East to seize the Holy Land of Jerusalem, at that time controlled by Muslims. These bloody battles were intermittent, lasting from 1096 to at least 1291, and the Europeans never fully succeeded in their mission of permanently capturing the Holy Land. After their bloody excursions, though, crusaders brought back luxuries rarely available to medieval Europe, including spices, silks, and gems. Before long, Europeans deemed these goods invaluable (especially the spices). The Italian merchants who supplied these goods grew fabulously wealthy and began to yearn for greater autonomy and freedom from the feudal system.

**The Black Death.** The **Black Death**, or bubonic plague, which started to spread in 1346, also advanced the decline of the feudal system. It did so in two principal ways. First, it caused the death of one-third of all Europeans, and it did not discriminate by class, meaning that feudal lords died at the same rate as did the poorer members of the continent. Second, the death of so many farmers meant that those who survived became more valuable; this forced feudal lords to grant them more allowances, including greater personal freedom, in order to maintain their loyalty.

**The Hundred Years' War**. The fourth reason for the decline of feudalism was rooted in politics. The **Hundred Years' War**, waged between France and England in the fourteenth century, was, at its core, a battle over who controlled the French throne, but it is significant for two reasons.

First, it prodded Italian and Iberian merchants to find water routes that connected southern and northern Europe, as they could no longer safely travel by land through France. This spurred several technological advances that would make possible the exploration of North America.

Second, the war allowed the kings to further consolidate their power at the expense of the feudal lords, leading to the rise of several large kingdoms. By the fifteenth century, kings who had long been subjected to the whims of the feudal lords and who did not possess the financial or military power to become absolute rulers began to assert themselves and respond to the mercantilists' demands for organization and protection. The kings did this with considerable popular support; few feudal lords had endeared themselves to their subjects. By the end of the fifteenth century, three strong dynasties had emerged: the Tudors in England, the Valois in France, and the Hapsburgs in Spain. As the power of feudal landlords diminished and that of the kings increased, one idea gained currency: that a person could belong to or identify with a unified nation. This, in some ways, was when the idea of nationalism was born.

ally prompt them to look outward and expand from Europe, sparking an Age of Discovery that would lead to sustained contact with the "New World."

## Society

Socially, most Europeans in the fourteenth and fifteenth centuries still lived in an agrarian society on remnants of the feudal system, although towns and even some great cities had developed since the eleventh century. To ensure a regular food supply, all the members of European villages usually shared their year's crops. As with any society based on agriculture, there were gendered roles in European society. Unlike some African and Indian cultures, women rarely participated in a town's political life or tilled the fields (but they did have lighter duties in the fields, as did children). Women's power was mostly limited to their influence on their husbands, children, and servants. In contrast, some women in religious orders (Catholic nuns) operated abbeys and wielded significant power in that realm.

Perhaps the greatest change during the thirteenth through fifteenth centuries was the expansion of European cities, where intellectual life prospered. Cities demanded surplus agriculture, which could be supplied only when rural farmers expanded their production to bring food to the market. This development further challenged feudal society because it gave serfs the ability to earn money at the market and thus purchase their freedom from the declining feudal lords.

## The Renaissance

By the late fourteenth century, the forces of economic expansion and the development of urban life allowed for a high level of material well-being in the great European cities and the general decline of closed-off feudal living. It was this wealth and expansive mindset that engendered the **Renaissance**, an intellectual and artistic reconnection to the age of Greco-Roman antiquity, when humankind was considered to be more cosmopolitan and not merely a source of labor for feudal fiefdoms. Central to Renaissance artists and thinkers was the idea of humanism, which lionized the individual and therefore directly challenged the declining feudal system.

## The Decline of Catholic Europe

If the system of feudalism was declining in the fourteenth and fifteenth centuries, **Catholicism** was still the undisputed religious force in western Europe. Indeed, the artists of the Renaissance usually used Christian images to celebrate the new, more open atmosphere. The Church exerted its greatest power amid the divided feudal society as the sole institution with moral authority and even political power over all of Europe. The later medieval years witnessed Catholicism's greatest thinker, Thomas Aquinas (1225–1274), and its most powerful popes, Innocent III (pope from 1198 to 1216) and Boniface VIII (pope from 1294 to 1303). Catholicism covered Europe like a cloak, unifying many disparate feudal lands.

## Change

By the first quarter of the sixteenth century, two impulses collided to challenge the authority of the Catholic Church. The first occurred in this world: a new attitude toward humankind brought about by the slow urbanization of Europe, the consolidation of monarchical powers, and the rise of popular piety. Merchants did not like priests moralizing about their profits, and rulers did not like their authority challenged. In addition, the Church's total incapacity to confront and respond to the crises of the fourteenth century, which included famine, plague, and the Hundred Years' War, prompted several movements of popular piety. Together, these challenges led to the development of **Christian humanism**, defined as a renewed belief in the importance of the singular individual as opposed to the institution of the Church. Optimism, curiosity, and emphasis on naturalism were components of the humanistic worldview. These factors led to renewed interest in the sciences, which began to challenge Christianity as a worldly authority.

The second event concerned humans' relationship with God, and the Church itself helped invite this second challenge. Beginning during the

**mercantilism**
Theory that a nation or state's prosperity was determined by the total volume of its trade

**Crusades**
Series of campaigns in which Europeans marched to the Middle East in an effort to seize the Holy Land of Jerusalem, which at the time was controlled by Muslims; battles lasted from 1096 to at least 1291

**Black Death**
Bubonic plague, which started to spread in 1346 and eventually killed one-third of all Europeans

**Hundred Years' War**
War waged between France and England in the fourteenth century over who controlled the French throne

**Renaissance**
Intellectual and artistic reconnection to the age of Greco-Roman antiquity, starting in the fourteenth century, that lionized the individual

**Catholicism**
Central religious force in western Europe; sole institution with moral authority and political power over all of medieval Europe

**Christian humanism**
Belief in the importance of the singular individual, as opposed to the institution of the Church; characterized by optimism, curiosity, and emphasis on naturalism

**selling of indulgences**
Practice of popes using their authority to limit the time a person's soul spent in purgatory, in exchange for cash

**Protestant Reformation**
Movement that challenged the Catholic Church to return to its unornamented origins; protesters criticized Church rituals, including the Mass, confession rites, and pilgrimages to holy sites

**printing press**
Invention of the 1440s using metal letter faces to print words on paper, allowing for the quick, widespread dissemination of ideas, opinions, and scientific findings

Crusades of the eleventh century, the Church had grown increasingly secular in its discipline; it had even begun to sell its favors. For instance, some popes used their authority to limit the amount of time a person's soul spent in purgatory; the cost of this divine favor was usually cash. This practice, which grew throughout the thirteenth and fourteenth centuries, was called the **selling of indulgences**.

## The Reformation

These dual challenges sparked the **Protestant Reformation**. At its core, the Reformation was a movement that challenged the Catholic Church to return to its unornamented origins. In addition to questioning the selling of indulgences, the leaders of the Reformation were critical of Church rituals, including the Mass, confession rites that reinforced the hierarchy by putting absolution at the discretion of a priest, and pilgrimages to holy sites. In short, the reformers felt it was faith in God that led to salvation, not the works one did to demonstrate that faith. As protesters (root of the word *Protestant*), the leaders of the Reformation sought a simpler church defined by an individual's relationship to God and the Christ. In Protestantism, the central authority was the Bible; in Catholicism, authority lay with the Bible but also with tradition as espoused by the hierarchy of the Church.

>> Martin Luther took advantage of the invention of the printing press to advocate that scripture be read in local vernacular languages like German and English rather than Latin. Luther's ideas sparked the Protestant Reformation, which challenged the Catholic cloak over Europe, leading to numerous "Wars of Religion" and hastening the development of nationalism.

The leaders of the Reformation, most importantly Martin Luther (the moral conscience of the movement) and John Calvin (its great organizer), took advantage of the invention of the **printing press** (developed in the 1440s, although not used widely until the 1450s) to advocate that scripture be read in local vernacular languages like German and English rather than Latin. See "The reasons why . . ." for an overview of the significance of the Reformation for the future of Europe.

## Europe in 1492

By 1492, Europe was a dramatically different continent from that of just a century earlier. Europeans had fundamentally altered their political, social, economic, and religious structures. Feudalism, headed by hundreds of feudal lords and vassals, had collapsed, and nations, headed by a handful of kings and queens, had become the most powerful political structures on the continent, covering vast territories and allowing for the easy movement of

**The Reformation is important for our purposes for at least two reasons:**

**Nationalism.** It hastened the development of nationalism by fragmenting the unity of Catholic authority over Europe. Freed from that yoke, European nations began to develop unique identities and consolidate wealth, which, in the creed of mercantilism, spurred aggressive attempts to expand in search of greater wealth. This would lead to the Age of Discovery and to sustained contact with both Africa and the New World.

**Religious conflicts.** The Protestant Reformation triggered several vicious battles over religion, many of which bled over into the New World and provoked people to leave Europe in search of greater religious freedoms.

goods and peoples. Spain was the most powerful nation in Europe at the time, France was the largest, and Portugal had the advantage of superior nautical craftsmanship. Reformers, meanwhile, challenged the righteousness of Roman Catholicism, creating schisms and, eventually, new religious traditions. And in 1492, Spain took control of the city of Granada, ending the northward spread of Islam for at least five hundred years. Merchants had arisen as a powerful force across the continent too, paving the way for capitalism to flourish and for the market to penetrate more deeply into society than it ever had before. The printing press, invented in the 1440s and developed throughout the 1450s, helped democratize knowledge, allowing scientists to share discoveries and news in many vernacular languages.

England was not as powerful as most of the rest of the countries at the time, mainly because it had been divided by internal religious wars for several decades, as Catholics and Protestants brutally vied for control of the country. It would become a powerful force only later, after Queen Elizabeth muted religious conflict, stabilized the economy, and prepared the country to challenge Spain as the most powerful nation in Europe. All that would take place after 1492.

## And in the end . . .

At the end of the fifteenth century, three societies, long separated from one another and uniquely developed, stood on the verge of sustained contact. The location of this contact would be the "New World," which included Native North America, as well as Central and South America. Europeans would be the principal catalysts, as their world was in the middle of dramatic changes that led to outward expansion. But the peoples of West Africa and Native America would struggle to shape the outcome of sustained intercultural contact. The battle, both physical and ideological, would begin in earnest in 1492.

### What else was happening . . .

| | |
|---|---|
| **C. 200,000 B.C.E.** | The earliest humans appear in Africa. |
| **16,000 B.C.E.** | The last Ice Age reaches its coldest point; people in Asia, across Beringia, live in huts made from wooly mammoth bones. |
| **2500 B.C.E.** | Age of the Egyptian pyramids. |
| **0 C.E.** | Rise of the Roman Empire, birth of Christ. |
| **1023** | Paper money is printed in China. |
| **1300** | Corsets for women are invented. |
| **1300s** | The Aztecs make "animal balloons" by creating inflated animals from the intestines of cats and present them to the gods as a sacrifice. |
| **1489** | The symbols + (addition) and − (subtraction) come into general use. |

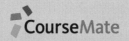

Visit the CourseMate website at www.cengagebrain.com for additional study tools and review materials for this chapter.

# CHAPTER 2

# Contact *and* Settlement,
## *1492–1660*

## Learning Outcomes

*After reading this chapter, you should be able to do the following:*

LO **1**    Explain the reasons for Europeans' exploring lands outside Europe, and trace the routes they followed.

LO **2**    Describe the founding of European nations' first colonies in the New World.

LO **3**    Trace the expansion of England's holdings in the southern colonies.

LO **4**    Outline the reasons for and timing of England's founding of colonies in New England.

© The Mariners' Museum/CORBIS

**"At first, the results of contact were generally bad: the tale is mostly one of hunger, disease, and death."**

In the collision of cultures that took place in the New World, Europeans were the initiators. Their desire to find wealth and spread Christianity brought Indians, West Africans, and Europeans into sustained contact for the first time. At first, the results of contact were generally bad: the tale is mostly one of hunger, disease, and death. After this difficult start, however, the seeds for a new nation were planted.

## LO¹ Exploration and Discovery

Beginning in the fourteenth century, Europeans took advantage of the new technologies developed during the previous century, especially the nautical advances made during the Hundred Years' War, when large parts of central Europe became battlegrounds that required circumvention. They did so for at least two reasons: (1) to alleviate a trade deficit and (2) to spread Christianity (see "The reasons why . . .").

## { *The reasons why . . .* }

### Europeans sought to explore lands outside Europe primarily for two reasons:

**To alleviate a trade deficit.** After the Crusades, many Europeans began to consider spices and other luxuries from the Middle East, India, and parts of Africa true necessities. To reach Europe, the goods had to be shipped from the Far East, through Middle Eastern and then Italian traders. This sequence of middlemen drove prices up, leading to a problem: Because the Europeans had few commodities to trade in return, they had to use gold to pay for the goods, and gold supplies subsequently diminished. This trade deficit led to a depression throughout Europe, as a great deal of money was going out and very little was coming in. The depression sparked a scramble to find another way to obtain the desired goods; namely, a cheaper route to the Far East that would avoid Muslim and Italian middlemen.

**To spread Christianity.** The second factor in European expansion was the mission to spread Christianity, initially Catholicism, around the world. Like many other religions, Christianity has a missionary message within it, and many of the first explorers thought they could simultaneously search for riches and spread the gospel. Competition from the rapidly growing Islamic faith provided further motivation for spreading Christianity, as did the continuing battles between Catholics and Protestants that began during the Reformation. An important consequence of Christianity's messianic message was that Europeans sought not only trade relations with those whom they came into contact, but also dominion over them.

## The Eastern Route: The Portuguese

The search for riches and for lands not already in the hands of Christians drew European explorers to several locations around the globe, many of which they encountered quite accidentally. (Indeed, the Americas were perhaps the largest pieces of land ever discovered by mistake.) In 1298, the adventurer Marco Polo wrote that the Orient was the source of many desired goods and that there might be a western route there across the Atlantic Ocean. Others still believed in the existence of an eastern route, through Africa. Both beliefs propelled explorers into the unknown.

Portuguese leaders were among those who still believed that an eastern route could be found. Led by Prince Henry the Navigator (1394–1460), Portuguese sailors traveled down the western coast of Africa searching for the dramatic left turn that would lead them to India and the Middle East. After several failures, in 1498 they finally succeeded. In that year, Vasco da Gama (1469–1524) reached India by rounding the Cape of Good Hope in southern Africa, then heading back north to India. His success made Portugal a wealthy nation throughout the sixteenth and seventeenth centuries (see Map 2.1).

> **❝ Plenty of rubies, plenty of emeralds! You owe great thanks to God, for having brought you to a country holding such riches! ❞**
> —*Vasco da Gama*

## The Beginnings of European Slavery

Before da Gama's success, however, Portuguese sailors in the 1440s had probed West Africa and made a discovery that would be critical for the development of future relations between cultures. African kings wanted to trade with the Portuguese along the shore, and both sides benefited from the trade in goods. But in the process, the Portuguese also bartered for African slaves. They carried them back to Portugal as living novelties, thus introducing the system of African slavery to Europe during the fifteenth century.

By the 1490s, the Portuguese had taken control of a previously uninhabited island off the west coast of Africa called São Tomé. São Tomé had the perfect soil for growing sugar, a product much in demand in Europe. Sensing profits, in the 1500s the Portuguese began using African slaves to harvest sugar in São Tomé, thus establishing the first modern economy dependent primarily on slave labor.

 Read a firsthand account of Vasco da Gama's travels.

>> **Fifteenth-century exploring ship.**

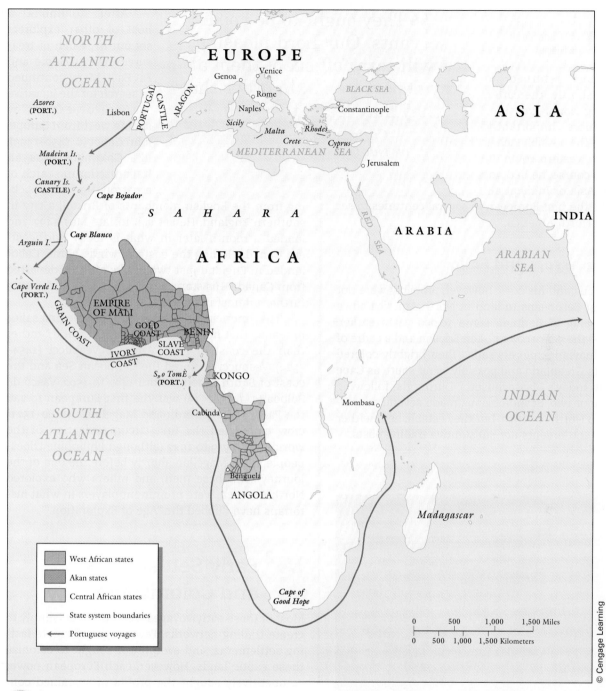

Map 2.1. Routes of Early Exploration

## The Western Route: The Spanish

With Portugal's numerous successes, rival Spain acted like a jealous neighbor, and Spanish sailors began advocating the search for a western route to the Orient. After years of delay, the Spanish monarchy finally agreed to fund the costly venture. The first voyage that Spain reluctantly funded, in 1492, was that of Christopher Columbus (1451–1506), a Portuguese-trained Italian sailor. The Spanish monarchs, Ferdinand and Isabella, sent him westward with three small ships, the *Niña*, the *Pinta*, and the *Santa Maria*. On October 12, 1492, Columbus and his crew sighted land in the present-day Bahamas. Thinking this was an outlying portion of Asia and India, he called the local inhabitants "Indians."

Columbus returned to Spain shortly thereafter, bringing some treasures and, more importantly, tales of the possible riches via the western route. In fact, of course, he had not found Asia or India at all; he was the first European in several centuries to set foot in North America.

> **"They ought to be good servants. Our Lord pleasing, I will carry off six of them at my departure . . . in order that they may learn to speak."**
> —*Christopher Columbus, on Native North Americans*

## Predecessors and Followers

Columbus and his crew, however, probably were not the first Europeans to land in North America since the closing of Beringia some 10,000 years earlier. Around the year 1000 C.E., Leif Ericson and a cadre of Scandinavian explorers sailed their brightly colored ships to Greenland and possibly as far south as Cape Cod, in today's Massachusetts. During the following decade or two, Scandinavians made several expeditions to North America, but they established neither lasting settlements nor substantive trading posts.

**Christopher Columbus.**

Image Copyright © The Metropolitan Museum of Art/Art Resource, NY

After Columbus, a host of other explorers set out in search of treasures in the Middle and Far East. Many continued to search for the lucrative "passage to the Orient" by sailing west from Europe. John Cabot (c. 1450–1499), like Columbus, was an Italian sailor in search of a patron. He found backing from the English merchants of Bristol, a city in southern England. He set sail in late May 1497 and landed a month later in what is today northeastern Canada. Riding the easterly winds home, Cabot landed in England just two weeks after he departed from Canada. His stories and his rapid return fueled further interest in exploration.

The Americas got their name from the first sailor to realize that he had reached a "new world," rather than the coast of Asia: Amerigo Vespucci (1454–1512). Vespucci explored the Caribbean Sea and the coast of South America from 1497 to 1502. Vasco de Balboa (c. 1475–1519) was the first European to sail the Pacific (1513). Ferdinand Magellan's (1480–1521) crew completed the first circumnavigation of the world from 1519 to 1522 (although Philippine tribespeople killed Magellan shortly before the end of the journey). All these men, and others who explored North America, were prominent players in what historians have dubbed the "Age of Exploration."

# LO² Early Settlements and Colonization

Most of these early voyages were intended simply to create trading networks. Few sought to create lasting settlements, and even fewer sought to colonize these exotic lands. However, each European power competitively sought the profits of sustained contact, and this competition for wealth drove them to create encampments that would enable them to defend their claims to those faraway natural resources.

## Portuguese

After Columbus's voyage, Spain claimed possession of all of North America. Predictably, the Portuguese would have none of it. They protested Spain's claim. To prevent open conflict between the two Catholic nations, Pope Alexander VI intervened. In 1493, he drew a line on a map that extended from north to south, proclaiming that all land east of the line belonged to Portugal, all land west of it to Spain. The effect of this line, called the **Line of Demarcation**, was to grant all of Brazil to Portugal, while Spain had claim to Central and North America. In 1500, the Portuguese explorer Pedro Cabral accidentally landed in Brazil, beginning what would be Portugal's most profitable colonial venture. As perhaps the first act of modern European colonialism, the pope made his arbitration with no consideration of the peoples already inhabiting the land (see Map 2.2).

## Spanish

Despite Portugal's early ambition, it was the Spanish that established the first colonies in North America. In the process, they began one of the bloodiest chapters in the world's history, as disease and warfare nearly vanquished the native populations of the Caribbean, Mexico, and North and South America. The advent of disease was so bad that perhaps as many as one in five people then

> **Line of Demarcation**
> **Line drawn by Pope Alexander VI through a map of the Western Hemisphere; granted the eastern half to Portugal and the western half to Spain, in what could be considered the first act of modern European colonialism**

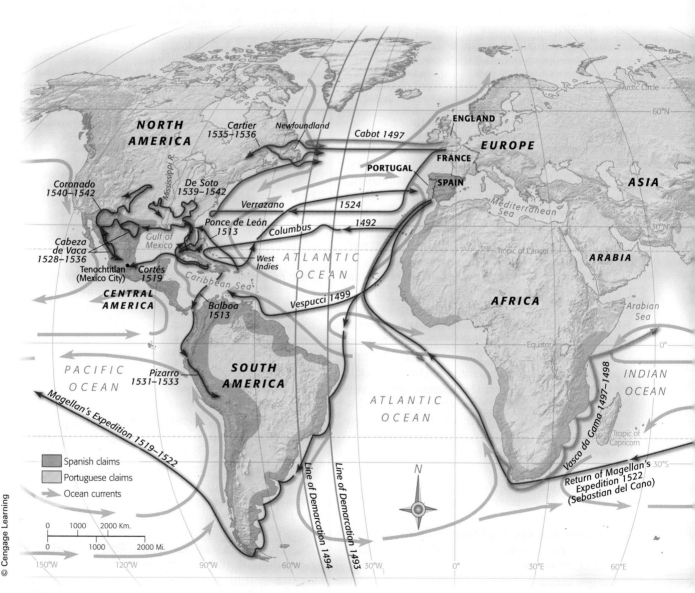

 Map 2.2. Exploration in the New World, 1492–1542

**conquistador**
One of the Spanish noblemen who sailed to the New World with small armies to vanquish kingdoms there

**encomienda**
Tribute, usually payable in gold or slaves, demanded of conquered Indian villages by the conquistadors

**viceroy**
Representative of the Spanish crown who governed conquered Indian villages

living on Earth died in the fifteenth and sixteenth centuries. Furthermore, Spain, searching for gold and other sources of wealth, brutally abused the native populations, often enslaving them and forcing them to work in gold mines to increase Spain's vast wealth. Just two decades after Columbus first crossed the Atlantic, the Spanish had established permanent settlements in Hispaniola, Cuba, Puerto Rico, Jamaica, and Panama. By 1513, the enslaved natives of Hispaniola were producing $1 million worth of gold annually. It would be only a few years before the Spanish expanded their settlements into the interior of North America in search of greater riches.

## Spanish Expansion into North America

The system the Spanish used to develop their colonies was distinct. In the early sixteenth century, Spanish **conquistadors**, mostly minor noblemen, led private armies to the New World. These armies were relatively small, usually made up of fewer than one thousand men, but they devastated indigenous populations with weapons and disease wherever they went. Once they had overpowered a kingdom, it became known as an **encomienda**, in which Indian villages were obliged to pay a tribute, usually in gold or slaves, to the conquistadors. This, in essence, enslaved the Indians in Spanish-controlled lands, although no one actually owned another human being. (In doing this, the Spanish were adapting the system that had been enforced by the North African Muslims to control the Spanish when they conquered Spain.) As the number of encomiendas grew, **viceroys** reporting directly to the Crown began to govern them.

Their growth also inspired a stern opposition to the brutal manner in which the conquistadors exerted their control. Of these critics, Bartolomé de las Casas, a Spanish priest, is the most famous. His book, *A Short Account of the Destruction of the Indies* (1552), serves as a key beginning point for humanitarian concerns about the potential for cruelty inspired by imperialism.

Despite protests like that of de las Casas, Spanish imperialism continued. The most successful of the conquistadors were Hernán Cortés (1485–1547) and Francisco Pizarro (c. 1475–1541), whose adventures sparked widespread interest in the New World.

*Cortés and Mexico.* Between 1519 and 1521, Hernán Cortés led an expedition of six hundred men against the Triple Alliance (better, if incorrectly, known as the Aztecs) in Mexico and their ruler, Montezuma. Four weapons allowed Cortés and his men to overrun the huge civilization: horses, which allowed mobility; firearms, which terrorized their victims; the support of other Indian tribes who had suffered under Aztec rule; and, by far the most important weapon, disease. Smallpox was first introduced to the New World by one of Cortés's men and by 1520 had decimated the Aztecs. Under assault from these four weapons, the great civilization of the Aztecs fell into Spanish hands within two years of Cortés's arrival, and, to Cortés's delight, so did the Aztecs' gold and silver reserves. The Spanish built Mexico City on the ruins of the Aztec capital, Tenochtitlán. Hoping to find the same plunder that Cortés had found, Spanish colonists soon arrived in large numbers, and Mexico City became the largest "European" city in America.

Read firsthand descriptions of Cortés's first contact with the Aztecs.

Experience the battle between Aztecs and Cortés's men through the simulation "Colonial Expansion."

*Pizarro and Peru.* By the 1530s, Pizarro, well aware of Cortés's triumph, explored the western coast of South America from a base he established in Panama. In 1532, he and his army of just 168 men (mostly untrained soldiers) encountered the tremendous Inca Empire of Peru. Initially, like the Aztecs, the Incas welcomed the army, but the relationship quickly soured. Many of the Inca soldiers were off at battle with another tribe because the ravages of smallpox, which had spanned the continent less than a decade after being introduced by Cortés's men, had created political strife for the Incas. In the meantime, Pizarro kidnapped the Inca leader, amassed a huge fortune by ransoming his life, killed him anyway, and seized the Inca capital of Qosqo. With the Inca warriors away, Pizarro faced only mild resistance from what would have been formidable foes. When the Inca soldiers returned, Pizarro and his men were already entrenched in the empire. Pizarro founded the city of Lima as his capital in 1535 and ruled from there until his death in 1541. Again, internal battles within the Indian populations and especially smallpox contributed to the decline of what had been a vibrant civilization.

**price revolution**
Inflationary event, such as the huge influx of silver to Spain in the mid-1500s, that causes the price of goods to surpass the wages paid to laborers and landless agricultural workers

soldiers to drive out the French pirates. In 1565, in order to secure the region, the Spanish conquered the city of St. Augustine from the French. Once established, Florida was a low priority for the Spanish because it did not contain the riches of Mexico, Peru, or other parts of Central America, but it was important as an outpost guarding against attack. St. Augustine, now a part of Florida, is the oldest continually occupied European-established city in the continental United States. Under Spain's control, it was largely a town ruled by military leaders and Catholic clergymen, serving as an anchor for Spain's northernmost imperial designs.

Read an account of the capture of St. Augustine.

*The American Southwest.* The Spanish also explored the American Southwest, heading north from Mexico as far as present-day Colorado. As with St. Augustine in Florida, the Spanish occupied the town of Santa Fe to secure the region against intruders but had little other use for it.

Read more about the founding of Santa Fe.

In 1598, Juan de Onate, a Spanish conquistador, became the first European governor of a future American state—New Mexico.

## Results of Spanish Conquest

By the middle of the 1500s, Spanish conquistadors controlled numerous areas surrounding the Gulf of Mexico. There were five principal results of this initial Spanish conquest: (1) financial, (2) biological, (3) racial, (4) religious, and (5) geopolitical.

*Financial.* Financially, the economic impact of the flow of silver from the mines of these lands was enormous. The influx of minerals made Spain one of the wealthiest nations in the world. Spain could now afford to defend a three-way trade between West Africa, the Americas, and Europe. But the sudden abundance of silver also meant that many people had access to money, causing prices to rise. The result was an inflationary **price revolution**, which badly hurt European

>> The sacrificial practices of the Aztecs were scarcely more brutal than their treatment at the hands of Cortés and his men.

© North Wind Picture Archives/Alamy

*The Caribbean.* Throughout the sixteenth and seventeenth centuries, the Caribbean islands were some of the most prized New World possessions. From the time of Columbus, Europeans had attempted to subjugate the local Caribbean Indians to mine gold, search for food, and, in the case of the Spanish, serve as sexual companions. When sugar production began in earnest in the mid-1600s, Europeans devoted vast amounts of resources to grow the valuable cane. By the late 1600s, huge numbers of African slaves worked in the Caribbean.

*"Victory! Victory! The French fort is ours!"*
*—from The Founding of St. Augustine*

*Florida.* In today's United States, the Spanish developed settlements in Florida and the Southwest. The Spanish initially had little interest in Florida, but when French adventurers began to use eastern Florida as a base from which to attack Spanish ships traveling to Mexico and Peru, Spain sent

**Columbian Exchange**
**Biological crossover of agricultural products, domesticated animals, and microbial diseases from Europe to the New World and vice versa**

laborers and landless agricultural workers, whose wages could not keep up with increasing prices throughout Europe. Increased numbers of impoverished Europeans were driven to emigrate to the Americas in search of a new life.

© Réunion des Musées Nationaux/Art Resource, NY

*Biological.* The most important result was the **Columbian Exchange**, in which agricultural products, domesticated animals, and microbial diseases crossed over from one civilization to the other, creating a vast "exchange" that would forever change the world, for good and for ill. As more Spanish came to the New World, they unknowingly carried with them microbes for several diseases to which Indians had not been exposed, smallpox being the most destructive. The direct result of the spreading of these microbes was the death of perhaps as much as 95 percent of the Indian population. The numbers tell the story. Historians estimate that more than

25 million people lived in central Mexico before Cortés arrived; fifteen years after his arrival, more than 8 million had perished. Within a few generations, diseases eliminated two-thirds of the native population. And a century after first contact, the Indian population of central Mexico was around 700,000. It took less than one hundred years for this population to fall from more than 25 million to 700,000.

Diseases also spread far from the location of their initial inception, debatably stretching as far north as New England. This is perhaps one reason why English explorers found so few Indians when they first landed on the Atlantic coast in the 1600s, although diseases affecting New England's tribes may also have come from contact with European fishermen off the coast of Canada. For their part, Indians may have introduced syphilis to Europeans, but even if syphilis did originate in the New World, it was hardly as deadly as smallpox or measles proved to be. Lest this part of the exchange be used to induce latter-day guilt in Europeans or European-Americans, most historians believe that, due to complex genetic dispositions within the Indian population, there would have been no way to prevent this microbial transmission. Furthermore, the recent work of Mexican epidemiologist Rodolfo Acuña suggests that many Indians in today's Mexico might have died from a disease called cocolitzli, which had nothing to do with smallpox and which was likely not imported from Europe.

If the exchange of microbes had horrifying ramifications, the mutual transfer of plants and animals led to a more positive biological exchange between the Americas and Europe. Contact allowed the cultures to expand the kinds of food they could grow and the animals they could domesticate. Horses and livestock were introduced to the Americas by the Europeans; maize, tobacco, tomatoes, chocolate, and potatoes, all of which had been first cultivated by Indians, came to Europe. The development of sugar plantations in the Caribbean Islands was also a product of the Columbian Exchange, although their dependence on slaves was a corrosive element of the exchange. The number of foods and animals that traversed the globe for the first time is truly astounding.

*Racial.* Another component of the Columbian Exchange concerns race, as Spanish exploration began the process of mixing various races of

© AAA Photostock/Alamy

>> "How Indians Treat Their Sick," from *Neue Welt und Americanische Historien* by Johann Ludwig Gottfried.

people. For one, the Spanish explorers procreated with Indian women. For another, their diseases had greatly depopulated Native America, a circumstance that expedited the introduction of African slaves as a labor force in the New World. By 1600, the multiracial character of the New World was firmly established.

*Religious.* To convert the Indians, the Spanish often destroyed Indian temples and replaced them with Catholic cathedrals. Catholic friars tried to use the religious symbols of the Indian religions to teach the lessons of Catholicism. But often the Indians transformed Catholic saints into spiritual likenesses of their preexisting gods and goddesses. The most famous example of this religious meshing was the Indian corn goddess and the Virgin Mary. Many Indians were able to accept the Catholic faith on their own terms once it had been hybridized in this way.

*Geopolitical.* Geopolitically, the Spanish successes meant that other European nations became hungry for conquest. Rivalries grew as nations sought resources they lacked at home. Of the five major results of the Spanish conquest, geopolitical concerns were the most significant in bringing the French and the English into New World exploration.

## French

Like the Spanish and the Portuguese, French explorers, too, had been searching for the fabled route to the Orient. They focused on looking for the Northwest Passage that would lead them through today's Canada to the Pacific Ocean. The French never found this nonexistent route, but they did find valuable products, mainly furs, that they could return to France.

The result was the creation of several encampments in present-day Canada that served as French trading posts in the New World. The largest was Quebec, founded in 1608. At these encampments, the French traded for furs with the Indians and spread Catholicism. However, the French were beleaguered by disease, by warfare with the Iroquois (who resented the Frenchmen's successful trade with the Algonquians), and by the weather of the Northeast. Thus they remained a small but sturdy presence in North America, with holdings that extended great distances but vanished quickly after challenges from the more entrenched English throughout the 1700s. In the mid-1600s, there were only about four hundred French colonists in North America.

## English: Planting Colonies, Not Marauding for Wealth

The English were slow to enter into New World exploration because the Tudors were still consolidating their Crown in the early 1500s, when Portugal, Spain, and France were busy traveling abroad. Furthermore, the Tudors at this time were closely allied with Spain (both were still Catholic) and did not want to challenge Spain's dominance in the New World. Also during the early 1500s, the English textile industry was booming, so wealthy individuals invested in textile businesses rather than in high-risk overseas ventures.

By the middle of the 1500s, this English disinclination toward exploration began to change. There were religious, social, economic, and geopolitical motives for this transition (see "The reasons why . . ." on the next page).

Despite hopes to the contrary, England (and all other European nations other than Spain) did not find great wealth through quick plundering of existing civilizations in the Americas. England's wealth from the New World came instead through prolonged colonization, the development of substantial economies, and the exploitation of agricultural resources. As illustrated by Sir Walter Raleigh's explorations, it would take time and experience for the English to learn to focus on such endeavors. The desire for quick riches has persisted as a human flaw through the ages.

### Sir Walter Raleigh and Roanoke

Sir Walter Raleigh was the first Englishman to found a New World colony. Raleigh received a royal patent to claim New World lands in the name of the queen, who was eager to check Spain's colonial expansion. In 1585, he established his first colony, using the Spanish conquistadors as his model. Like the Spanish adventurers who had conquered the Aztecs and Incas, Raleigh and his men sought gold and silver, and he planned to exploit native labor to mine these treasures.

But there was a hitch in Raleigh's plan. Hoping to avoid conflict with the Spanish, Raleigh decided to focus his search to the north of Spain's territories in Mexico and South America. He and his men established their base at Roanoke, on the outer banks of modern-day North Carolina, a region lacking mineral wealth. Frustrated in their search for New World gold and silver, Raleigh's men abandoned the colony within a year and returned to England.

After the first Roanoke settlement failed, Raleigh decided to continue his efforts on a different basis.

## {*The reasons why . . .*}

**There were four key reasons why the English became more interested in exploration in the mid-1500s:**

*Religious.* After several contentious decades during which Catholics and Protestants fought bitterly over whose faith was the rightful inheritor of the Bible, Protestant Queen Elizabeth I came to the throne. Queen Elizabeth's support of the Reformation suddenly turned England into Europe's leading opponent of the increasingly powerful Catholic Spain. Their rivalry increased after Spain supported two unsuccessful Roman Catholic plots to assassinate Elizabeth for her support of the Reformation (whether Pope Sixtus V was aware of these attempts remains an open question). Making things worse, in 1588 Spain tried unsuccessfully to invade England. This intense rivalry meant that the English were unwilling to allow Catholic Spain to convert all the non-Christians of the New World without competition from the surging English Protestants.

*Economic.* The second motive for English expansion was that the textile markets of Antwerp, Belgium, failed in the late 1500s, a development that left English producers without this market for their cloth. As a result, many wealthy individuals stopped investing in textiles and looked for new opportunities, such as New World exploration. In addition, the English economy was burdened by importing large quantities of raw materials, which created a dangerous trade imbalance. The New World had the potential to supply the English with these raw materials at cheaper prices.

*Social.* Meanwhile, the enclosure of farms and the inflationary price revolution created a glut of impoverished Englishmen seeking to escape poverty by leaving England. But the poor were not the only English affected by limited economic possibilities. The English gentry was growing, and after the Church of England separated from the Catholic Church, traditional opportunities for the younger sons of nobles to serve in the Catholic Church were closed. With little unsettled land remaining in England, many members of the English upper class were willing to seek their fortune in the colonies.

*Geopolitical.* Fourth, Queen Elizabeth's durability as a monarch, reigning for over fifty years, stabilized the Tudor throne, meaning that England could now participate wholeheartedly in New World ventures. The bitter relations between Spain and England had erupted into war after Elizabeth knighted the British pirate Francis Drake for his raids on Spanish treasure ships from 1578 to 1580. The Anglo-Spanish war, most noted for the defeat of the Spanish Armada, led to an English victory. For our purposes, the Anglo-Spanish war is significant for two reasons. First, it established England as ruler of the sea, prompting it to begin exploring the New World, and second, it signaled the decline of Spain as a world power. Now other nations could more successfully capitalize on the promises of the New World.

---

**plantation**
Large farm staffed by an entire family in an agricultural economy

**lost colony of Roanoke**
Second settlement by English colonists at Roanoke; deserted sometime before 1590

**joint stock company**
Company that sold stock to numerous investors in order to raise large sums of money

 Do a CSI Roanoke where *you're* the crime scene investigator.

He returned to the same region because he still wanted to avoid the Spanish, but this time he declared that he would not seek easy treasure. Learning from his initial failure and drawing on the experience of English settlements in Ireland earlier in the century, Raleigh decided that his second colony would consist of **plantations**. Instead of sending conquerors, he sent whole families to the New World, hoping to recreate English society and its agricultural economy. Poor English farmers would perform the labor on the plantations, while transplanted gentry would perform their traditional functions of land ownership and governance.

But Raleigh's second Roanoke colony ultimately failed as well. Voyages to resupply the colonists were delayed, and by the time a ship finally reached Roanoke in 1590, the outpost was deserted, perhaps after an attack by a local Indian tribe. The fate of the roughly one hundred settlers has never been conclusively determined, and the second Roanoke settlement came to be known as the **lost colony of Roanoke**.

### Lessons of Roanoke

Although Roanoke was a catalogue of failures, it did teach the English two lessons. First, Raleigh had discovered that the formula for successful English colonization would not be quick strikes for gold but rather a plantation model that would create self-sustaining settlements. Second, Raleigh's efforts demonstrated that more than one person needed to fund such ventures—the demands were too great to be borne by a single purse. This realization resulted in the expansion of **joint stock companies**, or companies that sold stock to numerous people in order to raise large sums of money. At first, the English used joint stock companies to finance trade; then, in the second half of the sixteenth century, English

>> **What became of the colonists left at the stockade on Roanoke Island? No one knows.**

## Virginia: Jamestown

Despite 115 years of contact, the year 1607 is often regarded as the first year of American history. It was in that year that the English established their first lasting colony in the land that would become the United States: **Jamestown**, in present-day Virginia.

Begun by the Virginia Company of London (a joint stock company), Jamestown began with 104 colonists, some of whom favored the plantation model of settlement, others of whom favored the conquistador model. Failure bedeviled them, however, mainly because of a harsh drought and because this group of settlers included too many English gentlemen who had little desire either to work the soil or to build fortifications. Most notably, John Smith attempted to unite this first group of settlers, but his rise to power insulted many of the gentleman explorers, who had him shipped back to England. The first years for these settlers were difficult, as disease, lack of food, poor management, and hostile relations with Indian tribes took a toll. Historians now call the winter of 1609–1610 the **starving time**, when food supplies were so scarce that at least one colonist resorted to cannibalism. Only the continued arrival of new colonists kept the settlement functioning. From 1607 to 1609, more than 900 settlers arrived in Jamestown. Only 60 survived the first few years.

**Jamestown**
**English settlement of 1607 in present-day Virginia**

**starving time**
**Winter of 1609–1610 in Jamestown, when food supplies were so scarce that at least one colonist resorted to cannibalism**

Read John Smith's *Generall Historie of Virginia.*

Take a tour of Jamestown.

> 66 From 1607 to 1609, more than 900 settlers arrived in Jamestown. Only 60 survived the first few years. 99

investors started a number of joint stock companies for ventures in the Old World. In 1553, the Muscovy Company traded for furs and naval stores in Russia; in 1581, the Levant Company was founded for trade with the Turkish Empire; in 1585, the Barbary Company focused its attention on North Africa; in 1588, the Guinea Company traded in West Africa; and in 1600, the East India Company formed to trade in Asia. Many of these companies were highly successful, and they encouraged many English investors to consider establishing colonies overseas by the early 1600s.

## LO³ England Founds the Southern Colonies, 1607–1660

These two lessons observed, if not always adhered to, the English began to expand their holdings in the New World. Between 1600 and 1660, more than 150,000 English people left for the New World. Most went to the West Indies, and perhaps slightly less than a third crossed the Atlantic to settle the eastern coast of North America.

### Jamestown Finally Succeeds

Jamestown eventually succeeded, and its success depended on two things: Indian relations and tobacco.

*The Powhatan Confederacy.* First, the English settlers, badly in need of food, relied on a group

**Powhatan Confederacy**
Group of six Algonquian villages in present-day Virginia, named after its leader

**cash crop**
Agricultural product grown primarily for sale. Examples include sugar and tobacco harvests

**indentured servitude**
System of labor whereby farmers paid the Atlantic passage for English and Irish workers in exchange for four to seven years of their work on farms or plantations

**head right**
A grant by the Virginia Company of 50 acres of land to any individual who paid his or her own passage across the Atlantic; put more property in private hands

**"seasoning"**
Period of several years during which indentured servants were exposed to the New World's microbes; many did not survive

of six Algonquian villages known as the **Powhatan Confederacy** (named after its leader). Powhatan and his tribe saw the English settlers as allies who would accept food in return for knives and guns, which would help Powhatan secure his confederacy against other tribes. This was likely a difficult decision, because the Indians had little idea of what the colonists had in mind regarding the kind of life they wanted to develop in the New World. Other tribes deemed it less troublesome to simply attack and kill the newcomers. The relationship between Powhatan's tribe and the Virginians was often difficult and sometimes violent, especially when crops were limited. But the tribes of the Powhatan Confederacy did assist the settlers throughout their struggling early years.

*Tobacco.* Second, in the early 1610s, the English settlers hit a jackpot: They successfully cultivated tobacco. The Spanish had introduced the crop to Europe in the late 1500s after first encountering it in the Caribbean. Tobacco had been a tremendous success in the markets of Europe, making it, along with sugar, one of the most profitable **cash crops** of the New World. By 1612, the Virginia settler John Rolfe (best known for making peace with the local tribes by marrying Pocahontas, the daughter of a local chieftain) had successfully cultivated an imported strain of tobacco in Jamestown. The colonists shipped the first crop to England in 1617, and by 1620 they had delivered 40,000 pounds of the cured plant back to England. Within a few years, shipments had climbed to 1.5 million pounds. Virginia was about to boom.

## Jamestown Grows

The success of tobacco made Jamestown a more appealing place to be. But cultivating tobacco requires labor. To meet this need, early tobacco growers attempted to follow the Spanish model and force Indians to work in their fields. Such efforts were hampered by several problems: Indians objected to the concept of growing surplus crops for cash; language barriers made it difficult for English planters to explain their demands; and, chiefly, the colonists lacked the military force required to enslave Indians. In 1619, Dutch traders imported a small number of Africans to Jamestown, who performed much of the backbreaking work of establishing a town. However, due to cost considerations, the institutionalized importation of Africans was slow to progress throughout the seventeen century.

The result was the expansion of a system of labor called **indentured servitude**, in which English and Irish poor sold their labor for four to seven years to a farmer who would fund their voyage across the Atlantic. To encourage their importation, the Virginia Company offered a **head right** of 50 acres to individuals who paid their own passage, which put more property in private hands. Throughout the 1600s, almost 80 percent of the immigrants to Virginia were indentured servants, most of whom were young lower-class males. These servants had to endure several years of **"seasoning,"** a period of time during which they were exposed to the New World's microbes. Many did not survive.

 Read Rolfe's firsthand account of conditions in Jamestown at the end of its first decade.

 Read more about the economic aspects of colonial tobacco culture.

 Read a contract of indenture.

> > **Tobacco was a currency, also used to pay fines and taxes. For example, persons encouraging slave meetings were to be fined 1,000 pounds of tobacco; owners letting slaves keep horses were fined 500 pounds of tobacco; if a person wanted to become married, he had to go to the rector of his parish and pay the man so many pounds of tobacco.**

## Consequences

Jamestown continued to grow in size and in population. This expansion had three major consequences: (1) increased hostility with Indians, (2) change in leadership of the colony, and (3) the introduction of African slavery.

*Increased hostility with Indians.* Local Indian tribes were leery of the growth of Jamestown, which was rapidly encroaching on lands to which they had previously had access. After Powhatan died in 1618, his successor, Opechancanough, began planning an attack to expel the colonists. A fierce assault in 1622 resulted in the death of 357 English colonists, or one quarter of the Jamestown settlement. Angered, the settlers felt the attack gave them justification to destroy every Indian they encountered. Hostilities brewed.

*Change to royal control.* A second result of Jamestown's growth was a change in who controlled the colony. Opechancanough's attack of 1622 wiped out vital infrastructure and subsequently bankrupted the Virginia Company of London, which had had a grant for the land from the Crown. This, combined with internal conflicts within the company, led England's King James I to seize the colony and place it under royal control. Virginia thus became a **royal colony**, with a governor chosen by the king. But the colonists fought for their liberties and forced the governor to work with an assembly that would be chosen by the landholders (a democratic method carried over from the Virginia Company). This assembly was called the **House of Burgesses**. Although the king maintained control, the colony enjoyed self-government and had its own political body within which it could air grievances. America's struggle for political liberty had begun.

*Introduction of African slavery.* The third major result of Jamestown's growth was the introduction of African slavery into the colonies that would become the United States. Throughout the 1600s, indentured servitude remained the preferred source of labor, but slaves were a small, significant part of the labor force as early as 1619. However, slavery did not become legally defined or a dominant source of labor until late in the seventeenth century.

## Maryland: Founding and Politics

Following Virginia's success, in 1632 the king of England granted the region that we now call Maryland to George Calvert, a lord whose royal name was Lord Baltimore. Lord Baltimore created the first of the **proprietary colonies**, or colonies overseen by a proprietor who was allowed to control and distribute the land as he wished. The king granted Lord Baltimore the land in part to end a religious problem, because Lord Baltimore was a prominent English Catholic looking for a haven for members of his faith. The first settlers landed in Maryland in 1634, with large numbers of Catholics but an even slightly larger number of Protestants. Learning from the mistakes of Roanoke and Jamestown, the colonists under Lord Baltimore developed an economy based on the plantation model, raising corn and livestock for food and tobacco for profit.

Although Lord Baltimore and his sons at first attempted autocratic rule over Maryland, they

**royal colony**
English settlement whose governor was chosen by the king

**House of Burgesses**
Assembly of landholders chosen by other landholders, with which the royal governors were forced to work

**proprietary colony**
Colony overseen by a proprietor who was allowed to control and distribute the land as he wished

Pocahontas (c. 1595–1617) 1616 (oil on canvas), English School (17th century) / Private Collection / Peter Newark American Pictures / The Bridgeman Art Library

>> At the age of twenty-one, Pocahontas visited London, where she was presented to King James I and the court. In March 1617, she and her husband, John Rolfe, departed for home, but it soon became clear that Pocahontas would not survive the voyage. She died of pneumonia or tuberculosis and was taken ashore and buried far from her home.

quickly opted to create a legislature in the model of the House of Burgesses, which allowed the colonists a good amount of self-rule. Self-rule had its problems, though: As more Protestants came over from England and openly rebelled against being ruled by Catholics, Lord Baltimore realized that he must protect his fellow Catholics. The result was one of the major landmarks in the history of liberty: the **Toleration Act of 1649**, which granted freedom of worship to anyone who accepted the divinity of Jesus Christ. The act did not end religious disputes between the colonists, as Protestants continued to battle Catholic rule in the colony. But it did prevent legal action from being taken on account of one's faith. Christians, whether Catholic or Protestant, could not be imprisoned for their faith.

## Life on the Chesapeake

Although Maryland and Virginia prospered, mainly due to tobacco, life on the Chesapeake was generally miserable. Virginia and Maryland remained a collection of tiny villages made up of numerous small farms worked by indentured servants (Map 2.3). Three quarters of those who came over were young males, and most died during their seasoning period. Families were unstable: Marriages were fragile, childbirth risky, and growing up with both parents a rarity. In this atmosphere, the population was slow to establish churches and schools. Most homes were crudely built, with few partitions, and the quality of life could adequately be described as bleakly rustic.

 Read the Toleration Act.

# LO⁴ Founding the New England Colonies, 1620–1660

Despite the harsh reality of life in the colonies, the promise of wealth and freedom fueled England's desire for more colonies, for two main reasons.

© H. ARMSTRONG ROBERTS/ClassicStock/The Image Works

The first were financial. The English had seen the wealth that successful cultivation of a cash crop like tobacco could generate, and this furthered investors' interest in colonial development.

There were religious reasons as well. In 1559, Queen Elizabeth reestablished the Church of England as a body distinct from the Catholic Church. Nevertheless, several groups in England felt she had not gone far enough in freeing Christianity from the yoke of the Catholics. One of these groups was the **Puritans**, who wished to reform, or purify, the Church of England by removing its hierarchy, its emphasis on work as payment to God, its allowance of prayers for communal salvation, and its promotion of missions. Another dissenting group was the **Separatists**, who wished to separate completely from the Church of England because they believed it was irrevocably corrupted. Both these groups were buttressed by England's social problems, which created a large number of poor people who feared the power of an overarching institution such as the Church of England.

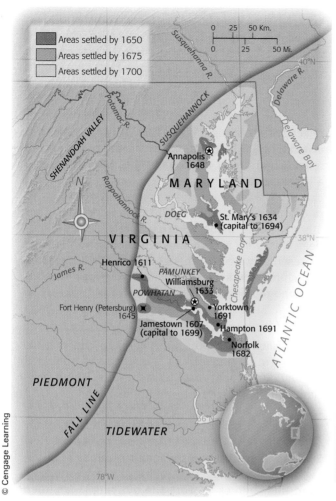

**Map 2.3. Settlement of the Chesapeake**

governing once they landed, they signed an agreement that bound each member to obey majority rule and to promise to defend one another from potential eviction. This was the **Mayflower Compact**, an agreement that set a precedent, in rhetoric if not always in reality, for democratic rule in Massachusetts. It was also grounded in the notion of Christian unity, lending a messianic fervor to the mission: In their minds, they were there because God wanted them to be there. One year later, in 1621, they secured from the Crown a patent to the land.

## Settlement

After a difficult first winter in 1620, during which half of them died or returned to England, the Separatists established farms and developed a fur trade in today's Maine. The local Wampanoag Indians viewed their presence—and all European presence—as a short time to enjoy trading with the Europeans, after which the Indians would expel the Europeans. By 1621, however, the Wampanoags had been ravaged by disease and needed help fend-

> **Mayflower**
> Ship containing Separatists who sailed from Holland and landed in Plymouth, in present-day Massachusetts, in 1620
>
> **Mayflower Compact**
> An agreement that bound each member of the Separatist group in Plymouth to obey majority rule and to promise to defend one another from potential eviction; set a precedent for democratic rule in Massachusetts

## Massachusetts

In order to escape the Church of England and worship according to their understanding of the Christian faith, a group of Separatists departed from England. First, they went to Holland; then, after receiving a land grant from the Virginia Company of London, they sailed on the ship *Mayflower* in 1620, destined for Virginia. The winter winds caught them, and they were blown off course, landing in present-day Massachusetts on a site they called Plymouth. Weakened by the crossing and fearful of storms, they decided to establish their pure Christian community there. The Plymouth colony was born.

These Separatists had no title to land this far north, however, and they knew this would be a problem if other settlers arrived with a proper patent. To remedy this problem, and to establish ground rules for

 Participate in a simulation of the founding of a new colony.

>> **Replica of the *Mayflower*.**

ing off their rivals in the interior. The Wampanoag leader thus made a decisive deal: They would allow the European visitors to stay if they would agree to ally with the Wampanoags. Once the agreement was settled, a harvest festival enjoyed by the two peoples in 1621 became the symbol for the event we today know as Thanksgiving. The settlers were bound to be permanent residents.

In 1623, the settlers divided their land among the people, rewarding those who were willing to work hard. The ingenuity and drive of these early settlers, in addition to some help from London benefactors, helped them pay off their debts to the Virginia Company by 1627, a remarkably quick repayment that encouraged others to migrate to Massachusetts. They also had stable governmental self-rule, as one of the new settlers, William Bradford, ruled with a strong, level hand and consulted numerous colonists before making decisions.

 Learn more about Plymouth.

## Expansion

Encouraged by the developments at Plymouth, English Puritans (not Separatists) sought to formalize Massachusetts as a royal colony. This was done in 1629 under the name of the Massachusetts Bay Company. Its charter was special, however, in that it did not stipulate that decisions about the colony had to be made in England, thus implying that those who lived under the charter would enjoy self-rule. The charter encouraged a larger group of Puritans, who were under increasing assault in England for their religious beliefs, to migrate.

Led by John Winthrop, 1,000 Puritans set out for their religious haven of Massachusetts; between 1630 and 1640, 25,000 more followed. Their success, supported by the cultivation of cereals and livestock, made the Puritans believe that "God hath sifted a nation"—that God had wished the Puritans to settle the Americas as the world's Promised Land. As John Winthrop told them before they arrived, "We shall be as a city upon a hill [and] the eyes of all people are upon us." Their so-called "errand into the wilderness," as it was described in a 1670 sermon, was an attempt to form an exemplary religious community, one that would inspire reform in Old England.

## Politics

Politically, the Puritans were not democrats, believing instead in a state that forced all of its inhabitants to hold a specific religious orthodoxy within an established church. This unity of belief, combined with the fact that most of the immigrants came as families, allowed the development of tightly knit communities based on a less rigid hierarchy of labor exploitation than that found in the Chesapeake.

By 1634, the people of Massachusetts began to reject the absolutism of Puritan control (it had not lasted long), although the colonists did not reject the religious nature of the colony. They also demanded a legislature, which had been approved in the royal charter. The legislature was composed of two separate houses: one an elite board of directors, the other a larger house made up of popularly elected deputies. This was a less-than-representative form of representative government, though: Only selected church members were allowed to vote for the deputies who represented them.

## Society

As Massachusetts prospered through the cultivation of grains and cereals, small towns appeared throughout present-day Massachusetts, Maine, New Hampshire, Connecticut, and Rhode Island (see Map 2.4). Small villages composed of several families were the central institution of Massachusetts. They dotted the New England coast and the central New England rivers. Large farmlands surrounded the villages, and the villagers would trudge each morning from their homes to work the outlying lands, then return to the central village at nightfall.

The town's land was parceled out to families depending on each family's size and needs. Successful families were expected to give back to their community by helping out the poor or the unlucky. Importantly, the tightly knit nature of these sparse communities and the priority placed on families meant that disease was much less of a problem than in the Virginia and Maryland colonies. Infant mortality in Massachusetts fell below that of Europe, resulting in a remarkable population boom during which the population doubled every twenty-seven years.

Even the most successful of the colonists often remained less powerful than the town's minister, however, as biblical orthodoxy was demanded of all settlers. Single men and women were required to live with a family so as not to appear promiscuous. In response to a need for religious education, the Puritans founded Harvard College in 1636. New England also was fertile ground for famous writers and poets during this period.

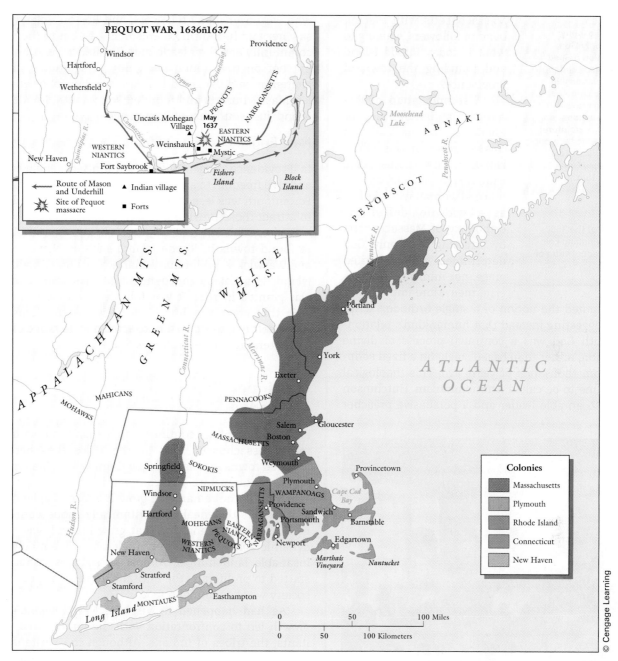

**PEQUOT WAR, 1636–1637**

Legend:
— Route of Mason and Underhill
✴ Site of Pequot massacre
▲ Indian village
■ Forts

**Colonies**
- Massachusetts
- Plymouth
- Rhode Island
- Connecticut
- New Haven

© Cengage Learning

Map 2.4. New England in the 1640s

## Rhode Island

In Massachusetts, the persistent demands of religious orthodoxy rankled some settlers, and one of the biggest troublemakers was Roger Williams, the minister of Salem, Massachusetts, who hoped for a "purer" form of religion than even the Puritan founders had institutionalized. Most importantly, he suggested that there should be a clear division between the practice of religion and the politics of state. He believed that politics necessarily impeded the soul's progress toward perfection. Williams's teachings obviously contradicted the Puritan notion of a commonwealth based on devotion to God, and Williams was expelled from Massachusetts. He left

**Antinomianism**
Theological philosophy stressing that only God, not ministers, determined who merited grace and that humankind's relationship with God was a continual process of divine revelation and not dependent on a single orthodox scripture; Anne Hutchinson led a group of Antinomian dissenters and was banished from Massachusetts for these beliefs

**Pequot War**
Bloody battles of the 1630s between New England colonists and the Pequot tribe of Indians

Massachusetts with a small band of followers, walking to what is today Rhode Island and founding the town of Providence.

A second group of dissenters was also destined for Rhode Island. The leader of this second group was a charismatic woman named Anne Hutchinson. Hutchinson, a married woman who worked as a midwife, defied the orthodoxy of Massachusetts by stressing that only God determined who merited grace, not ministers or powerful men. More importantly, she disputed the notion of a single orthodox scripture, suggesting instead that humankind's relationship with God was a continual process of divine revelation, rather than based solely on a fixed scripture from thousands of years ago. This theological turn came to be called **Antinomianism**. Hutchinson was also an able leader and a persuasive preacher

who won over many followers, and Boston's clergy saw her and her Antinomianism as a threat to their community and their leadership. To silence her, they put her on trial, found her guilty of sedition and contempt, and banished her. She and her followers left Massachusetts and founded Portsmouth, Rhode Island, just southeast of Providence.

## New England in the 1660s

In Providence, Roger Williams promised religious and civil freedom to all settlers. Hutchinson's town of Portsmouth was less tolerant, although it continued to attract those unwilling to follow Massachusetts's orthodoxy. This encouraged other religious "heretics" to found towns in Rhode Island, such as Newport and Warwick. A preliminary charter founding Rhode Island as a colony independent of Massachusetts was granted in 1644. It was followed by another in 1663 that granted political and religious freedoms to the settlers; this charter attracted a wide range of dissenters from other colonies and Europe.

## Continued Expansion and Indian Confrontation

Puritan dissenters continued to expand outward from Massachusetts, and by the 1630s they had founded towns in what are now Connecticut, Maine, and New Hampshire. The combination of these dissenters and the remarkable growth of New England meant that the ideal of puritanically pious communities was untenable. What grew instead was a dynamic agricultural society fueled by a seemingly insatiable land hunger. Almost as soon as it had started to proliferate, the Puritans' hope of a "pure" society was beginning to fade.

As had happened in Virginia, New England's growth led to confrontation with the land's inhabitants, the tribes of Indians. Although the Puritans had several Indian allies, John Winthrop had prepared New Englanders quite early for the possibility of conflict, agreeing to train all male colonists to use firearms, forbidding Indians' entering Puritan towns, and forbidding Puritans' selling firearms to Indians.

During the first years of settlement, conflict was sporadic and light, no doubt in part because European diseases had killed off as much as three quarters of the Indian population before the colonists arrived at Plymouth. In fact, the Puritans viewed this dying as the work of God, who, they felt, divinely wished to transform New England's wilderness into a shining work of the Lord. One tribe remained strong, however, and by the 1630s conflict between the

© North Wind Picture Archives/Alamy

>> **Anne Hutchinson's trial.**

New Englanders and the Pequots became inevitable. The result was a series of bloody battles collectively called the **Pequot War**, in which the supposedly pious New Englanders effectively exterminated the tribe, gruesomely killing men, women, children, and the elderly. With the Pequots now removed from power, the colonists were assured control over all the southern tribes of New England. The blood shed during the Pequot War foreshadowed the dark nature of Indian-colonist relations that was just over the horizon.

# And in the end . . .

Historians still debate the legacy that modern America inherited from this initial phase of colonial development, but some parallels are clearly visible.

 Learn more about what life was like in 1628 New England.

For instance, the freedom to worship as one pleased had its origins in both Maryland and Rhode Island during a time when that level of tolerance was unknown elsewhere in the world. There was a considerable expansion of political freedoms and self-rule that one would never have encountered in England. And economically, it was plausible and possible that one could work one's way out of one's class and become a landholding farmer. This

>> New Englanders effectively exterminated the Pequot tribe in the bloodbaths of the 1630s.

## What else was happening . . .

| | |
|---|---|
| 1300s | The Aztecs make "animal balloons" by creating inflated animals from the intestines of cats and present them to the gods as a sacrifice. |
| 1405–1433 | Chinese explorer Zheng He goes on seven expeditions to Arabia, East Africa, India, and Indonesia. |
| 1489 | The symbols + (addition) and − (subtraction) come into general use. |
| 1492 | The Spanish peso is first put into circulation. |
| 1498 | The first toothbrush is made from hog bristles in China. |
| 1540 | The first horses arrive in North America, when Spanish explorer Francisco Vasquez de Coronado, traveling through Kansas, lets about 260 of them escape. |
| 1551 | What is now the National Autonomous University of Mexico is founded. |
| 1585 | Sir John Harrington invents the first flushing toilet and puts one inside the palace of Queen Elizabeth, who deems it too loud. |

sense of economic mobility also transcended any similar experience one might encounter in Europe.

On the other hand, each of these democratic impulses had considerable limitations. In religion, every colony besides Maryland and Rhode Island had restrictions on what faith one could hold by 1660; the two exceptions existed because minority sects had begun them to find freedom from harshly restrictive colonial magistrates or the dangers of popular opinion. In politics, the right to participate in political life was limited to landholding farmers or orthodox religious adherents (depending on whether one lived in the South or the North). Economically, although there was some mobility, one had to endure tremendous hardships to realize it. Most who came seeking great wealth were promptly disappointed. Nevertheless, with the Chesapeake in the South and New England in the North, these were America's colonial beginnings. They would only grow, as we will see in the next chapter.

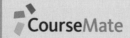
Visit the CourseMate website at www.cengagebrain.com for additional study tools and review materials for this chapter.

# Expansion *and* Its Costs, *1660–1700*

## Learning Outcomes

*After reading this chapter, you should be able to do the following:*

**LO 1** Describe the changes in European development of North America during the period from 1660 to 1700, and analyze the four distinct areas that began to emerge.

**LO 2** Discuss the English colonists' experiences up to 1700 with Native American tribes.

**LO 3** Discuss the English colonists' experiences up to 1700 with African slaves.

**LO 4** Discuss the European wars that had an impact on North America.

> ❝*No matter where one lived, daily life in the early colonies was grueling.*❞

During the hundred years between 1660 and 1763, the English colonies in North America not only scratched out a living in a harsh environment, but also grew and expanded into a sizeable power central to the British Empire. In 1660, England had only a few colonies in the land that would become the United States. They were just a tiny part of Europe's New World holdings, vastly overshadowed by colonial holdings in the Caribbean and South America. They were in New England, with its numerous small towns, and in the Chesapeake, in its large tobacco-producing farms sprawling along the region's riverbanks. In total, there were about 70,000 people of non-Indian origin living in these regions. There was not much commerce between these European settlements, and no matter where one lived, daily life in the early colonies was grueling.

One hundred years later, the landscape had changed considerably. By 1763, there were thirteen English colonies in four distinct regions: New England, the Middle Colonies, the Chesapeake, and the Southern Colonies. Each of these regions enjoyed a vibrant economy based on commerce, agriculture, and industry. Intellectually and culturally, English colonies on American soil had begun to develop a style all their own. The colonial non-native population reached 1 million by 1750, with colonists pushing toward lands in the west that would accommodate their growing numbers.

This chapter explores this development from 1660 to 1700, paying particular attention to the expansion of British America, the decline of the Indian populations along the Atlantic coast, and the subtle transition from indentured servitude to race-based slavery. It also examines how the growing North American colonies became crucial players in the "Wars for Empire" between the European powers. Chapter 4 will focus on the solidification of the four distinct colonial regions, the development of the American slavery system, and the attempts by the British Crown to reassert control over colonial America, efforts that would ultimately trigger the Revolutionary War.

## What do you think?

When the first Africans arrived in the North American colonies, they were not treated badly.

| Strongly Disagree | | | | | | Strongly Agree |
|---|---|---|---|---|---|---|
| 1 | 2 | 3 | 4 | 5 | 6 | 7 |

## LO¹ Expansion of English Holdings in North America, 1660–1700

### English Motives for Further Expansion

There were several reasons for England's further expansion. Some related to the English civil war, others to the issue of royal control, and still others to financial concerns.

**commonwealth**
A kingless republican government

**Restoration**
Period of English history when the Stuarts were restored to the throne (1660–1685)

**Navigation Acts**
Regulations that dictated where colonial producers could ship their goods, stipulated that colonists must transport their goods in English ships, and listed a group of products that colonists were permitted to sell only to England

**enumerated articles**
Goods (tobacco, sugar, cotton, indigo) listed in the Navigation Acts that colonists were permitted to sell only to England

**proprietary colonies**
Colonies owned and ruled by an individual or a private corporation, rather than by the Crown

## The English Civil War

The initial impetus for English colonial expansion came from the homeland. In 1649, revolutionaries led by Oliver Cromwell executed the English king, Charles I, igniting a civil war that lasted a decade and a half. The revolutionaries intended to create a kingless republican government called a **commonwealth**, founded on concepts like taxation only with representation, limited government, and antimonarchical beliefs—all of which would become central ideas of the American Revolution more than a century later. Because English Puritans formed the backbone of the revolutionary forces, the civil war greatly slowed Puritan migration to Massachusetts.

When he died in 1658, Cromwell's commonwealth dissolved into chaos, leaving the revolution without a leader. Conservative military men took control of the country, and, in 1660, a group of generals invited Charles II to fill his late father's position as king of England. After twelve years of civil war, the Stuarts (the family that had controlled the throne since 1603) regained power. This period of English history is called the **Restoration** (1660–1685), and it was significant for colonial North America because King Charles II used the colonies to tighten control of his initially unstable leadership and to pay off debts incurred during his fight to recover the throne.

## Tightening Royal Control

To reinforce control over the colonies (which, in general, had been sympathetic to Cromwell and which had engaged in more trade with the Dutch because of the decline in English trading), Charles II first enacted strict trade regulations. Passed by Parliament in 1651, the first of these regulations, known collectively as the **Navigation Acts**, dictated where colonial producers could ship their goods, stipulated that colonists must transport their goods in English ships, and listed a group of **enumerated articles** (tobacco, sugar, cotton, indigo) that colonists were permitted to sell only to England. The goal of these measures was to prevent the transfer of resources from England to its rivals, France and the Dutch Republic. They were also intended to curb the growth of colonial North America, which the Crown saw as a potential threat to English producers.

## Paying Off Debts

The Navigation Acts meant that the colonies could be lucrative for those who controlled them, because the acts ensured an English monopoly on the first sale of all colonial goods. Thus, to pay off his debts, Charles II offered land in the New World to his supporters, where they could establish colonies called **proprietary colonies**, which were colonies owned and ruled by an individual or a private corporation, rather than by the Crown. If the proprietors ruled them successfully, they could become extremely wealthy.

## The Creation of Colonies during and after the Restoration

Proprietary colonies were the chief means of colonial expansion between 1660 and 1700, and it was through them that the large gap of land unsettled by Europeans between Massachusetts and Virginia, as well as the lands between Virginia and Florida, were colonized (Map 3.1). During the Restoration, friends of Charles II created five proprietary colonies: Carolina (present-day North and South Carolina), New York, Pennsylvania, and East Jersey and West Jersey (later joined to become New Jersey). The proprietary colony of Georgia was founded after the Restoration. The proprietors of these colonies were free to establish governments as they wished, so long as their laws did not contradict those of England. Given this freedom, each of the proprietary colonies developed quite differently from one another. The expansion of colonial America had begun.

### Carolina

Three years after returning to his father's throne, Charles II granted the vast territory of Carolina to a group of eight noblemen who had supported him during the commonwealth. According to the grant, the Carolinas extended from Virginia south to the northern tip of today's Florida, and west all the way to the

>> **Tobacco ships in the James River, Virginia Colony, 1600s.**

Map 3.1. English Settlement between 1660 and 1700

Pacific Ocean. The eight proprietors set up elaborate rules (in a constitution drafted by the philosopher John Locke) and encouraged the establishment of large plantations. Two-fifths of each county was to be set aside for the proprietors, thus ensuring the continued wealth of the founders.

*The failure of proprietorship.* Things did not turn out as Carolina's proprietors had hoped. Basically, they misunderstood that the American context of abundant land would not accommodate the hierarchical society of England with its noble titles and

haughty proprietors. Many of the earliest settlers of Carolina came from the Caribbean rather than England, because a temporary dip in sugar prices made the Caribbean islands less appealing. These settlers were accustomed to self-rule, not the hierarchical society the proprietors intended to emulate. They also brought slaves with them, meaning that, from its earliest history, Carolina was powered by small-scale entrepreneurs and slave laborers. It later had the distinction of being America's first colony dependent on slave labor. Charles Town (later Charleston) was founded in 1670 after the decimation of Indian tribes in the area, but Carolina was considered highly undesirable; its weather was hot and humid, and tobacco did not thrive in the colony's soil. Everything was going badly.

*Rice.* The colony's fortunes reversed in 1693, when Carolinians discovered from their African slaves that rice could be grown easily in the fertile soil. Rice culture spread rapidly, making Carolina lucrative and suddenly creating an urgent need for more labor. This labor crunch meant that by 1720 the southern part of the colony, where the soil was most fertile, was populated by twice as many slaves as European freemen or indentured servants. Most of these slaves had been imported from Barbados, in the West Indies, which had become a key marketplace for the worldwide slave trade. The large number of slaves in Carolina made Charlestown the center of North America's early slave trade, which would begin to prosper in the 1680s and 1690s.

*Life in Carolina.* Few Europeans lived in the southern part of Carolina because life there was so miserable. Diseases spread rapidly, and population growth remained low. Despite the proprietors'

> *Carolina had the distinction of being America's first colony dependent on slave labor.*

hopes for a harmonious existence with the Indians, before rice made Carolina lucrative its principal export was captured Indian slaves who were sold in New England and the West Indies. This meant continued warfare with Indian tribes—yet another reason to avoid the southern part of Carolina. Within the first three decades of the colony's founding, the two largest tribes on the Carolina coast were largely extinct.

In the northern part of the colony there were fewer diseases and lower humidity, which led to the development of a different kind of society. Tobacco farmers from Virginia developed small farms and advocated self-rule there. Although slavery existed, it never became the main labor supply. By 1698, the differences between the south and the north had become so marked that the proprietors chose to divide the colonies in two; they became South Carolina and North Carolina in 1712.

## New York

New York was also a proprietary colony, but from the beginning it was polyglot and diverse and developed much differently than Carolina did.

© The Image Works Archives

>> A Carolina rice field.

**The New York Dutch.** New York began as a Dutch colony, founded long before the Restoration in 1624, when the Dutch claimed New Jersey and New York. The Dutch based their claims on the voyage of

 Take a virtual tour of New Netherland.

Henry Hudson in 1609 and Peter Minuit's purchase of the island of Manhattan for a small amount of trinkets and jewelry. They called their territory New Netherland. This was a bold move because the English were

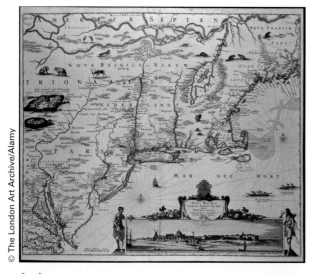
© The London Art Archive/Alamy

>> Map of New Netherland, by N. J. Visscher, 1650–1651, based on a manuscript map compiled by Adriaen van der Donck in 1648.

developing colonies south of New York in Virginia and north of it in New England.

During the early 1600s, the Dutch had moderate success trading furs with the Iroquois. But their biggest success lay in the port town of New Amsterdam (later New York City). There, a multicultural group of traders gathered to trade and barter near the Atlantic. None was more impressive than Adriaen van der Donck, a Dutch lawyer who became an eager advocate for and political leader of New Amsterdam and the New World more generally. He created maps, wrote travelogues, and paid to have colonists come to Manhattan. By 1660, the population of New Amsterdam reached 10,000.

**The English take over.** Competition over commerce led to bitter relations between the English and Dutch, and three small "Anglo-Dutch" wars broke out between the two nations, fought mostly in the English Channel, between 1652 and 1675. In 1664, England's Charles II wrested New Amsterdam from the Dutch and granted it to his brother, the Duke of York. Renaming the colony New York, the duke ruled it severely and autocratically for two decades. But his attempts to restrict the rights of New Yorkers were resisted by the diverse mix of settlers and traders, who fought to keep New York free for commerce and expression. No matter who was in charge, though, New York did allow slavery. By 1703, 42 percent of New York's households had slaves, a percentage that was the second highest of any North American city at the time, bested only by Charleston, South Carolina.

## Pennsylvania

Outdoing even New York's polyglot character, William Penn established the most diverse of the proprietary colonies. Penn was named after his father, a royal courtier to whom the king had become indebted because of gambling losses. When the elder Penn died, the younger William Penn inherited claim to the debt. And when Charles II began imprisoning religious minorities in the 1670s, Penn, a newly converted Quaker, traded the debt for a North American colony.

*Quakers.* The **Quakers** were Protestants who believed that God's will was directly transmitted to people through "the inner light" of divine knowledge that a person possesses within his or her being. This belief was in opposition to the Protestant mainstream, which made the Bible the center of the religious experience. The Quakers also rejected the concepts of Original Sin and predestination, further alienating them from the Protestant core.

In the 1600s, there were also social differences between Quakers and Protestants. Quaker meetings employed no professional ministers (whom they derisively called "hireling ministers"), relying instead on laypeople (nonordained faith-community members). Quakers, sometimes called the Society of Friends, rejected class distinctions as well, which prevented them from deferring to social superiors. Furthermore, the Quakers argued that any believer was as capable as any other of transmitting the truth about God's will, including women, a policy that threatened traditional Christian distinctions between the sexes. In an era of religious intolerance and political instability, the Quakers were distrusted and even outlawed.

*Fleeing England.* In 1674, Penn, along with ten other Quakers, purchased the proprietary rights to West Jersey. Penn drafted an egalitarian constitution for the colony that protected the right of trial by jury, prohibited capital punishment, allowed almost all free males the right to vote, and sought to ensure good relations with the Indians. His

>> William Penn meeting with Native Americans on the site of the city of Philadelphia.

constitution required settlers to purchase any land taken from Indian inhabitants and extended the right of trial by jury to Indians (with the stipulation that juries in the trial of an Indian would be half Indian, half English).

Although many considered such policies radical, Penn enjoyed good relations with both Charles II and the Duke of York. In 1681, Charles granted him Pennsylvania ("Penn's wood")—which he had named after Penn's father. The sale of "Penn's wood" relieved the king of two things: his gambling debt to Penn's father and the Quakers. In 1682, the Duke of York sold Penn three additional counties from his own vast New World landholdings. In time, these counties would become Delaware.

*Creating Pennsylvania.* Recruiting settlers was the key to creating

> **"** Colonies then are the Seeds of Nations begun and nourished by the care of wise and populous Countries. **"**
> —*William Penn*

Penn's idyllic vision. Penn's promotion of the colony rested on two factors: religious freedom and a liberal land policy that allowed easy access to land. Penn dispatched agents throughout Europe to advertise the colony, and the response was overwhelming. In 1682, the population was about 1,000; two years later, it had grown to 4,000; by the end of the 1680s it had risen to 12,000. Although not yet as large as the Massachusetts Bay colony, Pennsylvania's population continued to grow. Penn was also successful in promoting peaceful relations with the Indians; Indian refugees migrated to Pennsylvania from other lands where they had faced violence from colonists.

 Read Penn's "Some Account of the Province of Pennsylvania."

Penn did permit slavery. He owned slaves personally and allowed other colonists to do the same. Like most northern slaves, slaves in Pennsylvania were Africans used primarily as domestic workers. Although some Quakers spoke out publicly against slavery as early as 1688, slavery lasted in Pennsylvania until the 1780s.

## New Jersey

The Duke of York granted the southern portion of his colony to two friends, one of whom sold his portion to a group of Quakers. This led to the creation of East Jersey, which bordered New York, and West Jersey, which bordered Pennsylvania. Although they retained certain differences, by 1702 both areas had developed substantially, earning a single royal charter. To attract settlers, the proprietors of New Jersey promised both generous land grants and a limited freedom of religion. For these reasons, Puritan New Englanders and Dutch New Yorkers migrated there, prompting significant growth by 1726. The two colonies were united and renamed New Jersey.

## Georgia

Georgia was founded after the Restoration as a proprietary colony. The chief motives for its settlement were to create a buffer between Spanish Florida and the Carolinas, as well as a haven for English debtors and persecuted English Protestants, a place where they could live comfortably. James Oglethorpe, the utopian lead proprietor, led the first settlers to Savannah in 1733. It was his vision, as an opponent of Britain's policy of imprisoning those who could not pay their debts, that fashioned Georgia as a colony where the "worthy poor" could start anew.

The colony grew slowly because the charter stipulated that no one could own enough land to develop a large-scale plantation. Furthermore, slavery was initially prohibited because of Oglethorpe's vision for the colony and because the Spanish in Florida had promised freedom to any slave who would serve in their military, which would have meant a collection of slaves eager and able to desert Georgia for Florida. It was only in the 1750s that the Crown, to whom the proprietors had returned the charter, succumbed to local demands from English planters and allowed slavery.

**Pueblo Revolt**
An uprising of several villages spanning several hundred miles across the New Mexican landscape in 1680, led by the shaman Popé

 Read the story of the semi-utopian James Oglethorpe and Savannah.

## Where Were the Spanish?

As the English planted deeper roots in colonial North America, the Spanish were pulling their roots out. Their main limitation was an unwillingness to develop colonial settlements, preferring instead to bring home quick profits after a brief period of having conquered and controlled resource-rich lands. They established some settlements, like those founded by Catholic friars eager to convert Indians, although these permanent settlements frequently conflicted with local Indian tribes and persuaded Spain that permanent settlement was not worth the investment. Their colonial conflicts thus tended to be about labor relations and faith, rather than land, which was paramount with the English.

## New Mexico

In New Mexico, for example, the Pueblo people rejected the forced piety of the Spanish Catholic friars, and in a dramatic 1680 rebellion, a shaman named Popé led the **Pueblo Revolt**—an uprising of several villages spanning several hundred miles across the New Mexican landscape. The villagers burned Spanish farms, destroyed churches, and killed half the friars. Reeling from the revolt, the Spanish left the Southwest for more than a decade. They returned in the 1690s with a more tolerant outlook, and the Pueblo people welcomed them only because they felt they needed European weaponry to fight their tribal enemies.

 Read a letter written by the governor of New Mexico during the Pueblo Revolt.

## Florida

The Spanish faced similar resentments in Florida. But here the resentments were compounded by the proximity of colonial competitors, the English and the French. When England and France went to war in the War of Spanish Succession in 1701, British Carolinians attacked Spanish Florida (the British feared that Spain and France were becoming too closely allied). The result was the devastation of all Spanish strongholds in Florida except St. Augustine. And, because English colonists outnumbered Spanish settlers, the Spanish were slow to resettle Florida. By 1700, the Spanish presence in the future United States was limited to a few Catholic missions and a few increasingly smaller settlements.

> **❝I received information that a plot for a general uprising of the Christian Indians was being formed and was spreading rapidly. This was wholly contrary to the existing peace and tranquillity in this miserable kingdom, not only among the Spaniards and natives, but even on the part of the heathen enemy, for it had been a long time since they had done us any considerable damage.❞**
>
> —*Don Antonio de Otermin, governor of New Mexico during the Pueblo Revolt*

 Read more about the origins of Florida.

## Conclusion

Between 1660 and 1700, Britain had crafted the beginnings of a large colonial empire in North America. It had seeded permanent colonies and established itself as the European nation claiming the biggest stake to the land, ahead of the Dutch, French, and Spanish, whose primary colonial interests lay elsewhere. These English colonies were not wholly stable yet, nor were they unified. Furthermore, each colony comprised a mix of people, including Europeans from different countries, Indians from many tribes, and, increasingly, slaves.

## LO² Indians

As Britain's colonial holdings expanded into the American interior, they encroached on lands that were already inhabited. The initial encounters between Europeans and the tribes of Native America had mixed outcomes. In their search for gold and other riches in the 1500s, the Spanish annihi-

lated many tribes with violence and disease. The French, without a large settled presence in the New World, had mostly positive trade arrangements with the tribes near Quebec. The English had at first cautiously engaged the Indian tribes for trade and protection, but as their settlements expanded, suspicion and enmity between the two groups increased. In Jamestown, for instance, relations between the Powhatan Confederacy and the first settlers were generally nonviolent until the expansion of Jamestown provoked Powhatan's successor, Opechancanough, to attack. In New England, the Pequot War symbolized the violent direction that relations were taking.

These first encounters had elements of both trust and suspicion, but the situation worsened over time. By the beginning of the 1700s, it had become clear that the two peoples would not share the New World. Most English colonists believed that any Indian who stood in their path to settlement could be exterminated. Indians responded in kind to this threat. Competition for land was the key motive. Violence, disease, and the market economy were the principal means of effecting change.

### What Went Wrong?

There were several reasons why the situation deteriorated so drastically after 1660 (see "The reasons why . . ." box).

### The Middle Ground

Although the decimation of Native America is the most significant story of Euro-Indian relations, positive interactions occurred during the colonial era as well, usually over trade. In this "middle ground," where trading took place, the two groups operated as equals. Indians and Europeans shared rituals, such as tea and rum drinking, gift giving, and pipe

Read more about the "middle ground" at Chicago.

smoking. This middle ground was noticeable whenever colonists encountered large groups of Indians, meaning that the groups meeting were close to equal in number, and it allowed contact that benefited both Indians and colonists. These middle grounds existed most prominently around the Great Lakes and the upper Mississippi River basin.

>> In an area historians have called "the middle ground," Indians and Europeans shared rituals, such as tea and rum drinking, gift giving, and pipe smoking.

**Beaver Wars**
Intertribal battles in the 1600s in which the Iroquois forced the Hurons out of the Northeast

## Colonial Land Lust, Colonial Democracy

But the central story of Indian relations with the colonists is one of violence. In the first half of the 1600s, most outbreaks of violence between English colonists and Indians were short-lived. The deadlier conflicts occurred between Indian tribes seeking to win the European trade. The bloodiest of these intertribal battles were the **Beaver Wars** (1640–1680s), in which the Iroquois, seeking beaver pelts to trade with the French, forced the Hurons and their supporters out of the Northeast altogether, leaving the Iroquois Confederacy as the single most significant collection of tribes between northern Canada, southern Virginia, and the Mississippi River. They decimated their competition and forced the survivors to flee across the Mississippi River.

By the 1670s, enough English settlers had moved to the colonies that colonists and Indians could engage in prolonged wars. These wars established a pattern of violence that would last for the duration of contact between the two groups. Although highlighted by several large-scale battles, conflict between Indians and North American colonists was continual, making every outing a potentially perilous adventure. Two events of the 1670s,

{ *The reasons why . . .* }

There were four general reasons why relations between British colonists and the various Indians they came into contact with dissolved into violence:

**Land lust.** Land lust of the English colonists grew as the initial colonies succeeded, prompting perpetual incursions on lands occupied by Indians.

**Religion.** Religious differences between the two groups prevented each group from having a common understanding of the other and led to each one seeing demons and devils in the other.

**Culture.** Cultural differences about land use, gender roles, and language created further misunderstandings and resentments.

**European alignments.** Perhaps most important, the European powers were viciously protective of their lucrative New World holdings. Throughout the 1700s the Europeans fought several wars to defend them, and the battleground of this "great war for empire" (as historians have called these wars) was often the New World, forcing colonists and Indians to take sides. In the short term, Indians could profit from the situation by selling their support to one European power or the other. But as England pursued increasing world dominion, the tribes of Native America could no longer play one side off the other, and England (and eventually the United States) could subject the Indians to their will, at times violently.

**Metacom's War**
First large-scale conflict between colonists and Native Americans, waged in Plymouth, Massachusetts Bay, Rhode Island, and Connecticut (1675–1676)

**King Philip's War**
British colonists' name for Metacom's War, because they referred to Wampanoag leader Metacom as King Philip

however, greatly influenced colonist–Indian relations: Metacom's War and Bacon's Rebellion.

## Metacom's War (King Philip's War), 1675–1676

The first large-scale conflict was **Metacom's War** (sometimes called "**King Philip's War**"), which broke out in Plymouth, Massachusetts, in 1675. "King Philip" was the name the English gave to Metacom, the son of the Wampanoag chief, Massasoit. Massasoit had befriended the Plymouth settlers in the 1620s (his generosity thus giving Americans the model for today's Thanksgiving), but by the 1670s, the English settlement in Massachusetts had grown to 50,000. The New Englanders had expanded onto Indian territories and forcibly subjected the Wampanoags

and other tribes to English law. The settler's cattle trampled native cornfields, demonstrating the differences in concepts of land use between the two peoples and the arrogance of some New Englanders, who felt God had granted them the land to cultivate. The younger generation of Indians had had enough.

The result was war. Many tribes joined Metacom in battling the settlers, although several tribes that had converted to Christianity sided with the English. Over a period of fourteen months in 1675 and 1676, Metacom and his followers attacked fifty-two of the ninety Puritan towns, destroying thirteen of them completely. They attacked towns in four colonies: Plymouth, Massachusetts Bay, Rhode Island, and Connecticut (Map 3.2). Before the tide of battle had turned, Metacom's forces had pushed the area of English colonization almost back to the coast. The story of Mary Rowlandson, a young New England settler, dates from King Philip's War. Metacom's forces kidnapped her and held her hostage for three months before ransoming her back to her family; she wrote a wildly popular account of her tribula-

© North Wind Picture Archives

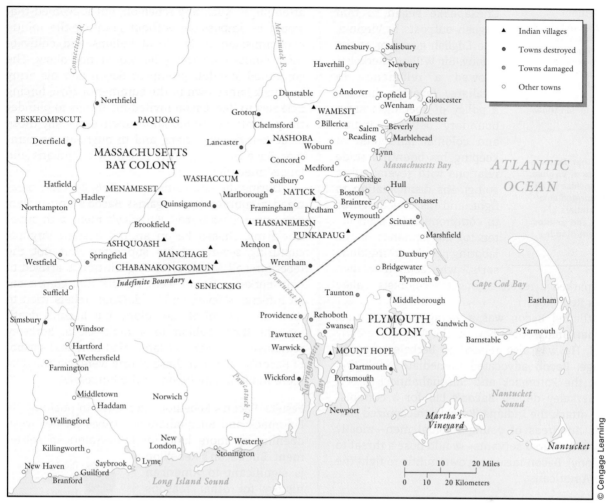

Map 3.2. New England During Metacom's War, 1675–1676

tions, giving many colonists a firsthand look at Indian life.

The tide of war turned against the Indians in 1676. The English retaliated against them for Metacom's assaults, and the colonists' most significant victory came after a New England boy escaped captivity, returned home, and then led the colonists to the exact location of the tribes. The fighting ended in 1676 when Metacom fell in battle at the hands of an Indian who was acting as a scout for the colonists. The colonists placed Metacom's head on a stake and let it stand in Plymouth town square for twenty-five years.

 Read Mary Rowlandson's account of her capture.

New England's Indians paid a heavy price for their resistance. Algonquian communities were decimated from Narragansett Bay to the Connecticut River Valley. Many died from disease and starva-

tion, in addition to the thousands who were killed in battle. Both sides suffered: Metacom's War killed one in ten of New England's colonists. It also led to a further decline of Puritan leadership, as many colonists viewed the war as a sign of God's displeasure. More obviously, the war exposed a ferocious undercurrent of racism among the English colonists, many of whom were eager to attack and kill any Indian. Metacom's War also showed an early, if uneven, willingness of Indian tribes to unite to fight colonists.

## Bacon's Rebellion, 1676–1677

The impact of Metacom's War was felt beyond New England. Metacom's message of pan-Indian resistance to English settlement spread (aided by the fact that all Indians faced the same frustrations as Metacom had), and in 1676 warriors from the Potomack and Susquahannock tribes of the

Chesapeake began to raid English outposts in Virginia. The English governor of the colony, Sir William Berkeley, showed a reluctance to retaliate, favoring instead a policy of keeping a strict boundary between Indian and colonial land (and of keeping his bountiful trade relations with several tribes going). His disinclination to fight, and his unwillingness to compromise (or even listen to) the demands of the laboring people, or "middling sorts," who aspired to own land, sparked a revolt among the colonists, called **Bacon's Rebellion.**

Nathaniel Bacon was a young, well-educated, and charismatic member of the Virginia colony council. He was also related to Berkeley through marriage. Bacon advocated immediate retaliation against the Potomack and Susquahannock tribes. After Berkeley denied Bacon's bid for a commission to attack the Indians (Berkeley recognized that arming hundreds of young colonial men—mostly former indentured servants—would pose a threat to the colony), Bacon raised his own militia to fight the Native Americans.

*Bacon's laws.* Bacon's militia quickly vanquished the Indians in the area. Fearful of where Bacon might go next, the governor dispatched three hundred militiamen to stop him. Bacon was captured and released, and then continued to seek a commission to attack the tribes. Berkeley resisted. A series of standoffs ensued, with Bacon variously being imprisoned or on the run. In the process, Berkeley became acutely aware of Bacon's wild popularity among the settlers and, to quell the potential uprising, passed a series of laws that democratized the politics of Virginia. Commonly called **Bacon's Laws**, the new rules granted the franchise to all freemen, inaugurated elections of the members of the legislature (rather than offering legislators lifetime appointments), and granted greater representation in taxation. In sum, Bacon's Laws reduced the influence of the ruling elite in Virginia, setting a precedent for free white man's democracy. This was a meaningful step in the expansion of colonial liberty.

It was also an attempt to win back some of the popularity Bacon had attracted. After the passage of Bacon's Laws, Berkeley persisted in his attempts to quell any rebellion, but it seemed that would be impossible without granting the militia a commission to kill local Indians and cultivate their lands—something he would not allow. The continued standoff prompted Bacon and his army to attack Jamestown in the summer of 1676, forcing Berkeley to flee. Bacon invited his troops to plunder the plantations around Jamestown, especially those of Berkeley's supporters, and throughout the summer, Bacon's ragtag army fought with Indians and Englishmen alike.

During the late summer of 1676, Berkeley organized a counterattack against Bacon's anti-Indian, anti-upper-class forces. Berkeley's men, with superior arms, chased Bacon around eastern Virginia, capturing several of his supporters but not the rebel himself. When 1,100 English troops arrived to help Berkeley, Bacon went on the run, contracted an infectious fever, and died. Other rebels tried to maintain control of the colony, but Bacon's death brought the rebellion to a rapid close. Berkeley remained in power and later tried to repeal several of Bacon's Laws, but these efforts were overruled by more moderate members of the Burgesses.

*Results.* Bacon's Rebellion succeeded in pushing the Potomack and Susquahannock tribes farther west, opening up more land for Euro-American settlement. But Bacon's Rebellion is significant to American history for other reasons as well (see "The reasons why . . ." box).

Read Governor Berkeley on Bacon's Rebellion.

# LO³ The Expansion of American Slavery

Europe's slave trade with Africa began in the 1400s and increased in the 1500s and 1600s as a means of relieving a labor shortage in the areas surrounding the Mediterranean. Labor needs arose in the New World during the late 1500s and 1600s after Europeans realized that sugar could be grown easily in the West Indies and South America. (Europeans had discovered sugar in their travels during the Crusades, and it became so popular and expensive in Europe that it was among the first items Columbus transported from the New World, in his second voyage of 1493.) Cultivating sugar is incredibly labor intensive, though, and once Europeans had exhausted and exterminated native populations in the West Indies and South America, their search for labor led them to African slaves. This was made

**Bacon's Rebellion is significant to American history for at least three reasons:**

**Land lust.** Bacon's Rebellion reflected the land lust of the growing colonial population.

**Demonstrable violence.** It demonstrated that the settlers were willing to use violent means to gain that land, usually against Indians, but sometimes against the English gentry.

**Rise of slavery.** It made wealthy colonists less willing to import indentured servants, who, as the rebellion proved, would do nearly anything to get land once they were freed from their condition of servitude. This was one factor that led to a rise in the importation of African slaves. It also initiated an upper-class proclamation of the similarity of all men perceived to be white; by importing more slaves and creating a racially divided population, the upper classes of Virginia sought to limit class conflict by prioritizing racial differences. This was a turning point in the history of North American race relations that buttressed a trend toward the expansion of the American slave system and the decline of indentured servitude.

---

easier by the fact that the established trade routes between Europe and Africa had made Africans eager for European goods, especially guns. Thus, in a mutually beneficial trade system, beginning in the early 1600s West African kingdoms competed with one another to supply slaves to the Europeans in return for European goods.

But what began so easily was not so easily stopped. As the Atlantic slave trade grew, West African kingdoms grew leery of supplying Europeans with more slaves because they were fearful of the overwhelming demand. Some Europeans resorted to kidnapping slaves from West African villages.

## Why the Transition from Indentured Servitude to Slavery?

In the early 1600s, the North American colonies relied mainly on European (and some African) indentured servants for labor. At least 70 percent of those in the Chesapeake came as indentured servants from England. By the 1680s, however, African slaves had begun to replace indentured servants as the colonists' preferred labor source, and by the early 1700s, there were few indentured servants in the colonial labor pool.

Despite the variety of benefits of indentured servitude (the ability of landowner and laborer to communicate easily, similarities in culture and religion between the two), it posed several problems in North America. First, many servants ran away once they landed in the New World, and, as Europeans, once they escaped they blended in easily. Second, most of those who did remain confronted the wet climate of the Chesapeake, which was so unhealthy that many servants died shortly after arriving in America.

Those who survived were habitually sick and unable to work. And third, indentured servants also earned their freedom once their term of indenture (usually seven years) expired. At that point, some of them acquired land and began competing with their former masters, a situation that most masters did not welcome, as proved by Bacon's Rebellion. Finally, as England's economy improved, fewer people signed up to become indentured servants in the first place.

By the 1680s, the practice of indentured servitude diminished rapidly. In need of labor, North American colonists tapped into the slave trade system that had developed during the 1600s.

## Africans Transition from Servants to Slaves

In 1619, when the first Africans arrived in Virginia, they were treated like indentured servants, which meant not generously, but not inhumanely either. They lived alongside European colonists in their landowner's house, and some earned their freedom after their term of service. But as the number of Africans in the Chesapeake increased during the 1680s, European and Euro-American colonists began to craft a slave-based society, developing laws that would make slavery an enduring, race-dependent institution.

By the late 1630s, colonists had already begun to differentiate between indentured servants and slaves, but the first major law specifically regarding slavery emerged in Virginia in 1662. It stipulated that the condition of the mother determined the condition of the child; if a mother was a slave from Africa—or had African heritage—her child was to be a slave as well. This allowed male slaveholders to exploit African American females and, at the same time, produce new slaves.

In 1664, Maryland enacted an "anti-amalgamation" law, which outlawed interracial sex and marriage, rendering any relationship between a male colonist and a female slave illegal, and any relationship between an African American male slave and a female colonist intolerable. Virginia followed suit, declaring in 1691 that any colonist who married a "Negro, mulatto, or Indian" would be banished from the colony. In 1682, Virginia passed a law that used specific racial differences to differentiate between servants and slaves, thus ensuring that African Americans and Euro-Americans were treated differently by the law. Thus, even before the rapid expansion of slavery in the 1680s and 1690s, colonial laws differentiated people by strict racial classifications. These differences grew markedly after slaves were brought to

the American colonies in greater numbers throughout the 1700s.

## Slave Codes

Slowly race became the central factor determining who was perceived as a freeman worthy of "natural rights" and who was not. In 1705, Virginia codified the racial orientation of the new system of labor with a series of **slave codes**. These codes meant that, in most areas, especially in the Southern Colonies and the Chesapeake, it became impossible for an African American to live as a free person. The codes declared that all "Negro, mulatto, and Indian" servants brought into the region were slaves, or "real estate." This guaranteed slaveholders *permanent* ownership of the black bondspeople they purchased. It also allowed masters to punish their property, and, because no one would deliberately destroy his own property, Virginia lawmakers said there was no need to enact laws prohibiting slaveholders from

## { *Some Slave Codes . . .* }

INTRODUCTION OF SLAVERY.

© North Wind Picture Archives/Alamy

### Virginia, 1639
**Act X**. All persons except Negroes are to be provided with arms and ammunitions or be fined at the pleasure of the governor and council.

### Maryland, 1664
That whatsoever free-born [English] woman shall intermarry with any slave . . . shall serve the master of such slave during the life of her husband; and that all the issue of such free-born women, so married shall be slaves as their fathers were.

### Virginia, 1667
**Act III**. Whereas some doubts have arisen whether children that are slaves by birth . . . should by virtue of their baptism be made free, it is enacted that baptism does not alter the condition to the person as to his bondage or freedom; masters freed from this doubt may more carefully propagate Christianity by permitting slaves to be admitted to that sacrament.

### Virginia, 1682
**Act I**. It is enacted that all servants . . . which [sic] shall be imported into this country either by sea or by land, whether Negroes, Moors [Muslim North Africans], mulattoes, or Indians who and whose parentage and native countries are not Christian at the time of their first purchase by some Christian . . . and all Indians, which shall be sold by our neighboring Indians, or any other trafficking with us for slaves, are hereby adjudged, deemed, and taken to be slaves to all intents and purposes any law, usage, or custom to the contrary notwithstanding.

killing their slaves. The codes stated that slaves needed written permission to leave their plantation, would receive severe physical punishments for any wrongdoing, and no longer had any legal standing. Virginia's slave codes served as a model for other states to emulate, which they readily did. English colonists were constructing a legalistic slave society based entirely on perceived racial distinctions.

# LO⁴ Wars for Empire

Propelled by the desires of landless young men and attracted by the potential profits of a slave-based economy, the English colonists pushed west into North America. There, they ran into an obstacle other than Indians: the French. Beginning in the late 1600s, the French recognized the rich potential of North America and fortified their posts from the Great Lakes to New Orleans, traveling down the Mississippi River and usually developing friendly relations with Indian tribes along the way, especially the Algonquians. Their only significant settlements, however, were at Quebec and New Orleans. Nevertheless, the increased French presence brought them into conflict with the English. When France and England had disputes in Europe, their battles had New World ramifications. Beginning in the late 1600s, European wars had North American fronts as well as European ones.

## King William's War and Queen Anne's War, 1689–1713

The first of these carryover battles lasted from 1689 to 1697, and its most significant theaters were in Europe and the Caribbean. But it also reached the North American mainland, where it was called **King William's War**. King William's War began when New York's governor, Thomas Dongan, goaded the Iroquois into attacking tribes that were friendly with France. The French fought back by attacking the Iroquois and, eventually, English colonists in northern New England and New York. England in turn attacked various French outposts, with minimal success. The New World front had stalemated without significant gains for either side.

Nevertheless, King William's War was influential for three reasons. First, it prompted the French to fortify their New World position, creating a stronghold of settlers for the first time. Second, it demonstrated the ways Europeans manipulated Indians (and vice versa) in efforts to conquer the land. And third, in its wake, the Iroquois established better relations with the French and agreed to remain neutral in future conflicts.

The second English-French war started four years later, when the French king angled to put his grandson on the newly vacant Spanish throne. The other European powers rejected this power play and attacked France. This was the War of the Spanish Succession, called **Queen Anne's War** in the New World. Twelve years of battle between the Spanish in Florida, the French in the North American interior, the English along the coast, and the various Indian tribes friendly to one group or another finally ended with an English victory.

Queen Anne's War was significant for two reasons. First, success gave the English a base on the Hudson Bay, further promoting their expansion westward, into the interior of America. Second, it ushered in a period of relative peace in Europe, which allowed France and England to fortify their positions in the New World, so that when later battles came, both sides were better entrenched. Over time, the increasing economic and social strength of English colonies threatened the French, who feared that the alliances they had built with the Indians would falter.

## Salem Witchcraft Trials

It should also be noted that historians have recently attributed the Salem witch trials to fears triggered by the Indian Wars. Because these witch trials were prosecuted during Queen Anne's War, they suggest how the European Wars for Empire were felt in even the smallest of New World hamlets.

Trouble began in 1692 when two girls were playing with an older female slave who taught the girls African voodoo tales. The girls later became seized with fits, and soon other girls in Salem were behaving strangely as well. Searching for an explanation, the town's leaders accused the female slave and two other women of practicing witchcraft. Soon, the village elders accused several others of being witches, too. Once started, accusations flew wildly.

Before long it became apparent that divisions relating to social class, gender, commercial profession, and religiosity determined who was accused and who was not, as the poor were accused more readily than the wealthy, as were those who had

**King William's War**
Battles between the Iroquois, French, and English colonists (1689–1697)

**Queen Anne's War**
The New World name for the War of the Spanish Succession; twelve years of battle between the Spanish in Florida, the French in the North American interior, the English along the coast, and various Indian tribes

fallen away from the church. Recent research demonstrates that unmarried women of property were prominent targets as well. Before the accusations slowed, twenty people had been executed. The strangeness of the Salem witchcraft episode reveals the anxiety of the time, sparked mostly by wars with Indians. It also reflects the widespread willingness to believe in witches, spirits, and ghosts, a prominent feature of what one historian has called the colonial "worlds of wonder."

## And in the end . . .

By 1700, then, the North American colonies had developed into established, but not yet prospering, outliers in Britain's colonial web. They were stably situated along the Atlantic seaboard, and it seemed inevitable that they would continue to settle farther into the interior of the continent. It was also clear

| What else was happening . . . | |
|---|---|
| 17th century | The average British colonial woman in America gives birth to thirteen children. |
| 1655 | The Dutch of New Amsterdam use lotteries to raise money for the poor. |
| 1666 | The Great Fire destroys three-fourths of London, killing only sixteen and helping halt the spread of the bubonic plague. |
| 1670 | Paris café starts serving ice cream. |
| 1686 | Christian Gabriel Fahrenheit invents the thermometer. |
| 1688 | The start of the Japanese Edo Renaissance, a cultural flowering that saw the development of Kabuki theater. |

that Europeans (and especially the English) would not blend into the lands of Native America or mix with its inhabitants, but would seek dominion over the areas they controlled. Also by 1700, the colonists had established slavery as the primary system of labor in the New World. From these roots, a system of racialized slavery would expand on American soil.

These trends would only continue from 1700 to 1763 as the colonies developed economically and socially. The four distinct regions became stronger and more established, so that when later "Wars for Empire" broke out, the North American colonists could ponder independence. But in 1700 those thoughts were still years away.

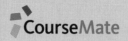 Visit the CourseMate website at www.cengagebrain.com for additional study tools and review materials for this chapter.

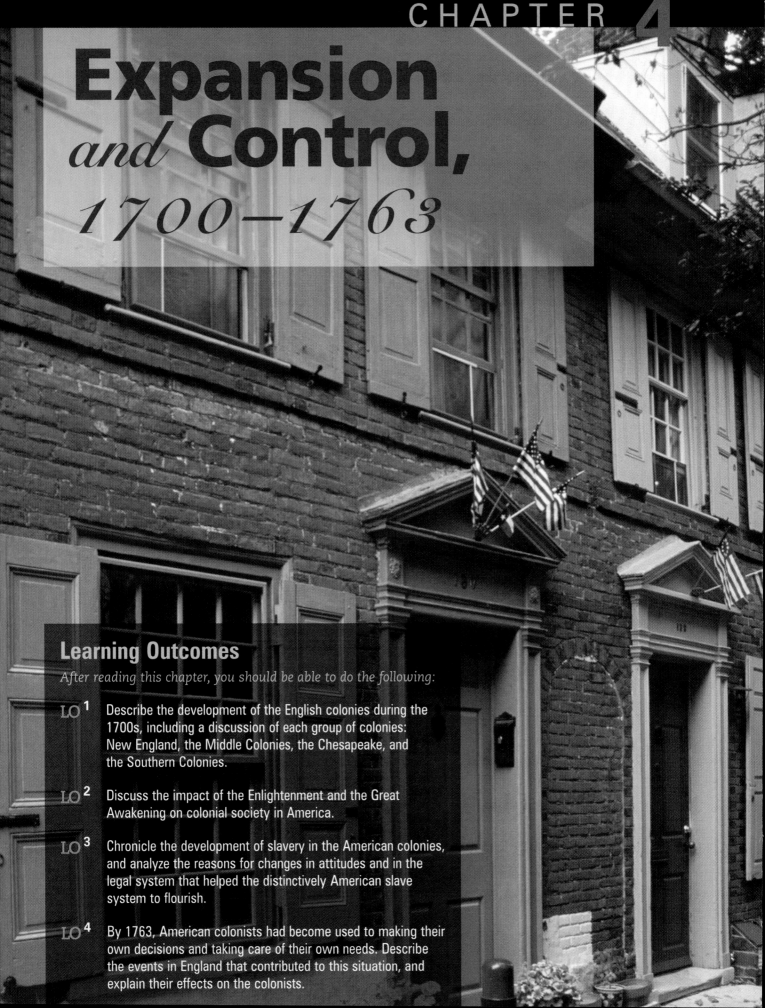

# CHAPTER 4

# Expansion
## and Control,
### 1700–1763

## Learning Outcomes

*After reading this chapter, you should be able to do the following:*

**LO¹** Describe the development of the English colonies during the 1700s, including a discussion of each group of colonies: New England, the Middle Colonies, the Chesapeake, and the Southern Colonies.

**LO²** Discuss the impact of the Enlightenment and the Great Awakening on colonial society in America.

**LO³** Chronicle the development of slavery in the American colonies, and analyze the reasons for changes in attitudes and in the legal system that helped the distinctively American slave system to flourish.

**LO⁴** By 1763, American colonists had become used to making their own decisions and taking care of their own needs. Describe the events in England that contributed to this situation, and explain their effects on the colonists.

© Paul S. Bartholomew/Alamy

**"One historian has called this developing society 'an empire of goods' because of the large number of goods newly available for purchase."**

As the last chapter discussed, British colonial America gradually evolved into four unique regions. This chapter explores the development of these regions from 1700 to 1763, the expansion of an intellectual and cultural life distinct from that of Britain, and the ways in which African slavery became ingrained in the life of colonial North America. It concludes with Britain's attempts to regain control of its increasingly feisty and independent-minded colony, an effort that would eventually foster a revolution.

**diversified farming**
System in which a single home could farm various crops to sustain the household throughout the year

## LO¹ Expansion of Colonial Economy and Society, 1700–1763

As colonial society grew, by 1700 four distinct regions had developed: New England (Massachusetts, Rhode Island, New Hampshire, Connecticut), the Middle Colonies (New York, New Jersey, Pennsylvania, Delaware), the Chesapeake (Virginia and Maryland), and the Southern Colonies (North Carolina, South Carolina, Georgia) (see Map 4.1). Each region had a unique economy based on its geographical location and its founding ideology, and each region's society developed in response to those two factors. The idea that all colonists possessed "natural rights" as Englishmen was perhaps the only unifying feature in colonial North America. Otherwise, the colonists lived incredibly distinct lives, based largely on the region in which they resided. These regional distinctions would remain significant, and would perhaps even lead to the American Civil War nearly a century later.

### New England

New England's terrain, climate, and founding ideology encouraged the development of certain types of agriculture, business, trade, and society.

### Economy

Like most other colonists, most New Englanders were farmers. New England's hilly land and a short growing season encouraged **diversified farming**, a system in which a single home could farm many different crops that would sustain the household throughout the year. Farmers lived in towns and walked each day to their fields to tend their crops. Livestock was allowed to graze on community-owned land, such as the town common. New Englanders were consistently alert to new economic opportunities. They grew surplus agricultural goods to trade for tools and other finished goods such as furniture. At first their surplus was limited to grains and cereals, but by the early 1700s New Englanders were trading meat, dairy, and orchard products as well. In the mid-1600s and throughout the early 1700s, New Englanders also maintained an active trade in furs, fish, and timber.

In this highly agrarian society, New Englanders often produced their own furniture and agricultural implements, and spun their family's flax and wool to make clothing. Over time, some small industries developed around New England's two principal products: fish and lumber. New Englanders used local timber to establish a shipbuilding industry, and by the mid-1700s, one-third of all ships used by England were built in New England, a truly remarkable statistic.

Developing industries require money, salesmen, and trade routes, and the merchants who met these needs became prominent players in the development of New England from 1700 to 1763. They brought in capital and managerial expertise, and when land opened up in the west, the commercial leaders of New England were some of the first speculators, originating the practice of western land speculation around 1670.

These commercial adventurers also participated in a pattern of trade that came to be called the **Triangular Trade**, although it was much more complicated than a simple triangle. The New England colonies traded fish and grains to England and to southern Europe in return for wine, spices, and gold. They also sold their goods to the West Indies in return for sugar and molasses. The New Englanders then distilled the molasses to make rum and traded it, along with other manufactured goods, to Africa in return for slaves and gold. The gold from this trade allowed New Englanders to purchase manufactured goods, tools, and linens from England, which in turn bought New England's manufactured ships. By 1763, this was a thriving arena of commerce that gave the colonies a good deal of economic independence, which later supported their insistent demands for increased political independence. New Englanders had also established a diversified economy that possessed but was not dependent upon slave labor.

## Society

In 1660, New England had a population of more than 30,000 people of European descent. These people lived a mostly provincial life in small, family-centered towns. By 1700, the population had tripled to 90,000, and by 1760 it had reached 450,000. Still, most of these people lived in small towns.

>> By the mid-1700s, one-third of all ships used by England were built in New England.

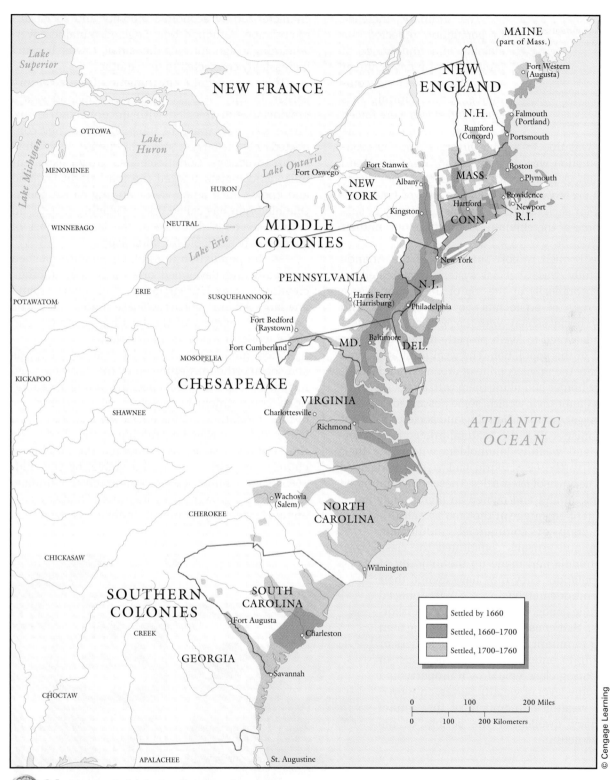

Lake Superior

Lake Huron

Lake Michigan

OTTOWA

MENOMINEE

WINNEBAGO

NEW FRANCE

Lake Ontario
Fort Oswego

HURON

NEUTRAL

Lake Erie

ERIE

POTAWATOM

SUSQUEHANNOOK

MOSOPELEA

KICKAPOO

SHAWNEE

CHICKASAW

CREEK

CHOCTAW

MAINE
(part of Mass.)

Fort Western
(Augusta)

NEW
ENGLAND

N.H.

Rumford
(Concord)

Falmouth
(Portland)

Portsmouth

Fort Stanwix

Albany

NEW
YORK

Kingston

Boston

MASS.

Plymouth

Hartford

Providence
Newport

CONN.

R.I.

MIDDLE
COLONIES

New York

PENNSYLVANIA

N.J.

Harris Ferry
(Harrisburg)

Philadelphia

Fort Bedford
(Raystown)

Fort Cumberland

MD.

Baltimore

DEL.

CHESAPEAKE

VIRGINIA

Charlottesville

Richmond

ATLANTIC
OCEAN

Wachovia
(Salem)

CHEROKEE

NORTH
CAROLINA

SOUTHERN
COLONIES

SOUTH
CAROLINA

Wilmington

Fort Augusta

Charleston

GEORGIA

Savannah

APALACHEE

St. Augustine

Settled by 1660

Settled, 1660–1700

Settled, 1700–1760

0        100       200 Miles

0     100     200 Kilometers

© Cengage Learning

Map 4.1. British Settlement by 1760

The dramatic increase in population reflected the stability and importance of families and an environment hospitable to life and commerce. Some immigrants came, and slaves were forced to come, but most of the growth was due to a high birthrate. This burgeoning population was the impetus for rapid westward expansion. A family with six sons could not divide its land six ways and bequeath a plot of land large enough for each son to ensure his prosperity or success. Some of the children had to strike out on their own.

One English import that crossed the Atlantic successfully was a social system demarcated by class. Theoretically at the top of the system was a small group of aristocrats—governors, judges, and wealthy businessmen with English backgrounds—who endeavored to live a properly refined life above the rest of the population. The wealthiest attempted to recreate the privileged life of urban England, building large homes and filling them with English furnishings. To flaunt their wealth, some possessed slaves.

A bigger group in New England society was what the colonists called the "natural aristocracy"—merchants and wealthy landholders who made their fortunes in the New World and were not deemed special because of their titles. These men dominated economic affairs and owned an increasingly larger and larger percentage of the area's wealth.

A group of commercial middlemen, farmers, and artisans constituted the class in the middle and made up the majority of the population. They may have owned their own farms or small businesses that produced handmade goods. Beneath them was a laboring class that consisted mostly of young men waiting to inherit land from their fathers or preparing to enter a craft. In time, most of this laboring class would own property and enjoy some level of wealth. Slaves, employed by the wealthiest members of the natural aristocracy, dwelled at the bottom of the social structure.

## Life in New England

With the growth that occurred between 1660 and 1763, the now-idealized image of an agricultural and religiously orthodox New England receded into the past. In its place emerged an increasingly commercialized society characterized by economic mobility and social differentiation. Although New England remained overwhelmingly agricultural, the small towns became increasingly connected to one another.

This was a significant transition from a century earlier. In the 1660s, colonial New England was a provincial land freckled with unconnected towns. There were few roads in the 1660s, and they connected only the largest towns. By the 1700s, this had begun to change. Commerce had grown exponentially, as colonists tracked the markets in England and knew which ships were carrying which goods. One historian has called this developing society "an empire of goods" because of the large number of goods newly available for purchase.

As the population multiplied, colonists pushed westward and developed one town after another, creating a large half-circle of small towns around any large Atlantic port city. These hinterland towns lay on the margins of the bustling economic and social world of New England's cities.

Such robust growth meant that the religious and social orthodoxy enforced by the Puritans could not last. Prosperity weakened the younger generations' commitment to the strict religious practices of their forefathers. Ministers slowly lost stature, no longer defining New England life as they had when the Puritans first arrived. Although the number of church congregants remained stable, by the mid-1660s some church leaders attempted to stimulate membership growth. They instituted "**halfway covenants**," whereby baptized individuals who had

© North Wind Picture Archives

>> By 1760 New England no longer looked like the Puritan ideal. Instead it looked a lot like England, though with greater economic and social mobility and a higher rate of literacy.

never had a personal conversion to Christ were counted as partial members of the church and were allowed to have their children baptized as well. These "halfway" members were usually brought to the front of a church, where members could watch to see if they were about to experience a conversion. By 1700, Puritan ministers had also begun to rely on the **jeremiad**—a long speech emphasizing society's fall from purity and grace to its current, depraved state—as a way to stir up congregations.

Despite the decline of the church's importance, the slow growth of the cities, and the rise of New England, commerce helped New Englanders maintain their commitment to family life. If all else was changing, these values remained constant. The sexual division of labor continued (as imported from England): women remained in charge of "indoor affairs" (raising children, preparing food, cleaning house, doing laundry) and men took charge of "outdoor affairs" (cultivating fields, chopping wood, and conducting the daily business transactions, such as buying horses and selling crops). In sum, New England consisted mostly of stable, agriculturally based families, an expanding economy that led to the growth of some cities, and a rapid westward migration to accommodate the growth of the population. And of course there continued to be the presence of Indians, who although being pushed west, still occupied significant terrain in all the colonies.

## The Middle Colonies

The warmer climate and distinct foundings of the Middle Colonies created some important differences from New England.

### Economy

In the Middle Colonies, farms were larger than in New England, and farmers lived on their farms rather than in the village. Many of the Middle Colonies' farms achieved relative self-sustenance, and some were so bountiful that they exported goods. Fruit, livestock, and wheat were the principal exported crops of the region, wheat being the biggest export. Indeed, by the early 1700s, New York and Pennsylvania were sometimes known to English traders as the "bread colonies." Agricultural production grew 2 to 3 percent every year from 1700 to 1770, and the best farmers in the Middle Colonies could afford to bring nearly 40 percent of their produce to market, meaning that this area rapidly grew wealthier than New England as money from England poured in.

As in New England, families in the Middle Colonies produced their own furniture and agricultural implements and spun their family's flax and wool to make clothing. Clay from the riverbeds allowed them to build houses of brick, usually two stories high. Unlike the many small towns of New England, commerce focused on the two hubs of the Middle Colonies: New York and Philadelphia. The chief industries of the Middle Colonies developed around corn and wheat, and mills built alongside rivers ground these grains into flour. Nearly all of these goods passed through New York or Philadelphia to be traded overseas. If you lived in the Middle Colonies during these years, it is likely you would have either lived on a wheat farm or in the commercial cities of New York or Philadelphia.

The success of the mills allowed the Middle Colonies to participate in the Triangular Trade by supplying wheat, grain, and excess fish to England and southern Europe, where they were traded for wine and gold. They traded other surplus items, such as meat and horses, to the West Indies in return for sugar and molasses. As in New England, they turned the molasses into rum, which they shipped with other goods to Africa in return for slaves and gold.

Some families were slaveholders, and by the 1760s slavery was generally well established in the Middle Colonies, although most families owned only small numbers of slaves.

## Society

In 1660, just 5,000 non-Indian people lived in the Middle Colonies. In 1710, that number had grown to 70,000, and by 1760 it was 425,000. The high rate of childbirth fueled this growth as well as (unlike New England) continued immigration from Scotland, Ireland, Germany, and England.

In the Middle Colonies, several members of the natural aristocracy owned enormous tracts of land. These people grew wealthier and wealthier throughout the 1700s as they sold some of their extensive lands. Below them socially were urban merchants and small family farmers, who comprised the majority of the population. Below these groups were tenant farmers who rented the farms they worked. And in the cities there was a growing number of poor. There were also around 35,000 slaves in the Middle Colonies in 1770, most of whom worked in the agricultural areas of New York, usually cultivating wheat. Slavery was also visible in the cities, usually because the wealthiest colonists liked to have a servant in tow to show off their wealth. By 1750, New York City was a major hub of the American slave trade.

## Life in the Middle Colonies

Life in the Middle Colonies can be differentiated by looking at the big cities (Philadelphia and New York) on the one hand, and everywhere else on the other. Family farms owned and worked by one family produced huge amounts of grain. In New York, however, large landowners owned baronial estates and had tenants work their lands. As in New England, the population boom propelled youngsters off family plots and farther west. Some tried to purchase farms, and some were reduced to tenant farming. In most areas, the sexual division of labor continued, with women controlling indoor activities and men controlling outdoor activities. Families remained generally stable, and, in the absence of large villages, the number of people living on a farm grew.

The cities were booming as well. In 1765, almost one out of every five Pennsylvanians lived in a size-

>> The wealthiest colonists liked to have a servant in tow to show off their wealth.

able town. A professional class of lawyers, craftsmen, and millers emerged. The populace founded urban institutions such as centers of public education, newspapers, theaters, fire departments, and libraries. More so than the other colonies, the Middle Colonies' thriving population was diverse. In New York City and Philadelphia, many languages were spoken, and people often grouped together by language. In general, the laboring people of the Middle Colonies exerted an impressive amount of control over civic life, as a ruling elite was slow to emerge. This civic input combined with devotion to family and to individual happiness and formed the cornerstone of Middle Colonies society.

*Tobacco was king of the Chesapeake.*

## The Chesapeake

The Chesapeake, with more fertile soil than either New England or the Middle Colonies, had fewer towns and more land devoted to a single crop: tobacco.

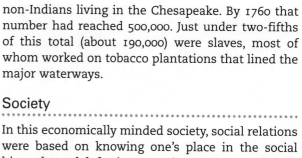

>> In most areas, the sexual division of labor continued, with women controlling indoor activities and men controlling outdoor activities.

## Economy

Tobacco was the chief product of the Chesapeake area, and, rather than developing a diversified economy, farmers in the Chesapeake remained tied to this single lucrative crop. For instance, in the late 1600s, tobacco generated 90 percent of the enormous wealth in Virginia and Maryland. Flour and grains came in a distant second as exports, growing in importance only in the mid-1700s. From 1660 to 1763, tobacco was king of the Chesapeake, its production influencing everything else in the colony.

Because people lived on huge stretches of land that grew tobacco, there were few towns and hardly any developed industries in the Chesapeake. Virginia did mine some iron ore, and after 1730, when grain became profitable, mills sprang up along the rivers. Indeed, just before the American Revolution, the Chesapeake's mills had developed into one of the strongest sectors of the economy. But this was a late development. The Chesapeake relied on its staple crop for its wealth, and the anemic growth of other industries would suffer because of it.

Cities, too, failed to develop. By the middle 1700s, the Chesapeake had only one sizeable city in Baltimore, which was developed as a port town for the area's grain. Other than that, most of the Chesapeake's cities (such as Norfolk) were little more than small towns.

Instead of living in cities or towns, the people of the Chesapeake settled on farms. Key to a farm's success was access to a riverbank where product could be transported to market. Thus, a developmental map of the Chesapeake would show a number of large farms moving farther and farther up the major rivers. In 1660, there were around 35,000

non-Indians living in the Chesapeake. By 1760 that number had reached 500,000. Just under two-fifths of this total (about 190,000) were slaves, most of whom worked on tobacco plantations that lined the major waterways.

## Society

In this economically minded society, social relations were based on knowing one's place in the social hierarchy and deferring to one's superiors. At the top of the structure were the few families with access to public land who profited from selling tobacco and grain. They increased their wealth throughout the 1700s, constructing a visible structure of leadership and power and modeling their lives after those of the landed English gentry, not wealthy Londoners. By setting themselves up as an elite with social responsibilities, they gained total control over political and religious institutions. By the mid-1700s, commentators were noting the extravagance and indulgences of this elite. They sat high above the less affluent free colonists, who were usually small landholders and who were, in turn, socially above the slaves.

## Life in the Chesapeake

The majority of the people in the Chesapeake lived on widely scattered farms and plantations. Because settlements were scattered, individual households grew larger and larger in size, and it was common to live with one's siblings for most of one's life. Throughout the 1700s, kinship networks among neighbors prospered.

As roads slowly developed, settlements began to spring up farther from the rivers. Horses provided the main mode of transportation. By the 1750s, the Chesapeake supported a rural commercial network along these roads, where merchants, innkeepers, and traders could hawk their wares. Life was slowly moving away from being entirely agricultural, although in contrast to New England and the Middle Colonies, urban life in the Chesapeake was nonexistent.

Until 1700, there were many more men than women in the Chesapeake. This meant that many people married late and that women possessed ample power. The region

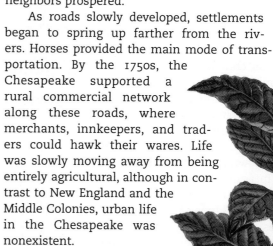

> >>The governor's palace at Williamsburg, Virginia, the seat of royal power in the colony, exemplified the standard to which wealthy Virginia families aspired.

© PCL/Alamy

eventual decline of a class of free white people, who would have constituted the region's middle rung of society. Because of the growth of slavery, this middle rung remained narrow in the Chesapeake; there was little middle class to speak of.

For women, this meant a changed domestic life, and a less influential one. Following the model of the landed English gentry, Chesapeake society viewed men as benign patriarchs presiding over their flock of dependents. The result was that women's roles in the region declined in importance from 1660 to 1760.

As opposed to the variety of religions in the Middle Colonies and, increasingly, New England, throughout the 1700s the Anglican Church became entrenched in the life of the Chesapeake. Unlike Puritans, Anglicans did not demand strict adherence, and the Chesapeake institutions remained generally secular. This situation was aided by the fact that there were few ministers in the growing region, and the gentry did not care to pay for more to come.

Throughout the 1700s, then, the Chesapeake developed a strongly aristocratic social structure and a largely rural, English model of living. This stood in contrast to New England, which featured small towns and social mobility. It also stood in contrast to the Middle Colonies, which relied on New York and Philadelphia as central urban hubs to support the many middle-rung farmers. Life in the Chesapeake was more deferential regarding status, more rural, and, at the top, more luxurious and comfortable.

suffered from high death rates, economic inequality among free people, and weak social institutions, such as churches (where a sense of community could develop). This began to change around 1700. A temporary lull in tobacco prices slowed the rush of new arrivals, allowing Chesapeake society to settle down as its sex ratio evened out. In addition, after 1675 slavery replaced indentured servitude as the preferred type of labor. By 1720, slaves made up 25 percent of the population, a percentage that stabilized at about 40 percent by 1760, when almost 50 percent of families owned slaves, usually in small numbers. The declining number of indentured servants meant the

66 By the mid-1700s, commentators were noting the extravagance and indulgences of the Chesapeake elite. They sat high above the less affluent free colonists. 99

## The Southern Colonies

Impressive as it was, the wealth of the Chesapeake could not compete with that of the Southern Colonies. Like the Chesapeake, the Southern Colonies relied overwhelmingly on a few staple crops, but life was generally so miserable that few colonists resided there permanently. Only two towns of any size were established, and no social models of leadership developed. The wealthy landowners enjoyed the profits, but they chose to live elsewhere.

### Economy

The staple crops of the Southern Colonies were tobacco, rice, and indigo, and they dominated the region's economic life. Cotton would become significant only after 1793, when Eli Whitney invented the cotton gin, which allowed the cultivation of the crop on lower-quality land, thus expanding the amount of cotton that could be grown. By the early 1700s, however, large plantations started springing up to grow those staple crops. Slave labor was the key to their development, allowing a few successful farmers to develop large plantations of over a thousand acres.

There was little industrial development in the Southern Colonies. Local artisans and their apprentices developed small establishments for manufacturing guns and other ironware. For the most part, however, the people of the Southern Colonies relied on trade with England for their industrial goods. This led to the creation of well-developed routes of commerce along waterways. It also allowed the Southern Colonies to participate in the Triangular Trade, shipping their tobacco, rice, and indigo to England in return for manufactured goods.

## Society

Because of the miserable living conditions, including the heat, humidity, and insects, the Southern Colonies were slow to grow in population. In 1660, there were very few non-Indian settlers. In 1710, there were 26,000, and in 1760 there were just 215,000, about 95,000 of whom were slaves. The social structure reflected this differentiation. Plantation bosses were heads of large fiefdoms. Under them was a tiny middle class of lawyers, merchants, and skilled workers who usually lived in the region's few small towns or worked in the lumber mills of North Carolina. The bulk of the working class was made up of slaves imported from Africa.

## Life in the Southern Colonies

There was a difference in lifestyle between the upper and lower Southern Colonies. In the lower colonies (today's South Carolina and Georgia), life expectancy continued to be perilously short. Few people lived to be sixty, and many died before they were twenty. This meant that, for the most part, those who could live elsewhere did.

Nevertheless, the lucky and the entrepreneurial amassed great wealth in the Southern Colonies. The commercial gentry who enjoyed this wealth lived a stylish life, usually in the manner of the English elite, enjoying West Indian accent pieces for their home's furnishings. They customarily owned two homes: one on their plantation (where they spent little time), and one in either Charleston or Savannah. To make use

>> Town homes in Charleston, South Carolina.

of the gentry's wealth and leisure time, these two cities developed such institutions as libraries, theaters, social clubs, and concert houses.

In the Southern Colonies, communities were not always based around families, mostly because there was no certainty that parents would survive long. Law enforcement was slack, depth of religious commitment was shallow, and interest in public education was limited. The wealthy frequently sent their children to England to be educated.

In dramatic contrast to this pleasant life they were leading, white Southerners developed draconian slave codes to govern the lives of their slaves. Punishment for slave insurrections was severe, travel for slaves was limited, and accumulation of wealth denied. Yet, there were few slave revolts, probably because most slaves did not yet work in gangs. The single major uprising, the Stono Rebellion of 1739 in South Carolina, was put down brutally and spurred the reinforcement of strict slave codes (see page 75).

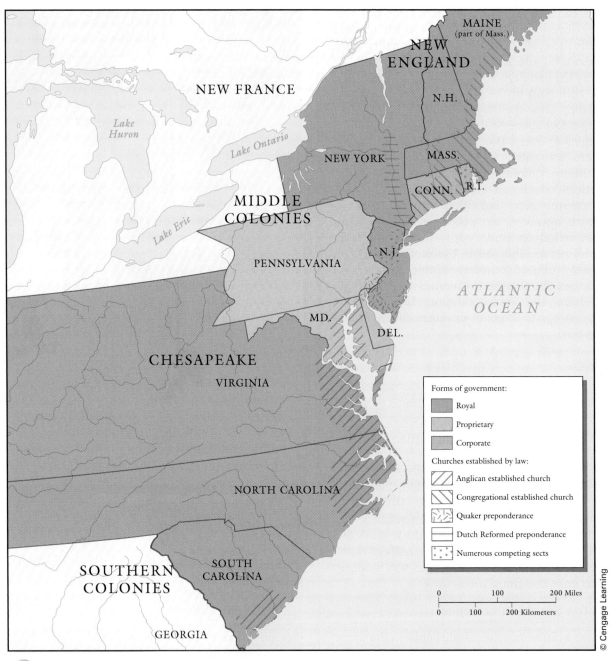

Forms of government:
- Royal
- Proprietary
- Corporate

Churches established by law:
- Anglican established church
- Congregational established church
- Quaker preponderance
- Dutch Reformed preponderance
- Numerous competing sects

© Cengage Learning

Map 4.2. Forms of Government and Religions in the Colonies, 1720

However, because of the high rates of white absenteeism from their plantations, there was little owner oversight, meaning that slaves actually led a slightly freer life than the laws dictated.

# LO² Expansion of Colonial Intellectual and Cultural Life

The expanding economic and social life of the 1700s gave some people the time and inclination to engage in intellectual and cultural pursuits. It also allowed Americans to participate in a monumental transition affecting much of the Western world, a movement away from medieval thought toward that of the Enlightenment. This was important for American history because Enlightenment ideals played a substantial role in the American Revolution and in the development of the American political system that was to come.

## The American Enlightenment

The American **Enlightenment** stemmed from the European Enlightenment, which was a movement to prioritize the human capacity for reason as the highest form of human attainment. In the early 1600s, most people of the Western world believed (1) in the unquestioned primacy of rulers (spiritual and secular); (2) in humans' incapacity for social change; and (3) that our time here on earth is a temporary interlude on our journey toward either eternal salvation or damnation. In the 1500s, European scientists, most notably Copernicus, began to question these beliefs, and by the 1600s educated people were postulating whether natural laws (not divine ones) governed society and the universe, and whether these natural laws were accessible to humans through the use of reason.

The most prominent of these thinkers were John Locke and Jean-Jacques Rousseau. Locke argued that one's environment was more significant than divine decree in the development of one's character, and Rousseau contended that individuals had "natural rights" to life, liberty, and property, which even a king or a pope could not deny. The key Enlightenment economist was Adam Smith, who postulated a natural balance in the economy determined by laws of supply and demand. Each of the central ideas put forward by these thinkers implied that progress was possible as people achieved more and more of their natural rights and that people had a stake in their own life and were entitled to reject authority if certain rights were denied.

> **Enlightenment**
> A movement to prioritize the human capacity for reason as the highest form of human attainment

## The American Enlightenment and Religion

These ideas inspired both harmony and conflict with religious leaders, and many of the most consequential American intellectual outpourings from the colonial period are either rejections of or support for the Enlightenment. Cotton Mather, for instance, produced important sermons as he refined a Puritan theology that articulated the centrality of God to an individual's well-being. William Bradford, John Winthrop, and Edward Johnson wrote histories of New England, giving special testament to the sacrifices made to religion by the colonial founders, but also hedging a bit toward the Enlightenment by praising the individual fortitude of those founders. And religion animated the poems of Anne Bradstreet, Edward Taylor, and Michael Wigglesworth. The American Enlightenment did not produce many atheists or agnostics, but it did begin a process whereby religious thinkers tried to find a balance between science and religion.

## Education

The necessity of training ministers, especially in New England, led to the creation of an educational system, and the Enlightenment ideals of individual progress and human reason prodded the slow democratization of the system over the course of the seventeenth and eighteenth centuries. Reflecting this balance between religious and secular ideals, America's first college, Harvard, was founded in 1636, not as an official church school, but under the prevailing Puritan philosophy and with a mission to create a literate ministry. In 1642, Massachusetts passed a law requiring parents to teach their children to read. In 1647, it passed a law requiring towns to maintain a primary school. Although they did so more slowly than New England, the Middle Colonies also launched endeavors in public education.

Over time, the presence of schools grew, especially in New England. Secondary schools opened there in the 1700s. They would not be established southward in significant numbers until after the revolution. Nine colleges were founded during the colonial period, four of them in New England. All, like Harvard, were in some way church schools.

 Read Cotton Mather on the need for education.

>> Harvard College, founded in 1636.

## The Secular Press

At the same time, Enlightenment ideals took hold with many laypeople, as did the secular practices of politics and commerce. This trend was reflected in the expansion of nonreligious newspapers throughout the 1700s, especially in New England. The first newspaper was published in Boston by Benjamin Harris in 1690, and the first regularly published paper was the *Boston News-Letter*, begun in 1704. By the middle of the 1700s, every major town had its own newspaper (although they published more about events in Europe than about those in the colonies). In 1741, Andrew Bradford published the first magazine, the *American Magazine*. The title alone reflects the unity that the colonists were beginning to feel.

The freedom encouraged by Enlightenment ideals also led to expansion of liberties, as in the case of John Peter Zenger, a New York newspaperman who was arrested after publishing an attack on the governor. Zenger was acquitted of the crime (because his attack was factually correct), setting a crucial precedent for freedom of the press; truth became a legitimate defense against a charge of libel, no matter how elevated in rank the alleged libel victim was.

 Take an interactive look at the trial of John Peter Zenger.

Illustrating the deep anti-authoritarianism that ran through the case, the jury, in coming to its decision, defied the wishes of the judge.

## The Great Awakening

During this expansion of Enlightenment ideals, American churches experienced a revival. A combination of Enlightenment ideals and a general unhap-

>> John Peter Zenger's trial.

© George Whitefield preaching, Collet, John (c. 1725–80)/Private Collection/The Bridgeman Art Library

piness with social and economic developments bred dissatisfaction with the direction American life was taking. Many colonists felt that the established religions had overly accommodated the Enlightenment, allowing rationalization too much free rein in the spiritual world; many colonists had also begun to feel alienated from the mainstream establishment and the traditions that ensconced them in power.

In response, ministers and laypeople alike originated a Protestant revival that emphasized the notion that individuals could find heaven if they worked hard enough (not just if they were predestined to go) and that allowed—even invited—emotional expressions of religion. Ignoring tradition, this new group of preachers stressed that all were equal in Christ. The result was the growth and development of several new Protestant denominations that invariably emphasized the laity's role in matters both spiritual and temporal, as well as a more emotional type of religion. Called the **Great Awakening**, it was America's first large-scale religious revival.

 Read Jonathan Edwards on the Great Awakening.

### Old Lights versus New Lights

Jonathan Edwards was the intellectual leader of the Great Awakening, although itinerant evangelical preachers such as George Whitefield played a considerable role in fomenting the revival. These itinerants advocated an emotional style of religion and sometimes attacked local ministers. By the time it had run its course (by about 1745), the Great Awakening had opened a tremendous rift among Protestants. On one side were the **Old Lights**, who condemned emotionalism and favored a more rationalistic theology favored by elements of the Enlightenment; on the other were the **New Lights**, who supported evangelism, the new methods of prayer, and equality before Christ. The revival slowed during the 1750s, but it is significant for at least five reasons (see "The reasons why . . ." on the next page).

> 66 The congregation was extraordinarily melted by every sermon; almost the whole assembly being in tears for a great part of sermon time. 99
> —*Jonathan Edwards on Great Awakening preacher George Whitefield's sermons*

## LO³ African Slavery

Alongside the American Enlightenment and the Great Awakening, an intricate and harsh slave system developed. Although slavery existed everywhere in colonial North America, it was especially brutal in the Southern Colonies. Numerically speaking, the colonies that would become the United States were a tiny part of a much larger **Atlantic slave trade**, a huge system of trade and migration that brought millions of slaves to the New World and Europe and that served as a pillar in the economy of one of the earliest forms of globalization. Europeans and colonials forced perhaps as many as 12 million Africans to cross the Atlantic. Many died during the arduous passage, masking the true number of forced migrants.

**Great Awakening**
America's first large-scale religious revival, originated by preachers who stressed that all were equal in Christ

**Old Lights**
Protestant leaders who condemned emotionalism and favored a more rationalistic theology favored by elements of the Enlightenment

**New Lights**
Protestant leaders who supported evangelism, the new methods of prayer, and equality before Christ

**Atlantic slave trade**
Huge system of trade and migration that brought millions of slaves to the New World and Europe in the 1600s and 1700s

About 75 percent of slaves came from West Africa, and the other 25 percent came from Southwest Africa. A majority of the Africans went to colonies controlled by Spain or Portugal: about 2 million to Brazil and 3 million to the West Indies, usually to work on sugar plantations. Roughly 350,000 Africans, less than 5 percent of the total, came to the future United States. Of this 350,000, Europeans forced 10,000 Africans to come during the 1600s and the remainder during the 1700s. Although some would become free after earning enough money to purchase their freedom, more than 95 percent of colonial Africans remained slaves for life.

## Enslavement

Enslavement was a brutal process in all three of its stages: initial capture in Africa, the middle passage across the ocean, and the period of adjustment to the New World.

## Capture

The process by which the captured slaves came to North, South, and Central America was rationalized by the profits to be made. Acquired either through barter between a European slave trader and an African kingdom or through kidnapping, the enslaved Africans were bound at the neck in a leather brace. The slave trader connected a gang of slaves together by chains attached to these neck braces. Then the chained gang was marched to the coast, a journey sometimes as long as 550 miles, which could take up to two months. Once on the African coast, the traders herded their captives into stucco pens to be inspected and sorted by desirability. Some traders branded the slaves with hot irons to mark their property. Then the slaves waited in captivity for cargo ships to arrive.

## The Middle Passage

When the ships arrived, slave traders forced the slaves from their pens and onto canoes and then paddled them out to the larger ships. At this point, some slaves jumped overboard, keeping themselves under water long enough to drown.

Once aboard the transport ship, slaves faced the "**middle passage**," their horrible journey across the Atlantic. Traders packed the ships until they were overfilled. They cuffed the slaves and kept them below decks, away from fresh air. The captives were denied access to latrines, and the stench in the holds became unbearable. Many captives vomited in response, making the stench even worse. The Europeans also fed the slaves paltry food and threw sick slaves overboard to try to prevent the spread of diseases. They force-fed with a mouth wrench those who sought to commit suicide by starvation. Because the slaves came from varied tribes, it was likely they did not speak one another's language, cutting them off completely from the life they once knew. The middle passage took between four and eight weeks,

## { *The reasons why . . .* }

**The Great Awakening was significant for at least five reasons:**

***Growth of churches.*** As ministers formed new sects to meet the demands of the population, they greatly increased the number of churches in colonial America.

***Rise of lower churches.*** Many of these new churches emerged from evangelical sects, such as the Baptists, who became prominent in the Chesapeake and sought to overturn the aristocratic social structure.

***Development of colleges.*** Seeking to train all these new ministers, many religious orders established several colleges, many of which still exist today (for example, Princeton, Brown, Rutgers, and Dartmouth).

***Religion and science.*** In the North American colonies, the Great Awakening aligned nicely with the Enlightenment, demonstrating the persistence of religion in conjunction with Enlightenment ideals in America.

***Decline of authority.*** The Great Awakening also severed colonial ties to established structures of authority (religious authority, in this case), serving in some ways as a precursor to revolution.

>> To meet the labor demands of the New World, European merchants developed the Atlantic slave trade, which would eventually force as many as 12 million Africans to cross the Atlantic where they would work as human property. Of this huge number, roughly 5 percent came to land that would eventually become the United States.

 Read a doctor's account of the middle passage.

and more than one in four captives died along the way. In the seventeenth and eighteenth centuries, any trans-Atlantic journey was perilous and potentially fatal, but especially so for the captured Africans.

## To a New Life

Once in the New World, slave traders auctioned off their cargo in public squares, chiefly in New York and Charleston, but in several other cities as well. Potential buyers inspected the captured men and women's teeth, underarms, and genitals. Strong young men were the most valuable, but women of childbearing age were also prized because they could have children who, by law in the 1700s, were also the slaveholder's property. Then the buyer transported the slaves to what lay ahead: a life of ceaseless labor. In total, the journey from African village to New World plantation routinely took as long as six months.

This process began in the 1600s and continued into the 1800s, although the 1780s were the years of the Atlantic slave trade's peak. Before the American

>> Slave traders packed their ships tightly to maximize profits.

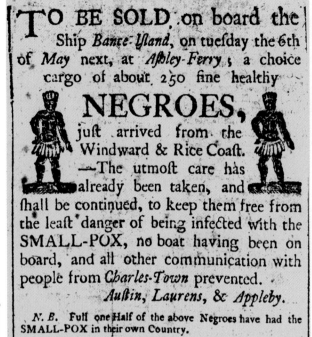

>> A 1780s newspaper ad for a slave auction held near Charleston, South Carolina.

Revolution, there were only a few scattered movements to protest the slave trade and the practice of slavery (primarily by the Quakers, the Mennonites, and a few other religious groups). Much of European society simply accepted the horrors of slavery as a necessary cost of colonial expansion.

## The Spread of Slavery

Tobacco, rice, and indigo—the three staple crops of the Southern and Chesapeake colonies—all demanded significant labor, and by the late 1600s, the favored form of labor in the American colonies was rapidly becoming African slaves. Between 1680 and 1700, the average number of slaves transported on English ships rose from 5,000 slaves a year to more than 20,000.

Although slavery was most common in the Southern Colonies and the Chesapeake, it was legal in *all* English colonies in America. In the North, slaves worked as field hands on farms and as domestic servants, dockworkers, and craftspeople in cities. But because of their labor-intensive cash crops, the market for slaves was much more lucrative in the South and the Chesapeake. Nevertheless, many northerners were involved in the trade. Northern traders, especially from Massachusetts, New York,

and Rhode Island, engaged in and profited from the slave trade before the United States outlawed the importation of slaves in 1808.

## Life Under Slavery

The daily life of a slave in colonial America depended on where he or she lived. In New England, where only about 3 percent of the population was African during the colonial era, slaves worked as field hands on small farms, as house servants for wealthy colonists, or as skilled artisans. Slaves could be isolated from one another (and most were), or they could live in a port town like Newport, Rhode Island, where slaves made up 18 percent of the population.

In the Middle Colonies, some slaves worked as field hands on small farms, while smaller numbers worked in cities in nearly every labor-intensive occupation. Neither of these regions relied on gang labor.

In the Southern Colonies and the Chesapeake, most slaves were field hands who grew sugar cane, rice, tobacco, or cotton. Some were house servants who cooked, cleaned, and helped care for children. A very few were skilled artisans. As arduous as the southern labor system was, however, plantation life allowed for development of a slave culture. This was possible because of the large number of slaves who could gather together after working hours.

### Plantation Life

The plantations where slave life developed most fully were entirely in the South, especially in the lower South, where slaves outnumbered other colonists. Many slaves here spoke Gullah, a hybrid language of several African tongues. They preserved several African religious traditions, such as a couple's jumping over a broomstick to seal a marriage. Over time, these traditions merged with Christianity in the same way that Catholic images merged with the traditional beliefs of Native America.

For slaves, family life was unpredictable, fragile, and subject to the arbitrary whims of their owners. Children typically stayed with their family until they were eight, at which time they were sometimes sold. Masters occasionally raped or coerced female slaves into sexual relations, further demonstrating their limitless power over their property. Nevertheless, families did struggle through, and wherever possible, strong family structures emerged. The hazards and difficulties inherent in the process of sustaining a family life under these conditions led slave men and women to take on roles different from those of their masters. Slave women, for instance, worked both in the field and in the home. Slave men, meanwhile, took on occasional domestic duties.

### Rebellion and Resistance

Despite the horrific nature of slave life, slave rebellions were infrequent, principally because slave owners had taken such drastic measures to maintain control over their slaves. The few slave rebellions that did arise met with violent resistance and led to even tighter controls. One planned insurrection in New York City in 1740 ended with the burning of thirteen slaves and the hanging of eighteen others (along with four white allies).

The most notable slave revolt of the 1700s—the **Stono Rebellion**—occurred in Stono, South Carolina, in 1739, when, on a quiet Sunday morning, a group of mostly newly arrived slaves marched into a firearms shop, killed the colonists manning the shop, stole several firearms, and marched south, probably in an effort to get to Florida, where the Spanish government promised England's slaves freedom. After traveling only a few miles, the number of slaves had grown to more than one hundred. They marched from house to house, murdering slave owners and their families as they went. After 10 miles, the band was met by an armed militia, which killed at least thirty of the rebelling slaves and captured almost all of the rest. Nearly all who were captured were killed.

 Learn more about the Stono Rebellion.

In response to the rebellion, South Carolina passed the **Negro Act**, which consolidated all of the separate slave codes into one code that forbade slaves from growing their own food, assembling in groups, or learning to read. This sharp response to the Stono Rebellion continued a pattern of harsh legal retributions for slave insurrections.

### Slavery and Racism

In the end, slavery promoted the rise of extreme, sustained racism against African Americans in North America. Since their arrival in the Chesapeake in 1619, dark-skinned people had been considered of lower status by Europeans. But because until the 1680s there were so few African slaves in the American colonies, they were generally not treated harshly. During this early period, a few slaves broke the bonds of enslavement and became landowners and politically active freedmen. Yet as the cost of indentured servants went up and that of slaves went down (for the reasons why, see Chapter 3), slaves were employed as the central labor force of the South and the Chesapeake.

As the number of slaves rose, so did restrictions on Africans and African Americans. Rabid manifestations of racism emerged out of owners' growing fears. The result was the creation of a caste-like system of segregation in which African Americans were considered inherently inferior to Europeans and Euro-Americans, and sometimes less than human. At the same time, religious writers, philosophers, scientists, and lay writers (among them, Thomas Jefferson) concocted theories about the "inferior" nature of African Americans, thus creating an intellectual framework to support the economic reality. Slavery lasted until the Civil War, and elements of this racial caste system have persisted well into the present day.

 Explore a wide variety of images and documents

## LO⁴ Attempted Expansion of English Control

Slavery was, of course, a huge part of the economic expansion of the early 1700s—an expansion that led to increased interest in the colonies by the British Crown. Most importantly, the exceptional production of raw materials had propelled the colonies into a second stage of economic development, whereby manufacturing and industry began to prosper (and not just the creation of raw materials). This stimulated economic competition between the North American colonies and England, which the Crown could not tolerate.

> *Religious writers, philosophers, scientists, and lay writers (among them, Thomas Jefferson) concocted theories about the "inferior" nature of African Americans.*

## Salutary Neglect

Any attempt by the Crown to reassert control of the colonies would aggravate the colonists because they had become accustomed to a hands-off style of relations between the Crown and the colonies, a relationship labeled **salutary neglect**. The principle developed in the late 1680s, when, upon King Charles II's death in 1685, his brother, James II, became king and promptly attempted to make England Catholic once again. This change created such a severe rift within England that it almost fell into civil war. Unlike the Cromwellian revolution of the 1650s, however, this second revolution was bloodless, and in the so-called **Glorious Revolution of 1688**, Protestant factions forced James II to flee England. His exit left the Crown to his Protestant daughter and son-in-law, William of Orange and Mary II, more commonly referred to as William and Mary.

For the colonists, the result of the Glorious Revolution was looser governance by the Crown and the removal of many of the proprietors who had founded the colonies. William and Mary continued to have a definite economic interest in the colonies, establishing a Board of Trade to oversee affairs and collect data. They also established a privy council to administer colonial laws. But, in general, royal administration over the colonies grew much looser with the decline of the proprietors.

The colonists loved, advocated, and fought for the loose system of oversight that came to be called salutary neglect. The concept is simple: the Crown would essentially ignore governance of its colonies and enforcement of its trade laws so long as the colonies continued to provide England with sufficient cash and produce. Politically, this system gave colonial assemblies a high level of legitimacy, which was accomplished at the expense of the royal governors. Of course, the risk of salutary neglect was that, if England ever decided to enforce the laws on its books, a serious conflict was inevitable. This is exactly what would happen in the French and Indian War, yet another of the "Wars for Empire" that occurred from 1754 to 1763.

## The French and Indian War, 1754–1763

The truce from Queen Anne's War lasted nearly thirty years, but the battles between the European powers were not over. In **King George's War** (1744–1748) England and France continued their New World spat, but the war ended with resolutions concerning only Europe; the exact New World ramifications remained unclear.

Meanwhile, English colonists pushed deeper into the Ohio Valley, further infuriating the French, who were already established traders there. Eventually the French attempted to build a series of military strongholds that would intimidate the English, the largest of which was Fort Duquesne in today's southwest Pennsylvania. They wanted to keep the English out. Virginian colonists who were speculating on lands in the west retaliated by building Fort Necessity nearby. When the Virginians sent an inexperienced young militia colonel named George Washington to deter the French from building more forts, a skirmish between the French and the English ignited yet another war, with more consequences than before.

George Washington was swiftly forced to surrender, and it seemed that the French were going to control trade relations in the American interior for the foreseeable future. But English merchants in London lobbied to use this backwoods dispute to forge a war that would eject the French from North America once and for all. Without the French, London merchants would have a monopoly on much of the New World trade, which promised to be incredibly lucrative. They succeeded in their lobbying, and a hesitant Crown used this minor provocation to start a major war. It was in this contrived way that a skirmish on the Pennsylvania frontier exploded into a world war that involved France, England, Austria, Russia, Prussia, Spain, and numerous Indian tribes. In Europe, the war was called the **Seven Years' War**; in North America, it was the **French and Indian War**.

## The Albany Congress

The coming war put the English colonists on high alert. To discuss the matter, seven of the colonies sent representatives to Albany, New York, in the summer of 1754. The meeting, called the

>> Model of Ft. Duquesne.

**Albany Congress**
Meeting of representatives from seven colonies in Albany, New York, in 1754, the first time the mainland English colonies met for a unified purpose

**Albany Plan**
Concept for the first-ever colonial union, drafted by Benjamin Franklin

**Treaty of Paris**
1763 agreement between Spain, England, and France that made the Mississippi River the boundary between England's holdings and Spain's, and evicted France from North America

**Albany Congress**, represented the first time the mainland English colonies met for a unified purpose.

## The Albany Plan

Part of their purpose was to convince the Iroquois to join the English side in the battle, but the Iroquois chose to remain neutral to preserve their trade routes. Another part of the colonists' strategy was to develop what would have been the first-ever colonial union under the **Albany Plan**, drafted by the printer, scientist, and, later, politician Benjamin Franklin. The plan would have placed all of England's colonies in America under a single president-general, appointed by the Crown, whose responsibility would be to manage all activity on the frontier and handle negotiations with Indians. It also would have created a single legislature, made up of representatives from each of the colonies, whose number would depend on how much in taxes each colony paid.

The union failed to materialize, however, mainly because the colonists felt allegiance only to their particular colony and (to a lesser extent) to the Crown. They did not yet fully identify with their fellow colonists. England was unhappy with the prospect of colonial unity, but slowly, the colonists were beginning to perceive the need for it. The French and Indian War did much to solidify the feeling that the English colonies along the Atlantic Coast would share one fate and should, perhaps, unite.

## Results

As the colonists had foreseen, war came, and under the leadership of General James Braddock, the English fared badly. Braddock's attempts to raise money from the colonists to help supply his troops provoked colonial ire, and his patronizing attempts to work with Indian tribes also failed. Worse, he bumbled his way from one military defeat to another. Within three years, two-thirds of his troops were dead, including Braddock himself.

In 1758, the English began to take the conflict more seriously and sent a large army under the leadership of Jeffrey Amherst to take over military operations. What followed was warfare marked by extreme brutality on all sides. After a year, the English were prevailing, and a year later, in 1760, hostilities largely ended. In 1763 the three warring nations (Spain, England, and France) signed the **Treaty of Paris** (Map 4.3), which laid out the so-called Proclamation Line giving England the western interior of North America, Canada, and Florida. Spain received Louisiana from France, and the Mississippi River became the boundary between England's holdings and Spain's. France had been evicted from North America.

The French and Indian War was significant for several reasons (see "The reasons why . . ." box).

## Pan-Indianism

With all the lands east of the Mississippi River now belonging to England, Indian tribes had to adapt. No longer could one tribe negotiate with one group of colonists and play the European nations off against one another to win concessions. Now Indian–colonial relations were centralized in London. The Indians recognized this transition and began to realize an increased unity between tribes in opposition to the English. Simply put, in the aftermath of the French and Indian War, many of the tribes of Native America shifted from favoring a tribal identity to assuming a racial one, or **pan-Indianism**. This was especially true in the Northwest, between the Great Lakes and the Appalachian Mountains, where contact with the colonists was most sustained.

### Neolin

In the late 1750s and 1760s, **Neolin**, a Delaware prophet, began preaching a return to old Indian ways, as they were before Europeans had come to America. Central to this revitalization movement was the notion of purging all European habits, such as reliance on material goods, use of alcohol, and belief in Christianity. Neolin traveled to several tribes preaching his message of pan-Indianism and anti-Europeanism.

### Pontiac's Rebellion

By 1763, several Indians had followed Neolin's advice and come together to present a unified front against the colonists. Under the leadership of Pontiac, chief of the Ottowa, they were ready to protest English intrusion into their lands and attempt to drive the colonists back across the Appalachians. The resulting battles in **Pontiac's Rebellion** were brutal, with the English attempting to introduce smallpox into Indian communities (through infected blankets) and Indians deliberately poisoning English troops' drinking water (by putting rotten meat in springs upriver from English camps). The English troops were better equipped for warfare, however, and the tribes of Native America, without the French available to help, could not withstand the English armies. They were beaten back, pushed farther west in yet another battle of what one historian has called "the long war for the west."

# And in the end . . .

Little did England suspect that, although it had won the Wars for Empire, it had done so at great cost:

$\left\{ \textit{The reasons why . . .} \right\}$

## The French and Indian War was significant to the colonies for several reasons:

***France removed and Indians lose a strategy***. France was forced to give up its land claims in Canada. This was disastrous for Indians in the north, because they had been surviving by playing one European power off another. Freed from competing with the French, the English could dictate the terms of trade and land possession. The Iroquois, for instance, tried to maintain their trading power but were suddenly without leverage now that the French were gone.

***Colonial ire toward England***. During the war, the colonists gained experience dealing with the English army. They disliked its hierarchical style, especially after having experienced extensive self-rule in the colonies. For their part, the English saw the colonists as ragtag and undisciplined, and contempt between the two peoples increased.

***Colonial unity***. The French and Indian War allowed the English colonies to see themselves as a united body distinct from England. The Albany Congress proved to be the first demonstration of an increasingly unified colonial identity.

***The British financial burden***. The war was costly for England, and its attempts to recoup its losses through taxes on the colonies led directly to the Revolution.

***French anger***. The French would greatly want revenge against the British for this battle, a chance they would get by helping the Americans during the American Revolution.

***Pan-Indianism***. The French and Indian War led to increased feelings of pan-Indianism against white settlers.

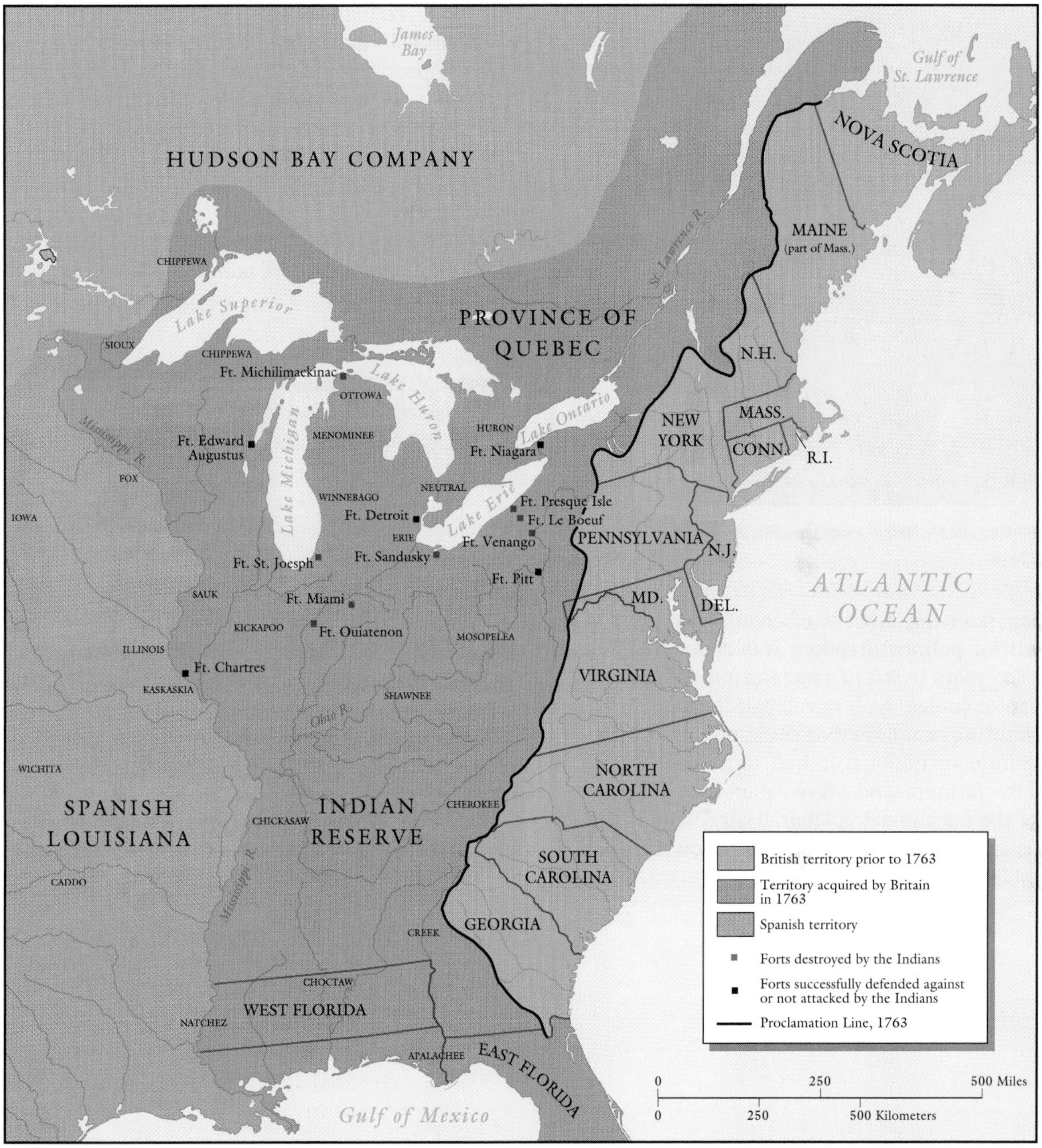
James Bay
Gulf of St. Lawrence
HUDSON BAY COMPANY
NOVA SCOTIA
MAINE
(part of Mass.)
CHIPPEWA
Lake Superior
PROVINCE OF QUEBEC
St. Lawrence R.
SIOUX
CHIPPEWA
Ft. Michilimackinac
Lake Huron
OTTOWA
Lake Ontario
N.H.
MASS.
NEW YORK
CONN.
R.I.
Mississippi R.
Ft. Edward Augustus
MENOMINEE
Lake Michigan
HURON
Ft. Niagara
FOX
WINNEBAGO
NEUTRAL
Lake Erie
Ft. Presque Isle
Ft. Le Boeuf
IOWA
Ft. Detroit
ERIE
Ft. Venango
PENNSYLVANIA
N.J.
Ft. St. Joesph
Ft. Sandusky
Ft. Pitt
SAUK
Ft. Miami
MD.
DEL.
ATLANTIC OCEAN
KICKAPOO
Ft. Ouiatenon
MOSOPELEA
ILLINOIS
Ft. Chartres
KASKASKIA
VIRGINIA
SHAWNEE
Ohio R.
WICHITA
NORTH CAROLINA
SPANISH LOUISIANA
INDIAN RESERVE
CHEROKEE
CHICKASAW
SOUTH CAROLINA
CADDO
Mississippi R.
CREEK
GEORGIA
British territory prior to 1763
Territory acquired by Britain in 1763
Spanish territory
Forts destroyed by the Indians
Forts successfully defended against or not attacked by the Indians
Proclamation Line, 1763
CHOCTAW
WEST FLORIDA
NATCHEZ
APALACHEE
EAST FLORIDA
0
250
500 Miles
0
250
500 Kilometers
Gulf of Mexico

© Cengage Learning

Map 4.3. Territories after the Treaty of Paris, 1763

>> Pontiac and his Native American allies visit British officer Major Gladwyn.

it had sparked the process of colonial unification. The fight for political freedom was about to begin. During the years between 1700 and 1763, the North American colonies had developed into a stable, manufacturing economy that could potentially rival many European nations. It had large numbers of free white farmers and slave laborers performing much of the backbreaking labor. It also had a growing class of merchants and wealthy landowners who provided leadership and governance.

As the French and Indian War was fought on American soil, many colonists began to feel themselves a people apart from their Mother Country. The initial and uncertain itching for political independence had begun. Many colonists could not, or would not, fathom the idea of independence—they had too much to lose. But many outspoken colonists felt that if England persisted in proclaiming the end of salutary neglect, and intended to intrude upon colonial affairs more pointedly, there would be trouble.

| What else was happening . . . | |
|---|---|
| 1709 | Bartolomeo Cristofori invents the piano. |
| 1712 | The last execution of an accused witch takes place in England. |
| 1751 | Benjamin Franklin sends up a kite during a thunderstorm and discovers that lightning is a form of electricity. |
| 1752 | The first eraser is put on the end of a pencil. |

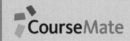

Visit the CourseMate website at www.cengagebrain.com for additional study tools and review materials for this chapter.

# Toward Revolution, *1763–1775*

## Learning Outcomes

*After reading this chapter, you should be able to do the following:*

**LO¹** Explain Britain's main reasons for attempting to overturn salutary neglect.

**LO²** Explain how the colonists responded to the new acts, and trace the evolutionary process that brought the colonies closer to rebellion.

**LO³** Trace the path to revolution from the Townshend Acts of 1767 to the meeting of the First Continental Congress.

**LO⁴** Explain how the American Revolution began, and describe the

> 66 *The British came to see the colonists as not only resisting the demands of their mother country, but also as getting free armed protection from the world's most powerful army.* 99

Getting the colonies organized for the French and Indian War revealed a number of problems for Britain, the most serious of which was the lax enforcement of royal policies in the colonies, the principle labeled salutary neglect (for more on salutary neglect, see Chapter 4). The tradition of salutary neglect meant that

## What do you think?

Simple boycotts of British goods were meaningful because they radicalized the population, forcing colonists to choose sides.

*Strongly Disagree*                  *Strongly Agree*
1       2       3       4       5       6       7

the colonies were slower to mobilize when the British demanded adherence to their dictates. It also meant that the colonists paid few taxes. After the expensive French and Indian War, the British came to see the colonists as not only resisting the demands of their mother country, but also as getting free armed protection from the world's most powerful army. The British, meanwhile, were being taxed pretty stiffly, in part to help secure American economic development. The colonists, the British pointed out, also benefited from having had that army remove the colonists' most powerful competition (the French) from the land. Should the colonists not pay for these benefits?

As the French and Indian War came to a close in 1763, Britain decided to remedy these problems through a series of reforms that tightened control over the colonies and limited the areas where colonists could settle. The colonists resisted these encroachments, however, for they had become accustomed to the self-rule implied in salutary neglect. In addition, since the Enlightenment, Englishmen had sought to protect their "natural rights" from encroachment by their rulers. It did not matter if the ruler was a king or a parliament: if either institution violated one's rights to life, liberty, and property, all Englishmen felt they could reasonably rebel. From the colonists' perspective, they hoped that England's King George would protect them from what they saw as the enmity of a jealous Parliament. The English, on the other hand, saw the colonists as a bunch of headstrong upstarts, demanding rights without assuming the responsibilities inherent to them. As this rhetoric escalated, conflict escalated as well. And it all began during the French and Indian War.

 Explore an interactive module showing life on the eve of the American Revolution.

## LO¹ British Attempts to Rein in the Colonies

The British plan to reform colonial relations had three main goals: (1) to tighten control by eliminating absenteeism and corruption of royal officials in the colonies and by limiting smuggling, by which colonists were avoiding taxes, tariffs, and regulations; (2) to limit the areas where colonists could settle; and (3) to raise greater revenue.

© American School/The Bridgeman Art Library/Getty Images

## Tightening Control

England began its attempts to rein in the colonies in 1760, shortly before the end of the war with France. In that year, the **Privy Council**, which advised the Crown on various matters, issued the "Orders in Council," which required absentee officials to occupy their posts instead of collecting the salary and then paying a substitute to occupy the post. The Privy Council also rewarded officers and crews of naval vessels for seizing smuggling ships. There ought to be no more absentee colonial leadership, and smugglers were to be punished for avoiding taxes.

## Limiting Settlement

The next major reform was the Proclamation of 1763, which did three things: (1) placed a moratorium on government sale of western lands; (2) put trade with Indians under royal control; and (3) forbade settlement west of the Proclamation Line, which followed the crest of the Appalachians (see Map 4.3). The Proclamation's thrust was to control British settlement and push the colonists into the newly acquired colonies of Canada and Florida. Royal officials also believed that the policy would protect British manufacturing, because if colonists moved too far from the Atlantic coast, they would develop their own manufacturing industries rather than import British goods.

Many colonists who were merely frustrated by the Orders in Council were infuriated by the Proclamation. After all, in their minds, the French and Indian War had been fought so that the colonists *could* move farther west. Many colonists had celebrated the British victory, believing that the removal of the French from the region would make westward colonial expansion a possibility. King George's proclamation directly contradicted this belief. Ultimately, the Proclamation of 1763 was impossible to enforce. Settlers moved across the line anyway, and the royal government lacked the resources to stop them.

## Raising Revenue

The final piece of reform was George Grenville's plan for paying off Britain's debt. The British had tried to prevent the colonists' evasion of royal taxes earlier in the 1700s, most notably with the 1751 Writs of Assistance, which gave British officials the right to inspect not only places of work, but also private homes. The colonists fought this infringement on their liberties, although they did not persuade the Crown to reverse the decision. Grenville, who became England's prime minister in 1763, contributed to these woes. He convinced Parliament to pass several specific acts in the 1760s that significantly increased the Crown's interference in the economy of its colonies. It was these revenue acts as much as anything else that signaled the end of salutary neglect.

The first of these acts was the **Sugar Act of 1764**, which was technically a *cut* in taxes on molasses and sugar brought into the colonies from non-British colonies in the West Indies. But it was troublesome to the colonists because, even though it reduced the assessment on sugar, it increased enforcement of tax collection. Furthermore, the act taxed items besides sugar, including indigo, pimento (allspice), some wines, and coffee. Britain was now evidently looking to the colonies as a source of direct revenue.

© North Wind Picture Archives/Alamy

>> The English saw the colonists as a bunch of headstrong upstarts.

>> Many colonists rioted in protest of the passing of the Stamp Act. No one paid more dearly than Thomas Hutchinson, shown here fleeing his house.

>> British soldiers were harassed by colonial boys.

The next intrusive act, the **Quartering Act of 1765**, required the colonies to feed and house British troops stationed in their territory. Colonists bristled at the idea of British soldiers living in their houses, and the colonial assemblies often refused to provide the money required to feed and house these soldiers.

Most disruptive of all, however, was the **Stamp Act**. Passed by Parliament in 1765, the Stamp Act mandated the use of stamped paper for all official papers, including diplomas, marriage licenses, wills, newspapers, and playing cards. The stamp, embedded in the paper (not a topical stamp), indicated that a tax had been paid on the document. Grenville insisted that revenues from the tax go directly to soldiers protecting the North American colonies. He also mandated that those who avoided using taxed paper would be tried in a Crown-operated vice admiralty court, rather than by a trial of one's peers. Not only had the Crown declared its intention to raise revenues from the colonists, but it had also indicated it was ready to enforce its actions.

**Quartering Act of 1765**
This act required the colonies to feed and house British troops stationed in their territory

**Stamp Act**
Passed in 1765, this act mandated the use of stamped (embedded) paper for all official papers, including diplomas, marriage licenses, wills, newspapers, and playing cards

**circular letter**
Communication among a number of interested parties that was sent from colony to colony to keep the disparate colonies together, or united; a primary form of communication for the colonies during the revolutionary period

**Stamp Act Congress**
Gathering of colonial leaders from nine states in New York City in October 1765 to discuss resistance to the Stamp Act; one of the early instances of collaboration between colonies and of identifying Parliament as the opposition rather than the king

**Daughters of Liberty**
Group of colonial American women who organized boycotts of tea and other imported British goods and who produced homespun clothes as a protest of British imported clothing

# LO² Beginnings of American Resistance

The Sugar Act was widely unpopular. New Englanders in particular saw that the new regulations threatened their profitable (though now illegal) rum trade. And the Quartering Act seemed wildly intrusive. But the Stamp Act provoked a much stronger backlash than the Sugar Act had, for three reasons (see "The reasons why..." box).

## The Stamp Act Congress

To try to force Parliament to repeal the Stamp Act, opponents in Massachusetts initiated a **circular letter** inviting all of the colonies to send representatives to a congress to discuss resistance to the Stamp Act. This was a radical move; convening an intercolonial congress without British authorization was an illegal act. Nevertheless, the **Stamp Act Congress** convened in New York City in October 1765, with representatives from nine colonies in attendance.

Although it began as an act of defiance, the Stamp Act Congress was largely conciliatory to the Crown. It acknowledged that the colonies were "subordinate" to Parliament in matters of administration, but it maintained that the colonists' rights as Englishmen were infringed upon when Parliament levied taxes without providing the colonists with representation in Parliament. Resolutely noninflammatory, the Stamp Act Congress avoided words like *slavery* and *tyranny*, which were common in editorials of the day. Nevertheless, it did declare that taxes had never been imposed on the colonists by anyone other than colonial legislatures. It also differentiated between the Crown, to which the Stamp Act Congress pledged allegiance, and Parliament, to which it acknowledged a grudging "subordination." In the end, the congress showed the colonists' increasing tendency to collaborate as a single unit; it also began a pattern of finding fault with Parliament rather than with the king.

 Learn more about (and read) the Resolutions of the Stamp Act Congress.

## Boycotts

In addition to these legalistic declarations, there were other, more potent forms of protest. In Boston, New York, Philadelphia, Charleston, and smaller ports, merchants signed agreements not to import British goods until the Stamp Act was repealed. In New England, women's groups called **"Daughters of Liberty"** organized local boycotts against cloth and tea imported from Britain. These women also held "spin-

*The very clothes that people wore became a form of protest.*

# {The reasons why...}

**The Stamp Act provoked a stronger colonial response than the Sugar or Quartering Acts for three principal reasons:**

***An educated resistance.*** The Stamp Act applied to the kinds of goods used by merchants and lawyers, which stirred up an educated and powerful opposition.

***Time to organize.*** Although Parliament passed the Stamp Act in March, the act did not go into effect until November 1, 1765. This gave colonists time to organize.

***Undermining colonial self-rule.*** The Stamp Act was a direct tax on the colonists (instead of a regulation of trade), and the proceeds were meant to pay the salaries of colonial officials, something the colonists themselves had done in the past. Taxing the colonies so that the Crown could pay these salaries undermined colonial control over royal officials and seemed to indicate that Parliament was limiting colonists' liberties.

>> Tax stamp.

ning bees" that encouraged American women to show loyalty to the resistance by producing home-spun cloth. Locally produced clothing was a sign that one was a "patriot," and colonial women like Abigail Adams and Deborah Sampson Franklin were the key to making it happen.

The boycott proved effective, especially in New York, where boycotters shut down the port. British exports to the colonies declined, and the opposition party in Parliament began to advocate repealing the Stamp Act. The boycotts were also meaning-ful because simple participation in a colonywide boycott radicalized the population, forcing them to choose sides. This was becoming larger than a protest of elite lawyers. The very clothes that people wore became a form of protest.

## Rioting

Although the Stamp Act Congress and boycotts proved fruitful, rioting proved to be the most effec-tive means of protest. To coordinate the riots, sev-eral colonists formed groups called the **Sons of Liberty**. Typically led by men of wealth and high social standing (such as Samuel Adams), the Sons of Liberty served as leaders in organizing protests and intimidating stamp officials. Mobs in Massachusetts, New York, Rhode Island, and South Carolina burned the homes of stamp officials and hanged effi-gies of tax collectors, occasionally even tarring

and feathering them. As a result of this intimidation, all known stamp officials resigned before the Stamp Act went into effect on November 1, 1765. When the Crown offered the positions to others, they refused the jobs. Furthermore, when the stamps and stamped paper arrived in America, colonists sent them back to England, destroyed them, or locked them away.

> **Sons of Liberty**
> Groups of colonial leaders who organized protests and intimidated stamp officials; their actions caused the res-ignation of all known stamp officials
>
> **Radical Whigs**
> Political activists and pam-phleteers who vigorously defended the rights and liberties of Englishmen and who coined the phrase "no taxation without representation"

## Ideological Opposition

In addition to these physical forms of protest, several colonial assemblies sent Parliament written protests, called "resolves." The wording of the resolves was usually influenced by British political pamphlets that circulated at the time. Both the pamphlets and the resolves are significant because they articulated the ideas of liberty that positioned the colonists against Britain all the way to the Revolution.

The central drafters of the pamphlets called themselves **Radical Whigs** (which referred to the opposition party in England, the Whigs). Radical Whigs in England cast a suspicious eye on any infringement of personal liberties, and Radical Whigs in colonial America, such as James Otis of Massachusetts, argued that, because the colonists were not represented in Parliament, Parliament had no authority to tax them. These men coined the phrase "no taxation without representation." The Radical Whigs claimed that the principle that taxation required representation had precedent in British law (in the Magna Carta) and was one of the basic English liberties.

**external taxes**
Duties designed to protect the British Empire; part of Parliament's right to regulate trade, as argued by Benjamin Franklin and Daniel Dulany

**internal tax**
Duties that directly affected the internal affairs of the colonies; according to Benjamin Franklin and Daniel Dulany, this internal legislation threatened private property

**virtual representation**
Theory endorsed by Parliament that said the House of Commons represented the interests of all the king's subjects, wherever they might reside; this was the pretext for rejecting the colonists' demand for actual representation

**deputy representation**
The practice of the people's interests being advocated by a deputy; also known as actual representation

Read some of Patrick Henry's *Resolutions Against the Stamp Act.*

In Virginia, Patrick Henry followed this same line of reasoning. He argued that the Stamp Act was unconstitutional because only the Virginia legislature had the authority to tax Virginians. He introduced a series of *Resolutions Against the Stamp Act* to the Virginia Legislature and asserted that anyone who supported the Stamp Act was an enemy to Virginia. Several of his *Resolutions* were passed by the Burgesses and forwarded to Parliament, indicating the level of radicalization provoked by the Stamp Act.

John Adams of Massachusetts framed another argument against Parliament's right to tax the colonists. In his *Instructions of the Town of Braintree to Their Representative*, Adams argued that allowing Parliament to tax the colonists without their consent threatened the sanctity of private property and personal liberty. If Parliament could seize colonists' property, Adams argued, then colonists were dependents of Parliament and not free men. Furthermore, Adams railed against Parliament for creating the specific courts (called vice admiralty courts) that denied the colonists the right to a trial by a jury of one's peers. More than anything else, Adams argued, the colonists wanted liberty; they did not want to become slaves to the whim of a Parliament over which the colonists had no control.

Benjamin Franklin and Daniel Dulany (a celebrated Maryland attorney) promoted another argument against the Stamp Act. They insisted that colonists accept Parliament's right to regulate trade through the use of duties—a form of taxation they called **external taxes**. What the colonists objected to, according to these writers, was the Stamp Act's imposition of an **internal tax** that directly affected the internal affairs of the colonies. Dulany and

Read Adams's *Instructions of the Town of Braintree to Their Representative.*

View a short film about Benjamin Franklin's life.

Franklin feared that internal legislation threatened private property. Both the Crown and many colonists questioned the validity of this distinction between the two forms of taxation. Although this was a milder argument than that of Adams, who rejected all taxes, it also demonstrated strong opposition to the Stamp Act.

## Opposition to the Opposition

Not all colonists agreed with these dissenters. In fact, a large portion of colonists did not care one way or another about the Stamp Act. Meanwhile, some, such as James Otis, opposed the Stamp Act *and* resistance to it, favoring instead to advocate for a Parliamentary repeal. Still others, such as Lieutenant-Governor Thomas Hutchinson of Massachusetts, defended the Stamp Act as a fair policy. Hutchinson personally disliked the Stamp Act but believed that, because Parliament was the supreme legislative body in the Empire, everything it did was constitutional. Hutchinson said that no matter how inconvenient the Stamp Act was, duty and law required obedience. Hutchinson became a focal point of the rioters, who viewed him as a stooge of the Crown. They sent Hutchinson fleeing, and a mob eventually pulled the roof off his house and trashed all of his possessions. In 1765, resentments were heating up.

In Britain, few people accepted any of the colonists' arguments. Since they shouldered a heavy tax burden already, most of them felt that the colonists were asking for a better deal than British subjects living in the mother country received. The British regarded the colonists' arguments as mere rationalizations to avoid paying taxes.

Members of Parliament also rejected the opposition to the Stamp Act. They argued the dubious point that the House of Commons represented the interests of all the king's subjects, wherever they might reside. This theory of **virtual representation**, they said, was vital to Parliamentary legitimacy because many regions within England were not directly represented in Parliament. In addition, in some areas that *were* represented in the House of Commons, the people had no say in who represented them. Instead, the local nobility or the king selected their representative. King George himself owned the right to appoint more than fifty members to the House of Commons—more than 10 percent of the entire body. Under this theory, Parliament rejected the colonists' demand for actual or **deputy representation**.

## Repeal of the Stamp Act

A trade recession that gripped the British economy in late 1765 ended the bitter dispute. With a downturn in the economy, the king withdrew his tacit support of the Stamp Act for fear that the opposition to it would damage revenues too much. His withdrawal of support doomed the Stamp Act, and Parliament eventually repealed it. In repealing the act, however, Parliament stated that it was yielding not to the colonists' demands, but to the king's. To make this clear, on the same day it repealed the Stamp Act, Parliament passed the **Declaratory Act**, which affirmed its authority to legislate for the colonies "in all cases whatsoever." Although it was largely symbolic, the Declaratory Act became one of the nonnegotiable claims that Parliament was unwilling to relinquish throughout the struggle. Its leaders would rather go to war than have Parliament lose authority.

News of the Declaratory Act perplexed American leaders, leaving them to wonder whether Parliament had accepted the distinction between internal and external taxation. If the distinction was not accepted, the Declaratory Act asserted Parliament's raw power over the colonies because it gave no concessions on the issue of representation. Most colonists, however, overlooked such abstruse concerns and simply celebrated the Stamp Act's repeal. When Parliament passed few new taxes in 1766, many colonists believed that the crisis was over. They were wrong.

# LO³ Taxation without Representation, 1767–1773

In 1766, Charles Townshend, a British politician who believed it was fair for England to tax the colonies "to provide their own safety and preservation," was installed as Britain's chancellor of the Exchequer. The first act he sponsored did not impose a new tax on the colonies, but it did alert colonists that their struggle with Parliament was not over. In the **Restraining Act**, Townshend suspended the New York Assembly for failing to comply with the Quartering Act. This bred suspicions that Townshend would deal harshly with the colonies. It also pushed the debate beyond mere revenue issues, such as taxation without representation. Now Parliament was infringing on the colonists' self-government and self-rule.

> ❝ No freeman should be subject to any tax to which he has not given his own consent. ❞
> —*John Adams, 1765*

John Adams.

**Declaratory Act**
Passed by Parliament in 1766, this act affirmed its authority to legislate for the colonies "in all cases whatsoever"; largely symbolic, it became one of the nonnegotiable claims that Parliament was unwilling to relinquish throughout the struggle

**Restraining Act**
In this act, chancellor of the Exchequer Charles Townshend suspended the New York Assembly for failing to comply with the Quartering Act

**Townshend Acts**
These acts of 1767 instituted duties on glass, lead for paint, tea, paper, and a handful of other items

## The Townshend Acts of 1767

Townshend confirmed the colonists' worst fears in the summer of 1767, when he steered new taxes through Parliament. Townshend considered the colonists' distinction between internal and external taxes invalid, but he saw how he could use it to his advantage. He intended to raise revenue with new, *external* duties on the goods that the colonists imported from Britain. The resulting **Townshend Acts** laid duties on glass, lead for paint, tea, paper, and a handful of other items. The Townshend Acts also demanded the collection of duties and bolstered the importance of colonial governors who were friendly to the Crown. Once again, they threatened the previous status quo of salutary neglect and signified that England would not give up its control so easily.

### Opposition

Opposition to the Townshend Acts followed the pattern of the Stamp Act opposition—although

© Stock Montage/Stock Montage/Getty Images

more slowly, largely because of internal splits among merchants. But many colonists eventually began to boycott British goods again. Women stopped wearing silks and satins or serving tea and wine, making fashionable what they saw as a modest, patriotic life. By 1769 the boycotts were effective in every colony, having been spread by colonial newspapers, which shared information and important essays.

One essay, published in all but four colonial newspapers, offered a distinctive ideological protest to the Townshend Acts. Posing as a simple country gentleman resisting a corrupt government, the prominent lawyer John Dickinson wrote a series of essays called *Letters from a Farmer in Pennsylvania*—published in both Britain and America. Dickinson

Read Dickinson's twelve short letters.

explained that the colonies had tolerated earlier duties because they accepted the idea that Parliament should regulate trade. The purpose of the Townshend duties, however, was not regulation, but revenue. Dickinson considered this unconstitutional. This was yet another argument against Britain's attempts to overturn salutary neglect.

## The Boston Massacre

Opposition to the Townshend Acts triggered rioting as well. Radicals in the Massachusetts legislature drafted a circular letter rejecting the Townshend Acts that was sent to all the colonies. Written primarily by Samuel Adams, the letter urged all merchants to enforce the boycott. In one case, colonist John Hancock's sloop *Liberty* arrived in port in Boston with a cargo of wine. Colonists held the customs official hostage as the wine was unloaded without payment of the required duties. Similar protests followed in other towns. In response, the British sent troops to restore order, and by 1770 British troops were quartered in New York, Boston, and other major towns. The conflict was growing increasingly tense.

On March 5, 1770, a crowd of Boston rebels began throwing snowballs, oyster shells, and other debris at a British sentry in front of the Customs House, prompting the British captain to order more guards outside. When a stick hit one of the soldiers, he fell, and someone shouted, "Fire!" prompting a British guard to shoot into the crowd. Hearing the report,

>> A color print of the Boston Massacre by Paul Revere, used as propaganda to spur on the cause of colonial rebellion.

© Eon Images

*The British regarded the colonists' arguments as mere rationalizations to avoid paying taxes.*

other soldiers shot into the crowd, and in the end, five colonists lay dead and six were wounded. The colonists called this the **Boston Massacre**. Nine British soldiers were tried for the act, and two were convicted of manslaughter (they were all defended by the future president John Adams). The "Massacre" served as important propaganda for the colonial agitators, despite the fact that the English had followed the rule of law and that most of the soldiers were found innocent in a colonial court of law. Furthermore, responses to the "Boston Massacre" sparked a vigorous debate

Read an eyewitness account of the Boston Massacre.

within the colonies about how far rebellion should go. Many colonists remained on the side of the soldiers.

## Repeal

The same day as the Boston Massacre, Parliament repealed most provisions of the Townshend Acts. But, as a symbol of its continued control, it left the tax on tea in place; the colonists accepted the tea tax and dropped their boycott, claiming victory in the conflict.

But this sort of compromise meant that Parliament and the rebelling colonists had not reached a clear agreement, leaving the situation ripe for future conflicts. For the next several years, no major issue emerged to galvanize colonial opposition, lulling many in Britain and in the colonies into the belief that the crisis was over. This was a relief to the Crown, as well as to the many colonists who were content with the colonies' relationship to the royal government. Furthermore, royal officials in America did their best to foster this pacified view, asserting that subordination of the colonies had finally been achieved. This, however, was merely the surface view.

## Local Conflicts, 1770–1773

If unified colonial opposition declined between 1770 and 1773, local conflicts continued, demonstrating that colonists remained assertive and that royal control was tenuous.

### The *Gaspée* Incident

The most noteworthy local conflict was the **Gaspée incident**. In Rhode Island, colonists from Providence boarded and burned an English naval vessel, the *Gaspée,* that had run aground while in pursuit of a colonial ship accused of smuggling. This was quite a radical move. Britain assembled a royal commission of British officials in America to identify the perpetrators and remand them to England for trial. The local commission, however, shortly became the target of colonial protest. **Committees of correspondence**, or organized groups of letter writers, coordinated opposition to the extradition of the suspects, and, as a result, the perpetrators of the *Gaspée* incident were never identified or tried.

### Committees of Correspondence

Massachusetts's colonists also continued their resistance to royal policies. In 1772, several Bostonians set up a committee of correspondence to inform other Massachusetts towns and other colonies of their grievances, "as Men, as Christians, and as Subjects."

This organization aimed to stir up dissent and unite the colonists in their opposition. Several other colonists from towns outside of Boston joined these committees, creating a method for the relatively quick transmission of information between the colonies. As letters circulated from one committee to the next, they passed along information, helping to unify colonial opposition to the Crown.

> 66 Women were the key players in reducing tea consumption, while men were the staunchest advocates of using violent means. 99

*Gaspée* incident
**Conflict that occurred when colonists from Providence boarded and burned the English naval vessel *Gaspée***

committees of correspondence
**Organized groups of letter writers who would provide quick and reliable information throughout the colonies**

## Choosing Sides

Although local opposition to Crown policies was significant between 1770 and 1773, it was not as widespread as the protests that emerged in response to the Stamp Act or the Townshend Acts. And, although some colonial leaders tried to transform local concerns into colonywide grievances, most issues never achieved more than local prominence, mainly because most colonists were reluctant to engage in a full-on confrontation with the Crown.

Within cities like Boston, New York, and Philadelphia, wealthy people remained mostly supportive of the Crown, while artisans and merchants, who had been financially stung by several economic acts passed by the Crown, were the most avid patriots. Many people did not favor conflict and could not imagine rebellion. New England's slaves, meanwhile, attempted to use the language of political freedom to their benefit, and in 1773 and 1774 they petitioned the colonial government for their freedom. When the legislature passed a bill on their behalf, the royal governor vetoed it. Regardless, the slaves made it clear that whoever promised to free them would earn their support.

In the Southern Colonies and the Chesapeake, many of the most powerful families remained supportive of the Crown, whose policies had enriched them in the first place. Meanwhile, those living in rural areas were more supportive of the rebels, mainly because they felt slighted by the meager amount of self-rule that the colonial elite granted them. These internal cleavages would persist through the Revolutionary War, although between

1770 and 1773, they were less visible because no single issue stoked the fires of dissent. In 1773, however, an issue emerged that would prod more and more colonists toward open opposition to royal control.

## The Tea Act, 1773

In 1773, Parliament passed the **Tea Act**. The act was designed not to anger the colonists, but to give the East India Company a monopoly on the sale of tea to North America (the company was badly in debt and had influence in Parliament).

### Provisions of the Act

The Tea Act had three provisions: (1) it lowered the colonists' duty on tea; (2) it granted the East India Company the monopoly; and (3) it appointed royal agents who were to pay the duty in England and then sell the tea to the colonists. This last provision meant that colonial merchants could no longer sell tea. Prior to the Tea Act, most colonists had bought smuggled Dutch tea because it was cheaper than the English variety. The Tea Act was designed to bring British tea to the colonies at a lower price, thus undercutting the illegal Dutch trade. Because tea was the most common beverage consumed by the colonists, Parliament and the East India Company hoped that the colonies would be pleased with the measure and buy more tea.

### Colonial Response

This was not the case, for two reasons. Naturally, powerful colonial tea merchants were upset at losing the business. In addition, the timing of the act meant that many colonists interpreted it as yet another move to establish Parliament's authority. Radical Whigs pointed out that until 1773 the duty on tea had been paid in Britain. But now, under the Tea Act, the duty would be collected from British agents who had collected the revenue from the Americans. Instead of a tax laid in England and collected in England, it was a tax laid in England and collected in America.

The colonists responded as they had before, only more violently. They published protests and pressured anyone concerned with the enforcement of the law to send tea back to Britain. They forged a campaign of intimidation by threatening anyone who tried to enforce the Act. In short, the colonists planned to nullify the Tea Act by refusing to comply with it. Women were the key players in reducing tea consumption, while men were the staunchest advocates of using violent means.

### The Boston Tea Party

Most of the tea-bearing ships that encountered resistance simply returned to England. But in Boston, the tea issue was especially sensitive because Governor Thomas Hutchinson's son was one of the major consignees, and Hutchinson was determined to support his son's enterprise. In addition, Hutchinson viewed the Tea Act as a chance to demonstrate his fidelity to the Crown in the face of the most rebellious colony in North America. Thus, when Bostonians pressed to have the tea returned to England, Hutchinson said that was fine, so long as they paid the tax on the tea first.

The rebelling colonists refused, and in this impasse, the ship simply sat in Boston Harbor. The deadlock could not last: by law, the tax had to be paid within twenty days, which, in this case, meant it had to be paid by December 17, 1773. Governor Hutchinson vowed to have the tea unloaded and the tax paid on the day of the deadline. To prevent this, on the night of December 16, an organized squad of roughly sixty colonists dressed as Mohawk Indians boarded the ship and dumped the entire cargo—342 chests of tea—into Boston Harbor. Historians are unsure why they chose that particular disguise to commit their act of protest. Perhaps it was to distinguish themselves from others? Perhaps costumes promoted unity? Perhaps Native Americans symbolized both savagery and radical democracy, freed from the constraints of British "civilization"?

For Boston radicals like the Sons of Liberty, the **Boston Tea Party** was momentous. Bostonians were proud that they had made a powerful strike against the Crown, and they noted that discipline among their ranks was maintained. Beyond the tea, the squad did not commit vandalism or destroy any other property.

But they also recognized that they had pushed the conflict to a new level. After the destruction of British property, colonists could only speculate on how the British government would react to this new provocation. Refraining from buying tea was essentially a passive protest; destroying an entire ship's worth was something altogether different.

 Read a participant's eyewitness account of the Tea Party.

> **❝I immediately dressed myself in the costume of an Indian, equipped with a small hatchet . . . and a club, after having painted my face and hands with coal dust in the shop of a blacksmith, I repaired to Griffin's wharf, where the ships lay that contained the tea.❞**
> —*Eyewitness to the Boston Tea Party*

 Read the Coercive Acts.

## The Coercive and Quebec Acts, 1774

Parliament's response came quickly. A few members of Parliament argued that the Tea Party's ringleaders should be arrested. The majority disagreed, recalling the failure of the government to bring to trial the perpetrators of the *Gaspée* incident. To avoid the difficulties of prosecuting the individual Bostonians, Parliament opted to pass punitive legislation—the so-called Coercive Acts—in 1774.

### The Coercive Acts

The laws that came to be called the **Coercive Acts** actually comprised four separate acts, most of which attempted to punish Massachusetts for the Tea Party. Parliament thought it could attack Massachusetts and thus divide the colonists in order to reconquer them. The four acts were (1) the Boston Port Act, which closed Boston's harbor until the town paid for the destroyed tea; (2) the Massachusetts Government Act, which terminated most self-government in the colony; (3) the Administration of Justice Act, which dictated that any British official charged with a capital offense in the colonies could be tried in Great Britain (this issue had arisen after the trials that resulted from the Boston Massacre); and (4) the Quartering Act, which applied to all the colonies and allowed the British Army to house troops wherever necessary, including private buildings.

### The Quebec Act

A fifth act followed the same year. The Quebec Act straightened out several legal issues in Canada but

>> **This nineteenth-century image of the 1773 Boston Tea Party highlights the Indian costumes worn by the radical protestors.**

also did two other things: (1) it guaranteed French Canadians the right to practice Roman Catholicism, which appalled the colonists, especially in New England, where almost everyone was a Protestant unaccustomed to accommodating other religions; and (2) it declared that much of England's holdings across the Proclamation Line of 1763 (everything west of the Appalachian Mountains) would be governed from Quebec. The colonists were infuriated that the Crown was governing this land from the north rather than the east. After all, many colonists felt they had fought for possession of this land during the French and Indian War. The colonists' widespread anti-Catholicism and their land lust led them to link the Quebec Act and the Coercive Acts, referring to them together as **Intolerable Acts**.

## Colonial Response

The various acts were intended to break the colonists' spirit, to dissolve colonial unity, and to isolate Massachusetts. But the actual consequences were different. At the most basic level, Bostonians refused to pay the penalties required by the Port Act. A small number of pro-British merchants offered to pay the fines on the city's behalf, but a group of rebellious colonists threatened them, too. The rejection of the offer was a strong measure of the colonists' convictions because the port closure inflicted considerable suffering on the people who depended on trade to maintain their economic well-being.

Through committees of correspondence, colonists everywhere heard of Massachusetts's plight. Virginia, South Carolina, and Connecticut sent food. Thus, rather than isolating Massachusetts, the acts unified the colonies.

## The First Continental Congress

This colonial unity is best seen in the meeting of the First Continental Congress. In May 1774, Rhode Island, Pennsylvania, New York, and Virginia called for an intercolony congress to address the growing crisis (doing so without consent from the Crown, which was still illegal). In September, delegates from twelve colonies met in the **First Continental Congress** at Philadelphia to consider the American

response to the Coercive Acts. Only Georgia was absent, principally because Creek Indians were actively fighting Georgians over western expansion, and the colonists there felt they needed British defensive support.

The delegates considered several plans of action. Ultimately, the congress created the **Continental Association**, which supervised a boycott of British trade. The association was prefaced with a "Declaration of Rights" that asserted the natural-rights foundation of the colonists' resistance, affirming the trio of natural rights put forward by John Locke—"life, liberty, and property." This was not yet independence, though. The delegates to the first Continental Congress tried to maintain a balance between supporting colonists' rights and affirming the role of the Crown. In 1774 they were pursuing autonomy, not independence. They agreed to meet again the next year.

# LO⁴ The Shot Heard 'Round the World

Meanwhile, back in Boston, local militias were preparing for battle. Parliament, these men felt, had pushed far enough; they would no longer tolerate more infringements on their liberties. Furthermore, who knew what the Crown would do next to plague their economic existence? Indeed, by mid-1774 colonists in western Massachusetts had essentially taken over the towns and evicted British officials. Like many colonists, they really did believe the British were coming to take away their freedoms.

## Militia Preparations

To ready themselves for battle, Massachusetts colonists stockpiled guns in several locations outside Boston, while militia groups drilled defiantly in town squares. They also developed a "Provincial Congress" that assumed the role of a colonial government outside the Crown. Other Massachusetts counties organized conventions to unify the resistance. In some areas, colonists opposed the Administration of Justice Act by closing courts rather than permitting the governor's appointed judges to sit.

Other colonies followed Massachusetts's lead, organizing their own provincial congresses, committees, and conventions. Patriots near urban centers formed committees of correspondence to circulate news, information, and instructions throughout the colonies. Although not all colonists were so enthusiastic for war, especially outside the cities that were affected most by Britain's policies, there was a growing sense that the conflict between Britain and its North American colonies might result in a full-scale rebellion.

## Britain's Response to the Preparations

The colonists' military preparedness became evident to the British in September 1774, when Massachusetts' patriots responded to false rumors that the royal governor had ordered the British Army to seize colonial gunpowder and that British troops had fired on the people of Boston. Roughly 3,000 colonists responded to the "Powder Alarm" by converging on Boston, a city of approximately 15,000 inhabitants. Many more patriots were on the road to Boston when news came that the rumors were untrue. The governor, Thomas Gage, realized that his army was outnumbered and that the colonists were prepared to actually fight. In response, he ordered the construction of fortifications across the small strip of land that connected Boston to the mainland (see Map 5.1) and asked Parliament for 20,000 more British troops.

## Lexington and Concord

By the spring of 1775, tensions were at a fever pitch. Feeling threatened, the British secretary of state pressured Gage to curb the colonists' military planning. So, in April 1775, Gage sent troops to the town of Concord, about 20 miles northwest of Boston, to capture the colonial military supplies hidden there and to arrest the patriot leaders John Hancock and Samuel Adams.

The British soldiers were thus armed and resolute when they left Boston on April 18, 1775. Despite the soldiers' efforts to move quietly, Boston patriots detected the troop movement and sent Paul Revere, William Dawes, and Samuel Prescott on horseback to alert the colonists in the countryside between Boston and Concord (only Prescott made it all the way to Concord; the others were captured on the way). On the morning of April 19, a militia assembled in Lexington to halt the British before they reached Concord. The British, still the most powerful army in the world at the time, did not back down. The American militia captain ordered his men (called "**Minutemen**" because they supposedly were ready on a minute's notice) to retreat after the much stronger British forces ordered them to disperse. As some of the rebelling colonists retreated, some-

one fired a shot (both sides later claimed the other fired first), and the British soldiers began firing on the militia. The colonists suffered eighteen casualties (eight killed and ten wounded), while the British suffered only one, after this, the supposed "shot heard 'round the world."

After the British rout of the Minutemen, the British marched to Concord, but by the time they arrived, Hancock and Adams had fled, and it is uncertain whether the cautious British would have exacerbated the already explosive situation by carrying out the capture of these two prominent colonists. Instead, when they took their position at one end of the North Bridge in Concord, they were met by another armed militia that positioned itself at the opposite end of the bridge. The militia fired on the British troops and forced them to alter their route back to Boston. This was the first time Americans had fired against the British Army (colloquially referred to as the Redcoats) in a formal confrontation. It was also the first time the Redcoats had been forced to retreat in the face of an American enemy.

The Minutemen made the Redcoats' return to Boston a nightmare. Militiamen gathered from surrounding towns to pursue the British the entire way, firing from behind stone walls and trees. The British suffered heavy casualties and, once in Boston, found themselves besieged by thousands more militiamen. Over the course of the day, the Americans suffered 95 casualties, while the British suffered 273, includ-  Watch a film about Lexington, Concord, and the "shot heard 'round the world."

ing 73 dead. This was a marked escalation of the colonial conflict; for the first time, Americans had killed British soldiers in battle.

## Colonial Response to Lexington and Concord

Following the battles of Lexington and Concord, the colonists had to determine what their best response might be. Had an all-out war begun? What about the many colonists who did not support the rebellion?

On May 10, 1775, the **Second Continental Congress** gathered in Philadelphia to answer this question. The congress enacted several policies,

**Minutemen**
Nickname for American militia soldiers because of their reputation for being ready on a minute's notice

**Second Continental Congress**
Gathering of colonial leaders in May 1775 to determine the colonies' response to the battles of Lexington and Concord; they passed resolutions supporting war that included a sharp rejection of all authority under the king in America

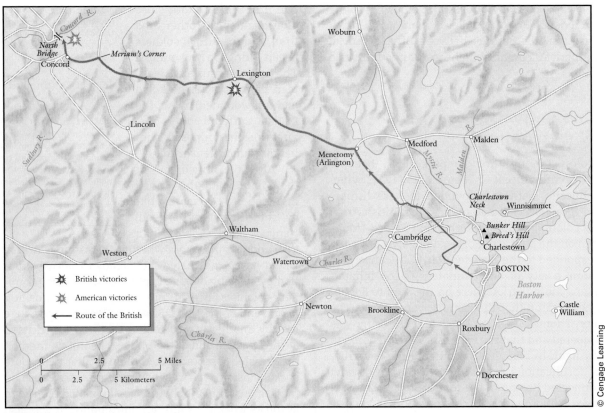

 Map 5.1 Lexington, Concord, and Boston, 1775

Olive Branch Petition
**A 1775 declaration to King George III that the colonists were still loyal to him and imploring the king to seek a peaceful resolution to the conflict**

including acknowledging the militia companies surrounding Boston as the core of a new "Continental Army" and appointing as its general a Virginian, George Washington. (The selection of a Virginian was meant to balance the predominance of Massachusetts militiamen in the army, thus showing colonial unity.) The Second Continental Congress passed resolutions supporting war, which included a sharp rejection of all authority under the king in America. It also adopted the "Declaration of the Causes and Necessity of Taking Up Arms." These were bold, brave actions, although no one was sure whether this was a battle over grievances against Parliament or one with a goal of independence.

Regardless, without formally declaring the colonies' independence, the Continental Congress was beginning to behave more like the government of an independent nation than that of a territory

within an empire. The congress remained cautious about the word *independence*, though, and in July 1775 it approved the "**Olive Branch Petition**," written by John Dickinson, which declared that the colonists were still loyal to King George III and implored the king to seek a peaceful resolution to the conflict. The king ignored the petition, viewing the colonists as insubordinate subjects of the Crown.

## The Battle of Bunker Hill

Within weeks, the hesitancy shown at the Second Continental Congress vanished. Local battles inspired this eagerness, especially the biggest battle, which occurred in Boston. After Lexington and Concord, thousands of men from throughout the colonies joined the Minutemen around Boston to besiege the British military. On June 17, 1775, the British Army sent troops across the Charles River to capture the colonists' cannons located on Breed's Hill, which overlooked Boston and was connected to nearby Bunker Hill by a saddle of land. The

*For the first time, Americans had killed British soldiers in battle.*

>> This nineteenth-century representation of the Battle of Concord highlights the struggling but valiant patriots fighting the large and organized Redcoats.

colonists had fortified Breed's Hill because they could fire their cannons at British ships in Boston Harbor from there. The ensuing battle was fought primarily on Breed's Hill but came to be known as the **Battle of Bunker Hill**. It was the first all-out battle of the Revolutionary War. Although British troops forced the patriots to abandon their hilltop position, the colonists inflicted heavy casualties on the British. In one particularly brutal episode, the British lost 1,000 men in an hour. The British killed around 400 Minutemen.

## And in the end . . .

When news of the Battle of Bunker Hill spread through the colonies and reached Britain, it had two key effects. First, it prompted thousands of additional colonists to join the opposition to Britain, as small conflicts spread across the land. Second, it convinced Britain that many colonists, not just a handful of troublemakers, were part of the rebellion. Because of this realization, Parliament issued the **American Prohibitory Act**, which declared the colonies to be "in open rebellion," forbade commerce with the colonies by blockading their ports, and made colonial ships and their cargo subject to seizure as if they were the property "of open enemies." Now that Parliament had declared the colonies to be in rebellion, this meant that any leaders who were caught could be tried for treason and executed. This raised the stakes dramatically. A rebellion was turning into a revolution. What had begun in the early 1760s as the Crown's attempt to tighten control over its North American colonies had led those colonies to unite in order to claim their independence.

**Battle of Bunker Hill**
Outbreak of fighting on June 17, 1775, near Boston Harbor; the first all-out battle of the Revolutionary War

**American Prohibitory Act**
This act declared the colonies to be "in open rebellion," forbade commerce with the colonies by blockading their ports, and made colonial ships and their cargo subject to seizure as if they were the property "of open enemies"

| Chronology | |
|---|---|
| 1763 | French and Indian War ends |
| 1764 | Sugar Act |
| 1765 | Quartering Act |
| March 22, 1765 | Stamp Act passed |
| Summer/Fall 1765 | Colonial protests and riots |
| August 1765 | Sons of Liberty |
| October 1765 | Stamp Act Congress meets |
| March 1766 | Stamp Act repealed |
| 1767 | Townshend Acts |
| 1770 | Boston "massacre" |
| May 10, 1773 | Tea Act passed |
| Dec. 16, 1773 | Boston Tea Party |
| Spring 1774 | Coercive, or Intolerable, Acts |
| May 1774 | First Continental Congress |
| April 19, 1775 | Lexington and Concord |
| May 10, 1775 | Second Continental Congress |
| June 17, 1775 | Battle of Bunker Hill |

## What else was happening . . .

| | |
|---|---|
| 1700s | American innkeepers think nothing of requesting that a guest share his bed with a stranger when accommodations become scarce. |
| 1760s | Because the British Macaroni Club's members are known for having affected manners and long, curled hair, "macaroni" becomes a slang term for "dandy." The song "Yankee Doodle" is invented by the British to insult American colonists. The section where Doodle puts a feather in his cap and calls it macaroni is a slap at the ragged bands of American troops. |
| 1769 | Shoelaces are invented in England. |
| 1772 | Joseph Priestley invents soda water. |
| 1773 | Seamstress Betsy Ross and her husband, John, begin renting the Philadelphia house where she will sew the first American flag. |
| 1774 | Empress Catherine II's Russian troops defeat Turkey, adding the Southern Ukraine, the Northern Caucasus, and Crimea to the Russian Empire. |

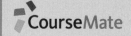 **CourseMate**

Visit the CourseMate website at www.cengagebrain.com for additional study tools and review materials for this chapter.

# CHAPTER 6

# The Revolution

## Learning Outcomes

*After reading this chapter, you should be able to do the following:*

LO **1**   Describe the long-term causes and more immediate events that led the colonists into a true revolution against Britain.

LO **2**   Discuss the various phases of the American Revolution, and analyze the circumstances that eventually helped the colonists win a conflict that Britain, by rights, should never have lost.

LO **3**   Assess the significance of the American Revolution to the following groups: colonists, slaves, native populations, and women.

© iStockphoto.com/Sean Locke

# "Ostensibly, the battle was between freedom and tyranny (if you were a patriot), or about the responsibilities of being an Englishman (if you were a Loyalist)."

After the "long train of abuses" leading up to the Declaration of Independence, from 1776 to 1783 American patriots fought a long and difficult war with Britain. Ostensibly, the battle was between freedom and tyranny (if you were a patriot), or about the responsibilities of being an Englishman (if you were a Loyalist). In reality, choosing sides was much more personal, depending, for instance, on whether your landlord was a Loyalist or a patriot, whether you thought political freedom would improve your business, or whether you felt the earnings you made from a slave-based economy were threatened. All colonists, of course, were forced to choose sides, although many remained ambivalent about each position. Loyalists were scorned, but revolutionaries would be punished brutally if their side lost the war. Choosing sides was no small matter, and the consequences could be deadly.

But the war and the political independence that followed made up only one of several revolutions that took place during these years. The revolutionary war brought with it fundamental questions about freedom and liberty, and about what kind of society Americans wanted. How far would the American Revolution go in promoting equality? Would economic and educational differences be eradicated by a leveling state? Would slavery be abolished? How different would the new society look compared with the old?

## What do you think?

**By the end of 1775, the colonists had no choice but to seek full independence from England.**

| Strongly Disagree | | | | | | Strongly Agree |
|---|---|---|---|---|---|---|
| 1 | 2 | 3 | 4 | 5 | 6 | 7 |

# LO¹ From Rebellion to Revolution

As in most revolutions, the American Revolution had long-term, underlying causes that finally came to a head because of short-term, precipitating events.

### Underlying Causes

Between 1660 and 1763, the colonies had formed a unique society distinct from that of England. Perhaps most importantly, they had developed a dynamic economy in manufacturing and developing goods, as well as supplying raw materials to trading partners in both the Old and New Worlds. In other words, the colonies were not just a primary economic supplier (supplying raw materials to a mother country), but a well-rounded economic system unto themselves. Of course, many wealthy southerners owed their fortunes to slave-based cash crops that were then traded with England, so these colonists shied away from confrontation with the Crown. Nevertheless, large sectors of the North American economy were becoming increasingly independent of England.

**Hessians**
German soldiers hired by Britain to fight against the rebelling American colonies

Along similar lines, property ownership was more common in the colonies than in England. This meant that, with the notable exception of slaves, the people working the land owned it, which gave them something to fight for should their position be threatened. The colonies also had developed without the titled aristocracy or widespread poverty found in England, two further factors in making the colonies an entity unique from England. And, in fact, each colony had developed a self-elected government, something they were not willing to give up easily.

## Precipitating Events

These long-term causes could not have detonated into a war without several precipitating sparks. Three were substantial: (1) increased local conflicts; (2) the uncompromising attitude of Britain; and (3) a shift in opinion among the colonists—toward revolution.

### The Widening War

At the local level, the war's scope was widening even before any official declaration of war. In 1775, for instance, Ethan Allen and his "Green Mountain Boys" attacked and captured Britain's Fort Ticonderoga and Crown Point in backwoods New York. The Continental Army invaded Canada and captured Montreal but failed to capture Quebec. In Charleston, patriots beat back an attack by a British fleet. In Boston, patriots surrounded and laid "siege" on the city after the British had taken control after the Battle of Bunker Hill. Virginians meanwhile forced the royal governor, Lord Dunmore, to retreat from the mainland to a British warship in the harbor at Norfolk. These local conflicts, organized without the assistance of any unified colonial body, indicated a widening war between England and the colonies.

Lord Dunmore's actions are significant, however, for another reason. After retreating to an offshore ship as he awaited British military support, Dunmore issued a proclamation offering freedom to any slave who agreed to fight for the British. His program, "Liberty to Slaves," angered the colonists, who would later cite Dunmore's actions in the Declaration of Independence. To many colonists, liberty was meant only for Europeans and Euro-Americans, and it stung that the governor was offering it to slaves. Within weeks of Dunmore's call, between five hundred and six hundred slaves responded, and before the war was over, several thousand more fought for Britain and for their freedom. This is in contrast to the colonial army, whose commander George Washington refused to use black soldiers during the first years of the war. Indeed, only during the final months of the war were colonists forced to press slaves into service, delaying doing so mostly because they feared arming them as enemies.

 Learn more about Lord Dunmore and read his proclamation.

### Uncompromising Britain

As the war widened, King George III grew increasingly angry at the colonies for their continued insubordination. He rejected the "Olive Branch Petition" of the Second Continental Congress and in August 1775 denounced the colonists as rebels. He also hired mercenaries from Germany, called **"Hessians,"** to fight the colonists. And in December 1775 he closed all American ports. This last action was particularly significant because it made independence absolutely necessary to open trade with other countries. The king's uncompromising attitude presented the colonists with few options other than revolution.

>> The king's uncompromising attitude presented the colonists with few options other than revolution.

## The Shift in American Opinion

Finally, popular opinion had gradually shifted toward independence. The decline of salutary neglect and the spread of local violence led many colonists to side with the revolutionaries. These economic and social events pushed the war of ideas about freedom and sovereignty into the lives of everyday Americans, and the more the Crown proved uncompromising, the more American opinion shifted toward revolution.

## Choosing Sides

There was, however, never unanimity, and thus, in addition to this being a revolutionary war, it was also very much a civil war.

### The Loyalists

Why remain loyal? In the end, somewhere between one-fifth and one-third of the colonists remained loyal to Britain throughout the war (see "The reasons why..." box). Most prominent in this group were wealthy landholders and slave owners, who had the most to lose in a revolution. Furthermore, a large percentage of colonists remained indifferent to both the British and the revolutionaries.

Although all the colonies had some pro-Crown families, geographically most Loyalists lived in the southern colonies and New York.

## The Revolutionaries

Why revolt? Each rebelling colonist had a different motive for supporting a break with England, and these reasons were just as complicated as those for remaining loyal.

Personal and commercial considerations were vitally important. But perhaps most influential was the ideology of **republicanism**, the idea that government should be based on the consent of the governed and that the people had a duty to ensure that their government did not infringe on individual rights. The American Revolution was the first serious modern attempt to craft a government based on these principles.

Republicanism set down deep roots in England before it flowered on American soil. The British Radical Whigs of the 1600s, for example, harked back to the classical Roman ideal of a "republican society," in which governmental power was curtailed by the actions of the people, who were presumed to be virtuous and willing to sacrifice for the public good. Drawing on these Roman ideals,

**republicanism**
The theory that government should be based on the consent of the governed and that the governed had a duty to ensure that their government did not infringe on individual rights

© Powered by Light/Alan Spencer/Alamy

---

## { *The reasons why ...* }

**Colonists were reluctant to withdraw from the British Empire for at least six reasons:**

***Personal connections in Britain.*** Many still felt a strong attachment to Britain and the king, and many still had family and friends there.

***Economic ties.*** Many also had strong commercial ties with Britain (the slave-based economy of the southern colonies was particularly dependent on such trade). To rebel was to risk their present and future wealth.

***Geo-political concerns.*** Some feared that France or Spain might take over if Britain were driven out of the colonies, and they preferred British rule to that of some other European nation.

***Fears of what American independence might mean.*** Some of the smaller religious groups felt that Britain had protected them from more powerful denominations that could potentially flourish if the new American state adopted a national religion.

***Personal motives.*** Economically, it was often a matter of settling small scores. If, for instance, your landlord was a revolutionary, you were likely to be a Loyalist; if your landlord was a Loyalist, you were likely to be a patriot.

***Uncertainty about American success.*** Some colonists doubted the colonies' ability to throw off British rule. After all, Britain was the most powerful nation in the world, with the mightiest army.

the Radical Whigs outlined a theory according to which a government was legitimate only when it was based on an agreement between the members of a society and government. In this formulation, the members of society would agree to sacrifice a degree of liberty and the government would maintain security and order, but otherwise avoid infringing on a person's life, liberty, or property. Any ruler who transgressed natural laws was a tyrant, and under tyranny the rebellion of a people was justifiable. (Republicanism was different from liberalism, which viewed any government as an unwanted infringement on individual liberty.)

Republican ideas spread throughout the colonies in the 1700s, mainly by the work of two English authors—John Trenchard and Thomas Gordon—who wrote a short book called **Cato's Letters**. In America, *Cato's Letters* and other Radical Whig writings were quoted every time Britain attempted to raise taxes after the French and Indian War.

But the best-known expression of republican ideas in revolutionary America was corset maker Thomas Paine's political pamphlet **Common Sense,** published in January 1776. Its simple wording of republican ideals nudged the colonists further toward independence. Paine asserted that the king never had the welfare of his subjects in mind and

that he was entirely concerned with his own exercise of power. Paine also argued that independence was the only answer to this problem, using language so powerful that it made any other course of action seem absurd. He set forth a vision of America as a dynamic, independent nation, growing in population and prosperity, with a kindly government doing a substantial amount of economic and political leveling to ensure equality. Pointing to the tremendous growth of the American colonies in the eighteenth century, Paine argued that America was more than just capable of maintaining independence from Britain; America was so strong, he claimed, that independence was inevitable.

Explore an interactive module on choosing sides in the American Revolution.

Read *Common Sense.*

Paine's pamphlet was enormously influential in changing the minds of those who had opposed independence. Emerging just as local conflicts spread, *Common Sense* was reprinted several times; in total, 150,000 copies were distributed throughout the colonies—a number equivalent to 15 million copies being distributed in the United States today.

## The Declaration of Independence

The increase of local conflicts, Britain's inflexibility, and the spreading of republican ideals made a break with Britain inevitable by 1776. But independence was expedited further by events on the ground. In March 1776, the Continental Army forced the British to evacuate Boston, ending the eleven-month siege of the city that had begun after Lexington and Concord and the Battle of Bunker Hill. Rather than sail for home, however, the British Army headed for New York, where more Loyalists resided than in any other colony. Choosing not to establish their base where the colonists were united in opposition (Boston), the British hoped to divide the colonies by setting their base of operations in an area less committed to independence.

© North Wind Picture Archives

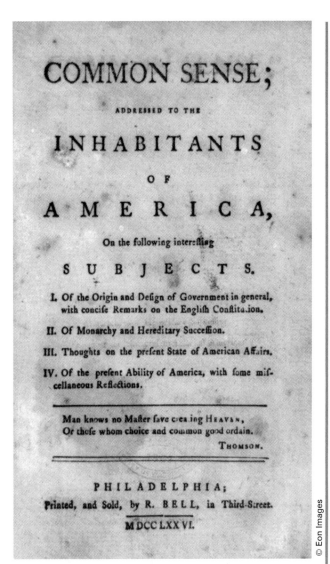

COMMON SENSE;

ADDRESSED TO THE

INHABITANTS

OF

A M E R I C A,

On the following interesting

S U B J E C T S.

I. Of the Origin and Design of Government in general,
with concise Remarks on the English Constitution.

II. Of Monarchy and Hereditary Succession.

III. Thoughts on the present State of American Affairs.

IV. Of the present Ability of America, with some mis-
cellaneous Reflections.

Man knows no Master save creating HEAVEN,
Or those whom choice and common good ordain.

THOMSON.

PHILADELPHIA;

Printed, and Sold, by R. BELL, in Third-Street.

MDCCLXXVI.

>> **Common Sense** was reprinted several times; in total, 150,000 copies were distributed throughout the colonies—a number equivalent to 15 million copies being distributed in the United States today.

### The Drafting

With this crisis at hand, Richard Henry Lee, a Virginia delegate to the Continental Congress, proposed, on June 7, 1776, that the colonies officially declare their independence. With regional balance in mind, the Congress created a committee to draft a declaration. The committee consisted of John Adams

 View a film about the drafting of the Declaration of Independence.

 Read the Declaration.

of Massachusetts, Roger Sherman of Connecticut, Robert R. Livingston of New York, Benjamin Franklin of Pennsylvania, and Thomas Jefferson of Virginia, who was selected as the principal draftsman. After the committee made minor revisions to Jefferson's first draft, the committee presented the **Declaration of Independence** to the Congress on June 28, 1776.

### The Declaration

The document consisted of two parts: (1) a preamble justifying the revolution on the basis of natural rights, as espoused in the language of republicanism; and (2) a list of grievances accusing George III of tyranny and therefore justifying revolt.

### The Signing

Once the Congress had read the Declaration, they debated it and made several major changes (the most important one was deleting Jefferson's tortured assertions that England had been responsible for implanting the evil institution of slavery in the New World and then, through Lord Dunmore, provoking slave rebellions). Then the Continental Congress unanimously approved the Declaration of Independence on July 2, 1776, by a vote of 12 to 0. (The delegation from New York abstained from voting because it had not received instructions from its colony legislature, but the delegates themselves stated that they were in favor of independence.) Two days later, on July 4, John Hancock, as president of the Congress, may have signed the edited document; other delegates added their signatures to a clean copy of the Declaration in early August.

> **Declaration of Independence**
> Statement adopted by the Second Continental Congress declaring that the thirteen American colonies, then at battle with Britain, constituted a free and independent state; drafted primarily by Thomas Jefferson and adopted in 1776

## LO² The War for Independence

With the Congress's July 2, 1776, Declaration, the Revolution now had a goal—political independence

**bills of credit**
Currency printed by the Continental Congress during the Revolutionary War; printing these bills in huge numbers and without any backing led to high inflation

for the American colonies. What had begun as a struggle to secure the rights and liberties that the colonists felt they deserved as British subjects had become a war to secure American nationhood.

## The Opposing Sides

The colonists had declared their independence, but now they would have to fight for it. But how could they? They had long been protected by the British, and, other than a few small colonial militias, they had no standing army.

### The Continental Army

Efforts to build an army began in earnest even before the Declaration of Independence. It was an uphill battle. The army of the patriots, called the Continental Army, was often ill equipped, undermanned, and hungry. From the beginning, recruitment was a problem. Many colonists wanted freedom, but not many wanted to give their lives for it. The Continental Congress had to offer large bounties of land to induce men to enlist, and eventually it reduced the term of service to just three months. Although the Congress set enlistment quotas for all the new states, the states rarely met them. At any given time, there were usually 10,000 poorly trained troops in the Continental Army. They were usually hungry and unpaid, but the

> 66 The main way they raised money was simply to print it and hope people would accept the bills. 99

Continental Congress could not help because it did not have much money itself. As fighting progressed, the army had to live off the kindness of surrounding farmers (hoping they were patriots and not Loyalists).

The Continental Army acted under the orders of George Washington, a patrician Virginia tobacco farmer whose wealth came from his wife's family. He believed in the republican ideology to the very marrow

 View a film about the life of George Washington.

of his bones. And he had a brilliant grasp of the war's military strategy. He recognized that, because of the ideological nature of the Revolution and the nature of his ragtag army, his chances would be better if he did not try to win every battle. Indeed, if he refused to engage the British at all and made them wear themselves out in pursuing him, he could win simply by surviving. This strategy, of course, also depended on nonmilitary colonists continuing to resist and harass the British governors and troops. Without this grassroots support in colonial cities and towns, the British might have simply starved the colonists into submission.

### The Revolutionary Government and Finances

Washington received his orders from the Continental Congress, the only centralized authority in the colonies, although it had no legal standing or charter document. The Continental Congress could only request assistance from the various states, which had no obligation to grant those requests. Although the revolutionaries planned a national government in 1777, its founding charter (the Articles of Confederation) was not completed until 1781. Throughout the Revolutionary War, then, the revolutionaries had no official central authority.

This hindered them organizationally, and worse, it meant that the revolutionaries could not easily raise money. They had neither the power to levy taxes nor the infrastructure of a treasury. The main way they raised money was simply to print it and hope people would accept the bills. The Continental Congress issued these **bills of credit** throughout the war. The states issued their own money as well, almost all of which was generally more stable than the Continental dollars. Toward the end of the war, the phrase "not worth a Continental" became

© iStockphoto.com/Mark Grenier

>> The army of the patriots was often ill equipped, undermanned, and hungry.

George Washington.

© George Washington in the uniform of a Colonel of the Virginia Militia during the French & Indian War (1755–63) (colour litho), Peale, Charles Willson (1741–1827) (after)/Private Collection, Peter Newark American Pictures/The Bridgeman Art Library

© iStockphoto.com/Lee Pettet

common, suggesting the centralized currency's lack of buying power and the widespread lack of faith in it. Only after 1781, when Robert Morris became superintendent of finance, did monetary conditions improve, mainly because he could borrow from friendly European nations. But throughout the war, the United States endured the highest inflation in its history. This took a tremendous toll on consumers, which is to say, all colonists.

Read more about how the revolutionaries paid for the war.

## The British Army

The British, on the other hand, had the most powerful army in the world, supremacy of the seas, and an organized hierarchy of authority that extended all the way to the king. But they also had the more difficult military task of trying to destroy Washington's army, which was adept at running up hills and into forests to avoid being captured. The Crown sent seasoned British troops who were well armed and accustomed to large battles on vast battlefields. It also had hired German mercenaries, the Hessians, to fight the revolutionaries. Many times, the British outnumbered the revolutionaries and were better trained and better armed, but they confronted three insurmountable problems: (1) Britain could never supply its troops adequately, especially as Washington prolonged the war by constantly retreating inland, away from places where British ships could easily resupply British troops; (2) Washington avoided directly engaging the British troops, so the regimented British army was subjected to unaccustomed guerrilla warfare as it chased him around the countryside; and (3) other European nations (notably France) eventually supported the revolutionaries. These other nations were only too glad to see mighty Britain humbled by upstart New World backwoodsmen.

## The First Phase of the War, 1775–1779

The first half of the war took place in the North (see Map 6.1 on page 109). The second half was fought in the South. Generally speaking, the Americans' strategy was to run and survive. They attacked only when they were convinced of victory.

### Early British Successes

After evacuating Massachusetts in March 1776, the British Army repositioned on Long Island and pressed to drive patriot forces from New York City. Their goal was to isolate New England (which it saw as the center of resistance) by taking control of New York City and the Great Lakes, then subduing the South, leaving Massachusetts stranded in its revolutionary fervor.

In July 1776, 34,000 British troops delivered a crushing defeat to the patriots on Long Island and forced the revolutionary army of 18,000 to give up New York City. The patriots withdrew all the way to New Jersey, then to Pennsylvania. Fleeing was militarily embarrassing and bad for morale, but it was tactically sound: so long as the Continental Army remained intact, the colonies were still fighting for independence.

## Crossing the Delaware

This loss at New York was a terrible blow to morale. Recruitment suffered, and Washington realized he needed a victory. Furthermore, most of Washington's soldiers were enlisted only through the end of 1776, so Washington feared that without a victory before the end of the year, the majority of his soldiers would not reenlist. Washington decided on a bold, brilliant action. On Christmas night 1776, the army crossed the ice-filled Delaware River and captured Trenton, New Jersey, which at the time was held by 1,500 Hessian mercenaries working for the British

Army. The American victory at Trenton had little strategic significance, but it boosted morale and energized the Revolution.

## Reversal of Fortune

Because the loss at Trenton was of minor strategic importance, the British let it go, and, in 1777, British leaders planned a two-pronged invasion that they hoped would finish off the war. British general John Burgoyne was to lead his army south from Canada. At the same time, General William Howe was to capture Philadelphia, the seat of the colonial government, and then sail up the Hudson River to join Burgoyne, completely isolating New England and testing the revolutionaries' unity.

At first, the plan was successful. Burgoyne's army captured outposts in New York (Fort Ticonderoga) and began moving south. Meanwhile, Howe drove the patriots from Philadelphia on September 26, 1777 (forcing the Continental Congress to flee the capital), and headed north.

Then the British faced obstacles. General Burgoyne's troops were slowed by assorted Loyalists seeking protection from the revolutionary fervor of the northern states, which allowed guerrilla fighters and an organized camp of the Continental Army to catch up and harass the British troops. By the time Burgoyne neared the Hudson River, the Americans had forced him to halt, and, while he waited for reinforcements, he found himself surrounded by 6,000 Continental soldiers. Recognizing their advantage, the Americans attacked.

 Read a secret "spy" letter from Howe to Burgoyne.

At the end of the fighting, Burgoyne surrendered all 5,700 men who remained of his army. This was the **Battle of Saratoga**. The American victory there proved two things: (1) that the patriots could defeat sizeable regiments of the larger British Army and (2) that, if the British were to win this war, it was going to be a long, expensive affair.

## The French Alliance

The Battle of Saratoga was also significant in that it convinced several European powers, including Spain and the Dutch, to fight against the British. Obtaining the support of France, how-

© Eon Images

>> **The American victory at Trenton, after Washington's crossing the Delaware, had little strategic significance, but it boosted morale and energized the Revolution.**

>> From the perspective of the winter at Valley Forge, the Revolutionary War would not last long.

ever, was key. The French allied themselves with the Americans for two reasons: they wanted to help weaken the British Empire, and they wanted access to New World trading posts, which they had lost in the French and Indian War. Up until this point, the French had been reluctant to advocate a losing cause, however, and the Saratoga victory helped alleviate these concerns.

In addition to France's backing, the Americans also received aid from an influential Frenchman. The Marquis de Lafayette, a nineteen-year-old nobleman committed to the Republican cause in France, volunteered for the American fight. Lafayette became an instrumental leader in the American Army and played a key role in several pivotal American victories. The youngest of all the generals in the war, he successfully lobbied the French to more fully support the patriots' cause.

In the end, French support was vital. The French naval fleet battled Britain's mighty navy in both the eastern (European) and western (American) Atlantic. The French also fought naval battles in the West Indies, the Mediterranean, and India, further diverting British efforts from the American Revolution.

With the French involved, the British now had to defend their entire empire. By 1780, French armies were actively fighting alongside Washington's army, giving a considerable boost to the revolutionaries.

## The War in the West

In the American West—in land west of the Appalachian Mountains, south of the Great Lakes, and east of the Mississippi River—the Revolutionary War was a brutal and violent "Indian War," where the British and the revolutionaries vied for Indian allies and control of the various forts European settlers had built since first contact. Like the colonists, the Indians were greatly divided as to which side to support, and the stakes for them were incredibly high, considering their already plummeting fortunes in North America. If they picked the wrong side, they could easily be destroyed for their allegiance. Several major tribes, including the Iroquois, Cherokees, and Shawnees, divided into factions over which side to support. The Iroquois who sided with the British were eventually destroyed by the American military, and their lands were torched as a punitive lesson.

The British, in general, had more success finding allies and establishing forts near the Great Lakes, and they often used those forts as staging grounds for raids into western New York and Pennsylvania. Again, as they advanced, they encountered a variety of Indian tribes and settlers, and they never could be quite sure whose side these people were on. This uncertainty made the war in the west a violent and unstable concoction.

In Ohio country, the Virginian George Rogers Clark sought to end British control in Detroit and in other vital throughways to the west. In 1779, Clark captured some key British and Indian troops and controlled parts of Ohio territory. Despite this advantage, a decisive victory proved ephemeral, and uncertainty reigned.

In perhaps the most horrific example of the brutality of the war in the west, in 1782, more than 150 Pennsylvania militiamen were on the hunt for enemy warriors. Instead, they came across nearly 100 Delaware Indians who had converted to Christianity and were noncombatants. The Indians were starving and were in an unexpected location searching for food. Uncertain of the veracity of the Delaware Indians' story, the militiamen held a council and voted to massacre the whole lot, leading to the execution (they were scalped) of 28 men, 29 women, and 39 children. Two boys escaped the vicious execution, telling the story of what has come to be called the Gnadenhutten Massacre, named after the Pennsylvania town in which it occurred. Several militiamen refused to participate in the slaughter, but the violence and uncertainty that surround it suggest the frightful and violent nature of the war in the west.

## The Winter of 1777–1778

Aside from the victory at Saratoga and the French commitment to enter the conflict, the Americans were slowly losing the war. General Howe's forces were continually besting George Washington's troops, enabling the British to capture Philadelphia and other locations. And Washington, keeping with his chief tactic, kept on running. As a result, while Howe's army wintered in the comforts of Philadelphia, Washington and his army stayed 20 miles away in the wilderness of Valley Forge, Pennsylvania. It was a harsh winter, and Washington's men were close to starvation. They were poorly equipped, and, although the country had enjoyed one of its best harvests ever, the Congress had allowed the military supply system to deteriorate into chaos. The men's clothes were threadbare and the troops were losing heart. From the perspective of the winter at Valley Forge, the Revolutionary War would not last long.

## The Second Phase of the War, 1778–1781

But the victory at Saratoga reemerged to stimulate the revolutionary fervor once again. When the snow finally melted, the colonists realized the British had changed tactics. The patriots' victory at Saratoga meant that Britain had to commit more troops to America, and to do this it needed to raise money, most plausibly by raising taxes in England. This was unpopular in England, and the people's resistance to increased taxes forced Parliament to make a peace offering to the revolutionaries. Parliament's offering would have maintained the colonial status of America but abandoned British attempts to tax the colonists—returning things to the way they had been in 1763. To the patriots, this offer was unacceptable; they now wanted freedom.

> **"I saw several of the men roast their old shoes and eat them, and I was afterwards informed by one of the officers' waiters, that some of the officers killed and ate a favorite little dog that belonged to one of them."**
>
> —*Joseph Plumb Martin, Continental soldier, on northern campaigns of the winter of 1780*

## Giving Up on New England

So instead of attempting the costly venture of replacing Burgoyne's troops in an effort to capture New England, the British planned to contain New England by holding New York while harassing the coastline and the South (see Map 6.2, page 110). They also aimed to demoralize the patriots and break the will of the fighters. For example, the British recognized that the American treasury had little to offer its generals, so they tried to "buy" major American leaders, hoping that the defection of prominent patriots would spread disaffection. The purchase of General Benedict Arnold in 1779 (for more than £10,000) was their chief victory on this front. Arnold had been a revolutionary hero, serving in many of the war's major battles, including Ticonderoga and Saratoga, where he had been badly injured. After having invested his personal fortune in the war effort, he was then somewhat suddenly charged with corruption by political adversaries and was investigated by the Congress. He thus was a ready, bitter target for bribing. But aside from Arnold, Britain's bribery policy proved unsuccessful.

## Britain's Southern Plan

Meanwhile, the British prepared to invade the southern colonies. Understanding that the South possessed more abundant natural resources than the North, they sought to preserve their claim to at least that region. They also believed that Loyalists were abundant in the South, so they hoped to exacerbate divisions along Loyalist–patriot lines. They had several reasons to believe this, the main one being that, in the South, the Revolutionary War really was a civil war between frontiersmen, who generally favored independence, and landholders, who usually sided with the British to protect their assets. These two factions had battled among themselves during the early years of the war in countless backwoods battles.

The British miscalculated in their estimation of Loyalist support in the South, however. For one thing, Loyalists lacked the fervor and militancy of the patriots. For another, Loyalists were not as prev-

## Map 6.1. Revolutionary War in the North

alent as British leaders had hoped. The British plan was doomed from the beginning.

In 1779, the British landed a large army at Charleston. Commanded by General Sir Charles Cornwallis, the army speedily captured Savannah, Georgia, and Charleston, South Carolina. Through 1780, Cornwallis continued to capture southern towns, and he planned to march north to subdue the rest of the colonies, particularly Virginia, which he viewed as crucial to holding the South.

## Washington and Greene's Strategy for Victory

In 1780, the Continental Army in the South, now led by Nathanael Greene, attempted to counter Cornwallis's successes by fleeing inland and thus sucking the British Army farther into the continent, away from the coast and easily accessible British support. This approach served two purposes: it stretched British supply lines, and it countered British attempts to rally Loyalist opposition. By

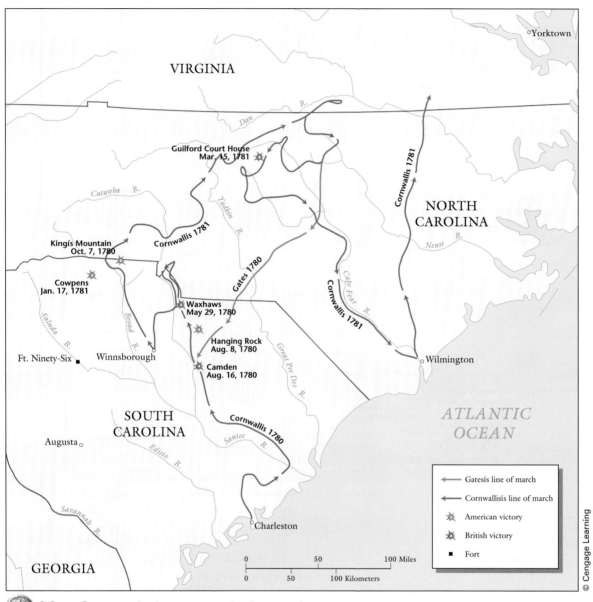

VIRGINIA

°Yorktown

*Dan* R.

Guilford Court House
Mar. 15, 1781 ✳

*Catawba* R.

Cornwallis 1781

NORTH
CAROLINA

*Yadkin* R.

*Neuse* R.

King's Mountain
Oct. 7, 1780

Cornwallis 1781

Gates 1780

Cornwallis 1781

*Cape Fear* R.

Cowpens
Jan. 17, 1781

Waxhaws
May 29, 1780

*Broad* R.

Hanging Rock
Aug. 8, 1780

*Great Pee Dee* R.

Ft. Ninety-Six ■  Winnsborough

Camden
Aug. 16, 1780

*Saluda* R.

SOUTH
CAROLINA

Cornwallis 1780

*Santee* R.

ATLANTIC
OCEAN

Augusta °

*Edisto* R.

*Savannah* R.

°Charleston

GEORGIA

| | |
|---|---|
| ← | Gates's line of march |
| ← | Cornwallis's line of march |
| ✳ | American victory |
| ✳ | British victory |
| ■ | Fort |

0    50    100 Miles
0    50    100 Kilometers

© Cengage Learning

Map 6.2. Revolutionary War in the South

· · · · · · · · · · · · · · · · · · · · · · · · · · · · · · · · · · · · · · · · · · · · · · · · · · · · · · ·

drawing the British away from their supplies, Greene hoped to force them to "live off the land," a military euphemism for stealing food from the populace. Greene and Washington expected that any support for the British would evaporate as hungry British soldiers began to raid farms.

Their plan succeeded. For several months, Cornwallis pursued the Continental Army across the Carolinas (note Cornwallis's movements in Map 6.2). British supplies gradually ran low and, just as Washington and Greene had predicted, the troops began stealing from once-sympathetic farmers. On top of this, when the two armies actually fought, the Continental soldiers inflicted major casualties on the British. Although the British won most of the engagements, meaning that they took control of the territory being fought over, the Continental strategies made British victories costly.

In early 1781, Cornwallis was forced to cease his pursuit and take his army north, into Virginia, to

Read a Continental soldier's account of his experiences in 1780.

await reinforcements. Faced with mounting casualties, he planned to reunite with his naval fleet at Chesapeake Bay.

### Yorktown and Victory

The problem with Cornwallis's plan was positioning: while Cornwallis waited for the British fleet (which the French had forced to retreat to New York), his army was stranded at the tip of the Yorktown peninsula in Virginia. Seizing the opportunity to attack, Washington moved a combined force of American and French troops across the lower peninsula; the American victory was complete when the French naval fleet arrived just before the British fleet could rescue Cornwallis's 27,000-man army.

After a night of bombardment, on October 19, 1781, Cornwallis turned his sword over to Washington. More accurately, an emissary for Cornwallis handed it to American general Benjamin Lincoln, whom Washington appointed to accept the surrender when he learned that the British commander had refused to offer his sword personally. When news of Cornwallis's surrender reached England, King George III grudgingly accepted defeat. The surrender ended six long years of battle.

### Newburgh Conspiracy

It took more than a year after the last major battle before a peace treaty was crafted, however, and while negotiations were ongoing, the armies remained mobilized. Unpaid and undersupplied, several American military leaders proposed a coup, seeking to take control from the relatively impotent Continental Congress in order to implement a tax to pay for unpaid expenses, including their own salaries. The Continental Army was at the time positioned in Newburgh, New York, about 60 miles north of New York City, which was still occupied by the British, and thus the plan became called the Newburgh Conspiracy.

With the British in close striking range, any hint of turmoil within the Continental Army might have provoked Britain to resume hostilities. But Washington rapidly quashed the proposed conspiracy, principally by demonstrating the costs of the war on him personally. The generals were not the only ones who had suffered during the war, he said, reminding them that independence was more consequential than worldly gain. Washington's words derailed the revolt, but the unrest demonstrated the significance of the peace treaty that was to come.

### Peace Negotiations, 1782–1783

With battle over, the American team of negotiators—Benjamin Franklin, John Jay, and John Adams—found themselves in a difficult situation. They traveled to Paris for the talks in 1782, with instructions to consult with the French. However, the Americans knew that both France and its ally, Spain, had territorial goals of their own in the New World, goals that the Americans did not want to encourage. As a result, Franklin, Jay, and Adams determined that it was in their best interest to negotiate with the British separately and deal with the French later.

### The Treaty of Paris

The treaty that Franklin, Jay, and Adams fashioned in 1782 included so many provisions favorable to the Americans that it has frequently been called the greatest triumph in the history of American diplomacy. To guarantee that France did not have the best trading rights to the New World, Britain offered generous terms to the Americans in terms of land and trading rights. America and Britain signed a treaty in November 1782. In doing so, Franklin, Adams, and Jay violated one of the provisions of the Franco-American Alliance of 1778: namely, that neither France nor America would negotiate a separate peace with the British. Nevertheless, the French were eager to end the war, and on January 2, 1783, preliminary treaties were signed between Britain and France and Britain and Spain, and on February 4 hostilities formally ceased. All parties signed the Treaty of Paris in September 1783.

There were five major parts to the Treaty of Paris of 1783: (1) American independence; (2) American expansion west to the Mississippi River and north to the Great Lakes (a much greater area than Americans had thus far settled); (3) freedom of all parties to travel the Mississippi River; (4) Spanish control of Florida; and (5) "no lawful impediment" placed on British merchants seeking to recoup debts from America.

 View a map of America after the Treaty of Paris.

# LO³ Significance of the War

The six long years of the Revolutionary War were filled with suffering. A doctor in the Continental Army suggested that American losses totaled 70,000, but the number of war-related deaths was more likely 25,000, with perhaps another 25,000 injured. Disease and infection killed off many more. Indeed, the war took place in the midst of a widespread smallpox epidemic, which may have killed as many as 130,000 colonists. (Washington wisely had his troops inoculated, perhaps his smartest move in the entire campaign.) But it was nevertheless a long war, longer than the Civil War, World War I, or World War II.

Furthermore, the war had divided the colonists between Loyalists, rebels, and those who were indifferent to either side. It had also greatly disrupted daily life, as soldiers were recruited to join the army and leave their families for extended periods of time, women were asked to shoulder a heavier burden in their household and in civic life, and slaves contemplated their future in a new American republic, one that showed little sign of granting them freedom. Beyond this tremendous disruption of daily life, the American war for independence had six major results.

## The Impact on Politics

Politically, the American Revolution was the first world conflict whose winners embraced the promise of the Enlightenment. In promising the "natural rights" of life, liberty, and property, the American Revolution served as an ideological model for later revolutions in France and in Central and South America, among others.

But the Revolution was a bellwether of not only liberty but also of republican democracy. The American revolutionaries hoped that their struggles would curb the system of Old World aristocracy. They no longer wanted to be ruled by a few powerful people with long-entrenched methods of perpetuating their wealth and status. Many also did not want an established church that denied the freedom of belief. No one was sure what would arise in the place of Old World aristocracy, but they knew that, after the revolution, the old system was dead.

Eventually, this awareness would lead to the formal separation of church and state and limited (but growing) access to the ballot. During the revolutionary era, access to the ballot was still dependent on owning property, which usually excluded women and African Americans, but the Revolution geared up the machinery for a more expansive democracy in the future.

## The Impact on American Nationalism

Before the American Revolution, the colonists living in what became the United States did not think of themselves as having a national culture fundamentally unique from England's. In terms of nationality, most colonists considered themselves as their great-grandfathers were, English. But the French and Indian War and the American Revolution unified the colonists under a new, ideological definition of what it meant to be an American. A nation is composed of people who recognize that they share certain qualities that set them apart from other nations, whether those qualities are ideological, political, linguistic, religious, cultural, racial, or historical. For Americans, in the revolutionary era and after, a strong belief in democracy and the experience of fighting for their political independence were the impetus for the mounting tide of patriotism that followed the Revolutionary War.

Explore an interactive module about building a new nation through symbols.

## The Impact on Slavery

The Revolutionary War also illustrated the contradiction between slavery and liberty, and it triggered the abolition of slavery in the North. During the

© American School/The Bridgeman Art Library/Getty Images

>> The experience of fighting for their political independence was the impetus for the mounting tide of patriotism and patriotic imagery that followed the Revolutionary War.

war, slaves participated in the fight on both sides, although the British welcomed them more willingly than the revolutionaries. Cornwallis himself employed 5,000 slaves, promising to free them after the war. Many slaves simply fled their masters during the confusion of battle. In all, there were about 50,000 fewer slaves after the war than before it. Some former slaves went to New England, some went to Canada, and many stayed in the South to live free.

After the war, the progress of formal abolition was slow and gradual, but it was progress nonetheless. Some advances were even made in the South, where the vast majority of slaves lived (see Map 6.3). Virginia and Maryland made it easier for owners to **manumit** (or willingly free) their slaves, and many revolutionaries chose to do so. By 1800, one in ten African Americans in the Chesapeake region was free. This meant there were large communities where escaped slaves could hide in the growing cities of the Chesapeake. Nevertheless, slavery had not been abolished in the South, and leaders like Thomas Jefferson, who were well aware of the contradiction between the practice of slavery and the rhetoric of independence, never freed their slaves.

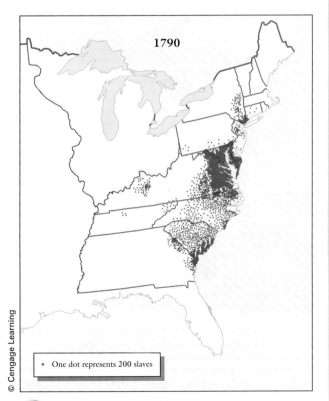

Map 6.3. **Distribution of Slave Population, 1790**

One dot represents 200 slaves

The most dramatic changes occurred in the North when abolition was set in motion legally. Vermont outlawed slavery in its first constitution in 1777. In Massachusetts and New Hampshire, slaves sued for their freedom—and won. In the Middle States, where the slave population was larger, progress was slower, but both Pennsylvania and New York favored gradual emancipation, which, in Pennsylvania's case, meant that all slaves born in 1780 or later were free when they turned twenty-one. Throughout the North, five states allowed African Americans to vote, and in total, by 1810, three-quarters of the 30,000 African Americans living in the North were free. By 1840, there were only 1,000 slaves in the North, and the freed slaves and their children had developed large social institutions, including various sects of historically black churches and numerous fraternal organizations, such as the African American Masons.

Perhaps most importantly, however, by 1790, all states except Georgia and South Carolina had outlawed the importation of slaves from abroad. As Americans began to consider the political meanings of liberty and freedom, they were confronted by the obvious contradiction of having freed themselves of the Crown while others lived in slavery. After the Revolution, only compromise would keep the issue of slavery at bay, as the North and South took different tactics in handling the contentious issue.

Read one Quaker's attempt to point out inconsistencies between American freedom and slavery.

**manumit**
**To willingly free one's slaves**

## The Impact on Native America

The war also greatly affected the fate of Native Americans, who were generally worse off after the war than before it. By the time of the Revolution, there were few tribes still living on the Atlantic coast, as disease and violence had decimated the tribes of that region. The most powerful tribes in contact with the colonists lived between the Appalachian Mountains and the Mississippi River, where the Iroquois dominated in the North and the Choctaw, Seminole, Creek, and Cherokee dominated in the South. The battles throughout Native America were unspeakably harsh, as the war often served as a pretext to remove Indian tribes and empty Indian land for land-hungry colonists. Anyone could become a casualty on the frontier. By the end of the war, nearly one-third of the Iroquois nation was dead. Their supremacy in the land between the Appalachians

© Cengage Learning

and the Great Lakes did not survive the war.

In addition to these violent encounters, with the war over, the tribes of Native America had to contend with an expanding nation of settlers who respected no practical western boundary and answered to no governmental authority preventing them from moving farther west. This portended a grim outlook for American Indians.

## The Impact on Women

Women played key roles during the Revolution. They enforced boycotts, sewed clothing made of nonimported fibers, raised impressive funds for the Continental Army, and sometimes even engaged in battle. This was a significant shift from the colonial era, when women only rarely protested their total exclusion from politics. New Jersey's constitution of 1776 opened the franchise to "all free inhabitants" who were worth at least fifty pounds, thus allowing many New Jersey women to vote for the first time.

But immediately after the war, women generally lost out politically as the new nation decided how far it would extend the rewards of citizenship. In many states, women were not eligible to own property. And, in every other state besides New Jersey, there is no evidence that women were ever offered the vote. In 1807, even New Jersey rescinded its offer of the franchise.

Men confined women's role to that of "Republican motherhood," which historians now describe as a double-edged identity—one that put women in charge of raising young male republicans through a demanding path of education, religious adherence, and political engagement but that also confined women's role to familial relations outside the realm of direct intervention in the public sphere.

## The Impact on Religious Minorities

Many historians have pointed to the Great Awakening of the 1730s and 1740s as laying part of the foundation for the revolutionary events of the 1760s and 1770s. With its emphasis on personal religious experience rather than the authority of the ministers, and as one of the first events to create a shared experience for people from New England to the southern colonies, the Great Awakening has been viewed as an early form of revolutionary activ-

ity. Colonists were also afraid that, around 1763, Parliament was planning to establish a bishop of the Anglican Church for America. They feared that any such appointment would extend England's official church to the colonies.

Two American actions after the war reflected their concerns about an established church: (1) Most of the new state constitutions included some guarantee of religious toleration, although a few of the states that already had an official church (like Massachusetts) moved more slowly toward disestablishment; and (2) the democratic ideals of the Revolution called into question public financial support of churches that were not attended by everyone.

The best-known representation of these ideas came in 1786, when the Virginia legislature passed a Thomas Jefferson-drafted bill that called for the disestablishment of the Episcopal Church. Jefferson's **Virginia Statute on Religious Freedom** was one of the accomplishments that Jefferson himself was most proud of. The statute said that no Virginian

>> Molly Pitcher: fact or fiction? It is true that women played a significant role in the Revolution. One in particular, however—nicknamed Molly Pitcher—has achieved legendary status for taking her husband's place in battle when he was incapacitated. It is not clear whether the New Jersey woman known as Molly Pitcher was based on Mary Ludwig Hayes, who was praised for her courage at the Battle of Monmouth, or Margaret Corbin, who similarly fought at the Battle of Fort Washington.

See numerous primary sources connecting the Revolution with religion, including a revolutionary flag.

 Read the Virginia Statute of Religious Freedom.

would be "compelled" to go to any church or form of religious worship against their will, and that all Virginians were free to profess their own opinion "in matters of religion." It immediately influenced several state constitutions, and several states made their ratification of the United States Constitution in 1787 contingent on an amendment promising that the federal government would not infringe on religious liberties.

At the same time, the Revolution led to the creation of several divisions of American churches, such as the Methodist Episcopal Church of America and the Presbyterian Church of the United States. Two "freedom churches" also opened, both of which stressed the brotherhood of man and the freedom of conscience: the Universalist Church (1779) and the Unitarian Church (1785). Thus, not only did the Revolution inspire laws mandating the separation of church and state, but it also encouraged the creation of two major antidogmatic sects.

## What else was happening . . .

| | |
|---|---|
| July 4, 1777 | The United States celebrates its first birthday. Ships lined up on the Delaware River discharge thirteen cannon shots in honor of the thirteen states. |
| 1778 | New Orleans businessman Oliver Pollock creates the $ symbol. |
| 1784 | A new trade route opens for Americans when the *Empress of China* sails from New Jersey around Cape Horn in South America to China. |
| 1787 | The first U.S. penny, designed by Benjamin Franklin, is minted. |
| 1789 | The French Revolution begins, initiating a long battle in France over "liberty, equality, and fraternity." |
| 1790 | The cornerstone of the mansion known as the White House is laid. |

# And in the end...

The war generated a bewildering mix of emotions and warnings. It set the patriots free from English control, but it also drew boundaries that the future nation would have to observe when it created its new government and society. It set in motion the ideals of the Enlightenment, but it also provoked the question of how far republican democracy would extend—not just politically, but socially and economically as well. Many revolutionary leaders feared that too much freedom might lead to chaos: if everyone were free, who would ensure order? On the other hand, too little freedom might trigger a second revolution.

With the war over, the leaders of the new nation confronted yet another daunting task: forming a new nation that embodied the revolutionary spirit without letting that spirit extend to anarchy.

## Chronology

| | |
|---|---|
| 1763 | End of salutary neglect |
| 1775 | Local conflicts escalate |
| January 1776 | Tom Paine's *Common Sense* |
| July 1776 | Declaration of Independence |
| December 25, 1776 | Crossing the Delaware |
| Sept.–Oct. 1777 | Battle of Saratoga |
| 1778 | France enters war on the side of the United States |
| 1779 | Britain invades the South |
| 1780 | Inland battles force British away from supply lines |
| Oct. 1781 | Yorktown and American victory |

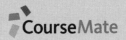 CourseMate

Visit the CourseMate website at www.cengagebrain.com for additional study tools and review materials for this chapter.

# Confederation *and* Constitution, *1783–1789*

## Learning Outcomes

*After reading this chapter, you should be able to do the following:*

**LO¹** Describe the first state constitutions written and adopted after the United States declared its independence.

**LO²** Analyze the federal government as it existed under the Articles of Confederation.

**LO³** Describe the most significant issues that the United States had to deal with under the Articles of Confederation, and explain how the Articles failed to live up to the needs of the new country.

**LO⁴** Explain the need for the Constitutional Convention that met in Philadelphia in 1787, and describe the process of writing the Constitution.

**LO⁵** Describe and explain the major provisions of the Constitution created by the Philadelphia convention, especially concerning the separation of powers and the rights given to individual states.

**LO⁶** Explain the procedure established for ratification of the Constitution, describe the actions of its supporters and its opponents, and explain how and when ratification was eventually achieved.

# "Could Americans design a government able to provide liberty and strong enough to protect that liberty?"

By 1783, the nation was officially independent, but it had three immediate problems: (1) it had amassed a huge debt from fighting for independence; (2) it suddenly had vast lands to control in the west; and (3) it had to recreate a system of trade after England's protections had been withdrawn. These problems were intensified because the ideology that had propelled the revolution—republicanism—strenuously warned against a strong central authority, and most Americans were repelled by the idea of a home-grown authoritarian yoke. They wanted their day-to-day freedoms. They wanted the liberties promised in the Declaration of Independence. Which begs the obvious question: What were those freedoms and, just as important, what price were people willing to pay for them? Could Americans design a government able to provide liberty and strong enough to protect that liberty?

This was a primary concern from the moment the colonists declared their independence in 1776. Their first attempt to find an appropriate balance (through a government established under the Articles of Confederation) proved unsuccessful. The Articles made the federal government too weak to address the nation's pressing needs. By 1787, Americans had scrapped the Articles and designed an entirely new structure of government. This new government, as defined in the United States Constitution, placed more power in a central authority than most Americans had anticipated or wanted. But a Bill of Rights protected the liberties Americans sought to preserve. Although not perfect, what they created in the Constitution has served the nation for more than two hundred years.

This chapter explores the development of the American government between 1783 and 1789. It begins by examining the state constitutions that served as testing grounds for the federal constitution; then it examines the strengths and weaknesses of the Articles of Confederation before addressing the current U.S. Constitution and its Bill of Rights.

## What do you think?

The framers of the Constitution intended it to be an adaptable document.

| Strongly Disagree | | | | | | Strongly Agree |
|---|---|---|---|---|---|---|
| 1 | 2 | 3 | 4 | 5 | 6 | 7 |

## LO¹ State Constitutions, 1776–1780

Between 1776 and 1780, while the fighting continued, all of the thirteen states except Connecticut and Rhode Island drafted their own constitution. Most changed their constitution several times, meaning that there was a good deal of experimentation going on. The ideas laid out by John Locke, Jean-Jacques Rousseau, John Trenchard,

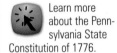
Learn more about the Pennsylvania State Constitution of 1776.

Thomas Gordon, the English Parliament, and the colonial legislatures were put to the test at the state level during these years. These state constitutions worked out ideas that would influence the federal system.

## Content

Most of the state constitutions had several common elements. For instance, all were attempts to fashion a government that offered some form of representation. They almost all shared three other things that were particularly important: bills of rights, limits on participation, and separation of powers.

### Bills of Rights

Each state constitution included a **bill of rights** that protected the "natural rights" that many Americans felt were threatened by England's prerevolutionary laws. Most of the bills of rights guaranteed the freedom of the press, the right of popular consent before being taxed, and protections against general search warrants. Most states guaranteed the freedom of religion, although some limited political participation to Christians only.

### Limits on Participation

Almost universally, the state constitutions broadened the base of people who could participate in government by relaxing property-holding qualifications. Pennsylvania, for instance, gave the vote to anyone who paid taxes. And New Jersey opened the vote to "all free inhabitants" worth at least fifty pounds. Nevertheless, each state maintained limits on who could vote and who could hold public office. These limits usually concerned owning property or adhering to a particular religion. Women and teenagers were almost universally excluded from voting, except, sometimes, when they owned property.

### Separation of Powers

As they tinkered with various forms of government, each state recognized that creating several different branches of government and giving each of them different responsibilities prevented one person or one body from becoming overly tyrannical or exerting an excess of authority. This was called the **separation of powers**. In the 1780s, John Adams of Massachusetts developed the theory behind separation of powers, one he called "mixed government." Most of the states operated according to separation of powers, in that they had a weak elected governor, a powerful legislature that changed membership frequently, and courts whose judges were named for life to ensure they were beholden to no one. Despite the ideal of separation of powers, the legislative branches were almost always more powerful than the executive and judicial branches.

© The London Art Archive/Alamy

>> New Jersey's constitution of 1776 opened the franchise to "all free inhabitants" who were worth at least fifty pounds, thus allowing many New Jersey women to vote for the first time. Note that there is also an African American man waiting to vote.

## Results

The various state constitutions were valuable forums for working out different types of government. Many worked well for their citizens. However, none addressed the issue of how the states would participate in and contribute to a national body. They were jealous of their powers. And anyway, most Americans were leery of a large national government, uncertain it could prevent itself from becoming increasingly powerful.

# LO² The Articles of Confederation, 1777–1787

Americans managed to fight more than half the Revolutionary War without any legitimate federal government. That was unsustainable, and the problem was rectified by 1777 with the Articles of Confederation.

## Origins

In the absence of a federal government, the Continental Congress had assumed a number of rights and responsibilities, such as creating the

© North Wind Picture Archives/Alamy

>> Carpenters' Hall in Philadelphia was chosen as the site for the Continental Congress.

Continental Army, printing money, managing trade, and dealing with debt. But it had done these things without having been granted authority by the people or some other sovereign power. Feeling the need to legitimate their actions and define the colonies' collective sovereignty, the revolutionaries realized they had to form a governing body. So between 1776 and 1777 the Continental Congress drafted the **Articles of Confederation**. The following year, it presented the document to the states for ratification, and, by July 1778, eight states had ratified the document. But full unanimity of the thirteen states, which was required before it could go into effect, would not be reached until 1781.

The experimentation that had taken place in the states did not affect the Articles of Confederation, which were drafted too early to be substantially influenced by the state constitutions. Thus the Articles did not innovate; they basically codified the way things were in the late 1770s. John Dickinson, the prominent lawyer who had drafted the ideological tract *Letter from a Farmer in Pennsylvania*, was the principal author of the Articles. Although he initially voted against independence (he felt the colonies were ill prepared), the Continental Congress invited him to draft the new system of government.

> **Articles of Confederation** Document that defined the colonies' collective sovereignty; drafted by the Continental Congress between 1776 and 1777, then ratified by the thirteen states by 1781

## Division of Powers

Fundamentally conservative, the Articles provided for each state's independence, granting very little power to the overarching federal government. The central government was simply an administrative agency that provided a meeting place for debate and enacted some very minimal, hard-to-enforce rules.

### Powers Reserved for the Federal Government

Dickinson's Articles placed all governing power in a single legislature, which was the system followed under the Continental Congress. This meant no separation of powers. There was no president, monarch, or prime minister to serve as the executive power. Instead, there was a "Committee of the States," in which one representative from each state was seated. This was the most centralized authority, and its powers were minimal. The Continental Congress, on the other hand, had five powers under the Articles: (1) to declare war and make peace;

(2) to make international treaties; (3) to control Indian affairs in the west; (4) to establish a currency; and (5) to create and maintain a postal service.

### Powers Reserved for the States

The states, meanwhile, maintained the all-important rights to (1) levy taxes and (2) regulate commerce. Unfortunately, these were perhaps the two most pressing needs of a nation conducting a war, precisely because they are the actions that keep money rolling in. If the states would not provide enough funds to fight a war, what could the federal government do? Under the Articles of Confederation, it could do nothing.

## Achievements of the Articles

We can already begin to guess at the flaws and limits of the Articles, but they also represented significant achievements. From a philosophical perspective, two stand out: (1) the Articles established the United States as a government of laws that placed limits on the government's authority, and (2) the Articles created a national citizenship, which gave equal rights to qualifying members. There would be no titles or codification of classes in America. These were both major accomplishments well within the ideals of republicanism.

## Weaknesses of the Articles

But the weaknesses of the Articles outweighed their achievements. Three stand out: (1) the inability to raise funds; (2) the need for unanimity to make changes; and (3) the lack of authority over internal trade.

### Inability to Raise Funds

The war had sunk the new nation badly in debt, and the Articles declared that Congress could not levy taxes. Furthermore, with a massive debt, it was hard to find creditors. This combination spelled immediate trouble for the new nation. For instance, how could it afford to pay an army? Who would regulate currency? Who would maintain credit?

### The Need for Unanimity to Make Changes

In 1781, nationalists in Congress chartered a national bank to help consolidate the national debt and facilitate credit. In order for the bank to operate, however, Congress needed capital to create a system of reserves. To get that capital, Congress passed a bill that put a 5 percent tax on all imported goods.

However, the Articles of Confederation required that all bills receive unanimous approval before becoming law. Tiny Rhode Island, reliant on foreign trade for its economy, would not assent to the tax. Without Rhode Island, the bill died, as did these early plans for a national bank. In matters legislative, the need for unanimity was a clear problem.

### Lack of Authority over Internal Trade

Finally, commerce between the states suffered because there was no centralized authority to manage it. Because each state had its own currency, its own levels of inflation, and its own taxes, it was difficult to transport goods across state lines or engineer large programs that would encompass an entire region. The Articles provided no national policy on commerce, and throughout the first half of the decade, delegates from southern states resisted efforts to devise one. They feared that such a policy would allow northern merchants to monopolize the trade of southern agricultural products, bypassing southern merchants and traders. The way in which each region had developed as a colony helped dictate its outlook on a federal state.

 Learn more about (and read) the Articles of Confederation.

# LO³ Day-to-Day Operations of the Confederation

In addition to these constitutional problems, the government under the Confederation faced three other significant challenges: (1) managing the western expansion, (2) foreign relations, and (3) debt. These further underscored the Articles' strengths and weaknesses.

## The Western Problem

The most pressing challenge concerned land in the west. During and after the Revolution, Americans continued their seemingly perpetual push westward, and in the 1780s large numbers of Americans moved to western Pennsylvania, Kentucky, and the Nashville region. They were slowly populating the area between the Appalachian Mountains and the Mississippi River. But as these pioneers moved west, they began to enrich the states that had charters in the west. (Recall that many of the original colonial charters specified northern and southern boundaries but usually made the western boundary

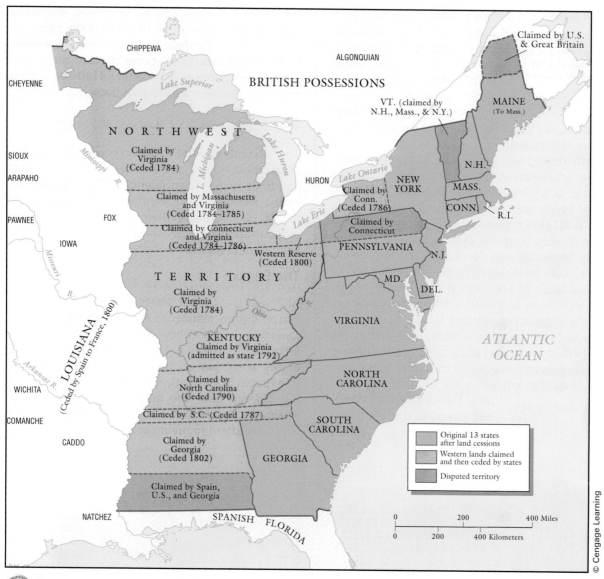

Map 7.1. Western Land Claims After the Revolution

the Pacific Ocean.) These stipulations bred jealousy among states that had no claims on western land. Maryland, in fact, refused to ratify the Articles of Confederation until the largest western landholder, Virginia, ceded its western holdings to the federal government (Map 7.1).

## Land Cessions

In 1784, Congress finally persuaded Virginia to cede much of its land to the federal government. But Virginia and other large landholders did so only on the condition that they be allowed to keep small "reserves" of land for later use, a condition the Continental Congress had to grant. By 1802, eigh-

teen years later, all states had ceded their western lands to the federal government. The inability of the federal government under the Articles to make this happen sooner showed it could not bully the states into doing what it wanted, even if what it wanted was best for the young nation.

## Organizing Territories

With continued westward migration and calls for the federal government to oversee that expansion, Congress devised several plans to organize the western territories. The Land Ordinance of 1785, which surveyed the immense western territory, divided it into townships 6 miles square and set prices for its sale to individuals. This plan favored wealthy speculators because small farmers could not afford an entire "township," thus requiring speculators to act as intermediaries, which drove prices up. These speculators, not small farmers, were the real beneficiaries of this system.

Furthermore, two years later Congress passed the great achievement of the government under the Articles of Confederation, the **Northwest Ordinance of 1787**, which established territorial governments in the Great Lakes region and set a pattern for future western development. The Ordinance crafted boundaries for territories and developed laws by which a territory could be included in the nation. When the male population of a territory reached 5,000, it could elect a legislature and send a delegate to Congress. When the population reached 60,000, the territory could enter the Union as a state, on equal status with all other states, including the original thirteen. The Northwest Ordinance also contained something absent from the Articles: a bill of rights. In addition, the Ordinance prohibited slavery in the territories, a point that would become

 Read the Northwest Ordinance.

increasingly contentious as westward expansion continued throughout the first half of the 1800s.

Overall, the Confederation enabled easier access to western lands. But because it could not fund a standing army, the government had little capacity to protect the settlers who moved there.

## The Problem of Foreign Relations

The second important issue confronted by the government under the Articles of Confederation had to do with foreign relations. Most significantly, with a weak federal government, Americans found it difficult to secure their borders. Three groups took advantage of this weakness: the English, the Spanish, and pirates.

### The English

Although the United States had won its independence, Britain retained a few forts along the U.S.-Canadian border. They did this to protect their lucrative fur trade and to ensure that the United States would pay off its loans to British creditors. The United States badly wanted these forts removed but did not have the muscle to push them out. Again, the United States had no standing army and could not afford to maintain one.

Library of Congress, Prints & Photographs Division, LC-USZ62-2766

>> Like other images of the American west, this "Plan of an American new cleared farm" from 1793 helped entice Americans to move further west, something the federal government sought to control with the Northwest Ordinance of 1787.

## The Spanish

From a foreign relations perspective, there were three main problems with Spain: (1) The Treaty of Paris was unclear about who controlled a piece of land called the Yazoo Strip, which was the boundary between Spanish Florida and American Georgia; (2) the Spanish controlled the mouth of the Mississippi River and were able to close off this central access point to the American interior, should they ever wish to; and (3) the Americans wanted access to Spanish traders in the West Indies, but Spain was reluctant to allow this access because it did not want the United States to become dominant in the Western Hemisphere.

In 1784, Spain made a proposition to the United States: Spain would grant Americans access to the Spanish West Indies (which would benefit American traders), but it would cut off access to the Mississippi River (so that Spain could limit the amount of goods that came down the Mississippi into the open market). Needing nine votes in Congress to pass the measure, the treaty floundered, winning only seven. It was revealing that all seven votes came from northern states, infuriating the South, which would be hurt economically if the Mississippi River were closed off to American traders. The Spanish eventually reopened the Mississippi but charged high duties to American merchants.

## Pirates

In the 1780s, American forces were also impotent in the face of Mediterranean pirates, who preyed on American trade ships in the Atlantic and the Caribbean. Without the capital to maintain a strong army or navy, the government under the Articles could do little to stop the marauding of American ships and pillaging of American goods.

## The Debt

Despite these two serious issues (the west and foreign relations), the overarching problem facing the new nation was debt. This had three visible political ramifications: (1) Those who held the debt wanted to be repaid; (2) the rank-and-file of the army grew angry when the government could not pay all the back pay it owed the soldiers; and (3) farmers grew angry because inflation had priced them out of the life to which they were accustomed.

## Promissory Notes and Bonds

To finance the Revolutionary War, the American government had sold bonds, which had to be repaid, plus interest, at a certain time in the future. Furthermore, the government had issued several promissory notes, mostly to farmers and usually after the army had seized farmers' property in order to wage battle. Both types of these debt-holders wanted to be paid back to prevent them from defaulting on their own loans.

## An Angry Army

The problem escalated when, shortly after the war, it became evident that the government could not pay its soldiers their back pay. Officers petitioned on behalf of the soldiers' grievances, sometimes threatening violence if the payments were not made. In one standoff, troops protested in front of Philadelphia's Independence Hall, forcing the Continental Congress to abandon Philadelphia (it moved to Princeton, New Jersey, until the threat quieted down). Only George Washington's words could soothe the troops. But this signaled troubles to come; after all, the Continental Congress was still unable to raise revenue, and the soldiers were angry.

## Angry Farmers

Meanwhile, inflation continued to rise, meaning that prices increased dramatically. Farmers were hit the hardest. They had enjoyed rising prices for their goods during the war and had increased their spending, sometimes to the point of indebtedness. After the war, with no army to feed, markets suddenly shrank. At the same time, Britain prohibited American ships from trading in the West Indies, further limiting the size of the market.

As a result, American agricultural goods flooded American markets, lowering prices and dropping farm wages by as much as 20 percent. When creditors demanded payment from the farmers in gold or silver (a form of payment called **specie**), most farmers were unable to pay their debts. Although most of the farmers' debts were small, foreclosure threatened many. Some were about to lose their farms or were imprisoned after being convicted in debtors' court.

## Shays's Rebellion

The financial burden seemed unbearable to those who had just fought for independence. In Massachusetts, a tax increase compounded these problems. In 1786, rural towns in Massachusetts petitioned its state assembly for a moratorium

> **specie**
> Gold or silver, which has intrinsic value, used as payment instead of paper money, which has extrinsic value

on taxes and on lawsuits against debtors. In doing so, they relied on the republican revolutionary language that had fueled the revolution in 1776. When the assembly rejected their petitions, angry crowds gathered at several county courthouses to stop the courts by force. Daniel Shays, a former Continental Army officer, emerged as the leader of the protesters.

Fed up with the Massachusetts government's failure to address the problem of inflation and with its apparent favoritism toward coastal merchants who did not require the large and costly infrastructure that farmers did, on January 26, 1787, Shays led 1,200 men to seize control of the federal arsenal in Springfield, Massachusetts. This potential coup was formally called **Shays's Rebellion**.

The Massachusetts government, however, had prepared for such a move (after protesters had stormed the debtors' courts), and a force of 4,400 soldiers from New England was ready to defend the arse-nal. Tellingly, these troops were funded and led into battle by East Coast merchants, not country farmers. The troops opened fire on Shays's army. Six died. This seemed to be the beginning of a civil war between the commercial class and the farming class, the wealthy and the poor. But, unprepared for formal combat, Shays's followers quickly abandoned their siege, and during the next few weeks Shays's Rebellion waned.

Despite the rebellion's dissolution, unrest continued to haunt leaders in Massachusetts and other states. Shays's Rebellion was a warning that the federal government would have to address the problem of debt to prevent a lower-class uprising. Under the Articles it was impossible for it to do so. Shays's Rebellion was also a warning about the dangers of true democracy, dangers that made many leading intellectuals of the time incredibly nervous. How could order be preserved in a country that lionized liberty?

## The Failure of the Articles of Confederation

Despite these underlying problems with the Articles of Confederation, a financial collapse was the last straw. In 1783, England banned all American ships from the West Indies and put limitations on specific competitive items. Few other countries granted protective treaties with the United States, knowing that America was too weak to honor them. Meanwhile, the individual American states began to levy their own tariffs to raise money. The result was that the states with the lowest tariffs received the most trade, which led to hostile competition between the various states within the Union. The federal government's attempt to pay off its debt by simply asking the states for help was not working and was in fact promoting further discord. With a single veto, both New York and Rhode Island rejected proposed revenue-raising tariffs. Change had to come.

### Calls for Change

At the urging of Virginia and Maryland, in 1786 (months before Shays's Rebellion), congressional representatives made plans to meet in Annapolis, Maryland, to discuss the problem of commerce. Only five states sent delegates, but several prominent figures were there, including James Madison, Alexander Hamilton, and George Washington. The convention's main success was in reaching a consensus to call a general meeting of delegates for the purpose of amending the Articles of Confederation. They agreed to meet again in May 1787, in Philadelphia.

>> Shays's Rebellion was a warning that the federal government would have to address the problem of debt to prevent a lower-class uprising.

# LO⁴ The Constitutional Convention

Although it started out as an effort to amend the Articles of Confederation, the meeting in Philadelphia rapidly became a Constitutional Convention, aimed at creating an entirely new government. There were substantial differences of opinion, however, and the Constitutional Convention debated these issues throughout the summer of 1787. The goings-on were kept secret, thus allowing each member to speak his mind without fear of political retribution. Only through participants' notes, most notably James Madison's, do we know what happened at the Convention.

## Membership

One matter on which there was complete agreement was that George Washington should be the president of the Convention. Washington's reputation and integrity protected the Convention from accusations that it had usurped the authority of the Congress.

In addition to Washington, fifty-four other delegates attended. The states had elected members to go to the meeting who were, for the most part, members of the social and educational elite. Most were young (average age: forty-two), wealthy, and wanted to strengthen the national government to protect trade and promote economic and social stability. They were leery of democracy, however, because Shays's Rebellion had demonstrated that democracy could be messy. Most of the delegates were also lawyers (more than half were college graduates), which meant they would respect and honor the rule of law.

## Preliminary Plans

There were several key divisions at the Convention (northern states versus southern, merchants versus farmers), but none was as important as that between the large states and the small ones. Two plans, prepared before the Convention even began, highlighted the differences between the two.

### The Virginia (Large States) Plan

James Madison of Virginia was clearly the star of the Convention. A thirty-six-year-old Princeton graduate, Madison was well read in political science. He came to the Convention with an agenda, summarized as the Virginia Plan. The **Virginia Plan** sought to (1) scrap the Articles of Confederation; (2) create a Congress with two houses; (3) establish a federal judiciary; (4) establish a president who was elected by Congress; and (5) in general create a centralized system of government in which Congress had veto power over the actions of the states. Membership in Congress would be determined by population, which would clearly favor the large states.

### The New Jersey (Small States) Plan

For obvious reasons, smaller states objected to the Virginia Plan. Under the Articles of Confederation, all states had received an equal voice in Congress, regardless of size. To counter the Virginia Plan, New Jersey delegate William Paterson proposed an alternative—the **New Jersey Plan**—which called for revising the Articles of Confederation rather than replacing them altogether. Paterson's plan strengthened the federal government in many ways, but it proposed giving each state equal representation in a bicameral legislature, defined as a legislature with two houses with differing rules regarding responsibilities and duration of a member's term.

> **Virginia Plan**
> **This proposal, known as the large states plan because it favored those states, sought to scrap the Articles of Confederation and create a Congress with two houses, with representation in Congress being determined by population**
>
> **New Jersey Plan**
> **This proposal suggested revising the Articles of Confederation rather than replacing them altogether**

© Eon Images

>> Most delegates were young (average age: forty-two), wealthy, and wanted to strengthen the national government to protect trade and promote economic and social stability.

## Drafting the Constitution

The Convention was dead-locked over apportionment of representatives until Roger Sherman of Connecticut came up with a compromise.

### The Great Compromise

Sherman suggested granting each state equal representation in the upper house (to be called the Senate) and representation that was proportional to population (1 representative for every 30,000 people) in the lower house (the House of Representatives). This plan was ultimately approved (after Benjamin Franklin reproposed it and conceded to the larger states the power to have all funding bills originate in the lower house). Sherman's plan is called the **Great Compromise** because it broke a stalemate that could have been fatal to the development of a new federal constitution.

### Slave State versus Free State

The large states–versus–small states debate was only one of the many divisions that bedeviled the Convention, and indeed, the Great Compromise had raised another problem. How do you count the population of each state? Should only voters count? Only taxpayers? Should women count toward the total? Although the conventioneers had ready answers for many of these questions, the issue became volatile when it touched on slavery.

In the early 1780s the Atlantic slave trade was at its height, and southerners were on the defensive over the issue. The spread of abolitionist ideas in the North threatened their labor supply. In addition, southerners feared that freed slaves would seek vengeance against their former masters. The southern delegates wanted a constitutional guarantee that slavery would be legal in the new nation, and they needed political power to ensure that slavery would continue. Thus, in a stroke of historical irony, this demand meant that

>> James Madison of Virginia was clearly the star of the Convention.

southerners wanted slaves to be included in the counting of their population, which would grant the South more representatives in the House. Northerners objected, arguing that, because slaves would not have an active political voice, their numbers should not be included.

Yet another compromise emerged, allowing southerners to include three-fifths of their slave population for both representation and the apportionment of federal taxes. This **"three-fifths clause"** demonstrated that, despite the new nation's stated commitment to freedom and equality, African Americans still were treated as far less than equal by white Americans—and that this inequality would be enshrined in the American Constitution.

Delegates also had to forge a compromise regarding the slave trade. Some southerners threatened to secede if the slave trade was abolished, but many delegates (both northern and southern) considered the trade inhumane.

> 66 George Mason, a Virginia slaveholder himself, predicted that slavery would cause 'the judgment of heaven' to fall upon the nation. 99

George Mason, a Virginia slaveholder himself, even predicted that slavery would cause "the judgment of heaven" to fall upon the nation. But the majority of delegates felt that the survival of the nation was at stake and agreed to yet another compromise. Ultimately, antislavery delegates agreed to permit the slave trade for twenty more years, until 1808. In exchange, proslavery delegates granted Congress the authority to regulate commerce with a simple majority (rather than the two-thirds vote desired by most southerners).

### East versus West

The final compromise of the Convention was made between eastern and western states. Easterners were afraid that western expansion would allow the government to be controlled by agricultural interests rather than commercial ones. To compromise, the Convention granted Congress (and not the president) the power to admit new states to the nation, which meant that the eastern states that were already a part of the nation would have the power to regulate the number of new (western) states that could enter.

## LO$^5$ The Constitution

Once these compromises were agreed upon (after the Convention had gone on for four hot summer months), the Convention established the structure of the new government in a constitution. The U.S. Constitution developed mostly out of

Learn more about the Constitutional Convention and read Madison's original notes.

© iStockphoto.com/Bonnie Jacobs

the Virginia Plan, although considerable concessions were made to small states, southern states, and eastern states. The Convention created a government of three branches—executive, legislative, and judicial—granting unique powers to each branch.

## The Powers Given to Congress

The Convention allocated several specific powers to Congress. Its intention was to make Congress the most powerful branch, allowing it to do five vital things: (1) collect taxes and raise revenue; (2) regulate commerce, both foreign and domestic (except on the issue of slavery, where compromise meant that it could not touch the issue until 1808); (3) declare war; (4) maintain an army; and (5) make any changes necessary to pursue these powers. By controlling the government's purse strings and by demanding that all laws originate in Congress, the Constitutional Convention wanted to ensure that no single authority would possess too much power. This was a testament to the republican ideology of the war, although somewhat tempered by the compromises made at the Convention.

## The Executive Branch

The Convention also created an executive branch, consisting of a president and his cabinet.

### How Elected

Because of their experience with King George III, most Americans initially favored keeping power in the hands of elected legislators. Yet, after the failure of the Articles of Confederation, those at the Constitutional Convention realized that this system did not work. As an alternative, the Virginia Plan proposed to have Congress elect the president. Another plan would have the president serve a life term. A third plan would have three presidents serving simultaneously. Finally, Gouverneur Morris, an influential delegate from Pennsylvania, insisted that the executive should not depend on Congress for his office. Instead, Morris proposed to have him elected directly by the people to two terms of substantial length.

Although this plan certainly had its merits, the framers of the Constitution remained fearful of true democracy. They remembered Shays's Rebellion. So in the Constitution they created an **Electoral College** that was composed of delegates from each state equal in number to its total apportionment in Congress (number of senators plus number of representatives). The college was to ensure that only qualified candidates, not populist hooligans, got elected. Each delegate in the Electoral College was to vote for two people. The person who received the most votes would be president; the one with the second most votes would be vice president. Anticipating that several people would run for president (and not anticipating the two-party system), the House of Representatives would decide the president if no one received a majority of the votes.

### Powers

The Constitution also gave the president the power to do five important things (although perhaps not as important as the powers granted to the legislature): (1) make treaties, but only if two-thirds of the Senate approved them; (2) oversee the army and navy as commander-in-chief; (3) name diplomats with the consent of the Senate; and, most important, (4) execute the laws passed in Congress and (5) veto acts of Congress that he did not feel were constitutional (or, as it was understood after Andrew Jackson, in the country's best interests). The president was to be powerful, but also somewhat deferential to Congress.

## The Judicial Branch

The Constitution also provided for a federal system of courts, headed by a Supreme Court and several regional courts. The president was to name the judges to the courts to serve lifetime appointments. The judges had jurisdiction over constitutional questions, cases in which the United States itself was a party, and cases between two or more states or between the citizens of two or more states. The framers also included a "supreme law of the land clause" (or Supremacy Clause), which made the Constitution supreme over state laws in all legal matters.

## Federal and State Powers

Conscious of the necessary balance between state and federal powers, the framers of the Constitution forbade states from making their own money, levying customs, or infringing on the obligation of contracts (all things that the states had done during the era of the Articles of Confederation). Other than that, states maintained significant power. By design, if a power was not specifically given to the federal government, the states controlled it.

## Relationship of the Government and the Governed

There were other transitions as well. Under the Articles, the central government was not permitted  Read the U.S Constitution. to reach the individual—that was the sovereign right of the states. But under the new Constitution, the federal government could rule individuals directly. Perhaps the most significant change in this regard was granting the federal government the power of taxation. The revolutionary commitment to representation was not abandoned, however, as the legislative branch of government, which represented the people most directly, held the exclusive right to tax.

# LO⁶ The Ratification Debate

In September 1787, the framers of the Constitution presented their work to the states for ratification. The Constitution needed the states' approval to become the law of the land. Otherwise, the Articles of Confederation would still rule. The convention-eers urged each state to hold a special convention to discuss ratifying the new document, and they voted that approval by nine states was enough for the Constitution to take effect—deliberately avoiding the need for unanimity.

## A Slow Start

A few states ratified the Constitution almost immediately: smaller states, such as Delaware, Connecticut, and New Jersey, supported the Constitution because it promised to strengthen their position in conflicts with their larger, more populous neighbors. The Great Compromise had secured their votes. Georgia ratified quickly as well because it felt threatened by Indian conflicts and the Spanish presence in Florida. The people of Georgia needed protection. But the only large state to ratify the Constitution before the end of winter 1788 was Pennsylvania. In the other states with a large pop-

ulation—particularly New York, Massachusetts, and Virginia—concerns about the loss of sovereignty generated opposition. They wanted to ensure they kept the rights they felt they had won during the Revolution.

## The Federalists

Factions speedily formed. It was never a foregone conclusion that the Constitution would be passed, especially after reflecting that the Revolution had been fought to get rid of an overarching government. In an effort to undercut opposition, supporters of the Constitution took the name **Federalists** and began openly campaigning for the Constitution's ratification. The Federalists emphasized that the new government would not end state autonomy. They also contemplated a bill of rights that would prevent the new centralized government from infringing on what were considered natural rights.

To influence the debate in the key state of New York, in 1787 the Federalists John Jay and Alexander Hamilton wrote a series of essays that came to be called the **Federalist Papers**. The essays appeared in pamphlets and were condensed in newspapers. Soon James Madison of Virginia added his own essays to the series. The Federalist Papers were to become the most important tool in the ratification debate, as well as America's most significant contribution to political theory. They defended the Constitution article by article and addressed many of the complaints of opponents, such as the concerns about the size of the new nation. The papers were a tool of ideological warfare in the name of the new Constitution.

The Federalists' choice of a name was meaningful too. Supporters of the Constitution emphasized that the new government was designed around the principle of **federalism**, which is the philosophy of government in which states and nation share

**Federalists** Framers of the Constitution who emphasized that the new government would not end state autonomy; they also contemplated a Bill of Rights that would prevent the new centralized government from infringing on what were thought of as natural rights

**Federalist Papers** Essays written by John Jay, Alexander Hamilton, and James Madison in 1787, meant to influence the Constitution ratification debate in New York State; the essays defended the Constitution article by article and addressed many of the complaints of opponents, such as the concerns about the size of the new nation

**federalism** Philosophy of government in which states and the nation share the responsibility of government, with no one group or agency possessing sufficient power to dominate the other

 Read the Federalist Papers.

the responsibility of government, with no one group or agency possessing sufficient power to dominate the other. This was an attempt to assuage notions that the new government would slide into tyranny.

## The Anti-Federalists

The name *Federalists* impelled opponents to take the name *Anti-Federalists*. The **Anti-Federalists**, who included many prominent patriots, including Patrick Henry, John Hancock, and Samuel Adams, preferred a weaker confederation of states and a more direct democracy. They sought to protect the "spirit of '76," the language they used to make sure democracy was preserved despite the obvious need to govern. In fact, Anti-Federalists did not really oppose federalism, but they did object to the concentration of power in a centralized government regardless of how it divided power. They believed that centralized governments threatened the sovereignty of the states and the liberties of individuals. At the very least, the Anti-Federalists wanted an explicit bill of rights to safeguard those liberties. Because of their steadfast defense of individual rights, historians often view the Anti-Federalists as idealistic patriots concerned about how much liberty they would have to sacrifice to earn federal security.

## The Debate

The Federalists attempted to address the concerns of their opponents by arguing that the rights of the states and of individuals were adequately protected by state bills of rights. However, the Anti-Federalists maintained that, if the Constitution were the supreme law of the land, its provisions would have preeminence over any state legislation. Thus, Anti-Federalists—especially those from the powerful states of Massachusetts, New York, and Virginia—insisted on the addition of a federal Bill of Rights before they would consent to ratification. The Federalists, on the other hand, resisted any amendments because they knew that the addition of new sections to the Constitution meant that the entire process of ratification would have to start over.

Compromise ultimately broke the deadlock. In Massachusetts, the Anti-Federalist leader, John Hancock, changed his position after Federalists promised him that the insertion of a Bill of Rights in the Constitution would be the first order of business for the new government. Such conditional ratification provided New York and Virginia with an acceptable formula for their own voting; they shortly consented to the new Constitution, although the voting remained incredibly close. Virginia passed the Constitution by a vote of 89 to 79. New York's vote in favor was 30 to 27 (see Table 7.1).

The compromise came just in time. In June 1788, New Hampshire voted to ratify the Constitution,

Table 7.1 Ratification of the Constitution

| Date | State | Votes Yes | Votes No |
|---|---|---|---|
| December 7, 1787 | Delaware | 30 | 0 |
| December 12, 1787 | Pennsylvania | 46 | 23 |
| December 18, 1787 | New Jersey | 38 | 0 |
| January 2, 1788 | Georgia | 26 | 0 |
| January 9, 1788 | Connecticut | 128 | 40 |
| February 6, 1788 | Massachusetts | 187 | 168 |
| April 28, 1788 | Maryland | 63 | 11 |
| May 23, 1788 | South Carolina | 149 | 73 |
| June 21, 1788 | New Hampshire | 57 | 47 |
| June 25, 1788 | Virginia | 89 | 79 |
| July 26, 1788 | New York | 30 | 27 |
| November 21, 1789 | North Carolina | 194 | 77 |
| May 29, 1790 | Rhode Island | 34 | 32 |

There were at least four reasons why the states ratified the Constitution:

***Small states got apportionment.*** Several small states, such as Delaware, Connecticut, and New Jersey, supported the new Constitution immediately, mainly because the Constitution strengthened their position relative to the larger, more populous states. The Great Compromise had secured their votes.

***Georgia needed protection.*** Georgia supported the Constitution quickly too, mainly because it needed protection from the Spanish in Florida and the Indians to its south and west.

***The persuasive Federalist Papers.*** The Federalist Papers, drafted by John Jay, Alexander Hamilton, and James Madison during the ratification debate in New York, argued that the new Constitution would not abridge the "natural rights" that were fought for and thought to be secured by the American Revolution. More than just a series of polemical pamphlets, the Federalist Papers addressed many of the most important questions in political theory at the time, including how much liberty should be sacrificed for the protection of a governing state, how the rights of minority groups could be protected in a democracy, how the Constitution could prevent one of the three governing powers from growing too strong, and how a nation could expand its borders without sacrificing the liberty of those already members. The Federalist Papers are perhaps the most important contributions in political theory ever to emerge from the United States. Their arguments swayed many state delegates, especially in New York.

***The promise of a Bill of Rights.*** And fourth, impelled by the writers who came to be known as the "Anti-Federalists," who were afraid the Constitution would make the national government too strong, the framers agreed to attach a Bill of Rights to the Constitution, which ensured that some of the liberties deemed sacred would be protected in the Constitution. By agreeing that the new government's first order of business would be to draft a Bill of Rights, the framers of the Constitution won the support of the three most important states at the time: Massachusetts, New York, and Virginia. The state legislatures in each of these three states, however, still endured incredibly close votes.

becoming the critical ninth state and putting the Constitution into functional operation. But it was crucial for the new government to have the support of the larger states of Massachusetts, New York, and Virginia if it was going to succeed. With these larger states now supporting the document, by the end of the year, twelve states had accepted the Constitution (Rhode Island finally ratified the Constitution in 1790). The new United States government was launched.

## The Bill of Rights

Massachusetts, Virginia, and New York had all agreed to ratify the Constitution only if Congress hastened to the task of drafting a Bill of Rights that would

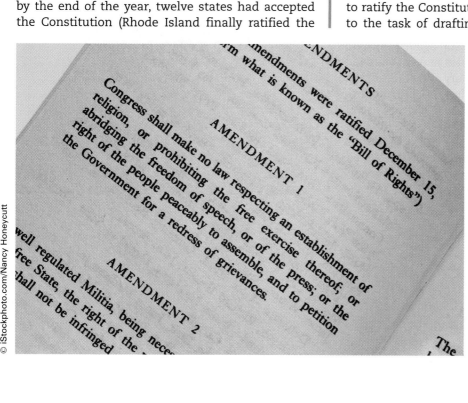

>> Congress pondered a dizzying number of protections as part of the original Bill of Rights. In the end, twelve were proposed, and ten passed.

protect individual freedoms from the threat of potentially tyrannous federal government. It began the task of crafting these rights even before the Constitution was fully ratified. Congress pondered a dizzying number of protections, many of which were borrowed from the various state constitutions. In the end, twelve were proposed, and ten passed.

The first two amendments, which specified the number of constituents of each representative and compensation for congressmen, respectively, did not pass. The remaining ten became the Bill of Rights.

We can see in each amendment a specific grievance that emerged during the "long train of abuses" that led to the Revolution, including the fear of an established church, abridgements to free speech and peaceful gatherings, attempts to disarm the people, the quartering of soldiers in private homes, the forcible removal of private property, unreasonable searches by the federal government, the denial of a trial by one's peers, and the suspension of protections under the law. The First Amendment's prohibition against establishing a national religion was especially important because of the sectarian battles happening between the various Protestant denominations. The Congregationalists in New England were afraid the Anglicans in the South might win federal power, while the Anglicans were equally afraid of the Congregationalists. The Baptists, meanwhile, were bitter that some states maintained control over certifying who could become a minister, making them fearful that one day they might be disallowed from practicing their faith. The First Amendment ended many of these debates and assuaged most of these fears, at least at the federal level.

The Bill of Rights was to defend against the kind of tyranny that the revolutionaries had encountered in the runup to the Revolutionary War. Indeed, the final amendment making up the Bill of Rights pronounced that any power not delegated to the federal government by the Constitution was reserved for the states, thus ensuring a balance of power between the new government and the state governments.

 Read the Bill of Rights.

## And in the end . . .

The Constitution has survived, relatively unchanged, as the basis of the United States's republican government for more than two hundred years. The first ten amendments—the Bill of Rights promised by the Federalists—were added in 1791. Since then, only seventeen more amendments have become law. Some of the fundamental debates, including the question of the balance of power between the states and the federal government, continue today. Interpretations of the framers' intentions have changed over time, but the American frame of government created in 1787 has demonstrated impressive flexibility and longevity.

More than just a political document, the Constitution also sparked essential debates that would continue to preoccupy the American nation. What would be the role of African Americans? Was America a nation only for white people? And what about women as citizens? Was there any justifi-

| What else was happening . . . | |
|---|---|
| 1785 | Frenchman J. P. Blanchard is said to be the first to actually use a parachute by dropping a dog in a basket, to which the parachute was attached, from a hot-air balloon. The dog survived, but fourteen years later, Blanchard suffered a heart attack, fell from one of his own balloons, and died of his injuries. |
| 1787 | Mozart composes his opera *Don Giovanni*. |
| 1788 | Australia is first settled by Europeans as a penal colony. |
| 1789 | Mutiny takes place on *H.M.S. Bounty*. |
| 1793 | Reign of Terror begins in France, as rival revolutionary factions battle over the proper ways in which "liberty, equality, and fraternity" can be implemented in a modern nation-state. Between 15,000 and 40,000 French lose their lives during the fourteen-month Terror, many by the blade of the guillotine, which earns the nickname "National Razor." |

cation for their exclusion from voting? How long would that justification be sustainable? And what would be the nature of the relationship between the Americans and the Indians, both of whom had good reasons to think of the land as theirs? Who would decide? The Constitution took a stand on many of these issues, coming out in ways that make it look anything but democratic. Slaves were to be counted as merely three-fifths of a person, women were not explicitly granted the right to vote, and Indians were not made citizens.

Through amendment and custom, though, the American nation would slowly achieve greater democracy. The initial steps were taken in the first years of the new nation, a period that historians today call the Federalist era.

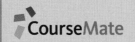 Visit the CourseMate website at www.cengagebrain.com for additional study tools and review materials for this chapter.

# Securing *the* New Nation,

## *1789–1800*

## Learning Outcomes

*After reading this chapter, you should be able to do the following:*

**LO 1** Describe the creation of the federal government under the new Constitution.

**LO 2** Describe how disagreements over how the United States should be governed led to political divisions, and discuss some of the individuals who took strong stands on each side.

**LO 3** Outline the country's development of a two-party political system.

**LO 4** Discuss the issues of John Adams's presidency, and explain how he and the country dealt with them.

**LO 5** Explain the convoluted political process that made Thomas Jefferson president in 1800, including the constitutional change designed to mend the problem.

# "*A blueprint is not a building.*"

Although the war had been won and the Constitution ratified, the debate about the size, shape, and duties of the federal government continued. A blueprint, after all, is not a building. Some, like New York's Alexander Hamilton, were worried that common people could not handle democracy and would be confused by the challenges of running a modern nation. Others, like Thomas Jefferson, were concerned that a powerful centralized federal government would likely take away coveted liberties.

The stakes were high, as the unformed nation struggled to establish itself on the periphery of the European economic system. Daily life went on, of course: people went to school, got married, had families, bought slaves, moved west, and built new homes. But they did so during a time of heightened worries about the political stability of their new nation. Was American independence going to be temporary? Could the country's leaders pull the nation together? Politics of the 1790s was fraught with questions, anxiety, and passion. It led to disagreements, and even duels. And the social life of the new nation would not change dramatically until the 1810s and the Market Revolution (which appears in Chapter 10).

In the end, the political center held, but not in a way that anyone had predicted. Nearly all the founders disliked political partisanship, yet they helped usher in the two-party system that we know today. They also preached the virtues of liberty and equality but went to great extremes to safeguard both the practice of slavery and the continued seizure of Native American lands. Thomas Jefferson advocated a rural, agrarian republic, yet the stability enjoyed and the land acquired during his presidency helped foster an economic revolution—one that we will encounter in the following chapters. But, first, to the decade following the ratification of the Constitution, when the central role of the federal government was to secure the new nation. This chapter examines the development of the new government, the rise of the two-party political system, and the first peaceful turnover of power in the "bloodless revolution" of 1800.

## LO¹ Creating a New Government

From 1789 to 1800 the federal government was remarkably small. In 1800, the Department of State had only three employees, plus representatives in London, Paris, Madrid, Lisbon, and The Hague. The entire Treasury had a total of about seventy-five employees. The War Department consisted of the secretary of war, two clerks, and a messenger. The Post Office numbered seventy-five offices. The legislative branch had only twenty-six senators and

*From 1789 to 1800 the federal government was remarkably small.*

**Naturalization Act of 1790**
Legislation which declared that, among immigrants to the U.S., only "free white persons" could become citizens of the United States

**patronage**
System of granting rewards for assisting with political victories

>> **Federal Hall in New York City, the first capitol building of the United States, on the day of George Washington's inauguration as first president.**

sixty-four representatives. For a nation suspicious of centralized power, a small federal government was appropriate.

As the new government began operations in 1789, it became clear that, although the Constitution outlined a framework of government, the exact roles of its three branches were not clearly defined. Establishing precedents would be the mission of the first group of federal politicians.

## The First Citizens

According to Article 4, Section 2 of the Constitution, the states dictated who was and was not a citizen. They more or less confined citizenship to white, property-holding males, although there were a few exceptions to this generalization. Immigrants could become citizens as well, and in the **Naturalization Act of 1790**, Congress declared that, among immigrants, only "free white persons" could become citizens of the United States. This obviously limited black people, Native Americans, and Asians. (These restrictions continued for almost a century, until 1870, when African Americans were allowed to become citizens.) White women also had few property rights, and, once married, anything a woman owned became the property of her husband. It was not until 1920 that women were granted full citizenship.

 Read the Naturalization Act of 1790.

## The First Congress

The first federal election under the new Constitution was held late in 1788. Most of the men elected were sympathetic to the arguments laid out in the Federalist Papers. At its first meeting in the capital city of New York, the first Congress had four major tasks: (1) setting up a system of federal courts; (2) securing the Bill of Rights that had been promised during the ratification period; (3) establishing the executive department; and (4) raising revenue. By addressing these pressing issues in a relatively tidy manner, the first Congress demonstrated its strength compared to the Continental Congress under the Articles of Confederation. The new government seemed to be working.

### Courts

The Judiciary Act of 1789 created three circuit courts and thirteen district courts to accompany the Supreme Court established by the Constitution.

### Rights

James Madison proposed to Congress seventeen amendments to the Constitution, twelve of which Congress approved and ten of which the states later ratified. These ten amendments are known as the Bill of Rights.

### Executive Department

Congress created five executive posts: (1) the secretary of state, (2) the secretary of war, (3) the secretary of the Treasury, (4) the attorney general, and (5) the postmaster general. These positions were to be filled by the president, meaning that the president would control **patronage**, defined as

Take a virtual tour of the activities of the First Federal Congress.

the granting of rewards for assisting with political victories (although, in these early years, these jobs were not viewed as lucrative because the federal government was so small). Under President George Washington, these positions (except that of postmaster general) would serve as his cabinet of advisors.

### Revenues

James Madison, who had played an essential role at the Constitutional Convention, was elected to the House of Representatives from Virginia. His work was equally indispensable during the first term of Congress. In 1789, he persuaded Congress to pass the **Hamilton Tariff of 1789**, which imposed a 5 to 10 percent tariff on certain imports. This act's success freed the federal government from constant worry about economic shortfalls.

## The First President

The least surprising outcome of the nation's first election was installing George Washington as president. His stature as an honest war leader made him the obvious choice to lead the new government. He never ran for the office,

> **❝It was not until 1920 that women were granted full citizenship.❞**

and indeed, had retired from public life altogether before he was elected. Washington had to be talked into coming back and serving his country once again.

As he formulated his approach to the office, Washington was aware that he had no contemporary role models; the American republic was truly an experiment. "I walk on untrodden ground," he said. "There is scarcely any part of my conduct which may not hereafter be drawn in precedent." Washington established several important precedents while in office. Three of the most significant concerned the presidential manner, the cabinet, and relations with Congress.

### The Presidential Manner

Washington displayed a dignified and formal manner as president. In the debate about how people should address him, Washington remained quiet. Federalists proposed calling him "His Excellency" or "His Highness," but Anti-Federalists rebuffed the proposal, favoring a less lofty title. Without any insistence from Washington himself, he came to be called simply "Mr. President." This endowed him with importance, but not regal entitlement. Washington also dressed formally (never in military attire, always in American-made suits), conducted affairs in a formal manner, and decided not to use his veto power unless he deemed a law unconstitutional. He wanted people to take the office of president seriously, but without encouraging the office to usurp the will of the people as expressed by Congress.

**Hamilton Tariff of 1789**
Act that imposed a 5 to 10 percent tariff on certain imports to fund the new government

>> **Washington in retirement at Mount Vernon after the war. He would have to be persuaded to reenter public life and become the new nation's first president.**

## The Cabinet

Washington's second important precedent concerned his cabinet. Congress voted to create several departments within the executive branch, but the Constitution did not explicitly outline the responsibilities of these departments (which were collectively known as the president's "**cabinet**"). With the cabinet's role open to interpretation, Washington assembled this group with an eye toward gathering differing viewpoints. He hoped that including a range of opinions within the government would keep leaders working together in the nation's interests rather than fighting among themselves for power.

Washington appointed Thomas Jefferson the first secretary of state. In addition to heading American diplomatic relations, Jefferson's office was also in charge of the census, patents and copyrights, public lands, and the mint. Washington's Treasury secretary was Alexander Hamilton, a close friend who had served as his aide-de-camp during the Revolution. Henry Knox was secretary of war, as he had been under the Continental Congress during the 1780s. Knox commanded an army of 5,000 men, most of whom were deployed for defense against Native Americans in the western territories. Samuel Osgood was the postmaster general, in charge of mail delivery. Edmund Randolph was the attorney general, who met with the cabinet as Washington's personal advisor.

Reflecting the balance of perspectives that Washington sought, Hamilton and Knox favored a strong centralized government, whereas Jefferson and Randolph favored greater power at the state level. Jefferson and Randolph were from Virginia, Hamilton from New York, Knox and Osgood from New England. When Washington began consulting them on official matters (or, more commonly, asking Randolph to solicit their opinions), the cabinet system was born.

Read Washington's First Inaugural Address.

Explore Washington's life in a series of interactive modules.

### Relations with Congress

The Constitution required that the executive branch draft treaties with the "advice and consent" of the Senate, but the first time Washington endeavored to make a treaty, the resulting bickering with Congress led to an inconclusive treaty. From then on, Washington decided to negotiate treaties first and then submit them to Congress for approval. This established a precedent. Washington also took seriously his role of informing Congress of the state of the union once a year, thus demonstrating that he was ever attentive to the will of the people.

# LO² Political Divisions

During its first decade, this small government had serious problems to confront, and the confrontations sparked factionalism. Whose side you chose in the debate depended on your vision for the nation. Some, like Washington,

© North Wind Picture Archives

Hamilton, and Adams (who, as a political group, would come to be called the Federalists), wanted a strong federal government that would assist merchants and industry in order to create a buoyant, market-based nation. Others, like Jefferson and Madison (who would come to be called the Democratic-Republicans), preferred a weaker federal government that would allow the preservation of "natural rights" and of slavery. Two issues illustrated these competing visions—problems over government finance and foreign policy.

## The Problem of Finance

During the Revolutionary War, the Continental Congress had taken out loans to fund the war. Foreign investors held $12 million worth of notes; domestic bondholders were owed $48 million. To establish good credit and to maintain authority over the states, the federal government had to pay off the loans.

### Hamilton's Financial Plan

As Treasury secretary and an author of the Federalist Papers, Alexander Hamilton promoted economic policies aligned with his vision for a strong, centralized government. He proposed an economic plan that favored the interests of the commercial and mercantile elite. His plan had four key components: (1) consolidating the loans that Congress took out during the Revolutionary War into one national debt, which would importantly commit the wealthy people who were owed money to the success of the federal government; (2) consolidating the individual states' loans into the national debt, making the states beholden to the federal government and thus strengthening its authority; (3) raising revenue through the sale of bonds, the sale of public lands, the establishment of tariffs, and the imposition of an excise tax on whiskey; and (4) creating the First Bank of the United States, which would hold the government's revenue and issue bank notes (paper money) that would be legal tender throughout the country.

The bank was the linchpin of the plan. It would benefit the business classes, who could capitalize on the stability provided by a bank. It would organize the loans and the debt as well. But it would also expand the power of Congress and, therefore, of the federal government. A national bank was not mentioned in the Constitution, but the Constitution did grant Congress the power to do anything "necessary and proper" to carry out its delegated powers. If

Congress could successfully charter a bank (which it did in 1791), it would assume a vast amount of **implied powers** through a loose interpretation of the words in the Constitution—a position called **loose constructionism**. This would in turn make the federal government much more powerful. Some of the founders had envisioned this all along, while others had not, thus making the "original intent" of the founders difficult if not impossible to decipher.

## Opposition to Hamilton's Plan

Thomas Jefferson and James Madison led the faction that immediately opposed Hamilton's policies. Because Jefferson was a towering figure in the new government, this faction came to be called the Jeffersonians, although they preferred to be called the **Democratic-Republicans**. The Democratic-Republicans had three problems with Hamilton's plan (see "The reasons why..." on page 140).

Jefferson, Madison, and their supporters envisioned an agrarian nation made up of independent farmers, not laborers and industrialists who were dependent on others. Their plan for an agrarian nation, of course, also allowed for, indeed depended on, the perpetuation of slavery. (Hamilton, meanwhile, ardently opposed slavery, believing that it denied individual liberty and favored the established aristocracy of the South over the merchants of the North.)

**implied powers**
Congress's power to do anything "necessary and proper" to carry out its delegated powers, even if those actions are not explicitly named in the Constitution

**loose constructionism**
Interpretation of the Constitution suggesting that the Constitution should be flexible to accommodate new demands

**Democratic-Republicans**
Faction that coalesced in opposition to Alexander Hamilton's economic policies and Jay's Treaty; led by Virginians like Thomas Jefferson and James Madison; also known as the Jeffersonians

© iStockphoto.com/Stefan Klein

## The Democratic-Republicans had three problems with Hamilton's plan:

**Speculators would benefit.** The Democratic-Republicans thought that honoring all debts was unfair because many of the Americans who had purchased bonds to fund the Revolutionary War—often widows and soldiers—had been forced to sell their bonds for less than their face value during the hard economic times of the 1780s. Commercial speculators bought the bonds from them at low prices, and Hamilton's plan would reward these speculators unfairly.

**Some had already paid off their debts.** They also believed that nationalizing the state debts was unfair because some states (especially southern states like Jefferson's Virginia) had already made headway in paying off their debts by selling western lands. If the debts of all states were pooled together, the residents of the states that had already reduced their debts would have to pay a disproportionate share of the national debt.

**A fear that financiers were given preferential treatment.** Creating a bank was contentious because many Americans—particularly southerners—argued that the creation of a national bank would serve the interests of only financiers and merchants. They believed it would offer little aid to farmers and plantation owners. The Democratic-Republicans considered these groups the most virtuous citizens of an agrarian republic. Arguing that the creation of a bank was not within the purview of the federal government, the opponents of Hamilton's plan favored a more literal interpretation of the Constitution—a position called **strict constructionism.**

## Congressional Impasse and Washington, D.C.

The deadlock over Hamilton's plan was ultimately broken by a compromise on an entirely separate issue: the location of the national government. Between 1789 and 1793, the federal government of the United States was in New York City. In 1793, the government moved south to Philadelphia, but southern leaders wanted the government to be located even farther south, in Virginia. They also wanted it to be located *outside* a big city, because many of Jefferson's supporters considered big cities sinkholes of corruption.

Over dinner and wine one night, Jefferson and Hamilton struck a deal: Hamilton would instruct the supporters of his economic plan to favor relocating the seat of government along the Potomac River, and Jefferson would allow Hamilton's plan to pass through Congress. With this compromise, the economic legislation passed, the First Bank of the United States was created (it lasted until 1811), and the stage was set for the national government to move to Washington, D.C.

## The Whiskey Rebellion

Opposition to Hamilton's economic policies was not limited to Democratic-Republicans in the govern-

>> **The bank was the linchpin of the plan.**

©iStockphoto.com/Robert Dodge

### The Difference between Jefferson and Hamilton

| | Jefferson | Hamilton |
|---|---|---|
| **Party** | Democratic-Republican | Federalist |
| **National vision** | An agrarian republic of independent farmers | A capitalist, industrial power |
| **Federal government** | Small, subservient to states | Strong and centralized |
| **Labor** | Free and enslaved | Free |
| **National bank** | Against | For |

ment. In western Pennsylvania, Hamilton's decision to tax whiskey proved divisive. Before railroads or canals were built, western farmers depended on slow, halting, horse-based transport and had difficulty transporting their crops without spoilage. They found it easier to distill their grain to whiskey and ship it in that form. A tax on whiskey was thus a serious threat to their livelihood. To make matters worse, Hamilton's plan taxed small producers of whiskey more than it did large producers, in part because the tax was an effort to demonstrate to small farmers and westerners the government's authority to tax them. This gave rise to accusations of East Coast elitism.

In 1794, many westerners attacked the tax men who tried to collect the whiskey tax. When Washington and Hamilton attempted to bring some of the rebels to justice, they chose whiskey producers in western Pennsylvania as their test case. The rural Pennsylvanians fought back, eventually rioting and overrunning the city of Pittsburgh, where they were to be tried for tax evasion. This was the **Whiskey Rebellion**. Alarmed by the direct refusal to adhere to the dictates of the federal government, George Washington issued a proclamation declaring the farmers in rebellion and sent a newly organized army of nearly 13,000 to quell the revolt. Washington himself at times led the troops. But by the time the army reached western Pennsylvania, the rebels had gone home. Washington ultimately pardoned the two men who were captured in the dispute.

There were two main results of the Whiskey Rebellion. First, from this time forward, the western provinces were firmly Anti-Federalist, favoring the small-government approach of the Democratic-Republicans. But second, Washington's message was clear: The national government would not allow extralegal protests to effect change. In a nation of laws, change would come only through peaceful means.

## The Problem of Foreign Policy

Through the 1790s, there were still no formal political parties, but clear divisions were apparent. Both politicians and everyday Americans had to determine what kind of nation they wanted. In the Whiskey Rebellion, the Pennsylvania farmers sought to defend their idea that the federal government should not reach too deeply into the pockets of everyday Americans. They lost that particular battle, but the sympathy they aroused from the future Democratic-Republicans showed that their complaints did not go unheard.

As a new nation, the United States also had to travel the often-treacherous terrain of foreign policy. And here too, almost every decision made by the federal government was liable to be framed in divisive language. Would the nation support other Enlightenment-based revolutions, like the one taking place in France? Would it challenge England when it infringed on American liberties in the seas? Plus, there were still divisions in the west, with the Spanish still in control of the Mississippi River and Florida, the British still possessing forts in the western hinterlands and Canada, and Indians still living on and claiming lands throughout the vast terrain. The answers to these questions only increased political divisions.

**strict constructionism**
Literal interpretation of the Constitution, arguing that the original meaning of those at the Constitutional Convention should not be adapted to fit more recent times

**Whiskey Rebellion**
Conflict in which Pennsylvania farmers fought a tax on whiskey, eventually rioting and overrunning the city of Pittsburgh in 1794, where they were to be tried for tax evasion

>> Washington, D.C., in 1800.

## The Pinckney Treaty

In one rare instance, the **Pinckney Treaty of 1796** (also called the Treaty of San Lorenzo) was an accomplishment everyone could celebrate. The tax on whiskey remained after the Whiskey Rebellion, but opposition to the policy cooled when the treaty with Spain gave Pennsylvania farmers an easier way to get their crops to market. The Pinckney Treaty opened the Mississippi River to American shipping and allowed Americans the "right of deposit" at New Orleans, which meant that American merchants could warehouse goods in the city. The Pinckney Treaty was popular, a notable foreign policy achievement in a decade of political controversy. Other foreign policy decisions, however, divided American leaders in the 1790s. In particular, government officials clashed over the French Revolution and the conduct of trade with certain foreign nations.

## The French Revolution and the Citizen Genêt Affair

In 1789 in France, growing discontent with the king spurred the French people to overthrow their monarchy, inciting the French Revolution. Most Americans were initially pleased with the news, thinking that they themselves had been on the front line of an inevitable transition to republican governments around the world. But by the early 1790s, the news from France grew worse: The country had

erupted into violence, and one leader after another had been deposed, creating chaos and a reign of terror. The French could not agree on what liberty was, who was deserving of it, or how it could be governed fairly.

Public opinion in America was divided over the French Revolution. The disorder in France alarmed many Federalists, and criticism increased when the revolutionaries executed the former king, Louis XVI, and his wife, Marie Antoinette, in 1793. At the same time, many Federalists (especially in New England) viewed England as the United States's natural trading partner. When Britain declared war on France in 1792 (other European nations saw France's chaos as an opportunity to make territorial gains, prompting Europe-wide battles), many New Englanders were concerned that too much support for France's revolution would sour trade relations with England. On the one hand, the Democratic-Republicans continued to sympathize with the revolution, supporting its attempt to create a republican government. On the other hand, Federalists in New England supported Britain.

In the United States, the conflict came to a head when an ambassador from the revolutionary French Republic, Edmond Genêt, arrived in the United States on April 8, 1793. Genêt's mission was to raise support for the new French government, particularly because the revolution had brought France into conflict with England and Spain, key trading partners of the United States. Genêt received a mixed reception. Many Americans remembered the French contribution to the American Revolution and welcomed him. Others pointed out that America's alliance had actu-

FAMOUS WHISKEY INSURRECTION IN PENNSYLVANIA.

**>>** George Washington sent a newly organized army of almost 13,000 to quell the Whiskey Rebellion.

ally been with the now-deposed French king, not the new French Republic. To avoid entanglement, Washington issued a neutrality proclamation two weeks after Genêt's arrival, on April 22, 1793.

Genêt ignored the proclamation and very publicly tried to recruit American soldiers and advocate American attacks on British ships. Since this was a direct challenge to Washington's stance on neutrality, the president issued a proclamation in August 1793 that France recall Genêt. (Genêt was allowed to stay in America, however, after a new French government demanded his arrest and Washington became aware that Genêt would likely be executed if he returned to France. Washington opposed Genêt's methods, not Genêt himself.)

Besides creating a diplomatic nuisance, the Genêt affair was significant because it delineated further distinctions between Washington's Federalists and Jefferson's Democratic-Republicans. Jefferson opposed President Washington's neutrality and realized that Washington had started looking more to Hamilton for advice on foreign affairs than to him. Recognizing his loss of influence, Jefferson resigned as secretary of state in July 1793, a sign of the growing divisions within American political leadership.

### U.S. Neutrality and Jay's Treaty

The rebuke of Genêt did not end Washington's problems maintaining neutrality. Indeed, neither France nor Britain respected American neutrality, with the British sometimes performing the terrible act of **impressing** (capturing and forcing into service) American sailors into its navy. Other British policies, unrelated to the war with France, also aggravated Americans. For example, the treaty that ended the American Revolution decreed that the British evacuate their forts on the American frontier, but a decade after the agreement was reached, Britain still occupied the forts. In addition, Britain closed its ports in the West Indies to American ships.

To address these issues, in 1794, Washington sent New York's John Jay to Britain. Jay had served as the first chief justice of the Supreme Court and helped negotiate the treaty that ended the American Revolution.

In 1795, Jay returned with **Jay's Treaty**. In it the British agreed to evacuate military posts along the frontier in the Northwest Territory and make reparations for the cargo seized in 1793 and 1794. But Jay made several concessions; for instance, the United States lifted duties on British imports for ten years. Furthermore, the treaty avoided addressing other important issues, such as the impressing of American sailors.

Jay's Treaty brought the conflict over foreign relations (whether to support France or England) to a boiling point. Jefferson's partisans were brutal in their attacks on the Federalists, claiming that Jay's Treaty was a betrayal of the 1778 alliance with France and a humiliating capitulation to the British. At public rallies, protesters burned Jay in effigy. The vehemence of the opposition caused Washington to hesitate in signing the treaty, although he did sign it eventually. Nevertheless, Jay's Treaty indicated growing divisions within American politics, passionate divisions over the direction of the nation that would contribute to the rise of a two-party political system.

## Indian Relations

If problems of finance and foreign policy were crafting two political factions, both parties could at least agree on the policies toward Indians. Once again, it was the Americans' westward expansion that provoked conflict.

### Indian Resistance in the Northwest

In 1790, a huge coalition of Indian tribes (including the Chippewa, Ottawa, Shawnee, Delaware, Pottawatomi, and others) attacked American settlers north of the Ohio River, in what is today Ohio. Buttressed by British promises of support, the Native Americans were successful in defeating several American battalions until 1794, when the American Army finally secured a victory in the Battle of Fallen Timbers. President Washington intended to clear the Ohio River Valley for settlement and had finally done so at that battle. The result was the **Treaty of Greenville** (1795), which forced the Indian tribes of the Old Northwest westward across the Mississippi River (Map 8.1). This development signaled peace in the Ohio River Valley and white settlement there for two decades.

### The South

At about the same time, the Creeks near Georgia were battling to prevent further American encroachment on their lands. The Spanish were the real

**impressment**
Practice of capturing and forcing sailors from other nations into naval service

**Jay's Treaty**
Treaty in which the British agreed to evacuate military posts along the frontier in the Northwest Territory and make reparations for the cargo seized in 1793 and 1794 while the United States lifted duties on British imports for ten years

**Treaty of Greenville**
Agreement that forced the Indian tribes of the Old Northwest westward across the Mississippi River in 1795

beneficiaries of the Creek war, because the Creeks served as a buffer between Spain's Florida territory and the American settlers in Georgia.

Anxious to avoid continued attacks by the Creeks, George Washington called the Creek leader, Alexander McGillivray, to New York to pursue a treaty. The parties agreed to terms that legitimated the Creek presence and ended hostilities until 1792, when McGillivray accepted better terms from the Spanish. Small wars continued in the South and Southwest until 1794, at which time Tennesseans, hoping to establish Tennessee as a state, successfully pushed the Creeks farther west and south.

### A New Policy

The continuing violence led the United States to revise its Indian policy. In 1790, Congress passed the first of the **Indian Trade and Intercourse Acts**, which made it illegal for Americans to trade with Native American tribes without formal consent from the federal government. The acts also made it illegal to sell land to or buy land from Native Americans without similar federal consent. This last part began the process of defining "Indian territory," the lands where Indians could live and work. The acts once again made it clear that the United States had no intention of integrating Indians into their new nation.

# LO³ The Rise of Two-Party Politics

Despite the factions' willingness to come together to fight Indians, by 1795, after the uproars caused by the Citizen Genêt affair and Jay's Treaty, the two major divisions of opinion had crystallized into political parties: the Democratic-Republicans and the Federalists. Each party considered itself the inheritor of America's revolutionary ideology and viewed its opposition as illegitimate.

## The Democratic-Republicans

The Democratic-Republican Party (often called the Republican Party or the Jeffersonian-Republicans) coalesced in opposition to Hamilton's economic policies and Jay's Treaty. James Madison and a few other Virginians were the architects of the new organization. They transformed a loose collection of "Democratic-Republican societies" into a disciplined party whose members voted with consistency. In 1792, Thomas Jefferson assumed the party's leadership.

In general, the Democratic-Republicans favored limited government. They opposed the national bank and other measures that enhanced the power of the federal government, and they sided with France over Great Britain because of the feeling of shared republican brotherhood with France. It should be noted, however, that their sense of self-rule also included the right to own slaves if one so desired. Jefferson found supporters among southern landholders and among free workers and laborers everywhere.

## The Federalists

The **Federalist Party** grew out of the faction of American leaders that endorsed Hamilton's economic policies and Jay's Treaty. They supported Washington's presidency and helped John Adams succeed him in 1796. In general, the Federalists supported the stability provided by a centralized government and were suspicious of the whims of the populace. The Federalists supported a strong governmental role in economic affairs and the stability of trade with Britain. They were mostly wealthy merchants, large property owners, or conservative farmers. New England and the Middle Colonies were Federalist strongholds.

### Slavery

Aside from finance and federalism, another issue caused a rift between the two parties: slavery. To be sure, most Federalists were not abolitionists, but many of them were less committed to the continuation of slavery than the Democratic-Republicans. This division was illuminated in each party's reaction to the Haitian Revolution.

### The Haitian Revolution

In 1791, slaves in Santo Domingo, Haiti, a Caribbean island nation just south of Florida, revolted, killing planters and burning sugar plantations. Led by Toussaint L'Ouverture, the slaves declared independence from their French overlords. In America, the Federalists supported the revolution (in this

Map 8.1. The West, 1790–1796

instance, *they* were the ones mindful of their own republican roots). George Washington kept up trade relations with Haiti and sought to recognize the independent nation that was made up mostly of former slaves.

Democratic-Republicans were aghast at Washington's actions. The Haitian Revolution had forced a flood of white landholders to decamp to America's southern states, who told of the vio-

lence they had witnessed and warned against the potential creation of a black republic near the coast of America. When Thomas Jefferson became president in 1800, he reversed the nation's position on the Haitian Revolution and supported French attempts to crush the slave rebellion. (The French lost this effort in 1803, and Haiti became the first black republic and Latin America's first independent state.)

There were three results of the Haitian Revolution in the South. First, southern lawmakers tightened black codes, citing fear of slave insurrections in America. Second, the revolution also hardened planters' conviction that the South was meant to maintain slavery. This reliance on slavery had deepened after the invention of the cotton gin in 1793, which made labor-intensive cotton profitable in much of the South. Finally, the revolution underscored France's increased reluctance to maintain its possessions in the New World, a sentiment that led to the Louisiana Purchase of 1803 (see Chapter 9).

### Gabriel's Conspiracy

Yet another result of the Haitian Revolution was the spread of revolutionary fervor among American slaves, which sparked **Gabriel's Conspiracy** in 1800. After the American Revolution, New York and Philadelphia became havens for free black people, and nearly all of the northern states developed plans to free their slaves. The opposite was happening in the South, where slavery was becoming more and more entrenched.

In 1800, several churchgoing African Americans learned of the events in Haiti and planned a similar attack on Richmond, Virginia. They intended to burn the town and capture the governor, James Monroe. After heavy rain postponed the attack, several conspirators leaked the plan. State leaders hanged twenty-six rebels, including the leader, a slave named Gabriel. A second attack in 1802 (led by a slave named Sancho) was also preemptively stopped. These two attempts to overthrow the system resulted in the continued tightening of the laws governing slaves. Most significantly, all postrevolutionary talk of emancipation in the South ended due to white fears of black insurrection. The harsh mea-

See documents related to Gabriel's Conspiracy.

sures were meant to stifle slaves' hopes of escaping the system, and the measures worked.

## LO⁴ Adams's Presidency and Dealing with Dissent

George Washington easily won reelection as president in 1792, but as the election of 1796 approached, Washington decided not to run for a third term. Exhausted by his years as president and by the continual attacks of the Democratic-Republican press, Washington encouraged Americans to come together under a nonpartisan system.

Read Washington's Farewell Address of 1796.

His hopes were not realized. The Democratic-Republicans and the Federalists both began organizing local meetings of their supporters. In his heartfelt Farewell Address, Washington rued these divisions, but both parties were sufficiently well organized to field candidates in the election of 1796. The two-party political system was born.

### Adams's Election

When Washington's vice president, Federalist John Adams, announced his candidacy for president, the Democratic-Republicans nominated Thomas Jefferson to oppose him. After a particularly partisan campaign, rife with intense bickering and dissention, Adams received seventy-one electoral votes and became president. According to the Constitution, the candidate with the second highest number of electoral votes was to be vice president, and, by previous arrangement among Federalist electoral voters, Adams's running mate, Thomas Pinckney of South Carolina, was meant to receive the same number of votes as Adams less one, with one supporter withholding his vote. This would have given Pinckney seventy

> **"** Adams's opponent, Thomas Jefferson, became his vice president. From 1797 to 1800, there would be no harmony in the federal government. **"**

votes and the vice presidency. Confusion and trickery muddled the plan, though, and, communications were slow. No one was sure who was supposed to hold back his vote for Pinckney, and so several did. The result was that, instead of Pinckney, it was Jefferson who took second place, with sixty-eight electoral votes. Thus, Adams's opponent, Thomas Jefferson, became his vice president. From 1797 to 1800, there would be no harmony in the federal government.

## The XYZ Affair

Upon entering office in 1797, Adams immediately faced a foreign policy crisis called the **XYZ Affair**, which further divided the two factions. The French had interpreted Jay's Treaty as an indication that the United States was siding with Great Britain in the trade wars, and they retaliated by raiding American merchant ships. France was angry at what it saw as a rebuke to the clan of republican brotherhood. Adams sent three envoys to France to defuse the situation, and the French foreign minister sent three agents to meet them (designated X, Y, and Z in official French documents). It became evident that X, Y, and Z's real purpose was to extort money from the Americans as a prerequisite for negotiations. When news of "the XYZ Affair" reached the United States, Americans were outraged at France's galling lack of respect.

### Result—The Quasi-War

Meanwhile, the French continued to raid American ships. The Adams administration responded to these raids by repudiating America's 1778 alliance with France, and a so-called "quasi-war" erupted between the two nations. From 1798 to 1800, the naval fleets of both countries openly plundered each other's ships. As Franco-American relations deteriorated, Adams feared the outbreak of a full-scale war between the two nations. This was significant because it put Adams on the defensive regarding dissent within the American government. In his mind, America was on the verge of an international war.

*Lyon retaliated by spitting in Griswold's face, and the two men began wrestling on the floor of the House of Representatives.*

## The Alien and Sedition Acts

Adams's concerns about dissent became problematic because partisanship had continued to escalate during his term. For example, in 1798, a fight broke out on the floor of the House of Representatives when Matthew Lyon, a pugnacious Democratic-Republican congressman from Vermont, declared that aristocratic Federalist representatives were perpetually duping the people. Roger Griswold, a Federalist representative from Connecticut, asked Lyon if he meant to defend the people with a wooden sword. (Griswold was referring to the fact that, during the American Revolution, Lyon had been court-martialed for cowardice and forced to wear a wooden sword as punishment.) Lyon retaliated by spitting in Griswold's face, and the two men began wrestling on the floor of the House of Representatives.

Attempting to bring such bitter conflicts under control, Adams pushed a series of measures through Congress known collectively as the **Alien and Sedition Acts**. They turned out to be his undoing.

© Eon Images

>> "Cinque-têtes, or the Paris Monster," an outrageous contemporary political cartoon on the XYZ Affair, shows staunch Americans resisting threats and demands for money from revolutionary France, depicted as happily devouring frogs, guillotining aristocrats, and supporting the Haitian Revolution (notice Toussaint L'Ouverture seated at the far right).

**Virginia and Kentucky Resolutions**
Declarations written by Thomas Jefferson and James Madison and adopted by the legislatures of Virginia and Kentucky, proclaiming the Sedition Act to be an infringement on rights protected by their state constitutions and that states had the right to nullify federal laws within their borders

The Alien and Sedition Acts consisted of three separate acts, the third of which would have the biggest impact on Adams's future: (1) The Alien Enemies Act authorized the deportation of the citizens of enemy nations; (2) the Alien Friends Act allowed the government to detain and deport noncitizens for almost any cause. Because many of the most active Democratic-Republicans were recent British immigrants, the Alien Friends Act was regarded as a deliberate assault on the party; and (3) the Sedition Act set fines and prison sentences for anyone found guilty of writing, speaking, or publishing "false, scandalous and malicious" statements against the government.

The two Alien Acts had little impact, but the Sedition Act was explosive. Several Democratic-Republican newspaper editors were jailed for violating the new law. Federalists used the law to jail Matthew Lyon, the Democratic-Republican representative who had wrestled on the House floor. Not only did the act make political martyrs out of the jailed Republican-Democrats, but it also provoked their party colleagues to fight back.

Calling the Alien and Sedition Acts a violation of the First Amendment's guarantees, Thomas Jefferson and James Madison collaborated anonymously to pen a set of resolutions denouncing the acts. In 1798, the legislatures of Virginia and Kentucky adopted resolutions—called the **Virginia and Kentucky Resolutions**—proclaiming the Sedition Act to be an infringement on rights protected by their state constitutions. The resolutions declared that each state had the right to nullify federal laws within its borders.

This bold challenge to federal authority was called the **doctrine of nullification**. No other state endorsed the resolutions, and several openly rebuked them, but they provided the intellectual framework for sectional divisions that were to come. They also set the stage for the bitter election of 1800.

# LO⁵ The "Bloodless Revolution" of 1800

The candidates in the election of 1800 were the same as those in 1796, Jefferson and Adams. Four years of controversy, however, had intensified the bitter rivalry between the two men. Citing the Alien and Sedition Acts, Democratic-Republicans accused Adams of harboring monarchical ideas and called him a slave to British interests. Federalists castigated Thomas Jefferson as an atheist (he had composed his own personal copy of the Bible by cutting out everything but the words spoken by Christ) who would follow the lead of the French revolutionaries and instigate a reign of terror in the United States. The campaigning was vitriolic, to say the least.

### The Mistake

John Adams gave his opposition unexpected help by reopening negotiations with France. In terms of international relations, the negotiations were a success; they resulted in a peace treaty that brought the quasi-war to an end. In terms of Adams's candidacy, because most of his fellow Federalists were pro-British, his efforts to smooth things over with France divided his own party. The Federalist Party had already suffered in the controversy over the Alien and Sedition Acts. Now they were divided over whether the United States should negotiate with France.

### The Election

As the election of 1800 approached, the Federalists were too divided to give Jefferson any real competition. Hamilton, in fact, jockeyed to get the Federalists to dump Adams as their candidate. In contrast, the Democratic-Republican Party was well organized, and the final tally in the Electoral College gave Jefferson and his running mate, Aaron Burr of New York, a clear margin of victory.

### Results

The assumption of power by the Democratic-Republicans did not go off without a hitch, however.

Ironically, the Democratic-Republicans were, in a way, *too* organized. Jefferson and Burr received seventy-three votes apiece in Electoral College voting. This was a problem because the Constitution did not provide for a two-person ticket (with one designated as president and the other as vice president). Rather, it stated that the candidate with the most electoral votes became president and the candidate with the second most votes assumed the vice presidency. In the event of a tie, the decision was placed in the hands of the House of Representatives.

In the election of 1800 (Map 8.2), Democratic-Republican candidates had also won control of both houses of Congress, but the new Congress did not sit until after the presidential election was settled. Therefore, it was the **lame-duck** (or, soon-to-be-out-of-office) Federalist Congress that would make the decision. Some Federalists decided to support Burr and deny Jefferson the presidency, and, although Burr did not openly support this movement, he also did not denounce it. Hamilton, however, distrusted Burr more than he disliked Jefferson. Using his influence among the Federalists, Hamilton helped his old rival Thomas Jefferson to victory on the thirty-sixth ballot. To ensure that the shenanigans of the

**doctrine of nullification**
The theory that each state had the right to nullify federal laws within its borders

**lame duck**
Politician who is not returning to office and is serving out the rest of his or her term with little influence; a soon-to-be-out-of-office politician or Congress

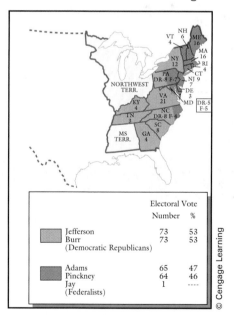

**Map 8.2. The Election of 1800**
The presidential election of 1800 witnessed the first transfer of power from one political faction to another. This "bloodless revolution" was vital in ensuring the survival of the young nation.

1800 election would never be repeated, in 1804 the United States adopted the Twelfth Amendment to the Constitution, allowing electors to vote for president and vice president separately.

# And in the end . . .

Although party politics had increased tremendously between 1796 and 1800, the election of 1800 was valuable in demonstrating that an opposition party could defeat the party in power without causing a total breakdown of government or a civil war. This was a tremendous accomplishment. When Adams and the Federalists handed over the reins of power peacefully, optimism ran high that the nation had passed a critical test. Jefferson himself declared in his Inaugural Address, "We are all Republicans. We are all Federalists," thus suggesting that the survival of the nation should trump political differences. After 1800, opposition became a cornerstone of the American system of government, as did the two-party system. The so-called bloodless revolution of 1800 paved the way for active, peaceful political dissent in American life.

| What else was happening . . . | |
|---|---|
| 1791 | Early bicycles are made in Scotland. |
| 1791 | France begins using the metric system. |
| 1795 | Tula Slave Rebellion in the Dutch Caribbean colony of Curacao lasts a month before finally being suppressed. August 17 is still celebrated in Curacao as a day of freedom. |
| 1798 | The first soft drink is invented. |
| 1800 | Worcestershire sauce is invented. |

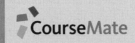

Visit the CourseMate website at www.cengagebrain.com for additional study tools and review materials for this chapter.

{ More Bang for Your Buck }

"I like the lower cost, the size of the book, the lighter reading, and the interactive games and quizzes on the website."
– Jillian Basiger, Student at Lakeland Community College

HIST has it all, and you can too. Between the text and our online offerings, you have everything at your fingertips. Make sure you check out all that HIST has to offer:

- Chapter in Review Cards
- Online Quizzing with Feedback
- Robust eBook
- Primary Source Exercises
- Flash Cards
- Interactive Maps
- And More!

Visit CourseMate to find the resources you need today!
Login at **www.cengagebrain.com**.

# CHAPTER 9

# Jeffersonian Democracy, *1800–1814*

## Learning Outcomes

*After reading this chapter, you should be able to do the following:*

LO **1**   Define Jeffersonian Democracy, and explain how Jefferson's presidency both defined and contradicted that political philosophy.

LO **2**   Discuss the reasons for and results of the War of 1812.

# "Democratic-Republicans brought politics to the people in a new, more personal way."

Jefferson's election in 1800 marked a reversal in American politics. Jefferson's apprehension of an overly strong centralized government led him to advocate a vision of a farmers' republic, led by an agrarian upper class. He hated cities, thinking they were "sores" on the body politic, places where corruption and vice would tarnish the purity and benevolence earned by a farmer who labored in the earth. His vision was of a nation of small farmers who were economically self-sufficient, personally independent, and beholden to no one.

To realize this vision, Jefferson attempted to roll back several of the Federalist policies, although he did not go as far as many of his supporters hoped. At the same time, Jefferson dramatically expanded the boundaries of the nation to allow for continued westward expansion. All this occurred during a similarly dramatic expansion of America's social and economic life, which is the subject of Chapter 10. This present chapter, however, examines Jefferson's presidency, the meaning of "**Jeffersonian Democracy**," and the rule of the Jeffersonians through the War of 1812.

## What do you think?

Jefferson's attempts to create an idealized agrarian republic proved disastrous.

| Strongly Disagree | | | | | | Strongly Agree |
|---|---|---|---|---|---|---|
| 1 | 2 | 3 | 4 | 5 | 6 | 7 |

**Jeffersonian Democracy** Innovation introduced by Jefferson's Democratic-Republicans when they eagerly cultivated popular opinion by campaigning at the grass roots

## LO¹ Jefferson's Presidency

In addition to being the beneficiaries of the country's first bloodless revolution, the Democratic-Republicans were instrumental in transforming the political culture of America. This new political culture earned the name "Jeffersonian Democracy."

### Jeffersonian Democracy

Since George Washington, the Federalists had never relished the notion of making appeals to the public, preferring instead for the people to call on their leaders to act on their behalf. In contrast, Jefferson's Democratic-Republicans eagerly cultivated popular opinion. They founded highly partisan newspapers that spread throughout the country. They campaigned at the grass roots, staging political barbecues and clambakes. They also led virulent attacks on their Federalist opponents. The Federalists never mastered this aggressive art of politicking, a failure that made them appear increasingly out of touch with the people. Thus, although the vote remained restricted to white male property holders over the age of twenty-one, the Democratic-Republicans brought politics to the people in a new, more personal way. This is what historians mean by Jeffersonian Democracy.

**Marbury v. Madison (1803)**
Court decision declaring that William Marbury deserved his appointment but that the Court could not force the president to grant it because a federal law was unconstitutional; first U.S. Supreme Court decision to declare a law unconstitutional

**doctrine of judicial review**
Right of the courts to judge the constitutionality of federal laws; this established the Supreme Court as the ultimate interpreter of constitutional questions

# Jefferson's Domestic Policies

Jefferson's domestic policies focused on (1) reducing the size of government, (2) expanding what he saw as the agrarian republic, and (3) navigating the development of the first national court system.

## Reducing the Size of Government

Although Jefferson and his supporters changed America's political culture, they retained much of Hamilton's ambitious economic plan. However, Jefferson did seek to make the small federal government even smaller. He proposed two major cutbacks. First, he repealed many of the taxes Hamilton had imposed, which allowed Jefferson to reduce the number of federal employees (especially the hated tax assessors). Under Jefferson's plan, tariffs from trading partners, not internal taxes, would fund government operations. Second, Jefferson cut back the military, maintaining just a small army on the western frontier and a tiny navy that could protect only America's coast. He would pay a substantial price for these two changes, but there was no way for him to know this during his first term. The Federalists, having lost both houses of Congress, could do nothing to prevent these actions, despite the fact that many New England Federalists were concerned that their shipping industry would be jeopardized by the weakened naval fleet. Perhaps taking pity on their powerless status, Jefferson refused to use the Alien and Sedition Acts against the Federalists, as he was legally entitled to.

## The Courts

Federalists still had power in the courts, though. This situation birthed two of the most important developments in U.S. judicial history: (1) judicial review, which gave the courts the right to declare an act of Congress unconstitutional and therefore make it void; and (2) the idea that partisanship was not a crime.

*Judicial review.* The first of these developments emerged in 1800, when the outgoing president, John Adams, made a number of last-minute "midnight appointments" of Federalist judges. Adams hoped to ensure that the Federalist Party could retain a strong position in the judiciary. But Jefferson and his Democratic-Republicans swiftly repealed the appointments. William Marbury, one of the frustrated judges, sued James Madison (Jefferson's secretary of state) for denying his appointment. This dispute reached the Supreme Court as **Marbury v. Madison (1803)**.

Chief Justice John Marshall, a Federalist, headed the Supreme Court from 1801 to 1835. Marshall, suspecting that Jefferson would ignore his decision whatever it might be, issued a decision, in 1803, declaring that Marbury deserved his appointment but that the Court could not force the president to grant it. He said that the original Judiciary Act of 1789, which supposedly gave the Court the right to enforce appointments, exceeded the powers granted to the Court in the Constitution. Thus, the original Judiciary Act of 1789 was unconstitutional.

In this roundabout way, Marshall ultimately declared that the courts had the right to judge the constitutionality of federal laws, a right called the **doctrine of judicial review**. Based on that ingenious decision, the Supreme Court refused to engage in the partisan bickering of the time, while at the same time carving out its position as the ultimate interpreter of constitutional questions.

*The legality of partisanship.* The second important judicial precedent was established when Jefferson sought to impeach the most politically biased Federalist judges. To Jefferson's chagrin, in 1805, the Senate refused to convict Federalist judge Samuel Chase on purely political grounds. This set the precedent that partisanship was not a crime and that, once appointed, judges could be as partisan as they wished in their decisions without facing rebuke or retribution.

## Expanding the Agrarian Republic

Given the republican belief that farming provided the moral basis for good citizenship, Jefferson felt it essential that the United States continue to open new territory to settlement. Without access to new land, Jefferson reasoned, crowding would pressure people into working for others as urban wage laborers. In contrast, territorial expansion allowed every American the chance to be a self-sufficient farmer. Jefferson believed the new nation was likely to expand and should continue to do so, dislodging Spanish claims to territory in Florida and northern Mexico and French claims in the Mississippi.

UNDER MY WINGS EVERY THING PROSPERS

>> **Panorama of New Orleans in 1803.**

*The Louisiana Purchase.* The first step Jefferson took to realize this vision was to purchase the city of New Orleans from France. New Orleans was a vital port city at the mouth of the Mississippi River, and the Mississippi was the country's main north-south inland waterway, providing a means of transportation from the Gulf of Mexico to present-day St. Paul, Minnesota. The United States could never guarantee control of the Mississippi unless it controlled New Orleans as well.

In 1803, Jefferson sent emissaries to France to negotiate the purchase of New Orleans. Much to Jefferson's surprise, the French emperor, Napoleon Bonaparte, wanted to sell not only New Orleans, but the rights to all of Louisiana, which was at the time a huge tract of land that stretched from the Mississippi River to the Rocky Mountains, land that was of course occupied and claimed by a variety of Native American tribes but which was nevertheless laid claim to by the French. The French treasury was nearly empty, and another war between France and Britain loomed imminently. In addition, after the Haitian Revolution (see Chapter 8), France had learned how costly it was to maintain colonial possessions. Napoleon asked only $15 million for the claim to 830,000 square miles of Louisiana.

> *The Lewis and Clark expedition inspired generations of Americans to move westward.*

**Louisiana Purchase**
Tract of 830,000 square miles that stretched from the Mississippi River to the Rocky Mountains; Jefferson bought the rights to it from Napoleon for $15 million in 1803

The Constitution did not give the president power to buy new territory, but Jefferson pushed ahead with the **Louisiana Purchase**. Although he claimed to believe that federal power was dangerous and that the Constitution had to be followed strictly, Jefferson was willing to bend his own rules to expand America's western boundary all the way to the Rockies (Map 9.1). The purchase nearly doubled the geographic size of the nation.

*Lewis and Clark.* Jefferson took responsibility not only for acquiring new territory, but also for exploring it. In 1803, before the Louisiana Purchase was completed, Jefferson sent his private secretary Meriwether Lewis with William Clark as co-commander on an exploratory mission to the Pacific. In 1804, Lewis and Clark, along with forty-eight other men, left St. Louis and journeyed northwest toward the Rockies. With the help of Sacajawea, a Shoshone Indian woman who served as their guide, Lewis and Clark traveled to the Pacific. In 1806, the expedition returned to St. Louis with an immense amount of information about the American West. Their journey inspired generations of Americans to move westward and lay claim to the nation's interior.

 Take an interactive journey with Lewis and Clark.

 Read Lewis and Clark's journal.

*Land policies.* Jefferson also made access to western lands easier through a revised land policy. The Land Act of 1800, signed by President Adams, had set up land-selling offices in the West, made the parcels smaller (and more affordable), and allowed for payment over time (rather than in a single large lump sum). In 1804, the Democratic-Republicans again reduced the minimum amount that could be purchased, making western land even more affordable. In a sense, the federal government had become the real estate agent for the nation's interior. And, as always, increased westward expansion meant increased contact, and battles, with Native Americans.

>> **William Clark's diary of the Lewis and Clark expedition.** To peruse the journals, visit the following website: www.pbs.org/lewisandclark/archive/idx_jou.html

## Tecumseh and the Prophet

In the early 1800s, two Shawnee brothers, Tecumseh and the Prophet, proposed to unite tribes from the Old Northwest (in Ohio and Michigan) and the South (Georgia) to

*The Louisiana Purchase nearly doubled the geographic size of the nation.*

resist the perpetual encroachment of American settlers. The brothers toured across the land preaching a revival of old ways in a **revitalization movement** reminiscent of Neolin's (Chapter 4). The brothers opposed the acceptance of European and American habits, including whiskey and guns.

They set up pan-Indian towns across Indiana, the most famous of which was called "Prophetstown" by the surrounding American settlers and was situated alongside the Tippecanoe River. As white Americans moved further west they would eventually run into a united force of Indians.

## Reelection

Taking advantage of the new culture of politics, the expansion of the nation, and the good economic times of the early 1800s, Jefferson coasted to an easy reelection in 1804. The Federalists had once again been beaten badly, and some Federalists were so dismayed at their reversal of fortune that they persuaded Aaron Burr to run for governor of New York and then, if victorious, to separate New York and New England from the rest of the nation. This, in 1804, was the country's first serious plot of secession. Alexander Hamilton—ever the nationalist—learned of the plot and politicked against Burr in New York, leading to Burr's defeat.

© Eon Images

>> **Tecumseh and the Prophet,** Shawnee Indian brothers who led a revitalization movement among tribes of the Old Northwest, saw their movement decimated after the Battle of Tippecanoe at Prophetstown.

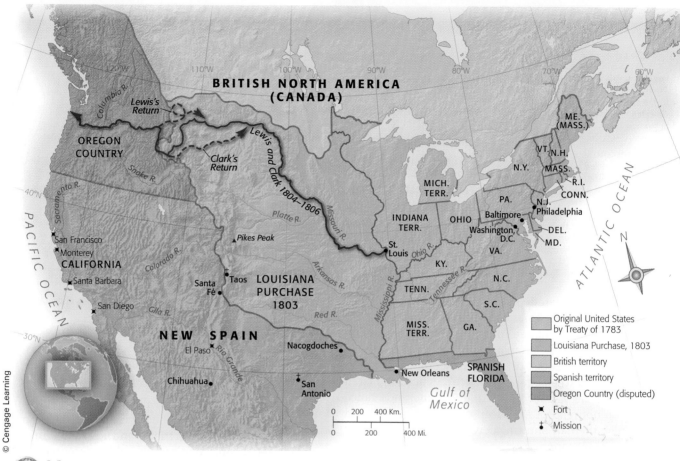

© Cengage Learning

🌐 Map 9.1. The Louisiana Purchase

In his fury, Burr challenged Hamilton to a duel. In the duel, Burr shot and killed Hamilton, who, disapproving of duels, had fired his gun into the air. Burr subsequently lost all political respectability because most Americans believed that politics was meant to occupy the realm of discussion and law, not violence and vigilantism. Cast out from political society, Burr moved west, plotting further secession attempts, until he was tried for treason in the nation's first "Trial of the Century." He was found not guilty by Chief Justice John Marshall, but his widespread unpopularity prompted him to decamp to Europe.

Although Burr is an extreme case, his actions illustrate the bitter divisions between the Federalists and the Democratic-Republicans. His very extremity and singularity, however, also demonstrate that, despite partisanship, the new nation was a nation of laws.

## Jefferson's Foreign Affairs

While the new nation was weathering the few internal storms that arose (and enjoying good economic times), international events seized attention during Jefferson's two terms.

## Jefferson's Problematic Diplomacy

Shortly after the Louisiana Purchase, the long-expected war between France and Great Britain erupted. At first, the United States benefited. With Britain and France fighting each other, America (as a neutral power) took control of the shipping trade between the Americas and Europe. Many American traders grew wealthy. Soon, however, the United States found itself caught in the middle.

England controlled the seas, and France controlled the continent of Europe. With no land to fight on, each nation attempted to starve the other into submission. They restricted other nations from trading with their enemies, raided ships, and prevented them from entering European ports. American shipping was particularly punished. By 1807, about eight hundred American ships had been raided by French and British fleets. Meanwhile, the British began impressing American sailors into the Royal Navy, much as they had in the early 1790s. Estimates of the number of Americans eventually impressed range from 4,000 to 10,000. After one highly publicized attack on the U.S.S. *Chesapeake*, Americans were so angered that some called for war, but it was not to be, for the simple reason that Jefferson had

**Embargo Act of 1807**
Legislation that stopped American exports from going to Europe and prohibited American ships from trading in foreign ports

**Non-Intercourse Act**
Legislation passed in 1809 that allowed American ships to trade with all nations except Britain and France and authorized the president to resume trade with those countries once they began respecting America's neutral trading rights

dismantled the U.S. military and was sure to lose any such battle.

*The right of neutrality.* Eager to save face, Jefferson reiterated the rights of a neutral party and initiated a program of "peaceable coercion," which he hoped would get both England and France to stop tormenting America's shipping industry. His plan turned out to be his administration's biggest mistake.

The plan centered on the **Embargo Act of 1807**, which stopped American exports from going to Europe and prohibited American ships from trading in foreign ports. Jefferson reasoned that depriving France and Britain of American commerce would force them to recognize America's neutral rights. In essence, he was saying that, if England and France would not respect American rights, Jefferson would punish them by shutting down a large portion of the American economy.

*Results.* The Embargo Act was a disaster. Europe was not deprived of very much, and British ships took over the Atlantic sea trade. The act imperiled the American economy, though, especially in the Federalist stronghold of New England, where shipping was a major part of the local economy. Angered by the embargo, American traders began smuggling goods out of the country, an act the Democratic-Republicans denounced.

Despite the policy's shortcomings, Jefferson refused to admit his mistake. All of these frustrations bubbled into the presidential election of 1808.

# LO² James Madison and the War of 1812

The Federalists hoped to capitalize on the unpopularity of the Embargo Act to reclaim the presidency in 1808, but, despite solid support in New England, they did not have the national strength to defeat the Democratic-Republicans.

>> Burr assassinated Hamilton, who, disapproving of duels, had fired his gun into the air.

## The Election of 1808 and Declaration of War

Like Washington, Jefferson had chosen not to run for a third term. Instead, he ensured that the nomination would go to his friend and fellow Virginian, James Madison. Madison handily defeated the Federalist candidate, Charles Pinckney, but Pinckney did better than projected, worrying the Democratic-Republicans, who became aware of the widespread anger stirred up by Jefferson's Embargo Act.

### The Repeal of the Embargo Act

To prevent the Federalists from gaining ground on the issue of the Embargo Act, Congress repealed it in 1809, shortly before Madison became president. In its place, Congress passed the **Non-Intercourse Act**, which allowed American ships to trade with all nations except Britain and France, and authorized the president to resume trade with those countries once they began respecting America's neutral trading rights.

### France Makes Amends

In a brilliant tactical move, France's emperor, Napoleon, announced that he would respect America's neutrality rights, whereupon Madison resumed trade with France and vehemently prohibited trade with Britain. With British trade banned from both continen-

66 The Embargo Act was a disaster. Europe was not deprived of very much, and British ships took over the Atlantic sea trade. 99

>> **Ships lie idle, and grass grows on the wharves in Portland, Maine, during the embargo.**

tal Europe and the United States, the British economy suffered a depression. On June 16, 1812, the British vowed to respect American neutrality. But it proved to be too little, too late.

## In the West

It was events in the West that proved determinate, though. Tecumseh and the Prophet had grown popular with young Indians, and the few British who remained in the American West encouraged the growth of the revitalization movement, hoping it would prove too formidable for the American frontiersmen and curb further expansion. But the American settlers had a strong presence in Indiana. In 1811, Indiana governor William Henry Harrison attacked Prophetstown, setting the town ablaze.

## Declaration of War

Madison had been incensed by Britain's refusal to recognize American neutrality. Moreover, he had been influenced by westerners who wanted war with Britain because they felt the British were to blame for increased Indian violence in the Midwest. These westerners, led in Congress by Kentuckian Henry Clay, were called "war hawks." They wanted the British evicted from the West, and they hoped to annex Canada as well. Their influence meant that the war would be fought against both the British in the Atlantic and hostile Indians to the west.

Under these pressures, James Madison went to Congress on June 1, 1812 (two weeks before Britain pledged to honor America's neutrality), to ask for a declaration of war. Congress split over the question along party lines, with Democratic-Republicans favoring war and Federalists condemning it. Federalists were convinced that war would only hurt American trade further. They believed an expansionist war would not address the problem of impressments or the violation of neutrality rights. In contrast, Democratic-Republicans were convinced that a "second war for American independence" was necessary before Britain would recognize America's rights as a neutral nation. Despite Federalist opposition, the Democratic-Republicans carried the vote, and the United States declared war against Britain on June 14, 1812. (For more, see "The reasons why . . ." on the next page.)

The regional support for the war emerged a few months later, in the presidential election of 1812. Madison and the Federalist candidate DeWitt Clinton split the votes of all the eastern states, while the five western states voted solidly for Madison, catapulting him to a second term.

## There were four reasons why the War of 1812 began:

***A violation of neutrality rights.*** In 1803, Britain and France began fighting what came to be called the Napoleonic Wars. At first the United States benefited from a battle between two of its primary economic competitors, and it remained officially neutral in the war. These benefits dissipated, though, once both sides began restricting American ships from trading with their enemy. The British raided and attacked American ships bound for France, and France did the same to ships bound for Britain. The United States was an unwilling participant. Its rights as a neutral power were being violated.

***Impressment.*** Furthermore, in need of soldiers, the British began forcing Americans into British naval service, an act called impressment. Americans were obviously angered by the practice. The British impressed between 4,000 and 10,000 Americans in the buildup to the War of 1812.

***Napoleon's smarts.*** In a brilliant tactical move, the French emperor Napoleon Bonaparte saw the increasing American resentment against the British and recognized that France would benefit if Britain were distracted by a war with the United States, so he announced that he would respect America's neutrality rights, leaving Britain as the lone violator of American neutrality rights.

***Battles for the West.*** In the West, meanwhile, the British offered encouragement to a pan-Indian revitalization movement led by Tecumseh and the Prophet in the Indiana territory. Expansive-minded Americans were unimpressed, and western congressmen such as Henry Clay from Kentucky became known as "war hawks" because they saw a potential war against Britain as a way to remove the British from the American West and from Canada too.

## The War of 1812

With Britain still embroiled in conflict with France, many Americans expected to win the War of 1812 handily. In reality, winning the war proved more difficult.

### Early Defeats

Jefferson's reduction of the American military had left the United States poorly prepared. Nevertheless, American forces initiated an assault on British-controlled Canada in 1812, hoping to conquer it quickly and make it one of the United States (Map 9.2).

The invasion of British Canada was a complete fiasco. Instead of striking directly at the St. Lawrence River—the lifeline that linked Canada's principal cities to the Atlantic Ocean—the Americans split into three forces, each too small to crush the opposition. They were further handicapped by Britain's willingness to sign treaties with Native Americans if they would fight against the Americans.

### Surprising Victories and Indian Decimation

The following year, the picture brightened for the United States. American forces held their own against the British and won a crucial naval battle at Put-in-Bay on Lake Erie. American naval control of the waters in the region made defense of the area north of Lake Erie impossible for the British. The British defeat spelled disaster for a group of Indian tribes that had united with the British to fight for tribal rights, as the victorious Americans now felt entitled to plunder their villages.

In the South in 1813, a frontier army under Andrew Jackson defeated the Creek Indians (who viewed the War of 1812 as an opportunity to take advantage of a distracted American army and finally secure land in Georgia). At the Battle of Horseshoe Bend, in today's Alabama, in March 1814, Jackson's troops forced the Creeks to accept a treaty that ceded their best lands to the Americans. The Creeks had divided over the issue of who to support in the war, leading to a civil war between the Upper Creeks and the Lower Creeks. This division did not matter much to Jackson, though, who, upon winning, took the land of all the Creeks, including those who had helped him at Horseshoe Bend.

 Take an online course on the Battle of Horseshoe Bend.

### Culmination

Just as the Americans had seemed to turn the tide of battle, their position teetered when the British forced the abdication of Napoleon, briefly ending European hostilities and freeing the British to focus on their war with the United States. British leaders planned a three-pronged strategy: attacking Lake Champlain, Washington, D.C., and New Orleans.

At Lake Champlain, in September 1814, the British ground force of 15,000 men faced stiffer-

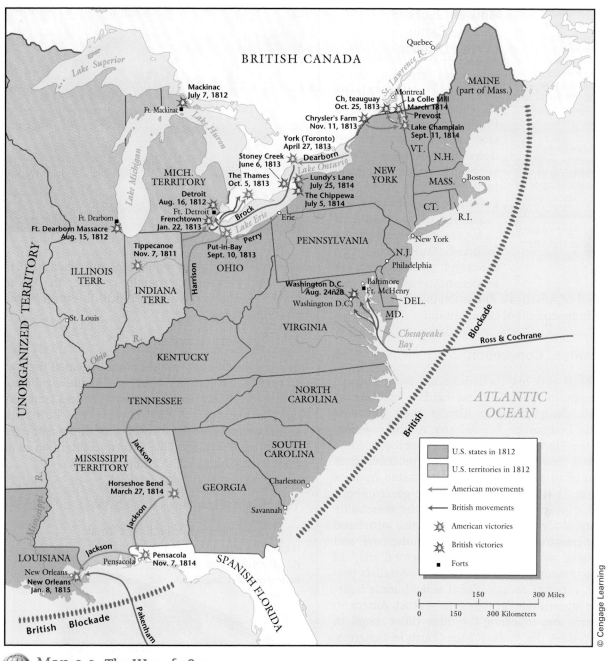

**Map 9.2. The War of 1812**

than-expected resistance from American advance units, while U.S. naval forces under Captain Thomas Macdonough defied all expectations and destroyed the British fleet as they waited for ground support. The British assault on Washington, D.C., was more successful. The U.S. militia was overwhelmed and essentially vanished during the fight, leaving only a small force of American soldiers and sailors to serve as the region's defense. President Madison and his wife Dolley were among those compelled to flee the city. The British burned the White House, the Capitol, and other government buildings, but the ultimate objective of the invasion—to capture the port city of Baltimore—eluded them. During the failed invasion of Baltimore, Francis Scott Key wrote the poem "The Star-Spangled Banner." Later set to the tune of an English drinking song, this became the national anthem.

Read the lyrics to "The Star Spangled Banner."

## Andrew Jackson and the Battle of New Orleans

The most startling upset took place at New Orleans in January 1815, where the British bungled their invasion plans and were mowed down by American troops serving under Andrew Jackson. The Americans suffered only twenty-one casualties in the Battle of New Orleans, but the British incurred more than two thousand. Jackson became an instant national hero and a symbol of America's determination to be permanently independent of Great Britain.

## The Hartford Convention

As Jackson and his men defended New Orleans, Federalists in New England held a meeting at Hartford, Connecticut, to discuss their problems with the Democratic-Republicans. At the meeting, called the **Hartford Convention**, Federalist leaders expressed their frustrations with the proceedings of the War of 1812, which they had protested from its inception. They were fed up with the government's economic policies, which had hurt the mercantile interests of New England. They had also witnessed their increasing alienation from southerners and westerners, as indicated in the electoral map of 1808. To remedy this problem, some Federalists proposed a series of constitutional amendments limiting the government's ability to restrict American commerce and repealing the three-fifths clause in order to limit the power of the South in Congress. Some representatives even broached the idea of seceding if these measures failed.

Jackson's victory, followed by an announcement that the United States and Britain had negotiated terms for peace, made a mockery of the Hartford Convention. The Federalist Party was immediately tainted with treason, and nearly all support for the party vanished. The nation's first two-party era was over, as only the Democratic-Republicans remained viable. The period of nonpartisan politics that followed became known as the **"Era of Good Feelings."** This lasted a few years, and, although the

 View a satirical cartoon poking fun at the Hartford Convention.

seeds of factionalism would blossom again in 1819 and 1820, historians generally consider the Era of Good Feelings to have lasted until the presidential election of 1824.

## The Treaty of Ghent

In 1814, the Treaty of Ghent formally ended the War of 1812, but it did not settle any of the significant issues, principally naval impressments and America's right to neutrality. It did, however, end hostilities, which was a relief to both sides. With the war over, the United States was able to turn its attention away from Europe and back to affairs at home.

## The Significance of the War of 1812

The War of 1812 was significant for at least four reasons: (1) in politics, it affirmed the importance of a strong national

government; (2) it vacated the British from the West; (3) it shaped America's role in world affairs; and (4) it unified the nation and boosted American patriotism.

*Political changes.* Politically, the War of 1812 demonstrated the weakness of the Republican-Democrats' insistence on a small federal government. It prompted four immediate changes from James Madison: (1) he recognized that having a stronger standing army and navy would have served the country better than the scanty forces that had eked out a victory against Great Britain; (2) he recognized the need for a new national bank to centralize banking, which he chartered as the Second United States Bank in 1816; (3) he agreed to new protective tariffs designed to support the growth of American industries; and (4) he realized the need for a system of national improvements, such as roads and canals to facilitate transportation between the newly settled West and the East Coast. Each of these lessons (some of them very Hamiltonian and Federalist) would play an integral role in the future development of the United States.

*Vacating the West.* In the West, the War of 1812 produced decisive defeats against the most powerful Native American tribes in the Southwest (in today's Tennessee and Arkansas) and the Northwest (in the Ohio River Valley). The conclusion of the war also meant that Britain would no longer impede settlement in the American interior, leaving the United States free to expand in the West—at the continued cost of Native Americans, who were running out of room further to the west.

*America's role in the world.* The War of 1812 also showed the European powers that the United States was a relatively strong, modern nation. Twice in three decades the United States had defeated Britain. The United States had earned greater respect and entered a prolonged period of relative isolation, safe from invasions and incursions from abroad.

*American patriotism and American culture.* And fourth, pride in their victory in the War of 1812 generated a strong urge to define the United States as fundamentally different from England. Hatred of the British prompted some to propose that the United States make German its official language. This movement obviously did not succeed, but during the course of the 1800s, Noah Webster developed a more practical solution. He noticed that a new American idiom had arisen over the 150-year colonial period; in 1828 he codified this new idiom in his Webster's *American Dictionary of the English Language.* Webster's dictionary included such uniquely American words as *skunk* and *squash*, and replaced British spellings, such as *colour*, with American versions, such as *color*.

At the same time, a group of poets called the "Hartford Wits" became the first well-known creative authors on American soil. The most prominent of the Hartford Wits was Francis Scott Key. Other "Wits" composed such enduring songs as "Hail Columbia."

**>>** John Trumbull's The Signing of the Declaration of Independence (1819) reflects the rise in American nationalism during the aftermath of the War of 1812.

>> Thomas Jefferson's home, Monticello.

© iStockphoto.com/Cheng Chang

At the same time, the first American magazine of note—the *North American Review*—began publication in 1815. The very title of the magazine denoted Americans' attempt to separate culturally from Europe.

In the graphic arts, talented painters in early America crafted pictures with patriotic themes, expressing their gratitude for liberty. The best remembered are the portraits of the founding fathers, many of them painted by Gilbert Stuart (1755–1828) and John Trumbull (1756–1843). Trumbull was also known for his patriotic images, the most popular of which is *The Signing of the Declaration of Independence* (1819), which today appears on the back of the two-dollar bill.

The most notable artistic expression of early American nationalism developed in architecture, as American architects, identifying with the ancient republican Romans, revived  classical architecture styles and motifs. Both Thomas Jefferson, who designed the University of Virginia and his home, Monticello, and Charles Bulfinch, who designed the Massachusetts State House in Boston, excelled in this flourishing realm. Pierre l'Enfant, the French architect commissioned to design the capitol

View more pictures of the classical revival in America.

buildings in Washington, D.C., also participated in this revival, which explains the plethora of classical architecture found today in Washington, D.C.

## And in the end . . .

With the rise of the Democratic-Republicans in the early 1800s, the American nation had survived its first significant transfer of power. The Democratic-Republicans had also introduced a new, livelier style of politics into the political culture, one that focused on courting voters and asserting a specific kind of patriotism.

### What else was happening . . .

| | |
|---|---|
| 1808 | End of legal slave importation in the United States. |
| 1810 | Peter Durand invents the tin can. |
| 1810 | Father Miguel Hidalgo begins the movement for Mexican independence. |
| 1811 | Steamboat service begins on the Mississippi River. |
| 1815 | Battle of Waterloo ends the Napoleonic Wars and the reign of Napoleon. |

But Jefferson's attempts to create an idealized agrarian republic proved problematic. By curbing the size of the military and limiting federal income to only tariffs, Jefferson exposed the nation to a variety of geopolitical upheavals taking place in Europe. Only heroic fighting and some good luck during the War of 1812 kept the young nation politically solvent.

Shortly thereafter, the nation would turn another corner and embark on a period of economic growth that ran counter to the image idealized by Jefferson and his followers. In place of an agrarian republic governed by large landholders who disdained city life, the nation developed into a trading center, bustling with markets and commerce. America was still largely a nation of farmers, but these farmers became more intent on bringing their product to market than on merely remaining self-sufficient. Although the Democratic-Republicans established much of the political and diplomatic security for the new nation, their vision for the nation would not carry the day. It is to the Market Revolution and its manifestations that we now turn.

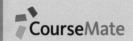

Visit the CourseMate website at www.cengagebrain.com for additional study tools and review materials for this chapter.

# CHAPTER 10

# *The* Market Revolution

## Learning Outcomes

*After reading this chapter, you should be able to do the following:*

LO **1**   Describe the economic system known as the American System.

LO **2**   List the three specific parts of the Market Revolution in early-nineteenth-century America, and evaluate how America developed during this era.

LO **3**   Describe the growth of America's middle class during the first half of the 1800s, and discuss some of the stronger movements toward reform during the era.

# "*The American System of economics was a fantastic success.*"

In the years following the War of 1812, America became relatively isolated from Europe. It focused inward. There was a strong feeling that the United States needed to strengthen its economy to protect itself against further incursion from outside powers. This view took tangible form as politicians and citizens designed what they called an "American System" of economics that focused on keeping American goods within the United States.

## What do you think?

The social and economic changes that occurred between 1812 and the 1860s were as much of a revolution as the political changes that had taken place in the 1770s.

Strongly Disagree          Strongly Agree
1     2     3     4     5     6     7

The American System of economics was a fantastic success, and it facilitated so many economic and social changes between 1812 and the 1860s that historians see this period as the social and economic equivalent of the political revolution of the 1770s. They describe all these transitions under the umbrella term **Market Revolution**. Aided by numerous transportation, communication, and technological innovations, the Market Revolution refers to the time when an increasing number of farmers willingly turned away from the ideal of being self-sufficient to focus on a single crop that could be sold at market. This change encouraged specialization and the growth of a dynamic string of market hubs within the United States. The United States had always been a part of the colonial world market, and between 1810 and 1860 the markets moved closer to home. Instead of American commerce focusing on transactions between the Atlantic seaboard and Europe, it shifted, focusing now on transactions between the East Coast and the lands extending to and beyond the Mississippi River.

The rise of localized, commercial agriculture changed the way Americans lived their lives. It moved them closer to the world of the marketplace and allowed many to leave the world of agriculture altogether. At the dawn of the 1800s, more than 80 percent of the American labor force worked in agriculture. By 1850, that figure had declined to 55 percent. By the 1880s, less than half of America's work force was engaged in farming. Local markets needed local salesmen, lawyers, factories, marketers, economists, and bookkeepers. The changes associated with this transition affected nearly every American, and America in 1860 looked dramatically different than it did in 1810.

This chapter examines the Market Revolution, its causes and effects, and the variety of responses to it.

> **Market Revolution**
> Umbrella term for the many economic and social changes that took place between 1812 and the 1860s

## LO¹ Economic Nationalism

The second generation of American politicians (James Monroe was the last American revolutionary to be president, serving from 1817 to 1825) did not have the distrust of

**American System**
Economic plan based on the idea that the federal government should encourage economic enterprise

**internal improvements**
Building of roads and canals by the federal and state governments

**Second Bank of the United States**
National bank established in 1816 to curb rampant currency speculation

## The American System

The American System came from a surprising source: young Democratic-Republican politicians from the West, the South, and the Middle Atlantic states who had superficially embraced Jefferson's vision of a small federal government but in fact eagerly sought the patronage that a large federal government could dole out. Henry Clay from Kentucky and John C. Calhoun from South Carolina led this group. Together, they advanced a vision that the federal government should encourage economic enterprise in three ways: (1) by creating roads and canals, collectively called **internal improvements**; (2) by developing secure economic institutions, such as banks; and (3) by providing for the security of America's economic interests through high tariffs. After seeing the weaknesses of Jefferson's vision of a disparate collection of states, the leaders of the American System wanted to strengthen the nation and secure centralized authority that characterized the revolutionary era. Several men of this younger generation developed a nationalist program for economic growth similar to the one proposed by Alexander Hamilton during the Federalist era. Updated to fit the demands of the 1810s and 1820s, they called this economic plan the **American System**.

the advancement of the West through the creation of tremendous public works projects.

## A New National Bank

One of the key components of the American System was the creation of a national bank. When Congress, before the War of 1812, refused to recharter the First National Bank in 1811, the states chartered their own banks, offering a bewildering variety of credit and currencies. More than four hundred banks were operating in 1818, each offering its own form of currency and credit. Speculation ran rampant, as investors attempted to pick which currency would appreciate the quickest. Fortunes were won and lost very quickly, and investors had little idea which currencies would be the most durable.

To end the mayhem and strengthen the national government, proponents of the American System designed the **Second Bank of the United States**. In a bill drafted by Calhoun, the Second National Bank was established with support from western and southern congressmen. New Englanders, who had adequate and secure banks in the North, opposed the creation of the bank. With Democratic-Republicans mostly supporting a national bank and former New England Federalists opposing it, times had changed since the Federalist era; now each party was advocating what it had opposed just two decades prior. The new bank was chartered in 1816. Ironically, the loose credit offered by the newly rechartered bank, and then a sudden tightening of that credit, led to a major economic recession, the Panic of 1819 (discussed in Chapter 11).

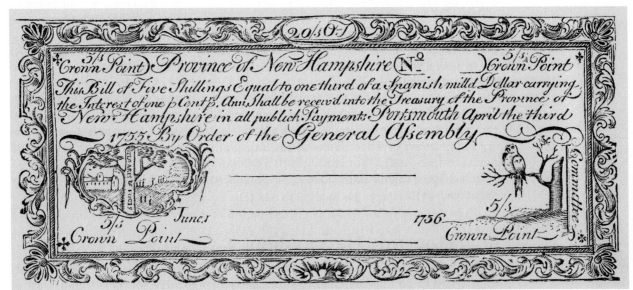

>> The states chartered their own banks, offering a bewildering variety of currencies and credit.

## A Protective Tariff

Calhoun and Clay also supervised the passage of the Tariff of 1816, which taxed all incoming goods at the stiff rate of 25 percent. They designed the tariff to limit consumption of foreign goods in the United States and to encourage the development of American commerce and industries. This meant that the goods in the American System were to be American.

## Court Cases

During these years, the Supreme Court issued a number of decisions that advocated economic growth at the expense of the states or of previous contracts. One of the most consequential cases was *Dartmouth College v. Woodward* (1819), which forbade state legislatures from altering college charters in order to gain control over them, because a corporation (the university) had drafted the charter. This decision prioritized the rights of a corporation over those of the state, thus clearing the path for increased economic development. In *Gibbons v. Ogden* (1824), a steamboat operator named Aaron Ogden argued that his business license from the state of New York entitled him to a monopoly on transporting commerce along the New York coastline. The U.S. Supreme Court disagreed, however, arguing that Thomas Gibbons, whose steamboat company had been chartered by the U.S. Congress, could navigate there as well, suggesting that the federal government's power to regulate commerce overruled that granted by states.

## A Protected Hemisphere

The War of 1812 and the economics of nationalism also allowed the United States to assert its dominance throughout the Western Hemisphere. In 1818, it established a northern boundary at the 49th parallel between the United States and British Canada, and in 1819 it won from Spain both Florida and lands extending nearly to today's Oregon, all in exchange for parts of Texas. Now the United States extended from the southern tip of Florida to the current-day northern boundary with Canada, and from the Atlantic almost to the Pacific (although it still did not claim today's American Southwest).

The new dominance was expressed most clearly in the **Monroe Doctrine** of 1823. This doctrine declared that any European nation attempting to colonize Latin America would be treated as a party hostile to the United States. President James Monroe announced that the Western Hemisphere was the domain of the United States and was to remain separate from the affairs of Europe. At the same time, Monroe agreed to refrain from any interference with existing European colonies or with the internal affairs or wars of the European powers. Although the Monroe Doctrine was little noted at the time, it later became a foundation for American foreign policy, used to justify American expansion into and involvement with the countries of Latin America.

> **Monroe Doctrine**
> Declaration of 1823 proclaiming that any European nation attempting to colonize Latin America would be treated as a party hostile to the United States; President James Monroe announced that the Western Hemisphere was the domain of the United States and was to remain separate from the affairs of Europe

## Opponents of the American System

Not everyone favored the American System. Some southerners saw it as merely an attempt to wrangle taxes from wealthy cotton planters and give the money to northern and western business interests. Others liked the American System well enough when the money was spent in their home state but opposed it when resources were spent elsewhere. War-hero-turned-politician Andrew Jackson at first enjoyed the fruits of the plan but eventually came to see it as a vehicle for corruption. Despite these mounting complaints, which would increase throughout the first half of the 1800s, the American System was the prevailing economic plan for the nation until the 1830s and 1840s.

>> **James Monroe.** Although the Monroe Doctrine was little noted at the time, it later became a foundation for American foreign policy.

**Erie Canal**
Artificial river connecting the New York State cities of Buffalo and Albany; provided a continuous water route from the shores of the Atlantic to the Great Lakes; measured 364 miles long and 40 feet wide

# LO$^2$ The Market Revolution

Combining tariffs, internal improvements, and a national bank, the American System of economics facilitated the Market Revolution. Farmers, more than ever before, could focus on producing what they produced best, bring their goods to local American markets, and purchase the items they could not grow or make themselves. The result was a change in people's notions about their role in the economy, leaving behind the idea that they had to be self-sustaining farmers. Instead, they began to think of themselves as participants in the national and international marketplace. This made them more accepting of commercial and capitalist goals, for they were becoming not only producers, but also *consumers*. For the most part, the Market Revolution had to do with commercialized agriculture and not with industrialization (although the beginnings of the Industrial Revolution can be identified in this period).

The Market Revolution was made up of three parts, in roughly this order: (1) a transportation and communications revolution, (2) a transition to commercialized farming, and (3) industrialization. Each transition provoked significant social changes.

## The Transportation and Communications Revolution

Along with friendly government policies, the Market Revolution could not have happened without a revolution in the way people and goods moved around and the way people communicated with one another. Since the start of European settlement in North America, long-distance travel had meant using rivers or the sea. Water offered the quickest and most reliable means of moving goods from their place of origin to a market where they could be sold. However, America's rivers run primarily from north to south, making travel from east to west difficult. For instance, there was not a single navigable river connecting the northeastern cities of New York, Philadelphia, or Boston to the farmlands of the Ohio River Valley.

Recognizing the importance of speedy transportation, in the years after 1800 some states began internal improvements. They financed, for the most part through tax dollars, the construction of toll roads, canals, and other modes of transportation. This funding sparked four eras of transportation innovation: (1) the turnpike era, (2) the canal era, (3) the steamboat era, and (4) the railroad era (Map 10.1).

### The Turnpike Era

The first improvements were roads and turnpikes (private roads with tolls), and the 1810s were the turnpike era. Between 1800 and 1825, hundreds of miles of toll roads crisscrossed the nation. The Cumberland Road was the best known, extending from Maryland to West Virginia. But these early roads were mostly unpaved, and huge ruts and tree stumps made them dangerous. The roads were too unpredictable for Americans to use reliably to transport large amounts of commercial goods.

### The Canal Era

To solve this problem, human ingenuity provided the country with something that nature had not—a series of east-to-west canals—and the 1820s were the canal era. New York led the way in 1817, when the New York legislature paid for the construction of the **Erie Canal**, an artificial river connecting Buffalo—on the shore of Lake Erie—to Albany. Because Albany was linked to New York City by the Hudson River, the Erie Canal provided a continuous water route from the shores of the Atlantic to the Great Lakes. This was an immensely complex project. At the time, the longest canal in the world was 28 miles long. The Erie was 364 miles long and 40 feet wide. New Yorkers completed construction in eight years. When it was

>> These early roads were mostly unpaved, and huge ruts and tree stumps made them dangerous.

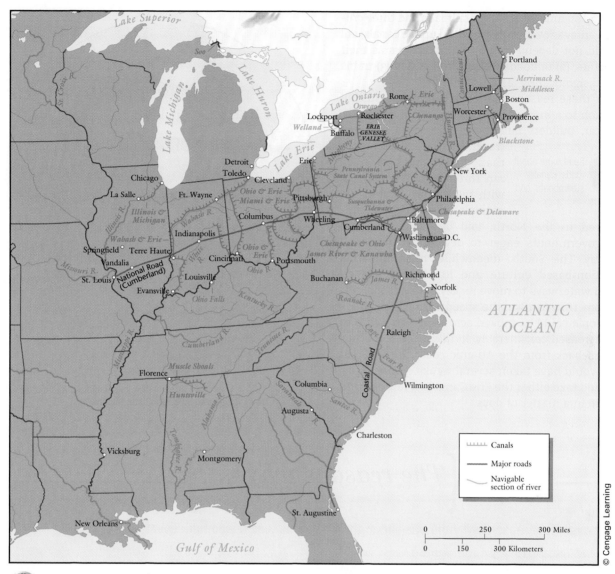

## Map 10.1. Rivers, Roads, and Canals, 1825–1860

**The first fifty years of the nineteenth century witnessed four separate revolutions in transportation: the turnpike era, the canal era, the steamboat era, and the railroad era. All but the steamboat era were concentrated in the North and the West.**

done, mules on paths along the shore could tow with a rope a barge filled with more than a ton of goods. The barge moved as fast as the mules. The Erie Canal opening was a landmark event for four reasons (see "The reasons why . . ." on the next page).

### The Steamboat Era

Despite the general reluctance of the South to invest in transportation improvements, there were innovations in the South and the West as well. There, steamboats, developed in the early 1800s, proved to be effective transport on the regions' broad rivers.

By the 1830s, they carried much of the commerce in those regions and succeeded in reducing cargo rates across the country. Their fabulous success made many southerners consider funding other internal improvements unnecessary.

### The Railroad Era

The most transformative new form of transportation was the railroad, which became the cornerstone of the American transportation revolution of the 1840s and 1850s. The development of railroads further extended the transportation improvements begun during the canal and steamboat eras, but railroads had three crucial advantages over water travel: (1) unlike canals, rail lines did not depend on natural waterways as their end points; (2) railroads did not freeze; and (3) trains traveled significantly faster than mules.

For these reasons, railroads completed the full transition to a market-based economy. In the 1830s, American builders laid more than 3,000 miles of track. By the 1860s, more than 30,000 miles of track ran through the country. As with the canals, most of the nation's railroads were concentrated in the North, laid by merchants and state governments eager to develop a diversified economy. The South, meanwhile, maintained its plantation-based culture and its dependence on natural waterways to move its key staple crops.

 Read more about roads, canals, steamboats, and railroads.

From 1810 to 1850, the speed with which goods and people could be moved across vast stretches of land increased considerably. In the 1810s, a journey via horseback from the Atlantic coast to the Great Lakes would have taken several weeks. In the 1850s, one could take either the Erie Canal or a railroad and be there in a matter of days.

>> **Trains traveled significantly faster than mules.**

# { *The reasons why . . .* }

There were four reasons why the opening of the Erie Canal was a landmark event:

*Financial.* First, the project was a tremendous economic success. The cost of moving one ton of goods from Buffalo to New York City dropped from nineteen cents per mile to a little more than one cent. The canal cut the time it took to move goods between Buffalo and New York City from twenty days to six. The state of New York charged tolls on the canal, which yielded a huge profit.

*Copycats.* Second, these profits pushed other states to invest in transportation. Many states chartered private corporations to build those internal improvements, which greatly politicized the role of corporations in American life. This process became political because it was profitable to run a canal, so winning a charter to build one was comparable to winning the lottery. Significantly, all but three of the largest canals were built in the North, signifying a northern commitment to the Market Revolution. Southern leaders, who were usually wealthy landowners, remained content to rely on the rivers that transported cotton and other staple crops.

*Creating a major metropolis.* Third, it spurred the growth of New York City. As the major trading link between the interior of the United States and the Atlantic Ocean, New York City became the nation's major economic center.

>> **The Erie Canal provided a continuous water route from the shores of the Atlantic to the Great Lakes.**

*A change in farming.* Fourth, the creation of a cheap way to move goods to market made it more enticing to farmers in the interior to produce only the few items that would be the most profitable.

## The Communications Revolution

At the same time, Americans were inventing and incorporating new methods of communication. The key development was Samuel F. B. Morse's successful transmission via the first telegraph, which used electric wires to send a message nearly instantaneously from one place to another. Now news about politics, the price of goods, and arrival of new products could be known throughout the nation in a matter of seconds. The telegraph facilitated nationwide commerce and lowered the cost of communication. It also symbolized the energy of the era, when, for the first time in human history, communication was set free from the realm of physical transit. Americans at the time were unaware of the kinds of communications that would emerge in future years, but they were aware that they were living at a transformative time in human history. Morse emphasized this notion when he chose the first words to be transmitted: "What Hath God Wrought?"

## Commercialized Farming

The transportation and communications revolutions caused a transition in how farmers (that is, most Americans) farmed their land. No longer did each family have to produce almost everything it consumed. This transition was not entirely new to farmers in the South and in areas of the Middle Colonies, where colonial-era farmers had already oriented their production around staple crops. But the rest of the nation had concentrated on self-sufficiency and diversified farming, and this market transition led to dramatic changes in the South, the West, and New England.

### Changes in the South

Before 1793, southern agriculture consisted of the staple crops of tobacco and rice, but farmers had added a few more varieties of crops during the 1700s. After 1793, when Eli Whitney promoted a new invention called the cotton gin, everything changed. The cotton gin allowed for the profitable cultivation of cotton even in land with poor soil by allowing the harvesting of "short staple" (or hard-to-reach) cotton. This meant that cotton was easy and profitable to produce throughout the South (not just in areas rich in nutrients), and cotton production rapidly took over southern agriculture and the southern economy. By 1825, the American South was the world's largest producer of cotton. Between 1816 and 1840 southern cotton constituted more than half the value of all American exports.

>> "What Hath God Wrought?" —Samuel F. B. Morse

This created obvious opportunities for white southerners. If you could get a little land and a few slaves, you could earn huge profits. The ease with which wealth could be generated spurred a large westward migration throughout the South, as small farmers searched for land to grow cotton. The development of the cotton gin also reinforced the farmers' dependence on slaves, because it made their labor even more valuable (slaves could be used profitably on even poor land). At the same time, slavery moved west with the cotton farmers, making the slave trade profitable even after the importation of slaves from Africa had stopped in 1808, per the agreement reached in the U.S. Constitution. These farmers revived the domestic slave trade. Any ideas that emancipation might be plausible in the South during these years vanished after the introduction of the cotton gin.

This cotton boom had two other key outcomes. First, cotton impeded any significant internal improvements in the South because wealthy southerners considered waterways sufficient to transport cotton.

Read more about cotton production in the South.

This hurt small farmers, who could not afford land along waterways, and it stalled the development of any major railroad lines in the southern states. Second, the roaring success of cotton, in combination with the Market Revolution elsewhere in the nation, hindered southerners from developing a diversified economy. They could rely on other parts of the nation for the goods they needed. This meant that if the South's cotton production was ever threatened, the southern economy would be in trouble.

### Changes in the West

The Market Revolution also meant that farmers in the Midwest (Ohio, Indiana, and Illinois) could

**Land Act of 1820**
**Legislation that promoted settlement west of the Appalachians by setting affordable prices for manageable plots of land**

**Tallmadge Amendment**
**Proposal that would have enforced gradual emancipation in Missouri**

**Missouri Compromise**
**Arrangement brokered by Henry Clay that set 36°30′ as the divider between free and slave territories and that allowed Missouri to enter the nation as a slave state if Maine were allowed to enter as free**

take maximum advantage of the land's rich soil and plentiful rain. Reflecting the Market Revolution's transition to commercialized agriculture, a wheat belt stretched from western New York to Wisconsin, a corn belt reached from Ohio to Illinois, a tobacco belt extended from Kentucky to Missouri, and a cotton belt spread from Georgia to Mississippi. Each area continued to grow a diverse range of crops, but each increasingly specialized in what it grew best.

The commercial development of these regions prompted a huge shift of the American population (Map 10.2). With the **Land Act of 1820**, the federal government helped promote settlement of land west of the Appalachians by setting affordable prices for manageable plots of land. This prompted one of

the largest internal migrations in American history. In 1789, two-thirds of all Americans (about 3 million people) lived within fifty miles of the Atlantic Ocean, while only 5 percent lived west of the Appalachians. By 1840, one-third of the population (more than 5 million people) lived in new states west of the Appalachians. Several new areas applied for statehood, almost all of them as a result of westward migration: Indiana (1816), Mississippi (1817), Illinois (1818), Alabama (1819), Maine (1820), Missouri (1821), Arkansas (1836), Michigan (1837), Florida (1845), Texas (1845), Iowa (1846), and Wisconsin (1848). During these years, between 5 and 10 percent of all Americans moved each year.

## The West and Slavery

Westward migration provoked another significant question: what to do about slavery? In 1819, Missouri sought entry into the union as a slave state. Its request provoked a debate in Congress that Congress wished desperately to avoid. Even the aging Thomas Jefferson wrote that the issue of slavery frightened him like a "fire bell in the night."

The issue of whether slavery would be allowed in Missouri was pivotal for two reasons: (1) Missouri lay along the same latitude as several free states, and its entry into the Union as a slave state would move slavery northward; and (2) the admission of Missouri as a slave state would upset the congressional balance of eleven slave states and eleven free states. Northerners, mindful of the ideals of the Revolution and intent on avoiding a large black population in the North, sought to keep slavery in the South. Southerners sought to expand the development of cotton, which, they felt, required the labor of slaves.

When Representative James Tallmadge, Jr., proposed the **Tallmadge Amendment**, which would have enforced gradual emancipation in Missouri, a vicious debate broke out on the floor of Congress. Henry Clay brokered a compromise: Missouri could enter as a slave state if Maine could enter as a free state. In addition, Clay drew a line at the latitude of 36°30′. Territories north of the line would remain free, south of it could maintain slavery. This was the **Missouri Compromise**, passed in 1820, which would dictate the spread of slavery in the West for the next thirty years.

## The New England Transition

New England farmers had since colonial times developed diversified farms that could fulfill many of their families' needs, while local markets provided the items that could not be grown or manufactured

© iStockphoto.com/Oktay Ortakcioglu

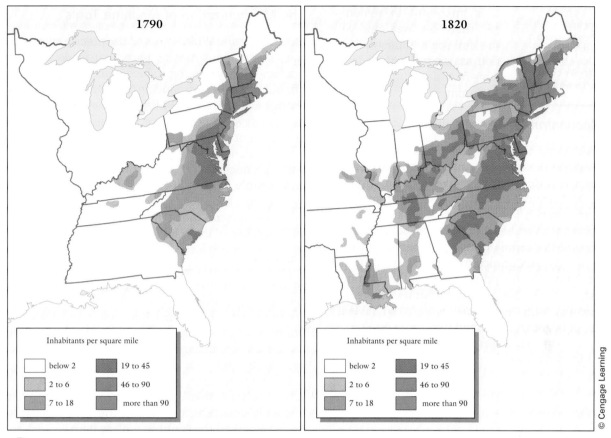

1790

1820

Inhabitants per square mile

below 2     19 to 45

2 to 6     46 to 90

7 to 18     more than 90

Inhabitants per square mile

below 2     19 to 45

2 to 6     46 to 90

7 to 18     more than 90

© Cengage Learning

Map 10.2. Population Density, 1790–1820

easily. The Market Revolution (combined with soil exhaustion) slowly eroded this lifestyle. Rocky, cold New England had never been a great place to farm, and access to cheap western agriculture furthered the decline in farming during the 1820s.

Without a central profitable crop to turn to, New Englanders reorganized their economy. Giving up on corn and wheat, New Englanders began to grow garden vegetables, fruit, dairy products, meat, eggs, and other perishable goods that could sustain growing urban markets. They took advantage of the new methods of transportation to get their goods to market. In 1820, about one-third of all New England produce was sent to market. By 1850, that percentage had jumped to about half.

The result was dazzling success—for those who owned land. Those who did not own land confronted rising land prices. Many headed west, where land

*The aging Thomas Jefferson wrote that the issue of slavery frightened him like a "fire bell in the night."*

was cheaper. Others worked as wage laborers on farms, hoping one day to earn enough money to buy land of their own.

Women's output was similarly affected. Many women stopped weaving clothes, because store-bought cloth was cheaper. They churned butter and made cheese instead, participating in the new market economy by selling these dairy products at market.

## Industrialization

The transportation revolution and the conversion to commercial agriculture required machines. Railroads needed machinery to fabricate engines, cars, and tracks. Cotton crops required factories to turn the raw product into cloth. Specialized farming in the West demanded large reapers and tough plows. Thus, the third aspect of the Market Revolution was the rise of industrialization and the creation of factories.

It is important to remember that this was not yet the full-scale industrialization associated with today's large factories. But it was the beginning of that process.

## The Mechanization of Agriculture

Cyrus McCormick's development of the reaper in 1831 was the most significant industrial development in agriculture. A twenty-five-year-old Virginia farmer, McCormick created a machine that harvested grain much faster than manual labor could. This was a boon for the western states, because they had miles of flat farmland that was perfect for the reaper. In 1837, McCormick moved his factory from Virginia to Chicago, the principal city of the booming Midwest, and sold his reapers to farmers there. In the same way, John Deere's steel plow (1837) made it easier to plow tough fields, and the cotton gin (1793) sped up the process of separating short-staple cottonseed from its fiber.

>> The cotton gin easily separated cotton fibers from the seed, a mechanizing process that led to the dramatic expansion of the cotton industry.

## The Mechanization of Machine Tools

McCormick and Whitney noted the precise specifications of the many moving parts that made up their machines. They then reproduced those parts in large quantities, thus introducing the system of interchangeable parts. Eli Whitney was chiefly credited for this development (more than he deserved) and won government contracts to develop muskets that used interchangeable parts. With interchangeable parts, producers could make products more quickly and cheaply instead of handcrafting each item one by one. Watches, clocks, and locks—all luxury items in 1800—became inexpensive household goods by 1840 because of interchangeable parts.

## Factories

Factories were the most efficient way to produce the large quantities of goods that were needed to accommodate the Market Revolution, but they did not prosper as quickly as one might imagine. Before 1800, most production was done in a decentralized system of family- or artisan-based manufacturing. Large manufacturers would pay one family to perform one task, then pass the item on to the next family or artisan to perform the next task. This was called the **"putting out" system**.

The rise of the factory in the 1820s altered this system by bringing nearly all aspects of production under one roof. Samuel Slater was the first to develop the workings of a factory on American soil, designing in 1789 a factory that spun cotton into thread. Within its first ten years of operation, Slater's textile mill hired more than one hundred people, mostly women and young children. The amount of thread produced by Slater's mill prompted a rise in the volume of thread-based goods (mainly clothes, but also towels and curtains) and a drop in their price.

Entrepreneurs opened other factories, and these new factories continued to improve production. Slater could not weave thread into cloth at his mill, for example (he still had to "put out" his thread to home workers for this task). In 1813, Boston merchants developed a power loom to weave cloth. Headed by Francis Lowell, the new factory brought all the processes of cloth-making under one roof. This quickened the pace and cheapened the price of production. Between 1820 and 1860 textile mills sprouted all over the northern and Middle Atlantic states, harnessing the power of swift-moving rivers. Americans began purchasing their clothing rather than making it, which boosted the rise of retail clothing stores. Other manufacturing industries, such as shoemaking and clockmaking, followed.

## Social Changes Associated with the Market Revolution

The Market Revolution had many social ramifications. The six most significant were (1) the growth of cities, (2) the impact on the environment, (3) the changing face of the labor force, (4) an increase in religious divisions, (5) the beginnings of a working class and a middle class, and (6) increased protest movements.

### The Growth of Cities

The expansion of markets and the growth of factories led to a slow process of urbanization. In 1830, only 5 percent of Americans lived in towns of 8,000 people or more. By 1850, that number had more than tripled, to 16 percent. With the development of the Erie Canal, New York City solidified its position as the largest city in the nation, with a population in 1840 of more than 300,000. Philadelphia, Boston, and Baltimore experienced robust growth as well. Of the ten largest cities in 1860, only one, New Orleans, was in the South.

### Environmental Costs of the Market Revolution

There were significant environmental costs of the Market Revolution as well. Steamboats and early railroads burned wood as a source of power, which caused rapid deforestation in the Northeast. Similarly, as the transportation revolution enabled more people to move west, new settlers cleared land and chopped wood, destroying animal habitats and western landscapes. Sawmills and textile mills, relying on waterways for their power, interrupted the paths of spawning fish. These costs would only increase as industrialization expanded through the rest of the century.

### Women and Immigrants in the Labor Force

There was also a dramatic change in the composition of the labor force. Setting a pattern followed by other factory owners, Francis Lowell hired single women from New England farms to work in his clothmaking factory. He needed cheap labor, and young women would work for lower wages than men. To present a wholesome image to the farm families who might send their daughters to work there, Lowell built boarding houses for his "mill girls," where they were taught Christian ethics and monitored by chaperones. This was called the **Lowell System**. Factory life was harsh for these workers, however, and most sought to return home to start families after a short tenure in a Lowell mill. Most stayed just five years. They worked without insurance, wage guarantees, or legal protections of any kind, and when times were hard, these factory workers were the first to suffer.

For the most part, working in a factory was arduous, and wages were low. People often worked fifteen-hour days, six days a week, and usually an entire family had to work in order to get by. Men, women, and young children spent long hours in the hot, noisy factories.

But mill owners were not obligated to listen to complaints; they could always find eager replacements. After 1840, the number of immigrants arriving in the United States suddenly soared, causing the nation's population to increase a whopping 36 percent in the 1840s. Roughly two-thirds of these new arrivals were Irish, fleeing years of miserable poverty and hunger that peaked during the **Great Irish Famine** of 1845–1851. The majority of Irish immigrants settled in northeastern cities and worked at industrial jobs, replacing New England women and children. By the 1860s, half of the employees in most American factories were immigrants, most of them Irish. The Irish became a distinct underclass in the nineteenth-century United States.

 Read a firsthand description of the Lowell mills from one young female worker.

### Challenges to the Protestant Consensus

Along with a willingness to work for cheap wages, the Irish immigrants brought Roman Catholicism. Catholicism had been present in the United States since the first European settlements, but Catholics had always been a small minority compared to the Protestant majority (roughly 1 percent at the time of the Revolution). With the wave of Irish immigrants, Catholics formed the first sizeable religious minority in American history. Many Protestant Americans feared this development, believing that rising

**Lowell System**
A labor and production model for manufacturing textiles that, for the first time, brought all stages of textile production under one roof, with employees living near the factory in employee housing, away from their families; featured mostly female employees, young women seeking to earn wages before getting married

**Great Irish Famine**
Years of miserable poverty and hunger in Ireland that peaked during 1845–1851 and led millions of Irish to the United States

levels of Catholic immigration threatened the character of America, which they considered a "Protestant nation." Catholics, most nineteenth-century Americans believed, were too bound to the teachings of the pope to behave like free and independent republicans. They were also prone to the excesses of drinking and licentiousness, or so claimed Protestant nativists.

To counteract the growing Catholic presence, some Protestants began seeking an official proclamation of Protestantism as the official religion of the nation. Such efforts did not succeed, but they stirred controversy. For instance, the efforts of Protestant educators to introduce Protestant religious study into the curriculum of the nation's public schools prompted the development of the first Catholic parochial schools.

## A New Working Class

In their new jobs, Irish workers earned little pay. Indeed, what made Irish laborers so attractive to factory owners was their willingness to work for low wages. Moreover, as urban land prices skyrocketed, the Irish were forced to accept the worst housing available. Irish families crowded together in basement apartments or in attics, and Irish slums became hotbeds for diseases like cholera and tuberculosis. To the eyes of native-born Americans, these conditions served as unhappy notice that the squalor of Britain's industrial towns had been transplanted to America. In fact, the Irish slums were simply a part of the new working class that worked in the factories, earned day wages, and were increasingly removed from the fruits of their labor. Over the course of the 1800s, these laborers would begin to feel aligned with one another, creating a sense of belonging to a particular class.

## Protest Movements

Several movements arose to protest the living and working conditions experienced by the working class. Protest movements of the early nineteenth century were usually one of two kinds: (1) an organization of middle-class reformers seeking to safeguard the morality of workers or (2) laborers fighting for economic and work-related protections, such as a shorter workday. The two movements often opposed each other, sometimes because the middle-class reformers were anti-immigrant, while the labor movement was made up of Irish and non-Irish immigrants. Furthermore, the federal and state governments firmly supported economic development, so ceding to the demands of laborers did not seem to offer immediate gains for the economy.

Despite these hurdles, the laborers enjoyed some successes. Neighborhood groups began to meet up in citywide trade assemblies that delved into politics and rallied to elect politicians sympathetic to their cause. They then attempted to unify the citywide assemblies into nationwide unions. One such union, the **Workingmen's Party**, was formed in 1828 and spread through fifteen states. It was surpassed in 1834 by the **National Trades Union**,

>> "The early millgirls were of different ages. Some were not over ten years old; a few were in middle life, but the majority were between the ages of sixteen and twenty-five." —Harriet Hanson Robinson, Lowell mill girl for fourteen years, starting at age ten

© The London Art Archive/Alamy

which is usually regarded as the nation's first large-scale union. And, although the power of the trade unions varied depending on the economy, in 1840, President Martin Van Buren instituted the ten-hour day for federal employees, yielding to one of the long-standing demands of the laboring classes.

# LO³ Reformers

But the most influential reform movement of the early nineteenth century emerged from the middle class. Spurred by a religious revival known as the Second Great Awakening, a large group of middle-class social reformers attempted to control the changes brought about by the Market Revolution. The men and especially the women who led the reform movement promoted a vision of a more caring nation, one more considerate of human life. In doing so, these reformers broached some of the most consequential issues the nation would face during the next two hundred years, including racism, the rights of workers, and the rights of women.

## The Creation of the Middle Class

Where did these reformers come from? As more and more unskilled laborers transitioned to factory work, a need arose for paper-pushing bureaucrats who could manage others, balance the books, and sell goods. This was new. In 1800, a shoemaker would have made shoes himself, selling them at his own shop. By 1860, however, many "shoemakers" did not actually make shoes at all. Rather, they supervised a group of semiskilled or unskilled laborers, each of whom completed a part of the shoemaking process. Similarly, large factories needed bookkeepers, accountants, salesmen, and clerks.

This management class formed the backbone of an emerging middle class. Before 1800, Americans had hardly ever used the term *middle class*. By 1850, the term was part of the popular vocabulary. The middle class began to develop a culture distinct from that of the elite property owners or that of the workers. In the middle class of the mid-1800s, men were presumed to be the sole income earners, usually working outside the home. Their wives, meanwhile, transitioned from income providers to guardians of the home and family, a concept that came to be called the "cult of female domesticity." Middle-class women developed their own social and cultural outlets. Manufacturers were quick to recognize this trend, providing products exclusively geared to women, in a feminization of consumer-

ism. Publishers introduced a "ladies" literature, a feminization of culture. But a woman's first priority was making the family home a sanctuary for her laboring husband, a "haven in a heartless world."

## The Second Great Awakening

For most people, and especially for women, new evangelical churches lay at the center of middle-class culture. More than any other group in American society, the middle class—the shopkeepers, clerks, and managers—was most active in the evangelical sects that developed in the 1830s and formed the center of what historians call the Second Great Awakening. The Second Great Awakening was a Protestant religious revival that began in the West but shortly moved to the Northeast and the South. It lasted from the 1790s to the 1840s, and reached its high tide between the 1820s and 1840s.

### The Theology

The central theological idea behind the Second Great Awakening was that an individual's soul could be saved through human agency (meaning hard work) and his or her acceptance of responsibility for

>> A woman's first priority was making the family home a sanctuary for her laboring husband, a "haven in a heartless world."

**burned-over district**
Area in upstate New York that had many converts who had been inspired by the fiery orators speaking the Word of God during the Second Great Awakening

**Transcendentalists**
Group of thinkers and writers in the Northeast who believed that ultimate truths were beyond human grasp

**lyceum circuit**
Schedule of lectures in which clergymen, reformers, Transcendentalists, socialists, feminists, and other speakers would speak to large crowds in small towns

a sinful nature. This meant that divine revelation was not the only path to salvation. This stood in contrast to Jonathan Edwards's and George Whitefield's theology of relying on divine benevolence for salvation, which was paramount during the First Great Awakening. The ideas behind the Second Great Awakening were that humans could achieve a level of perfectibility—both individual and social—by doing good works and by promoting what they understood to be God's intent. Action was the key. Humans had the power to choose good or evil and, by choosing good, they could eventually alleviate sin or, put another way, become perfect. The name for the idea that humans can accept or reject divine grace is Arminianism.

## How It Spread

The Second Great Awakening spread through a series of three- or four-day revivals orchestrated by itinerant preachers. The most prominent was Charles G. Finney, a New York lawyer who gave up the law in 1821 to convert souls. Finney was a spellbinding orator whose sermons were particularly effective in the towns that had experienced the most changes during the Market Revolution. One area in upstate New York had so many converts it was called the **burned-over district**, having been penetrated by fiery orators speaking the Word of God. Many people genuinely believed God had touched them, and the habits they developed because of their faith—thrift, sobriety, obedience—led them to succeed in the new market-based economy. In the South, women and African Americans were particularly moved by the Christian message of salvation and hope. American Catholics and Jews responded to the newfound fervor as well, usually by upgrading the importance of the sermon in their worship ceremonies. Alas, this awakening of the mainstream did not extend to that mainstream accepting the beliefs of Catholics and Jews. The Methodists and the Baptists, both reform-minded low-church traditions, capitalized on the religious fervor to the greatest extent. By the 1820s, both denominations had surpassed all others to become the two

Learn more about the burned-over district.

largest churches in America. Meanwhile, the Second Great Awakening led to a "Christianization" of African Americans, both free and enslaved, during this era.

## Why a Revival?

Some historians have argued that middle-class interest in religion stemmed from a desire for economic security. As the American economy became more competitive, those who aspired to succeed embraced religion for a sense of hope and confidence in the future. In addition, evangelical religion promoted the values—frugality, sobriety, diligence, and zeal—that Americans needed to achieve their economic goals. More prosaically, church membership also bestowed social respectability, and those who joined were more likely to impress their superiors at work, which might lead to promotions. Both religion and the cult of female domesticity were central aspects of the emerging American middle class.

## The Transcendentalists

The theology of perfectibility appeared in secular form in writings by the **Transcendentalists**, a group of thinkers and writers in the Northeast who believed that ultimate truths were beyond human grasp. They believed that these truths "transcended" our capacity for understanding. This being so, they turned inward—to themselves and to their society— asking what could be done to improve the human condition. The best-known Transcendentalists were Ralph Waldo Emerson and Henry David Thoreau, two genuine celebrities of the time. Seeking to live by their ideals, Thoreau's attempt to return to nature was narrated in his book *Walden*. Telling the tale of his two-year journey living in the wilderness, the book demonstrated Thoreau's desire for self-sufficiency and for the conservation

Read portions of Thoreau's *Walden*.

of nature. He also protested slavery and war, and he advocated civil disobedience, starting a tradition that would influence later reformers like Martin Luther King, Jr. His friend Emerson, meanwhile, critiqued economic competition and social conformity.

The purity of their ideals struck a chord with their generation and with the generation that followed, whose luminaries included Nathaniel Hawthorne and Herman Melville. These writers debated in their fiction the perfectibility of humankind. Perhaps ironically, all of these thinkers were speakers on the **lyceum circuit**, a touring lecture circuit that was made possible only by the transportation breakthroughs of the Market Revolution.

>> A replica of Thoreau's cabin at Walden Pond, where he speculated about the changes wrought by the Market Revolution.

>> The revivals of the Second Great Awakening proved fertile ground for new religions, the largest of which is Mormonism, which began when Joseph Smith claimed to be visited by the angel Moroni, who led Smith to golden tablets upon which were written the Book of Mormon.

## Utopianism

Utopianism provided another response to the quest for perfectibility. After their inception in Europe, several "perfectionist" communities popped up in the 1840s and 1850s, mostly in the Northeast, but also in the Midwest. One was in Oneida, New York, where John Humphrey Noyes led a group of fifty-one followers to develop what he viewed as a perfect community. The Oneida community had open sexual mores, communal child rearing, a unique division of labor, and a therapeutic milieu where people freely offered constructive criticism of one another under the watchful eye of Noyes.

The Shakers, meanwhile, who developed from a group of Quakers, also believed in perfectionism and communal property. Their communities developed a tradition of rejecting commercial endeavors, one result being their creation of beautiful handcrafted furniture. There were many more of these groups. More than one hundred utopian communities were established between the

See a narrated slide show about the Oneida Community.

1820s and the 1850s, mostly in the Northeast and Midwest.

## The Latter-day Saints

Creating a utopia was not for everyone. Some preferred to anticipate the Second Coming of Christ, when perfection would reign for the chosen. The most significant group was the Mormons, founded by Joseph Smith, a Protestant convert who witnessed one of Charles Finney's revivals. After his conversion in the burned-over district, Smith claimed to have been visited by the angel Moroni, who showed him several golden tablets that revealed the foundations for a new religion based on the lost tribe of Israel. According to Smith, these tablets contained *The Book of Mormon* (he said he returned the tablets to the angel after he had transcribed them, so no one has seen them). Smith asserted that the tablets possessed an ancient revelation of God that predicted the "endtimes," making the Mormons "saints" called out by God to usher in the new millennium; this is why

Read more about Mormonism.

Mormons called themselves the Latter-day Saints.

Smith's vision appealed to a growing number of people who were either convinced by Smith's vision and/or dissatisfied with the new social order unfolding during the Market Revolution. Chastised as heretics, Joseph Smith led his congregation to Ohio, then Missouri, then Illinois, in an attempt to avoid persecution. By 1844, Smith was tried for treason and, facing persecution once again, the Mormons headed west in 1846, ultimately settling in the territory of Utah. (For more on the Mormons, see Chapter 13.)

## The Reform Impulse

While movements striving for perfectibility continued to blossom throughout the first half of the 1800s, most Americans preferred more subtle attempts at reform.

### The Benevolent Empire

Instead of drastically altering the entire society, most Americans sought to change one element at a time. This led to a series of single-issue reforms. Many of the reformers felt that, all together, their various efforts would create a "Benevolent Empire" on American soil. Led by individuals like Arthur and Lewis Tappan, evangelical brothers who advocated numerous reforms, the reformers of the 1820s, 1830s, and 1840s sought social change with a messianic fervor. In their advocacy, they sometimes patronizingly questioned the morality of impoverished immigrants and non-Protestants, but they claimed to do so only in an effort to improve American society.

### Female Reform Societies

The reforming impulse was particularly meaningful for nineteenth-century women. Politics were thought of as men's arena, but social reform was considered within women's sphere, and thus activist women played a large role in the movement for social reform. This was most dramatically illustrated by the **American Female Moral Reform Society**, which by 1840 had more than five hundred local chapters throughout the country and had successfully lobbied for legislation governing prostitution.

### Temperance

By far the largest reforming effort went into moderating the consumption of alcohol in America. In 1800, Americans per capita drank five gallons of alcohol every year (today we drink about two gallons per capita). Booze was especially integral to the new culture of politics, but it permeated the rest of American culture too. At the same time, the Irish immigrants who streamed into the country in the 1840s brought with them a tradition of alcohol consumption and of gathering in saloons.

View an online exhibition of the American Temperance Society.

Female reformers attacked the habit, claiming that men who drank often beat their wives and children. They maintained that drinking also affected their work habits, sometimes forcing families into financial hardship. In 1826, temperance workers founded the **American Temperance Society**, and by the middle of the 1830s, 5,000 local and state temperance organizations had appeared. In 1851, Maine prohibited the sale of alcohol. By 1855, temperance and prohibition laws spread throughout New England and the Midwest. The temperance movement also played a prominent role in the presidential elections of the 1840s and 1850s, as temperance workers vigorously promoted candidates who shared their ideals.

© From the Collection of the Oneida Community Mansion House, Oneida, NY

**>> Even routine chores, such as shelling peas, were communal activities at Oneida.**

## Education

Between 1800 and 1860, free public education expanded across parts of the United States. Overcoming the mainstream perception that free schools were only for poor people, reformers such as Horace Mann and Henry Barnard fought to establish the public elementary school as a fixture in antebellum America. By the 1820s, public secondary schools had increased in number, although they were generally reserved for those interested in a profession. Schools expanded in every region, with the South being the slowest to adopt the institution.

 Read more about Horace Mann.

A few state-supported colleges also opened in these years. Women gained access to public education as well, highlighted by the founding of a series of coeducational colleges. Most schools took for granted America's Protestant majority and subsequently instituted courses in Protestant moral theology and Bible readings from the King James, or Protestant, Bible.

## Prison Reform

Prisons also attracted significant attention from middle-class reformers. Before 1800, punishment was usually doled out financially (in fines) or physically (in lashes). But during these reform years, reformers designed a criminal justice system whereby criminals were incarcerated for a fixed period of time. Solitary confinement—another old-time punishment—was limited to extreme cases. Inmates were allowed (mostly forced) to work together in the daytime, a practice thought to bring about personal reform. The reformer Dorothea Dix was crucial in focusing public interest on the criminal justice system and in removing large numbers of the mentally ill from prisons.

## Abolition

Of deeper importance was the small but growing movement for abolition. The moral perfectibility preached during the Second Great Awakening openly exposed the greatest sin of the nation: slavery. And, as the cotton gin enabled cotton production to expand westward, slavery became firmly established in the expanding South during the first quarter of the 1800s.

Free African Americans had long advocated abolition, and in the 1820s they accelerated their protests. Richard Allen, head of the African Methodist Episcopal Church, and David Walker, a vocal pamphleteer, advocated immediate emancipation. Walker's essay *Appeal to the Coloured Citizens of the World* (1829) serves as the strongest statement from an African American during the era; it provoked many small slave riots across the South.

While African Americans advocated immediate emancipation, most white Americans favored gradual emancipation, or gradualism. In the North, slavery had been phased out after the Revolution, and the problem seemed less pressing to northern white reformers. Some white Americans demonstrated racism in other ways, however, most significantly in founding the **American Colonization Society**. The society advocated sending all black Americans to Africa, and it even established the colony of Liberia on the West African coast for this purpose in the 1820s.

## Garrison and *The Liberator*

Public opinion began to shift in 1831, when William Lloyd Garrison, a white journalist advocating immediate emancipation, began publishing the antislavery newspaper *The Liberator*. *The Liberator* served for thirty years as the central voice of the abolition movement. It drew together a group of antislavery advocates, many of whom were evangelical preachers affiliated with the Lane Theological Seminary in Cincinnati (men like Lyman Beecher and Theodore Weld). The ideas of the Second Great Awakening prodded these leaders to advocate immediate emancipation, although many other northern white churches were slower to adopt the cause of emancipation, prompting Garrison to attack them for their complicity. Garrison was clearly the most steadfast in his pursuit of abolition: at one point, he publicly burned a copy of the U.S. Constitution, suggesting that it too was complicit in allowing slavery (which, of course, it was). This action, and others like it, alienated Garrison from many white abolitionists who favored gradualism. In 1833, Garrison founded the **American Anti-Slavery Society**, an organization that served as a point of contact for escaped slaves like Frederick Douglass and Harriet Tubman. His secretary, the dynamic Maria Weston Chapman, edited *The Liberator* when Garrison was off doing other work.

> **American Colonization Society**
> Group that advocated sending all black Americans to Africa; it established the colony of Liberia on the West African coast for this purpose in the 1820s
>
> **American Anti-Slavery Society**
> Organization founded by journalist William Lloyd Garrison in 1833 that served as a point of contact for escaped slaves like Frederick Douglass and Harriet Tubman

 Read a selection from Walker's *Appeal*.

 View a Library of Congress exhibit about the American Colonization Society.

Read Garrison's remarks from the Anti-Slavery Convention.

## Resistance to Abolition

Abolitionists faced fierce, stubborn resistance in both the South and the North. In northern states like New York and Illinois, merchants and laborers challenged abolitionists mainly because they were afraid that poor black people would be willing to work for low wages, thus depressing the economy. In 1837, vigilantes in Illinois even murdered the minister and journalist Elijah Lovejoy for perpetually publishing abolitionist tracts. In the South, southerners also sometimes violently prevented abolitionists from distributing antislavery tracts. Georgia offered a $5,000 reward to anyone who delivered Garrison to state authorities.

## Congressional "Gag Rule"

Abolitionists continued to fight, though, sending thousands of petitions to Congress. In an effort to prevent Congress from discussing slavery (and therefore threatening the free state/slave state balance established by the Compromise of 1820), the House of Representatives adopted, in 1836, what opponents called the **"gag rule."** This was a legal provision that automatically tabled any discussion of abolition. Under this law, slavery was not open for discussion in Congress. Former president John Quincy Adams, now a representative from Massachusetts, repeatedly protested the rule, but persistent opposition frustrated his efforts for eight years, when Congress finally rescinded the rule.

By the 1850s, the movement for abolition was growing, and so was its opposition. As the debate became increasingly polarized, more and more people had to weigh the costs associated with slavery.

## The Women's Movement

Women, both black and white, were some of the most ardent abolitionists. The sisters Angelina and Sarah Grimké, Lydia Maria Child, Maria Chapman, and Lucretia Mott were all active in the crusade. For many of these women, advocating the rights of African Americans highlighted the absence of basic civil rights for women. In one notable instance, the Grimké sisters were criticized for their abolitionist activism by Congregationalist ministers who circulated a letter outlining the "proper" duties of women in the church. This quite pointedly turned the Grimkés' attention to the condition of women. In response, in 1838, Sarah Grimké published *Letters on the Equality of the Sexes and the Condition of Men* and Angelina Grimké published her *Letters to Catherine E. Beecher*, both landmark tracts in the struggle for women's equality. Together, these works brought together a group of like-minded reformers interested in the place of women in American society. They found eager constituents in the women who had found their voices during the Second Great Awakening and in the new occupations generated during the Market Revolution.

Elizabeth Cady Stanton and Women's Rights

In 1848, several women, including the leading abolitionists mentioned previously and Elizabeth Cady Stanton, organized the Women's Rights Convention at Seneca Falls, New York, normally called the **Seneca Falls Convention**. The convention adopted a Declaration of Sentiments, which was modeled after the Declaration of Independence and articulated the injustices that women faced in American society. As a political tactic, the women's movement put securing the vote for women atop their list of demands. But they faced two challenges: (1) from men reluctant to admit women into the raucous world of nineteenth-century politics, and (2) by the rising issue of racial equality, which would culminate in the Civil War and make all other attempts at social reform seem less pressing. The movements for justice by African Americans and women have always been linked (for example, Frederick Douglass spoke at the 1848 Seneca Falls Convention), but the thorny issue of whether to concentrate on establishing African American rights or women's rights perpetually divided the various women's movements, at least until the latter half of the twentieth century.

 Read more about Seneca Falls.

## And in the end . . .

Between 1812 and the 1860s, the nation's social and economic life had changed dramatically. With the American System of economics as a model, the United States became increasingly market oriented. Production was implemented on a larger scale and became more and more mechanized. The transportation and communications revolutions altered the way people thought of the vast expanse that was their nation. And urbanization and the creation of a sizeable working class served as reminders that certain advances come with costs.

The significant changes associated with the Market Revolution provoked various reactions, from the perfection seekers of the Second Great Awakening to calls for social reform from the working class, American Catholics, African Americans, and women. A new form of politics also arose during these years, years that are usually associated with one dynamic character. It is to Andrew Jackson and the politics of the Market Revolution that we now turn.

### What else was happening . . .

| | |
|---|---|
| 1815 | John Roulstone writes the first three verses of "Mary Had a Little Lamb" after his classmate Mary Sawyer comes to school followed by her pet lamb. |
| 1823 | The game of rugby is invented. |
| 1833 | Britain outlaws slavery in response to the continued efforts of evangelical Christians and the politician William Wilberforce. |
| 1838 | Massachusetts prohibits the sale of liquor. One man gets around the law by painting stripes on a pig and advertising that, for 6 cents, a person could see the pig and get a free glass of whiskey. |
| 1847 | Hanson Gregory, a New England mariner, invents the donut. |

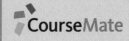 **CourseMate**

Visit the CourseMate website at www.cengagebrain.com for additional study tools and review materials for this chapter.

# CHAPTER 11

# Politics of the Market Revolution

## Learning Outcomes

*After reading this chapter, you should be able to do the following:*

**LO¹** Describe the changes that took place in American politics during the first decades of the 1800s, and explain reasons for these changes.

**LO²** Explain how Jackson's approach to the "spoils system," the nullification crisis, the National Bank, Indian removal, and the Panic of 1837 reflect his vision of federal power.

**LO³** Explain the development of America's second two-party political system, the parties being the Democrats and the Whigs.

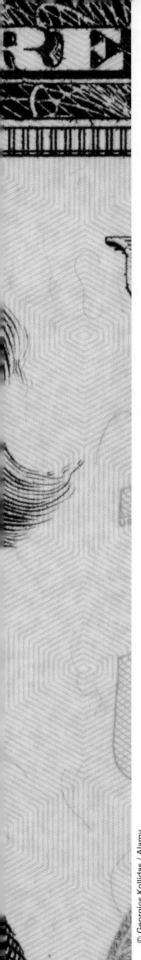

© Georgios Kollidas / Alamy

> **"Despite what his appearance on today's $20 bill might suggest, Andrew Jackson ruined the national currency, which did not revive again until the Civil War."**

The first half of the 1800s saw political developments almost as momentous as the social and economic changes brought on by the Market Revolution. While the American economy was booming and busting and booming again between 1814 and 1850, American politics

were becoming more and more democratic. The politics of deference—in which people were expected to defer to the wisdom of the more educated elite—were dying out. Historians have called it "the era of the common man," in which politics expanded beyond its elite origins and the vote was extended to more and more of the population.

To be sure, the America of the early 1800s considered the "common man" to be white and, quite literally, a man. However, while racial minorities and women were still excluded from the franchise, many states ceased requiring property ownership as mandatory for full citizenship. This meant that a much higher percentage of Americans could vote in 1840 than in 1790. Large political parties arose to woo the new voters. The result was a vibrant, sometimes raucous political life for men that featured the rise of two new parties to replace the Federalists and the Democratic-Republicans from the Founding Era. These new parties—the Democrats and the Whigs—mostly argued about the best way to manage the economy during the Market Revolution. Because Andrew Jackson symbolized this new style of politics, the period is often called the Age of Jackson.

# LO¹ Politics in the Age of Jackson

## A New Kind of Politics

Four factors contributed to the rise of a new kind of politics in the 1820s and 1830s: (1) economic booms and busts caused Americans to feel that the government should be more responsive to their needs; (2) the expansion of the franchise, or vote, allowed greater numbers of American men to participate in politics; and (3) the contentious presidential election of 1824 led the entire nation to become increasingly political, which (4) drove the rise of mass parties and the second two-party system.

### The Panic of 1819

As we saw in the last chapter, during the first half of the nineteenth century, the United States became a more market-driven society, with increasingly rapid communications and transportation. At the same time, Americans were on the move, settling western lands and building railroads to connect the new settlements with eastern cities. The South was booming as well, becoming Europe's principal supplier of cotton. With these developments, many Americans felt they were destined to reap continued economic success.

Such optimism did not last. In 1819, global demand for American agricultural production (particularly cotton) plummeted, in part because of Europe's recovery after the end of the Napoleonic Wars in 1815. At the same time, the Second Bank of the United States tightened credit, due to fears about overinvestment in factories and land. With fewer people buying American goods and with credit tightened, the United States entered its first major economic depression. Land values tumbled across the nation, and the demand for goods and foodstuffs slackened. Every bank south and west of Pennsylvania failed except two. Thousands of people declared bankruptcy or were sentenced to debtors' prison.

The Panic of 1819 deeply affected the average American. Farmers in the West were particularly hard pressed. Having bought their farms on credit, many could not make their payments. This led banks to foreclose the loans. In desperation, people turned to their state governments, demanding financial assistance during these tough times. In Kentucky and other states, voters agitated in vain for the government to declare a moratorium on the collection of debts. In general, Americans began to feel that the government should protect its constituents from economic disaster and, more importantly, from the topsy-turvy nature of a market-based economy.

## Expansion of the Franchise

This push to make government more responsive to the common people coincided with the opening up of the political process. In the first years after the Revolution, most states limited the vote to white men who owned a certain amount of property. Such requirements were designed to place political power in the hands of men who were considered to have a "real stake" in society.

These limits did not last long. During the first part of the 1800s, almost every state removed property restrictions on citizenship. By 1824, most states had liberalized their laws so that every free white man was allowed to vote. After 1824, only Rhode Island, Virginia, North Carolina, and Louisiana maintained property restrictions.

As they expanded the franchise to all white men, legislators of the early 1800s also developed restrictions that prevented African Americans from

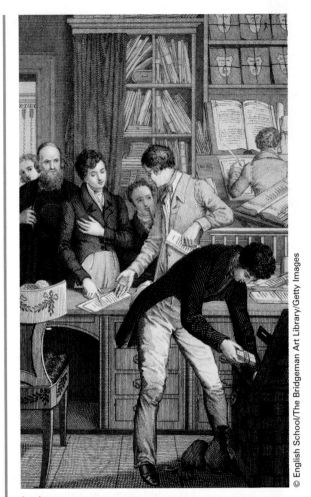

>> Depositors run on the bank. During the Panic of 1819, every bank south and west of Pennsylvania failed except two.

voting. If slavery had slowly departed from the North, racism had not. For example, the New York Constitution of 1777 did not mention race at all, but in 1821, the revised New York Constitution restricted the vote to all white men and to wealthy African Americans. Women and poor black men were specifically excluded. The world of politics was becoming more democratic, and more people were allowed to participate, but it still maintained significant limits to participation.

## The Election of 1824

Nowhere was this new politics better reflected than in the election of 1824 (see Map 11.1 on page 190). Since the Federalist Party fell apart in the late 1810s (after contemplating secession at the Hartford Convention), all national politicians of the 1820s considered themselves Democratic-Republicans. Five Democratic-Republicans were nominated to the presidency in 1824, for example, and each had strong regional support. Yet no single candidate was able to muster a majority.

Per the Constitution, the election was handed over to the House of Representatives, which was, by law, instructed to consider only the top three candidates. They were Andrew Jackson, John Quincy Adams, and William H. Crawford. The candidate who had come in fourth place (and was thus no longer on the ballot) was Henry Clay. Clay instructed his backers to support Adams—an action that infuriated Jackson, who had won the most popular and electoral votes. With Clay's support, then, John Quincy Adams, the son of former president John Adams, was elected president of the United States on the next vote of the House.

When Adams shortly thereafter appointed Clay his secretary of state (a frequent stepping-stone to the presidency), Andrew Jackson and his followers protested that there had been a **"corrupt bargain"** between the two men. Jackson and his supporters vowed revenge, and revenge they would get.

The split between Clay and Adams on the one hand and Jackson on the other was the key step in the development of the **second two-party system**. By 1824, the followers of Jackson called themselves the Jacksonians, and they advocated a strong executive branch, perpetual westward expansion, and an aggressive democratization of the political process, especially opening the franchise for white men. A few years later, the followers of Clay and Adams chose to be called the National Republicans. They later changed their name to the Whigs, in honor of Britain's Whigs, who had protested the authoritarian actions of the king of England (thus insinuating that Jackson yearned to be a dictatorial king). And they advocated a strong legislature, government-funded internal improvements, economic protectionism, and the American System of economics.

But the more immediate effect of the "corrupt bargain" was to stimulate partisanship and get more people interested in politics. In the election of 1824, national voter turnout was just 24 percent. By 1840, turnout was nearly 80 per-

cent. National parties had developed in the intervening years to capitalize on and profit from the newfound interest in politics.

## A New Culture of Politics

These national parties fed a new culture of politics in the 1820s and 1830s. Between the increased number of eligible voters and the expansion of political parties, popular interest in politics soared. Because most "common men" now had the right to vote, political candidates had no choice but to mingle with the masses and earn their respect and attention. As a result, politics for the first time became mass entertainment. Partisan newspapers flourished. Campaigns were conducted to appeal to popular tastes and featured public rallies, picnics, and elaborate parades with marching bands. Alcohol flowed freely at these events. What better way for a candidate to prove to be a man of the people than to raise a glass of whiskey to their health? In this jovial atmosphere, no one charmed the people better than Andrew Jackson.

 Use historical evidence to evaluate how corrupt the "corrupt bargain" truly was.

## Andrew Jackson and the Politics of the "Common Man"

Resentful of the "corrupt bargain," in 1828 Jackson and his newly emerging Democratic Party set out to mobilize voters and achieve the presidential victory he felt he deserved.

### The Election of 1828

They had a busy four years between 1824 and 1828, barnstorming all twenty-two states. Jackson's opponent in 1828 was the incumbent president, John Quincy Adams, an old-style, patrician politician in the mold of his father. He made

> **"What better way for a candidate to prove to be a man of the people than to raise a glass of whiskey to their health? In this jovial atmosphere, no one charmed the people better than Andrew Jackson."**

**"corrupt bargain"** Alleged deal between John Quincy Adams and Henry Clay to manipulate the voting in the House of Representatives to install Adams as president and Clay as his secretary of state in 1824

**second two-party system** Evolution of political organizations in 1824 into the Jacksonians and the Whigs

Andrew Jackson on the campaign trail. Note his roughly worn attire and his engaged, aggressive stance.

Hear music for an Andrew Jackson campaign song, and be sure to read the lyrics!

no effort to reach out to the people, relying instead on his record as president, which mostly included a series of internal improvements in the West. In his platform, he proposed even more internal improvements, funding explorations of the western interior, and leveraging American manufacturing in order to win votes, but he did so from the White House, not the campaign trail.

Jackson took a different route. Instead of focusing on specific issues, he used a campaign strategy all too familiar to American voters today: mudslinging. While Jackson defamed the personal character of his political adversaries, his fellow Democratic

leaders organized rallies and barbecues to attract and mobilize voters. The Democrats amplified Jackson's biography as a hero of the War of 1812, and his biography changed slightly depending on where he campaigned. He was most successful with three groups: (1) southerners, who appreciated the fact that some of the Indians he had killed were Florida's Seminoles, who were hated by southerners because the tribe had invited slaves to escape to freedom in Seminole lands; (2) westerners, who viewed him as a hearty frontiersman (his supporters avoided revealing the fact that his frontier lifestyle depended largely on the hundred slaves he owned); and (3) the working classes of the North, who had come to resent what they called the "elitism" of the Federalists and their political offspring. Jackson won the election of 1828 (Map 11.2) by a wide margin—all the more impressive because the total number of voters had tripled in just four years. He did not make the customary visit to President John Quincy Adams before taking office, and, to return the snub, Adams refused to attend Jackson's inauguration, a rollicking affair that was open to the public (for the first time) and that led to significant damages to the White House.

## A New Style of Politics

The election of 1828 marked a major turning point in American political history. A new style of politics had emerged, characterized by pandering to the masses. Style over substance became the rule. Moreover, new techniques of mass mobilization, such as campaign leaflets, public speeches, and

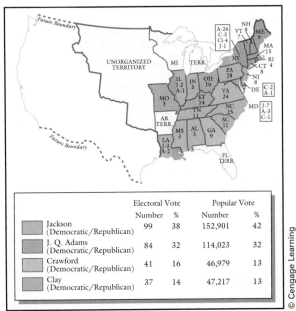

| | | Electoral Vote | | Popular Vote | |
|---|---|---|---|---|---|
| | | Number | % | Number | % |
| | Jackson (Democratic/Republican) | 99 | 38 | 152,901 | 42 |
| | J. Q. Adams (Democratic/Republican) | 84 | 32 | 114,023 | 32 |
| | Crawford (Democratic/Republican) | 41 | 16 | 46,979 | 13 |
| | Clay (Democratic/Republican) | 37 | 14 | 47,217 | 13 |

Map 11.1. The Election of 1824

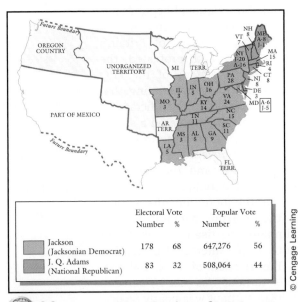

| | | Electoral Vote | | Popular Vote | |
|---|---|---|---|---|---|
| | | Number | % | Number | % |
| | Jackson (Jacksonian Democrat) | 178 | 68 | 647,276 | 56 |
| | J. Q. Adams (National Republican) | 83 | 32 | 508,064 | 44 |

Map 11.2. The Election of 1828

>> John Quincy Adams made no effort to reach out to the people, relying instead on his record as president.

other kinds of political propaganda, became essential to running a successful campaign. The election of 1828 signaled the beginning of the kind of political culture that persists in America today.

## White Male Democracy

Jackson's ascendance to the presidency is often described as the dawning of the age of the common man, or the revolt of westerners and southerners against a northeastern elite. Both interpretations are somewhat misleading. Jackson was a successful lawyer and a wealthy slaveholder and, in political acumen at least, he was far from common. And, in the 1828 triumph, he won sections of large northern states such as New York.

Nevertheless, it was Jackson's appeal to the American masses that got him elected in 1828. More than anyone else, Jackson symbolized the power of the people in the new political system. He was the first president from the West (Tennessee) rather than from the aristocracy of New England or

Virginia. He was supported by a coalition of western frontiersmen, southern planters, and the northern working class who supported manhood suffrage (extending the vote to all white men regardless of property ownership) and opposed anyone they considered an aristocrat, even if those aristocrats were interested in extending rights to other, less privileged minorities.

Read Andrew Jackson's First Annual Message, and see what might have appealed to the "common man."

## Racism in the North

One group that did not support Jackson, largely because they did not have the legal right to do so but also because of the racism of Jackson's supporters, was African Americans. Slavery remained legal in the South, and although Jackson did not design any policies specifically against free blacks, the Democrats were hostile to any suggestion of improving the condition of free blacks living in the North. These northern free blacks were usually denied basic civil rights. Often they could vote, but only in Massachusetts, for example, could a black person sit on a jury. Worse still, Ohio, Indiana, and Illinois passed laws that prohibited free blacks from settling within their borders. By custom, segregation was the rule in the North. Blacks had to sit in separate sections on railroads, steamboats, and stagecoaches. They were barred from entering many hotels and restaurants. Thus, although the North had abolished slavery during the first quarter of the 1800s, society-wide racism made blacks an underclass, separate from the "common men" whom Jackson came to represent.

# LO² Jackson as President

He may have symbolized the "common man," but Andrew Jackson's presidency was anything but common. Four issues dominated his presidency: (1) patronage, (2) the nullification crisis, (3) the Bank War, and (4) Indian removal. The way he handled each of them had long-lasting ramifications, some of which we live with today.

## Patronage

When Jackson and his followers came to power, they sought to exact revenge on Adams, Clay, and their supporters. Following the advice of the masterful New York politician Martin Van Buren, Jackson took control of the federal government through a

**patronage**
Exchange of a government job in return for political campaign work

**nullification**
Assertion that the United States was made up of independent and sovereign states; states did not agree to give up their autonomy; and every state reserved the right to reject any federal law it deemed unconstitutional

system of political **patronage**. Patronage is defined as the direct exchange of a government job in return for political campaign work. This means that, rather than seek out the best-qualified person for a job, a politician simply awards the job based on the campaign support one has given him. This system was routinely called the "spoils system," as in "to the victor go the spoils." Upon his victory in 1828, Jackson fired many federal workers and replaced them with committed Jacksonians, surrounding himself with like-minded men.

The one non-Jacksonian who could not be fired was Vice President John C. Calhoun, a former senator from South Carolina and a strong advocate of states' rights. The battles between Jackson and Calhoun were legendary, especially during what came to be known as the nullification crisis.

## The Nullification Crisis

By far, the most serious crisis Jackson confronted—in fact, the most serious crisis in the nation between the Revolution and the Civil War—developed around the concept of states' rights and whether or not a state could "nullify" a federal law. Nullification emerged as a major issue during Jackson's first term.

### The Context of Nullification

By the time Jackson was elected president in 1828, the Panic of 1819 was just an ugly memory, but Americans were still anxious about economic matters. The economy was changing so rapidly during the Market Revolution that many Americans felt they could hardly keep up. This was especially true in South Carolina, where the cotton market had been hit hard by the depression and by soil depletion. South Carolinians focused the blame for their economic problems on the high tariff placed on their goods.

### Tariffs

Congress had begun increasing America's tariffs in 1816 to protect American industries, especially the newly mechanized textile industry taking root in New England, which used southern cotton as its raw material. This was a key component of the American

System. The western states also benefited from the tax on imported goods because taxes on European wheat, hemp, and other agricultural products made them more expensive; with the tariff, Americans would buy American goods. The South, however, felt left out. American tariffs did not affect southern staple crops because Europeans did not grow competing crops. As southerners saw it, they were forced to pay higher prices for goods to subsidize the economic development of the North and West.

When Congress raised these tariffs in 1824, South Carolina and other southern states vigorously objected. Despite these complaints, Congress narrowly approved the tariff. Then, in a move that backfired, in 1828, Jackson, running for president against Adams, advocated a ridiculously high tariff, assuming it would not pass. Jackson's promotion of the tariff would have gained him the support of the West and the North (which might otherwise have supported Adams), while the South would be content that no tariff had been passed. Jackson's support was intended to be a political ploy.

To Jackson's shock, the Tariff of 1828, which came to be known as the "Tariff of Abominations," passed in Congress. Adams, the outgoing president, did not veto the measure, leaving Jackson with a tariff that made many of his supporters unhappy. The South was furious and, in response, the South Carolina legislature issued a document called the *South Carolina Exposition*. The anonymous author of this document was John C. Calhoun, Jackson's incoming vice president.

### What Was Nullification?

The *South Carolina Exposition* gave voice to a new political idea: **nullification**. Calhoun's concept of nullification was designed to answer a serious problem of political theory: how to protect the rights of a minority in a government based on the rule of the majority. (This is something we have seen before, in Jefferson's Virginia and Kentucky Resolutions of 1798.) Calhoun's theory of nullification asserted that the United States was made up of independent and sovereign states. In joining the Union, Calhoun argued, states did not agree to give up their autonomy. Therefore, every state reserved the right to reject any federal law it deemed unconstitutional.

In 1828, South Carolina did nothing more than articulate the idea of nullification, but in 1832, after Congress failed to revise the Tariff of Abominations, South Carolina actually put nullification into prac-

Read South Carolina's Ordinance of Nullification.

tice. The state legislature authorized the election of delegates to a popular convention, and, in November 1832, that convention passed an ordinance declaring the tariffs of 1828 and 1832 null and void in South Carolina, effective February 1, 1833.

### Jackson's Response

As an ardent nationalist, President Jackson was not about to let South Carolina challenge the authority of the federal government. In his Proclamation on Nullification, delivered in December 1832, Jackson emphasized that the states of the Union were not independent and that, therefore, no state had the right to reject a federal law; only the Supreme Court had the authority to do that. Moreover, Jackson declared that the Union was perpetual. By this logic, Calhoun's assertion that a state could withdraw from the Union was treason.

Read Jackson's Proclamation on Nullification (especially the last four paragraphs).

To demonstrate how seriously they took the threat, Jacksonians in Congress passed the Force Bill in March 1833, which confirmed the president's authority to use the army and navy to put down insurrection. But Jackson was wise enough to use the carrot as well as the stick. While threatening South Carolina with the possibility of force, Jackson also urged Congress to lower the tariff. By doing so, Jackson isolated South Carolina. No other state would defend South Carolina when the federal government was trying to be accommodating. As a result, Calhoun himself backed away from nullification and supported a compromise tariff bill. It went into effect on the same day as the Force Bill, March 1, 1833. South Carolina promptly repealed its nullification of the tariff, but, in a final display of spiteful defiance, it nullified the Force Bill. Jackson sagely ignored this and allowed the nullification crisis to die out. For the moment, Jackson's brand of nationalism had triumphed over the forces of nullification and secession.

### The Bank War

As strong as Jackson's sense of nationalism was, it did not prevent him from attacking and eventually destroying one major national institution:

> **"**On your undivided support of your government depends the decision of the great question it involves, whether your sacred Union will be preserved, and the blessing it secures to us as one people shall be perpetuated.**"**
>
> —*Andrew Jackson, Proclamation on Nullification, December 10, 1832*

the Second Bank of the United States. The crisis surrounding the charter of the Second Bank of the United States was the third issue that polarized the politics of the 1830s (along with patronage and nullification).

### The Bank

The Second Bank of the United States, located in Philadelphia, had been created by Congress in 1816 and been granted a twenty-year charter. During its first years, the Bank extended credit easily, helping grow the economy in the aftermath of the War of 1812. Americans were on the move, buying and cultivating new lands in the West, and credit from the Bank underwrote much of this economic activity. In 1819, however, the Bank reversed course and began calling in its loans, contributing to the Panic of 1819. People late on their payments now had to pay up. Many Americans went to debtors' prisons; others suffered bankruptcy. Although the Bank was not the sole cause of the panic, many citizens considered the Bank a dangerous institution.

In 1823, Nicholas Biddle, a Philadelphia businessman, assumed leadership of the Bank. Biddle believed that the Bank could serve as a stabilizing influence over the American economy by preventing the national credit supply from expanding too far or contracting too quickly. It is important to remember that America's monetary system in the nineteenth century was dramatically different from today's. Until 1863, there was no standardized national currency. Several forms of money existed, and payments were made in (1) specie (gold or silver); (2) barter (goods exchanged for other goods without the use of money); and (3) state bank notes (paper money issued by state-chartered banks). The problem with the paper money was that its value fluctuated depending on the status and solvency of the bank. When too many notes were in circulation, their value declined. Biddle promised to use the Bank to control fluctuations in the value of paper money by limiting the amount in circulation.

### Jackson's Opposition

Jackson personally distrusted the Bank. After losing his money in a bank in the 1790s, he viewed paper

>> **The Second Bank of the United States in Philadelphia.**

money as dangerous. In his eyes, only specie provided stability. Outright conflict between Jackson and Biddle erupted in 1832, when Biddle applied for a renewal of the Bank's charter four years before the charter was set to expire. Jackson presumed that Biddle was trying to make the Bank an issue in the presidential election of 1832. Already reeling from the nullification crisis, Jackson had no patience for Biddle's request and vowed to destroy the Bank altogether. Despite Jackson's objections, Congress renewed the Bank's charter in the summer of 1832. Undeterred, Jackson vetoed the charter. He justified his veto with a powerful message, arguing that the Bank was a nest of special privileges for the wealthy who were out to hurt America's humble poor. He also argued that the Constitution did not allow for the creation of a national bank or for the use of paper money. His veto was popular with the working classes, westerners, and southerners.

### Crushing the Bank

Once Jackson was reelected at the end of 1832, the Bank still had four years of its charter left. Jackson brashly resolved to crush the Bank before its charter expired. He ordered that all $10 million of federal deposits be withdrawn and redeposited in state banks. The Senate censured Jackson for defying its

wishes, but it could not prevent the Bank from going under. When the Bank's charter expired in 1836, the institution closed its doors for good.

### Wildcat Banking

The result was not what Jackson had anticipated. Jackson deposited all of the government's money in several state banks, many of which were owned by his friends. (This was another example of Jackson's controversial use of political patronage.) The absence of a central bank allowed for the rise of many state and local banks that had less than adequate credit and little government regulation.

Hundreds of paper currencies appeared, many of which were valueless. Counterfeiting was popular. Ironically, the only people who were knowledgeable about currencies were the commercial elite, reinforcing the notion that paper money only helped the wealthy. With no regulation, Jackson's rhetoric about the insecurity of paper money made sense, and some states, such as California in 1849, outlawed paper money entirely. But on the whole, the financial instability handicapped economic growth. Despite what his appearance on today's $20 bill might suggest, Andrew Jackson ruined the national currency, which did not revive again until the Civil War.

## Westward Expansion and Indian Removal

While all this was happening, Americans continued their perpetual move west. Soil exhaustion in the Southeast, a shortage of land in New England, and the alluring expanses of the Midwest drew Americans to the Great Plains. Southerners usually moved west to find land where they could grow cotton. Cotton growers moved through Alabama, Mississippi, and Arkansas, populating Texas (with free blacks and slaves) in the 1840s. Similarly, northerners moved in order to cultivate the fields of the Midwest, pushing as far as Iowa by the 1840s.

All this growth boosted the development of several cities that served as trading and transportation hubs for the growing West. Louisville, Cincinnati, Detroit, Chicago, and St. Louis grew into the largest cities in the region. Connected to the East Coast by a chain of steamboats, canals, or trains, these cities boomed as centers of America's westward expansion. Rapidly they, too, became industrial centers, with mills and factories lining their riverways.

## Indian Resistance

And, as before, the tribes of Native America were the chief obstacles to westward migration and settlement. Although the U.S. government pursued numerous treaties with the various tribes during the first part of the 1800s, such agreements proved untenable because the federal government would not keep its word. In addition, westward pioneers did not heed the restrictions placed on them; they often strayed into Indian territory. In some instances, Indians were invited to trade with the Americans at specified trading posts, but the result often plunged the Indians into debt, forcing them to sell their lands to find economic relief. The Choctaw, Creek, and Chickasaw tribes all succumbed in this way. And, as Americans moved west, they introduced disease. Smallpox wiped out the Pawnees, Omahas, Otoes, Missouris, and Kansas in the Midwest during the 1830s and 1840s. Where debt and disease did not crush Indian resistance, war did: for example, the small tribes in the Midwest were decimated in the Blackhawk War of 1832. This ended any significant Indian presence in today's Midwest.

## Indian Removal Act of 1830

In the South, the tribes were larger and better organized. Constant battles raged, and complete Indian removal became established U.S. policy. After some harsh political debate, Congress passed the **Indian Removal Act of 1830**, which allowed the federal government to trade land west of the Mississippi River for land east of the river. Citing the act, Jackson forced several tribes, including the Creeks and the Lower Creeks, to move west throughout the 1830s. This, however, would not happen so easily.

> **Indian Removal Act of 1830**
> Legislation that allowed the federal government to trade land west of the Mississippi River for land east of the river, allowing the federal government to move Indians further west

## The Cherokee Nation versus Georgia

The Cherokees had accommodated to the American way of life more than any other Indian tribe. They had adopted an American-style bicameral government, translated a Christian Bible into the Cherokee language, and adopted American rules regarding property and slaveholding. By 1833, the Cherokees owned 1,500 black slaves.

But when gold was discovered in western Georgia, white Georgians wanted the Cherokees removed so they could mine the gold. The white Georgians attempted to dissolve the Cherokee constitution and take away their property rights. To resist, the Cherokees sued the Georgians in federal court. And they won. In *Worcester* v. *Georgia* (1832), which followed a similar case from the year before, *Cherokee* v. *Georgia*, the Supreme Court ruled that the Cherokee nation was a sovereign nation and that the state of Georgia could not enter it without Cherokee permission. According to the court, if the U.S. government wanted to move the Cherokees, it would have to do so in a treaty, not through the Removal Act.

Amazingly, Jackson simply ignored the decision. One newspaper reported the president as saying, "[Chief Justice] John Marshall has made his decision: now let him enforce it." With the prospect of violence looming, a tiny faction of Cherokees (500 out

© *The Trail of Tears* (oil on canvas), Lindneux, Robert Ottokar (1871–1970)/ Woolaroc Museum, Oklahoma, USA, Peter Newark Western Americana/The Bridgeman Art Library

**>>** **The Trail of Tears.**

View an interactive account of Indian removal.

**Trail of Tears**
Forced removal of the Cherokee nation from Georgia to Oklahoma in 1838; the Cherokees were forced to walk more than a thousand miles

of 17,000) attempted to end hostilities by signing a treaty with Jackson. The treaty traded Cherokee land for land west of the Mississippi, and when Congress ratified the treaty (by a single vote, over the strenuous objections of Henry Clay and Daniel Webster), the Cherokees lost title to their land. (The tribe later murdered the Cherokee treaty makers, who were viewed by the majority as traitors.) After one American general resigned in protest, in 1838 General Winfield Scott invaded the Cherokee nation and forced the Cherokees to walk a thousand miles, from Georgia to Oklahoma, enduring hardship and death on what was called the **Trail of Tears.** About 4,000 Cherokees died along the way, and, when they arrived in Oklahoma, they faced conflict with the tribes that had already settled there. For more on why the Cherokee were pushed off their lands in Georgia, see "The reasons why . . ." box below.

### Was Jackson Anti-Indian?

Jackson had a complicated relationship with Native Americans. His Indian Removal Bill of 1830 forced all Native Americans to move west of the Mississippi, clearing their lands for white settlement. But he defended these actions under the guise of paternalism—the idea that Jackson was moving Indians for their own good, saving them from the ravages and greed of the white man. He put this idea into practice when he adopted a Creek Indian as a son after the Creek War. On the whole, however, the evidence begins to stack up against Jackson. He ultimately believed any Indian presence east of the Mississippi River was illegitimate, and, in fact, he believed the Indian people as a whole were destined for extinction anyway. His policies nearly made him correct.

### The Seminole Revolt

Jackson's paternalism had limited appeal for those who were being patronized, though, and Jackson's Indian removal plan and his attitude toward African Americans combined to provoke what may have been the largest slave revolt in American history. Seminole Indians in northern Florida had long provided a refuge for escaped slaves. Beginning in 1835, Seminoles had been fighting a perpetual war with American settlers over land in Florida. In 1836, the Seminoles and their free black population (called Black Seminoles) attacked at least twelve white-owned sugar plantations. Enslaved plantation workers joined the fray, striking back at their slave masters.

In the mayhem that followed, many slaves freed themselves and burned all the sugar plantations in the region. The residents of St. Augustine watched the smoke drift from the south as the plantations burned to the ground. Sugar was never again a viable product in northern Florida. The war between the Seminoles and the settlers lasted until 1842 without a clear victor.

Learn more about the Seminole Revolt.

## { *The reasons why . . .* }

There were four reasons why the Cherokee were pushed off their lands in Georgia:

*White land lust.* First, soil exhaustion in the Southeast sent farmers further west in search of land where they could grow staple crops such as cotton, which had been made considerably easier to do after the invention of the cotton gin in 1793.

*Racism.* Second, since the early colonial days, European colonists in North America (and later, white Americans) had rarely treated Indians with any decency, largely thinking of them as un-Christian, uncivilized dark-skinned heathens. By the 1820s and 1830s, many Americans, such as Andrew Jackson, simply felt the Indians were dying out, which would, of course, open land in the West for settlement by white Americans.

*Federal policy.* In light of these two long-standing propositions, the Indian Removal Act of 1830 made it established U.S. policy to move Indians west of the Mississippi River, pushing them further away from the settled parts of the United States.

*Andrew Jackson's ire.* After the Cherokee Nation sued the state of Georgia for allowing white Georgians onto their land while searching for gold, the Cherokees sued, claiming they were a sovereign nation beyond the bounds of the Indian Removal Act of 1830. The U.S. Supreme Court upheld the Cherokees' claims, but, citing a controversial treaty with a tiny faction of Cherokees, Andrew Jackson ordered the U.S. military to march the Cherokees from Georgia to Oklahoma, on what has come to be called the "Trail of Tears." One general resigned in protest of Jackson's order.

## The Panic of 1837

The westward push, the Indian policy, and Jackson's bank policy all combined to create a panic in the mid-nineteenth century.

### The Specie Circular

Once Indian removal became the official policy of the federal government in 1830, speculators began purchasing land in the West. And many of them used paper money from the wildcat banks that had emerged in the aftermath of Jackson's Bank War. This proved a bad combination because the cash was not stable, and it often lost much of its value. In an attempt to protect the settlers

> **❝**I have recommended them to quit their possessions on this side of the Mississippi, and go to a country in the west where there is every probability that they will always be free from the mercenary influence of White men, and undisturbed by the local authority of the states: Under such circumstances the General Government can exercise a parental control over their interests and possibly perpetuate their race.**❞**
>
> —*Andrew Jackson, in a letter to Captain James Gadsden, 1829*

**Specie Circular**
Executive order of 1836 requiring that the government cease accepting paper money as credible currency, accepting only gold or silver (specie) for all items, including public land

and to affirm his distrust of paper money, Jackson, in 1836, passed the **Specie Circular**, an executive order requiring that the government cease accepting paper money as credible currency, accepting only gold or silver (specie) for all items, including public land. The result of the federal government's saying it did not trust the value of paper money was to devalue paper money even further, abandoning settlers

**≫ In 1837, the United States plummeted into an economic depression that, ever since, has been rivaled only by the Great Depression of the 1930s.**

to worse economic trouble and sending much of America's specie west.

## The Panic of 1837

The Specie Circular could not have happened at a worse time. The rollicking economy of the Market Revolution experienced a boom in the early 1830s, mostly due to rampant speculation in the West along new transportation routes. The Specie Circular caused an immediate drop in demand for western lands and drained most of the specie from New York banks.

Unable to match its paper money with specie reserves, several hundred banks in New York City closed their doors in April. In May 1837, every bank in New York refused to accept paper money for specie. Paper money lost nearly all of its value, and nearly a quarter of all banks in the United States closed. After the Bank War, there was no central bank to control the economic contraction, and the United States plummeted into an economic depression that, ever since, has been rivaled only by the Great Depression of the 1930s.

# LO³ The Development of the Second Two-Party System

Jackson's contentious presidency stirred up a vibrant, flourishing opposition, and during the 1830s the second two-party system in American history took hold, pitting Jackson's Democrats against Adams's and Clay's Whigs.

## Jackson's Democrats

For their part, Jackson's Democrats were extremely nationalistic and believed it was best to keep the federal government small. They fashioned themselves as the heirs of Jefferson, who considered government as nothing more than a necessary evil. To Jackson's Democrats, the government was not supposed to control the way that people conducted themselves privately. This made them less aggressive in pushing America's economic development, viewing American society as being divided between two hostile camps: "the people" (farmers, planters, workers), who worked hard to make an honest living, and "the aristocracy" (merchants, bankers, financial agents), who manipulated markets for their own private enrichment. This, of course, did not preclude Jackson's Democrats from supporting America's westward expansion. Jackson's Indian Removal Bill secured much new territory for white settlement, and subsequent Democratic presidents would eventually push the boundaries of the United States all the way to the Pacific. Prominent Jacksonians included Andrew Jackson, Martin Van Buren, and James K. Polk.

## The Whigs

The Whigs, on the other hand, favored a more active federal government. They supported using federal funds to finance internal improvements like turnpikes and railroads. They also believed that government power could be used to promote the moral health of the nation through temperance laws or antislavery legislation. And the Whigs were more comfortable with market capitalism. As they saw it, economic development made people richer, increased popular demand for foodstuffs and other agricultural products, and created jobs. The Whigs denied that there was any conflict between the common people and big business. According to their view, banks were not evil; they were essential for controlling the flow of money. Many Whigs also opposed the expansion of slavery into new territory, but they did form alliances with southern states' rights groups. Prominent Whigs included Henry Clay, Daniel Webster, and William Henry Harrison.

## Constituencies

Although it is tempting to categorize the Democrats as the party of the poor and the Whigs as the party of the rich, this was not the case. Most Americans were farmers of the "middling sort" who were neither miserably impoverished nor impressively wealthy. It was true that most businessmen joined the Whig Party, but

BORN TO COMMAND.

OF VETO MEMORY.

HAD I BEEN CONSULTED.

KING ANDREW THE FIRST.

>> As this 1832 cartoon shows, the Whigs lambasted Jackson for his authoritarian style, styling his presidency as a return to the royalty overcome during the revolution.

the Whigs had several other key constituencies: farmers who wanted better methods to transport their produce to market; workers who believed they would benefit from economic growth; and planters who wanted the United States to have a stable bank system that would float loans. The Whigs also appealed to people concerned about the increasing numbers of Irish Catholics entering the country. In short, the Whigs did well in cities and rural areas that embraced market competition. Appealing to these various constituencies, and playing the new politics developed by the Jacksonians, the Whigs developed a solid party by the late 1830s, symbolized by William Henry Harrison's presidential victory over Martin Van Buren in 1840 (Map 11.3).

The Democrats, in contrast, attracted farmers and workers who felt alienated by America's increasingly commercialized economy, as well as small businessmen who hoped the Democratic Party would stand watch against monopolies and give "little guys" a chance to succeed. They also found a ready constituency in the Irish immigrants who immigrated in large numbers during the 1840s.

### Political Stability

By the election of 1840, Americans had succeeded in building a stable two-party system. Each party held together a coalition of northerners and southerners, and the party system helped relieve sectional tensions over slavery. (Basically, neither party wanted to talk about slavery and its westward expansion for fear of dividing their party.) As long as the second two-party system existed, hostilities between the North and South faded into the background. Such tensions never disappeared entirely, however, and territorial expansion in the 1840s set in motion a breakdown of America's second two-party system, leading to renewed sectional conflict and, ultimately, civil war.

## And in the end …

As the Market Revolution changed the economy and the ways of living associated with it, politicians sought to manage the changes and profit from them politically. They expanded patronage and developed a new political culture that was defined by race and gender. In one respect, the politicians were struggling to keep an increasingly disparate nation together through a series of political endeavors. At the same time, however, reformers were provoking questions that only increased sectional divisions, the most prominent of which was the slavery issue.

In the end, the economic tugs of the Market Revolution would be too strong to preserve this unity and, between the 1830s and the 1850s, America to a large degree fractured into a regionalized nation. This is the subject of the next chapter.

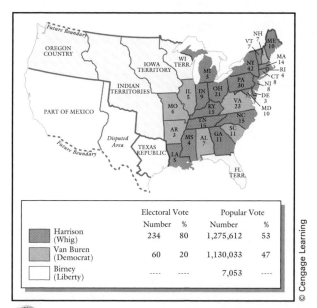

Map 11.3. The Election of 1840

| | | Electoral Vote | | Popular Vote | |
|---|---|---|---|---|---|
| | | Number | % | Number | % |
| ▣ | Harrison (Whig) | 234 | 80 | 1,275,612 | 53 |
| ▣ | Van Buren (Democrat) | 60 | 20 | 1,130,033 | 47 |
| ▢ | Birney (Liberty) | ---- | ---- | 7,053 | ---- |

© Cengage Learning

| What else was happening . . . | |
|---|---|
| 1821 | Mexicans finally win an eleven-year war for their independence from Spain. |
| 1822–1834 | English mathematician Charles Babbage proposes constructing machines to perform mathematical calculations: the Difference and Analytical Engines, forerunners of the modern computer. He runs out of money before completing either. |
| 1824 | Michael Faraday invents the first toy balloon. |
| July 4, 1826 | Both John Adams and Thomas Jefferson—longtime friends, rivals, and, in the end, correspondents—die, on the fiftieth anniversary of the Declaration of Independence. |
| 1830 | Simón Bolívar dies of tuberculosis in Colombia, after contributing to the independence of much of Latin America, including Venezuela, Colombia, Ecuador, Peru, and Bolivia. |
| 1837 | The first kindergarten, called "small child occupation institute," opens in Germany. |

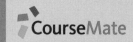 CourseMate

Visit the CourseMate website at www.cengagebrain.com for additional study tools and review materials for this chapter.

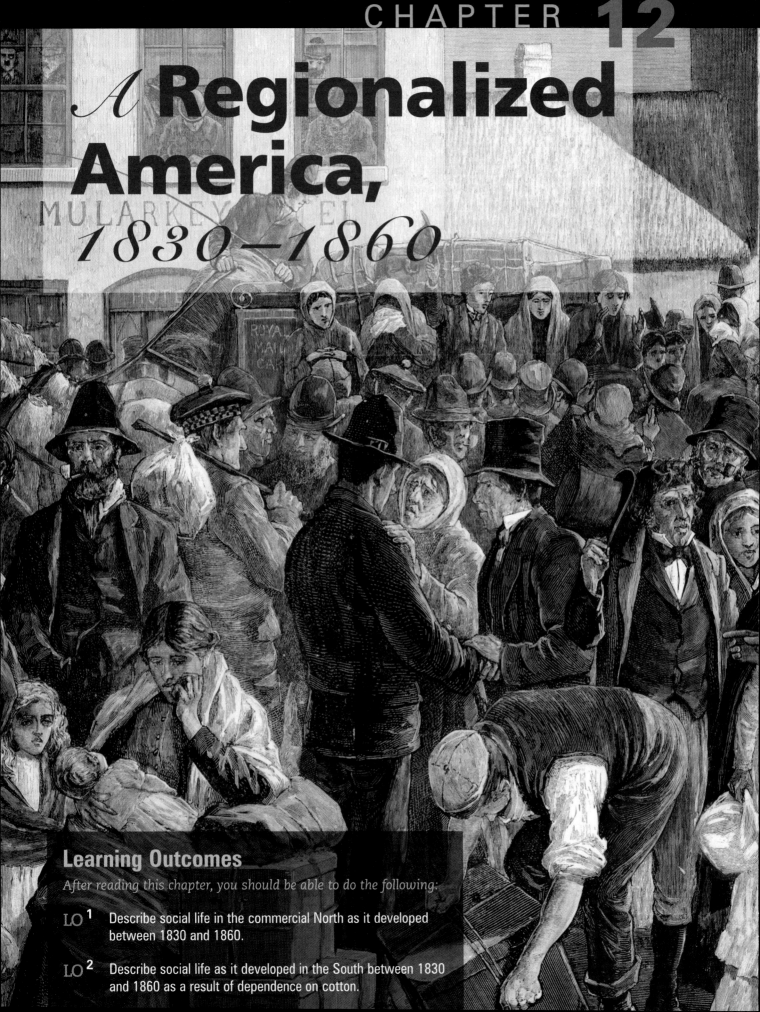

# CHAPTER 12

# A Regionalized America, 1830–1860

## Learning Outcomes

*After reading this chapter, you should be able to do the following:*

**LO 1**   Describe social life in the commercial North as it developed between 1830 and 1860.

**LO 2**   Describe social life as it developed in the South between 1830 and 1860 as a result of dependence on cotton.

# "Regionalized identities persisted despite the best efforts of politicians to bridge sectional gaps."

Between 1830 and 1860, American life became increasingly regionalized. Different ways of living emerged in the North, the South, and the West. Work relations were different, communities developed in different ways, and people often thought of themselves in regional terms. "I'm a northerner," they might say, "and I don't work for slave wages." Another might say, "In the West, we operate by a different law."

Slavery, western expansion, and commercial development were the vital issues that perpetuated regionalized identities, although the transportation revolution bound the West with either the North or the South. These regionalized identities persisted despite the best efforts of politicians to bridge sectional gaps (see Map 12.1).

This chapter describes social life in the North and the South as it developed during the Market Revolution. The next chapter describes life in the West, which had an identity all its own.

## LO¹ Social Life in the Commercial North

Three forces dramatically altered life in the northern United States in the three decades before the Civil War: (1) the Market Revolution, (2) massive immigration, and (3) urbanization.

### The Market Revolution

First, although some protested the Market Revolution (recall Thoreau and others from Chapter 10), most northerners accommodated and even promoted the transitions associated with it. The beginnings of an industrial urban sector, the opening of the farmlands of the West, and the interconnectedness of the different groups living in the North affected the social life of every northerner. For the most part, northerners acclimated themselves to these changes. Railroads crisscrossed the North. Commerce blossomed. The Market Revolution ignited the processes that made the North look like a modern society.

### Immigration

The second dramatic change was the massive wave of immigrants that came to the United States between 1830 and 1860. By 1860, about 20 percent of the total population of the North was foreign-born. Most of the immigrants came from Europe, and nearly two-thirds came from just two countries: Ireland and Germany. These immigrants settled

© North Wind Picture Archives/Alamy

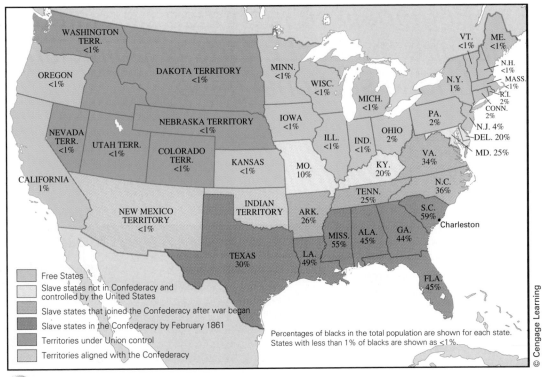

WASHINGTON TERR. <1%
OREGON <1%
DAKOTA TERRITORY <1%
MINN. <1%
WISC. <1%
MICH. <1%
VT. <1%
ME. <1%
N.H. <1%
MASS. <1%
N.Y. 1%
R.I. 2%
CONN. 2%
N.J. 4%
DEL. 20%
MD. 25%
NEVADA TERR. <1%
UTAH TERR. <1%
NEBRASKA TERRITORY <1%
COLORADO TERR. <1%
IOWA <1%
ILL. <1%
IND. <1%
OHIO 2%
PA. 2%
CALIFORNIA 1%
KANSAS <1%
MO. 10%
KY. 20%
VA. 34%
N.C. 36%
NEW MEXICO TERRITORY <1%
INDIAN TERRITORY
ARK. 26%
TENN. 25%
S.C. 59%
Charleston
TEXAS 30%
LA. 49%
MISS. 55%
ALA. 45%
GA. 44%
FLA. 45%

Free States
Slave states not in Confederacy and controlled by the United States
Slave states that joined the Confederacy after war began
Slave states in the Confederacy by February 1861
Territories under Union control
Territories aligned with the Confederacy

Percentages of blacks in the total population are shown for each state. States with less than 1% of blacks are shown as <1%.

© Cengage Learning

Map 12.1. Region and Race in Antebellum America

mostly in the North, creating distinct immigrant neighborhoods. As these immigrant groups became established and stable, they prompted new definitions of what it meant to be an American. These were not descendants of the American Revolution and thus had a different vision of what America meant.

## Urbanization

The third dramatic change to affect the northern states was urbanization. In 1860, the cities still housed a minority of the American population (most Americans were still farmers), but within their borders the dramatic interplay of America's obvious social divisions played out. Differences between black and white, rich and poor, and native-born and foreign-born all became flashpoints in early-nineteenth-century urban American life. Each of these developments contributed to a unique and tumultuous social life in the antebellum North. And the cities would only continue to grow.

>> A stone house typical of those built by the early German and Swiss immigrants to what is today called Pennsylvania Dutch country.

© iStockphoto.com/Dennis Guyitt

## Life in the Northern Countryside

These events had widespread ramifications for all groups, but life in the North varied depending on whether one lived in the cities or in the countryside.

### Communal Values

For the most part, communal values still prevailed in the northern countryside. Farm families gathered regularly to raise barns, participate in politics, and attend church. Social networks were strong. Sewing bees and apple bees brought communities together. Most farming families in the "Old Northwest" of Illinois, western Pennsylvania, and Indiana (areas west of the Appalachians but east of the Mississippi River) found a balance between their roles as consumers and as producers. Some, like the Shakers and the utopians, rejected these impulses, but most northerners adapted to them.

### Decreased Isolation

Nevertheless, change did come to the northern countryside. For one, the countryside was less isolated than it had been. Markets sprang up at railroad depots, and mail and news traveled rapidly from one part of the country to the next.

Meanwhile, the transportation revolution communicated new ideas to once-isolated areas. The itinerant ministers of the Second Great Awakening, for example, moved across the country on canals and, later, railroads. The countryside also enjoyed an active lyceum circuit, where clergymen, reformers, Transcendentalists, socialists, feminists, and other provocative speakers would speak. The North opened some public schools and enjoyed a burgeoning newspaper industry as well. The press, though, was heavily partisan, because it was usually financed by political parties. This meant that in almost every town there were at least two papers: one Democrat, one Whig. Meanwhile, the entire North, including the countryside, achieved almost universal literacy in those years. And at the same time, immigrants from Germany and Scandinavia moved into the Old Northwest to continue the farming life they had left behind in Europe. These newcomers slightly altered midwestern accents, politics, and social life, while upholding steadfast rural ideals. Descendants of these immigrant groups still have a significant presence in these areas today.

## City Life

City life in the North was changing much more rapidly than life in the country. The cities were growing at a tremendous rate. Between 1830 and 1860, the number of towns with 10,000 or more people quintupled, totaling ninety-three in 1860. There were seven towns in the North with more than 100,000 people. In 1830, there had been just one city that large, New York City, which had just over 200,000 inhabitants. By 1860, more than 814,000 people lived in New York, making it by far the nation's largest city. The Market Revolution had increased the importance of commercial hubs, making cities singularly important and vibrant.

### Immigrants

Immigrants contributed to much of the urban growth. In all, more than 5 million immigrants came to America between 1830 and 1860. The peak period of immigration came in the late 1840s and 1850s, when nearly 1 million Irish came to the United States to escape the potato famine. Many Germans came at this time too, especially in 1848, after a failed revolution in Germany forced many political dissidents to flee. Unlike the Irish, these German immigrants, called **the 48ers**, were educated and often financially well off.

The immigrants arrived in such numbers that they changed the nature of the cities. For example, more than half of all the inhabitants of New York City were foreign-born in 1855. More than a third of Bostonians were. Within the cities, immigrants usually created enclaves of ethnic neighborhoods, starting their own churches, leisure societies, sporting clubs, and charitable organizations.

While most of these new immigrants stayed in the Northeast, some moved to the Midwest. In 1855, for example, more than 60 percent of St. Louis was foreign-born. And many of the 48ers moved to the rural western provinces, where they could farm and where they could vote after just one or two years of residency. These new immigrants largely avoided the South because of its dependence on slave labor, which limited access to jobs.

> **the 48ers**
> Germans who came to the United States in 1848, after a failed revolution in Germany forced many political dissidents to flee

> **"Immigrants from Germany and Scandinavia moved into the Old Northwest to continue the farming life they had left behind in Europe."**

**Nativism**
Political identity that defined an American as someone with an English background who was born in the United States; supporters formulated a racial and ethnic identity that proclaimed the superiority of their group, usually labeled "native Americans"

## Racial and Ethnic Identities

With the arrival of these millions of immigrants, many Americans began to consider what it was that made someone an American. One response was to define an American as someone with an English background who was born in the United States. The most ardent supporters of these views formulated a racial and ethnic identity that differentiated the various immigrant groups and proclaimed the superiority of their own group, usually labeled "native Americans." They chastised the Irish, equating them with black slaves in the South. And they were offended by the German tradition of gathering at beer gardens on Sundays, which these "native Americans" considered a day of worship. The native American movement, sometimes called **Nativism**, moved into politics and into the social and economic life of America as well. Nativists placed restrictions on what fields of business the new immigrants could enter, where they could live, and where they could find work. The influential temperance movement also contained within it a large amount of anti-Irish and anti-German nativism. This was the era when the term *yankee* came to have meaningful social significance, differentiating

Read a song written by a recent Irish immigrant about his struggle to find a job.

between those whose family lineage predated the Revolution and those who arrived later.

Related to this racial and ethnic stereotyping was a brutal form of anti-Catholicism. The Irish were usually willing to work for lower wages than anyone else, which provoked anti-Irish sentiment from workers who felt threatened by this cheap labor force. Because the Irish were identifiable by their Catholicism, mobs, angry at how the nation was changing, sometimes attacked Catholic churches, convents, and priests. In Boston, where large numbers of Irish had settled, anti-Catholic riots broke out regularly. Public education became more visibly influenced by Protestantism in the 1840s and 1850s, prompting many American Catholics to establish alternative parochial schools.

Read a newspaper account of an anti-Catholic riot in Philadelphia.

But identity formation went both ways. Upon their initial arrival, Irish and German immigrants routinely referred to themselves by the town or county from which they came. But after just a short time in America these immigrants began to consciously think of themselves as "Irish" or "German" or "Swedish." A common language was one feature that bound certain groups together. Religion also helped newcomers feel part of a cohesive group, especially for the Irish. Restricted to certain neighborhoods, immigrant groups developed communities that embraced cultural forms harking back to the homeland. For instance, Milwaukee and St. Louis maintain extensive brewing industries today, a legacy of the German immigrants who settled in these cities during the middle of the nineteenth century. Several of these communities also still have *Turnvereine*, or turnvereins, gymnasiums founded in the spirit of the German liberation movement that erupted in 1848.

>> The immigrants arrived in such numbers that they changed the nature of the cities.

>> Milwaukee and St. Louis maintain extensive brewing industries, a legacy of the German immigrants.

## Class Consciousness

In addition to the formation of racial and ethnic identities, the combination of ethnic enclaves, middle-class professions, and the incredible wealth earned by canal builders and others led to highly visible social divisions. While most of the working class lived in small apartments, wealthy Americans were constructing large mansions. By the 1850s, affluent neighborhoods had access to indoor plumbing and gas lighting. The wealthy moved through the cities via horse-drawn cars, and they built neighborhoods away from industrial hubs. And the rich were getting richer: in 1845, almost 80 percent of New York City's individual wealth was owned by just 4 percent of the population. Poorer people had none of these luxuries and were often forced to live in the least desirable neighborhoods, near stockyards or slaughterhouses.

Take a virtual tour of a New York tenement.

Read about Beechwood, built in 1851 in Newport, Rhode Island, for a New York City merchant.

One result of these increasing economic distinctions was the creation of identities associated with being a member of a specific class. Although never totally distinct from ethnic, racial, and religious divisions, there was a growing commonality in how poor people talked, voted, and fought. Much of the lower-class consciousness developed not in the workplace, but in places of leisure, where workers felt most free. It was in these locations that organizers had success developing the political parties of the working class.

## Women and the Middle Class

Along with a slowly forming working-class consciousness, the cities also became crucibles of the middle class, made up mostly of managers, desk workers, and educators. This group of educated middlemen and their families cultivated a middle-class identity between wealth and poverty. Their children slept one to a bed, they owned several pieces of large furniture, and their sons often went to college. Women were central to the formation of the middle class, and indeed, one hallmark of a

**Uncle Tom's Cabin**
Antislavery novel published by Harriet Beecher Stowe in 1852; best-selling book of that period

middle-class family (in contrast to working-class families) was that its women rarely worked outside the home. As work moved out of the home and into factories and commercial centers, the home became idealized as a haven in a heartless world, and middle-class women were expected to cultivate and maintain this idealized perception. In serving as the moral centerpieces of middle-class society, women became the backbone of reform efforts designed to improve the moral character of the nation. Consequently, teaching became the main profession open to middle-class women. Catharine and Mary Beecher headed up efforts to ensure that middle-class women were prepared to teach middle-class children the proper disciplines.

## Leisure

Also during this period, several forms of leisure became commodities to be purchased rather than merely games to play. Although urban Americans still gathered at taverns and competed in physical contests, enterprising merchants developed networks of theaters and professional sports. Boxing, horse racing, track and field, and, in the 1850s, baseball, all evolved into professional sports during this era, attracting large crowds and meriting their own pages in the newspapers. In contrast to male-dominated professional sports, theaters provided social spaces for both men and women.

>> Teaching became the main profession open to middle-class women.

Towns routinely constructed theaters early in their development, featuring plays by Shakespeare and other luminaries. Perhaps the most popular form of entertainment was minstrel shows, featuring white men smeared with burnt cork (to make them look black) who lampooned slave life in the South. The joke was intended to be twofold, making fun of the South for its backward ways and also ridiculing African Americans for being, in the actors' minds, doltish and childlike. The most famous minstrel show featured an actor portraying a slave doing a silly dance and singing a song about "jumping Jim Crow." Despite the slow elimination of slavery in the North after the Revolution, northern racism held firm. The minstrel shows ran concurrently with Shakespeare's plays and other forms of what might today be thought of as high culture. Throughout the 1800s, audience participation was expected at plays, and the interaction between performer and audience made plays a democratic form of entertainment rather than a polished form reserved for the educated elite.

In the private spaces of their homes (and with increased access to indoor gas lighting), Americans also began to read more. The number of newspapers skyrocketed during these years (funded mostly by political parties), and American novelists flourished. Herman Melville, Nathaniel Hawthorne, and Fanny Fern were some of the most popular authors. The best-selling book of the period was Harriet Beecher Stowe's antislavery novel, *Uncle Tom's Cabin; or, Life Among the Lowly* (1852). Stowe and Fanny Fern were part of the growth of a

>> This 1835 watercolor depicts the American minstrel tradition, a tradition that often featured white men in blackface poking fun at the South's backwardness and at African American people in general.

Read reviews and other items about *Uncle Tom's Cabin.*

Read Chapter 1 of *Uncle Tom's Cabin.*

"ladies' literature" in which middle-class women used their leisure time to cultivate what historians have since called a "sentimental culture." Despite the dismissive title, Stowe's *Uncle Tom's Cabin* emerged from the sentimental culture but had far-reaching political ramifications, enlightening people across the country to the conditions of southern slavery. Many of the other works of ladies' literature were less politically engaged, more often propagating middle-class morality than espousing abolitionist ideology.

## Free People of Color

The cities of the North were also home to free people of color, albeit in small numbers. In all, there were about 500,000 free people of color in the United States in 1860, about half of whom lived in northern cities. The remainder lived in border states, especially in and around Baltimore, Maryland. These enclaves were important not so much for provoking nativist opposition (as the Irish did), but because they created lasting institutions that perpetually supported movements for freedom. One institution was the organization of African American freemasons named after its founder, Prince Hall.

The most influential institution for free people of color, though, was the black church. During the Second Great Awakening, a majority of African Americans became Christians. Barred from worshiping in several houses of the Christian religion, black Americans founded the **African Methodist Episcopal (AME) Church** in the 1790s. By 1816, there were enough branches to merit a national organization, and by 1824 the AME Church had several thousand congregants. More than just places of worship, the churches functioned as schools and community centers. Because white people were unwilling to block church development for fear they would be accused of preventing Christian worship, the churches developed a separate sphere of freedom for black Americans.

In the wake of the development of the black church, several African American voluntary groups appeared, promoting abolition, temperance, and other reform causes. Black social fraternities prospered as well. If free blacks could not successfully conquer white racism, they could create institutions that developed a class of black leaders and an ideology of independence. Leaders such as James Forten and Reverend Henry Highland Garnet became political advocates for the abolition of slavery during these years. And the educated members of this society began referring to themselves as "Colored Americans" rather than "Africans" in order to assert their membership in the American nation. Throughout the 1840s and 1850s, these black Americans swayed between optimism and pessimism about the place of black people in America,

> **African Methodist Episcopal (AME) Church** National African American Methodist religious denomination founded by Richard Allen and Absalom Jones in the 1790s; doctrinally Methodist, it was the first major religious denomination in the Western world to originate for sociological, not theological, reasons

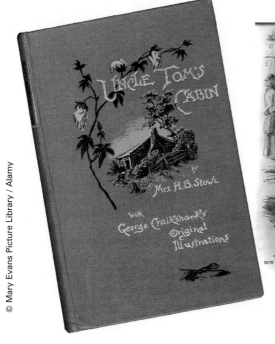

THE SEPARATION OF THE MOTHER AND CHILD.

" The old men of the company, partly by persuasion and partly by force, loosed the poor creature's last despairing hold, and, as they led her off to her new master's waggon, strove to comfort her."—Page 103.

>> *Uncle Tom's Cabin,* with one of George Cruikshank's original illustrations that helped stir reactions to the book's antislavery message.

© Mary Evans Picture Library / Alamy

© The Art Gallery Collection / Alamy

and with the Civil War, their struggle would become central to the nation's political agenda.

## Conclusion

In general, most Americans in the North accommodated the Market Revolution. The wealthy got wealthier, and the middle class created a unique and comfortable life for itself. Immigrants poured in, and, although the working class faced brutal working hours, painstaking labor, and few benefits beyond a paycheck, all they had to do was look south to see that they were much better off than the laborers there, a great majority of whom were enslaved and had no hope of freedom. Indeed, it was around the idea of "free labor" that many northerners, diverse as they were, united. All the symbols of the Market Revolution, including railroads, newspapers, the telegraph, and more, were created by "free laborers," meaning those who were free to work or not to work—in other words, those who were not enslaved. Impoverished as many were, they saw themselves as uniquely distinct from the slave society of the South.

# LO$^2$ Social Life in the Cotton South

Between 1830 and 1860, southerners experienced dramatically different developments than northerners. In every way, cotton became king. It constituted nearly half of the exports of the entire nation, and southerners knew that they could get rich if they could succeed as cotton farmers. But growing cotton required slaves and land, so southerners brought slaves and slavery with them into the southwestern territories of the United States. This ended any potential talk of gradual emancipation during this period. Furthermore, southerners had little need for big cities, and, without jobs to offer, they did not attract immigrants in the same numbers as the North. This was the period when southerners solidified their plantation economy and developed a vehement defense of it—one based on the superiority of the white race.

When we think of the antebellum South, we are prone to think of images culled from the novel and film *Gone with the Wind*, which portrayed the leisurely lifestyle of a landed and cultured white elite being served by willing and subservient black slaves. But three facts are vital in understanding how the actual prewar South contrasted with this image (see "The reasons why . . ." box on page 209).

## Southern White Society

While the North was notable for distinctions between the countryside and the city, there were no similar complexities in southern society, because there were so few cities. White southern society was stratified between yeoman farmers and wealthy planters. A group of landless white people ranked below the farmers (but above slaves), mostly working as laborers on farms or as frontiersmen settling the Southwest. But most white southerners were either wealthy planters or yeoman farmers.

### The Planters

The planters viewed themselves as paternalistic aristocrats managing preindustrial fiefdoms. They were deeply involved in national and international markets (for instance, the development of the telegraph in 1845 allowed them to monitor cotton prices in England). But they usually preferred to keep the marketplace at a distance. They spent their summers abroad and sent their children to be educated

>> The vision of the antebellum South presented in *Gone with the Wind* (1939) correctly identifies only a tiny percentage of southerners living during the era.

There are three main reasons why popular images of the antebellum South as portrayed in venues like *Gone with the Wind* are misleading:

***Most white Southerners did not own slaves.*** First, of the 8 million southern white people, only 338,000 owned slaves, meaning that a huge majority of southern white people had no direct connection to slavery. Most were isolated yeoman farmers seeking self-sufficiency.

***Most slaveowners owned few slaves.*** Second, of those 338,000 slave owners, most owned very few slaves. More than 60 percent of slave owners owned only five or fewer slaves, and only 3 percent owned twenty or more slaves.

***But most slaves lived on plantations.*** Finally, while a vast majority of southern white people had no connection to a plantation, the majority of slaves did. Indeed, the few massive plantations housed as many as half of all the slaves in the region. As such, plantations were vital in the development of a unique slave culture. But the wealthy plantation life of *Gone with the Wind* was lived by only a very small minority of white southerners.

in Europe and at the Ivy League colleges in the North. The planters also often entered politics, considering themselves the natural leaders of society. Financially and politically powerful, the planter class fought all attempts to make their society more democratic. It resisted funding public education through taxation and defeated similar attempts to create internal improvements that would have invited more commerce and industry to the South. Content with the society they had created, southern planters resisted change unless it could earn them greater profits.

© North Wind Picture Archives/Alamy

>> Content with the society they had created, southern planters resisted change unless it could earn them greater profits.

## Yeoman Farmers

Only a tiny minority of white southerners were planters; the majority were yeoman farmers. Yeoman farmers were largely self-sufficient, living with their families on remote farms or in small towns, and missing out on much of the Market Revolution. They were usually forced onto less desirable plots of land, and, most of the time, these farmers used most of their land to plant cotton and the rest to grow crops needed by the household. They used the money earned from cotton to purchase items that could not be grown in southern soil, such as coffee.

Most yeoman farmers remained largely isolated from markets. A few acquired large plots, bought slaves, and became wealthy, but this was rare. Social mobility was limited in the antebellum South, and when it did occur, it mostly pushed people downward. Thus, at some point during their lives, nearly one-quarter of white southerners were landless and thus forced to search for work on someone else's farm or push west in search of work. With few public schools, most yeoman farmers were also uneducated. (At least 20 percent of white adult southerners could not read.) Consumed by the work of their farms, they remained isolated in their culture, which was centered on family, church, and region.

## The Defense of Slavery

No matter what their station in society, nearly all white southerners were advocates of slavery. For the planters, this was an easy decision: slavery, while expensive to maintain, was profitable, and profits and social norms overcame any moral difficulties.

Read more about *The Confessions of Nat Turner.*

 Read Harriet Ann Jacobs's account of life in the South after Nat Turner's rebellion.

For yeoman farmers and landless white people, the existence of slavery ensured that there was always a class of people below them socially, that there was always one rung farther down the ladder. The presence of slaves kept alive their hopes that maybe one day they too might own slaves and become wealthy.

## Nat Turner

In the 1830s and 1840s, white southerners developed a more militant defense of slavery. In doing so, they were responding to one of the most violent slave revolts in American history. In 1831, Nat Turner, a Christian preacher, led a group of slaves through the Virginia countryside, brutally murdering sixty white people of both sexes and all ages during a two-day stretch. Turner's plan was to raise an army of freed slaves and lead an insurrection against the southern white planters. The white response was overwhelming and harsh. White militiamen attacked the group associated with Turner, but also indiscriminately killed slaves not involved in the insurrection. Perhaps more than two hundred slaves were killed in retaliation. Turner was eventually captured and hanged, but not before being interviewed by southern physician Thomas R. Gray, who published the interview as *The Confessions of Nat Turner.* The book sold well from its first publication, and it is one of the most haunting tales of American slavery.

> 66 The calm, deliberate composure with which he spoke of his late deeds and intentions, the expression of his fiend-like face when excited by enthusiasm; still bearing the stains of the blood of helpless innocence about him; clothed with rags and covered with chains, yet daring to raise his manacled hands to heaven; with a spirit soaring above the attributes of man, I looked on him and my blood curdled in my veins. 99
> —*Thomas R. Gray,* The Confessions of Nat Turner

## Legal Restrictions

Besides the violent damage done to black bodies, Nat Turner's insurrection also caused white southerners to pass further laws restricting black freedoms. Many states prohibited slave literacy. Others required all slave meetings to be supervised by whites. Slave behavior was monitored. In 1832, the Virginia legislature developed a plan that would simultaneously emancipate its slaves gradually and then deport them all to Africa. The plan did not pass, and no other open discussion of emancipation ever occurred in the South until the Civil War.

## A Sterner Defense

Beyond punitive and legal ramifications, the reaction to Nat Turner stimulated a change in the way slavery was understood in the South. In this period, southern writers developed a defense of slavery that suggested that slavery was good for both races, because black people were not equipped to take care of themselves and needed white, paternalistic masters to protect them. White slaveholders began to cite biblical references to slavery, suggesting that the institution was somehow sanctioned by God. Thomas R. Dew, George Fitzhugh, and J. D. B. DuBow all advocated the benefits of slavery in widely read publications. Through them, the South's understanding of slavery transitioned from being a "necessary evil" (as it was conceived during the revolutionary period) to being a "positive good."

>> Although photographed in 1940, this homestead looks much the same as a yeoman farmer's home would have appeared in the South before the Civil War.

## Slave Society

Certainly no slave would agree with the notion that slavery was a positive good. Life for slaves was arduous, a relentless grind of forced labor in uncertain social conditions, shadowed by the constant threat of abuse. Most slaves were field hands growing sugar, rice, tobacco, and especially cotton. Some were house servants who cooked and cleaned for their masters and helped take care of their children. Some were skilled artisans, such as blacksmiths, carpenters, or ironworkers. A few worked as longshoremen or shipbuilders in port cities such as New Orleans, Louisiana, and Charleston, South Carolina. Yet all were regarded as property, to be bought, sold, or bartered at the whim of their owners.

The law did not protect slave families. Husbands and wives, as well as parents and children, could be separated from each other permanently, without notice. Although there were official limits on the treatment of slaves (the murder or unjustifiable mutilation of slaves was illegal in most states, and state laws set minimum standards for the amount of food, clothing, and shelter that must be provided for slaves), such laws were unenforceable because slaves were prohibited from taking their masters to court.

Despite severely restricting the rights of slaves, many slave masters believed it was in their best interest to treat slaves decently—as long as the slaves remained obedient. Masters were generally profit-minded men who understood that healthy laborers were more productive than those who were sick or abused.

Owners also recognized that healthy slaves were more likely to produce healthy offspring. Slave reproduction mattered to plantation owners because the

United States had outlawed participation in the international slave trade in 1808. While Caribbean slaveholders frequently worked slaves to death only to replace them with new imports, this was impossible in the United States. Nevertheless, the fact that slaveholders had an interest in keeping their slaves alive did not mean that slaves were treated humanely in the antebellum South.

## Work

The work conditions endured by slaves were as varied as the tasks they performed, but plantation labor was usually organized in one of two ways. The first was the **gang system**. Under this system, masters organized slaves into groups of twenty to

>> A cartoon image revealing the idealized view of slavery that developed in the 1830s and 1840s. The caption reads:

Slaves: God bless you massa! you feed and clothe us. When we are sick you nurse us, and when too old to work, you provide for us!

Master: These poor creatures are a sacred legacy from my ancestors and while a dollar is left me, nothing shall be spared to increase their comfort and happiness.

**slavedriver**
Supervisor or overseer of slave labor, usually employed on a cotton plantation

**task system**
Work arrangement under which slaves were assigned a specific set of tasks to accomplish each day; often employed on rice plantations and in domestic service situations

twenty-five workers, supervised by a white overseer or a black **slavedriver**. This method of organizing labor was most commonly used on cotton plantations. During the major seasons of cotton cultivation, slaves labored in the fields for up to sixteen hours a day. Although most masters, in keeping with their Christian beliefs, gave their slaves Sundays off and required only a half-day of work on Saturday, working under the gang system was backbreaking.

The second major labor system was the **task system**. As the name suggests, this system assigned each slave a specific set of tasks to accomplish each day. Once slaves had accomplished these tasks, their time was largely their own. The task system was common on rice plantations, because rice did not require the constant care and toil that cotton did. Slaves working as domestic servants also commonly labored under the task system. Although the task system often gave slaves more freedom, slaveholders frequently set unrealistic expectations for slaves and then punished them for failing to finish their work.

Some slaves did not work in either of these two systems. Instead, they had special arrangements that allowed them an unusual amount of freedom. This was especially common among slaves living in the cities. Although urbanization did not occur as quickly as it had in the North, slave states had a small number of cities, including Baltimore, Richmond, Charleston, Mobile, and New Orleans. Each city housed large slave populations, and, even though urban slaves remained the property of their masters, owners could not exercise complete authority over their slaves in the city. For instance, a skilled slave carpenter needed the freedom to move about the city to reach job sites. Craftsmen, such as blacksmiths or jewelers, often worked independently, sharing a portion of their earnings with their master. As these slaves' experiences attest, slavery was an adaptable economic institution, working in a variety of agrarian and urban settings.

## Quarters

Despite the wide variety of possible slaving conditions, most slaves were owned by planters who lived on large plantations. In these conditions, most slaves lived in slave quarters, defined as a group of cabins set away from the master's home. The cabins were usually organized around families, who tended personal gardens and raised their own animals. On the largest plantations, slave quarters were significant-sized communities with ample freedom away from the watchful eye of the master.

## Community

In slave quarters, slaves created a culture far removed from that dictated by white southerners. From the beginning, Africans came to America with their own cultures, and the experience of slavery did not completely obliterate those cultures. The influence of African cultures was especially strong in the music, dancing, and verbal expressions that slaves used in their everyday lives and religious ceremonies.

Family lay at the center of slave culture. Although masters retained the right to separate spouses, siblings, parents, and children from each other, slaves remained determined to preserve a sense of family. Slave marriages were not legally recognized, but slaves entered marital unions with great joy and celebration. Some marriages were made by obtaining the master's verbal consent.

When possible, slaves maintained traditional nuclear families with a father, a mother, and children living together. Within this family unit, men and women followed traditional gender roles, although they worked side by side, doing the same work in the fields. At home, women usually did the indoor work, such as cooking, cleaning, sewing, and raising children, while men did chores outside the home, like hauling

> "I heard them [slaves] get up with a powerful force of spirit, clapping they hands and walking around the place. They'd shout, 'I got the glory. I got the old time religion in my heart.'"
> —*Mose Hursey, former slave from Red River County, Texas*

>> An unusual sight—five generations of a slave family, together, on Smith's Plantation, Beaufort, South Carolina, 1862.

 Learn more about slave religion.

 Research slave religion further.

maintained belief in benevolent spirits and in the practice of conjuring or foreseeing the future. Theirs was a jubilant faith, promising deliverance. Religious services in slave quarters included dancing, singing, and clapping. Spirituals were the most significant form of African American music developed during this period. For obvious reasons, the biblical lessons slaves emphasized were not those that commanded obedience and docility, but those that inspired hope for the future. The God they worshiped was one who would redeem the downtrodden and lift them up to heaven on Judgment Day. The master might be rich and powerful in this life, but many slaves took solace in the conviction that they would attain glory in the next one.

## Resistance and Revolt

Although several slave revolts are well remembered today, it is worth wondering why there were not more of them. Partly the answer has to do with the harsh reaction southern whites had after slave revolts. Still, the low number of slave revolts in American history should not be interpreted as a lack of resistance on the part of American slaves. Most slaves who wanted to buck the system simply found less overt ways of insulting or irritating their masters, especially considering that punishments for revolt were so severe. Slaves broke tools and machinery in order to slow production. Some feigned illness and injury to avoid work. Still others stole goods from their master to sell or trade for other goods. Even in their everyday demeanor, slaves occasionally outsmarted their owners. They could pretend to be ignorant and happy, as whites believed them to be, and use white stereotypes of them as a way to escape work. For example, intelligent slaves often faked confusion to avoid being assigned certain tasks or to explain why work was not completed. They were resisting their condition in a subtle, undetectable manner.

 Read an excerpt from *Narrative of the Life of Frederick Douglass*.

 Read other slave narratives.

 Take an interactive journey on the Underground Railroad.

water and gathering wood. Although premarital sex was common in slave quarters, at some point every slave was expected to choose a mate and settle down. Maintaining a two-parent family was not within their control, however. Whenever it was convenient or profitable, many masters sold off married slaves, leaving mates behind. One estimate suggests that, in the four decades preceding the Civil War, around 600,000 slave husbands and wives were separated from each other in this way.

Religion served as another pillar of slave culture. Most slaves arrived in America holding some form of West African religious belief. They usually believed in a Supreme God or Creator, as well as in the existence of a number of lesser gods. During the colonial period most slaves continued to practice their native religions, and slave owners did little to introduce their slaves to Christianity, fearing that if slaves became Christians they would have to be freed.

During the Second Great Awakening, however, most slaves became Christians. And despite the controlling efforts of the masters, slaves formed their own ideas about Christianity, melding their native practices with Christian beliefs. Many slaves also

Those who wanted to resist white authority in more dramatic fashion, but did not want to take the chance of organizing widespread revolts, had another option. They ran away. However, few slaves found permanent freedom in this way, especially if they were trying to flee states in the Deep South, defined as Alabama, Georgia, Louisiana, Mississippi, and South Carolina. Southerners organized slave patrols to watch for

 Library of Congress, Prints & Photographs Division, LC-B8171-152-A

runaways and used hunting dogs to track escaped slaves. Slave owners also used newspapers to alert whites across the South to be on the lookout for certain runaways. Because so few southern blacks were free (only about 8 percent), slaves on the run were easily sighted.

Despite the odds, many slaves did flee, and a few found permanent freedom. Some runaways found help from the **Underground Railroad**, defined as a network of men and women (white and black) who opposed slavery, sheltered runaway slaves, and expedited their journey to freedom. One slave who successfully escaped bondage and settled in the North was Frederick Douglass. After his escape, Douglass became one of the foremost figures in the abolition movement. He wrote about his experiences in his autobiography, *Narrative of the Life of Frederick Douglass* (1845), which traces his personal journey from slavery to freedom.

# And in the end . . .

By the 1830s, the North and the South had begun to develop divergent societies. The Market Revolution and slavery served as obvious battle lines. And indeed, these two societies were growing increasingly at odds with one another, both politically and culturally. For instance, although most northerners did not favor abolition, they generally agreed that slavery contradicted the way of life that the Market Revolution was bringing about, one that underscored the presence and importance of labor that was free to choose its manner and place of employment. The North was also becoming increasingly urbanized and industrialized, with a large population of landless (often immigrant) workers.

Southerners, meanwhile, had begun to articulate the concept that slavery was not shameful, but essential to the protection and improvement of the black race. The region remained a predominantly agrarian society that depended on slave labor for the cultivation of its most profitable crop, cotton. Many in the South viewed the growth of cities and commerce in the North as a move away from the values on which the country had been founded and toward materialism and greed. Northerners, in turn, tended to view the South as a region stuck in the past, venerating the kind of class system and aristocracy against which the revolutionary patriots had rebelled decades earlier.

In addition, the two regions had widely differing attitudes toward the role of the federal government. The North depended on the high tariffs of the American System to protect its growing manufacturing concerns, and the government used the income from the tariffs to finance the roads, canals, and other internal improvements that northerners needed to bring goods to market. Southerners opposed high tariffs. They did not need tariffs to

© iStockphoto.com/Rick Rhay

>> Runaways were told that they could recognize a "safe house," a stop on the Underground Railroad, by a lantern hung on its hitching post.

| What else was happening . . . | |
|---|---|
| 1848 | Revolutions occur throughout Europe protesting industrial disorder and aristocratic rule. Most fail. |
| 1848 | Karl Marx and Friedrich Engels publish *The Communist Manifesto*. |
| 1849 | The first safety pin is patented. |
| 1850 | Beer is first sold in glass bottles. Before that, patrons had their beer poured into a bucket or cup that they brought with them. |
| 1857 | The words and music to "Jingle Bells" are registered, under the title "One Horse Open Sleigh"—which didn't stick. |
| 1857 | Elisha Graves Otis demonstrates his passenger safety elevator at the Crystal Palace Exposition in New York by cutting the elevator's cables as it ascends a 300-foot tower. |

protect their cotton production, so tariffs accomplished nothing for southerners beyond raising the cost of the imported goods they wanted to purchase.

Until the 1830s, most northerners had been content to tolerate slavery outside their own state borders but, as the nation expanded geographically, Americans were repeatedly forced to confront the issue. Should slavery be allowed to move west? Over the next few decades, the question of whether or not slavery would be allowed into new western territories reappeared continually, and conflict over this question would lead to sectional tensions, political conflicts, and eventually, a civil war. What made the issue so pervasive was the continued move to the West, which had a culture and society all its own. This continued move westward is the subject of the next chapter.

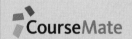

Visit the CourseMate website at www.cengagebrain.com for additional study tools and review materials for this chapter.

# CHAPTER 13

# *The* Continued Move West

## Learning Outcomes

*After reading this chapter, you should be able to do the following:*

**LO**[1]   Describe the conquest and development of the West between 1820 and 1850 by white Americans.

**LO**[2]   Explain how the expansionist spirit in the West led to political conflict at home as well as conflict with Mexico, even as it gave the United States its modern boundaries.

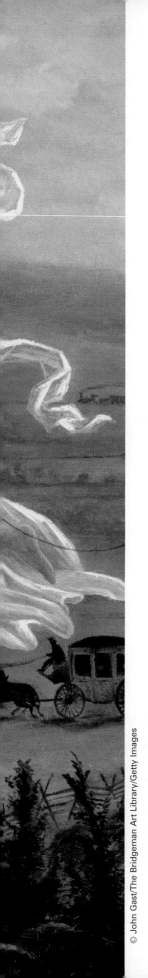

© John Gast/The Bridgeman Art Library/Getty Images

> **"*The 'opening' of the frontier kept alive the democratic promise that poor but free men could make it on their own.*"**

Beginning in the 1820s, white Americans began settling west of the Mississippi River for the first time. They did so for a variety of reasons, the three foremost being (1) to flee religious persecution, (2) to pursue greater social freedom, and (3), most often, to seek riches.

Between the 1820s and 1860, Americans' westward migration across the Mississippi occurred in two general phases. The first phase, which lasted from the 1820s to 1844, saw Americans move west without their government's consent or decree; they moved mostly for personal reasons. The second phase of westward migration began in 1844, after the election of President James K. Polk, an active evangelist for American expansion. On his watch, the American nation doubled in size. This second, deeply nationalistic phase was promoted under the banner of manifest destiny, the idea that America was destined by God to conquer North America and spread American civilization far and wide. The artist John Gast captured the image perfectly (to your left), showing an angel of the Lord carrying a school book (representing education and civilization) and telegraph wires (representing the Market Revolution) as she guides white Americans west, all while Indians back away, cowering under the power of God's divine plan. The reality of America's westward expansion was of course much more complicated, but the idea of "manifest destiny" was a powerful propellant pushing white Americans west.

The continued westward movement of Americans had at least four significant consequences: (1) the further decimation of Native America; (2) the continued expansion of the Market Revolution; (3) the "opening" of the frontier, which kept alive the democratic promise that poor but free men could make it on their own instead of subjugating themselves to capitalist chieftains; and (4) perhaps most important, the explosion of the slavery issue onto the American political stage. After decades of cobbled-together political compromises, the question of whether slavery would be allowed in the new territories of the West helped lead to a political breakdown that ignited the Civil War. But, first, to the great westward expansion between the 1820s and 1860.

## LO¹ Western Conquest and Development, 1820–1844

Americans developed four unique territories in the West between 1820 and 1844: Texas, Oregon, Utah, and California. Each territory was developed for a different reason, and each bore the imprint of its initial conquest long after the territory was settled.

## Texas

Before the late 1840s, the most popular destination of westward migrants was Texas. It was a Spanish colony until 1821, when it became part of the newly independent nation of Mexico. Americans seeking land for growing cotton had been hesitant to settle in Texas while it was a Spanish colony. But the new nation of Mexico seemed much less powerful than Spain, and Americans in the 1820s seized their chance to settle in Texas. During that decade, about 20,000 Americans streamed into the province, rapidly outnumbering the 5,000 Mexicans who were living there. A few Anglo-Americans assimilated to Mexican culture, but most chose not to. The new settlers continued to speak English, created separate schools, and conducted most of their trade with the United States. American cotton planters brought slaves along with them, ignoring Mexico's 1829 abolition of slavery.

By 1830, the Mexican government became worried that it was losing control of Texas. Objecting to the persistence of slavery there, it sought to curtail U.S. immigration to the region. It raised taxes there, built new military posts, and prohibited further American settlement. But it was too late. The floodgates had opened, and Americans, both free and enslaved, continued to pour into the province. Predictably, the new regulations frustrated the American immigrants, who eventually demanded autonomy from Mexican rule. When Mexico resisted, bitter conflict was destined to erupt.

### Mexican-American Hostilities

Mexico had other problems, though. Between 1829 and 1834, Mexico suffered a series of internal political coups, leading up to General Antonio López de Santa Anna's seizing power in Mexico City. He abolished the Mexican constitution and declared himself absolute dictator. He also intended to rein in Texas's autonomy. Led by Stephen F. Austin and William B. Travis, and with Sam Houston as commander-in-chief of the new Texas army, Texans rebelled, declaring their independence and creating an interim government. Santa Anna refused to tolerate this insurrection, and in 1836, he led 5,000 troops to San Antonio, attacking the American rebels at an abandoned mission called the Alamo. Some 187 Texans, including western pioneer legends Davy Crockett and James Bowie, were killed during the battle. But

before they lost the Alamo, the Texans had killed between 1,200 and 1,600 Mexican troops. Their stand became a source of inspiration for the Texas military, which continued to "remember the Alamo" during later battles.

Learn more about the battle of the Alamo.

### A Victory for Texas . . . and for Slavery

Two months later, Texans scored the decisive victory over Santa Anna when Sam Houston surprised the Mexican forces at San Jacinto, near today's city of Houston. Santa Anna himself was captured (while napping in his slippers), and the Texans forced him to sign treaties guaranteeing Texan independence. Soon after this victory, Texas drew up a new constitution that guaranteed its white citizens the right to own slaves and prohibited free black people from immigrating to the new nation of Texas. Texans formally petitioned the United States for immediate annexation. Many northern members of Congress feared that admitting Texas as a slave state would disrupt the Compromise of 1820, which had crafted

>> **The Alamo.**

© iStockphoto.com/Stephen Finn

a delicate balance between slave and free states. American leaders therefore rebuffed the appeals for annexation and left the new Texas Republic to make its own way as an independent nation. Despite this temporary rebuff (Texas would become an official part of the Union in 1845), settlers continued to flood into Texas, most often to develop cotton farms.

## Oregon and the Oregon Trail

The next region colonized by American settlers was Oregon. The U.S. government had asserted its sovereignty over Oregon ever since maritime merchant Robert Gray's expedition to the region in 1792, which helped inspire Jefferson to send Lewis and Clark on their expedition. But there were also prior British, Spanish, and Russian claims on the territory. In the early 1800s, as the Oregon fur-trade competition increased, American diplomats took steps to ensure that their merchants would not be excluded from trading in the region. Before 1830, only a few American citizens (usually Protestant missionaries) ventured into distant Oregon, because most of it was

>> A new route through the Rockies, called the Oregon Trail.

controlled by Native American tribes and British fur-trading companies.

As the area's beaver population dwindled, the British slowly withdrew. Their departure left the territory open to settlement, and in the 1830s and 1840s American settlers began to move into Oregon's Willamette River valley. Between 1842 and 1845, the number of Americans in Oregon increased tenfold, from about 500 to about 5,000.

### New Settlements and Indian Violence

Predictably, as the new settlements spread throughout the valley, tensions between Indians and settlers increased. Indians felt crowded, and many were dying from diseases imported by American settlers. In 1847, discontent erupted into violence when a group of Cayuse Indians killed fourteen settlers, including a white doctor who had been treating infectious diseases in white people but refused to treat Indians. The violent attack prompted outrage in Washington, D.C., and provoked Congress to establish more direct control over Oregon by organizing it as a formal American territory.

### Oregon Fever

Although violence persisted between Indians and American settlers, increased government control prompted a surge of new arrivals. After the opening in the early 1840s of a new route through the Rockies, called the Oregon Trail, more and more Americans moved to the territory. They farmed in the bountiful valley, and by 1850 there were 12,000 American inhabitants (see Map 13.1, page 221).

## Utah and the Mormons

Most American settlers in Texas and Oregon moved for economic reasons, but another group—the Mormons—went west seeking a haven from religious persecution. The Mormons found refuge in the area around the Great Salt Lake, in what would become the state of Utah.

### Joseph Smith and the Origins of Mormonism

In 1830, Joseph Smith organized a new religion called the Church of Jesus Christ of Latter-day Saints, known colloquially as the Mormons. Like other new religious communities founded during the Second Great Awakening, Mormonism emphasized a direct and ecstatic connection with God. It attracted people who both believed in Joseph Smith's divine visions and who wanted to renounce the sinfulness and social disorder they saw all around them. Mormonism gained converts by the thousands. But many Christians viewed Mormons with suspicion because of their community's isolated ways and curious practices, such as polygamy. Joseph Smith, for instance, was reputed to have had thirty-four wives between the ages of fourteen and sixty. Each time tension grew with neighboring "gentiles," the Mormons moved their headquarters, first from New York to Ohio, then to several locations in Missouri. In 1838, they settled in Commerce, Illinois, which they renamed "Nauvoo" (as it is known today).

For five years, the Mormon community grew and prospered in Nauvoo. But in 1844 trouble erupted after a local newspaper, fearful of Smith's growing power, published an exposé of the polygamy practiced by Smith and other Mormon men. As the mayor of Nauvoo and the head of its court and its militia, Smith demanded that the newspaper be suppressed. During the controversy, non-Mormons grew increasingly hostile toward the religion and appealed to state authorities to help drive the Mormons out. Soon after, Joseph Smith and his brother Hyrum were arrested for treason, and on June 27, 1844, a lynch mob entered the jail where the men were being held and shot them both dead. In 1845, in what was referred to as "the Mormon War in Illinois," Mormon opponents torched more than two hundred Mormon-owned buildings in Nauvoo. Rumors surfaced that the federal government was planning a raid, and the Nauvoo city charter was revoked. The Mormons, now led by Smith's successor Brigham Young, negotiated a truce so that they could leave Illinois peacefully.

## Brigham Young

From published journals celebrating the western frontier, Young learned of an inland sea—the Great Salt Lake—that lay north of New Mexico. Although surrounded by inhospitable deserts and mountains, the land immediately next to the lake seemed ideal for settlement. To Young, the area also appeared sufficiently remote to guarantee that the Mormons would not encounter persecution. In addition, Utah was still technically under Mexican control and therefore outside U.S. jurisdiction. This meant that the Mormons could function independently, following their own laws and customs. They set out to find their promised land on what came to be known as the Mormon Trek (see Map 13.1).

## To Utah

A dynamic leader, Young had little difficulty persuading most of his followers that the Great Salt

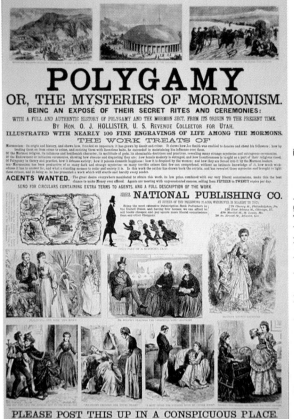

>> Joseph Smith was reputed to have had thirty-four wives between the ages of fourteen and sixty, prompting responses such as this anti-Mormon poster advertising a book critical of *Polygamy or, the Mysteries of Mormonism.*

Lake area would be their home. In 1847 and 1848, thousands of Mormons settled in the Salt Lake basin. There they developed an irrigation system, which expanded their acreage of arable land, and laid the foundation for today's Salt Lake City.

But the Mormon dream of settling beyond the reach of the U.S. government did not last long. The United States won control of Utah in February 1848 as part of the settlement of the Mexican-American War, thus continuing the contentious relationship between Mormons and the federal government for the next fifty years. From 1856 to 1858, relations soured over the issue of who controlled the Utah territory, leading to a brief "Utah War." One notable episode of this conflict was the Mountain Meadows massacre of 1857. In the massacre, more than one hundred California-bound migrants from Arkansas were slaughtered by a collection of Mormon militiamen and Paiute Indians, both of whom feared the continued presence of American settlers in their territory.

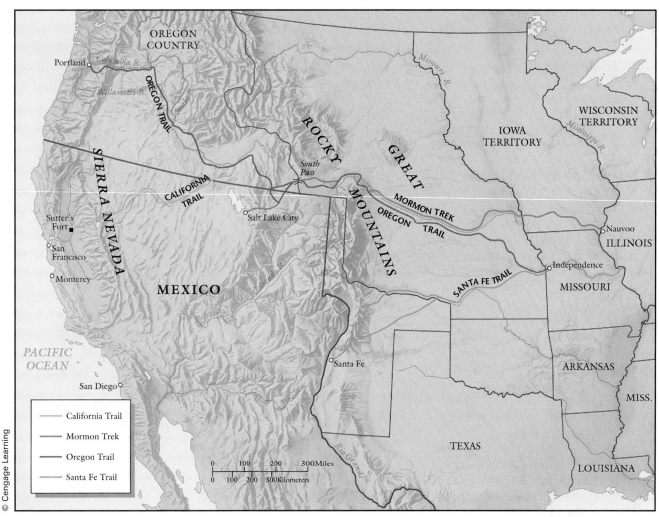

Map 13.1. Overland Trails, 1846

## California: Ranches and Gold

Still farther west, American citizens were beginning to settle the Mexican state of Alta California. In the early 1840s, new Republican leaders awarded huge land grants in California to a handful of its American citizens and retired Mexican soldiers. Word of California's bountiful, fertile lands spread quickly. With the opening of the Oregon Trail and its offshoot, the California Trail (Map 13.1), more and more Americans made their way to the distant Mexican state. By early 1846, about 800 Americans and about 8,000 to 12,000 *californios* lived there.

This all changed in January 1848, when gold was discovered along California's American River. Emigration to California suddenly exploded. In 1849, an estimated 80,000 fortune hunters reached California, half of them Americans, the rest immigrants from across the globe. For instance, gold was the key attraction for numerous Chinese immigrants, beginning a long-standing Chinese presence in the West. Regardless of country of origin, though, most of the miners were young, unmarried men who had no intention of settling in California; they wanted to get rich and return home. But whether or not mines "proved out" and produced the riches expected of them, many of these "forty-niners" ended up staying in California. They set up temporary businesses, such as saloons, stores, and brothels, which soon surrounded the hastily erected shacks of mining camps. They also treated with scorn the surrounding Indian tribes, viewing them as obstacles

 View a map of California Gold Country.

 Read a letter from a gold miner in Placerville, California.

to their riches. Once miners had exhausted the gold supply, they abandoned the area, looking for the next profitable mine. Most of the booming settlements of the gold-rush days later decayed into ghost towns.

## Tribal Conflicts

No matter where Americans went, they moved onto lands claimed by other parties. While Mexicans in Texas and British settlers in Oregon suffered from the American expansion, no group was more dislocated than Indians. Most dramatically, the hunters of the Western Plains—the Arapahoe, Blackfoot, Cheyenne, Kiowa, and Sioux Indians—depended on the migratory hunting of buffalo for food. White settlers moving through buffalo ranges disrupted the natural hunting process, threatening the livelihood of these tribes. The interference eventually prompted the Plains Indians (as these tribes are collectively called) to attack white pioneers on the emigrant trails, sparking many bloody battles. As for white settlers during the colonial era in New England and Virginia, conflict with the tribes of Native America was part of daily life for the westward bound.

The U.S. government's response to this increased Indian conflict was typical: as the number of white settlers increased, the U.S. government continued

>> In 1849, an estimated 80,000 fortune hunters from around the world ventured to California in search of gold.

to cajole or force Native Americans into giving up their land. In the 1851 **Fort Laramie Treaty** with Plains Indian tribes, the U.S. government agreed to make cash restitution for disruptions to the buf-

>> "There is a good deal of sin & wickedness going on here, Stealing, lying, Swearing, Drinking, Gambling & murdering. . . . Almost every public House is a place for Gambling. . . . Men make & lose thousands in a night, & frequently small boys will go up & bet $5 or 10—& if they lose all, go the next day & dig more. We are trying to get laws here to regulate things but it will be very difficult to get them executed." —S. Shufelt, gold miner

Read the Fort Laramie Treaty.

Read about some of the most famous mountain men.

falo grounds, while tribal leaders in turn agreed not to attack the large number of settlers moving through the area. But in 1854 yet another transportation corridor for white pioneers was carved out of land that was once set aside as Indian territory. Following the development of this new route, Indian tribes were relocated once again. As they were being shuffled from one area to another, the creation of a defined system of reservations for Native Americans was not far off.

> "... a very companionable man. In person he was over six feet tall, spare, straight as an arrow, agile, rawboned and of powerful frame, eyes gray, hair brown and abundant even in old age, expression mild and manners agreeable. He was hospitable and generous, and was always trusted and respected."
>
> —*Biographer Grenville Dodge, on mountain man James "Old Gabe" Bridger*

these years, coloring the image of the West as a dangerous and exciting place. Each of these mountain men married Native American women, but they also worked as scouts for the U.S. Army, which over time participated in the ongoing encroachment of Indian lands. And Beckwourth is today celebrated as one of the key African American mountain men of the Old West.

## Mountain Men

In addition to new territories, from the 1820s to the 1840s a new breed of Americans emerged. These so-called mountain men roamed the Rocky Mountains and the various trails carved out by settlers traveling across the harsh landscape. Mountain men were frequently employed as trappers, working for one of the fur companies that bought and sold beaver pelts. But their main occupation was exploration. Men like Jim Bridger, James Beckwourth, and Christopher "Kit" Carson are some of the best-known mountain men. Their names are largely remembered in either the names of mountain passes and Rocky Mountain locales or in the folklore of the West that blossomed during

>> **James "Old Gabe" Bridger, from a photograph.**

## Conclusion

Western settlement complicated matters reaching far beyond the lives of the settlers themselves. The haphazard manner in which westward movement took place forced politicians in the East to bring some form of governing order to the West. And independent-minded settlers, accustomed to managing their own affairs, did not welcome the imposition of eastern ideals. Friction was inevitable. Moreover, by taking responsibility for the actions of white settlers—particularly the rebels in Texas and the pioneers traversing Native American territories—government officials committed themselves to defending, and defining the course of, westward expansion. This led to westward expansion's second phase.

## LO² The Expansionist Spirit Rebounds

During the 1840s, America's official interest in acquiring western territory surged for five principal reasons (see "The reasons why ..." box). These arguments motivated the

## { *The reasons why . . .* }

There were five reasons why America's official interest in westward expansion surged in the 1840s:

**Route to China?** The Market Revolution created a desire to have access to the Pacific Ocean and thus to the fabled Chinese and other Asian markets. (Americans were already establishing connections in Hawaii.)

**Governmental interest.** The government had targeted land that it wanted and was willing to fight for.

**Politically popular.** Political leaders discovered that proposals to annex new lands were popular with American voters, despite the festering question of whether to allow slavery there.

**A new beginning.** The financial Panic of 1837 led many Americans to desire going west in order to start their lives over.

**National ambition.** The U.S. government sought a rapid expansion of its power, which meant owning as much land as foreign powers, if not more.

American government to aggressively resume the game of territorial expansion. Journalists and others who favored national expansion embraced an ideology justifying the sometimes brutal methods used to expand American civilization: manifest destiny.

## Texas and the Rise of James K. Polk

Because of Texas's substantial number of American settlers, annexing it was at the top of the U.S. government's agenda. But the task proved arduous.

### Texas and Slavery

The Texas Republic, upon winning its independence from Mexico in 1836, had already applied to become a U.S. state. But the Texas constitution guaranteed the perpetuation of slavery, so if Texas entered the Union, it would be as a slave state. President Andrew Jackson knew that this would disturb the balance in the Senate between free and slave states established by the Compromise of 1820. Moreover, U.S. annexation of Texas would surely start a war with Mexico, which had never recognized Texan independence and therefore still claimed Texas as a part of Mexican territory.

Jackson also refused to annex the Texas Republic because the 1836 presidential election was pending, and he badly wanted Vice President Martin Van Buren to succeed him. Annexing Texas might infuriate northern voters (because of the slavery issue), and Jackson was not willing to risk Van Buren's loss. Van Buren, who did win the election and served as president from 1837 to 1841, avoided discussions of Texas altogether during his campaign. In response to this official silence, Texans suspended all efforts to gain admittance to the Union and focused on developing their own political and economic institutions.

During the decade following Van Buren's election, the dilemma of whether to annex Texas loomed in the shadows of American politics. Foreign policy issues in the 1840s forced it back into the limelight. Britain considered establishing relations with the independent Texas to gain a stronger hold in North America. This prospect alarmed many Americans, and in 1843 Secretary of State John C. Calhoun signed a treaty with Texas that would admit it to the Union. President John Tyler (who became president in April 1841) then sent the treaty to the Senate for ratification. Would Texas finally become a state? Northerners in Congress reasoned that the excuse of foreign diplomacy was just a thinly veiled power play by southern slave owners. Swayed by this argument, the Senate defeated the proposed treaty. Texas would await statehood a little longer.

### Texas and the Whigs

Besides the threats from Britain, a second reason Tyler advocated the annexation of Texas was that he was seeking reelection in the 1844 presidential race. He knew the issue would attract voters. He had little support from his party—although he was officially a Whig, he opposed much of the Whig platform and had vetoed several measures passed by Whigs in Congress. Ultimately, despite his interest in annexing Texas, Tyler failed to attract much public support in his bid for reelection, and he dropped out of the race before the November vote.

## Texas and the Democrats

With Tyler out of the race, the Democrats were now in an ideal position to "steal" Texas annexation as *their* national campaign issue. They made overall territorial acquisition a key issue in their strategy to spread American civilization far and wide. They blustered on and on about how America's territorial growth would make it a first-class nation. Their platform called for the "re-annexation" of Texas and the "re-occupation" of Oregon up to a northern boundary of 54°40', an outrageous land grab that included nearly all of today's British Columbia, extending to the southern border of today's Alaska.

The Democrats' plan, though greedy, was perceptive. By offering to acquire both Texas and Oregon, they intended to give something to the North and to the South, thus unifying the nation and securing a Democratic victory. The party's presidential nominee was James K. Polk, a former Tennessee governor and congressman (whose nickname was "Young Hickory," aligning him with Andrew Jackson, who was called "Old Hickory"), and he became the loudest spokesperson for the benefits to be gained from American expansion.

## Texas and the Liberty Party

Henry Clay replaced Tyler as the new Whig candidate. Clay initially opposed annexing Texas. But midway through the campaign, he decided the issue was too popular to resist, and he needed the votes. Outraged at his reversal—and his political gaffe of not offering to acquire Oregon as well—a group of northern antislavery activists left the Whig Party. They created the **Liberty Party**, which opposed admitting any new slave territory to the United States. The Liberty Party nominated James G. Birney, who attracted voters who would otherwise have supported Clay. This division strengthened the Democratic Party and allowed Polk to win the election fairly easily. But the introduction of the Liberty Party revealed hairline fractures in the second two-party system—fractures that would steadily grow into an outright break.

 Read a dramatic antislavery letter by a member of the new Liberty Party.

## Tyler and Texas

Tyler, who had a few months left in his term before being succeeded by Polk, interpreted Polk's victory as a sign that the public did indeed support efforts to admit Texas. Thus, during his last months in office, in an effort to ensure himself a positive legacy, Tyler again pushed Congress to annex Texas

through a congressional resolution. (A resolution is similar to a treaty but requires only a simple majority to pass instead of the two-thirds majority needed for a treaty.) This time, the Senate, swayed by the public enthusiasm it had witnessed during the election, narrowly voted in favor of the resolution. On March 1, 1845, the United States formally offered Texas statehood, which Texas accepted in December.

In response to admission of Texas as an American state, Mexico broke off diplomatic relations with the United States, setting the stage for conflict between the two nations.

 Read more about Texas statehood.

# Oregon and American Dominance in the West

## Polk as President

Despite Tyler's role in granting Texas statehood, it was Polk who would become the nation's staunchest

James K. Polk.

Copyright © The Granger Collection, New York / The Granger Collection

**"Fifty-four Forty
or Fight!"**
Rallying cry referring to the
Americans' intended latitude
for the contested border
between the United States
and Canada; Britain was
willing to settle for the 49th
parallel

**Buchanan-Pakenham
Treaty**
Agreement of 1846 between
the United States and
Britain, agreeing on the
49th parallel as the border
between the United States
and Canada; the treaty gave
the United States uncon-
tested access to the Pacific

supporter of acquiring new territory. He was an avid believer that Americans were destined to control the West, and he had the personality, vigor, and power to be a strong cheerleader. However, when it came to the West, Polk was less concerned about slavery and more concerned about a surge in British influence in North America. Thus his first action as president was to snuff out any plans Britain had for reentering Oregon and California. Polk also had to live up to his campaign promise of bringing in a northern state to balance the recent addition of Texas.

## 54°40'

During Polk's presidential campaign, he pledged to fight for exclusive title to the Oregon Territory and to settle for nothing less than the entirety of American claims, which extended all the way up to a northern line of 54°40'—close to what is now the southern-most point of Alaska's border with British Columbia (see Map 13.2). Britain, however, would certainly not concede that the United States owned a territory that Britain had long explored and claimed. After his inauguration in early 1845, Polk softened his position and returned to the demand made by every president since James Monroe: the United States would be willing to settle for a border along the 49th parallel—Oregon's northern border today. Britain rejected the offer; it wanted to control the Columbia River, two hundred miles south of the 49th parallel. Angered at British stubbornness and inspired by the partisan cry of **"Fifty-four Forty or Fight!"** Polk returned to his more aggressive position. In early December 1845, he asked Congress to extend U.S. military protection to the Oregon Trail. He hoped that feigning military intervention would persuade the British to concede the vast Oregon Territory.

### 49th Parallel

His tenacious talk was merely a bluff. Polk had long believed that the land north of the 49th parallel, where few American settlers had reached, was not that important. What he really wanted was Puget Sound and access to the ports of California for trading. Britain's government, meanwhile, decided that its interest in the region, originally based on the once-robust fur trade, which was now rapidly declining, was not worth a war. In late December 1845, Britain and the United States reopened negotiations over the issue, intending to prevent what would have been the third war in seventy-five years between the two nations. The British proposed a treaty accepting the 49th parallel as a border, although it sought to retain the right to navigate the Columbia River. The Senate approved the resulting **Buchanan-Pakenham Treaty** in July 1846, and America now had uncontested access to the Pacific.

### Manifest Destiny

Amid the frenzy stirred by the Oregon and Texas statehood issues, a new expression of the spirit of an American

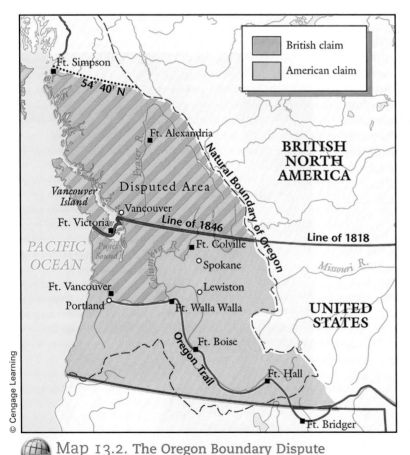

Map 13.2. The Oregon Boundary Dispute

empire was born. The term **manifest destiny**—meaning that the United States was *fated* to possess North America from the Atlantic to the Pacific—was coined by New York journalist John O'Sullivan. In July 1845, O'Sullivan wrote an editorial in his *United States Magazine and Democratic Review* urging Whigs and Democrats to join together in support of "the right of our manifest destiny to overspread and to possess the whole of the continent, which Providence has given us." Manifest destiny was popularized in political debates over Oregon, where it was used as an argument for why Britain should not block U.S. expansion. Soon the rhetoric made its way into American popular culture.

Though the term *manifest destiny* was newly coined, it reflected a much older American belief that divine providence was directing the nation. Many Americans felt that their country—by virtue of its strong Christian faith, its commitment to "civilization" and democracy, and the supposed "emptiness" of the West—would dominate North America as a great Empire for Liberty, thriving under God's benevolent guiding hand. The phrase was explicitly chauvinistic, implying the need to "subdue" and "fertilize" the "virgin land" of the West. It was also explicitly racist, referring to the God-given rights of the white man to conquer the "red man's lands." Manifest destiny interpreted the conquest of the West as a story of triumph in the cause of freedom rather than a saga of conflict, death, and destruction. The concept grew in popularity throughout the 1840s, justifying westward expansion.

## The Mexican-American War

When Texas won its independence from Mexico in 1836, the Mexican dictator General Antonio López de Santa Anna vowed that any move by the United States to annex Texas would be met with military force. When Texas did become the twenty-eighth state, in 1845, President Polk privately relished Mexico's threat. Polk hoped that by provoking Mexico to make good on its promise of war, the United States could crush the Mexicans and gain control of even more Mexican territory, particularly the far western prizes of California and New Mexico. During the next two years, Polk tried peaceful negotiations with Mexico for these territories (he offered to buy them many times), but all the while he was prepared to order a military strike if negotiations broke down.

 Read John O'Sullivan's "Annexation" essay.

### Polk Seeks a Fight

Polk's preparations for attack, however, seemed to be in vain. The Mexican officials, though they would not accept the annexation of Texas as legal, did not want to wage war over the matter. Instead, they chose to haggle over the precise boundary of Texas's southern border. Texas state officials insisted that the proper boundary between Texas and Mexico was the Rio Grande River. The Mexicans, however, considered the Nueces River (130 miles north of the Rio Grande) to be the border. Polk decided that the United States had a responsibility to defend Texas's land claims, and the first action he took as president was to station U.S. warships off the coast of Texas. In October 1845, Polk dispatched nearly 4,000 U.S. troops to the northern side of the Nueces River. By demonstrating American strength, Polk hoped to bully the Mexican government into ceding the disputed lands.

Despite these intimidation efforts, Mexico refused to respond. So, in November 1845, Polk took another approach, attempting to pressure Mexico into selling both New Mexico and California to the United States by sending an emissary to Mexico. Polk's tactics failed once again. Frustrated, Polk decided to make another show of force. In January 1846, he ordered General Zachary Taylor, the head of the U.S. Army encamped along the Nueces, to move into the disputed region between the Nueces and the Rio Grande. Polk hoped to provoke the Mexican army into firing on the Americans. If American lives were endangered, the president reasoned, it would be easy to declare war on Mexico.

He finally got his fight. On April 25, 1846, Mexican forces crossed the Rio Grande and attacked Taylor's men, killing eleven soldiers. Polk immediately declared that Mexico had "shed American blood upon the American soil." According to the president, Americans had no choice but to avenge the lives of their slain countrymen.

 Read President Polk's "Message on War with Mexico."

### Patriotic Fervor

On May 13, 1846, as patriotic fervor swept the country, Congress passed a declaration of war by an overwhelming majority. Volunteers responded en masse to fill the ranks of the army. The war was not universally popular, especially not among northerners

Read Whig senator Thomas Corwin's speech opposing the Mexican War.

 Read Democratic senator Donald S. Dickinson's speech justifying the U.S. acquisition of territory.

who considered it a strategy to expand slavery into new western territory. Leading intellectuals, such as Henry David Thoreau, Frederick Douglass, and William Lloyd Garrison, opposed the war, rightly viewing it as an unjust aggression against Mexico and an opportunity for slave owners to annex new land for their plantations. In 1847, a young congressman from Illinois named Abraham Lincoln offered a resolution to Congress (which did not adopt it) demanding to be shown the exact spot upon which American blood was spilled on American soil. Lincoln rightly thought the first shots had been fired on disputed territory, not American land,

*If American lives were endangered, the president reasoned, it would be easy to declare war on Mexico.*

and the proposal came to be called Lincoln's "Spot Resolutions." Nevertheless, these countervailing views were overpowered by the louder voices advocating America's "manifest destiny."

## California and New Mexico

Now that the battle with Mexico had begun, Polk also planned to seize Mexico's other northern states, California and New Mexico (Map 13.3). In June 1846, a small group of American rebels, flying a flag decorated with a bear and a red star, seized the California town of Sonoma (north of San Francisco) and declared the state an independent republic. John C. Frémont led an armed expeditionary group in what came to be called the "Bear Flag Revolt." The California Republic was, however, to be short-lived. By the end of July 1846, Frémont's men were inducted into the

The San Jacinto Museum of History, Houston

El Fandaangoé.

>> Inspired by patriotic fervor, seventeen-year-old Bostonian Sam Chamberlain joined the 1st Regiment of Dragoons and saw service in northern Mexico under the command of General Zachary Taylor. His illustrated account of the Mexican War, entitled "Recollections of a Rogue," has all the color of a young American's first experiences in a foreign conflict—not all of them military, as this watercolor of a Mexican dance hall demonstrates.

Map labels:

OREGON COUNTRY

UNITED STATES

UNORGANIZED TERRITORY

MEXICAN CESSION

Fremont 1846

Fremont 1845–1846

San Francisco

Sutter's Port

Monterey

Santa Barbara

Stockton 1846

Los Angeles

San Diego

Sloat 1846

Sacramento R.

Colorado R.

Gila R.

Kearny 1846

Ft. Leavenworth

Bent's Fort

Kearny 1846

St. Louis

Missouri R.

Arkansas R.

Final Boundary 1850

Santa Fe

Las Vegas

Socorno

DISPUTED BY U.S. AND MEXICO

El Brazio

El Paso del Norte

Doniphan 1847

Chihuahua

Chihuahua

Red R.

Sabine R.

TEXAS

Austin

San Antonio

Pecos R.

Nueces R.

Rio Grande

New Orleans

MEXICO

Corpus Christi

Taylor 1846

Saltillo

Monterrey

Matamoros

Scott 1846

Buena Vista

Gulf of Mexico

American Blockade

Mazatlán

Santa Anna 1847

San Blas

San Luis Potosi

Tampico

Pánuco R.

Scott 1847

PACIFIC OCEAN

La Manzanillo

Mexico City

Chapultepec

Cerro Gordo

Veracruz

© Cengage Learning

Legend:
■ Fort
✸ Battle site
◊◊◊◊ Blockade

Map 13.3. Principal Campaigns of the Mexican War, 1846–1847

U.S. Army as the "California Battalion." By August, the United States had taken control of California's key ports, and Frémont became a national hero.

Further south, a group of American troops marched through what is today New Mexico. In August, this force seized Santa Fé, the capital of the Mexican region, without firing a shot. By January 1847, the troops had finished their mission and had moved to the California coast. They arrived just in time to put down a Mexican revolt against American rule that had been raging in Los Angeles since the previous September. Relatively easily, and within about six months, Americans had taken control of the large territories of California and New Mexico. Now all that was left was formalizing the land grab.

### Invading Mexico

After the United States seized both territories, Polk was prepared to offer Santa Anna a deal. Overthrown in an 1844 coup, Santa Anna was now living in Cuba, plotting his return to Mexico. Polk offered him the chance to do so in exchange for a promise to end the war and to cede California, New Mexico, and Texas to the United States. Santa Anna agreed. Once he arrived in Mexico, however, Santa Anna reneged on this promise and rallied Mexican forces against the Americans.

To counter this revolt, Polk ordered his generals, Zachary Taylor and Winfield Scott, to invade Mexico from the sea. With this daring move, he hoped to take control of Mexico City, thus undercutting Santa Anna and his men, who had moved north to attack Americans along the border. In March 1847, after capturing the Mexican port of Veracruz, 14,000 American troops marched inland toward Mexico City, and, after numerous battles and several bouts with yellow fever, on September 13 the American troops entered the Mexican capital. Within three days, Santa Anna, flanked on both the north and the south, surrendered to the American forces.

### Treaty of Guadalupe Hidalgo

In February 1848, an American envoy named Nicholas Trist negotiated the **Treaty of Guadalupe Hidalgo**, which officially ended the Mexican War. The treaty gave the United States control of Utah, Nevada, California, western Colorado, and parts of Arizona and New Mexico, and it set the Mexican-American border at the Rio Grande River. This was everything the U.S. government wanted, all in exchange for $15 million. It also safely ignored several arguments that the United States should swallow the entire nation of Mexico.

Learn more about the Mexican War.

## And in the end . . .

The Mexican cession, comprising nearly 500,000 square miles of territory, turned the rhetoric of

| What else was happening . . . | |
| --- | --- |
| 1822 | A yellow fever epidemic leaves New York City with 16,000 corpses and no readily available space to bury them. |
| 1829 | Mexico abolishes slavery. |
| 1835 | The Liberty Bell becomes cracked. |
| 1840 | The saxophone is invented. |
| 1842 | The Treaty of Nanjing ends the First Opium War between Great Britain and China, which began when China protested the importation of opium by British merchants. The treaty mandates that China open trade relations with Great Britain, including the continued trafficking of opium, and it makes Hong Kong a British colony, which it remains until 1997. |
| 1845 | The New York Baseball Club plays the Knickerbockers in the first recorded baseball game, at Elysian Fields in Hoboken, New Jersey. |

manifest destiny into reality. With Texas's annexation and the acquisition of Oregon, New Mexico, and California, the United States had become an empire spanning the width of the continent—all within four short years.

But the struggle involved in taking all this land provoked the issue that no American politician wanted to engage: slavery. The issue of whether or not slavery should exist in the western territories would lead to the political crisis of the 1850s, which would ultimately bring about the American Civil War. It is to this impending crisis that we now turn.

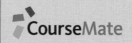

**CourseMate**  Visit the CourseMate website at www.cengagebrain.com for additional study tools and review materials for this chapter.

# CHAPTER 14

# *The* Impending Crisis

## Learning Outcomes

*After reading this chapter, you should be able to do the following:*

LO **1**   Describe the arguments that took place over whether slavery should be allowed to expand into the new territories, and explain how the Compromise of 1850 was supposed to settle the issue.

LO **2**   Explain how the Kansas-Nebraska Act affected the territories of Kansas and Nebraska, and describe the events that made "Bleeding Kansas" an accurate description for the region.

LO **3**   Discuss the events that propelled the United States into a civil war in 1861.

LO **4**   Explain why and how the southern states seceded from the Union, discuss President Lincoln's reaction, and describe the earliest physical conflict between the two sides.

© James Thomas Linnell/The Bridgeman Art Library/Getty Images

# "In the end, the election to the presidency of an antislavery northerner provoked southerners to withdraw from the Union altogether."

In the 1850s, the controversy over the spread of slavery to the West froze America's territorial expansion. The gains of the 1840s were impressive: the United States had acquired California, Texas, Oregon, Washington, New Mexico, and more. But in the 1850s, except for a small

stretch of land on the southern edge of today's Arizona (the Gadsden Purchase), the United States made no further territorial gains.

Nevertheless, the territorial expansion of the previous fifty years had made it nearly impossible for the two political parties to retain support from all the nation's various regions. In general, although northerners were not often hard-core abolitionists, they protested the spread of slavery in the West, favoring the expansion of free labor, in which men could choose the kind of labor they would perform. Most southern whites, meanwhile, fiercely supported the institution of slavery, seeing it as integral to the American economy and the cotton culture they had developed since the 1793 invention of the cotton gin. As for the political parties, neither Democrats nor Whigs could afford to alienate the South by appearing overtly against slavery or the North by seeming too supportive of the institution. The risk was that each party would become strictly regional or that they would implode in trying to find a balance.

This political conundrum provoked the development of splinter parties, and without the hedging and compromising of the two mainstream parties, the center of American politics could not hold. In the end, the election to the presidency of an antislavery northerner provoked southerners to withdraw from the Union altogether. Considering that people in democratic societies ideally intend to settle their differences without killing one another, how had things gone so wrong?

# LO¹ Arguments over Slavery in the New Territories

The Mexican War had, from 1846 to 1848, temporarily united the North and the South in a common enthusiasm for military conquest. But tensions between the two regions always lay just beneath the surface. During and after the war, American politicians became consumed with the issue of whether extensive territories won from Mexico should permit or prohibit slavery.

**Wilmot Proviso**
Legislation proposed in 1846 to prohibit slavery from any new territories that the United States might acquire from Mexico

**dough face**
Derisive name for a northerner who openly supported the South

**popular sovereignty**
Proposal for letting the settlers in the territories decide whether or not they wanted slavery

## *The Wilmot Proviso*

❝ Provided that, as an express and fundamental condition to the acquisition of any territory from the Republic of Mexico by the United States, by virtue of any treaty which may be negotiated between them, and to the use by the Executive of the moneys herein appropriated, neither slavery nor involuntary servitude shall ever exist in any part of said territory, except for crime, whereof the party shall first be duly convicted. ❞

## The Democrats' Response

Andrew Jackson's Democratic Party had always claimed to defend the rights of the "common man." Yet southern Democrats, by demanding that the new territories allow slavery, hardly seemed to be advocating policies that helped every common man. Indeed, many northerners of both parties argued that if slavery were allowed in Texas and other parts of the West, wealthy plantation owners would buy up all the new land, leaving little for less-affluent farmers. And southern Democrats were at a loss to reconcile their image as protectors of the common man with this argument.

### Racist, but Antislavery, Northern Democrats

More importantly, new plantations meant that the western territories would be populated with black people. Despite the fact that many northern Democrats were opposed to slavery, they shared the racist beliefs of the day and had no desire to live amid a large African American population. The belief in white supremacy led northern and southern Democrats to radically different conclusions. Many northern Democrats turned against slavery in order to avoid living and competing with black people in the western territories, whereas southern Democrats retained their proslavery stance in order to defend the plantation economy, which theoretically promised even the common man great wealth. This splintered the Democratic Party into southern and northern branches.

## The Wilmot Proviso and the "Free Soil" Movement

The splintering intensified in 1846 when one of the alienated northern Democrats, Pennsylvania congressman David Wilmot, proposed that slavery be prohibited from any new territories that the United States might acquire from Mexico. Wilmot was no abolitionist. He wanted slavery kept out of the West so the land would be available to average white farmers (who could not afford slaves) rather than to wealthy slave owners who would establish massive plantations. The **Wilmot Proviso** passed in the House of Representatives several times but was repeatedly rejected by the Senate, where southerners had the edge because of the support of several "**dough face**" senators, defined as senators from the North who supported southern slavery.

Meanwhile, each round of voting on the Wilmot Proviso exacerbated regional tensions. Many northern Whigs, such as Abraham Lincoln, joined northern Democrats in voting for the measure. At the same time, southern Democrats, such as John Calhoun (now a senator from South Carolina), argued that the Constitution guaranteed the option of slavery in federal territories, thus joining southern Whigs in voting against it. Now the Whigs were beginning to divide along regional lines too. Southerners from both parties advocated introducing slavery in the new territories, while northerners from both parties opposed such an effort.

### The Presidential Election of 1848

The presidential election of 1848 deepened these tensions. At first, the campaigners tried to ignore slavery altogether. When this proved impossible, Democratic nominee Lewis Cass hoped to sidestep the issue by proposing the idea of **popular sovereignty**, which meant letting the settlers in the territories decide whether or not they wanted slavery. The Whigs, meanwhile, who had nominated Mexican War hero Zachary Taylor (who had never voted before, much less held political office), made no mention of slavery in their platform.

### The Free Soil Party

Neither of these positions satisfied all Democrats or all Whigs, and disaffected Democrats launched a political movement under the banner of the **Free Soil Party**. The new party was headed by former Democratic president Martin Van Buren and advanced a platform centered on the Wilmot Proviso. The party was antisouthern, but not staunchly abolitionist. It argued that southern slave owners were blocking the development of northern progress. Southern congressmen, said the Free Soilers, refused to advance national programs for internal improvements, which would facilitate access to the West and extend the progress made by the Market Revolution. Free Soilers wanted western lands to be available to ambitious white farmers, and they wanted to save the land for white people.

In its platform, the party called for "free soil, free speech, free labor, and free men," focusing not on abolishing slavery where it already existed but on keeping slave-based plantations out of the West. Significantly, the Free Soil movement brought together all those who opposed slavery in the West. These groups opposed the expansion of slavery for different reasons. For instance, the abolitionists sympathized with the slaves, while the racists disliked African Americans and did not want to compete with them economically in the new territories. The Free Soil Party also brought together northern Democrats, such as Wilmot, with northern Whigs, who were unhappy about their party's nomination of slave owner Zachary Taylor.

Taylor and the Whigs cobbled together enough votes to win the election of 1848, but they failed to win a congressional majority, and in the long run, they were greatly weakened by the rise of the Free Soil Party. Democrats, too, had seen a split within their ranks that would grow in coming years. During the 1850s, the Free Soil Party and the slavery issue set the stage for a reconfiguration of American politics. The first instance of this would arise in 1850.

## The Compromise of 1850

California provoked the next round of compromises in Congress.

### California as the Problem

When Zachary Taylor took office in 1849, California, brimming with new settlers driven by the gold rush, applied for statehood. But would it enter as a free or a slave state? Either way, its statehood was destined to upset the balance between free and slave states that had held since the Compromise of 1820.

Taylor tried to address the crisis as soon as he took office. He hoped to simply bypass the slavery issue by granting immediate statehood to California and New Mexico without specifying whether they were free or slave states.

Southern politicians attacked Taylor's plan. They worried that once California was admitted, its citizens would vote to be a free state, thus setting a precedent for prohibiting slavery from all western territories. They also feared that someday slave states would be greatly outnumbered by free ones in Congress—an event that could lead to the permanent decline of southern interests and the permanent abolition of slavery.

### The Compromise of 1850

To allay these fears, Henry Clay, author of the Missouri Compromise of 1820 and now a powerful senator, stepped forward with yet another compromise. In January 1850, Clay proposed a five-part bill, which came to be called the **Compromise of 1850** (Map 14.1, page 238).

The Compromise of 1850 included five key components:

1. California would be admitted to the Union as a free state.
2. The remaining land won during the Mexican-American War would be divided into two new territories, New Mexico and Utah, and would remain open to slavery until they became states, at which time the state legislatures could vote on the issue.

**Free Soil Party**
Political movement started by disaffected anti-South Democrats and headed by former Democratic president Martin Van Buren; they wanted new lands to be made available to small, ambitious white farmers

**Fugitive Slave Law**
Law passed as part of Compromise of 1850 requiring that all runaway slaves be returned to their masters; those who willfully ignored the law were to be punished

**Compromise of 1850**
Five-part bill proposed by Henry Clay, which outlined specific arrangements that accommodated both antislavery northerners and slave-owning southerners

3. To mollify antislavery northerners, slave auctions (but not slavery itself) would be banned in the nation's capital, Washington, D.C.

4. Texas would receive $10 million in compensation but be prohibited from further influencing New Mexico, where it had hoped to extend slavery.

5. For southerners, the federal government would create and enforce a new and tougher **Fugitive Slave Law**. By punishing white northerners who helped slaves escape from the South, the measure sought to ensure that the North and the South would cooperate in protecting the slave system.

## The Controversy

The compromise contained elements to appeal to both sides, but it also set off a storm of political controversy. Opposed by hardliners on both sides of the slave-state issue, the compromise gave rise to the first focused talk of secession in the South. This alarmed President Taylor so much that he decided to oppose the compromise altogether. Months of impassioned arguments for and against the com-

 Read Calhoun's speech.

promise went on in Congress. The debates marked the last time that the great triumvirate of powerful senators, Clay, Calhoun, and Daniel Webster, would discuss the nation's fate with their formidable oratorical skills. Clay and Webster allied in favor of the compromise, and Webster's "Seventh of March" speech rallied northern opinion for the compromise. On the opposite side, Calhoun, dying of tuberculosis, watched his friend James Mason deliver Calhoun's last speech in the Senate against the proposed compromise. But the compromise remained in limbo.

>> "As much indisposed as I have been, Mr. President and Senators, I have felt it to be my duty to express to you my sentiments upon the great question which has agitated the country and occupied your attentions." —John C. Calhoun, debating the compromise in the Senate as read by his friend James Mason

## Becoming Law

When, in 1850, Zachary Taylor died of food poisoning and was replaced by Millard Fillmore, the compromise's chances of passing improved. Fillmore favored the plan. With Fillmore's support, Clay's political lieutenant in the Senate, Stephen A. Douglas of Illinois, set to work dividing the bill in five parts and finding majorities for each of its separate proposals. By September 1850, the compromise had become law.

The peace that ensued would prove ultimately unstable, however, as many northerners resented the tough Fugitive Slave Act. In fact, during the next decade many northern states passed **Personal Liberty Laws**, which were designed to protect escaped slaves—for instance, by prohibiting the use of a state's jail to restrain runaway slaves. Vermont, Rhode Island, and Connecticut passed Personal Liberty Laws in 1854. Maine, Massachusetts, and Michigan did so in 1855, followed by Kansas and Wisconsin in 1858, Ohio in 1859, and Pennsylvania in 1860. Reaction to the Fugitive Slave Laws also created the sympathy that propelled the success of Harriet Beecher Stowe's *Uncle Tom's Cabin*.

The debates of 1849 and 1850 only worsened the mutual distrust between North and South. But the Compromise of 1850 bought some time before the ultimate dissolution of the nation's political order.

## Western Destiny Deferred

### Buying Cuba?

As the debates over the Compromise of 1850 showed, admitting new states to the Union was bound to be contentious. In addition, southerners immediately noticed that there was more territory open for statehood in the North than in the South. Fearful of what this might portend, southern leaders sought to expand America's territorial holdings southward, by expanding into Latin America. Presidents Polk and Pierce, in fact, had both tried to buy the island of Cuba from Spain, thinking it could, perhaps, one day become a slave state. When Polk's offer was rebuffed, a group of Americans tried to invade the island in order to bring it into the Union. They failed, but the adventurers who attempted to take these lands came to be called **filibusters**, after the Spanish *filibustero*, for "pirate" or "freebooter." The term was subsequently adopted to describe attempts to extend debate over a legislative proposal in order to hijack it or delay its passage.

### The Slave Conspiracy

These reckless attempts to create more southern states heightened northerners' suspicions that the Democratic Party was plotting in league with slave owners. Abolitionists and Free Soilers viewed the Cuban plan as an indication that the South, rapidly being outpaced in population growth by the North, was desperate to acquire new slave states to maintain parity in the Senate. Sensing a conspiracy, northerners fought hard to prevent further accessions to slaveholders' power. Both sides were intensifying their opposition to the other.

# LO² The Kansas-Nebraska Act and New Political Parties

These sentiments erupted in the 1854 debate over the Kansas-Nebraska Act. And, again, it was expansion in the West that brought the issue of slavery to a head within the nation's corridors of power.

## Slavery in Kansas and Nebraska?

By the early 1850s, plans were under way to build the nation's first transcontinental railroad, and Senator Douglas of Illinois wanted Chicago to serve as the new railway's major hub. But Chicago could not serve as the hub if the unorganized northern portion of the Louisiana Purchase remained unorganized and unpopulated; it wouldn't make any sense to put a railroad where there were no people and where the United States had little political presence. To eliminate this problem, Douglas began to push for the creation of several new territories in that northern region, where today sit Kansas and Nebraska.

The problem with Douglas's plan was that, according to the Missouri Compromise of 1820, slavery was prohibited in the northern part of the Louisiana

Purchase. Southerners therefore resisted Douglas's efforts, fearing that when those territories eventually became states, they would become free states, tipping the balance of power in the Senate against the South.

### The Kansas-Nebraska Act

Douglas, a shrewd statesman, devised a compromise to ensure that southerners would support the development of the new territories. Douglas created two territories, Kansas and Nebraska (Map 14.1), and left the status of slavery in each territory open, to be decided by the popular sovereignty of those who settled there. In the end, this meant that the Missouri Compromise of 1820 did not

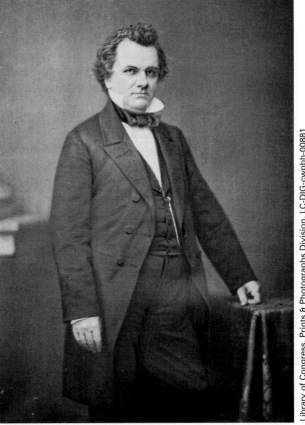

Library of Congress, Prints & Photographs Division, LC-DIG-cwpbh-00881

>> "Senator Douglas was very small, not over four and a half feet height, and there was a noticeable disproportion between the long trunk of his body and his short legs. His chest was broad and indicated great strength of lungs. It took but a glance at his face and head to convince one that they belonged to no ordinary man. No beard hid any part of his remarkable, swarthy features. His mouth, nose, and chin were all large and clearly expressive of much boldness and power of will." —Journalist Henry Villard, 1858

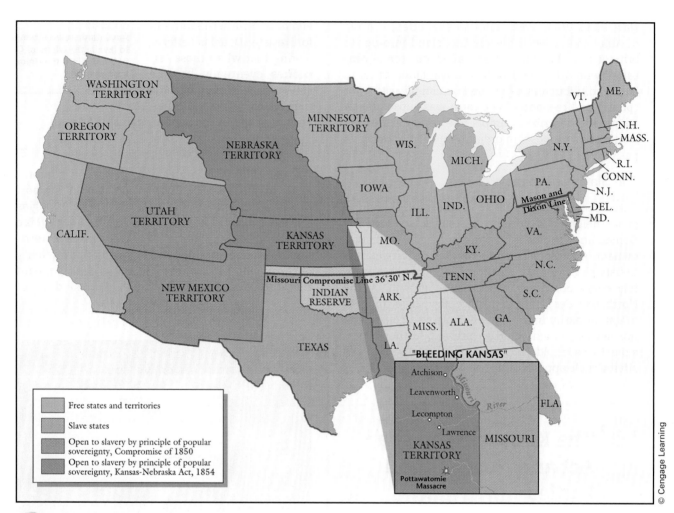

Map 14.1. Kansas-Nebraska and the Slavery Issue

**Kansas-Nebraska Act**
The 1854 act that created two territories, Kansas and Nebraska, and left the status of slavery in each territory open, to be decided by the popular sovereignty of those who settled there

Read the Kansas-Nebraska Act.

apply because slavery might have been allowed above 36°30', had the residents of Kansas or Nebraska so chosen. Many northerners were outraged at the prospect, but a coalition of northern Democrats (who wanted the transcontinental railroad) and southerners (who wanted a maintenance of slavery) passed the **Kansas-Nebraska Act** by a narrow margin.

## The Death of the Second Two-Party System

The passage of the Kansas-Nebraska Act had two direct results: (1) it contributed to the demise of the Whig Party, and (2) it sparked a race to populate Kansas, because the fate of slavery in Kansas would be decided by voters there. The race would lead to tension, then conflict, and, ultimately, violence.

But the first result to become visible was the fatal weakening of America's second two-party system, splitting both parties along regional lines. Northern Whigs found themselves at odds with southern members of the party; southern Whigs abandoned the party altogether to join the Democrats, who were more clearly supporting slavery. Many northern Democrats were increasingly sympathetic to parties like the Free Soilers. At the same time, several new political parties emerged, all of which spoke mostly for regional issues. By 1856, there were no longer any national political parties. The political system was crumbling over the issues of slavery and westward expansion.

## The Know-Nothing Party

One of the new parties to arise in the 1850s was the American Party, which built its base of support on anti-immigrant and anti-Catholic sentiment. The American Party was an outgrowth of a secret society called the Order of the Star-Spangled Banner. As a secret society, its members vowed to answer all inquiries about the Order with the response "I know nothing." Consequently, the American Party came to be known as the **Know-Nothing Party**.

Believing that "Americans should rule America," the Know-Nothings wanted to prevent the masses of new immigrants from gaining political rights. They advocated changing naturalization laws so that immigrants would be required to wait twenty-one years (as opposed to just five) before they could apply for citizenship, and they particularly targeted Irish Catholics. As they saw it, Catholics took their instructions from the pope and did not exercise the independence of mind necessary to function as democratic citizens. The Know-Nothings prided themselves on disdaining the very things the Irish stereotypically embraced: alcoholism, urban disorder, and poverty. The party appealed to middle-class and working men who saw immigrants as their main competition for industrial jobs.

Very quickly, the Know-Nothings won several elections, suggesting the appeal of Nativist ideas in mid-nineteenth-century America. Just a year after they formally established their party, in 1853 the Know-Nothings won important electoral victories in New York, Pennsylvania, Massachusetts, and Ohio, the states that had experienced the most dramatic influx of immigrants. By 1855, the Know-Nothings had more than 1 million voters enrolled in their various lodges. Although they were never a commanding national party, the rise of the Know-Nothings is significant not only as a testament to the appeal of anti-Catholic Nativism in the 1850s, but also because its rise killed off the Whig Party. Southern Whigs had deserted the party in order to join the Democrats, and many northern Whigs flocked to the Know-Nothings.

After its meteoric rise, the popularity of the Know-Nothings plummeted just as rapidly. When the Know-Nothings failed to achieve their goals of changing naturalization laws and restricting the political rights of immigrants, members became disillusioned. And by that time there were also other parties to join.

## The Republican Party

Most of the disaffected Know-Nothings joined another political party that was forming at the time, the **Republican Party**. Unlike any other party except the Free Soilers, the Republican Party was explicitly antislavery; its main goal was to prevent any further expansion of slavery in the West. Its platform included support for homesteading rights, a protective tariff, and internal improvements—most of the components of the American System.

**Know-Nothing Party**
**The American Party, a new political party of the 1850s that built its base of support on anti-immigrant and anti-Catholic sentiment**

**Republican Party**
**Explicitly antislavery party that emerged in the political turmoil of the 1850s; although not abolitionist, it favored "free-soil" movements to keep slavery out of the West**

Library of Congress, Prints & Photographs Division, LC-US262-19431

>> Popular music was on the rise during the 1850s, so it was inevitable that someone would compose a song for the new political party. Its sheet music cover is loaded with symbols of Americanism, from the eagle and flags to native pumpkins and corn.

The Republicans succeeded in unifying numerous antislavery groups, including the Free Soilers. They also drew support from northern Whigs and Democrats who were infuriated by the Kansas-Nebraska Act and the idea of popular sovereignty.

## Two Parties from Two Regions

The Republicans were a purely sectional party, drawing most of their strength from antislavery sentiment in the North. Because the North had a significantly larger population than the South, the Republicans expected that they could eventually win the presidency without courting southern voters. Therefore, by the late 1850s, after the downfall of the Know-Nothings, a new sectional party system was established, pitting antislavery northern Republicans against proslavery southern Democrats. This decline of national parties and the rise of sectional ones would accelerate the political crisis of the 1850s.

## "Bleeding Kansas"

So what would become of Kansas? Would it enter the Union as a slave state or a free one? Under the doctrine of popular sovereignty, voters in Kansas would decide.

## Popular Sovereignty

The problem was that there weren't many people in Kansas in 1854, so both parties (and their subsequent supporting groups) sent people to Kansas, just in time to vote in the election. Slaveholders in neighboring Missouri were fearful of having a free state just across their border. Being especially eager to see Kansas become a slave state, they encouraged slaveholding families to migrate to Kansas. At the same time, abolitionists sent northern settlers to Kansas. One effort, led by New Englander Ely Thayer, sent nearly 1,250 colonists to Kansas, where they established Lawrence as a strong antislavery town. The tension between the two settling groups was palpable and violence flared up with increasing frequency, each side trying to frighten the other away.

## The Stolen Election

With both sides actively working to promote their own interests, Kansas became a bitterly divided territory. When the first territorial legislature was elected in 1855, throngs of men from Missouri, who came to be known as "border ruffians," crossed the border for the day and stuffed the ballot boxes, electing a proslavery government. Only 2,900 registered voters lived in Kansas, but over 6,000 ballots were cast. The advocates of slavery had stolen the election.

Kansas's new proslavery government immediately set out to crush its opposition and make Kansas a slave territory. It expelled antislavery representatives from the legislature and made it a crime to publicly advocate Free Soil principles or help a fugitive slave. Opponents appealed to the White House, but President Franklin Pierce supported southern interests. His opponents called him a "dough face," that derisive name for a northerner who openly supported the South. Forced to fend for themselves, antislavery Kansans formed a rival government in the city of Topeka. For a time, there were two functioning state governments in Kansas.

Read a contemporary account of the "sacking of Lawrence."

## Bleeding Kansas

Inevitably, this bitterly contested conflict erupted into violence. In 1856, a mob of proslavery men sacked the Free Soil town of Lawrence. The town was put to the torch, but no one was killed. The violence enraged John Brown, a zealous abolitionist who considered himself God's executioner of justice. To avenge the attack on Lawrence, Brown and his sons entered the town of Pottawatomie Creek, Kansas, rounded up five proslavery advocates, none of whom was a slaveholder, and butchered them. Brown's acts inspired more vigilantism, and atrocities were met with counter-atrocities. As the newspapers reported, Kansas was bleeding.

## Kansas's Constitution

In June 1857, the people of Kansas elected another set of delegates to a convention in the town of Lecompton. The convention was charged with drawing up a state constitution. People opposed to slavery, however, boycotted the election on the grounds that the voting districts had been drawn so as to make it more difficult for them to elect antislavery representatives. Their boycott ensured that most of the men sent to the convention supported slavery, and predictably, they created a state constitution that made slavery legal in Kansas. Their constitution was called the **Lecompton Constitution**.

## Free Soilers Strike Back

In a provocative move, the convention refused to allow the citizens of Kansas a chance to challenge

>> Throngs of men from Missouri, who came to be known as "border ruffians," crossed the border into Kansas for the day and stuffed ballot boxes. Only 2,900 registered voters lived in Kansas, but more than 6,000 ballots were cast.

 Read the section on slavery from the Lecompton Constitution.

or reject the Lecompton Constitution. In the popular referendum that followed, Kansans were allowed to vote only on whether *more* slaves would be allowed into the territory, not on the legality of slavery itself. President James Buchanan, elected to succeed Pierce in 1856, was eager to satisfy the southern branch of the Democratic Party, so he backed the Lecompton Constitution despite what he knew about the antidemocratic convention that had created it. Senator Stephen Douglas, however, refused to support something so questionable, even though doing so angered the southern members of his party. President Buchanan pulled enough political strings to get the Senate to accept the constitution without Douglas's support, but he could not garner enough votes for it to pass in the House of Representatives. When no agreement could be reached on the issue, Congress sent the Lecompton Constitution back to Kansas for another vote by its people. This time, the Free Soilers participated in the vote and resoundingly rejected the proslavery constitution.

## Outcomes

Although the Lecompton Constitution was ultimately defeated, the shenanigans surrounding its creation disgusted northerners, and the controversy convinced many northern Democrats to switch to the Republican Party. With each new political crisis, the sectional divide between northern Republicans and southern Democrats became more and more profound.

## "Bleeding Sumner"

Events in the Senate only intensified the animosity. The reports from Kansas had caused emotions to run high among America's congressmen. No one was more vocal in his outrage than Charles Sumner, a Republican from Massachusetts who was perhaps the Senate's most outspoken opponent of slavery. Shortly before the burning of Lawrence (and John Brown's subsequent retaliation in Pottawatomie Creek), Sumner delivered a speech in Congress entitled **"The Crime against Kansas,"** which blamed slavery for all the violence. In addition, Sumner made personally insulting remarks about Andrew P. Butler, a proslavery senator from South Carolina, leading many in attendance to believe that Sumner was deliberately provoking an attack.

### The Caning of Sumner

Butler was not at the capitol to defend himself, and he was too old and feeble to do so anyway. But his nephew Preston Brooks, a South Carolina

> **"The Crime against Kansas"** Speech delivered in Congress by Charles Sumner, Republican of Massachusetts, that blamed slavery for the violence between pro- and antislavery activists in Kansas

SOUTHERN CHIVALRY — ARGUMENT versus CLUB'S.

>> With his first blow, Brooks opened a gash in Sumner's head and sent him careening to the floor. Brooks pounced on Sumner and continued to strike him in the head, even after his cane had shattered to pieces.

representative in the House, stepped in on Butler's behalf. Brooks himself had been a southern moderate before being galvanized by the events in Kansas. On May 22, 1856, just two days after Sumner delivered his vilifying speech, Brooks entered the Senate chamber and proceeded to beat Sumner senseless with his metal-topped cane. With his first blow, Brooks opened a gash in Sumner's head and sent him careening to the floor. Brooks then pounced on his victim and continued to strike him in the head, even after his cane had shattered to pieces. It took more than three years for Sumner to recover from his injuries.

In the opinion of many northerners, "Bleeding Sumner" came to match "Bleeding Kansas" as a symbol of southern barbarity. Certain southerners were proud of the caning, however, for its literal and symbolic value. Many of them mailed new canes to Brooks, with messages like "Hit Him Again." The episode captured in a moment the nation's breakdown of reason on the eve of civil war.

## The Election of 1856

### The Republicans

Bleeding Kansas and the caning of Sumner were featured as central images in the 1856 Republican presidential campaign. The Republican candidate, John C. Frémont, founder of the free state of California, ran on a platform that denounced slavery as a "relic of barbarism." Frémont called for Kansas to be admitted to the Union as a free state, as the most recent vote there had suggested. There were several central themes in the Republican agenda, including expanding internal improvements and embracing the Market Revolution. But none were more important than the promotion of personal independence and free labor. Blocking the expansion of slavery in the territories, argued the Republicans, was essential to giving free white men the opportunity to establish homesteads for themselves in the West.

### The Slave Power Conspiracy

The Republicans openly condemned the South's planter class. They argued that slaveholders were a minority group wielding a disproportionate amount of power. They believed that, in order to preserve slavery, southern leaders would be willing to attack and silence anyone who advocated against slavery. According to Republican propaganda, the **Slave Power Conspiracy** intended to outlaw free speech and make all Americans accept proslavery principles.

### The Election

Northerners comprised the majority of the American population, and the Republicans believed it was time for the northern majority to control the national government. In 1856, Republican rhetoric proved powerful at the ballot box, but not quite powerful enough. Out of the sixteen free states, Frémont won eleven. Millard Fillmore, the American Party candidate, managed to take only Maryland, a slave state. Meanwhile, the Democratic candidate, James Buchanan of Pennsylvania, won thirteen of the fourteen slaveholding states, as well as the five free states that eluded Frémont. It was just enough for Buchanan to get into the White House.

### Results

The election made two things clear: (1) American voters were divided into sectional parties, and (2) despite Buchanan's victory, the Republicans were close to having enough support in the North to win a presidential election without winning a single southern state. The South was politically outnumbered and knew it.

# LO$^3$ Three Events That Catapulted the Nation into War

In this heated atmosphere, three events pushed sentiments over the top: (1) the Dred Scott controversy, (2) John Brown's raid, and (3) the election of 1860. The events of the 1850s had pushed America to the brink of collapse. These three events would finish the job.

## The Dred Scott Controversy

On March 4, 1857, Buchanan was inaugurated as president, and just two days later, he confronted a controversial Supreme Court decision that threatened to intensify sectional tensions.

### Dred Scott

A Missouri slave named Dred Scott had been taken by his owner to live for a few years in Illinois and the Wisconsin Territory, where slavery was illegal. Eventually, however, Scott and his master returned to Missouri. With the help of antislavery advocates, Scott sued for his freedom on the grounds that his residence in a free state and a free territory had made him a free man.

The case forced the U.S. Supreme Court to rule on whether Scott's residence in Illinois and Wisconsin made him free. By a 7-to-2 decision, the Supreme Court ruled that Dred Scott was still a slave, despite his residence outside of Missouri. As Chief Justice Roger Taney explained, Scott had returned to Missouri before attempting to claim his freedom, and within Missouri he was a slave.

### Slavery as Law of the Land

But Chief Justice Taney used the case to do much more. Taney added remarks to his opinion that were intended to prevent black bondsmen from suing for their freedom ever again. In an incredibly bold statement, Taney asserted that the Missouri Compromise was unconstitutional because Congress had no right to prohibit slavery anywhere in the United States. A slaveholder could take his slaves anywhere he or she wanted within the Union, including free states, without losing title to them. By this logic, any attempt to restrict the westward march of slavery was prohibited by the land's highest court. This meant the Compromise of 1850, California's free-state status, and every state law prohibiting slavery ran afoul of the Constitution.

Republicans were outraged, interpreting the Dred Scott decision as proof that the Slave Power Conspiracy was as strong as ever. With the prohibi-

John Brown.

66 During the affair the negroes about H F were terribly alarmed and clung as closely as they could to master and mistress. One negro hid under a water wheel in the armory canal and didn't come out till Tuesday—and then was afraid Brown might catch him. 99
—*Charles White, eyewitness account of the 1859 raid on Harper's Ferry*

tion of slavery declared illegal by the Supreme Court, Republicans wondered if the South would attempt to renationalize slavery, as it had been before the Revolutionary War. Taney had, after all, declared slavery to be the law of the land.

Northerners could not accept this. Their fears made antislavery forces in the North all the more determined to reduce the South's political power in the country, deepening the sense of alienation and crisis between the two regions.

### John Brown's Raid

Following the Dred Scott decision, John Brown, the radical abolitionist who had provoked some of the violence in "Bleeding Kansas," intensified the sectional crisis again. In October 1859, with eighteen of his followers, he raided the federal arsenal at Harper's Ferry in northwestern Virginia. Brown envisioned that, after seizing the armory, he would rally the slaves in the surrounding area to join him in revolt against their oppressors.

To Brown's surprise, however, no slaves joined his side after he daringly seized control of the arsenal. Most were afraid Brown would be unsuccessful and did not want to risk their lives for the actions of a crazy man. Within three days, federal troops under the command of Colonel Robert E. Lee captured Brown and six of his cohorts. They were summarily tried for treason. Brown refused to give up the fight; throughout his trial, he spoke passionately against slavery and accepted his conviction and death sentence with the calm resignation of a martyr. On December 2, 1859, the state of Virginia hanged him.

Learn more about John Brown's raid.

## Results

John Brown's raid was a dismal failure that horrified even some northerners. A few high-profile northerners praised Brown in no uncertain terms, though. Ralph Waldo Emerson, the prominent philosopher and abolitionist, publicly proclaimed Brown a "saint." Although views like Emerson's were probably in the minority, southerners fixated on such remarks as evidence that the North was out to destroy slavery and crush the "southern way of life." Brown failed to arouse the revolt he had planned, but he did succeed in inspiring a keen sense of fear and loathing among the southern public. What the Dred Scott decision was to northerners, John Brown's raid was to southerners: an unfathomable, appalling episode that highlighted the gulf between the regions.

## The Election of 1860

The implosion of national party politics and the sense of isolation felt in the North and the South came to a head in the election of 1860.

## The Democrats

In April of 1860, the Democratic Party held its convention in Charleston, South Carolina, and the sectional divide between northern and southern members generated palpable tension. Stephen A. Douglas was a clear favorite for the nomination, but southern Democrats had become disgusted with his leadership after he refused to endorse Kansas's proslavery constitution. Moreover, to nominate Douglas meant accepting the idea of popular sovereignty, which Douglas still supported and which contained within it the chance that antislavery forces would carry the day. Douglas had articulated his advocacy of popular sovereignty in the 1858 **Lincoln-Douglas Debates**, when Douglas and his opponent for the U.S. Senate seat in Illinois, Abraham Lincoln, publicly debated the issue of slavery. After the Dred Scott decision, southern Democrats wanted their party to agree with the Supreme Court that slavery could not be barred from any U.S. territory. Douglas would not accede to such a demand.

Thus the Democrats could not agree on a candidate who would satisfy the party's northern and

Read the first Lincoln-Douglas debate on the spread of slavery.

Read Lincoln's powerful "House Divided" speech.

>> The Lincoln-Douglas debate at Charleston, Illinois, September 18, 1858.

© Art Resource, NY

southern members. They decided instead to adjourn the convention and reassemble in Baltimore in July. This second Democratic convention nominated Douglas, but the southern delegates refused the nomination and walked out. That move confirmed the long-standing divide within the party, and the Democratic Party officially split into northern and southern wings. The northern branch stood behind Douglas, and southerners backed the current vice president, John C. Breckinridge of Kentucky, on a platform that called for the creation of a national slave code protecting slavery everywhere in the Union.

## The Republicans

Meanwhile, the Republicans nominated Abraham Lincoln, who was an attractive candidate for two reasons. First, Lincoln had become known after the Lincoln-Douglas Debates as a moderate on the slavery question. Although he believed that slavery was an evil institution and he wished to keep it out of the western territories, he did not aspire to end slavery in the southern states where it already existed. Republican leaders felt that this position would appeal to the general public of the North, which hoped to avoid greater conflict if possible. Second, Lincoln was from Illinois, a state the Republicans had failed to carry in 1856. If the Republicans were to win in 1860, they needed to win Illinois.

## The Final Sectional Division

In addition to Republicans (who had nominated Lincoln), northern Democrats (Douglas), and southern Democrats (Breckinridge), a fourth party entered the race with hopes that a showdown between North and South could be averted. The Constitutional Union Party nominated John Bell of Tennessee as their presidential candidate. Its simple platform was to avoid all discussion of slavery in an attempt to raise the Constitution and the Union above all schisms.

Despite the best intentions of the Constitutional Union Party, the election was not really a national contest. In the North, only Lincoln and Douglas held any popular appeal; in the South, the race was between Breckinridge and Bell. When all the votes were in, Lincoln emerged with the most votes, but not a majority of them. But because his base of support was in the populous states of the North, Lincoln won 180 votes in the Electoral College, just enough to secure victory.

## Results

Lincoln won the presidency as a sectional candidate. He did not win a single southern state (Map 14.2 on page 247), and his platform revealed his intention to halt the westward expansion of slavery. Although Democrats still controlled Congress, the North's ability to dictate the 1860 presidential election outcome confirmed the southern states' worst fear: they had lost control of national politics. The institution of slavery was in peril.

 Read Lincoln's Inaugural Address.

# LO⁴ Secession and Civil War

In the eyes of many southerners, Lincoln's election spelled the end of the southern way of life as they knew it. Although Lincoln had actually affirmed the rights of the states in his campaign speeches, the South saw his opposition to the spread of slavery in the West as a serious threat. If all the western territories became free states, southerners assumed the Republicans would amend the Constitution and outlaw slavery everywhere. Many southerners believed it would be better to leave the Union before the horrors of abolition were inflicted upon them. (For more on slavery's role in the start of the civil war, see "The reasons why . . ." on the next page.)

Americans had considered secession in the past. Ever since the founding of the nation, defenders of "states' rights" had argued that any state should be able to "nullify" laws passed by the federal government and even withdraw from the Union should it so desire. In 1798, Thomas Jefferson claimed the right of nullification in his Kentucky Resolution; disgruntled New England Federalists threatened to leave the Union during the War of 1812; and South Carolina's great statesman John C. Calhoun had in the 1830s defended the South's right to "disunion" in order to protect it from what he called "northern aggression." In these prior cases, however, only the most hotheaded ideologues urged secession. Until 1860, southerners had held back from dividing the country. That changed with Lincoln's election.

## The Deep South Secedes

South Carolina took the lead. On December 20, 1860, a state convention repealed South Carolina's

# { *The reasons why . . .* }

There were at least four major reasons why slavery plunged the nation into civil war in 1861:

*Economics.* The New England and Middle Colonies in the North had developed differently than the Chesapeake and Southern Colonies in the South, with those in the South more reliant on staple crops and, after the decline of indentured servitude in the 1680s, on slavery as well. These differences only accelerated during the Market Revolution. In the first half of the nineteenth century, states and territories in the North embraced internal improvements and the communication and transportation revolutions of the time, while wealthy land owners in the South were slow to embrace such changes, content that their plantations' reliance on rivers would be sufficient to enrich the region. With slave-grown cotton at a premium during the period, they were right. However, this gamble made them reliant on cotton, and on the slaves that cultivated it.

*Westward expansion.* After the Revolution, many northern states began the long process of ending slavery in the North. They recalled the arguments they had made against England about the importance of liberty, and they were not as economically dependent on a handful of slave-grown crops, as was the case in the South. In the South, however, the invention of the cotton gin in 1793 made cotton easier to grow, and a farmer who owned a little land and a few slaves could become wealthy. Thus, any talk of abolition in the South ceased, and these smaller farmers began pushing west, looking for land on which they could grow cotton and bring their slaves. For their part, most white northerners wanted to keep slavery out of the West, not because they hated the institution of slavery (though some did), but principally because they did not want to compete against those with access to unfree labor.

*Political breakdown.* The westward expansion of slavery immediately created political problems. The House of Representatives and the Senate had agreed to develop a balance between slave states and free states, but with the proposed admission of new western states, the balance was threatened. A series of compromises in 1820, 1850, and 1854 allayed a few of the most problematic western additions, but the compromises took their toll on the various political parties, as many supporters would not abide by their party's compromises. By 1856, there were no longer any nationally unified parties, only sectional ones. After the newly formed Republican Party won the election of 1860 with support only from northern states, several states in the South seceded and attempted to drive American forces from the new Confederate States of America. Lincoln vowed to keep the nation together, and fought back.

*An enraged populace.* Not all northerners eagerly supported Lincoln, but many did. They did so because they viewed the South and slavery as barbarous and backward, and they were afraid that southerners wanted to renationalize slavery. If they were white, this "Slave Power Conspiracy" would limit their options as free white people, allowing slavery to sneak into areas in the West where they had the most to gain financially. They may not have been abolitionists, but they wanted to keep slavery from expanding. Many southerners, for their part, viewed the North as intent on ending slavery, and they were personally hurt by claims that they were backward and barbarous. These tensions led to violence in the West and even on the floor of the Senate. After the election of 1860, the enraged tempers meant that many people would be willing to fight for their side.

---

ratification of the U.S. Constitution and voted to withdraw from the Union. It did not want to be part of a nation in which it had no control. Over the next six weeks, several other southern states—Mississippi, Florida, Alabama, Georgia, Louisiana, and Texas—followed suit. Together, on February 7, 1861, they established the Confederate States of America: an independent, southern slave republic. The Confederate States of America elected Jefferson Davis of Mississippi as the new nation's first president.

## Lower South versus Upper South

Seceding was not a unanimous choice for these southern states. The planter class was the driving force behind the movement. Those counties that had

 Read South Carolina's declaration of the causes of secession.

a large number of slaveholding families tended to vote for secession in the secessionist conventions, while those

areas with few slaves typically voted against it. Therefore, the initial wave of secession was confined to the Deep South (Louisiana, Mississippi, Alabama, Georgia, South Carolina, Texas, and Florida), where slave-based agriculture was more fully established. The Upper South (Virginia, North Carolina, Arkansas, Kentucky, and Tennessee), by contrast, had a more diversified economy. Those states chose not to secede in the winter of 1860–1861.

## Conciliatory Efforts

A handful of attempts were made to prevent this situation from exploding in war, notably by John Crittendon and Abraham Lincoln.

### Crittenden Compromise

The first last-ditch effort at reconciliation was spearheaded by John Crittenden of Kentucky. Crittenden proposed that the Missouri Compromise line of 1820

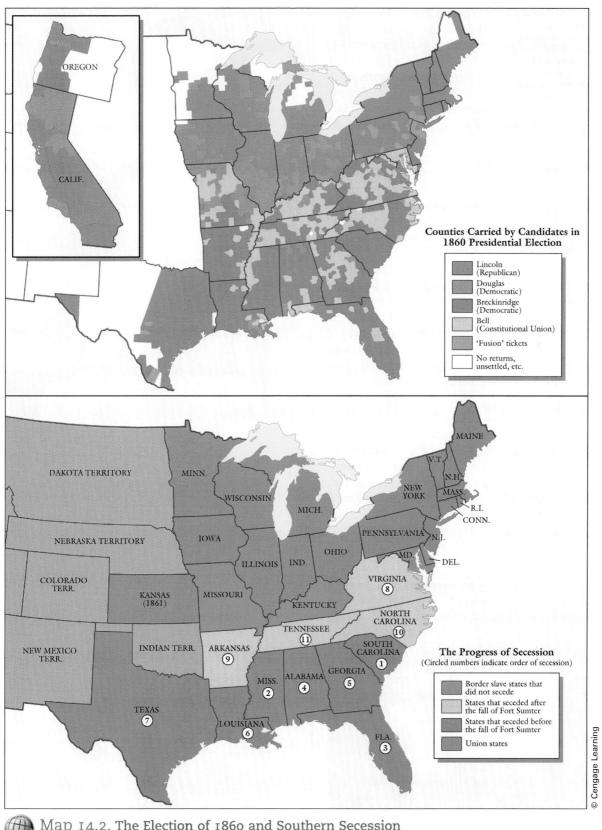

**Counties Carried by Candidates in 1860 Presidential Election**

- Lincoln (Republican)
- Douglas (Democratic)
- Breckinridge (Democratic)
- Bell (Constitutional Union)
- 'Fusion' tickets
- No returns, unsettled, etc.

OREGON

CALIF.

DAKOTA TERRITORY

MINN.

WISCONSIN

MICH.

MAINE

V.T.

N.H.

NEW YORK

MASS.

R.I.

CONN.

PENNSYLVANIA

N.J.

MD.

DEL.

NEBRASKA TERRITORY

IOWA

ILLINOIS

IND.

OHIO

COLORADO TERR.

KANSAS (1861)

MISSOURI

KENTUCKY

VIRGINIA ⑧

NORTH CAROLINA ⑩

NEW MEXICO TERR.

INDIAN TERR.

ARKANSAS ⑨

TENNESSEE ⑪

SOUTH CAROLINA ①

TEXAS ⑦

MISS. ②

ALABAMA ④

GEORGIA ⑤

LOUISIANA ⑥

FLA. ③

**The Progress of Secession**
(Circled numbers indicate order of secession)

- Border slave states that did not secede
- States that seceded after the fall of Fort Sumter
- States that seceded before the fall of Fort Sumter
- Union states

Map 14.2. The Election of 1860 and Southern Secession

© Cengage Learning

**Crittenden Compromise**
Reconciliation proposal advocating that the Missouri Compromise line of 1820 be extended all the way to the Pacific, excluding California, with all land north of the line free, all land south of it open to slavery; also included an "unamendable amendment" to the Constitution, guaranteeing the preservation of slavery in the southern states where it already existed

 Read the Crittenden Compromise.

be resurrected and extended all the way to the Pacific, excluding California. All land north of the line would be free, all land south of it would be open to slavery. Moreover, he recommended that an "unamendable amendment" be made to the Constitution, guaranteeing the preservation of slavery in the southern states where it already existed.

The **Crittenden Compromise** proved unworkable. Secessionists in the Deep South had no interest in returning to the Union. The Republicans, who had been elected to office on a platform that called for prohibiting the expansion of slavery, did not want to renege on their campaign promises. Thus, the Crittenden Compromise was a nonstarter, and the only question remaining was whether the states of the Deep South would be permitted to withdraw from the Union.

## Lincoln's Middle Course

After his inauguration on March 4, 1861, Lincoln attempted to chart a middle course. He sought to reassure southerners that he would not interfere with slavery in the states where it already existed. Slave states that did not secede would be allowed to maintain slavery. At the same time, Lincoln, like Andrew Jackson before him, maintained that the Union was perpetual and that no state could with-

>> The first flag of the Confederate States of America, called "the Stars and Bars," was flown from March 5, 1861, to May 26, 1863.

>> Abraham Lincoln circa 1860.

**"**A house divided against itself cannot stand. I believe this government cannot endure, permanently half slave and half free. I do not expect the Union to be dissolved—I do not expect the house to fall—but I do expect it will cease to be divided. **"**
*—Abraham Lincoln, June 16, 1858*

>> The bombardment of Fort Sumter.

draw from it. Furthermore, he insisted that federal property in the southern states (forts, arsenals, and customs houses) still belonged to the Union. Lincoln put the ball in the Confederacy's court. It was up to the southern states to either return to the Union or face civil war. He had invited them back and granted them slavery where it already existed, maintaining the status quo. What would the Confederates do?

## Fort Sumter

Army rations became the deciding factor. The deadlock was shaken when the federal garrison at

 Explore further information about Fort Sumter.

Fort Sumter, South Carolina, located just off the coast of Charleston (now a city in the Confederate States of America), ran low on food. Provisions needed to be sent to the U.S. troops there, or they would have to surrender the fort to the Confederacy. By March 1861, only six weeks of supplies remained.

In early April 1861, President Lincoln organized a relief expedition to the fort. Hopeful that war could be avoided, Lincoln assured the governor of South Carolina that the ships sent to supply Fort Sumter would contain only food, not guns or ammunition. Jefferson Davis, however, declared that any attempt to send provisions to Fort Sumter would be consid-

ered an aggressive act against the Confederacy. As a preemptive move, Davis ordered General Pierre Beauregard, the Confederate Army commander in Charleston, to demand Fort Sumter's immediate surrender. If the garrison of eighty-five men refused to surrender, Davis ordered Beauregard to open fire. On April 12, 1861, when Beauregard's demands

| What else was happening . . . | |
|---|---|
| 1842 | Abraham Lincoln accepts a challenge to a duel from James Shields, the Democratic state auditor. (The duel never takes place.) |
| 1845 | The rubber band is patented. |
| 1850 | Taiping Rebellion in China begins. This civil war, which lasts fourteen years, will see 20 million people die before the restoration of the Qing Dynasty. |
| 1853–56 | Crimean War pits Russia against Britain, France, the Ottoman Empire, and the Kingdom of Sardinia. It is considered the first "modern" war because of the tactical use of railroads and the telegraph. It is also the war in which Florence Nightingale pioneers modern nursing. |
| 1857 | Indian Rebellion, protesting British colonial rule, lasts a year before the British finally suppress the rebellion. |
| Feb. 11, 1861 | Both Abraham Lincoln and Jefferson Davis leave their homes to be inaugurated president. |

were rejected, Confederate batteries began shelling Fort Sumter. By the evening of April 13, the garrison capitulated.

## And in the end ...

In the wake of Fort Sumter's surrender, Abraham Lincoln called for 75,000 volunteers to put down the southern rebellion. Northerners eagerly rallied behind Lincoln and resolved to bring the secessionists to their knees. Lincoln had been savvy. By inviting the South to attack a U.S. fort, he had allowed a broad swath of northerners to support the suppression of the insurrection without forcing them to take a stand on slavery. The South was also coming together. In response to Lincoln's attempt to "coerce" the rebel states back into the Union, the Upper South states of Virginia, Tennessee, North Carolina, and Arkansas threw their lot in with the Confederacy.

Battle lines were now drawn. What was destined to become the bloodiest war in American history had begun. Later, in Abraham Lincoln's Second Inaugural Address, he said that "all knew" that slavery "was somehow the cause of the war." But it took time and a variety of factors before it became the driving force in the breakup of the Union. The political crisis of the 1850s, sparked by the question of whether slavery would be allowed in the West, finally erupted into civil war.

| Chronology | |
|---|---|
| 1846 | Wilmot Proviso |
| 1850 | Compromise of 1850 |
| 1852 | *Uncle Tom's Cabin* |
| 1854 | Kansas-Nebraska Act |
| 1856 | "Bleeding Kansas," "Bleeding Sumner" |
| 1857 | Dred Scott decision |
| 1859 | John Brown's raid at Harper's Ferry, Virginia |
| 1860 | Abraham Lincoln elected president |
| 1861 | Southern states secede |
| April 12, 1861 | Firing on Fort Sumter |

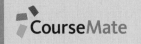 **CourseMate** Visit the CourseMate website at www.cengagebrain.com for additional study tools and review materials for this chapter.

# The Civil War

## Learning Outcomes

*After reading this chapter, you should be able to do the following:*

**LO 1**    Describe the areas of strength and advantage for each side at the beginning of the Civil War.

**LO 2**    Explain why both sides in the Civil War believed the war would be brief, and describe the early conflicts that made that outcome unlikely.

**LO 3**    Explain how preparing for and prosecuting the Civil War contributed to the transformation of the United States into a fully modern state.

**LO 4**    Describe the actions of those who opposed the war in the North and of those who opposed the war in the South.

**LO 5**    Discuss the events that occurred in 1863 and 1864 that demonstrated Lincoln's strong will and his eventual determination that the end of the war should bring a definite end to slavery.

**LO 6**    Describe and discuss the events that finally led to the utter defeat of the South and the end of the war.

**LO 7**    Assess the significance of the Civil War for the nation.

*© Michael Melford/The Image Bank/Getty Images*

> ❝*The war ended slavery and accelerated America's modernization, shaping the nation we live in today.*❞

In hindsight, we know the Civil War was four years of prolonged and bloody battles. At the outbreak of fighting, however, neither northerners nor southerners took the prospect of fighting one another all that seriously. Both sides expected a short war with few casualties. Southerners believed that northerners were effete cowards lacking the mettle to sustain a prolonged battle. They thought that once the northern armies caught a glimpse of the South's determination, northerners would drop their guns and let the South secede. Northerners, meanwhile, were certain that only southern slaveholders supported secession, and because they were a tiny minority in the South, their lack of support would quickly become evident. Northerners also considered southerners ill prepared and ill equipped to take on the U.S. Army. The North expected the South's will to fight to diminish rapidly.

As a consequence, northerners and southerners predicted that the war would not change their societies very dramatically. Southerners presumed that their plantation-based, slaveholding civilization would continue to thrive as it had for decades. Northerners imagined that the southern states would realize their error and return to the Union to resume amicable relations. Southerners would keep their slaves, most northerners thought, but slavery would be prevented from spreading westward.

All these predictions proved inaccurate. The fighting between North and South became fierce and vindictive, and casualties were high. In addition, when the North and the South emerged from the war in 1865, both were transformed from what they had been in 1861. In short, the war ended slavery and accelerated America's modernization, shaping the nation we live in today.

## What do you think?

**Lincoln's proclamation did not end slavery; slaves themselves ended slavery.**

| Strongly Disagree | | | | | | Strongly Agree |
|---|---|---|---|---|---|---|
| 1 | 2 | 3 | 4 | 5 | 6 | 7 |

## LO¹ Each Side's Strengths

### Northern Advantages

In some ways, northern expectations for a quick victory were reasonable, because the Union possessed overwhelming material advantages over the South. The North's primary advantages were (1) more people, (2) more materials, and (3) more industry.

## Population

In 1861, the total population of the Union was around 22 million, compared to 9 million in the Confederacy. This statistic becomes even more impressive when one considers that 3.5 million of the Confederacy's people were slaves, people clearly unwilling to fight on behalf of the perpetuation of slavery. In terms of military-age white males, the Union outnumbered the Confederacy four to one.

## Materials and Industry

The northern states had other advantages as well. The North had an existing navy and produced more firearms than the South. It also produced more of the essential provisions of war, including coal, textiles, corn, and wheat. By all estimates, the North was better able to outfit its men with weapons, clothing,

Read the results of the U.S. Census of 1860 (especially the last column).

shoes, and food. The North also had a more extensive network of railroad lines for transporting those supplies and a larger pool of money to finance its war effort. The Union possessed about $200 million in bank deposits, while the Confederacy had only $47 million.

## Southern Advantages

The Confederacy did have certain strengths, however, including (1) the will to fight, (2) the fact that it's easier to fight a defensive battle, and (3) a wealth of talented military leaders.

## Will to Fight

First, northerners severely underestimated the southern will to fight. While only slaveholders had taken the lead in the secession movement, by April 1861, most southerners supported the bid for Confederate independence, and they were willing to fight to win it.

## A Defensive Battle

The Union also had to wage an offensive war to occupy the South, while the Confederacy had the

> *In terms of military-age white males, the Union outnumbered the Confederacy four to one.*

> *Most men in the South were more comfortable with firearms than soldiers raised in the urban North.*

simpler task of fighting on the defensive. The Confederacy did not have to overwhelm or occupy the North; it merely had to frustrate northern efforts to conquer it.

## Military Leaders and Morale

At the beginning of the war, the South also had more well-trained military leaders and a stronger tradition of military service. Many of the West Point–trained officers in the U.S. Army, including Jefferson Davis, Robert E. Lee, Albert Sydney Johnston, Thomas "Stonewall" Jackson, and James Longstreet, sided with the Confederacy. In addition, living in a rural environment, most men in the South were more comfortable with firearms than soldiers raised in the urban North.

>> Filling cartridges at the U.S. Arsenal at Watertown, Massachusetts, 1861.

Library of Congress, Prints & Photographs Division, LC-USZ62-96445

>> The satisfaction and frivolity thought to be born of war—the Confederate soldier on the right wears a mess plate on his head—quickly gave way to the realization this would be a hard, long battle.

 Read a southern author's justification for southern independence, written in 1861.

And, in terms of morale, the Confederacy had the advantage of fighting for its existence.

# LO² The Fallacy of an "Easy War": 1861–1862

The fallacy of expecting a brief war became apparent at the first major battle of the Civil War.

## The Battle of Manassas (Bull Run)

On July 21, 1861, Union general Irvin McDowell moved 30,000 troops toward the Confederate soldiers clustered at Manassas Junction, just south of Washington, D.C. At the same time, civilians and congressmen from the capital packed picnic lunches and made the twenty-five-mile journey to witness the battle. After all, they anticipated fighting to be light and the battle to end shortly.

To the surprise of both sides, the Battle of Manassas, called the Battle of Bull Run by the Union (the North named battles after nearby creeks or rivers, the South after nearby towns), was hard-fought and bloody. Some 22,000 Confederate soldiers, led by General Pierre Beauregard, battled tenaciously against McDowell's men, and Confederate reinforcements under General Thomas "Stonewall" Jackson turned the tide decisively in the South's favor. When McDowell ordered a retreat, his troops panicked and stampeded from the fray.

## A Costly Confederate Victory

Although the Confederates had won the field of battle, they were not prepared to pursue the fleeing federal troops. The victory had been too costly. Each side had suffered nearly 10 percent casualties, with the northern forces having 2,896 killed, wounded, or missing, and the southern forces suffering 1,982 similar casualties. In light of such carnage, northerners and southerners alike were

 Learn more about the Battle of Manassas.

only would it deprive the South of food, clothing, and other supplies coming from Europe, but it would also demonstrate to the world that the South was unable to defend itself, thus keeping England and France from recognizing, and perhaps allying with, the Confederacy. These nations did, after all, need the South's cotton. In April 1861, Lincoln formally declared a blockade of the southern coastline.

Cutting the Confederacy off from sea-borne commerce proved difficult at first because the U.S. Navy had only forty-two ships to patrol 3,550 miles of Confederate coastline. After the first year of the war, however, blockading the South became easier, as the Union took control of several southern coastal locations, including Roanoke Island in North Carolina, the sea islands of South Carolina, and New Orleans. Taking New Orleans was a significant coup; it was the South's largest and richest city and its biggest port, and it opened the Mississippi River valley to invasion from the south. If the Union could not

*Read Stonewall Jackson's official report on the Battle of Manassas.* stripped of their assumptions about an easy war. The change in tone was especially marked in the North. After the defeat at Manassas, fearing that victorious southern forces would head straight to Washington, D.C., Congress authorized, and received, the enlistment of 500,000 volunteers. They were now preparing for a major armed conflict, a bigger war than anyone had predicted.

## Limited War

Although northerners no longer believed that the war would be won quickly, they clung to the idea that most southerners still loved the Union but had been pressured into fighting by a small clique of powerful slaveholders. They viewed it as a rich man's war and a poor man's fight.

In keeping with this view, the Union Army in 1861 and 1862 fought a limited war, which meant that, in attacking the Confederacy, Union troops were careful not to assault southern civilians or damage their property. Their goal was to occupy southern territory and defeat the Confederate Army. They were not aiming to subjugate the southern people. They attempted this strategy of "limited war" in three theaters: (1) the water, (2) the West, and (3) the East. See Map 15.1.

## The Naval Blockade

The imposition of a naval blockade of the Confederacy was a key part of the Union strategy. Not

>> Crew of the Union ironclad Monitor in front of their rotating turret.

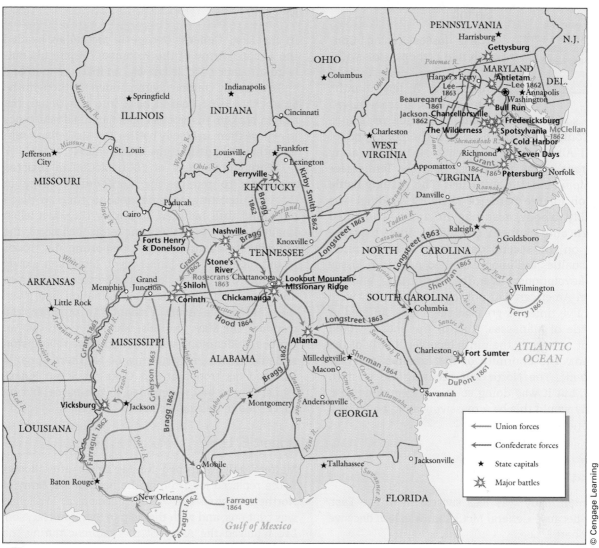

Map 15.1 Principal Military Campaigns of the Civil War

yet beat the Confederacy on the battlefield, it could prevent European goods from reaching it and eventually starve southerners into submission.

The blockade effort also stimulated the development of the ironclad battleship. Instead of wood, these ships used iron (later steel) siding and sat low in the water to ram targets more efficiently; one in particular, the U.S.S. *Monitor*, had a two-gun rotating turret on top. The first battle between ironclads, a four-hour barrage in March 1862 between the U.S.S. *Monitor* and the C.S.S. *Virginia*, ended inconclusively. But the news coverage it garnered signaled to the world a shift in military technology. Notably slow, however, the ironclads were only marginally successful in stopping Confederate blockade runners throughout the war.

## The West

### Some Union Successes

While the Union Navy was taking control of the southern coast, the Union Army achieved some success in the western theater of the war, located west of the Allegheny Mountains. Although the Confederacy won many of the battles waged in 1861 (including those at Wilson's Creek, Lexington, and Belmont), Union general Ulysses S. Grant earned the first decisive victories in the first half of 1862. In February 1862, with the support of Union gunboats, Grant's forces captured Fort Henry on the Tennessee River and then Fort Donelson on the Cumberland River.

## Shiloh

These losses forced Confederate troops to withdraw from Kentucky and Tennessee. A few months later, as Grant's army moved farther south, they encountered fierce resistance from Confederate troops under the command of General Albert Sydney Johnston. Johnston's army took Grant's men by surprise near the Tennessee-Mississippi border in April 1862. The ensuing **Battle of Shiloh** (or the Battle of Pittsburg Landing) was incredibly bloody, resulting in 23,000 combined northern and southern casualties. Grant took the victory on the second day, but at a heavy price. The casualties at Shiloh exceeded American losses in the Revolutionary War, the War of 1812, and the Mexican-American War put together, and they were almost five times as great as the losses suffered at the Battle of Manassas. And, in the end, it would turn out to be only the ninth bloodiest battle of the Civil War. The enormity of the fatalities was felt nationwide. The North was securing the western theater, but it was doing so at a tremendous cost. Not only would this be a massive war, it would be a tragic one as well.

## The East

The Union army was less successful in the East, mainly because General McClellan was less decisive than Robert E. Lee.

>> The casualties at Shiloh exceeded American losses in the Revolutionary War, the War of 1812, and the Mexican-American War put together.

## McClellan

In the East, General George B. McClellan headed the Union's Army of the Potomac. Despite his outward arrogance, McClellan was an insecure man and an excessively cautious commander. He thought the South should be coaxed back into the Union, not beaten back in. His troops appreciated his reluctance to expose them in bloody battles, but McClellan's self-defeating attitude hurt the Union cause.

Throughout most of 1861, McClellan resisted pressures to pursue the Confederate Army in Virginia, insisting that he needed time to discipline and drill his men. In spring 1862, McClellan finally decided to make a move on Richmond, the Confederate capital. After transporting his troops to the mouth of the James River, McClellan slowly made his way up the peninsula between the James and York Rivers. But his procrastination had given the Confederate Army a chance to organize and respond. On May 31, 1862, McClellan was within 5 miles of Richmond when General Joseph Johnston and the Confederacy's Army of Northern Virginia attacked his troops at Fair Oaks (or Seven Pines). Johnston was badly wounded in the battle, but he succeeded in halting McClellan's advance.

## Robert E. Lee

Matters only worsened for McClellan after Robert E. Lee replaced Johnston as the head of the Army of Northern Virginia. Lee was as audacious as McClellan was cautious, and with the help of Stonewall Jackson, Lee repulsed the Army of the Potomac during the Seven Days' Battles, which raged from June 25 to July 1, 1862. The Army of the Potomac was pushed north, out of Virginia.

With that defeat, Lincoln ordered the abandonment of McClellan's peninsula campaign, removed McClellan from his post, and put General John Pope in command of the Army of the Potomac. Pope was no more successful than McClellan had been. At the second Battle of Manassas, on August 29, 1862, Lee routed the Union troops and disgraced Pope. Despite McClellan's flaws, Lincoln reinstalled him at the head of the floundering Army of the Potomac. The Union armies were generally successful in the West and on the seas, but they were unable to beat their opponents where it mattered most—in Virginia, the heart of the Confederacy.

© Portrait of George Brinton McClellan (1826–85) (litho), Chappel, Alonzo (1828–87) (after)/Private Collection, Ken Welsh/The Bridgeman Art Library

>> "If General McClellan does not want to use the army, I would like to borrow it for a time." —attributed to Abraham Lincoln, 1862

## Results

Battles in these three theaters were hard fought, suggesting that the war would last longer than anyone had expected. War would require each side to mobilize its resources and, in the end, establish what is thought of today as a modern nation-state.

# LO³ Full Mobilization and the Making of a Modern State

In order to amass the manpower and money necessary to wage a serious prolonged war, northerners and southerners were forced to concentrate authority in the hands of their national governments. This process transformed the Union and the Confederacy into truly modern nations with intricate bureaucracies capable of controlling the resources of their states. The irony of this was felt strongly by Confederate president Jefferson Davis. After all, one of the principal reasons for southern secession was defending the rights of states over the rights of the national government. Yet in order to secure the South's independence, Davis found it necessary to concentrate power under a centralized authority. But northerners, too, felt the tightening grip of the federal government.

## Raising Armies

Nowhere was this truer than when it came to raising armies.

### The Confederacy

During the first year of the war, the Confederacy had only a small national army. Most soldiers volunteered for service through state militias controlled by state governors, not through the Confederacy. However, Jefferson Davis understood that engineering a strong war effort required greater coordination. So he convinced the Confederate Congress to implement a national draft in April 1862.

All men between eighteen and thirty-five became eligible for military service in the Confederate Army. Exemptions could be purchased, traded in return for supplying a substitute, or simply granted to wealthy landholders who owned twenty or more slaves. This **"20 Negro Law"** was designed to keep the planters producing their valuable cotton yield. The Confederate Conscription Act also contained occupational exemptions, whereby workers at gun and munitions factories would not be forced to leave jobs valuable to the war effort (the list of occupational exemptions immediately became political, such that, by the end of the war, the list of war-related jobs could not be contained on two finely printed pages). By 1863, the Confederate government, not the various state governments, had assumed control of the army.

### The Union

The North implemented a national draft in 1863. Like the Confederacy, the Union had initially relied on state armies to enlist soldiers, but the high desertion and low enlistment rates of state officers forced the federal government to establish a national conscription law, making all able-bodied men ages twenty to forty-five eligible for the draft. To ease

Read about life in the armies of the Civil War.

the burden of conscription, the Union also established volunteer quotas for each of its states. Only when a state failed to provide its allotted number of volunteer soldiers was the draft employed in that state.

Very few men were ever drafted; most volunteered. Others tried to fail medical exams in order to escape the war altogether. Similarly, under the conscription law, a person could be exempted until the next draft by paying a $300 **commutation fee**. The Union draft law, too, allowed men to be exempt from service by hiring a substitute to take their place. Some men, known as bounty jumpers, would receive a bounty to take another man's place in the army, then desert, only to do the trick again and again. Thus, in both the Union and the Confederacy, exemptions were made for rich men, who could afford to buy their way out of service, while ordinary workers and

farmers could not. The accusation that this was a rich man's war and a poor man's fight applied to both sides of the conflict.

## Suspension of Civil Liberties

The expansion of federal control also affected wartime civil liberties. In the first year of the war, both Union and Confederate governments suspended civil liberties.

### In the Union

Abraham Lincoln took the lead. From the start of fighting in April 1861, some northerners opposed the war and worked to hamper the Union's effort. For instance, on April 19, 1861, Confederate sympathizers in Baltimore destroyed telegraph lines, sabotaged railroads, and attacked Union soldiers who were passing through on their way to Washington, which was threatened after the Battle of Manassas.

To deal with the dissent, Lincoln used his authority as commander-in-chief to suspend the writ of habeas corpus in Maryland, which made it possible for Union soldiers to arrest any northern civilians suspected of disloyalty and imprison them without benefit of trial. Eventually, Lincoln suspended the writ in all other states, hoping to control disloyalty and dissent everywhere in the North. During the course of the conflict, roughly 14,000 people were arrested for undefined reasons.

 Read Lincoln's proclamation suspending habeas corpus.

### In the Confederacy

Jefferson Davis followed Lincoln's lead. As in the North, antiwar sentiment existed in the Confederacy from the outset, especially in poorer areas with few slaves. Several military losses in 1862 incited a level of dissent that provoked Davis to action. Unlike Lincoln, Davis himself did not suspend the writ of habeas corpus. Instead, he sought approval from the Confederate Congress, which granted the request and gave Davis the power to clamp down on citizens who opposed southern independence.

## Taxation

Both sides also exercised new controls over their national economies. Before the war, the federal government had depended mostly on tariff revenues and land sales to finance its operations. In fact, aside from the tariffs, the federal government had levied no taxes on the American people since the War of 1812.

A GREAT RUSH

Cost what it may, The Nation must be Saved!

TO JOIN THE

**36TH REGIMENT**

NEW YORK VOLUNTEERS,

Commanded by COLONEL W. H. BROWN.

This fine Regiment, one of the best in the Army of the Potomac, has been an active participant in the engagements on the Peninsula, and particularly distinguished itself during the "SEVEN DAYS' FIGHTING," having captured the Colors of the 14th North Carolina Regiment at the Battle of Malvern Hill. The term of enlistment of this Regiment will be out in

**NINE MONTHS.**

DON'T WAIT TO BE DRAFTED!

THE USUAL BOUNTY GIVEN.

Recruiting Office, No. 17 CENTRE STREET,

BETWEEN CHAMBERS AND READE STREETS.

Lieut. G. H. MOORE, Recruiting Office.

## Tariffs, Taxes, and Bonds in the Union

At the outbreak of hostilities in the Civil War, the U.S. Congress began raising tariff rates in order to pay for the war, and by 1865 the average tariff rate was an astronomical 47 percent. Despite these rates, tariffs failed to generate enough revenue to fully finance the military operation.

To compensate, Congress introduced direct taxation measures. During the first year of the war it enacted a 3 percent income tax. Then, in 1862, Congress enacted a graduated tax schedule to bring in more revenue from wealthier citizens. It also passed a comprehensive tax bill that levied new occupational and licensing taxes, corporate taxes, stamp taxes, insurance company taxes, dividend taxes, sales taxes, food taxes, and so-called sin taxes on alcohol and tobacco. To streamline the collection of these new levies, Congress created the Internal Revenue Service in 1862.

The U.S. government also tried to raise money by selling war bonds, or bonds that a person or corporation could buy that would earn interest over a fixed period of time. Bondholders could then redeem the bonds within five to twenty years for their initial investment plus interest (they were called **five-twenties**). New York banker Jay Cooke took the reins on this prospect and rapidly sold more than $500 million worth of bonds, to both large corporations and individual buyers.

>> The Confederacy preferred to finance the war by simply printing more and more paper money—a plan that succeeded only in creating runaway inflation.

© iStockphoto.com/Lee Pettet

## Inflation and Impressment in the Confederacy

At first, the Confederacy resisted creating a national system of taxation. It preferred instead to finance the war by simply printing more and more paper money— a plan that succeeded only in creating runaway inflation. The cost of living at the end of the war was an astounding ninety-two times what it had been before the war began. Only in 1863, once Confederate currency became nearly worthless, did the Confederate Congress institute a graduated income tax similar to the Union's. Nevertheless, while these types of taxes financed 21 percent of the Union's expenses, they furnished only 1 percent of the Confederacy's.

In addition, the Confederacy enacted a policy of impressment, authorizing armies to seize food, supplies, and even slaves for use in the war effort. Theoretically, citizens would be compensated, but many people complained that the government paid too little and that the payments were made in inflated and increasingly worthless Confederate dollars. The war was a financial disaster for the Confederacy, which never figured out the best method to pay for it.

## A Changing Nation

Between the new system of conscription, suspension of the writ of habeas corpus, and taxes, the Union and the Confederacy became powerful nation-states with great control over the lives of their citizens. Before 1861, Americans had little contact with their federal government. Most Americans encountered the federal government only when the U.S. postal service delivered their mail. By 1865, however, northerners and southerners lived under large and powerful national governments. After the war, the writ of habeas corpus was restored, but other powers assumed by the federal government were not rolled back. The Civil War established innovative and permanent changes in the scope of government authority in the United States.

## LO⁴ Dissent

These changes stirred dissent, and governments in both the North and the South found themselves confronted by those who opposed the war.

**five-twenties**
War bonds, or bonds that would earn interest over a fixed period of time; the bondholder could redeem the bond in anywhere from five to twenty years for the initial investment plus interest

## Dissent in the North

The entire body of Lincoln's policies came to elicit a great deal of opposition on the northern home front.

### Peace Democrats

For example, a minority of Democrats refused to support the war. These Democrats came to be called "Peace Democrats" or "Copperheads." They believed that secession was legal and that the Union had no right to force southern states to remain within it. Although their numbers were small in 1861, the Peace Democrats soon capitalized on popular dissatisfaction with Lincoln's leadership to become a formidable force in northern society.

### Lincoln the Tyrant

The Peace Democrats jumped on Lincoln's suspension of the writ of habeas corpus as proof that the president was a tyrant undeserving of popular support. Although the Constitution did allow the government to suspend the writ in times of national crisis, it had always been assumed that the power rested with Congress. Lincoln, however, acted without prior consent from Congress. This gave rise to the notion that Lincoln, like Jackson before him, was a dangerous tyrant, ready to sacrifice liberties in order to exercise and expand his own power.

### The Draft

Even more than suspension of habeas corpus, the draft became an important symbol of Lincoln's dictatorial ways that angered the Peace Democrats. Conscription seemed to contradict America's commitment to individual freedoms. In addition, the 1863 draft law seemed unfair to poor men, who, unlike the wealthy, could not afford to buy their way out of fighting.

### The New York Draft Riot

This inequity generated violence as well as political opposition. In July 1863, when the first national draft was about to be held in New York City, Democratic working men, most of them Irish, rampaged through the streets and shut down the draft office. They attacked  Take a virtual tour of the draft riots. anyone who was rich or a known pro-war Republican. The rioters also expressed hostility to the idea of fighting to free the slaves, and they acted most violently toward black people, who had recently been used to replace Irish longshoremen during a labor strike. It took four days before order was finally restored, and by then, more than one hundred people had been killed. This was the largest loss of life caused by any civilian riot in American history up to that point.

>> An engraving entitled "Sowing and Reaping" depicts southern women persuading their husbands to join in the rebellion (left) and the same women rioting for bread during the hard times of the war (right).

SOWING AND REAPING.

[SOUTHERN WOMEN HOUNDING THEIR MEN ON TO REBELLION.

SOUTHERN WOMEN FEELING THE EFFECTS OF REBELLION, AND CREATING BREAD RIOTS.

© MPI/Getty Images

>> The 7th New York Regiment firing into a crowd of draft rioters.

## Dissent in the South

The South faced its own problems on the home front.

### Economic Woes

The prospect of a long war had put the Confederate economy in desperate straits by 1863. With the institution of slavery disintegrating (as explained in the following pages), the women and men who remained on the southern home front were unable to maintain sufficient production of corn, grain, and other foodstuffs. The shortages caused the price of food to skyrocket. Manufactured goods also became scarce as the Union blockade of the Confederacy cut off the region from European suppliers. Merchants made matters worse by hoarding goods, which also drove prices up.

### Riots

In this economy, the average southerner could not afford basic necessities. High prices and food shortages provoked riots throughout the Confederacy in 1863. In April, in the Confederate capital of Richmond, three hundred women and children took to the streets armed with knives and pistols, broke into stores, and stole the items they needed but could not afford.

In the face of months of scarcity and starvation, many women on the Confederate home

66 The number composing this first mob has been so differently estimated, that it would be impossible from reports merely, to approximate the truth. A pretty accurate idea, however, can be gained of its immense size, from a statement made by Mr. King, son of President King, of Columbia College. Struck by its magnitude, he had the curiosity to get some estimate of it by timing its progress, and he found that although it filled the broad street from curbstone to curbstone, and was moving rapidly, it took between twenty and twenty-five minutes for it to pass a single point. A ragged, coatless, heterogeneously weaponed army, it heaved tumultuously along toward Third Avenue. 99

—*Journalist Joel Tyler Headley, Pen and Pencil Sketches of the Great Riots [of 1863], 1877*

**contraband**
Smuggled goods; during the Civil War, it also referred to runaway slaves who had fled to the Union Army

**Confiscation Act**
Legislation that officially declared that any slaves used for military purposes would be freed if they came into Union hands

 Read excerpts from Mary Boykin Chesnut's wartime diary from the South.

front started to lose their will to sacrifice for independence. Jefferson Davis and the other leaders of the Confederate States of America were ineffective in sustaining popular morale. This was not due to their personal qualities, but principally because the South's poor transportation networks, never fully developed during the Market Revolution, hindered leaders from making rallying trips across the land. In addition to this inability to communicate with its citizens, the government did little to alleviate their economic hardships. Focusing solely on the military problem of keeping the Union armies at bay, Davis made no attempt to provide his constituents with government assistance. Davis's wartime policies—the suspension of the writ of habeas corpus, conscription, and impressments—only increased popular dissatisfaction. As in the North by 1863, there was a full-blown peace faction in the South working to undermine Davis's leadership.

By the midpoint of the war, both the Union and the Confederacy had become bitterly divided societies.

# LO⁵ The Tide of Battle Turns, 1863–1865

Wars continue despite dissent, of course. During the Civil War, men fought brutal battles, combining ancient methods of fighting (using sabers and knives) with modern warfare (using long-range rifles, cannons, and other instruments that could kill opponents without ever having to see them up close). The conflict deepened, and by 1863 the war had turned from a "limited war" to an all-encompassing one.

Lincoln struggled to keep up morale in the North, and one way he did this was by performing a delicate political dance on the subject of slavery, leading ultimately to his powerful and eloquent Emancipation Proclamation. Seeking to outlaw slavery was a definitive move toward challenging the very existence of southern society.

## Slavery and Emancipation

Although slavery was clearly the root of the Civil War, Lincoln made no immediate move to end slav-

ery; he understood that in 1861 most northerners did not support broad emancipation. Northern people generally agreed that slavery was an evil institution, but they also balked at the thought of creating a large, free black population in the United States.

Lincoln also feared that immediate emancipation would alienate the four border states that remained within the Union; Missouri, Kentucky, Maryland, and Delaware all retained slavery but still sought to preserve the Union. In order to defeat the Confederacy, Lincoln knew he needed to keep those states relatively happy, something emancipation would undoubtedly jeopardize. Therefore, as part of the Union's limited war strategy, U.S. soldiers were initially instructed to leave southern slave property alone and return any escaped slaves who tried to hide behind Union lines.

## Overtures to Emancipation

As the war dragged on, however, Union practice gradually deviated from this policy. The South depended on its slaves to provide food and manual labor for the war effort, so in May 1861, General Benjamin Butler of Massachusetts began the practice of treating runaway slaves as **contraband** (smuggled goods), refusing to return them to their owners. Then, in August 1861, Congress passed its first **Confiscation Act**, which officially declared that any slaves used for military purposes would be freed if they came into Union hands.

Congress also freed the 2,000 slaves living in the nation's capital, providing compensation to their owners. At the same time, it banned slavery from all U.S. territories, officially putting an end to the issue of the expansion of slavery that had aroused sectional tensions in the 1840s and 1850s. And in July 1862 Congress passed the Second Confiscation Act, which stated that all slaves owned by rebel masters (not just those being used for military purposes) would be set free if they fell under Union control. With southerners absent from Congress, northern Republicans were making rapid strides toward eliminating slavery in the United States.

Although Lincoln signed the Second Confiscation Act, he generally ignored it. Lincoln wanted the slave states to choose emancipation, not to have it forced upon them. After the Second Confiscation Act became law, Lincoln summoned to the White House representatives from the border states of Missouri, Kentucky, Maryland, and Delaware, and presented them with a plan to free their slaves. Unfortunately, the border states resisted any suggestion that they end the practice of slavery.

 Read the Second Confiscation Act.

## Deciding on Emancipation

Eventually, Lincoln decided to initiate an emancipation policy himself, explicitly making slavery the central issue of the war. On July 22, 1862, Lincoln told his cabinet that he planned to issue a presidential proclamation freeing at least some of the slaves. Emancipation carried clear military benefits, he argued. For one thing, it would weaken the Confederacy by depriving southerners of slave labor. In addition, emancipation would earn moral support from the rest of the free world, making it difficult for nations such as Britain and France to ally with the Confederacy.

Taking the advice of his secretary of state, William H. Seward, Lincoln waited for a Union military victory before announcing his proclamation, in order to appear to speak from a position of strength, not desperation. Lincoln got his chance after the Battle of Antietam (Battle of Sharpsburg) on September 17, 1862, when the Union's Army of the Potomac forced Lee's Army of Northern Virginia to retreat from Union territory in Maryland back into the Confederacy.

## The Emancipation Proclamation

Five days after the Battle of Antietam, on September 22, 1862, Lincoln made his preliminary Emancipation Proclamation, which declared that all slaves within rebel territory would be freed on January 1, 1863, unless the southern states returned to the Union. To make the proclamation more palatable to white northerners, Lincoln justified it by saying he had given the order out of military necessity. Emancipation would weaken the Confederacy, he argued, and as commander-in-chief, he was obliged to initiate and enforce such policies. In addition, it would not free a single slave in the slave states that were already part of the Union. When the southern states failed to return to the Union as requested, Lincoln issued the formal Emancipation Proclamation on January 1, 1863. The North no longer fought for the reconstruction of the old Union. It was seeking the creation of a new Union, one without slavery.

Although undeniably bold, the proclamation was far from a comprehensive plan for emancipation. Lincoln exempted Missouri, Kentucky, Maryland, and Delaware (the border states), as well as Tennessee and areas of Virginia and Louisiana already under Union occupation. Only areas actively engaged in rebellion were affected. Moreover, those places where the proclamation was intended to free slaves were precisely those places where the Union lacked the power to enforce its policies.

## *A* Factor in the End of Slavery, but Not *the* Factor

Even before Lincoln issued the Emancipation Proclamation, however, slavery was disintegrating, as the dislocations of war made it impossible for southerners to maintain control over their slaves. As more southern men left their farms to enter the army, slaves took more and more liberties and, in some cases, openly challenged white authority. They shirked work, and attempts to impose discipline only made them more defiant. When word spread that the Union Army was nearby, thousands of slaves would run away and attempt to take refuge behind Union lines.

Learn more about the Emancipation Proclamation.

Read the Emancipation Proclamation.

Lincoln's proclamation thus did not end slavery; slaves themselves ended slavery—with the help of the Union Army. But the proclamation emboldened slaves to increase their resistance, and it offered hope that, if the Union won the war, slavery would be outlawed.

## Black Americans in the Union Military

Black Americans had been trying to volunteer for service in the Union Army all along, but, afraid of the effect on white soldiers' morale, Lincoln rejected them. This changed with the Emancipation Proclamation, which included an announcement that black Americans would be accepted into the U.S. Army and Navy. During the next two years, 180,000 black men, up to 80 percent of them runaway slaves, joined the Union military. They faced difficult conditions, however, serving in segregated units headed by white officers and receiving only half the compensation paid to white soldiers. Despite the prejudicial treatment, the Union's black soldiers signed up readily, and, in June 1864, Lincoln persuaded Congress to grant them equal pay retroactively. By the end of the conflict, 37,000 black servicemen had lost their lives in the battle for the Union.

## The Fort Pillow Massacre

Confederate soldiers resented the presence of African American troops in the U.S. Army. In one controversial incident, after a Confederate victory in the Battle of Fort Pillow, Tennessee, on April 12, 1864,

>> Harper's Weekly of March 14, 1863, illustrates a Union officer teaching black recruits how to use the relatively new French Minié rifle.

of tyranny. As they saw it, the government had no right to deprive anyone of his property. Moreover, the proclamation suggested that Republicans might actually allow black Americans to exist on a level of equality with white people in America. Given the depths of racism in the United States, the proclamation was hard for many northerners to accept, especially northern Democrats.

## Union Military Triumphs

In 1863 and 1864, while both Union and Confederacy dealt with rising dissent and the expansion of their governments, the Union military won a number of important victories. The turning point was Gettysburg.

### Lee's Hopes

Confederate forces under Robert E. Lee had won impressive victories at Fredericksburg, Virginia, in December 1862, and at nearby Chancellorsville in May 1863. With the momentum from these victories, Lee invaded the North with 75,000 troops. By invading the North, Lee (1) sought to allow the southern soil time to recuperate from months of battle; (2) was hoping that, strategically, a major victory in the North would buttress the Union's peace movement and force Lincoln to accept Confederate terms for peace; and (3) thought a major victory in the North would also compel the British to reconsider recognition of the Confederacy, thus giving the Confederacy a valuable partner in the war.

### Gettysburg

Despite Lee's intention of waging a northern battle in a major city, circumstances conspired to force a showdown at the small town of Gettysburg, Pennsylvania. Lee's Army of Northern Virginia had invaded Pennsylvania and had come close to taking Harrisburg, the state's capital. The Union's Army of the Potomac, however, now led by General George Gordon Meade, set off to chase Lee, ultimately confronting him in Gettysburg. The battle that ensued was one of the epic battles of the Civil War, and many historians consider it the turning point of the war.

Engagement was vicious and bloody. After two days of trying unsuccessfully to break the Union line, Lee made an ill-fated move on July 3. In an attempt to split the Union forces, he sent about 12,500 men in a charge into the well-entrenched center of the Union line. This attack is known as Pickett's Charge because General George Pickett was one of the three division commanders leading it. It was a disas-

Confederate soldiers, led by Major General Nathan Bedford Forrest (later the first leader of the Ku Klux Klan), massacred most of an African American regiment who may have been attempting to surrender. The interracial Union troops suffered defeat in the battle, and some witnesses said the Union troops were attempting to surrender when Confederate troops opened fire. Only about 20 percent of the black soldiers were taken as prisoners, while 60 percent of white soldiers were. The rest were casualties of war. The Fort Pillow Massacre became a rallying cry in the North at a pivotal time in the war.

Read the report from the congressional committee investigating Fort Pillow.

## Criticism of Lincoln's Proclamation

Although Lincoln's fellow Republicans generally supported the Emancipation Proclamation, many other northerners criticized it. Predictably, northern Democrats lambasted the proclamation as an act

trous move by Lee. Nearly two-thirds of the attacking Confederates were killed, wounded, or captured during the assault, and the Union took the victory. All told, Lee lost roughly 28,000 soldiers at Gettysburg (approximately one-third of his army) and never again had the manpower to go on the offensive. The federal losses numbered about 23,000, but the Union's great advantage in manpower made such losses easier to overcome than they were for the South. Indeed, in his Gettysburg Address, Lincoln memorably used the battle to motivate his side to continue the struggle under the belief that what they were doing was right, destined to give the nation a "new birth of freedom."

> **"**All that I had ever read in battle stories of the booming of heavy guns out-thundering the thunders of heaven and making the earth tremble, and almost stopping one's breath from the concussions of the air—was here made real, in terrific effect.**"**
>
> —*From "The Reminiscences of Carl Schurz," general at Gettysburg*

Read Lincoln's Gettysburg Address.

Read General Carl Schurz's impressions of Gettysburg after the battle.

### Victories in the West

Meanwhile, Union general Ulysses S. Grant continued to triumph in the West. On July 4, 1863, after a six-week siege, his troops forced the fortress town of Vicksburg, Mississippi, to surrender. Four days later, he captured Port Hudson in Louisiana. With those two victories, the Union controlled the entire Mississippi River, severing the Confederacy into eastern and western halves. The battle at Gettysburg received more public notice at the time, but Grant's victories on the Mississippi were perhaps more strategically important.

In light of Grant's success, Lincoln brought him east in March 1864 and made him commander of all the Union armies. From his new post, Grant prepared for an offensive against Lee in Virginia, while General William Tecumseh Sherman took over for Grant in the West.

### Northern Momentum?

While northern momentum was strong, the Union again faced the strategic problem of having to completely subdue and conquer its enemy in order to win. In May and June 1864, Grant relentlessly pursued Lee's army in a bloody campaign from the Rappahannock River to the city of Petersburg, south of Richmond, Virginia. Outside Petersburg, the two armies settled into opposing trenches. The siege there lasted more than nine months. Between May and July 1864, Grant lost 60,000 men, and news of these heavy casualties demoralized the northern home front. Northerners began to fear that the Union armies could never defeat the Confederacy. Despite northern military momentum, was it possible to win a war when the opposition never had to attack?

### The Election of 1864

In this atmosphere of uncertainty, the Union continued its pattern of predictable, regular elections as laid out in the Constitution and held a presidential contest. As the war stretched on, the impatience of the northern people during the summer of 1864 did not bode well for Lincoln. But, more than this, the election became a referendum on slavery and

© iStockphoto.com/Joanna Pecha

> ❝With malice toward none; with charity for all; with firmness in the right, as God gives us to see the right, let us strive on to finish the work we are in.❞
>
> —*Abraham Lincoln, Second Inaugural Address*

measure, so Lincoln concluded that once the war ended it would no longer be binding. Therefore, upon his electoral victory, Lincoln and his supporters moved quickly to secure the final, formal demise of American slavery.

Lincoln's Emancipation Proclamation. Did they want four more years of Abraham Lincoln and, potentially, of civil war?

## McClellan

In 1864, Lincoln's Democratic opponent was none other than the overly cautious George B. McClellan, the former general of the Army of the Potomac. If elected, McClellan promised to restore slavery in the South and negotiate peace with the Confederacy (perhaps leading to the recognition of Confederate independence). His party's slogan was "The Union as it was, the Constitution as it is, and the Negroes where they are." After three years of war, northerners were despairing of the casualties and fearful of the outcome, and even Lincoln did not believe he would be voted into office for a second term.

## Timely Military Victories

The Union military, however, saved the day for Lincoln. On August 5, 1864, the Union captured Mobile Bay in Alabama, and less than one month later, Sherman took control of Atlanta. After months of stagnation, the momentum had swung fully to the Union.

 Read Lincoln's remarkable Second Inaugural Address.

These victories heartened northern voters and gave them a renewed sense that the Confederacy could be beaten. On Election Day in November, Lincoln received 55 percent of the popular vote, giving him a landslide victory in the Electoral College.

# LO⁶ The Destruction of the South and the End of the War

Lincoln's reelection spelled the end of slavery. The Emancipation Proclamation had been made as a war

## The Thirteenth Amendment Abolishes Slavery

Lincoln used all of the influence he had in Congress to ensure the passage of a constitutional amendment freeing all the slaves in the United States without compensating their owners. On January 31, 1865, Congress passed the Thirteenth Amendment, and by the end of the year, enough Union states had ratified the amendment to make it part of the Constitution, abolishing slavery from the United States forever.

## The Destruction of the South

Lincoln's victory in November 1864 also marked the beginning of the end for the Confederacy, which now took a brutal punishing.

### Sherman's March to the Sea

With the Union now set to defeat the rebels rapidly, General Sherman waged his famous **"March to the Sea,"** mowing a path of destruction 60 miles wide and several hundred miles long, through Georgia. The March to the Sea stretched from Atlanta to the Atlantic. Sherman designed the move to encircle Lee's army, which was still in Virginia, and, more importantly, to prove to the southern people that the Confederate government lacked the ability to protect them. The soldiers burned fields, tore up vital infrastructure, such as railroad ties, and killed and consumed all the livestock they encountered. By Christmas 1864, Sherman's soldiers had reached Savannah. As much as the Union soldiers relished this punishment of the rebels, they relished even more the prospect of moving north and destroying South Carolina, the birthplace of the Civil War. After hitting the coast, Sherman's troops continued their march through South and North Carolina, heading north to join forces with Grant in Virginia, an act

The Art Archive / Library of Congress

>> **Richmond in ruins, 1865.**

the Union was fighting a total war, destroying railroads, bridges, cotton gins, and anything else that the rebels could use to support their war effort.

## The Southern Will to Fight?

The Confederacy's ravaged economy, the demoralization of its home front, and the dangers of the Union Army all combined to erode the southern people's will to fight. By the spring of 1865, more than half of Confederate soldiers had deserted. Meanwhile, Grant tenaciously attacked the Army of Northern Virginia, knowing that when Lee surrendered, the South would be forced to give up entirely. Lee finally capitulated on April 9, 1865, at Appomattox Courthouse, Virginia. Although there was sporadic fighting in the West until the end of May, with Lee's surrender the war was effectively over. For the reasons why the North won the Civil War, see "The reasons why . . ." box below.

that would encircle Lee's Army of Northern Virginia and end the war once and for all.

Sherman's March showed how much the war had changed since 1861. Having started with a strategy of limited war, intending to fight only against soldiers and leaving private property alone, by 1864

## {*The reasons why . . .*}

### The North won the Civil War for three principal reasons:

***The embrace of the Market Revolution.*** The North had integrated the breakthroughs of the Market Revolution better than the South had. With a well-developed manufacturing sector, varied agricultural supplies, a diverse labor force, and a transportation system able to move food, troops, and supplies rapidly, the North outmaneuvered, outpaced, and outproduced the South.

***Manpower supremacy.*** The Union simply had more men than the Confederacy, meaning that it could afford a long and costly war better than the South.

***Political organization.*** The political party system surrounding Lincoln provided him with an infrastructure to spread propaganda and garner widespread support. Jefferson Davis never had such an infrastructure and thus failed to create sustained enthusiasm for the war effort.

# LO⁷ Significance of the War

The four years of civil war were brutal for both the North and the South. One out of every twelve American men served in the war, and about 620,000 American men lost their lives, more Americans than were killed in World War I, World War II, the Vietnam War, and the Revolutionary War combined. For the Confederacy, of the roughly 1 million soldiers that fought, about 258,000 died from disease or battle. For the Union, its army of about 2,500,000 men lost around 360,000 men. In addition, for every 1,000 Union soldiers in battle, 112 were wounded. For every 1,000 Confederate soldiers, 150 suffered casualties. Of the 180,000 African American soldiers who fought, approximately one-third lost their lives. It was a brutal war indeed.

Beyond the grim number of dead, the American nation had turned into a battlefield. The various militaries had commandeered roads, pulled up enemy train tracks, destroyed factories, and killed livestock. The South bore the brunt of this destruction, but the entire nation felt the impact of the war. And there was more than just physical destruction. More than 4,000,000 men mobilized for war, meaning a major disruption of life back home. Labor relations had to be reworked and familial roles renegotiated. The large number of wartime dead also meant these transitions were often not temporary. For the soldiers who did make it home, roughly 50,000 returned with one or more limbs amputated, physical reminders of the devastations of war. Beyond this grim departure from daily life, the Civil War had at least six other long-lasting results.

## The Impact on Federal Government

First, fighting its first modern war greatly increased the size and the power of the federal government. While this occurred in both the North and, ironically, the South, it was the North's expansion that set the course for the nation after the war.

To pay for the war, for instance, the federal government began, for the first time, to collect an income tax. This brought the federal government into American lives in a whole new way. Rather than be charged a tax for goods purchased or imported, now everyone's annual income had a levy placed upon it. Meanwhile, the federal government consolidated the nation's money supply, ending the era of wildcat banking begun by Andrew Jackson. During the Civil War, the federal government became the sole issuer of paper money, solidifying its importance in the financial future of the nation and extending its reach throughout the various regions. The federal government also expanded its budget twenty-fold between 1860 and 1865, with the 1865 national budget exceeding $1 billion for the first time in the nation's history. It took an army of clerks and tax collectors to manage this new endeavor, and by 1865 the federal government was the nation's largest employer. With the Civil War, the federal government possessed greater power than ever before and had a much larger bureaucracy to manage that newfound power.

In addition, with no southerners in the wartime Congress, Lincoln's Republicans passed a series of laws furthering the reach of the national government. For instance, to spur agricultural growth and to populate the West with free laborers, Congress in 1863 passed the Homestead Act, which offered 160 acres of free public land to any settler (including slaves) who had never taken up arms against the federal government and who lived on the land for five years. In 1862, Congress passed the Morrill Land Grant College Act, which gave states free federal land if they promised to develop colleges for the state's residents. The federal government also made huge land grants for internal improvements, including, most famously, giving 100 million acres to the Union Pacific and Central Pacific Railroads to build a railroad that stretched to the Pacific Ocean. (Each of these developments will be discussed more fully in Chapter 17.) The federal government thus increased its power during the Civil War, and it used this new power to shape the nation in a free-labor vision. The West would no longer be contested terrain. It would be filled with landowning farmers who could educate their children at local universities and take transcontinental railroads to get from one coast to another, all subsidized by the newly expanded federal government.

## The Impact on Industry

But it was not entirely the free-labor vision that rose triumphant after the war. Rather, several leading manufacturers used the generosity of the federal government to create a vast industrial nation. Relying on profitable government contracts, several "captains of industry" consolidated their wealth during the Civil War, thus gaining a platform upon which they would plunge the nation into the Industrial Age of the late nineteenth century. Philip D. Armour, for instance, earned millions of dollars supplying meat to the Union Army during the war, using the exigencies of war to perfect the refrigerated railcar. He would become a major industrial magnate in the years after the war. Other industrial leaders, including steel baron Andrew Carnegie, oil magnate John D. Rockefeller, and financier J. P. Morgan, used the war to increase and consolidate their wealth, which allowed them to reshape the economy in the following decades. (These men too will be discussed more fully in Chapter 17.) The Civil War thus helped catapult the nation into the Industrial Age, allowing it to become one of the world's industrial powers.

## The Impact on American Nationalism

Somewhat ironically, the war also unified the nation, pulling together the various states to form a more unified country. It is commonplace to say that before the war, the country was called the United *States* of America and after the war it was the *United* States of America. With a stronger federal government serving as a yoke to keep the nation together, the Civil War, like most wars, served as a centripetal force, shifting people's identities from one associated with a particular state to one associated more fully with the nation. The expansion of the federal government only secured a deeper movement toward national identity, and American nationalism.

## The Impact on Women

The Civil War also greatly impacted women, both in the work they did and in the way they were viewed within democratic society. Some 400 women disguised themselves as men and fought during the Civil War. Many more worked with the various armies, serving as spies, cooks, and medical assistants. In addition to these battlefront contributions, the Civil War loosened up other opportunities for women. With millions of men off to fight, women in both the North and the South took jobs that traditionally had been defined as male work. Women worked in munitions plants, as clerks in government offices, and as a sales force in retail businesses. While some of these gains were temporary (such as in munitions plants), others were not (such as in retail).

>> During the Civil War, women took on many new roles, including becoming professional nurses. Clara Barton was one of the most famous, going on to found the American Red Cross.

Women also revolutionized the nursing profession during the Civil War, a profession that had been dominated by men before the war. In the North alone, more than 20,000 women served as nurses. Clara Barton was perhaps the most famous Civil War nurse, following troops into battle and working alongside doctors in makeshift battlefront hospitals. She once had a stray bullet go through her sleeve, killing the patient she was working on. After the war, Barton went on to found the American Red Cross.

Thousands of women in the North also served in the United States Sanitary Commission, the primary national relief organization, coordinating donations to the Union cause. While the national organization remained headed by men, women served as grassroots leaders, contributing directly to the ailing communities that were suffering due to the departure of millions of working-aged men, and emerging as community leaders.

At a more political level, while the war temporarily stalled the nascent women's suffrage movement, women's increased role in public life, especially in the North, provoked many women to announce that they would fight for access to the ballot once the war stopped. Fulfilling their promise, several leaders of the late-nineteenth-century women's suffrage movement claimed to have been both inspired by their wartime efforts and frustrated by the traditional roles ascribed to them after the war.

## The Impact on Religion

The war also changed the way people prayed, what denominations they belonged to, and how they viewed the Bible. Indeed, leading up to the Civil War, several large Protestant denominations split over the issue of slavery. Although the Bible clearly upholds the right to own slaves, several Protestant churches disagreed as to whether or not this was justifiable nearly 2,000 years after the life and death of Christ. Even more problematic, they disagreed about whether or not religious denominations had any right to enter into political debates without debasing their faith. Divisions over these questions led Presbyterians, Methodists, and Baptists to split along northern and southern lines in 1837, 1844, and 1845, respectively. These divisions foreshadowed the larger political split that was to come with the Civil War. Indeed, because the words of ministers often served as moral guidance for the rest of society, by placing the question of slavery in biblical terms church leaders made the sectional split appear cosmic in nature, demanding decisive, even destructive action. While Lincoln continually took a humble approach toward faith and the question of which side, North or South, God was on, both sides often claimed to be fighting for the righteousness of God. As one piece of evidence, the Civil War served to standardize the role and functions of military chaplains.

These divisions in turn foreshadowed a split that developed after the Civil War. Throughout the late nineteenth century, many northerners usually advanced a more liberal interpretation of the Bible, finding the institution of slavery to be vile and contrary to the spirit of the New Testament, thus placing great importance, they argued, on the spirit of the Bible. Southerners, on the other hand, held onto a more literal interpretation of the Bible, which clearly accepted the practice of slavery. This split between liberal Protestants and their more conservative counterparts would only grow during the course of the nineteenth century, with one historian describing these years as the formative years of what has come to be called "the Bible Belt" in the South.

For African Americans, the war was also religiously transformative. Hundreds of new churches opened up throughout the South, often with the help of northern missionaries. Utilizing their new status as freed people, African Americans eagerly filled the pews.

For Jews, who numbered around 150,000 in the United States, the Civil War exposed a deep vein of antisemitism in American life. Although about 10,000 Jews served in the war effort (on both sides) and many served in leadership roles (Judah P. Benjamin was secretary of state for the Confederacy), Jews were often used as scapegoats to explain the economic hard times many Americans experienced during the war. For instance, General Ulysses S. Grant expelled Jews from the areas of western Tennessee that were under his command. Although Lincoln quickly rescinded the order, Jews were expelled from several towns.

For Catholics, the vast majority of whom were recent Irish immigrants living in northern cities, the war provided them with an opportunity to assert themselves as Americans. Roughly 145,000 Irish Catholics served in the Union Army, and, while bishops preached a militant Catholicism that combated the varieties of Nativism they had experienced since their arrival, in the battlefield Catholic leaders sought to ensure that Catholics fought bravely and acted responsibly. They often did. On the home front, though, many Catholics resisted the intrusions into their daily life by a federal government that had at times been overtly anti-Catholic. It was, for example, mostly Irish Catholics that formed the mobs of the 1863 New York City Draft Riots.

## The Impact on Philosophy

While many northerners were accommodating themselves to a looser, nonliteral understanding of the Bible, still others grew disillusioned with any hard and fixed ideas. The passions invoked during the Civil War had led to violence, something democratic nations were not supposed to do. Thus the war discredited the beliefs and assumptions of the era that came before it, and there were very few guiding ideas to replace them. Oliver Wendell Holmes Jr. and William James would use this disillusionment to fashion, after the war, a new philosophy called pragmatism. Pragmatism holds that ideas are not out in nature waiting to be discovered by smart people, but rather are tools, like shovels and hammers, to be used by people to cope with the world in which they live. This is not to say pragmatism allows someone to grasp on to any convenient truth available, but rather that humans should be open to new "truths" that might emerge, evaluating them in conjunction

| 1861 | Serfdom is abolished in Russia. |
| --- | --- |
| 1862 | The first black troops are used in battle, at Island Mount, Missouri. |
| 1862 | The French go to war with Mexico after Mexican president Benito Juarez suspends interest payments to foreign countries. Mexican victory comes five years later, but the 1862 Battle of Puebla, an early Mexican victory, is now commemorated as Cinco de Mayo. |
| 1863 | Former Union nurse Louisa May Alcott (author of *Little Women*) publishes a collection of wartime letters, "Hospital Sketches." During the Civil War women enter the male-dominated profession of nursing in huge numbers. |
| 1864 | The *H. L. Hunley*, a Confederate submarine, is the first sub to sink an enemy ship. It sinks the U.S.S. *Housatonic* on February 17, only to find itself sinking that same night. |
| 1864 | Photograph of Lincoln is taken that appears on today's five-dollar bill. |

with their previously held beliefs. With this kind of flexibility, pragmatism's founders intended to create a worldview that made it harder for a nation to succumb to violence. Pragmatism, one of America's most important contributions to the world of philosophy, would be the predominant worldview in the United States until the middle of the twentieth century.

## And in the end . . .

Despite the reunification of the Union and the Confederacy after the war, exactly how northerners and southerners would come to live together again remained unclear. Reconstructing the nation would be a difficult process full of conflict and disappointment, and that is the subject of the next chapter.

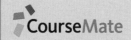

Visit the CourseMate website at www.cengagebrain.com for additional study tools and review materials for this chapter.

# CHAPTER 16

# Reconstruction,
## *1865–1877*

## Learning Outcomes

*After reading this chapter, you should be able to do the following:*

LO **1**   Describe the changed world of ex-slaves after the Civil War.

LO **2**   Outline the different phases of Reconstruction, beginning with Lincoln's plan and moving through presidential Reconstruction to Radical Reconstruction.

LO **3**   Explain how Reconstruction evolved at the individual states' level.

LO **4**   Evaluate and understand the relative success of Reconstruction.

# "Nearly 23 percent of the South's fighting-age men had died in the war."

Confederate soldiers returned home to a devastated South in 1865. While northern trains and cities began to hum with activity, the South's farms and factories, its railroads and bridges—its entire infrastructure—had been destroyed by war. Nearly 23 percent of the South's fighting-age men had died in the war. Thousands more bore the physical scars of battle. The physical rebuilding of the region began quickly and progressed rapidly, but reconstructing southern society was a much more difficult process, especially considering (1) the political questions about how to integrate rebel states back into the nation and (2) the social questions about how to integrate 4 million newly freed slaves.

The North was also vastly changed, albeit in another way. Northern politicians seized the opportunity to pass many of the laws that southerners in Congress had long resisted. During and shortly after the war, Congress passed laws supporting internal improvements, outlawing slavery, and expanding the developments of the Market Revolution. Indeed, some historians argue that the Civil War was crucial in turning the Market Revolution into the Industrial Revolution. Regardless of the term you use, the North after the Civil War was beginning to take the shape of what we think of today as a modern industrial society.

But, first, to the era of **Reconstruction**, the federal government's attempts to resolve the issues resulting from the end of the Civil War, which lasted from 1865 to 1877.

## What do you think?

Reconstruction had some significant achievements but was ultimately a failure.

| Strongly Disagree | | | | | | Strongly Agree |
|---|---|---|---|---|---|---|
| 1 | 2 | 3 | 4 | 5 | 6 | 7 |

**Reconstruction**
The federal government's attempts to resolve the issues resulting from the end of the Civil War

## LO¹ Freedmen, Freedwomen

After the Civil War, black Americans encountered a new world of opportunities. After years of enslavement, or at least the perpetual threat of enslavement if they had been already freed, African Americans confronted a new question: what does it mean to be free? What does one do after the bonds of slavery have been broken?

The first thing many freed people did was move. They often left the plantations upon which they had labored as slaves, or they sought to reunite with long-lost family members, who had perhaps been sold to another owner. The freedom of movement was the key.

This new mobility meant that black family life began to stabilize throughout the South. Men and women now had more control over their lives and their familial

© Dennis Brack / DanitaDelimont.com via Newscom

roles. Reflecting the priorities of nineteenth-century American society, ex-slaves often removed women from the fields so that they could occupy a "women's sphere of domesticity." Most black women still had to work for financial reasons, but they often began working as indoor domestics rather than as field hands.

Meanwhile, freed families often desperately sought to purchase land in order to continue the planting life they knew best, sometimes by simply purchasing a piece of the land on which they had labored before the Civil War. In their new communities, African Americans also expressed their religious independence by expanding the huge independent network of black churches that had been established since the Revolution. During the Reconstruction era, the number of black churches multiplied.

The newly freed people also sought the education that had been denied them during slavery. Schools for African Americans opened all over the South, for parents and for children. Learning to read meant learning to understand contracts, engage in political battles, and monitor wages, new experiences for those who had only recently been deemed chattel.

Politically, African Americans sought to vote. They marched in demand of it. They paraded to advocate for bills endorsing it. They lionized black Revolutionary heroes to establish their credentials as vote-casting Americans. And they held mock elections to show their capacity and desire to participate in the American political process. Life for the newly freed was tumultuous but exciting, filled with possibilities. It was a whole new world they encountered, full of promise and hope.

## The Freedmen's Bureau

While ex-slaves explored a life based on the free-labor vision, members of the defeated Confederacy sought to maintain as much of the old order as possible. To this end, they worked to prevent ex-slaves from acquiring economic autonomy or political rights. Although they had lost the war, ex-Confederates feared a complete turnover from the lives they had led before it. Indeed, one of the first organizations created after the war in the South was the Ku Klux Klan, founded in 1865 by six white Confederate soldiers concerned about the racial implications of black freedom. The Klan and other similar organizations, such as the Southern Cross and the Knights of White Camellia, served as quasi-military forces serving the interests of those who desired the restoration of white supremacy. Nathan Bedford Forrest, a Confederate general, was the Klan's first national leader.

To help mitigate this resistance, in 1865, Congress established the **Freedmen's Bureau**, a government agency designed to create a new social order by government mandate. Under the management of northerner O. O. Howard (after whom Howard University is named), Congress designed the Freedmen's Bureau to build and manage new

{ *What it means to be free . . .* }

After the Civil War, African Americans in the South demonstrated their freedom in numerous ways, large and small. Many bought dogs, some purchased firearms, and several held mass meetings without white supervision, all actions that were often denied them under slavery. Many quickly moved after the war, almost always traveling in search of lost relatives who had been sold to other plantations during the era of slavery, when slave families were secondary to profits. Many newly freed persons simply sought to be far away from the plantations on which they had been enslaved. Ex-slaves who traveled around the country demonstrated their freedom to make their own choices.

Library of Congress, Prints & Photographs Division, LC-DIG-cwpb-00468

>> "The Secretary of War may direct such issues of provisions, clothing, and fuel, as he may deem needful for the immediate and temporary shelter and supply of destitute and suffering refugees and freedmen and their wives and children, under such rules and regulations as he may direct." —Freedmen's Bureau Bill, 1865

schools, provide food and medical care to needy southern black and white people, and ensure equal access to the judicial system for southerners both black and white. It had some success with this Herculean task: the Freedmen's Bureau built 3,000 schools and expanded medical care throughout much of the South, paying particular attention to the freed slaves and the areas where they had settled.

Its task of redesigning economic relations would prove more challenging. Although Lincoln's Republicans in Congress succeeded in putting into the bureau's charter a provision that plantations be divided into 40-acre plots and sold to former slaves, that plan was upended by politicians intending to enforce their own plans for reconstructing the South. Because politics were vitally important in determining how Reconstruction would unfold, it is to politics we must turn.

Read the congressional act establishing the Freedmen's Bureau.

# LO$^2$ Political Plans for Reconstruction

Even before the war was over, President Lincoln had pondered what it would take to bring the South back into the nation. Unfortunately for him, many in Congress were more interested in punishment than in reconciliation.

## Lincoln's Plan for Reconstruction and His Assassination

In 1863, Lincoln issued his **Ten-Percent Plan**, which offered amnesty to any southerner who proclaimed loyalty to the Union and support of the emancipation of slaves. When 10 percent of a state's voters in the election of 1860 had taken the oath to the United States, they could develop a new state government, which would be required to abolish slavery. Then that state could reenter the Union with full privileges, including the crucial apportionment to the House of Representatives and Senate. Although requiring just 10 percent of a population to declare loyalty seems extremely lenient toward the opposition (besides the fact that it left out any role for the ex-slaves), Lincoln was attempting to drain support from the Confederacy and shorten the war by making appeasement look easy.

## Congress Bristles

Republicans in Congress, more interested in punishing the South than Lincoln was, bristled at Lincoln's leniency. In opposition to Lincoln's plan, they passed the **Wade-Davis Bill**, which would have allowed a southern state back into the Union only after 50 percent of the population had taken the loyalty oath. Furthermore, to earn the right to vote or to serve in a constitutional convention, southerners would have to take a second oath, called the **iron-clad oath**, that testified that they had never voluntarily aided or abetted the rebellion. The iron-clad oath was designed to ensure that only staunch Unionists in the South could hold political power. Lincoln vetoed the bill, but the battle about Reconstruction continued.

Read Lincoln's proclamation on vetoing the Wade-Davis Bill.

## Lincoln's Assassination

As this battle wore on between Congress and the president, the hostilities of the American Civil War finally ended. Although the South had lost the war,

**Ten-Percent Plan**
Plan issued by Lincoln in 1863 that offered amnesty to any southerner who proclaimed loyalty to the Union and support of the emancipation of slaves; once 10 percent of a state's voters in the election of 1860 signed the oath, it could create a new state government and reenter the Union

**Wade-Davis Bill**
Bill that would have allowed a southern state back into the Union only after 50 percent of the population had taken the loyalty oath

**iron-clad oath**
Oath to be taken by southerners to testify that they had never voluntarily aided or abetted the rebellion

a few disgruntled southerners would attempt to get revenge. Three days after Appomattox, John Wilkes Booth, a local actor and Confederate sympathizer,

 View a Library of Congress picture gallery about Lincoln's assassination.

shot and killed Lincoln during a play at Ford's Theater in Washington, D.C. Eleven days later, a Union soldier shot and killed Booth as he tried to escape from a burning barn. In the coming political showdown, Lincoln's deep empathy and political acumen would be missed, as the battle to reconstruct the nation now took place between defiant congressional Republicans and the insecure man who had stumbled into the presidency—Andrew Johnson.

## Andrew Johnson and Presidential Reconstruction

Upon Lincoln's assassination, Andrew Johnson became president. Johnson was a native southerner, born in North Carolina and then residing in Tennessee. He was also functionally illiterate. Throughout the war, however, Johnson proved a loyal Unionist, and he served as Tennessee's military governor after the state was taken over by the Union Army. Despite Johnson's being a Democrat, in 1864, Lincoln selected Johnson as his running mate because Lincoln

hoped to quiet dissent by running with a non-northerner and a non-Republican. While it may have helped him win the election, Lincoln's plan would ultimately backfire.

### Presidential Reconstruction, 1865–1867

Johnson was a lonely man who had a tough time handling criticism. Since his youth, he had looked up to the South's planter aristocracy and constantly sought its approval. Reflecting these insecurities, within a month of assuming the presidency, Johnson unveiled his plan for Reconstruction: (1) scrapping the "40-acres-and-a-mule" plan suggested in the charter of the Freedmen's Bureau and (2) creating a tough loyalty oath that many southerners could take in order to receive a pardon for their participation in the rebellion. However, Johnson added a curious caveat that Confederate leaders and wealthy planters—who were not allowed to take the standard oath—could appeal directly to Johnson for a pardon. Anyone who received amnesty through either of these measures regained his citizenship rights and retained all of his property, except for his slaves. Under Johnson's plan, a governor appointed by the president would then control each rebel state until the loyalty oath was administered to the citizens. At that point, southerners could create new state constitutions and elect their own governors, state legislatures, and federal representatives. Johnson showed no concern for the future of black people in America.

Southern states made the most of the leeway Johnson afforded them. Even Robert E. Lee applied to be pardoned (although his pardon was never granted during his lifetime). A line of southern planters literally appeared at the White House to ask Johnson's personal forgiveness; doing so allowed the southern elite to return to its former privileged status. In the end, Johnson granted amnesty to more than 13,000 Confederates, many of whom had been combative leaders in the Confederacy. Once Johnson had granted these pardons, he

*Even Robert E. Lee applied to be pardoned.*

>> The insecure man who had stumbled into the presidency—Andrew Johnson.

Read Johnson's Proclamation of Amnesty for the Confederate States.

ensured that there would be no social revolution in the South. With pardons in hand, they would not lose their land or their social control of the South.

## Black Codes

Most of the new southern state governments returned Confederate leaders to political power. These leaders then created **black codes** modeled on the slave codes that existed before the Civil War. Although the codes legalized black marriages and allowed African Americans to hold and sell property, freed slaves were prohibited from serving on juries or testifying against white people in court. Intermarriage between black and white Americans was also strictly forbidden. Some states even had special rules that limited the economic freedoms of their black populations. Mississippi, for example, barred African Americans from purchasing or renting farmland. Most states created laws that allowed police officials to round up black vagrants and hire them out as laborers to white landowners.

In the end, these new laws hardened the separation of black Americans from white Americans, ending the intermingling and interaction that had been more common during slavery. With the rise of post–Civil War black codes, black and white southerners began a long process of physical separation that was not

Read the Mississippi legislature's black codes.

present before the war, and that would last for at least a century. These black codes would also begin the process whereby black southerners after the Civil War were left with, in the words of one historian, nothing but freedom.

## Radical Reconstruction

Johnson did nothing to prevent the South from reimposing these conditions on the black population. In Johnson's eyes, reconstruction of the Union would be finished as soon as southern states returned to the Union without slavery. Conservative members of Congress agreed. The **Radical Republicans**, however, disagreed.

## The Radical Republicans

The Republican Party had never been squarely behind Lincoln's plan for Reconstruction, and in fact the Radical Republicans, known as the wing of the party most hostile to slavery, had opposed Lincoln's plans fiercely. Radicals in Congress, including Thaddeus Stevens of Pennsylvania, Charles Sumner of Massachusetts (of "Bleeding Sumner" fame), and Benjamin Wade of Ohio, had pushed for emancipation long before Lincoln issued the Emancipation Proclamation, and they considered Lincoln's lenient Reconstruction program outrageous. As they looked toward the end of the war, Radicals hoped to use the Confederacy's defeat as an opportunity to overhaul southern society. At the very least, they hoped to strip the southern planter class of its power and ensure that freed slaves would acquire basic rights.

## The Radicals versus Johnson

As we have seen, Johnson, considering himself somewhat of a moderate, took office intending to wrap up the process of Reconstruction quickly. Radicals in Congress, however, continued to devise measures for protecting the interests of the newly freed black population. With no southerners yet in Congress, the Radical Republicans wielded considerable power.

Read a *Harper's Weekly* editorial about the Civil Rights Bill.

Their first moves were (1) to expand the role of the Freedmen's Bureau, creating a stronger organization with greater enforcement powers and a bigger budget, and (2) to pass the important **Civil Rights Act**, which was designed to counteract the South's new black codes. The Civil Rights Act granted all citizens mandatory rights, regardless of racial considerations. Johnson vetoed both bills, but Congress overrode the veto on the Civil Rights Act, making it the first law ever passed over presidential veto.

> **"** Congress overrode the veto on the Civil Rights Act, making it the first law ever passed over presidential veto. **"**

**black codes**
Post–Civil War laws specifically written to govern the behavior of African Americans; modeled on the slave codes that existed before the Civil War

**Radical Republicans**
Wing of the Republican Party most hostile to slavery

**Civil Rights Act**
Bill that granted all citizens mandatory rights, regardless of racial considerations; designed to counteract the South's new black codes

Their willingness to override a presidential veto suggests the importance that Radical Republicans placed on a meaningful reconstruction effort. It was the first of many vetoes the Radical Republicans would override.

## The Fourteenth Amendment

Congress's success in circumventing Johnson's veto began a new phase of Reconstruction known as **Radical Reconstruction** in which Congress wielded more power than the president. Congress introduced a constitutional amendment in 1866 that (1) barred Confederate leaders from ever holding public office in the United States, (2) gave Congress the right to reduce the representation of any state that did not give black people the right to vote, and (3) declared that any person born or naturalized in the United States was, by that very act, an American citizen deserving of "equal protection of the law." This, in essence, granted full citizenship to all black people; states were prohibited from restricting the rights and privileges of any citizen.

To the frustration of Radicals like Thaddeus Stevens and Charles Sumner, the amendment, which became the **Fourteenth Amendment** to the U.S. Constitution, did not also protect the voting rights of African Americans. Nevertheless, Congress passed the amendment and it went to the states for ratification. Tennessee approved it and, in 1866, was invited by Congress to reenter the Union. Every other state of the former Confederacy rejected the amendment, suggesting that the Radicals' hopes for restructuring the South would not be realized easily.

 Read the Mississippi legislature's black codes.

*There was nothing worse than being part of a nation and having no say in how that nation was governed.*

## Radical Reconstruction, 1867–1877

Despite the strenuous labors of Andrew Johnson, the midterm elections of 1866 gave the Republicans a two-thirds majority in both houses of Congress, and they began to push their program of Reconstruction more vigorously. The election was vicious, as Johnson and his supporters went around the country on what was called the "swing around the circle" to castigate and even threaten the execution of several Radical Republicans. Despite Andrew Johnson's claim that Reconstruction was over, the Radical-led Congress easily passed (again over Johnson's veto) the **Military Reconstruction Act** in March 1867. This act divided the former rebel states, with the exception of Tennessee, into five military districts. In each district, a military commander took control of the state governments, and federal soldiers enforced the law and kept order. See Map 16.1.

Congress also made requirements for readmission to the Union more stringent. Each state was instructed to register voters and hold elections for a state constitutional convention. In enrolling voters, southern officials were required to include black people and exclude any white people who had held leadership positions in the Confederacy, although this provision proved easy to ignore. Once the conventions were organized, the delegates then needed to (1) create constitutions that protected black voting rights and (2) agree to ratify the Fourteenth Amendment. Only then would Congress ratify the new state constitutions and accept southern state representatives back into the national Congress. Holding a fair state election and agreeing to the Fourteenth Amendment became the litmus tests for reentry to the nation. Without doing so and thereby becoming full-fledged members of the Union again, the southern states would remain without congressional apportionment and under military control.

 Read the Military Reconstruction Act.

## The Second Reconstruction Act

At first, these provisions proved to be both too harsh and too lenient. The Military Reconstruction Act so outraged southerners that they refused to enroll the voters needed to put Reconstruction into

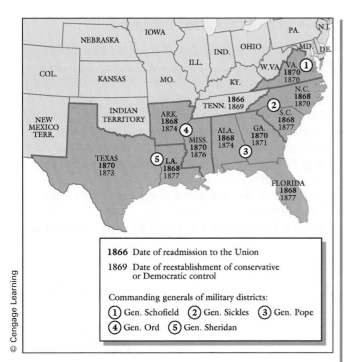

© Cengage Learning

1866 Date of readmission to the Union

1869 Date of reestablishment of conservative or Democratic control

Commanding generals of military districts:
① Gen. Schofield ② Gen. Sickles ③ Gen. Pope
④ Gen. Ord ⑤ Gen. Sheridan

Map 16.1. Reconstruction in the South

to force southerners to proceed with Reconstruction. President Johnson vetoed all these measures, but his vetoes were all overridden by Radical Republicans in Congress. He was helpless to stop Congress's actions.

Eventually, the southern states had no choice but to follow the Military Reconstruction Act's instructions. There was nothing worse than being part of a nation and having no say in how that nation was governed. They wanted congressional representation back and, in order to get it, they had to acquiesce to Congress's demands. In June 1868, Congress readmitted representatives and senators from seven states: North Carolina, South Carolina, Georgia, Florida, Alabama, Arkansas, and Louisiana. By 1870, the remaining three southern states—Virginia, Mississippi, and Texas—had also agreed to the required provisions and they too received permission to send congressmen to Washington. As more and more Confederate states came back into the Union, the Fourteenth Amendment became the law of the land in 1868.

 Read the Second Reconstruction Act.

motion. But southerners also preferred military rule to civilian control by those hostile to the South. In response to these various objections (and to the South's subsequent foot-dragging), Congress passed a second Reconstruction Act, authorizing the Union military commanders to register southern voters and assemble the constitutional conventions (since the southerners were not eager to do this themselves). The southern states continued to stall, so, in the summer of 1867, Congress passed two more acts designed

## Frustrations

Although the Radical Republicans in Congress had considerable successes, in many important ways they did not produce the social revolution they had envisioned: they did not redistribute land to freed slaves; they did not provide black people with guaranteed access to education; they did not forbid racial segregation; and they did not call for absolute racial equality for black and white people. The process of reconciliation meant that both sides had to give at least a little, and President Johnson's leniency at the outset of Reconstruction had caused Radicals the most consternation.

>> "The ponderous two-handed engine of impeachment, designed to be kept in cryptic darkness until some crisis of the nation's life cried out for interposition, was being dragged into open day to crush a formidable political antagonist a few months before the appointed time when the people might get rid of him altogether."
—Historian David Dewitt, referring to the Radical Republicans' impeachment of Andrew Johnson

## Johnson's Impeachment

Still stung by Johnson's initial act of granting pardons to the southern aristocracy, Radicals were equally stymied by his constant string of vetoes. Frustrated by all this, Congress took steps to limit the president's authority.

### The Tenure of Office Act

In 1867 Congress passed the Tenure of Office Act, which required the president to obtain the consent of the Senate before removing certain government officials from office. In essence, the law declared that Johnson could not fire anyone who had earned congressional approvals, especially Republicans who had been appointed by Lincoln. Johnson of course vetoed the act, but Congress once again overrode his veto.

### The Impeachment

A showdown over the new law occurred in August 1867, when Johnson wanted to remove from office Secretary of War Edwin M. Stanton. Stanton sympathized with the Radicals and had fallen out of favor with Johnson, so Johnson ordered his dismissal. The Senate, however, refused to authorize the firing. Undeterred, Johnson ordered Stanton to resign. When Republicans in the House of Representatives learned that Johnson had defied the Senate's Tenure of Office Act, they drafted a resolution to impeach Johnson. This could be the chance they had sought to eliminate a major obstacle to Radical Reconstruction. The House made eleven charges against Johnson, stemming mostly from his refusal to heed the Tenure of Office Act, and a majority of the representatives voted in favor of putting him on trial. This made Andrew Johnson the first president in the nation's history to be impeached.

Radical Republicans in the House of Representatives (especially Thaddeus Stevens) powered the vote for impeachment, but the Constitution dictates that impeachment trials must take place in the Senate and must be judged by the chief justice of the U.S. Supreme Court. Moderate Republicans and Democrats in the Senate refused to join the House Radicals in condemning Johnson, and, by one vote, the Senate lacked the two-thirds majority needed to convict the president and remove him from office.

Find out more about the impeachment of Andrew Johnson.

## The Fifteenth Amendment

In 1868, the Republicans nominated the war hero Ulysses S. Grant for president, hoping that Grant's tremendous popularity in the North would help them control the White House and propel their Reconstruction plans through the federal government. The Democrats nominated Horatio Seymour, the governor of New York. To the shock of the Republicans, the race between Grant and Seymour was relatively close. Although Grant obtained a majority in the Electoral College, he won the popular vote by only 300,000 ballots. Since an estimated 450,000 black people had voted for Grant, it was clear that a narrow majority of white Americans had cast their ballots for Seymour.

Recognizing the importance of their newest support base—and aware that their time in power might be limited—Republicans in Congress moved quickly to create a constitutional amendment guaranteeing the suffrage rights of black males. It became the **Fifteenth Amendment**, which was ratified and adopted in 1870. The Fifteenth Amendment prohibited any state from denying citizens the right to vote on the grounds of race, color, or previous condition of servitude.

Read the Fifteenth Amendment to the U.S. Constitution.

## Women's Rights

The Fourteenth Amendment introduced the word *male* into the Constitution for the first time, and the Fifteenth Amendment ratified the notion that voting rights were solely intended for men. Many women, who had often supported the fight for black civil rights, fought back. Historically, advocates for the rights of women have often first fought for the rights of racial minorities, especially black people. This was the case in the 1830s and 1840s, and again in the 1860s and 1870s. Viewing the overhauling of the U.S. Constitution as a moment ripe for extending various freedoms to women, Elizabeth Cady Stanton and Olympia Brown, two veterans of the struggle to expand women's rights, pushed for a constitutional guarantee of women's suffrage. Using new journals such as *The Agitator*, activist women also pushed for a reform of marriage laws, changes in inheritance laws, and, as always, the vote.

But they were frustrated at almost every turn. Even Republicans declared that Reconstruction was designed solely for black men. Women were torn about whether or not to support the Reconstruction amendments, even if they excluded provisions for women's rights. These bitter differences led to divisions within the women's suffrage movement that would last until the 1890s.

# LO³ Grassroots Reconstruction

With all the political jockeying within the federal government, Reconstruction at the state level was even more rancorous. Freed slaves exercised more muscle at the state level, ensuring that Republicans dominated all of the new state governments in the South. Newly freed slaves steadfastly cast their ballots for the party that had given them their freedom. To support this voter bloc, Republican politicians—from the North and the South—sought dramatic Reconstruction efforts. But at every turn they encountered strong opposition. Before long, it became evident that the process of reconstructing the South would be a process of two steps forward, one step back. And the most substantive change that could have happened—land and economic redistribution to the ex-slaves—remained perpetually frustrated.

## Black Officeholders

Even with the admission of black voters, the proportion of government positions held by black Americans was still smaller than their proportion in the population. They were rarely elected to high positions, and until 1990 no black person was ever elected or nominated to serve as governor. South Carolina was the only state where a black judge served in the state supreme court and, because the state was 60 percent African American, only in South Carolina did African Americans form a plurality of the legislature. Nevertheless, more than 2,000 black citizens gained political office in the Reconstruction South. Some were policemen, some were sheriffs, some were tax assessors. Their roles were important because they ensured that fairness would be enforced and that the rule of law would be upheld.

## Carpetbaggers and Scalawags

Yet white men held most of the offices in the new state governments, and many were Republicans supportive of protecting black rights. Some of these new officials were northern-born white men who moved south after the Confederacy's defeat. Southerners called these men **carpetbaggers** because they supposedly journeyed to the South with nothing more than what they could carry in a ratty old carpetbag. The carpetbag was meant to symbolize corruption and lowliness, as supposedly poor and pretentious northerners headed south seeking to capitalize on the region's fall from grace. Not all the so-called carpetbaggers were corrupt, of course. Many of them came to the South with a desire to improve the lot of America's black people.

Southern-born, white Republicans were given the name *scalawag*, originally a term used by cattle drivers to describe livestock that was too filthy for consumption, even by dogs. Although southern Democrats insisted that only the "dirtiest" citizens became scalawags, in reality, many elite men joined the Republican

**carpetbagger**
Northern-born white who moved south after the Confederacy's defeat

**scalawag**
Southern-born white Republican; many had been non-slaveholding poor farmers

 Analyze an image of the South Carolina legislature.

>> During Reconstruction, Hiram Revels of Mississippi (on the left) became the nation's first African American senator, while several other Southern states voted African Americans to the House.

Copyright © The Granger Collection, New York / The Granger Collection

THE FIRST COLORED SENATOR AND REPRESENTATIVES.
In the 41ˢᵗ and 42ⁿᵈ Congress of the United States.

Party, including Confederate generals Pierre Beauregard and James Longstreet. Most of the scalawags, however, had been nonslaveholding poor white farmers who worked and lived in the hill country. Many of these scalawags believed that participating in the Republicans' plan was the fastest way to return their region to peaceful and prosperous conditions.

## Southern Republican Successes

Although they faced considerable opposition from the old antebellum elite, southern Republicans managed to (1) construct the South's first public school system, (2) develop a system of antidiscrimination measures, (3) strengthen the rights and privileges of agricultural workers, and (4) begin efforts at internal improvements in the various states. Under the leadership of southern Republicans, for example, every state in the South financed a system of railroads and attempted to lure northern industries to the South. They met with mixed results, but they showed a newfound commitment to greater equality and to bringing the gains of the Market Revolution southward.

## Sharecropping

Despite the new opportunities put forward by southern Republicans, freed slaves had to struggle hard to enjoy their new liberty. There was no serious land reform and the Market and Industrial Revolutions were slow to move southward, so most black southerners had no choice but to accept work as agricultural wage laborers for white landholders, many of whom had been slaveholders before the war.

## The Battle of Labor

Many of these landowners attempted to recreate as much of the slave system as they could, closely overseeing their workers, forcing them to work in gangs, and even trying to use the whip to maintain discipline. The freedmen, however, refused to be reduced to slavery again. They insisted on working shorter hours, and they often refused to work in gangs. To limit the amount of surveillance, freedmen often built their own log cabins far away from the houses of their employers. Unless they were willing to go beyond the rule of law, most landowners could do nothing to stop them.

## The Sharecropping System

The power struggle between southern whites and the freedmen led former slaveholders to establish and develop the **sharecropping** system. As sharecroppers, families farmed a plot of land owned by someone else and shared the crop yield with the owner of the property. Typically, the farmer and the owner split the yield in half, but the owner often claimed an even larger share if he supplied the seeds or tools necessary for cultivating the crop or if he provided housing and food. Although black farmers had earned the right to work in a familial setting, as opposed to the gang labor system of the slave era, landowners had managed to curtail black freedom by preventing many of them from owning property.

Despite sharecropping's prominent place in southern black history, there were more white sharecroppers in the South than black. It was a sign of the South's poverty after the war. The sharecropping system offered little hope for economic or social advancement. Sharecroppers could rarely earn enough money to buy land, and they were constantly in debt to their landlords. The landlord was always paid first when crops were sold at market, so if crop prices were lower than expected, sharecroppers were left with little or no income. Although sharecropping was not slavery, it was still a harsh and limited form of economic existence that permeated

© Newscom

>> Many Southerners saw carpetbaggers as corrupt and lowly, although many came South with the intention of improving the life of America's black people.

the South after the Civil War. By 1900, 50 percent of southern whites and 75 percent of southern blacks lived in sharecropping families.

## Convict Leasing

Southern landowners and politicians also began the practice of convict leasing during these years, whereby the state leased out prisoners to private companies or landowners looking for workers after the demise of slavery. Convicts usually were not paid for their labor, and were often treated harshly. But the system was good for the state, which earned income from the practice, and the lessees, who exploited the labor of the prisoners. Convicts were used in railroad, mining, and logging operations, as well as on farms. And, although convicts of all colors were exploited by the system, African Americans were particularly targeted. During the three decades after the Civil War, the number of men in prison increased in nearly every state of the South, and the percentage of those prisoners who were black ballooned. Some historians see convict leasing as just an extension of slavery, with only a different name.

# LO⁴ The Collapse of Reconstruction

The reconstruction of the South had some significant achievements, including two new constitutional amendments, the passage of the nation's first civil rights law, and the abolition of slavery. These positive achievements could have continued to accumulate, but they did not, for two reasons: (1) growing northern disinterest in the plight of America's southern black population and (2) southern resistance to Reconstruction.

> ## Civil Rights Act of 1875
> **Act that forbade racial discrimination in all public facilities, transportation lines, places of amusement, and juries; it proved largely ineffective**
>
> ## Civil Rights Cases
> **Cases in which, in 1883, the Supreme Court declared all of the provisions of the Civil Rights Act of 1875 unconstitutional, except for the prohibition of discrimination on juries**

## In the North

On the whole, the eight years of Grant's presidency (1869–1877) were not marked by great strides for African American civil rights. Instead, Grant's term became infamous for economic chicanery and corruption. The president's personal secretary was caught embezzling federal whiskey revenues in the so-called "Whiskey Ring," while Grant's own family was implicated in a plot to corner the gold market. Charges of corruption even led to a split in the Republican Party, further draining support for Reconstruction efforts. As more upstanding political leaders became preoccupied with efforts to clean up the government and institute civil service reform, securing equal rights for black people in the South ceased to be the most pressing issue. Other things seemed to matter more. And, as Reconstruction moved into the background, northerners' racism—always just under the surface—became more visible.

Despite charges of corruption, Grant was reelected to the presidency in 1872, and during his second term, only one major piece of Reconstruction legislation was passed. Even that had several key limitations. The **Civil Rights Act of 1875** forbade racial discrimination in all public facilities, transportation lines, places of amusement, and juries. Segregation in public schools, however, was not prohibited. Moreover, there was no effort whatsoever to legislate against racial discrimination by individuals or corporations, so discrimination in the workplace remained legal.

In addition to these flaws, the Civil Rights Act proved ineffective anyway. The federal government did not enforce the law vigorously, so the southern states ignored it. And in 1883, in what would come to be called the **Civil Rights Cases**, the Supreme Court delivered a final blow to this last act of Reconstruction by declaring all of its provisions unconstitutional, except for the prohibition of discrimination on juries. In 1890, Henry Cabot Lodge, a Republican from Massachusetts, led the

The Collapse of Reconstruction **285**

**Panic of 1873**
Financial crisis provoked when overspeculation, high postwar inflation, and disruptions from Europe emptied the financial reserves in America's banks; many banks simply closed their doors; this emergency focused northern attention on the economy rather than on civil rights

House of Representatives in passing a Federal Elections Bill that would have revived protection of voting rights for African Americans, but a Senate filibuster prevented the piece of legislation from becoming law. It would be nearly seven decades before another civil rights bill made its way through Congress.

The failure of the Civil Rights Act of 1875 reflected a larger northern disinterest in Reconstruction. For many northerners, support for black rights had been an outgrowth of their animosity toward the South. In 1865, such feelings burned hotly, and northerners were willing to support federal efforts to guarantee the liberties of former slaves. As the bitterness of war faded, northerners were tired of the antagonism between North and South, so their interest in civil rights faded, too.

 Analyze a *Harper's Weekly* cartoon on the Civil Rights Act of 1875.

Instead, northerners became consumed with economic matters, especially after the United States entered a deep recession in 1873. The **Panic of 1873** erupted when numerous factors, including overspeculation, high postwar inflation, and disruptions from Europe, emptied the financial reserves in America's banks. Rather than honor their loans, many banks simply closed their doors, which led to a panic on Wall Street. Although Grant acted quickly to end the immediate panic, many businesses were forced to shut down. The Panic lasted four years and left 3 million Americans unemployed. In the years after 1873, Americans became concerned more with jump-starting the economy than with forging new laws to protect the needs and interests of black citizens.

The Republicans, meanwhile, took the blame for the nation's economic troubles, so, in the congressional elections of 1874, they lost 77 seats, thus losing control of the House. The party that had spearheaded civil rights legislation in America was no longer in a position to control federal policy. Instead, the Democrats were back.

 Analyze a *Harper's Weekly* cartoon on the Panic of 1873.

## In the South

The decline of northern support for Reconstruction emboldened southern Democrats, who worked to reclaim political control of their region. In order to create white solidarity against Republican rule in the South, the Democrats shamelessly asserted white superiority.

Racism proved to be a powerful incentive for the Democratic Party, especially to attract poor southerners worried about their economic fortunes. Keeping black people as an underclass in southern society was important to poor white people's sense of self-worth (and economic well-being), and Democrats promised to protect the racial hierarchy as it had been before the Civil War. Democrats earned the backing of the vast majority of white southerners—mostly by playing the race card.

### Intimidation of Black and Republican Voters

To control black votes, white Democrats often used economic intimidation. In the nineteenth century, voting was not done by secret ballot, so it was easy to know how every individual cast his ballot. Democratic landowners fired tenant farmers who voted Republican and publicized their names in local newspapers to prevent other landowners from hiring them. Thus the threat of starvation and poverty kept many black citizens from participating in elections and voting for the Republican Party.

More than economic intimidation, however, southern Democrats used violence to seize control of southern politics. A number of paramilitary groups, including the Ku Klux Klan, used violence to this end. They harassed black and white Republicans, disrupted Republican Party meetings, and physically blocked black southerners from casting ballots in elections. They even assassinated Republican Party leaders and organizers. Their goal was to erode the base of Republican support in the South and to ensure election victories for the Democratic Party, which promised to uphold white superiority. Prior to the presidential election of 1868, 2,000 people were killed or injured in Louisiana alone. In Texas, the federal military commander said murders were so common he could not keep track of them.

### Terror in the Heart of Freedom

In addition to these more purely political forms of repression, southern white males also used rape and sexual violence against African American women as a form of political terror. Because black women now had the right to accuse white men of sexual crimes, historians have been able to determine that white men often staged elaborate attacks meant to reenact the antebellum racial hierarchy, when southern white men were firmly in control. African Americans of course fought back, but as the Democrats grew increasingly powerful in the region, the claims of southern black women often went unheard. Most damningly, these crimes indicated how limited black freedom had become in the decade after the Civil War. Not only were African Americans losing their political and social rights, they were also losing the right to basic safeties, the right to organize their life as they saw fit, and the right to live comfortably in a democratic nation.

### Grant's Response

Although not known for its civil rights activism, the Grant administration did respond to the upsurge in southern violence by pushing two important measures through Congress: (1) the Force Act of 1870 and (2) the Ku Klux Klan Act of 1871. The new laws declared that interfering with the right to vote was a felony; they also authorized the federal government to use the army and suspend the writ of habeas corpus in order to end Klan violence. Grant proceeded to suspend the writ in nine South Carolina counties and to arrest hundreds of suspected Klan members. These efforts crushed the Klan in 1871 (although it would resurge in the 1910s and 1920s).

### The Mississippi Plan

Southern Democrats, however, did not always relent when faced with pressure from the federal government. In 1875, Democrats in Mississippi initiated a policy called the **Mississippi Plan**, which called for using as much violence as necessary to put the state back under Democratic control. Democratic clubs began to function much as the Klan had, terrorizing Republican Party leaders and the black and white citizens who supported them. This time, the Grant administration refused to step in to stop the violence. Most northerners no longer seemed willing to support federal intervention into southern strife.

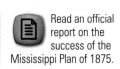
Read an official report on the success of the Mississippi Plan of 1875.

In 1876, the Mississippi Plan formally succeeded. By keeping tens of thousands of Republicans from casting ballots, the Democrats took charge of the state government. In the vocabulary of the time, Mississippi had been "redeemed" from Republican rule. In fact, it had been tortured into submission; official reports proclaiming as much were generally ignored.

### "Redeemers" Win the Presidential Election of 1876

The presidential election of 1876 put the final nail in Reconstruction's coffin. Through violence and intimidation, the Democrats had already succeeded in winning control of all the southern states except Louisiana, Florida, and South Carolina. They intended to use the Mississippi Plan to "redeem" those three states and win the presidency as well.

The presidential campaign pitted Ohio Republican Rutherford B. Hayes against New York Democrat Samuel Tilden, who had a reputation as a reformer and a fighter against political corruption. The election was a mess. Violence prevented as many as 250,000 southerners from voting for the Republican ticket, and, as southern Democrats had hoped, Democratic governors triumphed in Louisiana, Florida, and South Carolina. The Democrats in those states also reported that the majority of voters favored Tilden for the presidency. Republicans were suspicious, however, and did a canvass of their own. They claimed that the Democrats had used violence to fix the results. Louisiana, Florida, and South Carolina, the Republicans argued, should have gone to Hayes. These disputed states carried enough Electoral College votes to swing the entire election one way or the other.

### The Compromise of 1877

After receiving two versions of the final tallies, Congress needed help deciding what to do. It created a 15-member electoral commission, with 5 members from the Senate, 5 from the House, and 5 from the Supreme Court. The commission was composed of 8 Republicans and 7 Democrats, and, by a purely partisan vote of 8 to 7, the commission gave the disputed states of Louisiana, Florida, and South Carolina to Hayes, the Republican. The Democratic Party leaders were furious, but, in order to prevent further violence, Republican leaders proposed a compromise that became known as the **Compromise of 1877** (see Map 16.2).

In the compromise, Republicans promised not to dispute the Democratic gubernatorial victories in the South and to withdraw federal troops from the region. The white redeemers would be in control throughout the entire South. In return, the Republicans asked the Democrats to (1) accept Hayes's presidential victory and (2) respect the rights of its black citizens. The Democrats accepted these terms and, with that, Hayes withdrew the federal

**Mississippi Plan**
1875 Democratic plan that called for using as much violence as necessary to put Mississippi back under Democratic control

**Compromise of 1877**
Compromise in which Republicans promised not to dispute the Democratic gubernatorial victories in the South and to withdraw federal troops from the region, if southern Democrats accepted Hayes's presidential victory and respected the rights of black citizens

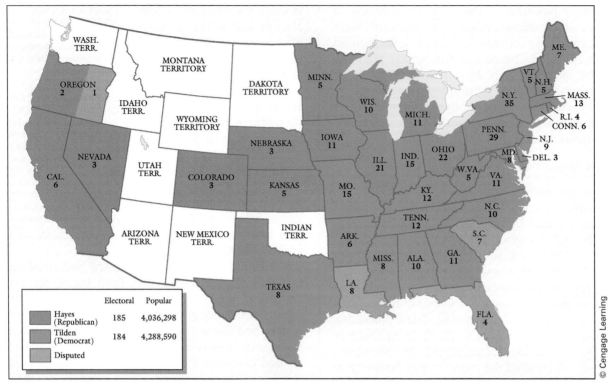

| | Electoral | Popular |
|---|---|---|
| Hayes (Republican) | 185 | 4,036,298 |
| Tilden (Democrat) | 184 | 4,288,590 |
| Disputed | | |

© Cengage Learning

Map 16.2 The Disputed Election of 1876

military from the South. Of course, without a federal military to protect black Americans, Reconstruction was over, and the South was left under the control of Democratic "redeemers" who used violence, intimidation, and the law to create the society they envisioned. Freed blacks lost whatever political and social gains they had achieved during the previous twelve years. This failure ensured that racial oppression would continue. In the words of one historian, Reconstruction was America's unfinished revolution, and a great chance to correct the colossal wrong that was slavery vanished. For more on why Reconstruction ended in 1877, see "The reasons why . . ." box on Reconstruction.

## And in the end . . .

Why did Reconstruction fail? So boldly stated, the question is perhaps unfair. There were some major accomplishments. Slavery was abolished. Federal laws were established that provided support for further political gains for America's black population. There have been only five black senators ever elected to the U.S. Senate, and two of them were elected during Reconstruction (Hiram Rhodes Revels and Blanche K. Bruce, both from Mississippi). About

Copyright © The Granger Collection, New York / The Granger Collection

>> The White League and other similar organizations were founded to use violence and intimidation to keep African American voters from the polls throughout the South.

{ *The reasons why . . .* }

There were three prominent reasons why Reconstruction ended in 1877, before equality could be ensured for southern African Americans.

*Northern indifference.* After the Panic of 1873, many northerners focused intently on economic matters. The passions inflamed by the Civil War had begun to fade by the early 1870s, and the economic turmoil provoked by the Panic led northerners to focus on their personal fortunes. Plus, with the Industrial Revolution ramping up in the North (see Chapter 17), northerners were even less likely to take big risks on behalf of black civil rights in the South.

*Southern recalcitrance.* With northern indifference becoming increasingly evident during the second presidential term of Ulysses S. Grant, white southerners increased the level of violence—political, physical, and sexual—they used against African Americans and Republicans more generally. The Democratic Party in the South prom-

ised white superiority, and throughout the 1870s it was beginning to deliver.

*National political ambivalence.* By 1876, northern politicians had more at stake in reviving the sagging economy than in fighting for the rights of African American southerners. When it became clear that the results of the presidential election of 1876 were going to be disputed, northern Republicans willingly negotiated with southern Democrats, securing the Republicans the presidency at the cost of pulling federal troops out of the South. Without northern oversight, southern whites were free to reclaim their social and political power, and that is exactly what they did.

---

a fifth of the 101 black Americans ever to serve in the U.S. House of Representatives were elected during Reconstruction.

But there was a dramatic decline of black political participation in the South (where a large majority of black people lived) beginning in 1876 and lasting until after

*Reconstruction was America's unfinished revolution, and a great chance to correct the colossal wrong that was slavery.*

the Second World War. There was an even more dramatic increase in physical segregation between America's black and white populations during and after Reconstruction. The failures are many. First, President Johnson's unwillingness to participate in a wholesale social revolution meant that land would not be redistributed in the South, signifying that, for the most part, the wealthy would remain wealthy and the poor would remain poor. The development of sharecropping as an institution further paralyzed black advancements, especially after the emergence of black codes limited black Americans' abilities to protest economic injustices. Finally, the violence used by the southern "redeemers" served as an emblem of the wrongs felt by white southerners, and, when northerners became more focused on the rollicking economy of the Industrial Revolution, there was no one left to monitor the henhouse. Plainly enough, most white southerners strongly opposed racial change, and after 1876, they were left in power to do as they wished.

## What else was happening . . .

| | |
|---|---|
| **1865** | William Bullock invents printing press that can feed paper on a continuous roll and print both sides of the paper at once. |
| **1867** | Bullock dies of gangrene after getting caught in his own invention. |
| **1867** | Benjamin Disraeli helps pass the 1867 Reform Bill in Britain, which extends the franchise to all male householders, including, for the first time, members of the working class. |
| **1869** | Opening of the Suez Canal in Egypt, connecting the Mediterranean Sea and the Red Sea, allowing water travel between Asia and Europe without having to navigate around Africa. |
| **1870** | First New York City subway line opens. |
| **1871** | Euphemia Allen, age sixteen, composes simple piano tune "Chopsticks." |
| **1873** | Mark Twain patents the scrapbook. |

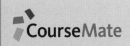 CourseMate

Visit the CourseMate website at www.cengagebrain.com for additional study tools and review materials for this chapter.

# *The* Industrial Age

## Learning Outcomes

*After reading this chapter, you should be able to do the following:*

LO **1**   Describe and discuss the development of the Industrial Revolution in America after the Civil War, concentrating on the major industries and their leaders.

LO **2**   Explain why the late 1800s in America have sometimes been called the "Age of Innovation."

LO **3**   Describe how America's regional and local markets merged into one truly national market, and how this influenced the consumer demand for products and services.

> **"***The world that had consisted of small farms, artisans' workshops, and small factories transformed into a full-scale industrial society.***"**

As the process of ensuring political, economic, and social rights of African Americans waned during the 1870s, most Americans turned their attention to another transformation brought on by the Civil War: the Industrial Revolution. During the half-century between 1865 and 1915, the

United States evolved from a relative economic backwater to become the most powerful economy in the world. Industrialization played a key role in the nation's advances, and both the Civil War and a core group of innovative, aggressive, farsighted, and opportunistic entrepreneurs were the main stimulants of growth. They embodied the optimism and inventiveness of the late nineteenth century, although they often pushed too far and engaged in practices we now see as unethical and corrupt, leaving wide gaps between the rich and the poor, between black and white, and between immigrant and native.

Like the Market Revolution of the first half of the century, the Industrial Revolution of the second half transformed the nation's economy, its social life, and its politics. During the nineteenth century, the nation's main energy sources shifted from human and animal power to mechanical power. Builders transitioned from using materials that one might find on the ground, such as stones and logs, to using manufactured materials, such as lumber, bricks, and steel. Smaller craft shops lost business to large specialized factories. Industrial cities grew dramatically as well, as mechanized public transportation allowed wealthier people to move away from the noisy city centers. And railroads made travel increasingly easy—even, by 1869, allowing people and goods to cross the continent speedily and safely. During the late nineteenth century, the world that had consisted of small farms, artisans' workshops, and small- or medium-sized factories at the beginning of the century transformed into a full-scale industrial society of large factories and polyglot urban hubs.

This chapter explores the contours of the Industrial Revolution of the second half of the nineteenth century, focusing on the industries, inventions, and actors that propelled the United States into the Industrial Age. These transformations sparked a host of challenges in the North, the South, and the West, and they directly challenged American politics at both a local and a national level. These broader changes are the subject of the following three chapters. But before we get to them, we need to understand the revolutions that brought on the Industrial Age.

## LO¹ The Industrial Revolution

The process of industrialization began well before the Civil War, and indeed, industrialization and improved communications sparked the Market Revolution during the first half of the nineteenth century. But after the Civil War, American material output increased dramatically, and big businesses extended their reach deeper into American life. Together, these events revolutionized the way Americans lived.

The **Industrial Revolution** can be defined as a transformation in the way goods were made and sold, as American businessmen between 1865 and 1915 used continuing technological breakthroughs and creative financing to bring greater efficiency to their businesses, which dramatically expanded their markets and their ability to produce goods. The effects of this transformation were felt outside the business world, resulting in two key social transitions: (1) more and more Americans left farming to

work in factories or retail, which spurred the rapid growth of cities; and (2) the American economy became dominated less by family businesses and more and more by large-scale corporate firms. Thus, many historians cite the late nineteenth century as the birth of modern industrialized America. One historian has pinpointed these years as the time when Americans physically and intellectually left behind the small, localized "island communities" that dotted the United States before the Civil War and confronted the large, polyglot nature of the American nation.

Why an Industrial Revolution in America? The Industrial Revolution had been launched in England in the 1750s, made its way over to the European continent by the early 1800s, and crossed the Atlantic well before the 1840s. But three reasons figure in its dramatic growth from 1865 to 1915 (see "The reasons why . . ." on American industrialization below).

# {*The reasons why . . .*}

## There were at least three reasons why American industrialization expanded when it did:

**The Civil War.** Production needs during the Civil War stimulated industrial development, particularly in the North. For example, the Union Army's high demand for food fueled the expansion of western farms. Clothing and shoe manufacturers were encouraged to produce more goods faster. And the government offered huge wartime contracts for uniforms, shoes, weapons, food, and other commodities, sparking breakthroughs in their manufacture.

**Government support.** Besides purchasing goods for its troops, Congress took advantage of the absence of southerners in the House and the Senate to pass a series of national internal improvement projects. The most majestic of these was the first transcontinental railroad. In July 1862, Congress offered enormous financial incentives to the Union Pacific Railroad and the Central Pacific Railroad companies to complete the expansive task. This transcontinental railroad was completed in 1869, and, over the next twenty years, legendary business moguls erected other transcontinental lines, often with financial incentives from the federal government. The federal government also supported scientific training and research, developed the first national currency and tax system, and made possible the construction of the first land grant universities (such as Michigan State University and Rutgers)—all evidence of the federal government's willingness to midwife the Industrial Revolution. In the end, government support of the building infrastructure allowed goods and information to travel more quickly and efficiently to wider markets.

**Technological breakthroughs.** An abundance of scientific developments also contributed to the expansion of big business, and again, the Civil War was the transitional moment. For example, the need to move meat from one place to

Vintage Images/Getty Images

another in order to feed Union soldiers prompted the creation of refrigerated railroad cars. By 1878, inventors had perfected the cars, which permitted long-distance transfer of numerous perishable goods. This, of course, allowed for the development of new towns in the West—so long as they were close to the railroad lines.

© Panoramic Images/Getty Images

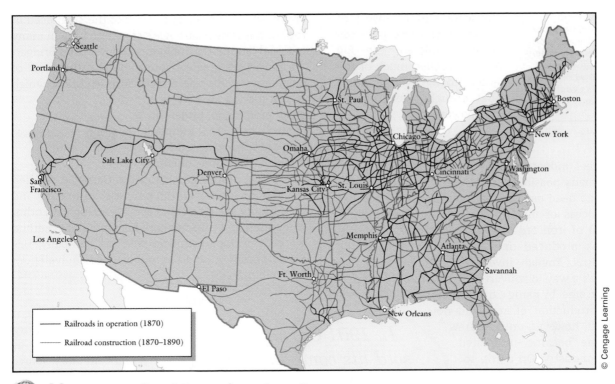

Map 17.1. Railroad Expansion, 1870–1890

## The Basic Industries

The central industries of the Industrial Revolution were railroads, steel, and petroleum. Each had leaders who took control of their industry's development. These "captains of industry" were also sometimes called "robber barons," depending on the perspective of the observer. Through these industries, Americans created a corporate society.

### Railroads

The expansion of the railroads was perhaps the one predictable development of the post–Civil War years. With the support of the federal government, between 1860 and 1915 total railroad development leapt from approximately 30,000 miles of track to more than 250,000 miles (see Map 17.1). By the eve of World War I in 1914, the national railroad network was basically complete, such that some historians say that all tracks built after 1890 were simply unnecessary. Railroads spanned the nation, making the movement of goods and products easy, cheap, and reliable.

Several ruthless and ingenious businessmen helped make all the growth possible. Leland Stanford, for example, was one of the "Big Four" captains of the railroad industry. With his partners, Collis Huntington, Charles Crocker, and Mark Hopkins, Stanford developed the railroad system in California and made the entire West easily accessible. All four men were New Yorkers who had headed to California during the Gold Rush. All four were Republicans and supporters of Lincoln during the war. Knowing that the war would promote the expansion of railroads, the four invested money and energy in creating a

>> Laying track for the Union Pacific Railroad.

**vertical integration**
The system by which a business controls all aspects of its industry, from raw materials to finished product, and is able to avoid working or sharing profits with any other companies

transcontinental network of tracks. Once these railroads were completed, the Big Four controlled much of the access to the West—control that brought great wealth and power.

## Steel

The steel industry made the massive expansion of railroads possible. As early as the Middle Ages, steel had been used to make weapons. But because the process of making steel—by burning impurities out of iron ore—was laborious and expensive, artisans produced only small quantities. In the mid-1850s, English inventor Sir Henry Bessemer invented a way to convert large quantities of iron ore into steel by using extremely hot air. Mass production of steel did not take off, however, until Andrew Carnegie became interested in the industry. On a trip to England in 1872, Carnegie saw the Bessemer process at work in a steel plant, and, amazed at its efficiency, he decided to open a steel plant in the United States. Rather than artisans, he could use cheap, unskilled laborers, who were willing to learn to operate the hot, dangerous machines for low wages. By 1900, he had built the largest steel company in the world and

*In 1901 Carnegie sold his company for more than $400 million—the equivalent of $9.8 billion today.*

produced more than 25 percent of the steel used in the United States. Carnegie's steel was used in many national landmarks, including the Brooklyn Bridge.

Carnegie's greatest contribution in the world of business was his use of **vertical integration**, which meant placing all aspects of steel production under his control, from the moment iron ore was extracted from mines to the time finished steel was shipped to customers. Carnegie realized that, by integrating all the processes of making and distributing steel, he could avoid working with other companies and thus increase his profits. His method worked: In 1901 Carnegie sold his company, U.S. Steel, for more than $400 million—the equivalent of $9.8 billion today.

Find out more about the steel business.

## Petroleum

In the mid-nineteenth century, petroleum use increased as both a lubricant and a source of illumination. In 1855, Professor Benjamin Silliman of Yale University discovered that kerosene, a formerly "useless" byproduct of crude oil (unrefined petroleum), was a powerful illuminant. Entrepreneurs then rushed to find greater supplies of crude oil. The Pennsylvania Rock Oil Company hired Edwin Drake, a speculator and promoter, to drill for oil in north-

© Hulton Archive/Getty Images

>> Bessemer converter in use at a Pittsburgh steel plant.

Library of Congress, Prints & Photographs Division, LC-USZ62-79048

>> The Brooklyn Bridge. "Hard! I guess it's hard. I lost forty pounds the first three months I came into this business. It sweats the life out of a man." —Steelworker at a Carnegie plant, circa 1893

western Pennsylvania. After two years of searching, on August 28, 1859, Drake successfully drilled for oil in Titusville, Pennsylvania. His find ushered in an American oil boom.

The next challenge was to figure out the best means of extracting crude oil, transporting it to refineries, packaging it, conveying it to cities and towns across the nation, and marketing the finished products. John D. Rockefeller essentially filled all of these niches. He consolidated refining operations in Cleveland, and then, by paying close attention to cost-cutting details, he ruthlessly drove down the costs of producing usable commodities. Much of Rockefeller's success can be attributed to his pioneering efforts at **horizontal integration**. In essence, he took over other oil companies or worked in combination with them to control competition, lower the cost of petroleum, and, of course, maximize profits. He practiced vertical integration as well, much like Andrew Carnegie in the steel industry. But he focused more intently on limiting competition with other businesses in the same industry. His legal advisors created a unique entity called "the trust," which acted as a board of directors for all the oil refiners. He intended to provide cheap petroleum and to make himself wealthy. He succeeded at both.

> Read Henry Demarest Lloyd's "The Lords of Industry."

## Harmful Business Practices

All this innovation came with significant costs. For most businessmen, the goal was to control the market; whatever it took to drive out competitors, they did. Thus, while several of the innovations of men like Stanford, Carnegie, and Rockefeller benefited the American population, often these men took things too far, engaging in harmful business practices, which, as we will see in the following chapters, eventually provoked a series of reforms. But those reforms would come later. First would come monopolization, manipulation, a bit of price gouging, and environmental damage.

## Monopolization

In the late 1800s, Rockefeller essentially controlled the drilling, refining, and transporting of most of the nation's petroleum. But that was not enough. He was determined to control the product's wholesale distribution and retail marketing as well. So he established regional outlets that ruthlessly undersold well-established companies for as long as it took to drive them out of business. Rich as he was, Rockefeller could absorb short-term losses much longer than his competitors. Once he had driven his rivals out of business, he was free to charge whatever he wished for his product (although he had to keep prices relatively low to keep international competition at bay). In 1879, his Standard Oil Company controlled 90 percent of all petroleum in the country.

Rockefeller also had his way with railroads. His petroleum shipments comprised the majority of the business of several rail lines. By threatening to take his business to other competitors, he forced several railroad officials to offer him rebates on every barrel he shipped. In this way, Rockefeller paid lower railroad rates than his competitors. Rockefeller also interfered with railroad lines that carried his competitors' products. He convinced officials that they were hurting his business whenever they shipped a competitor's products and that they should pay him a refund for each such barrel they shipped. Such business practices tested the limits of how much freedom politicians would allow businessmen to have.

> Read a contemporary piece chronicling Rockefeller's business tactics.

horizontal integration
**The system by which a business takes over its competitors in order to limit competition, lower costs, and maximize profits**

> ❝Mr. Rockefeller awakened a general bitterness.❞
> —*Ida Tarbell*, The History of the Standard Oil Company, *1904*

## Manipulating Stock Prices

Despite Rockefeller's ruthless tactics toward railroads, it is difficult to feel compassion for the railroad companies. The business practices of some of their leaders were particularly nasty and essentially corrupt. For example, from 1866 to 1868, in what came to be called "the Erie Railroad War," Cornelius Vanderbilt (another captain of industry) attempted to add to his already formidable railroad empire by taking over the Erie Railroad. Vanderbilt's plan was to buy up a majority of the Erie Railroad's shares. The Erie's leaders, however, gleefully printed "bogus" shares of Erie Railroad stock and flooded the stock market with them. Vanderbilt bought and bought, but more shares kept appearing. Vanderbilt's shares never gave him control of the company, but they did enrich the Erie leaders who were selling the bogus shares. The problem with their plan was that the Erie's value declined on the stock market, and, within a few years, it was forced to declare bankruptcy. Such manipulation of stock prices by "inside" operators affected many industries besides the railroads.

## Price Gouging

Railroads also engaged in price gouging. For example, in urban areas where demand was high, usually several railroads operated their lines. These railroads often had to provide competitive rates, and during the occasional price wars between their competitors, railroads sometimes cut prices below their own costs. To make up for these losses, railroads gouged customers in other places—usually small towns that were served by just one line. Railroad officials also increased rates for local service, provoking differences between "long haul" and "short haul" charges. For instance, farmers in the eastern Dakotas complained that it cost more to ship a bushel of wheat 400 miles to Minneapolis than it cost to send that same product to Europe, more than ten times as far. Once again, these practices would eventually motivate the government to act—but not for many decades.

## Environmental Damage

A fourth harmful business practice concerns what the Industrial Revolution did to the environment. Drilling for petroleum damaged the soil. The development of hydraulic mining was much more damaging to the land than the mining done by miners. Burning coal gave off damaging gases. And railroad tracks cut through lands that were largely untouched by sustained human development. Most

>> Oil gusher.

>> In 1892, John Muir began the Sierra Club in an effort to protest the environmental damage of the Industrial Age.

Americans did not express deep concerns for these types of problems, but a few did. The top preservationist of the period was John Muir, the founder of the American environmental organization the Sierra Club and an influential advocate of preserving the mountain lands between California and Montana. In 1872, the federal government created the first national park, Yellowstone National Park, which comprises parts of Wyoming, Montana, and Idaho.

# LO$^2$ The Age of Innovation

In addition to the dynamic developments of business leaders, numerous technological, financial, and legal innovations powered the Industrial Revolution. Indeed, this was the era of many of America's most far-reaching inventions and innovations.

## Technology

Perhaps no invention had more lasting impact than the incandescent light bulb, created by Thomas Edison in 1879. After years of experimentation, Edison harnessed the power of electricity and transmitted bright light for extended periods of time. The subsequent development of huge electrical power stations made this new form of energy cheap enough to allow middle-class homeowners to purchase it and businesses to operate after dark. Development of the first electric grids spread electricity throughout cities. In addition to light bulbs, Edison also perfected the motion picture camera, the phonograph, the microphone, and more. He set up the first industrial research laboratory in the world, developed solely to invent new things. It worked. In the United States alone, Edison held 1,093 patents. He possessed more abroad.

Separately, Alexander Graham Bell's invention in 1876 of the telephone, which also used electrical power, vastly sped up the flow of communications over long distances and enabled businesses to exchange information more efficiently. In architecture, major improvements in the design of blast furnaces allowed iron producers to manufacture stronger, more durable steel. Steel was the preferred building material of architects, who, dur-

>> After thousands of hours in the laboratory, Edison discovered that a carbon filament in an oxygen-free bulb lasted more than 40 hours.

Copyright © The Granger Collection, New York / The Granger Collection

ing this era, first designed skyscrapers that reached hundreds of feet into the air. And the mechanized elevator, invented by Elisha Otis in 1853, made all these skyscrapers useable. Before the elevator, few people would rent rooms above the sixth floor. At the same time, the typewriter was invented in the 1860s and marketed by Eliphalet Remington and Sons beginning in 1873. The typewriter created a number of office jobs that opened up to women during these years. In the otherwise patriarchal business world of the nineteenth century, the typewriter helped make women earners in an industrializing economy.

Invention bred still more invention. In the seven decades before 1860, the U.S. Patent Office issued 36,000 patent licenses. During the three decades after 1860, that number of patents grew to 144,000.

## Innovative Financing, Law, and Business Practices

To support the development of these technologies and the big businesses that marketed and distributed them, a new breed of financiers emerged. Such giants as Jay Gould and J. Pierpont Morgan specialized in forming groups of rich men (called syndicates) in order to provide huge amounts of capital to fund promising companies and start up new industries. Morgan and a handful of associates gathered investors from around the globe to underwrite and fund various investment opportunities. The advent of pooled funds allowed Morgan to broker the formation of one of the world's first billion-dollar corporations, the Northern Securities Company.

Beginning in the mid-1800s, federal and state governments made changes in corporate law that supported these financial schemes and encouraged growth. They provided corporations with the power to acquire and merge with other businesses, thus allowing corporations to accumulate the capital required to finance big businesses. They also provided a significant layer of protection between families' fortunes and the courts. Rather than relying on any single individual's fortune to raise money, corporate officers were allowed to sell their stock on the open market. In that way, the investors who bought shares of the stock would become "part owners" of the company. In the event that a corporation was sued successfully, investors holding stock limited their liability to just the number of shares they owned. During the Industrial Revolution, the number of corporations increased dramatically, creating a sizeable number of organizations with large amounts of money that were able and willing to buy up successful smaller companies and develop a national (and even international) market.

During this era, entrepreneurs also experimented with innovative business practices that allowed them to expand rapidly. For one, they streamlined operations. As businesses became larger, managers could not personally supervise all facets of their operations. So entrepreneurs established a hierarchy of managers and supervisors to coordinate schedules, keep track of shipments, and analyze the costs of each facet of the business. This development had two results: (1) It allowed corporations to control shops across a broad stretch of the nation, often centralizing control in one of the growing cities of the Midwest, such as Chicago; and (2) it created a class of managers that would figure prominently in the rapidly expanding middle class.

# LO³ The National Market: Creating Consumer Demand

By the late nineteenth century, with railroads spanning the nation and the process of replaceable parts making more and more goods available to a consuming public, the entire American nation became a marketplace. As wise businessmen capitalized on this development, they helped create the modern consumer culture.

## Advertising

One significant development in this regard was a revolution in advertising. Before the Industrial Revolution, businessmen notified people about the availability of goods simply by printing announcements in local newspapers or in leaflets handed out to customers. Because their companies served mostly a local market, such advertising techniques were effective. As the consumer economy evolved after the Civil War, however, businesses began to market goods more aggressively and across numerous regions. In newspapers, multiple-column, even full-page advertisements began to replace the single-column notices of earlier years. Celebrities

were featured wearing watches or hats. The number of advertising agencies expanded rapidly. Billboards and placards sprouted up everywhere.

## National Brands

Along similar lines, the first advertising agencies began rudimentary marketing surveys to identify potential consumers' preferences, and then applied the results to the marketing of individual products. For example, buying biscuits in the late nineteenth century was often problematic because they were stored in open containers; usually they became stale before they were bought. The National Biscuit Company (Nabisco) test-marketed a rather ordinary biscuit that had one difference from typical biscuits—a new, sealed package. Soon, consumers across the country demanded the product. The combination of technological and transportation innovations allowed the creation of truly national brands.

## Stores and Mail Order

Chain stores quickly followed. Essentially, chains began when successful storeowners decided to

© Bettmann/CORBIS

>> Nabisco's first ads featured a little boy in a rain slicker carrying a box of the specially packaged biscuits unharmed through the rain.

reach more customers by opening branches in separate locations. Large chain stores had the advantage of being able to negotiate lower wholesale prices because they could purchase items in bulk; often they passed on a portion of their savings to consumers in the form of lower prices. One of the largest grocery chains was the Atlantic and Pacific Tea Company, known as A&P. Frank W. Woolworth devised another type of chain based on the idea of selling lots of inexpensive goods at cheap, fixed prices. His Woolworth outlets were originally called "five and tens," meaning that almost all of the goods were priced at either a nickel or a dime. The growth of his stores was phenomenal. In 1859, Woolworth founded his first store; by 1915 he and his partners controlled around six hundred outlets.

The emergence of advertising and national chain stores helped create a consumer culture in the nation's cities. The wide availability of consumer goods prompted some entrepreneurs to open department stores, which quickly became the greatest symbol of the emerging desire for consumption. In ornate window displays, such as New York's Macy's (founded 1858) and Philadelphia's Wanamaker's (1877), a large selection of items dazzled passersby. The stores also provided employment to thousands of urban Americans, especially women.

Chain retail stores appealed to city and town dwellers, but to reach rural customers, farsighted entrepreneurs used catalogues. In 1872, Aaron Montgomery Ward set up a mail order business. Beginning with a single-page list of items, he expanded his lists until his catalogue was heavier than many magazines. Richard W. Sears and Alvah C. Roebuck were comparative latecomers to the mail order business, but they offered Ward stiff competition. By the late 1890s, the Sears catalogue numbered more than five hundred pages. Next to the family Bible, it was one of the few "books" considered indispensable by farm families.

## And in the end . . .

Between 1865 and the early 1900s, the American economy was transformed from one run by family shops and small factories to one generally controlled by large corporations. As these corporations con-

solidated their business practices, they helped improve access to food, material wealth, and new technologies. They also helped expand large urban centers, especially in the North, and pushed their innovations into the West and the South, creating what looked like the first national consumer culture to many Americans, where Nabisco crackers could be found in most American grocery stores and where the Sears catalogue could be found in all regions of the country.

Many of the inventions of the late nineteenth century did not seem particularly transformative to contemporaries. The *New York Times* reporter covering the 1882 story of Edison's first large-scale light bulb test, in New York City, passively described the test as "in every way satisfactory." He did not recognize the electric light bulb as something all that different from the gas bulbs that had illuminated the city before. But what the reporter missed was that the bulb required a grid of electrical power that could be extended for miles. He missed the fact that electric automation would lead to widespread electrification and spark hundreds of other inventions.

The inventions of the Industrial Age and the expansion of corporate America would influence the nation differently, depending on where one lived. In the North, they would transform society by inspiring the arrival of millions of immigrants and creating an urban society, along with a reactionary politics, as working-class laborers sought to make the government more responsive to their needs in the budding labor movement. It is these transitions in the North that we turn to next.

## What else was happening . . .

| 1868 | The world's first traffic light is used, in London, well before the automobile. |
| --- | --- |
| 1869 | Ives McGaffey invents his "sweeping machine"—the vacuum cleaner. |
| 1876 | Bass Pale Ale becomes the first product to bear a trademark. |
| 1895 | Lifebuoy soap trademark is registered. |

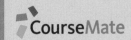

Visit the CourseMate website at www.cengagebrain.com for additional study tools and review materials for this chapter.

# Creating *an* Industrial Society *in the* North

## Learning Outcomes

*After reading this chapter, you should be able to do the following:*

LO **1** Describe the evolution of urbanization in the United States in the last decades of the nineteenth century, and the disparities of wealth that emerged within those cities.

LO **2** Discuss immigration to the United States that took place in the last decades of the 1800s, including where most immigrants came from, why they came, and what their experiences were after they arrived.

LO **3** Discuss the ways in which politics in American cities functioned during the late 1800s.

LO **4** Describe the early labor unions that were formed in the United States, including their goals, their activities, and their situations at the end of the nineteenth century.

*"Three developments— urbanization, immigration, and increasing disparities in wealth— were key components of the Industrial Revolution in the North."*

Most of the massive industries of the Industrial Age emerged in the North. There, because there was work, cities ballooned into metropolises. They attracted worldwide attention, and, for a variety of factors, the wealth of jobs in the industrializing North helped spur and sustain large-scale immigration from Europe, in a wave that dwarfed the immigration of the 1840s and 1850s. As the cities of the North expanded, economic disparities between the wealthy and the poor became more pronounced; the corporations of the Industrial Age generated enormous fortunes for a handful of people, leaving most industrial laborers in poverty.

These three developments—urbanization, immigration, and increasing disparities in wealth—were key components of the Industrial Revolution in the North. Unsurprisingly perhaps, the politics of the era were poorly equipped to handle all these challenges involved. In a society uncertain about the moral role of politics (especially after the bloody Civil War) and eager not to miss out on the economic possibilities of the new age, politics during the last third of the nineteenth century were characterized by high voter participation, extreme partisanship, and massive corruption.

By the early 1900s, three waves of reformers had emerged to demand that the government intervene to curtail the most oppressive practices of big business: (1) the labor movement, (2) the Populists, and (3) the Progressives. The first of these reformers—the labor movement—was the most radical. It emerged concurrently with the Industrial Age and focused on the working classes. Throughout the second half of the nineteenth century, urban workers sought to establish a politics of class by means of an increasingly vocal labor movement. During its first years, this labor movement was raucous and provocative, questioning America's commitment to capitalism and democracy. Socialists flourished in this environment, as did communists and anarchists. Each challenge to American democratic capitalism stirred fear among the American upper and middle classes, but that, of course, was the point.

This chapter examines the impact of the Industrial Age in the North, focusing on urbanization, immigration, and economic disparity, as well as the inability or unwillingness of politicians to manage these challenges. It concludes with an examination of the first grassroots demands for reform in the shape of the labor movement.

## What do you think?

If the government intervened to assist the weak and the incapable, it would pollute the business environment and prevent economic growth.

| Strongly Disagree | | | | | | Strongly Agree |
|---|---|---|---|---|---|---|
| 1 | 2 | 3 | 4 | 5 | 6 | 7 |

## LO¹ Urbanization

As businesses grew, manufacturers needed more workers. Displaced farmers, immigrants from Europe and Asia, and African Americans from the South all flocked to the job opportunities in northern urban centers. By 1900, more than a third of America's people lived in cities, and city populations were growing twice as fast as the population as a whole. Between 1870 and 1920, the number of Americans living in cities increased fivefold, from 10 million to 54 million. The population of New York City went from 800,000 in 1860 to 2 million in 1900. The population of Boston increased from 180,000 in 1860 to 600,000 in 1900. And Chicago grew from 109,000 in 1860 to 1.7 million in 1900. The cities were booming.

## Cities

Most of the people living in these growing cities were workers working in the new factories of the Industrial Age. For them, manufacturers sometimes provided company housing close to the factories so that the entire workforce could walk to work. For others, independent builders sought quick profits and got away with throwing up inferior houses

because few cities at the time had building codes. Developers also carved up previously built single-family homes into multiple-unit dwellings called **tenements**, which often had thin walls and frequently lacked windows as well. These kinds of close quarters led to communal childcare networks, and they also pushed people out into the streets, creating a raucous, lively, and sometimes dangerous street scene.

One effect of such rapid building was a dearth of parks in the new cities. Adequate plumbing was virtually nonexistent, and few pre-1900 workers' houses had an indoor water supply; most shared pumps and wells in back alleys. City governments began to build sewers after 1860, but these sewers were primitive; most ended at the nearest river or lake, where raw sewage was simply dumped into the water. Typhoid epidemics swept through city populations at a time when the connection between sewage and disease transmission was not widely understood. In 1900, the city of Chicago reversed the direction of the city's main river, diverting it to the Mississippi River in order to send the city's waste products away from Lake Michigan, its primary water source. The cities were growing tremendously, but the expansion was haphazard, and those at the bottom of the pay scale were often the most deprived of basic necessities.

Factory life was equally perilous. Between 1865 and 1915, working conditions in the nation's factories deteriorated. Before that time, the typical factory was little more than a large shop, often run by the individual who owned the business. It was likely that the owner knew the two to three dozen workers in his shop. A half-century later, workers in many factories were considerably more anonymous. Huge steel and textile mills and meatpacking plants employed thousands of workers. Workers spent ten-hour shifts on assembly lines, where machines hurled unfinished products at them, to which they were expected to add some part or turn some bolts. They repeated the same boring task, hour after hour, until the whistle finally blew at the end of the shift. Between 1880 and 1900 an average of 35,000 workers died each year on the assembly line. The work was grueling.

Many employers callously ignored the basic needs of their workers, most notoriously illustrated by the 1911 Triangle Shirtwaist Fire, in the New York City garment

>> Rival gangs of firefighting clubs sometimes fought each other while buildings blazed.

district, near Washington Square Park. Foremen at the **Triangle Shirtwaist Company** had bolted the fire escape door shut to prevent female workers from taking breaks. When a fire broke out in the front of their **sweatshop**—located several stories above the street—hundreds of employees were trapped in the back of the shop. They faced two choices: sure death from the fire or probable death by leaping from the window to the pavement below. Bystanders had lifelong nightmares from the sight of falling bodies thudding to the ground. The final death toll was 146 workers, most of them poor women.

 View an online exhibit on the Triangle Shirtwaist Company fire.

## Safety Hazards

Factory districts were smoky, noisy, unsanitary, densely populated areas that were prone to fires. Built of wood or brick, powered by coal-fired steam engines, and lighted by kerosene lamps or gas flames, early factories were particularly vulnerable. Factory fires, in places where fire escapes, drills, and other precautions were neglected, often caused fatalities. Before 1900, few cities had municipal firefighters. Instead, they depended on firefighting clubs, in effect youth gangs, who would compete to be first at the scene of a fire in the expectation of being paid for extinguishing it. Rival gangs of firefighting clubs sometimes fought each other while buildings blazed, and even firefighters with the best intentions were often thwarted by the lack of a sufficient high-pressure water supply.

*Between 1880 and 1900 an average of 35,000 workers died each year on the assembly line.*

## Wealthy Neighborhoods

While successful industrialists neglected the safety of their factories and workers' housing, they devoted enormous resources to the building of cultural institutions and the development of wealthy neighborhoods. Many had amassed huge fortunes and found novel ways to showcase their wealth. Fifth Avenue in New York, for example, was lined with mansions and townhouses. On New Year's Day, hostesses drew back the curtains of their mansions to reveal views of opulent interiors.

And this was just one symbol of their wealth. Successful businessmen made astonishing profits during this era. By 1890, the wealthiest 1 percent of the American population owned as much property as the remaining 99 percent. In the cities of the North, the leading industrialists ostentatiously displayed their fortunes. The Newport, Rhode Island, home of Pennsylvania coal magnate Edward Berwind, "The Elms," cost $1.4 million to build—more than $21.5 million today. The Newport home of William Vanderbilt, the grandson of Cornelius Vanderbilt, now called "Marble House," cost more than $11 million—a staggering $169.5 million today. "Diamond" Jim Brady, a wealthy New York City financier, was notorious for sitting two inches from his dinner table and continuing to eat until his expanding stomach touched the table. New York socialite Mrs. Stuyvesant Fish threw a party to honor her dog, which arrived wearing a diamond collar worth $15,000 (today, nearly $350,000). The wealthy of this era were extremely wealthy.

This gross materialism did not go unnoticed. Mark Twain and Charles Dudley Warner published a novel called *The Gilded Age* (providing the era with its most notable label) that satirically described the greed, materialism, and political corruption that accompanied the growth of industry and cities. Economics professor Thorstein Veblen, in his book *The Theory of the Leisure Class* (1899), called the behavior of the wealthy class "conspicuous consumption." He argued

 View pictures of The Elms, Marble House, and other Newport mansions.

>> A boy stokes a coal stove in a metal shop filled with young immigrant workers.

© George Eastman House/Getty Images

Read Andrew Carnegie's essay "Wealth."

that, ultimately, the selfishness of the rich harmed economic growth. Edith Wharton's novels, particularly *The House of Mirth* (1905), mocked the emptiness of the life led by the wealthy and the stifling social conventions that ruled their lives. Andrew Carnegie was one of the most conscientious of the captains of industry, and he described the problem of the Gilded Age as that of reconciling the wealthy and the poor in order to maintain a prosperous nation. In the burgeoning cities of the North, the two seemed to be living worlds apart.

## Suburbs

Often the middle classes would try to flee the polarities of the city, and in the late nineteenth century, suburbs began their initial growth. Street railways made it possible to live 4 or 5 miles from work (or farther), yet still get there fairly quickly each morning. Streetcar companies often built their lines beyond the edge of town in the confident expectation that housing developments would soon follow. They were often right; their lines formed the backbone of new suburban communities inhabited by the middle class. Slowly, city populations became increasingly stratified, with upper- and middle-class people living outside the noisy industrial districts, venturing as far away as bona fide suburbs, while the working classes and those enduring discrimination because of their race, religion, or country of origin lived in less desirable areas close to the industrial hubs.

## Entertainments

Cities had long been spaces of public entertainment, and in the nineteenth

>> New York socialite Mrs. Stuyvesant Fish threw a party to honor her dog, which arrived wearing a diamond collar worth $15,000 (today, nearly $350,000).

century they teemed with vaudeville houses, dance halls, and saloons. These spaces were often deemed immoral or improper by the upper classes. In the 1890s, entrepreneurs in the growing leisure industry found a more wholesome way to lure the city's masses: large, magnificent amusement parks. In 1895, New York's **Coney Island** opened, featuring roller coasters, water slides, and fun houses. Unlike other public amusements like vaudeville and saloons, amusement parks attracted both men and women because they were considered more respectable. For instance, Coney Island helped spur dating among working-class young men and women.

Attending professional baseball games was another way to relax, and baseball became a source of urban pride during these years. It began in 1876, with the formation of the **National League** by the Cincinnati Red Stockings (America's first professional team) and seven others. The league's success depended on reliable, intercity rail transport to carry the teams to each other's fields, as well as the telegraph lines along which rapid news of scores and results could be carried. The National League's success prompted the creation of the rival **American League** in 1901, and the two leagues competed in the first **World Series** in 1903, all due to the transportation and communications revolutions of the late nineteenth century, as well as the creation of a middle class with enough disposable income to enjoy an afternoon at the ballpark.

## LO² Immigration

Along with urbanization and the growing disparities of wealth,

>> "Grimy, gloomy . . . more suggestive of an enclosure for animals than a receiving station for prospective citizens of the United States." —*New York Tribune,* on Ellis Island, December 17, 1900

another important development in the industrializing North was immigration. Between 1880 and 1920, approximately 25 million people came to the United States. Unlike earlier arrivals, these new immigrants did not migrate from the British Isles or northern Europe; instead, they came predominantly from eastern, central, and southern Europe. They were Poles, Greeks, Italians, Bulgarians, Ukrainians, Czechs, Serbs, and Croats; they were Orthodox Jews, Eastern Orthodox Catholics, and Roman Catholics. For the most part, these different ethnic groups had only three things in common: (1) their status as new immigrants, (2) their lack of money and education, and (3) their reasons for leaving Europe. This new immigration was the result of at least four factors (see "The reasons why . . ." box on immigration below).

# { *The reasons why . . .* }

There were at least four reasons for the rise in immigration during these years:

***European population growth.*** Europe had experienced tremendous population growth during the nineteenth century, creating gaps between the number of workers and the number of jobs.

***Urban crowding in Europe.*** The Industrial Revolution in Europe drew people away from agricultural industries to cities, where the crush of newcomers made employment even harder to find.

***Antisemitism.*** A rise in antisemitism, especially within the Russian Empire, forced many Jews to flee.

***Economic opportunities.*** America served as a magnet because it promised economic opportunity and personal freedoms. Many who came planned only to acquire enough wealth to make a better life for themselves back in Europe. For example, between 1910 and 1914, more than 400,000 Italian immigrants left the United States. These immigrants were usually men who came to America alone, planning to return home and rejoin their families.

**greenhorns**
European newcomers to America

**Ellis Island**
Immigrant gateway to New York City from 1892 to 1954

 Explore the past of Ellis Island.

 Take a virtual tour of a Lower East Side tenement.

## The Immigrant Experience

Most of these new immigrants, who were often called **greenhorns**, faced a hard life in America. After successfully passing through well-known gateways like New York's **Ellis Island**, these immigrants struggled against tremendous adversity. America itself provided a tight labor market, and many immigrants came with limited knowledge of English, limited education, and limited work skills. Most stayed close to where they had landed, settling in such urban areas as New York City, Philadelphia, Chicago, and Boston. They found themselves on the bottom rung of the industrial hierarchy, working low-paying factory jobs.

By the end of the 1800s, immigrants made up a majority of the populations of most major American cities. By 1890, for example, New York's population was 80 percent immigrant. Chicago's population was a remarkable 87 percent immigrant. Most immigrants lived in crowded tenements that often lacked windows, heat, and indoor plumbing. Not surprisingly, poverty and overcrowding precipitated murder and other violent crimes, as well as theft. Some immigrant girls, driven by poverty and desperation, turned to prostitution.

## Working Conditions

Beyond the hardships and hazards of tenement life, immigrants often faced much more serious threats in the workplace. Jobs in factories locked this working class into a rigid, exhausting schedule. At the mercy of powerful machines that required them to perform the same simple task again and again, they worked ten to twelve hours a day, six days a week. As mechanization continued to decrease the need for skilled labor, and as employers kept searching for workers who would accept low pay, women and children entered factories in increasing numbers. By the turn of the century, 20 percent of the industrial workforce was female. The textile industry in particular relied almost completely upon women and children. Many states passed child labor laws by the end of the 1800s, but employers routinely ignored these laws, and the number of child factory workers remained high.

## Ethnicity, Assimilation, and the American Dream

Despite the struggle, immigrants also had their share of triumphs. Some even prospered, and many eventually gained a material stake in their new country by owning property. However, there was a fundamental tension at the core of the immigrant success story. Immigrants often sought to maintain a sense of connection to their native countries, but their status in America was inextricably tied to assimilation into American culture. New York and other major cities contained an amazing patchwork of different ethnic communities. These communities developed a variety of resources for comforting lonely and homesick immigrants, including foreign-language newspapers and fraternal and religious organizations. These were the years when America's cities evolved into complex mosaics of ethnic neighborhoods.

© CORBIS

>> "One of the sights which this coal side of our civilization has to show is the presence of herds of little children of all ages, from six years upward, at work in the coal breakers, toiling in dirt, and air thick with carbon dust, from dawn to dark, of every day in the week except Sunday. These coal breakers are the only schools they know. A letter from the coal regions in the Philadelphia 'Press' declares that 'there are no schools in the world where more evil is learned or more innocence destroyed than in the breakers. It is shocking to watch the vile practices indulged in by these children, to hear the frightful oaths they use, to see their total disregard for religion and humanity.'"
—Henry Demarest Lloyd, "The Lords of Industry," 1884

# LO³ The Politics of the Industrial Age

These kinds of dramatic changes required a new kind of politics to address growing economic disparities and the clannishness of the urban cities. But the politics of the late nineteenth century reflected the Industrial Revolution's devotion to business, not to the growing needs of the urban poor of the working classes. Indeed, politically, the devotion to the needs of business had two vital consequences: (1) It permitted a dramatic decline in attention to the treatment of African Americans, which had dominated the politics of the Reconstruction era; and (2) it sullied the image of politicians, who sometimes were guilty of blatant corruption as they prioritized the interests of business over those of other groups in the population. Federal, state, and local politicians gave massive land grants to their friends, offered government contracts only to their supporters, and accepted bribes for doing all sorts of "public works."

## Justifications of the Industrial Order

Three intellectual justifications for the social and economic order of the North emerged during the Industrial Revolution. Often they overlapped. Any reformer would have to overcome, or at least acknowledge, each of them before attempting to reform American politics.

### Mainline Protestant Morality

First, many of the leading industrialists of the late nineteenth century were sons of ministers, and they relied on a hard-line defense of Protestant individualism, arguing that economic problems stemmed from a particular individual's actions (or inactions) and that these problems were therefore not social in nature. There was a good bit of nativism in this argument too, especially considering that the vast majority of immigrants were Catholics and Jews from southern and eastern Europe. Furthermore, the industrialists firmly believed that their actions were improving the lot of humankind, which, despite some obvious contradictions, they were in fact doing. It was easy to argue that power grids, electric light, better transportation, and improved communications had increased the convenience and comfort of modern living.

### Social Darwinism

The second justification was **Social Darwinism**. Railroad tycoons like Charles Francis Adams Jr. believed that they were justified in their overbearing behavior because they had shown themselves to be the most successful competitors in an open market. Of course, because they had benefited from the federal government's actions to promote industrial growth through tariffs, subsidies, and cheap land sales, the successful capitalists' wealth was not as independently earned as they believed.

English philosopher Herbert Spencer promoted this Darwinistic perspective. After reading Charles Darwin's theories on biological evolution, Spencer coined the phrase "survival of the fittest" and applied Darwin's concepts to the contemporary economic environment. Spencer was attempting to account for differences in human ability in the business world by suggesting that economic progress would continue if the government kept its hands off free enterprise and allowed businessmen to do as they wished. If the government intervened to assist the weak and the incapable, he argued, such "softheartedness" would pollute the business environment and prevent economic growth.

Although very few Americans took Darwin's theory as far as Spencer did, businessmen occasionally borrowed those ideas that fit their needs. Later, Social Darwinism would be used by the Progressives to limit their willingness to challenge capitalism.

Social Darwinism also had a racialist tinge, providing intellectual justification for laws and social practices that kept African Americans, Indians, certain categories of immigrants, and women second-class citizens who were often denied the vote and a basic right to property ownership. This notion of a racial or cultural hierarchy of peoples was widely espoused in Gilded Age America; even the African American intellectual W. E. B. Du Bois relied on it when he argued that the vast majority of African Americans were ill equipped to be full citizens and instead should rely on a "talented tenth" to lead the way.

> **Social Darwinism** The theory that "survival of the fittest" extended to the business realm: tycoons believed they were justified in their overbearing behavior because they had shown themselves to be the most successful competitors in an open market

### The Myth of Success

Successful businessmen also perpetuated the belief that if you worked hard enough, you could become wealthy. This notion was popularized by many

> **"Where is the rich man who is oppressing anybody? If there was one, the newspapers would ring with it."**
>
> —*William Graham Sumner, in defense of Social Darwinism*

writers, none more ardently than Horatio Alger. An admired and prolific writer (he produced 135 pieces of fiction), Alger wrote virtually all of his stories with the same plot: a good person works hard and, with a little luck, inevitably succeeds. His protagonist, a young man with working-class roots, moves from a farm or small town to the city. Once there, leading a morally upright life, wholly committed to hard work, and, above all, showing loyalty to his employer, the hero literally rises "from rags to riches." Alger's formula was sometimes called "pluck and luck," because the hero always benefits from some fortuitous event (such as rescuing the boss's beautiful daughter from the path of a runaway fire truck). The (invariably handsome) young man sometimes then courts the daughter under her father's approving eye and advances swiftly up the company ladder.

Read a defense of Social Darwinism.

## Political Corruption

Supported by these intellectual justifications, many businessmen brought their probusiness agenda to politicians. Business interests quickly became the strongest lobby in the nation. As was the norm for lobbyists, their requests usually came with reimbursements. In order to obtain land grants, protective tariffs, tax relief, and other "favors," many businessmen exchanged cash or stock options with the era's politicians. The exchange of these favors occurred on both national and local levels.

### The Crédit Mobilier Scandal

The most damaging of these scandals was the Crédit Mobilier Scandal. In order to ensure an abundance of subsidies and land grants for their railroad, representatives from the Union Pacific offered federal lawmakers stock in the **Crédit Mobilier Company**. The problem was that this construction company had been set up by the directors of the Union Pacific in 1867 in order to build part of their transcontinen-

tal railroad—in essence, they were their own subcontractors. In these dual roles, they awarded themselves generous contracts (receiving between $7 million and $23 million). To avoid any interference from the government, officials at Crédit Mobilier awarded congressmen stock in the company. The corruption was so open and blatant that company proxies handed out shares on the floor of the House of Representatives. Recipients included the Speaker of the House, the minority leader, and Schuyler Colfax, vice president of the United States from 1868 to 1872. When the scandal became public, it led to a congressional investigation and sullied the image of many of the era's leading politicians.

### The Tweed Ring

Urban politics were equally corrupt, and none more so than New York's under "Boss" William

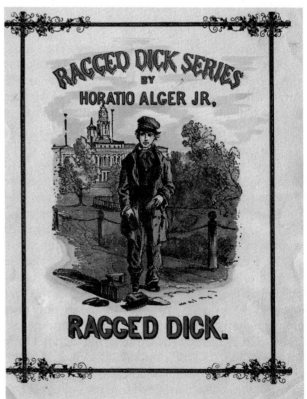

>> "He was above doing anything mean or dishonorable. He would not steal, or cheat, or impose upon younger boys, but was frank and straight-forward, manly and self-reliant." —Horatio Alger, description of the hero from *Ragged Dick*

© Bettmann/CORBIS

Learn more about Tammany Hall and "Boss" Tweed.

M. Tweed. Tweed's **Tweed Ring** of friends controlled **Tammany Hall**, a Democratic political organization known as a "machine" whose members regarded politics as an opportunity to get rich while providing favors to the urban underclass. Through his connections at Tammany, "Boss" Tweed was appointed to supervise the dramatic rebuilding of New York City's infrastructure during the formative years of the Industrial Revolution. Tweed profited from this rebuilding because he or his associates owned or had access to many of the subcontractors who did the labor. He also typically overcharged contractors and took tidy sums off the top for himself. Tweed was eventually exposed as a fraud in 1871 and was subsequently jailed and fined. After a dramatic escape, he was returned to jail, where he died in 1878. But Tammany Hall continued to exert influence on local politics until the early 1900s.

### The Appeal of Tammany

Despite its rampant corruption, Tammany appealed to recent Irish, Italian, and Jewish immigrants, who would provide Tammany politicians with their votes in exchange for preference in getting city jobs, free drinks on Election Day, and assorted social services.

One way local "bosses" established loyalty was to watch over neighborhoods and take care of short-term emergencies. George Washington Plunkitt, for example, a colorful Tammany boss who came to power after the fall of Tweed, told journalist William Riordan that if a family was made homeless by a fire, he went straight to the scene, found the family a temporary place to live, gave them money for immediate necessities, and ensured that they got back on their feet. What better way was there, he asked, to ensure voters' gratitude and loyalty? And what did it matter if, once empowered by the votes of those he "served," he took a little off the top?

Historians recognize that the machine system had its advantages, both in easing the transition to America for European newcomers and in dealing with short-term crises. But the system's reliance on above-the-law patronage also bred inefficiency, corruption, and cynicism, as unqualified people filled important government positions and as bribes raised prices for consumers.

**Tweed Ring**
Friends and cronies of New York's corrupt "Boss" William M. Tweed

**Tammany Hall**
A political organization known as a "machine," whose members regarded politics as an opportunity to get rich while providing favors to the urban underclass

 Read excerpts from William Riordan's *Plunkitt of Tammany Hall*.

## Political Divisions

Despite the corruption, or perhaps because of it, politics were vibrant at the national level, political parties dominated, and few major political programs were implemented (the battles were too fierce). Judging from presidential elections, the nation was almost evenly divided between Democrats and Republicans. But if the nation was evenly divided, the states were not, with Republicans controlling most of the northern states and Democrats controlling the South. Democrats also did well with urban immigrants. Rarely did the party of the president also control

WHO STOLE THE PEOPLE'S MONEY?" — DO TELL . N.Y.TIMES.  'TWAS HIM.

>> "'Who Stole the People's Money?' 'Twas him." One of cartoonist Thomas Nast's famous cartoons on the corruption of the Tweed Ring. Boss Tweed himself is pictured, far left foreground, with the full beard.

> **"There's an honest graft, and I'm an example of how it works. I might sum up the whole thing by sayin': 'I seen my opportunities and I took 'em.'"**
>
> —George Washington Plunkitt, from *Plunkitt of Tammany Hall, 1905*

Congress, and between 1876 and 1896, a series of one-term presidents occupied the White House. More than 80 percent of eligible voters turned out for elections, mostly because of the dynamism of the parties and their numerous supporting machines. Nevertheless, for the most part, the nation's leaders were either incapable of managing or unwilling to manage the many problems associated with the Industrial Revolution.

Moreover, after the trauma of the Civil War, the American people often shied away from such deeply emotional issues as social welfare or concern for minorities. In a brutal reminder of the way politics could inspire passion, in 1881, President James A. Garfield was assassinated by a fellow Republican who disagreed with the president over the issue of civil service reform. Spurred to act by the assassination, Congress passed the Pendleton Act in 1883, which for the first time created a class of federal jobs that was not entirely controlled by politi-

cal patronage. (Garfield's assassin had been fired from his post, not for incompetence, but based on the faction of the Republican Party he had supported during the election of 1880.) The act revealed divisions within the Republican Party, which was split between idealist reformers on the one hand and those supportive of machine politics and the spoils system on the other. Machine politicians mischievously labeled their Republican opponents **mugwumps**, meaning a Republican who supported Democratic candidate Grover Cleveland in the 1884 election only because the Republican candidate, James Blaine, was viewed as a product of machine politics.

## LO⁴ The Rise of Labor

For the first three decades after the Civil War, then, businessmen generally had their way in the political arena. They could count on friendly legislators to provide subsidies for promising new industries, and more mature industries might receive tariff protection against foreign competition. When workers went on strike, the government often intervened on the side of management by ordering troops to protect strikebreakers.

Nevertheless, workers still went on strike and fought for better working conditions, and one of the most important developments of these years was the rise of organized labor. For workers, industrial life held few guarantees. Every day, industrial workers faced danger, uncertainty, and a crushing workload. By

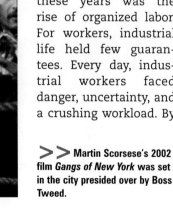

>> Martin Scorsese's 2002 film *Gangs of New York* was set in the city presided over by Boss Tweed.

© Miramax/courtesy Everett Collection

the turn of the century, accidents had caused more than 20,000 deaths and hundreds of thousands of injuries. Job security was nonexistent. Workers who became sick or injured risked being fired, and new inventions in machinery continually made certain jobs obsolete. And pay was minimal. Although the average wage for industrial work rose between 1870 and 1900, that wage in 1900 was still only 20 cents an hour, or less than five dollars today, hardly enough to pay for adequate food, clothing, and shelter.

In the late 1800s, men were not the only ones facing these long hours of toil; women and children worked too. In many instances, poor families simply could not survive without the added incomes of all able-bodied members, and it was not uncommon for young children to work twelve-hour days. In a chain reaction that punished all three groups, working women and children exacerbated labor dilemmas because they worked longer hours and for less pay than their male counterparts, who thus lost bargaining leverage.

## The Railroad Strike of 1877

Tensions caused by these conditions inevitably reached the boiling point, and the first labor conflict to come to national attention occurred in 1877, when railroad workers went on strike and froze most of the country's train traffic. The railroad industry had expanded enormously following the Civil War, and wage cuts during the Panic of 1873 created widespread resentment among workers.

Government intervention fueled working-class unrest. Word of the strike reached President Rutherford B. Hayes while he was dining in a train car with the president of the B&O Railroad, who argued that the strikers posed a serious threat to public safety. Hayes agreed and authorized the use of the National Guard to put an end to the strikes. Violence soon erupted in towns and cities across the country, and battles broke out in Baltimore, Chicago, San Francisco, and Pittsburgh. In St. Louis, striking railroad workers were joined by all other industrial workers in the city, shutting down all manufacturing establishments for four days. The city's industry was at a standstill.

Eventually, the National Guard defeated the strikers, railroad workers took pay cuts, and strike leaders were jailed. But more than one hundred people were killed nationwide, and there was astronomical property damage. Though the strike's carnage evaporated public sympathy for the workers, the conflict brought the issue of labor activism into the national consciousness.

## The Struggle over Union Expansion

As worker discontent grew, emerging unions of organized workers struggled to exert influence. But they faced an uphill battle. Business owners opposed them, had ample resources to do so, and could take advantage of ethnic, religious, and racial divisions among the workers themselves to weaken the unity of the working classes.

### Opposition of Business Owners

On a practical level, employers considered unions bad for business. To stay competitive, business owners were constantly seeking to keep costs down. Labor was one such cost, and a company whose profits were dropping might cut jobs and wages. Most owners also saw their union-busting tactics as a defense of the American way of life. For them, union organizing ran counter to the American virtues of independence and self-reliance, and they often justified the pitfalls of the capitalist system by citing the theory of Social Darwinism or the fact that their industries were propelling the United States toward building the largest economy in the world.

### Their Resources

Regardless of motive, American business owners had several resources at their disposal to fight against unions. They fired workers who joined unions and denied jobs to union organizers. Many workers had to sign a **yellow dog contract**, in which they promised, upon pain of termination, not to join a union. Employers also used the **blacklist**, a compilation of known union activists in a particular area. Employers shared these lists and refused to hire anyone whose name appeared on them. Also, by hiring a mixture of native-born Americans and immigrants of different backgrounds, employers tried to exploit ethnic divisions to forestall any feelings of worker unity, and they did so with considerable success.

Business owners were often just as successful in breaking strikes as they were in hindering union organization. To keep their factories and mines running, they hired **strikebreakers**, often unemployed immigrant workers from other areas who were hungry for jobs and had no stake in the union struggle.

**yellow dog contract**
Contract stipulating that an employee would not join a union

**blacklist**
A compilation of known union activists in a particular area; employers refused to hire anyone whose name appeared on one

**strikebreakers**
Workers who agreed to work while union workers were on strike

## Divisions among Workers

In addition to stiff opposition from business owners, union organizers also faced obstacles within the labor pool itself. Workers did not share the same levels of skill and pay, or the same occupations. More highly skilled workers enjoyed higher wages and better job security; for them, unions did not have much appeal. Immigrant workers also posed a problem to unity. They were isolated from one another by language and sometimes religion, and native-born Americans, who saw immigrants as a threat to their own jobs, often resented them. Many immigrants were in America only temporarily, to earn quick money to send back home; they had families to support and did not stand to benefit from a typical strike's long months of idleness. For these reasons, many labor unionists despised immigrants, seeing them as not committed to the cause. For example, it was the Workingman's Party of California that exerted political pressure for the passage of the Chinese Exclusion Act.

### Labor Solidarity

Despite the fractured nature of the American workforce, union leaders fought to create a sense of common purpose among its members. Arguing that it was the working class, not owners and managers, who produced America's wealth, union organizers tried to instill a sense of pride and camaraderie among union members. Some unions, especially those in urban areas with a large immigrant population, sought to overcome the inherent barriers between ethnic groups. The **International Ladies' Garment Workers' Union (ILGWU)** of New York City, for example, often conducted its union meetings in five different languages simultaneously.

### Roles of Government and the Middle Class

To achieve their goals, union leaders needed more than solidarity among workers; they also needed support from government leaders and the politically influential middle class. Such support was hard to find. In the last two decades of the 1800s, some middle-class reformers did address labor issues, and the government did take some actions to improve worker conditions. For instance, many middle-class

>> The Knights of Labor, led by Terence Powderly (center), sought to unite all the nation's "toilers," as indicated by the variety of laborers represented in each of the four corners of the image.

Americans participated in charitable reform efforts that sought to improve workers' living conditions. As a result of these efforts, Congress in 1868 mandated an eight-hour workday for federal construction projects, and in 1885 it passed the **Contract Labor Law**, which prohibited employers from forcing immigrants to work to pay off the costs of their passage to America. But these laws were exceptions. For the most part, the middle class and the government remained supportive of industry leaders.

## The Knights of Labor

At the national level, the Knights of Labor was America's first effective union, one that sought to unite all of America's "toilers" into a single organization that, through the power of its vast membership, could deliver workers from their plight. The Knights of Labor accepted farm hands and factory workers; it welcomed women, African Americans, and immigrants. (The union excluded lawyers, bankers, doctors, and liquor dealers, all of whom, from the union's perspective, were not toilers but white-collar workers.)

Founded in 1869 by a Philadelphia tailor named Uriah Stephens, the Knights of Labor rose to prominence in 1879, when Terence Powderly assumed

Read the original Knights of Labor platform.

leadership. Powderly opened the union's doors to almost all workers, and it became, for a brief time, the largest union in the country. In 1884 and 1885, the Knights of Labor entered the national spotlight when its members staged successful strikes against railroad companies in the Southwest. After the railroad strikes, membership in the Knights of Labor exploded; the union had approximately 100,000 members in 1884, and by 1886 its membership rolls had swelled to more than 750,000 workers.

## The Fall of the Knights

As quickly as it had grown, the influence of the Knights of Labor faded away. Ultimately, the Knights simply could not coordinate the activities of its members, who came from a variety of regions, industries, and ethnic backgrounds. Also, although the union owed much of its growth to the success of strikes, Powderly resisted using strikes because he believed, correctly, that they would jeopardize the union's public standing.

## The Haymarket Riot

Powderly's distrust of strikes proved to be well founded. Regardless of other problems plaguing the Knights of Labor, in the end it was a single event that caused the demise of the union. In spring 1886, workers demanding an eight-hour workday went on strike against the McCormick Harvester Company of Chicago. On May 3, four picketers were killed during a clash with the police. The next day a rally was held in Chicago's Haymarket Square to protest the police's actions. When police tried to break up this second gathering, someone threw dynamite at them. The explosion killed seven policemen and wounded dozens of others. Those police who were not injured then fired their guns into the crowd; four more people were killed, and more than a hundred others were trampled and shot at as they fled. The "Haymarket Affair," as it was called in the press, was believed to be the work of anarchists (who believed governments were unnecessary and should be abolished), and the incident created a state of hysteria among middle-class citizens, who mistakenly feared that all laborites were anarchists. Eventually, eight reputed anarchists were arrested for conspiring to kill the policemen, and although none of the men could be tied to the actual bomb, they were convicted, and seven received the death sentence.

After the Haymarket bombing, anti-union editorials appeared in newspapers across the country, and the Knights of Labor were a frequent target. One of the convicted men was a union member, and, although Powderly condemned the bombing, his organization became synonymous with anarchist activity. It could not

Read Terence Powderly's *Thirty Years of Labor.*

survive the mischaracterization, and by the early 1890s the union was gone, and, for a short time at least, its vision of a coalition of all workers disappeared with it.

>> **Woodcut of dynamite exploding among police ranks during the Haymarket Square riot, Chicago, 1886.**

> **"** My first step was thus taken in organized labor and a new influence fired my ambition and changed the whole current of my career. I was filled with enthusiasm and my blood fairly leaped in my veins. Day and night I worked for the brotherhood. **"**
>
> —*Eugene V. Debs, "How I Became a Socialist," 1902*

## Growth and Frustrations

Despite all the setbacks, in the late 1880s and throughout the 1890s, workers continued to organize, although usually on a smaller scale than the Knights of Labor. Particularly after 1893, when the country experienced a severe economic depression, union activity intensified. But the labor movement was no match for big business. In two important struggles, the Homestead strike of 1892 and the Pullman strike of 1894, business owners successfully called upon the full weight of the U.S. government to crush labor activism.

### The Homestead Strike

In 1892, the price of steel plunged. To reduce business costs, Andrew Carnegie and Henry Clay Frick, who managed Carnegie's Homestead Steel Factories outside of Pittsburgh, decided to cut wages and break the local union, called the Association of Iron and Steel Workers. When the union went on strike to protest the cutbacks, Frick fortified the plant with barbed wire and guns. He then sent a barge filled with detectives from the Pinkerton National Detective Agency down the Monongahela River to occupy the plant. Picketing strikers greeted the barge with gunfire and dynamite, and during the fourteen-hour battle that ensued, the detectives were defeated and forced out of town. But the union's success was short-lived. Responding to the violence, the governor of Pennsylvania brought out the state militia, which occupied the factory and allowed strikebreakers to enter. The union cause was further tarnished when an anarchist made an unsuccessful attempt to assassinate Frick.

 Read an excerpt from Andrew Carnegie's autobiography.

After four months, the hungry steelworkers abandoned the union and returned to the plant. The collapse of the steelworkers' union would mark the end of the labor movement in the steel industry for the next forty-five years.

### The Pullman Strike

In many respects, the story of the Pullman strike of 1894 is virtually the same as that of the Homestead strike. Once again, the government intervened in a hard-fought battle between a powerful business owner and a determined, well-organized union, tipping the balance in favor of the owner.

In the town of Pullman, outside of Chicago, George Pullman owned a factory that manufactured luxury railroad cars. Pullman was a company town; almost every worker in town was employed by the factory, bought goods on credit at the Pullman company store, and rented living quarters owned by the company. Pullman's adversary was the **American Railway Union (ARU)**, founded in 1893 by Eugene V. Debs, a former train fireman from Indiana and a Christian socialist, defined as someone who believes that the teachings of Jesus naturally lead to an advocacy of economic socialism. Debs believed that the means of producing and distributing goods should be owned by a centralized government that would then plan and regulate the economy. The ARU was America's first **industrial union**, meaning that it sought to bring together all the workers in a single industry (such as the railroad industry), rather than workers in a single occupation (such as the brakeman's union, which organized only brakemen).

In 1893, after a nationwide depression began shrinking the market for Pullman's luxury cars, Pullman fired a third of his workers and lowered by 25 percent the wages of those who remained. But he did not cut rents or company store prices. In May 1894, a local branch of the ARU struck the Pullman factory in protest. The struggle soon escalated to national proportions. Because the ARU was an industry-wide labor union, it paralyzed the nation's railroads when union members across the country refused to work on trains carrying Pullman cars. Pullman's managers challenged the strike by attaching U.S. mail cars to the Pullman cars, thereby making the strike an interference with the federal mail system. In response, President Grover Cleveland sent troops to break the strike's center in Chicago. In July, soon after the arrival of federal troops in Chicago, the union was in trouble. Violence between strikers and soldiers broke out, and Debs was arrested for contempt of court. With their union in tatters, the Pullman workers gave up their protests and returned to the factory.

## The Rise of the AFL

At the time of these highly publicized strikes, another union, the **American Federation of Labor (AFL)**, became the leading labor organization in America. Founded in 1881, the AFL gained momentum throughout the 1880s, as the Knights of Labor diminished, by pursuing a different strategy than the Knights of Labor and the ARU—one that made it more attractive to middle-class Americans. The AFL was a loose federation of roughly one hundred **craft unions** rather than a single national union. It was also avowedly antisocialist and anti-anarchist. Its leader, Samuel Gompers, coordinated the craft unions' actions without making any central decisions for them, and by arbitrating disputes, he ensured they stuck by each other. However, Gompers did not believe in organizing unskilled laborers, who were easily replaced by strikebreakers.

The AFL's successes helped offset failures like the Homestead and Pullman strikes. Its most important early achievement took place in 1890, when Gompers's own cigar makers' union established the eight-hour workday. Up until then, the typical

Read Samuel Gompers's congressional testimony regarding AFL unions.

workday had been ten hours or longer. In a pattern typical for the AFL, other AFL unions also demanded the shortened workday, and before long, printers, granite cutters, and coal miners were also working fewer hours per day. By the 1890s, the AFL had replaced the Knights of Labor as the most important labor lobby in the nation.

## Labor and Politics

Despite the AFL's victories, by the turn of the century government favoritism toward big business had convinced many labor leaders of the need for political solutions. But the labor movement was far from united in how to do this. The AFL's Samuel Gompers argued that entering the political arena was too costly and that labor's best strategy was to focus on winning individual concessions from owners.

Other laborites chose to enter the political arena by creating new parties. In 1901, socialists formed the **American Socialist Party**, led by Eugene Debs. The party fielded candidates in both national and local elections, with some success. It sought to help workers by replacing the nation's capitalist system, but through involvement in the democratic process.

More radical forms of political protest also emerged, among them those employed by the **International Workers of the World (IWW)**. Founded in 1905, the IWW grew out of a collection of militant mining unions in Colorado and Idaho, where workers scorned the AFL's exclusiveness. Under the leadership of "Big Bill" Haywood, the "Wobblies," as IWW members were called, pursued **anarcho-syndicalism**, which sought to use labor activism to overthrow the capitalist system.

## The Mainstream

Most labor leaders, however, followed the AFL's example and avoided challenging the country's political establishment. Nonetheless, union leaders did begin to see that influencing government officials through the political process could be beneficial to their cause. For example, when President Theodore Roosevelt arbitrated a coal miners' strike in 1902, he forced mine owners to make concessions to the union. During the years following 1902, laborites became active participants in the nation's politics—a role they would continue to play throughout the twentieth century.

**American Federation of Labor (AFL)**
The leading labor organization in America, founded in 1881 by Samuel Gompers and composed of craft unions rather than a single national union

**craft union**
Union of skilled laborers, the type of union assembled under the American Federation of Labor

**American Socialist Party**
Political party formed in 1901 and led by Eugene Debs that advocated replacing the nation's capitalist system

**International Workers of the World (IWW)**
A collection of militant mining unions founded in 1905 in Colorado and Idaho; sought to use labor activism to overthrow the capitalist system

**anarcho-syndicalism**
A radical form of political protest that advocates the use of labor activism to overthrow the capitalist system

Read Eugene Debs's "How I Became a Socialist."

# And in the end . . .

The development of the Industrial Age in the North during the last third of the nineteenth century was not always smooth. As new inventions and new ways of doing business expanded the power and purview of corporate leaders, wage disparities grew, urbanization introduced higher rates of crime and crowding in cities, and immigration provoked discussions about what it meant to be an American and about who belonged and who didn't. Meanwhile, the politics and politicians of the era were raucous, corrupt, and all too often unwilling to manage the transition into the modern industrial era. Those who attacked the new order most violently were usually shut down by the joint forces of industrial tycoons and national politicians.

The labor movement would live on, and it would continue to aid and assist in future movements for reform. But other calls for reform would be more successful during the turn of the twentieth century. Some of these calls would come from the South and the West, which had a completely different experience with the Industrial Revolution. It is to them that we now turn.

## What else was happening . . .

| | |
|---|---|
| 1876–1882 | The right arm and torch of the Statue of Liberty cross the Atlantic three times. |
| 1884 | N. Thompson, founder of Coney Island Luna Park, introduces the roller coaster, calling it Switchback. |
| 1886 | Statue of Liberty is dedicated. The statue, a gift from France intended to commemorate the two nations' founding ideal of liberty, will come to symbolize American freedom to millions of immigrants. |
| 1895 | Independent Labour Party founded in England. |
| 1896 | The first comic strip character—the "Yellow Kid"—appears in the *New York Journal*. |
| 1899 | Felix Hoffmann patents aspirin. |

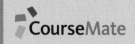 **CourseMate**

Visit the CourseMate website at www.cengagebrain.com for additional study tools and review materials for this chapter.

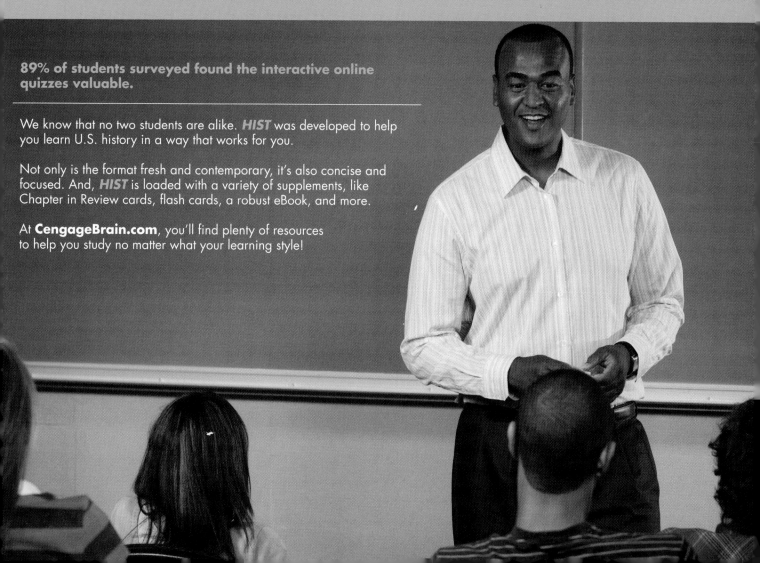

{ Learning Your Way }

**89% of students surveyed found the interactive online quizzes valuable.**

We know that no two students are alike. *HIST* was developed to help you learn U.S. history in a way that works for you.

Not only is the format fresh and contemporary, it's also concise and focused. And, *HIST* is loaded with a variety of supplements, like Chapter in Review cards, flash cards, a robust eBook, and more.

At **CengageBrain.com**, you'll find plenty of resources to help you study no matter what your learning style!

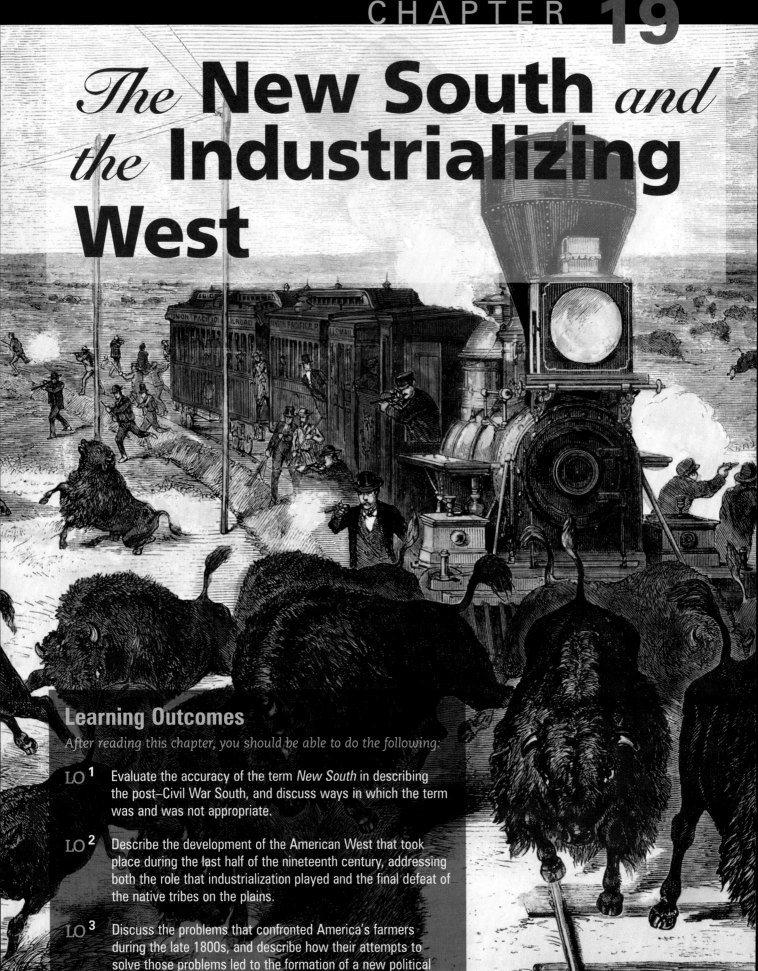

# CHAPTER 19

# The New South and the Industrializing West

## Learning Outcomes

*After reading this chapter, you should be able to do the following:*

**LO 1** Evaluate the accuracy of the term *New South* in describing the post–Civil War South, and discuss ways in which the term was and was not appropriate.

**LO 2** Describe the development of the American West that took place during the last half of the nineteenth century, addressing both the role that industrialization played and the final defeat of the native tribes on the plains.

**LO 3** Discuss the problems that confronted America's farmers during the late 1800s, and describe how their attempts to solve those problems led to the formation of a new political party.

> ## "Urban life had been part of the northern landscape since the colonial era. This was not the case in the newly developing South and West."

While the industrial North grew tremendously during the years after the Civil War, it had a foundation on which to grow. Factories were familiar sights in the North starting in the late eighteenth century, and urban life had been part of the landscape since the colonial era. This was not the case in the newly developing South and West.

In the South of the 1870s and 1880s, a collection of regional civic boosters attempted to harness the power of the Industrial Revolution to reshape the image of that region. In the antebellum era, the South was powered by a few crops (especially "King Cotton") and controlled politically and economically by a handful of wealthy families. And of course it was slaves who had done much of the laboring in that society. Post-Reconstruction civic boosters, however, made the argument that, after the Civil War, a "New South" had emerged, one based on economic opportunity, rich natural resources, and increased racial equality. While these hopes were sometimes met (some cities did in fact blossom), the promise of the New South was all too often frustrated. This frustrated promise was manifested in perhaps the deepest legacy of the New South: the system of racial segregation known as Jim Crow.

But even the South had more of an industrial foundation upon which to grow than the West. No region of the country was transformed more rapidly by the changes of the Industrial Age than the land west of the Mississippi River. During the final third of the nineteenth century, vast stretches of arable land were rapidly populated by millions of Americans who built great cities, decimated Indian populations, and created industries controlled by industrial magnates. (The cowboy, the most memorable image of the late-nineteenth-century West, was often working at the behest of a millionaire industrialist who was sending cattle to a slaughterhouse in one of the West's new great cities.)

But farming would remain central to both the South and the West, and the corporate-friendly politics whose unresponsiveness sparked the labor movement in the North provoked a rural movement for reform in the South and the West. Collectively called the Populist movement, it was often just as radical in its challenges to industrial capitalism as the labor movement, and it too would encounter more frustration than success. But these rural reformers put forward a platform that would succeed long after the Populists had exited the political stage.

This chapter examines the development of the New South and the industrializing West and then turns to the rural reform movement that emerged from, and sometimes unified, these two distinct regions.

# LO¹ The "New South"

Even before the Market Revolution, the South lagged behind the North in urbanization and industrialization, mainly because of its dependence on slavery and the domination of plantation owners in the state governments during the antebellum period. But after the war, southerners such as Henry Grady, the owner and editor of the *Atlanta Constitution*, argued that the South should improve its cities and provide for the growth of industry. It should partake in the Industrial Revolution and encourage economic relations with the North, including accepting northern loans. Grady's stirring speech "The New South" argued that the postwar South was a different world from the antebellum South, especially because it was not built on the subjugation of an entire race or the domination of a single industry like cotton. A spirit of enterprise characterized southern life in the late 1870s and 1880s, he argued.

Southern iron, steel, and textile industries all emerged during the thirty-five years following the Civil War, as did numerous cities. Still, despite Grady's celebration of cooperation between black and white southerners in the New South, blacks rarely benefited from any of these changes. Worse still, the era bore witness to the rise of the segregated society that would last until the 1960s and beyond. Thus, there were two components of the New South: (1) the halting and haphazard creation of an industrialized South, and (2) the quick and summary creation of a racial caste system. If many southerners shared the optimism, energy, and inventiveness that characterized the Industrial Revolution in the North, it nonetheless manifested itself far differently.

 Read Grady's "New South" speech.

## Southern Industries

Southern industry grew up around railroads, iron manufacture, and textile production. However, the South never developed a strong industrial base, at least not one comparable to what was taking place in the North.

> **"The New South is enamored of her new work. Her soul is stirred with the breath of a new life. The light of a grander day is falling fair on her face."**
>
> —*Henry Grady, "The New South," 1886*

## Railroads

Railroads led the South's industrial expansion, attracting capital from wealthy northern investors. The railroads also provided much-needed connections between the cities and towns of the South. Before the Civil War and up until about 1880, southern railroad development was very slow. But between 1880 and 1890—just one ten-year period—southern rails grew from 16,605 miles to 39,108 miles, an increase of more than 100 percent. Southern state governments poured resources into supporting rail companies, and northern rail companies began to expand into southern states, seeing an opportunity for profit and growth in the developing southern economy. By 1890, southern railroads had become a model for railroad development worldwide.

## Iron Production

The expansion of the railroads also helped foster the urbanization of southern cities and the growth of the iron industry. Many New South advocates hoped that iron production would become the central means for the South to compete with the North in industry. Because the demand for iron was high, especially in construction trades and in laying railroad lines, the iron industry seemed an ideal place to invest money and resources. As a result, it grew; the southern iron industry expanded seventeenfold in the 1800s.

## Cotton and Textiles

The easy transportation provided by railroads also allowed for the expansion of the southern textile industry. The industry grew fast in the South because of the abundance of cheap labor and the wide availability of cotton. Throughout the 1880s and 1890s, a mill-building craze swept the South. In 1870, about 10,000 people were employed in textile manufacturing. By 1900, nearly 100,000 people worked in the industry. The work was harsh, reflecting the typical labor conditions of the Industrial Age. It was not uncommon for a mill worker to work a fourteen-hour day.

## Industrial Failures

Despite the growth of the southern iron and textile industries, hopes of a new industrial South proved fleeting. The growth of the steel industry in Pennsylvania eventually surpassed southern iron production. Furthermore, although textile growth was impressive, the industry employed only a small percentage of southerners, and wages were as much as 30 percent lower than they were in the North, limiting the development of an expansive marketplace (because there were fewer dollars in circulation). Finally, although men like Grady had touted the contributions of African Americans, most black southerners were still barred from industrial employment. Poor white people were far more likely to be employed in railroads, iron, or textiles than African Americans, and these poor whites often resisted efforts at integration in their workplaces. Despite the industrial developments of the late 1800s, agriculture still led the southern economy.

## Southern Urbanization

For supporters of the New South, Birmingham, Alabama, became the symbol of southern urbanization. The city was ideally suited for growth because the Louisville and Nashville Railroad connected Birmingham with coal-mining towns all over Alabama, making it easy to ship the raw iron ore to the city's production facility. Birmingham became the center of the South's iron production in the late nineteenth century. Visitors from all over the world marveled at Birmingham's growth and its promise for future expansion. Many inves-

tors, including industrialist Andrew Carnegie, fueled this growth by pouring money into Birmingham's iron production.

Atlanta, Nashville, and Memphis all followed suit, taking precedence over Old South, water-centered cities like New Orleans and Charleston. But beyond them, similar cities were slow to grow in the South. There was simply not enough industry to merit continued expansion, in part because of southerners' unwillingness to increase wages for the South's black population, which would have expanded markets, encouraged growth, and made southern industry competitive. Immigrants, who could choose where to settle, chose the cities of the North over those of the South because of the depressed wages throughout the South.

## Segregation in the New South

Worse than low wages, though, was the southern drive to repeal political and social rights for black people. After the North retreated from military rule of the South in 1877, race relations became both rigid and violent, especially in areas where black and white Americans competed for economic opportunities. Southern white Democrats continued to deprive African Americans of their civil and political rights by passing laws that disenfranchised African Americans and separated blacks from whites. These efforts were coupled with an even more violent effort to block black citizens from participating in southern public life. Both efforts would prove only too successful. While the South did not have a monopoly on racism, it was where 95 percent of African Americans lived in 1865.

### Racial Disenfranchisement

Since the decline of Reconstruction, southern states had sought to disenfranchise African American voters. Formal disenfranchisement began in Mississippi in 1890. This **"Second Mississippi Plan,"** as it became known, established legal barriers to prevent African Americans from voting. The

> **"Second Mississippi Plan"** Plan that established legal barriers (the poll tax, literacy tests, and property qualifications) to prevent African Americans from voting in Mississippi; served as a legislative model for other states

© Hulton Archive/Getty Images

>> Workers from the blast furnace at Ensley, six miles from Birmingham, Alabama, where iron ore was converted into about 200 tons of pig iron per day in each of the three functioning furnaces.

plan served as a model for other states, and politicians across the South amended their state constitutions to deny blacks voting rights (South Carolina did so in 1895, Louisiana in 1898, and North Carolina in 1900). They did this through a series of questionable laws, such as the poll tax, which required voters to pay a fee to vote; literacy tests, which required voters to prove various levels of literacy; and property qualifications, which disqualified most black people, who were often too poor to own property. Eventually black citizens in every southern state effectively lost the right to vote. For example, in Louisiana, 95.6 percent of the state's black population was registered to vote in 1896, and more than half of them voted. In 1904, after the passage of these shady laws, only 1,342 of the state's black people were still registered— more than a 90 percent decline in just eight years.

## Jim Crow Segregation

Disenfranchisement occurred simultaneously with the development of other laws between 1890 and 1913 that segregated African Americans from white Americans in every public place in the South. These laws, known as **Jim Crow laws**, prevented African Americans from attending the same schools as white people or sitting in the same areas of restaurants. Citing these Jim Crow laws, one historian has called the 1890s the nadir of American race relations.

## *Plessy* v. *Ferguson*

Black people, of course, challenged these laws, but they were mostly frustrated in their efforts. The most important case emerged in Louisiana, when Homer Plessy, who claimed to be one-eighth black, challenged segregation on trains by sitting in a white car and announcing that he was black. Plessy intentionally violated the 1890 **Louisiana Separate Car Act** in order to support a local protest movement against the law. After his arrest, Plessy hoped that the courts would rule that the law violated the equal protection clause of the Fourteenth Amendment.

The case eventually went to the Supreme Court, which, in 1896, issued one of its landmark decisions. In *Plessy v. Ferguson*, the Court declared that segregation laws were constitutional, claiming that, as long as the accommodations were "separate but equal," it was legal to have separate facilities for black and white America. The nation's highest court had evaluated racial segregation and let it stand.

## Lynching

Violence was another form of political and social intimidation, and it was especially effective in areas where black and white Americans competed for similar jobs. Much of this violence came in the form of lynching, whereby a mob would gather to murder (usually by hanging, then burning) someone whom they believed to have violated a law or social custom. In the 1880s and 1890s, nearly 2,000 black men were lynched in the South. For more on why southerners created the system known as Jim Crow, see "The reasons why . . ." box.

 Read the *Plessy v. Ferguson* decision.

## African American Responses

Although every African American had thoughts on the rise of racial segregation in the South, there were two major responses from the African American community. The first called for black Americans to accommodate to their situation and not fight for political and civil rights, focusing instead on economic success. Booker T. Washington exemplified this accommodationist response. In Atlanta in 1895, he delivered a speech known as the **Atlanta Compromise**, encouraging black economic development and assuaging white fears of racial intermingling. Black and white people, Washington said, should remain as separate as the fingers on a hand, but they should work together to reach common economic ground. Economic progress, he

> *The nation's highest court had evaluated racial segregation and let it stand.*

# { *The reasons why . . .* }

There were at least four reasons why southerners created the racially segregated system known as Jim Crow during the decades after the Civil War:

**History of slavery.** The South, of course, was where the vast majority of American slaves lived before the Civil War, and the major underlying cause of the war was the perpetuation of slavery. Despite losing the war, many southerners sought to restore the South to what they idealized as its antebellum grandeur. This imperfect vision included, and indeed was predicated upon, creating a racist system as close to slavery as possible. The segregated social vision was, however, historically inaccurate, because slavery relied on relatively close proximal relations between black and white people, whereas segregation introduced social and spatial differences that were entirely new.

**Science.** The South did not have a monopoly on racism, though, and in most states throughout the nation black people could not vote and were denied many other basic rights. Indeed, the best science at the time openly advocated that the white race was superior and ranked the other races in descending order, with African Americans almost always at the bottom. Measurements of skulls and a variety of aptitude tests seemed to confirm the thesis. Using this **hierarchy of races**, white Americans in the North rebuked southern and eastern European immigrants (who were often not deemed "white"). White Americans in the West confidently lorded over Indians and Chinese. And white Americans in the South found justification for creating a social system that not only denied basic rights to African Americans but also segregated them from the rest of society. A large part of the fear, it must be noted, was that these evolutionary "lesser"

beings might try to improve their genetic stock by having sexual relations with white women, and interracial sex became a bogeyman behind much of the South's justification for segregation.

**Economics.** In 1865, about 95 percent of African Americans lived in the South. When the Industrial Age came south, the availability of black workers often kept wages low. This created tremendous animosity from much of the South's white working class. They argued that if black workers could be denied access to certain jobs, wages for white workers would go up. Indeed, the towns that had the highest number of lynchings in this period were those that had witnessed industrial growth and that had a competitive number of African American and white workers.

**Politics.** The Democratic Party shamelessly took advantage of all these factors, using its political power in the South to create the legal system of segregation known as Jim Crow. While claiming to be honoring southern history and using science as its justification, the Democratic Party secured votes by calling for racial solidarity within the white working class. When the Populist Party threatened to create an interracial working-class party, the Democrats fought back by calling for racial solidarity and by disenfranchising the "unfit" African American voters. By the 1890s, the legal system of segregation that would last until the 1960s was largely in place.

---

believed, could take place without racial integration. Washington believed that self-help within the African American community would stop the violence and allow for the progress of the race. Washington had

>> **Black and white people, Booker T. Washington said, should remain as separate as the fingers on a hand, but they should work together to reach common economic ground.**

enormous influence in the late nineteenth century, and his beliefs won wide support among white and black people into the twentieth century.

The other response from black America exemplified a refusal to compromise. For example, Ida B. Wells-Barnett, a writer and editor, led a crusade against lynching during the late nineteenth century after three of her friends were murdered in Memphis, Tennessee. In 1892, Wells-Barnett authored one of the most powerful antilynching pamphlets in the country, *Southern Horrors*. She became internationally famous for her protests.

W. E. B. Du Bois similarly criticized Washington's Atlanta speech. In the **Niagara Movement** (an

**Niagara Movement**
An attempt at political organization among black activists in the early 1900s. W. E. B. Du Bois drafted a "Statement of Principles," which declared that African Americans should fight for their rights rather than accept abuse and separation

 Read the "Atlanta Exposition Address."

attempt at political organization among black activists in the early 1900s), Du Bois drafted a "Statement of Principles" declaring that African Americans should fight for their rights rather than accept abuse and separation. Du Bois later played an important role in organizing the National Association for the Advancement of Colored People (NAACP). Formed in 1909, the NAACP led a decades-long assault on lynching and Jim Crow laws, continuously (and, for more than half a century, unsuccessfully) pressuring the government to end segregation and outlaw lynching. Du Bois and Washington openly debated black peoples' options, with Du Bois offering a stinging critique of Washington in Du Bois's famous book *The Souls of Black Folk* (1903).

W. E. B. Du Bois.

© The Art Archive / Culver Pictures

# Society and Culture in the Postwar South

The white South's brutal restrictions on the region's African American population gained greater popular acceptance in the late nineteenth century through a cultural revival that centered on the "myth of the lost cause." This myth tried to diminish the importance of slavery as a cause of the Civil War by lionizing the rebels of the Confederacy as avid defenders of "states' rights." Not only were many southerners attempting to reinstitute antebellum social practices, but many were also aiming to glorify the cause and culture of institutionalized slavery.

## The Myth of the Lost Cause

The myth of the lost cause provided cultural justification for the return of white political power. Associated with the defeat of the Confederacy, the myth was first presented in Edward Pollard's book *The Lost Cause* (1866). The war, as portrayed by Pollard, was a valiant effort fought against overwhelming odds to protect southern independence. Slavery, he argued, was not a cause of the Civil War; rather, it was northern aggression that disrupted the peaceful relationship between white masters and black slaves. Many organizations were established in the late-nineteenth-century South that defended this myth. These included the Southern Historical Society, founded in 1869 by a former Confederate general to promote a "proper" interpretation of the Civil War; the United Confederate Veterans Association, founded to establish a "Confederate Memorial Day"; and the United Daughters of the Confederacy, founded in 1895 to celebrate the southern war effort. Many northerners, racists themselves, were all too eager to accept this demotion of the importance of slavery as a cause of the war, and throughout the North historians reconceptualized the history of Reconstruction as a horror, characterized not by the violence of the Ku Klux Klan, but by corrupt black domination.

## African American Cultural Life

As white southerners variously confronted the impact of the Civil War and the meaning of the region's race relations, African Americans found ways to support their struggle for freedom and independence. For example, in Texas, black Americans celebrated their own holidays to keep the issues surrounding slavery and the Civil War alive. The celebration of **Juneteenth**, marking the date that slaves were formally freed in Texas (June 19, 1865), was

>> Forbidden from learning to read or write by pre–Civil War slave codes, African Americans made literacy and education a central priority after the war.

the most popular of these holidays, and it spread to black communities across the South. It is still celebrated in many southern communities today. But two other institutions reveal the central concerns of southern blacks in the late nineteenth century: (1) education and (2) the church.

## Black Literacy and Educational Institutions

One of the most important goals of African Americans after the Civil War was expanding educational opportunity. Forbidden from learning to read or write by pre–Civil War slave codes, African Americans made literacy and education a central priority after the war. As a result, black literacy rates grew dramatically in the late nineteenth and early twentieth centuries. Schools popped up, and

>> African American church in Washington, D.C., 1870s.

African Americans founded institutions of higher learning, such as Fisk University in Nashville (founded in 1866), Howard University in Washington, D.C. (1867), and Atlanta University in Georgia (1865).

The most prominent institution was Booker T. Washington's **Tuskegee Institute** in Tuskegee, Alabama (1881). Washington pioneered higher learning for African Americans and devoted his life to the growth of black education at all levels. However, he was often chastised for his belief that it would be better for black Americans to learn practical skills that would prepare them for industrial machine work than to seek other kinds of education, such as the arts and sciences, that might be perceived as challenging the white hierarchy. In this, as in so many other areas, Washington and Du Bois would spar over the relevancy of different kinds of education. Regardless, educational opportunities for African Americans in the South expanded, if in a segregated manner.

## Religious Life

The second central institution of black life in the South of the late 1800s was the church. After the war, the role of the black church quickly expanded in African American communities. The largest denominations were the Baptist Church and the African Methodist Episcopal Church. Churches became the central arenas of black social life after the Civil War because they were supposedly apolitical and therefore unthreatening to the South's white population. Churches did, however, host political meetings and develop social welfare institutions in an era before large-scale public welfare programs existed.

# LO² The Industrializing West

If the South remained burdened by the oppressions of history, including a commitment to racial inequality and the myth of the lost cause, the West carried different burdens. The main burdens of those moving west were getting the soil to produce food and keeping Indians and immigrants at bay. The federal government would turn out to be much more helpful in assisting with the latter development than with the former, although during and after the Civil War the federal government did make land readily available to those with the will to farm it.

> **Juneteenth**
> A celebration marking the date that slaves were formally freed in Texas: June 19, 1865

> **Tuskegee Institute**
> College established for African Americans in Tuskegee, Alabama, by Booker T. Washington in 1881

But the land of the Great Plains would prove far too dusty and poor for some, and many of these farmers struggled to make a living off their newly acquired land. As they did, large corporations sometimes bought them out, creating what were then called bonanza farms and what we would today call agribusinesses. The West of the late nineteenth century inspired the lore of the "Wild West," with its tales of cowboys and Indians. And indeed, there were components of the development of the West that were in fact wild. But for the most part, those most interested in the development of the West were corporate interests, usually with bases in the corporate capitals of the North. Like the South, which often depended on northern wealth to industrialize, the West too is sometimes referred to as a mere colony to the rest of the United States.

## Expansive Farming

The first American settlers in the West had always been farmers, and before the Civil War, most Americans in the region were involved in agriculture. They might have been grain elevator operators, agricultural commodities brokers, or farmers, but in general, most Americans in the West lived off the land. Chicago and St. Louis were booming towns, and most of their wealth was attributable to processing and distributing natural goods like lumber, corn, cattle, and wheat.

### The Homestead Act

This commitment to the land only accelerated during the Civil War, when northern congressmen took advantage of the absence of southerners in Congress and encouraged the expansion of a free-labor West by passing the **Homestead Act** in 1862. The Homestead Act awarded 160 acres to settlers who occupied the land for five years, and between 1862 and 1890 the Homestead Act led to the creation of almost 400,000 farms, on which some 2 million people eventually lived. African Americans seeking land, northerners seeking to avoid the industrialization of their cities, and new immigrants all came west.

## Industrial Farming

Despite the promises of the Homestead Act, the first homesteaders faced particularly severe trials. On the northern Great Plains, rainfall dwindled to as few as eight inches a year, and pioneers, or **sodbusters** as they were known, faced the ravages of locust swarms, tornadoes, hailstorms, and extreme temperatures. By the 1870s, however, life for Great Plains farmers had improved, mainly because of the Industrial Revolution. Between 1870 and 1910, eastern urban populations increased by 400 percent, stimulating demand for western wheat and other crops. In response to this new demand, the eastern plains from Minnesota and the Dakotas and south to Texas became the nation's wheat belt. Corn and hog production also spread throughout much of the West. In addition, the nation's growing rail network offered more, better, and cheaper connections to the markets of the East. Indeed, moving the western commodities was one of the principal reasons for railroad expansion throughout the nineteenth century.

Pioneer family pose outside their sod house, Kansas, c. 1860 (b/w photo), American Photographer (19th century) / Private Collection, Peter Newark American Pictures / The Bridgeman Art Library

>> Despite the benevolent promises of the Homestead Act, the first homesteaders faced particularly severe trials. Sodbusters faced the ravages of locust swarms, tornadoes, hailstorms, and extreme temperatures.

## Bonanza Farms

As technologies improved and markets grew, more and more speculators began growing wheat. Dwarfing the farms created by the original sodbusters, absentee owners built huge **bonanza farms** covering thousands of acres. Across the Great Plains, these "factories in the fields" operated with an economy of scale heretofore unknown to American agriculture. In the 1880s, a single bonanza farm in North Dakota's Red River Valley covered 13,000 acres and employed a thousand workers. By embracing the newest technologies, recruiting cheap laborers from Chicago and other midwestern cities, and securing lands from railroad companies, bonanza farmers increased farm yields dramatically and put greater economic pressures on the small farms.

## Industry in the West

Besides farming, three major industries shaped the post–Civil War western economy: railroads, cattle, and mining.

### The Railroads

During the Civil War, northern congressmen passed several internal improvement bills, including several that assisted the development of railroads in the West. Their efforts were just the beginning: During the 1800s, Congress awarded various railroad companies more than 223 million acres to encourage the construction of lines connecting East and West. The arrival of a railroad depot spurred the creation of towns. If an established town lay far from the newly built railroad lines, that town usually dwindled into nonexistence. As a boy, Thomas Edison's family was forced to leave Milan, Ohio, after the railroads bypassed the town.

> **bonanza farms**
> Giant farms on the Great Plains, covering thousands of acres and employing hundreds of workers

### The Cattle Industry

Cattle was one of the industries that railroads developed the most (see Map 19.1). Beginning in the 1860s, cowboys began to lead mass cattle drives from Texas, where most cattle were, to various cities along the railroad lines, especially Abilene, Kansas. Abilene was the nation's first "cow town," or town developed in order to facilitate the movement of cattle from Texas and Oklahoma to other parts of the country. From places like Abilene, the cattle would then be moved via rail to Chicago's slaughterhouses and meatpacking plants, where the animals would be slaughtered and the meat packaged and sent in refrigerated rail cars to eastern markets. Cowboys (who were actually employees of large corporations working to supply the world's demand for beef) largely disappeared by the 1880s. Barbed wire, first patented in 1874 and spread through the West by the late 1880s, closed the open ranges on which the cowboys' long drives depended. Between 1865 and 1885, the work of being a cowboy attracted some 40,000 young men from a variety of ethnic and class backgrounds. Many were white, but about 30 percent of the West's cowboys were either Mexican or African American; hundreds were Indian.

### The Mining Industry

The third pillar of western industry was mining (see Map 19.1), mainly for gold, silver, copper, and coal. Mining had fostered much of the original settlement in the West, when the first California gold rush of 1849 established the rollicking, boom-and-bust cycle that defined the region's economy. Yet

>> **A single bonanza farm in North Dakota's Red River Valley covered 13,000 acres and employed a thousand workers.**

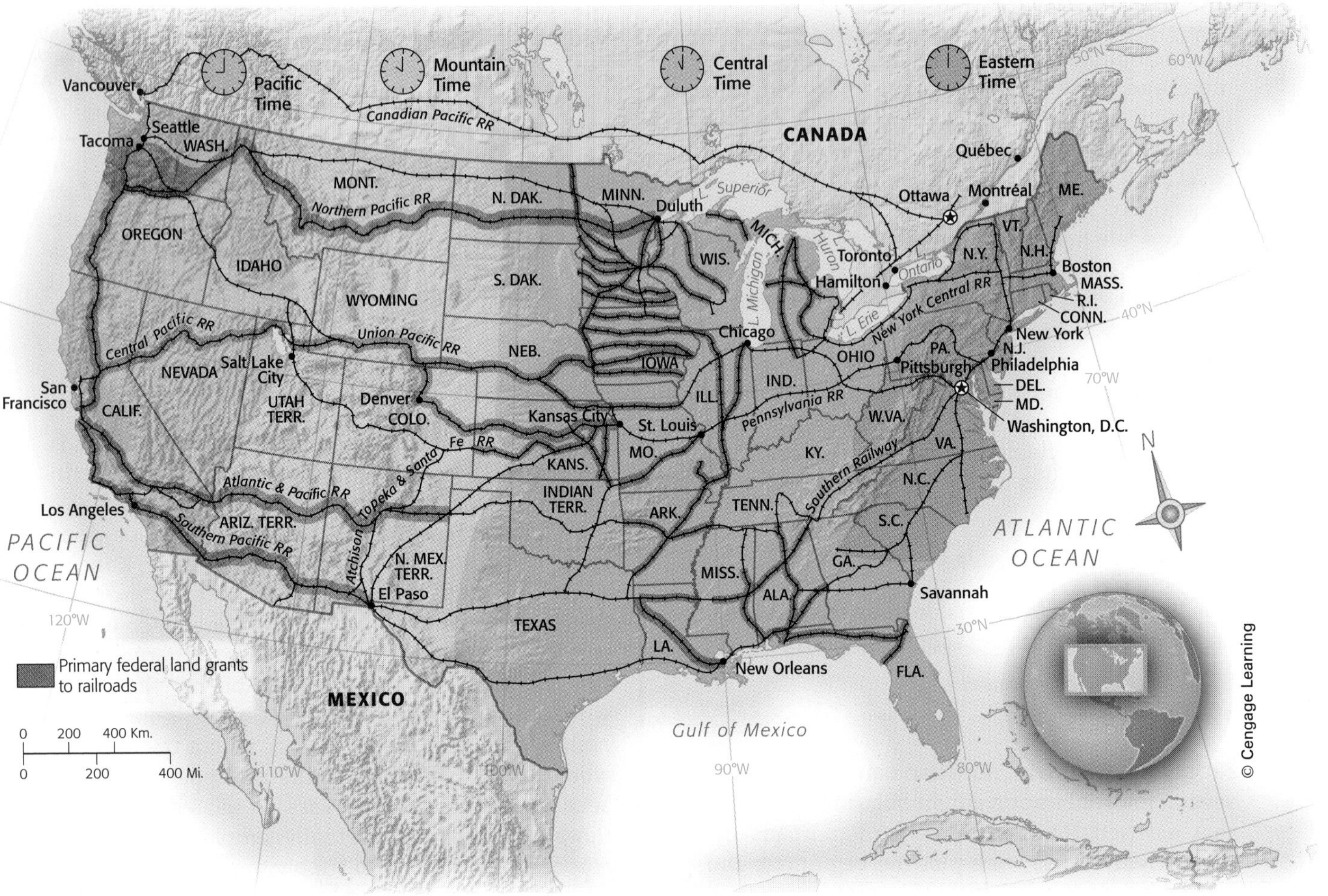

Map 19.1. **Primary Federal Land Grants and the Creation of Standardized Time Zones**

The map shows the United States with railroad lines, time zones (Pacific Time, Mountain Time, Central Time, Eastern Time), and states labeled. Key railroads include Canadian Pacific RR, Northern Pacific RR, Central Pacific RR, Union Pacific RR, Atlantic & Pacific RR, Southern Pacific RR, Atchison Topeka & Santa Fe RR, New York Central RR, Pennsylvania RR, and Southern Railway.

Legend: Primary federal land grants to railroads

the nature of mining changed dramatically after the Civil War, when most of the gold and silver deposits within reach of individual prospectors had been exhausted. Large investors with access to new technology displaced the roughshod world of the forty-niners. Unlike earlier rushes, the silver strike at Colorado's Leadville (1877) and the gold strike at Cripple Creek (1891) offered few opportunities for individual prospectors because big companies controlled access to the mines. As in the North and the South, large corporations controlled most of the wealth in the industrializing West.

## Western Cities

Farming, mining, and cattle were the lifeblood of the West, and that blood flowed through towns and cities. Western cities connected the natural resources of the West to urban centers in the East. Huge cities emerged rapidly in the West, humming with all the industries necessary to convert raw material into packaged goods ready for shipping. No city grew faster than the midwestern city of Chicago. With its busy train station and its avid business promoters, Chicago became the capital of western commerce. It developed meatpacking plants to turn cattle into cash and a stock market where speculators could bet on that year's yield. By 1900, 1.7 million people lived in Chicago. And Chicago was not alone. By 1890, a greater percentage of westerners lived in cities than in any other region in the nation. Cities like Dodge City, Kansas, transitioned from a fur-trading post to a cattle town to a stockyard city.

## Outsiders in the Industrializing West

The two groups that did not mesh with the way of life developing in the West were the American Indians and the Chinese; both were persecuted.

### Subjugating the Plains Indians

As always, westward migration entailed conflict with Indians. Like immigrants in the northern cities and African Americans in the South, American Indians suffered from the white Americans' racism, paternalism, and belief that the United States had a "manifest destiny" to control all the land between the Atlantic and Pacific Oceans (for more on manifest destiny, see Chapter 13). Although conflict was constant, violence between white Americans and Indians accelerated during the Civil War, as Union troops streamed into the West to put down various local Confederate revolts. During those travails, it was often difficult to tell where the Civil War ended and the escalating war against the Indians began.

These small "Indian Wars," as the U.S. Army called them, became commonplace throughout the second half of the 1800s. One conflict that epitomizes the violence is the **Sand Creek Massacre** of 1864. During the early 1860s, the Arapahoe and Cheyenne Indians

> 66 Their village consisted of one hundred and thirty Cheyenne and Arapahoe lodges. These, with their contents, were totally destroyed. 99
>
> —*Rocky Mountain News, 1864*

Chief Joseph.

clashed with white settlers who had been drawn to Colorado by the 1859 Pike's Peak gold rush. As white settlers began to demand the extermination of the Indians, a handful of chiefs sought peace. During one round of negotiation, a Cheyenne delegation near Denver was told it enjoyed army protection until negotiations were complete. The next morning, November 29, 1864, Colorado militiamen attacked the sleeping Indians. By the day's end, more than two hundred Cheyenne lay dead. As news of the massacre spread throughout the Great Plains, outrage turned to anger among Indians, and battles between Indian tribes and white settlers escalated.

The increasing violence between Indians and settlers inspired General William T. Sherman, of Civil War fame, to call for the extermination of all the Sioux. But, despite continuing conflict, U.S. government leaders in Washington, especially President Grant, still declared a desire for peace. In 1869, Grant initiated a so-called Peace Policy that consisted of empowering church leaders to distribute payments and food to the Indians. This "conquest through kindness" aimed to turn the Plains Indians, who had been offered open reservations to continue their traditional lifestyles, to the American ideals of private property, settled farming, and Christianity. Notwithstanding this paternalistic hope, Grant warned tribes that any Native Americans unprepared to make peace on his terms would be subject to continued military

**Sand Creek Massacre**
The 1864 massacre of over two hundred Cheyenne by Colorado militiamen during the "Indian Wars"

Compare editorials from the *Rocky Mountain News* with congressional testimony that followed.

**Dawes General Allotment Act**

Federal law, passed in 1887, declaring that lands held by tribes were to be divided among families, and the Indians were not allowed to sell their lands because the government held these lands in trust for twenty-five years, after which individual Indians were to receive title to the land and become U.S. citizens

action. In essence, he told them to accept his terms or face eventual destruction.

Unfortunately, many Americans did not follow Grant's Peace Policy, choosing instead to continue to invade lands guaranteed to Indians. One such example is the 1874 military expedition, under General George Armstrong Custer's command, into the Black Hills of present-day South Dakota. When Custer reported to eastern newspapers that there was "gold among the roots of the grass," American prospectors streamed into land not only considered sacred by the Sioux but also promised to them in an 1868 treaty. When the Sioux attacked some prospectors, Custer vowed to protect them. He was unable to do so. On June 25, 1876, his force came upon an encampment of some 2,500 Sioux and Cheyenne warriors, commanded by Chief Sitting Bull and his lieutenant, Crazy Horse. Despite Custer's belief that the Indians would cower to the white army, the two tribes annihilated Custer's division of some 200 troops along the Little Big Horn River, in today's southeastern Montana.

The Sioux victory at Little Big Horn was short-lived. The winter of 1876–1877 saw a massive counterattack that caused most of the Indian alliance to surrender. Chief Sitting Bull and some 50 Sioux escaped to Canada. However, cut off from bison, they had a difficult time finding food, and, in 1881, they too surrendered to U.S. forces. Other Indian efforts at resistance also failed. For example, in 1877, Chief Joseph and the Nez Percé tribe refused to be moved from their lands in Idaho to a reservation in Washington. Rather than fight, Joseph led a brilliant retreat to Canada with about 250 of his warriors and 450 noncombatants. The army followed Chief Joseph's party through 1,700 miles of mountains before catching up to them and demanding their surrender.

 Learn more about Chief Joseph's retreat.

> ❝ I do not come to fight the white men. If you leave me alone I will harm no one. I have been driven from my home by the white men and am going to the buffalo country to find another. ❞
> —*Chief Joseph, according to his biographer*

## The Dawes Act

By the 1870s, many reformers and U.S. policymakers decided that placing American Indians on large reservations might not be the best way to bring order to white-Indian relations. For one thing, reservations obstructed the routes of some planned railroads. Furthermore, reformers, such as Helen Hunt Jackson, criticized the U.S. policy on humanitarian grounds. Jackson wrote *A Century of Dishonor* (1881), which examined the treaties that the United States continuously broke with Indian tribes.

Arguments from these reformers led to the passage of the **Dawes General Allotment Act**, which became federal law in 1887. As with Grant's "Peace Plan," the act demonstrated an attempt to alter the tribal nature of Indians. It declared that lands held by tribes were to be divided among families and individuals. To prevent speculators from getting title to the lands, the act did not allow Indians to sell them; instead, the government held the land in trust for twenty-five years. At the end of the twenty-five years, individual Indians were to receive title to the land and become U.S. citizens. This was yet another attempt to wage peace by conversion. In the prevailing American view, Indians were capable of citizenship, but they were not quite there yet, so they needed to be treated as wards of the state until they learned the ways of American citizens.

As it turned out, the Dawes Act did not help Indians establish farms because the arid land of the northern Plains was unsuited to agriculture. In addition, despite the alleged safeguards, tribal lands were often lost by fraud or coercion, so that, by 1934, white Americans owned two-thirds of lands originally reserved for Indians. Most pointedly, the Dawes Act struck at Indians' greatest strength—their communal ethos—by dividing many of the reservations into individual plots of land.

 Read the Dawes Act.

## Dire Circumstances

In the midst of these efforts, conditions in the tribes became desperate. In particular, the loss of the bison proved devastating to the way of life that had sustained Indians since they first occupied the Great Plains. In 1865, the number of bison in the United States was some 13 million; by 1891, that number had dwindled to just 865. Railroads and commercial hunters were responsible for most of this decimation. Without bison to hunt, the Plains Indians had little means of subsistence. Confined to reservations, they obtained only a meager living from farming the barren lands provided by relocation treaties. The poor-quality food supplies from the U.S. government sometimes did not come at all because of the widespread corruption in the government's Bureau of Indian Affairs. Starvation and epidemics pervaded the tribes, making it even more difficult for them to defend themselves against further encroachment.

## Last Attempts at Resistance

With little hope left, some Indians attempted to participate in a revitalization movement similar to the one preached by Neolin before the Revolutionary War. The central ritual for the Plains Indians became the **"Ghost Dance,"** a dance lasting five days that, if done properly and at the proper time, would supposedly raise the Indians above the ground while the land below them was replaced with new land, effectively sandwiching the white men between the two layers of sod, removing them forever. But, when too many Indians began attending the mass meetings, they attracted the attention of the U.S. government, which sought to arrest several of the leaders. When an attempt to arrest a Sioux Indian who had fired at the army at Pine Ridge Reservation ended in a small battle, killing the Sioux chief Sitting Bull, a group of Sioux seeking to intervene agreed to the U.S. Army's command to encamp near the army at Wounded Knee Creek. On December 29, 1890, an accidental rifle discharge led soldiers from the U.S. Army to fire on the Sioux. After what became known as the **Wounded Knee Massacre**, 39 U.S. soldiers lay dead, while the Sioux suffered 146 deaths, including 44 women and 18 children.

Wounded Knee was the tragic and grisly end of the federal government's century-long war against the Indians. The next forty years witnessed continuing efforts to break up tribal sovereignty—most notably in Indian territories, where the government forced the liquidation of tribal governments. By 1900, the Indian population had reached its lowest point in American history, bottoming out at just 250,000. The "Wild West" of cowboy-and-Indian lore was gone.

>> San Francisco's Chinese quarter of the 1870s evolved into today's sprawling Chinatown.

## The Chinese Exclusion Act

In addition to subjugating the Plains Indians, white Americans in the West also targeted another population—the Chinese. In the 1850s, Chinese immigrants began traveling to the American West in search of gold and other lucrative minerals. Most never discovered those riches, but ample work for the railroads provided

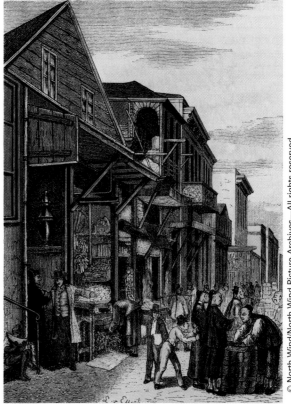

another impetus for migration, and by 1880, more than 200,000 Chinese immigrants had settled in the United States, mostly in California.

Accounts of their lives suggest that most white Americans initially saw them as hardworking people, but as the number of Chinese immigrants increased, many white Americans challenged their right to be in the United States. In the early 1850s, the California legislature passed a tax on "foreign miners," which led most of the Chinese immigrants to search for work outside of mining. Many found jobs in the railroad industry, which was booming after the Civil War. Indeed, Chinese laborers made up 90 percent of the laborers who worked on the western half of the first transcontinental railroad. Once the American system of railroad tracks was mostly completed, many Chinese immigrants moved to cities, such as San Francisco, and developed an expansive "Chinatown." Most of the urban Chinese worked as laborers and servants, but some rose to prominence and positions of leadership within their communities. These leaders often joined together to handle community disputes, place workers in jobs, and dispense social services.

In the workplace, however, Chinese laborers gained a reputation for working for lower wages than their white counterparts. This situation led to interethnic hostilities, especially among workers. Denis Kearney, an Irish immigrant who created the Workingman's Party of California in 1878, made the issue of Chinese immigration a political one. By the late 1870s, anti-Chinese sentiment extended along the entire Pacific Coast.

In 1882, Congress responded to Californians' demands that something be done to restrict Chinese immigration. At the behest of California's senators, Congress passed the **Chinese Exclusion Act of 1882**, which banned the immigration of Chinese laborers for ten years and prohibited the Chinese who were already in the United States from becoming citizens. The bill was renewed in 1892 and made permanent in 1902. It was the first repudiation of the United States's long history of open immigration. While the bill was most certainly racist, it is worth noting that, until 1917, there were few restrictions on wealthy Chinese immigrants, and in 1898 the U.S. Supreme Court ruled that the children of Chinese immigrants who were born in the United States were still American citizens.

# LO³ The Populists

If the politics of the Industrial Age seemed to favor business interests over others, this was certainly the sense of those who lived off the land in the South and the West. Farmers both western and southern felt squeezed by a system that seemed stacked against them. Vulnerable to falling crop prices, often saddled with debt, and unable to meet the forces of capitalism on a level playing field, during the 1860s, 1870s, and 1880s they formed organizations to protect their rural interests. There were many kinds of farm advocacy groups developed during these years, varying in objective, degree of racial liberalism, and political techniques. But in the 1890s, farmers joined together in the **Populist Party**, which championed the cause of farmers over what it saw as the entrenched powers of banking and credit.

## Problems Confronting Farmers

By the late nineteenth century, the business of farming had become a risky endeavor. In addition to the age-old threats of bad weather and poor crops, farmers now faced a host of new challenges. The greatest changes were in the West, where the Homestead Act of 1862 had prompted the cultivation of the Great Plains. But most farmers were deeply in debt from loans needed to purchase large-scale machinery. While the technological advances of the Industrial Revolution had made farming easier, they had also put farmers more in debt. Meanwhile, the great distances between western farms and the markets of the East increased shipping costs, a problem exacerbated by grain elevator owners and railroad companies, who often exploited their monopolies. Similarly, the increase in the amount of goods shipped to market from the expansive and bountiful Great Plains meant that prices plummeted. Farmers who had taken advantage of the Homestead Act were being stretched thin. They were in debt, and the cost of their product was declining.

### Sharecropping as a Problem in the South

In the South, sharecroppers faced additional problems. Sharecroppers usually bought their supplies on credit at a local store; because credit prices were rarely competitive, and because the sharecroppers' slim profits could not cover what was owed, every year they sank further into debt. Caught in this cycle of poverty, they were especially vulnerable to market changes, which could quickly wipe out their profits.

## Deflation

Whatever their specific difficulties, American farmers in the late nineteenth century all confronted the basic problem of falling crop prices. While overproduction played a part in pushing down prices, another, more insidious force was at work: deflation. Between 1873 and 1875, the federal government tried to erase its Civil War debt by putting the nation on a **gold standard**, taking most paper money ("greenbacks") and silver coins out of circulation and leaving gold as the primary form of currency. But when gold became scarce, the result was deflation, whereby prices fell because there was not enough money circulating in the system. This situation had a ruinous effect on farmers. As deflation pushed down the prices of all goods, including crops, farmers made smaller profits; meanwhile, their debts stayed the same as before.

## Farmers Unite

Initially, two movements arose in response to farmers' problems: the Grange Movement and the Farmers' Alliance.

© CORBIS

>> **An idealized view of the National Grange of the Patrons of Husbandry.**

## Emergence of the Grange Movement

The first movement to protest the farmer's plight emerged shortly after the Civil War. Founded in Washington, D.C., in 1867, the Grange (formally known as the National Grange of the Patrons of Husbandry) began life as a local fraternal organization. But by the early 1870s, as deflation plagued farmers, the Grange became a national movement that expressed farmer discontent. In seeking political solutions to the farmers' problems, it did achieve some limited success. Grangers demanded the regulation of railroad rates, for instance, and succeeded in having rate legislation passed in several states, including Minnesota, Iowa, Illinois, and Wisconsin. They also succeeded in having the Supreme Court declare, in the case of **Munn v. Illinois (1877)**, that states could regulate businesses within their borders if those businesses operated in the public interest. But internal divisions ultimately doomed the Grange, and in the late 1870s its influence waned.

### Rise of the Farmers' Alliance

In the late 1880s, another national movement known as the Farmers' Alliance emerged. The Farmers' Alliance was a network of smaller local alliances that first sprang up in the early 1880s in pockets of the South and Midwest and then spread to other farming regions. These alliances acted as cooperatives, meaning that they organized farmers into a unified front to gain bargaining power. Like labor unions, alliances hoped to find strength in numbers.

### The Turn to Politics

But the alliances failed to be effective because bankers and commercial interests often simply refused to do business with them. The Farmers' Alliance then sought a political remedy. In 1890, Dr. Charles W. Macune, the national movement's leader, lobbied members of the U.S. Congress to support his **Subtreasury Plan**. Under this plan, crops would be stored in government-owned warehouses and used as collateral for low-cost government loans to struggling farmers.

In 1890, when legislation to enact the plan was defeated in Congress, desperation among American farmers reached a fever pitch. With

**gold standard**
An economic plan using gold as the primary form of currency while taking paper money and silver coins out of circulation

**Munn v. Illinois (1877)**
A Supreme Court case that declared states could regulate businesses within their borders if those businesses operated in the public interest

deflation running rampant and crop prices continuing to fall, farmers suspected a conspiracy: Eastern bankers and capitalists, with the tacit blessing of the government, were deliberately keeping gold out of circulation. The farmers knew they needed to create a stronger, more powerful movement.

## Populism

The farmers thus entered the political arena with a national movement known as Populism. In 1892, a convention of farmers in Omaha, Nebraska, formed the People's Party (its members were called Populists) to advocate the farmers' concerns in local, state, and federal politics. In addition to addressing such issues as high storage and shipping rates, the Populists sought to reverse deflation so that crop prices would rise, which would enable them to pay down their debts. In particular, they wanted the government to **remonetize** silver or, in other words, turn silver into an acceptable currency. This would end the economy's reliance on gold, which had made currency hard to find and expensive, and put more currency in the marketplace, boosting prices.

 Read the Populists' 1892 election platform.

### A National Movement

Building from the national network of the Farmers' Alliance, the Populist Movement spread across the country. With its promise of relief for farmers, it overcame existing political and regional loyalties (white southerners were usually Democrats and preoccupied with race, whereas Midwestern farmers, owing their land to Lincoln's Homestead Act, were nearly all Republicans and were less opposed to the presence of black farmers in the movement). Tom Watson, a Populist leader from Georgia, argued that white and black sharecroppers alike were in danger of economic ruin, and he spoke to mixed-race audiences that were temporarily united by the Populist message. Some Populists even advocated bringing in industrial workers to fashion a working-class political party.

The Populists rapidly gained ground in the political arena. In 1892, James Weaver, the Populists' presidential candidate, won several western states, and the hard times that followed a financial panic in 1893 sparked widespread interest in the Populist demands for economic justice. Several Populist can-

didates won congressional elections in 1894. That same year Populist supporter Jacob Coxey led an army of roughly four hundred workers on a march from Ohio to Washington to demand government jobs for the unemployed. The year 1894 also saw the publication of *Coin's Financial School*, a national best-seller that made a dramatic appeal for the unlimited government purchase of silver, a plan commonly called "free silver."

### The Presidential Election of 1896

The mainstream popularity of currency reform, however, proved to be a double-edged sword for the Populists. In the 1896 presidential election (Map 19.2), Democratic nominee William Jennings Bryan was a charismatic thirty-six-year-old Nebraskan whose embrace of the free-silver position left the Populists in a quandary. As a member of one of the two traditional political parties, Bryan stood the best chance of winning the election, but beyond currency reform, he was not interested in Populist issues such as grain storage. Yet a separate Populist candidate would likely split the vote for Bryan, thus handing victory to Republican nominee William McKinley, who favored the gold standard. Faced with this prospect, the Populist Party nominated Bryan for president and Tom Watson for vice president.

The election was one of the most impassioned in American history and ended badly for the Democrats and the Populists. Bryan, whose free-silver "Cross of Gold" speech ("you shall not crucify mankind upon a cross of gold") is one of the most vivid political speeches in American history, never appealed to the largest voting bloc in the Northeast: urban immigrant workers. These workers actually benefited from deflation's low prices (they did not have large debts), and many were alienated by Bryan's evangelical Protestantism. Bryan carried most of the South and West, but Republican votes in the urban Northeast contributed to his stunning defeat. McKinley gained the presidency, beginning a fourteen-year Republican reign in office and ending the political stalemate that had marked the previous two decades.

### The Vanishing of the Populists

After 1896, the Populists' mass movement declined. At the local level, southern Democrats beat them back with calls for white solidarity. More importantly, the long deflationary trend for farmers that had been ongoing since the end of the Civil War finally broke in 1897, allowing many farmers to begin to prosper. When Bryan ran for president again in 1900, he lost even more emphatically than

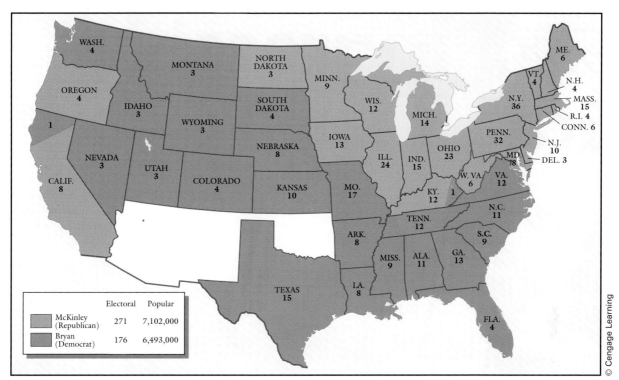

 Map 19.2. The Election of 1896

| | | Electoral | Popular |
|---|---|---|---|
| | McKinley (Republican) | 271 | 7,102,000 |
| | Bryan (Democrat) | 176 | 6,493,000 |

© Cengage Learning

 Was the original *Wizard of Oz* a Populist parable? Find out!

he had in 1896. In spite of their political decline, many of the less radical goals of the Populists were achieved in the twentieth century, including low-interest government loans for farmers, federal regulation of railroad rates, and regulation of the money supply.

## And in the end . . .

The Industrial Revolution affected each region of the United States differently. The North became one of the most industrialized regions in the world, confronting the challenges of immigration, urbanization, and the labor movement. Many southerners, meanwhile, attempted to transform their region into a smaller, more humane industrialized hub, but instead fell back into the racial disparities that had long been part of the region's identity. Americans in the West took more and more of that region away from American Indians, as homesteaders and corporate farmers tapped into the thin soil in order to provide much of the raw materials for the Industrial Age.

Like many of those in the North, southerners and westerners confronted numerous challenges in adapting to the new era. The land did not always prosper. Racism and fear of outsiders provoked reactionary political responses. And northern busi-

nessmen lost interest in the regions once they felt they had tapped their economic potential. Often frustrated by how state and federal governments were not addressing their economic needs, farmers from the West and South combined under the name of the Populists to challenge America's industrial order. The Populists did not carry out most of their goals, but the issues they brought forward would be central to the third wave of reformers responding to the Industrial Revolution. It is to those reformers, the Progressives, that we now turn.

### What else was happening . . .

| 1876 | A horse named Comanche is the only survivor from the losing side in the Battle of Little Big Horn. |
|---|---|
| 1885 | The first modern hamburger is made in Seymour, Wisconsin. |
| 1890 | Pharmacist Caleb Bradham produces "Brad's Drink" as a digestive aid and energy booster; in 1898 it would be renamed Pepsi-Cola. |
| 1893 | The melody for "Happy Birthday to You" is copyrighted. |

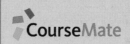 **CourseMate** Visit the CourseMate website at www.cengagebrain.com for additional study tools and review materials for this chapter.

# CHAPTER 20

# The Progressive Era

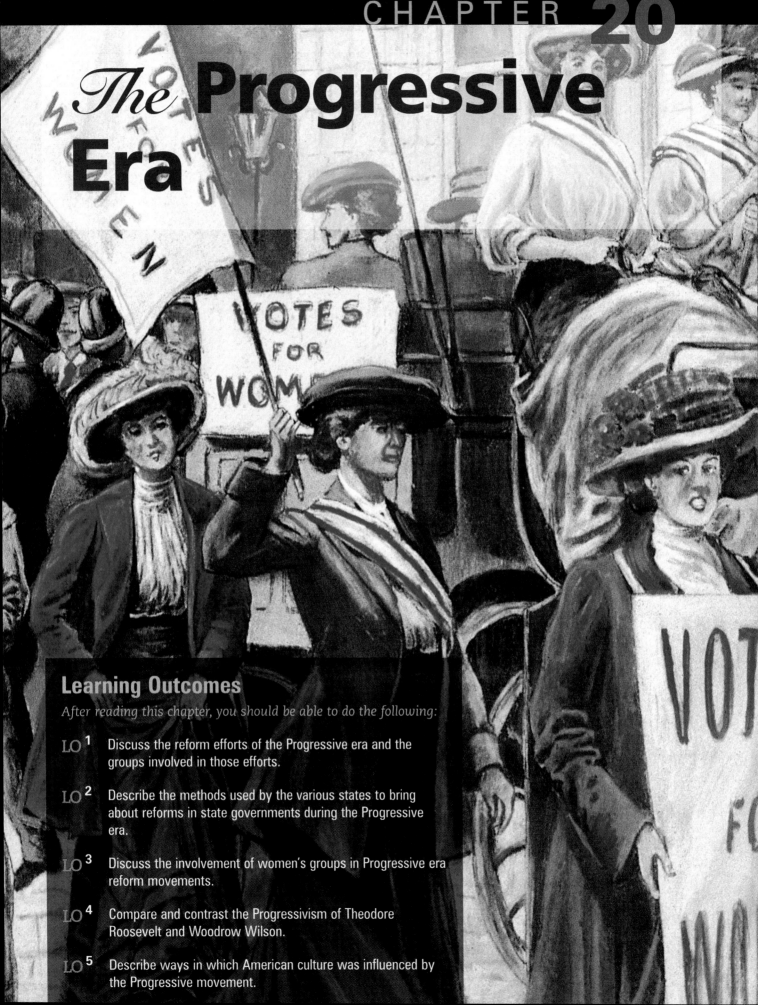

## Learning Outcomes

*After reading this chapter, you should be able to do the following:*

LO **1**   Discuss the reform efforts of the Progressive era and the groups involved in those efforts.

LO **2**   Describe the methods used by the various states to bring about reforms in state governments during the Progressive era.

LO **3**   Discuss the involvement of women's groups in Progressive era reform movements.

LO **4**   Compare and contrast the Progressivism of Theodore Roosevelt and Woodrow Wilson.

LO **5**   Describe ways in which American culture was influenced by the Progressive movement.

© Pictorial Press Ltd/Alamy

> **“If Populism was a rural response and unionization the working-class response to the Industrial Revolution, Progressivism is often seen as the middle- and upper-class response.”**

If Populism was a rural response and unionization the working-class response to the Industrial Revolution, Progressivism is often seen as the middle- and upper-class response. There is some truth to this generalization, but the reality was much more complicated. In fact, the ideas at the heart of Progressivism—

that benevolent government intervention could rectify the plight of the people, that the economic playing field needed to be regulated to ensure fair access for everyone, that American society could adapt to the advent of the Industrial Age without overthrowing democratic capitalism—became central to much of American social activism no matter what class proposed it. In this way, the ideas central to early-twentieth-century Progressivism have remained a fixture in modern American liberalism, defined most simply as the ideology that lionizes liberty and freedom, but which by the turn of the twentieth century came to mean the idea that the modern industrial age requires government to play a role in ensuring a fair distribution of wealth.

Turn-of-the-twentieth-century Progressivism began with a specific agenda: to clean up the nation's cities. But the social and political movement grew from there. Progressivism included reforms on state and national levels, including efforts to mitigate poverty, institute labor reform, create greater worker efficiency, and improve the unsatisfactory conditions of urban housing. Borrowing from the Populists, Progressives also worked to create a more democratic political process. They also sought greater government regulation of industry, the development of conservation efforts like the creation of national parks, and the use of experts to help solve persistent social problems. Indeed, the Progressives cast their nets so widely that some historians have debated the very utility of the word *progressive*. In general, it is an umbrella term for a host of changes demanded largely by the middle class to rein in the worst abuses of the Industrial Age. Its focus was on the search for stability, efficiency, and democracy within a rapidly changing world. The Progressives' demands propelled them into the political spotlight from the 1890s until the end of the First World War in 1918. Of the three initial waves of reform that emerged in the late nineteenth century, the Progressives were the most influential.

## LO¹ The Reformers

The Progressives were composed mainly of middle-class men and women, most of whom lived in Chicago, Philadelphia, and New York. Most were raised in deeply religious

>> By the late nineteenth century, many women were well educated, and many in this first generation of college graduates worked outside the home.

families, and they pursued social reform with the zeal of religious missionaries. As members of the middle class, many Progressives had money, time, and resources to devote to the cause of reform.

## Principal Reform Groups

Two groups were especially important: followers of the Social Gospel movement and women.

### The Social Gospel Movement

Beginning in the 1880s, Protestant ministers responded to the problems of industrialized society by fighting for social justice, concentrating on ending poverty and prostitution. Ministers like Washington Gladden and Walter Rauschenbusch became nationally known leaders of the Social Gospel movement, and their actions prompted many concerned middle-class citizens to fight for Progressive reform.

### Women

Progressive reform particularly attracted urban middle-class women. By the late nineteenth century, many women were well educated, and many in this first generation of college graduates ignored traditional social norms and worked outside the home. These women were schoolteachers, nurses, librarians, business clerks, typists, and doctors. However, there were fewer professional jobs for women. Participating in reform organizations was

a way to perform a public service and have a job. Furthermore, although since the early nineteenth century women's roles were supposedly confined to indoor domestic spaces (for this, see Chapter 10), with the rise of the Industrial Age it became apparent that the lives of children and families could be affected by government action, such as clean water sanitation, garbage collection, and education for poor children.

Women thus became involved in the public arena as part of their domestic responsibilities. One of the best-known Progressive reformers, Jane Addams, referred to her work as "municipal housekeeping." But Addams was not alone. Women were some of the most active reformers of the Progressive era. For example, nurse Margaret Sanger pushed to increase the advertising and availability of contraception. Journalist Ida B. Wells-Barnett led the antilynching crusade to stop violence against African Americans. And Alice Paul and others fought for female suffrage on the grounds that women's new role in the public world demanded that they have the right to vote.

## Reforming the Cities

The first target of Progressive reform was the nation's cities. From 1870 to 1900, the urban population of the United States grew from 10 million to more than 30 million. By 1920, the U.S. Census

Read Jacob A. Riis's *How the Other Half Lives.*

declared for the first time that the United States had more urban than nonurban dwellers. This rapid growth made it difficult for urban governments to provide basic services, such as street cleaning, garbage collection, and schools. Progressive reformers focused on fixing these problems and improving living conditions in the poor areas. If many middle-class people had not noticed the urban poverty of the era, journalist Jacob A. Riis's illustrated book about New York City's tenements, *How the Other Half Lives* (1890), shocked many Americans into "discovering" poverty.

## Settlement Houses

One of the most effective Progressive solutions to the problem of poverty was the creation of **settlement houses**, safe residences in poor neighborhoods where reformers could study local conditions. Much like a social scientist's fieldwork, living in the middle of these neighborhoods gave reformers a firsthand look at what needed to be changed. The settlement houses also provided a place for residents to hold meetings and receive free health care. Settlement houses became fixtures in many cities, including Chicago, Boston, and New York.

**Hull House** was the second but most renowned settlement house in the United States, founded in Chicago

in 1889 by Jane Addams. It exemplified the type of contribution reformers could make. Women made up the majority of its residents, and they lobbied the government to pass better construction and safety laws to improve the conditions in the surrounding tenement houses. The women of Hull House also established a new, more effective process for collecting garbage and fought to eradicate prostitution in the cities by closing red-light districts. Addams's book about her experience, *Twenty Years at Hull House* (1910), became a reform classic and expressed the moral tone of the Progressive era. Addams emphasized that it was not a matter of *noblesse oblige* that led her into the slums; she wrote that her own life was worthless before she undertook her mission and that the settlement house was as educational and therapeutic for her as its work was beneficial to the poor immigrants around her.

**Jane Addams of Hull House.**

 Learn more about Hull House and Progressive reform.

**settlement houses**
Safe residences in poor neighborhoods where reformers could study local conditions and where residents could hold meetings and receive free health care

**Hull House**
The second but most renowned settlement house in the United States, founded in Chicago in 1889 by Jane Addams; its residents lobbied the government to pass better construction and safety laws to improve conditions in the surrounding tenement houses

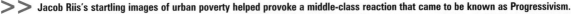

>> Jacob Riis's startling images of urban poverty helped provoke a middle-class reaction that came to be known as Progressivism.

## The Anti-Saloon League

Meanwhile, temperance advocates continued to attack the consumption of alcohol, thinking it had a negative effect on the working classes and on the stability of impoverished urban neighborhoods. Temperance workers also feared that the large number of immigrants from southern and eastern Europe, who by and large came from cultures that had long drinking traditions, were increasing America's dependence on alcohol. Thus, while the middle-class reformers may have had the best intentions in mind, they also suffered from paternalism and notions of Social Darwinism that were prominent at the time.

To influence legislation, temperance workers started the Anti-Saloon League in 1893, attempting to pass laws at local and state levels. Its interest in politics gave the Anti-Saloon League a higher profile than the Women's Christian Temperance League (WCTL), which continued to push for local,

mandatory temperance education. And, unlike the WCTL, the Anti-Saloon League was composed mostly of men (such as its founder, Howard Hyde Russell, and its most prominent national leader, Wayne Wheeler), who felt that the dirty work of politics should be carried out by men. The Anti-Saloon League became the first modern, single-issue lobbying group in the nation. As in the 1830s and 1840s, temperance was one of the major components of the reform impulse.

# LO² State Political Reform

Urban reform was just the beginning of the Progressives' battle to rectify the nation's problems. Progressives soon realized that improving conditions for the poor required a more democratic political system. They were determined to take the country back from, as they saw it, the corrupt and selfish interests that dominated politics. Many had been influenced by the **Galveston hurricane** of 1900, which utterly destroyed the once-booming island town of Galveston, Texas. Even though previous storms had barraged the city and its population of 42,000, local leaders did not heed the warnings to build a protective storm wall. After the hurricane killed more than 8,000 people, numerous factions began to reform local and state politics, attempting to give the general population a greater voice.

## Democratizing Trends

One way Progressive reformers empowered the masses was to change how senators were elected. Hitherto, senators had been chosen by state legislatures. Progressives proposed that senators be directly elected by citizens, enabling citizens to vote for a candidate they trusted. Many senators and businessmen opposed the idea; they both distrusted the voters' ability to select candidates and had no desire to campaign before the public. But, in 1913, after several years of agitation, the reform became law as the Seventeenth Amendment to the Constitution.

Another democratizing trend was illustrated by the **initiative** and the **referendum**. This device was designed to allow citizens more control over state law. Previously, those who sought to implement change had to create and maintain an expensive lobby in their state capital.

Library of Congress, Prints & Photographs Division, LC-USZ62-56439

>> Wreckage of the Galveston hurricane of 1900.

Initiatives and referendums allowed citizens to collect a few thousand signatures on a petition (or referendum) advocating their idea (or initiative) in order to get the initiative on the ballot. On Election Day, voters could give their direct opinion on the question. If a majority of voters favored the reform, it would become state law, even if a majority in the state legislature did not support the measure. Between 1900 and 1920, this new approach was adopted in numerous states, and it is still in use today.

Similar democratic reforms were the **primary** election and the **recall**. The primary is a preliminary election designed to let voters choose which political candidates will run for public office, rather than leaving the selection to potentially corrupt politicians plotting in "smoke-filled rooms." The recall is a device by which petitioning citizens can, with a vote, dismiss state officers, governors, and judges who are deemed to have violated the popular interest.

## Professional Administrators

In addition to the impulse to extend democracy to individual voters, reformers exhibited a somewhat contradictory impulse to get the right person in the right job. Sometimes this impulse meant that reformers sought to make certain government positions exempt from voting altogether. One chronic complaint against city political machines was that important administrative posts always went to friends of the "bosses" rather than to experts.

To get rid of cronyism, most Progressives supported the creation of a professional corps of administrators. The corps required anyone who wanted a government job to take a competitive exam. Only those who passed could get a job, and only those who excelled could rise to influential, decision-making positions. Ideally, no matter what political party won each new election, job-holders would be allowed to maintain their positions. This system ensured continuity and efficiency rather than a chaotic turn-over of personnel each time a new party came into office.

## Progress of Reforms

One by one, states adopted these various reforms, mostly beginning in the West and the Midwest. In Wisconsin at the turn of the century, Robert "Battling Bob" La Follette, the first Progressive governor of Wisconsin, created a Legislative Reference Bureau that became known as the "Wisconsin Idea." It was a board of experts such as Richard T. Ely, who ensured sound drafting of Wisconsin's laws for such things as worker's compensation, government regulation of railroad companies, and conservation of natural resources. The keys to reform were appointed commissions of experts working in the name of civil service.

New York City, where political machines remained strong, also changed local politics. In response to residents' complaints, and in the aftermath of the Triangle Shirtwaist Company Fire, leaders of Tammany Hall began to advocate moderate reforms. These included the abolition of child labor and the improvement of safety standards in the workplace.

# LO³ Women's Progressivism

Although women spearheaded many significant Progressive era reforms, they were still denied the right to vote. This became increasingly problematic once more and more women understood that individuals in the Industrial Age were buffeted by social and economic forces that were beyond their control and that required the involvement of the federal government. The denial of suffrage changed during the Progressive era, beginning in the western states (see Map 20.1).

Two main groups furthered the cause of women's suffrage: (1) the National American Woman Suffrage Association (NAWSA), founded in 1890, and

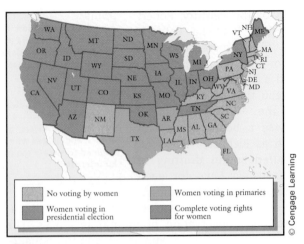

Map 20.1. Women's Suffrage before 1920

No voting by women
Women voting in presidential election
Women voting in primaries
Complete voting rights for women

© Cengage Learning

(2) the National Women's Party (NWP), founded in 1913 and led by Alice Paul. The NAWSA worked state to state (between 1911 and 1914 it achieved the vote for women in California, Oregon, Kansas, Arizona, Montana, and Nevada) to convince opponents that women were valuable assets to society and deserved the vote. Paul and the NWP, on the other hand, pursued a more aggressive national strategy. On the eve of President Woodrow Wilson's inauguration in 1913, Alice Paul organized a rally of 5,000 women to demand a federal constitutional amendment giving women the right to vote. She also held a six-month vigil outside the White House to protest restrictions of woman suffrage.

The combined efforts of these two groups ultimately led to victory. In 1920, just after the end of World War I, the Nineteenth Amendment was passed, and women won the right to vote.

Nonpolitical women's clubs were also vitally important to the Progressive cause. These clubs provided meeting places for African American and southern white women. They also organized social work, invited speakers to discuss topics of the day, and grew networks of women who discussed how issues uniquely affected women. Through these organizations, several women rose to national prominence. Margaret Sanger promoted reproductive rights for women, including advocating birth control. Charlotte Perkins Gilman's extensive writings exposed the inherent paternalism of early-twentieth-century America, especially the organization of its economic life.

Read Margaret Sanger's speech "The Morality of Birth Control."

# LO⁴ Progressivism in National Politics

Progressives had pursued reform at the city and state levels, but the real power of reform lay at the national level. The expansion of Progressivism into the federal arena came after the initial reforms at the state level in the late 1800s and continued under the presidential administrations of Theodore Roosevelt, William H. Taft, and Woodrow Wilson.

### Theodore Roosevelt, Reformer

During his eight years in the White House (1901–1909), President Theodore Roosevelt strongly advocated (from what he called his "bully pulpit" in the White House) Progressive reform and intervened more decisively in national affairs than any president since Abraham Lincoln. His larger-than-life personality had made him a celebrity. He built

Hulton Archive/Getty Images

Alice Paul.

Margaret Sanger.

Library of Congress, Prints & Photographs Division, LC-USZ62-29808

on this image during his presidency and developed what he called a "square deal" (a term he borrowed from his poker habit) because he offered an evenhanded approach to the relationship between labor and business.

Roosevelt believed that industrial society was threatened by the immorality of big businessmen, who were more interested in personal gain than in the good of society. Monopolies were the worst offenders, and yet Roosevelt did not believe in hastily breaking up concentrations of wealth and power. Rather, he hoped that large corporations or trusts could benefit the nation by providing more equitable employment and economic expansion. Thus, in 1902, he arbitrated a coal strike in West Virginia by finding a middle ground between the miners and the owners. Similarly, in 1903, he asked Congress to create a Bureau of Corporations to examine the conduct of businesses in America. As a result of the bureau's findings, Roosevelt prosecuted several companies for breaking the **Sherman Antitrust Act** of 1890, which was the federal government's first attempt to break up monopolies, but which was not widely used until Roosevelt took office.

Roosevelt also developed and used the **Hepburn Act of 1906**, which limited prices that railroads could charge and allowed the federal government to monitor the financial books of the large rail-

> **"When I say I believe in a square deal I do not mean to give every man the best hand. If the cards do not come to any man, or if they do come, and he has not got the power to play them, that is his affair. All I mean is that there shall be no crookedness in the dealing."**
>
> —*Theodore Roosevelt*

road companies. Roosevelt's actions showed that he was willing to put the force of the federal government behind antitrust laws, garnering him the nickname of **trustbuster**.

And, as a big-game hunter, Roosevelt shared the concern of most Progressives about the loss of the countryside and the conservation of nature. In particular, he was concerned about the nation's dwindling natural preserves. In response, he created five new national parks and fifty wildlife refuges designed to protect local animal species, preserving millions of acres—the greatest amount of land ever protected by a U.S. president. Roosevelt also supervised the creation of the **National Forest Service**.

## William Howard Taft, Reformer?

Roosevelt's successor, William Howard Taft, was a distinguished lawyer and later chief justice of the Supreme Court (1921–1930). He busted more trusts than Roosevelt, and he was key in bringing down the Standard Oil Company in 1911. But Taft was never as politically capable as Roosevelt, and on a few accounts he failed to continue Roosevelt's success in passing reform legislation.

 See a silent film of Roosevelt taking the oath of office.

In 1912, a dispute between Teddy Roosevelt and Taft over the issue of conservation led Roosevelt himself to form a third party, the **Progressive Party**, to win back the presidency from his successor. But in the end, Roosevelt and Taft split allegiances and lost to the Democratic candidate, Woodrow Wilson,

**Sherman Antitrust Act**
Passed in 1890, the federal government's first attempt to break up monopolies

**Hepburn Act of 1906**
An act that limited prices railroads could charge and allowed the federal government to monitor the financial books of the large railroad companies

**trustbuster**
A nickname for those in government advocating antitrust laws

**National Forest Service**
Government agency created by Theodore Roosevelt to preserve land and protect local animal species

**Progressive Party**
Political party created by Theodore Roosevelt in 1912 to win back the presidency from Taft

THE LAST ERUPTION OF THE GREAT AMERICAN VOLCANO.

>> **"The Last Eruption of the Great American Volcano"**—Roosevelt depicted as the engineer of corporate reform and trustbusting.

Read "The New Freedom."

**"The New Freedom"**
Woodrow Wilson's platform message pledging to use government power to destroy big businesses and give smaller ones greater ability to compete

**Clayton Antitrust Act**
Passed in 1914; outlawed unfair practices among businesses

**Federal Trade Commission**
A government agency charged with investigating unfair business practices

**Keating-Owen Child Labor Act**
Act that prevented the employment of children under sixteen

**muckrakers**
Investigative writers who exposed bad conditions in American factories, political corruption in city machines, and the financial deceit of corporations

who advocated parts of the Progressive mission with just as much zeal as Roosevelt.

## Woodrow Wilson, Reformer

Woodrow Wilson became president in 1913, when Progressive ideas were at their most influential. But Wilson did not trust big business as much as Roosevelt. In his platform message, entitled **"The New Freedom,"** Wilson pledged to use government power to destroy big businesses and give smaller ones greater ability to compete. He passed a series of laws that increased the size and power of the federal government, and he helped pass the Federal Reserve Act of 1913, which established a regional banking system under the control of the federal government. The act also included a massive tariff reduction, the first since the Civil War, known as the Underwood Tariff. Because Wilson believed that high protectionist tariffs were unfairly enriching America's industrialists, this tariff reduction served as a symbol of his suspicion of big business.

In 1914, Wilson assisted in passing the **Clayton Antitrust Act**, which outlawed unfair practices among businesses. Also in 1914, Wilson supported the creation of the **Federal Trade Commission**, a government agency that had the right to investigate business practices and issue rulings to prevent businesses from continuing such practices.

Wilson focused on Progressive reforms to regulate businesses, but he never fully supported the social reforms that other Progressives rallied for, such as child labor reform, women's suffrage, and regulation of laborer workdays. Because of the popularity of these ideas, however, Wilson eventually supported the passage of several bills, including the **Keating-Owen Child Labor Act**, which prevented the employment of children under the age of sixteen, and a bill that mandated a maximum eight-hour workday for American railroad laborers.

By the time he was reelected president in 1916, Wilson had fulfilled many of his Progressive goals, even some of the less benign ones. Claiming

to "clean up" federal government in behalf of the common good, for instance, Wilson allowed the racial segregation of a variety of federal departments within the nation's capital, including the Post Office and the Treasury. Wilson was, of course, a member of the Democratic Party, which, in the South at least, was premised on white supremacy. Thus, as conscientious as they were about the common good, most Progressives like Wilson were not beyond the common racial perceptions of the time.

## LO⁵ Progressive Influences on American Culture

Progressive reformers did not limit their efforts to improving urban conditions and reforming political systems. Their ideas influenced business and educational practices and attempted to improve the overall quality of life for many Americans. It was about more than just politics. (To understand why the Progressive era occurred when it did, see "The reasons why . . ." box.)

### The Muckrakers

In fact, Progressive ideas spread throughout the nation mainly through the voices of journalists, novelists, professors, and public intellectuals. Among the best remembered are the **muckrakers**, investigative writers who exposed miserable conditions in American factories, political corruption in city machines, and the financial deceits of corporations. Through diverse means, the muckrakers used these exposés to influence city dwellers to be active in flushing out immorality and to understand the positive effects of an urban democracy. Jacob Riis, Lincoln Steffens, Ida Tarbell, and Upton Sinclair were the best-known muckrakers. All wrote classic books in the Progressive tradition, including Riis's *How the Other Half Lives* (1890), Steffens's *The Shame of the Cities* (1904), Tarbell's *The History of the Standard Oil Company* (1904), and, most notable of all, Sinclair's *The Jungle* (1906), which told the harrowing tale of life in a Chicago meatpacking plant.

The details of Sinclair's factory were real, and middle-class meat-eaters, including President Roosevelt, were horrified. Sinclair described rats running over piles of rotten meat, embalming fluid mixed into the sausages to

Read more from *The Jungle*.

disguise the rot, and workers spitting tuberculosis germs into heaps of meat as it baked in the midsummer sun. Roosevelt's staff investigated these tales and found that the writer had not been exaggerating. This prompted Congress to pass, in 1906, the **Pure Food and Drug Act** and the Meat Inspection Act. The first national legislation of their kind, these acts gave the federal government responsibility for ensuring that meat would reach its customers fresh and disease-free.

## Progressivism in Business

In business, Progressives sought to improve working conditions and professional standards, but also to improve efficiency. While one of the first measures the Progressives undertook was to improve the relationship between owners and labor, these efforts often fell flat. For instance, the National Civic Federation, founded in 1900, sought to build a partnership between owners and workers. But the organization never accomplished its goal because there were simply not enough business owners who wanted to help their workers, and many workers did not trust the motivations of owners to help them.

Besides, many Progressives were more interested in improving efficiency, no one more so than the engineer Frederick W. Taylor. Like Progressives who sought to open the political process to more

> **Pure Food and Drug Act**
> Passed in 1906, this act, along with the Meat Inspection Act, gave the federal government responsibility for ensuring that meat would reach its customers fresh and disease-free

# { *The reasons why . . .* }

**There were four principal reasons why the Progressive era occurred when it did:**

*The Industrial Age.* The Industrial Age introduced a host of changes to the United States, including the tremendous growth of cities, the increasing plight of the industrial worker, and the close alignment of business interests and government. Toward the end of the nineteenth century, these problems became difficult to ignore, and a large swath of reformers attempted to address them.

*Growth of the middle class.* These industries also created an expansive middle class of bureaucrats, marketers, salesmen, and technical workers who possessed the wealth and leisure time to involve themselves in political causes. This was particularly true for middle-class women. The growing recognition that individuals are buffeted by social and economic forces beyond their control led middle-class women to embrace the notion that the outside world was encroaching on domestic space and thus entitled women to push for social and political change. Of course, only women with wealth and leisure were capable of undertaking these tasks, and so it was middle-class women who constituted much of the ground troops of the Progressive movement.

*Fears of radicalism.* Beyond simply cleaning up cities and making industrial life less dangerous, these reformers were also afraid that, if changes were not instituted, more radical calls for change would gain strength. Thus, while southern and western farmers embraced the potential radicalism of the Populists, and the urban working class formed a potentially radical working-class movement, the middle classes sought to redress the most egregious aspects of the Industrial Age to keep the more radical claims at bay.

*Scientific authority.* Finally, although the vast majority of Americans claimed to be religious adherents, during the late nineteenth century science rose as an authority with the potential capacity to answer most of society's needs. Thus Progressives embraced a scientific ethos that embraced the notion that, through study and experimentation, people could change the world in which they lived. Scientific knowledge, of course, changes over time, and the Progressives' attempts to harness scientific knowledge led them to embrace dubious positions, such as Frederick Taylor's theory of scientific management and, more damningly, eugenics. But their embrace of scientific rationality also introduced a variety of government regulations and a professional corps of administrators, which ensured that jobs upon which dollars and even lives depended on were not in the hands of unskilled political appointees.

Read Taylor's *Principles of Scientific Management*.

efficient methods, Taylor believed that businesses could also be made more efficient if they changed some of their practices. Taylor's key interests were **scientific management** (the detailed study of the best ways to schedule, organize, and standardize tasks) and **time-and-motion studies** (the study of exactly how factory jobs functioned). Using minute scrutiny, cameras, and stopwatches, he worked out the most efficient way to wield a shovel full of coal and showed business managers that systematic employment of his methods could boost productivity. He published his results in 1911. However, because these results were mostly fabricated, they led owners to make impossible demands of their workers. Thus, Taylor's efforts to improve efficiency made working conditions even more miserable.

## Progressive Education

Progressives also pursued efficiency in the educational system. They argued that, in order for citizens to work better in their jobs and participate in politics, they needed to be well educated. Thus, in cities and towns, Progressives helped build more schools and improved teacher education and salaries.

The most famous Progressive theorist of education was John Dewey, a philosopher at the University of Chicago. Dewey founded the Laboratory School for elementary and middle-school children, where Dewey pioneered child-centered educa-

© iStockphoto.com/Christine Balderas

tion. The idea was to allow students to pursue their own interests rather than force them to memorize a curriculum. Dewey argued that this approach taught children to live in a democracy and to make good moral and political choices for the rest of their lives. Eventually, Progressive educational ideas became so popular that, in 1919, Progressives formed the **Progressive Education Association** to support and advocate for these education reforms.

## The Role of Laws

Above all, the Progressives avowed a stern belief in laws as vital instruments of social change. Instead of using large social movements or force, Progressives sought to change the way Americans lived by crafting laws against what they saw as social wrongs. In addition to the many trustbusting, tariff, and voting laws they advocated, Progressives used the courts to limit the number of hours women and children could work and to end the most brutal forms of racial antagonism. They sometimes succeeded, as in the case of *Muller* v. *Oregon* (1908), which upheld a law limiting the number of hours that women could work in a day. Progressives were, however, unsuccessful in passing child labor laws and in promoting a federal antilynching law.

The Progressives' love of laws led in dark directions as well. In the name of improving human genetic qualities on behalf of the common good, some Progressives argued that it would be better to sterilize people with so-called less desirable qualities. This movement, called **eugenics**, was a worldwide phenomenon, led by the Briton Sir Francis Galton, who was Charles Darwin's cousin and who was infatuated with applying his cousin's ideas beyond the forces of biological evolution. In the United States, beginning in 1896, many states began prohibiting anyone who was "epileptic, imbecile, or feeble-minded" from getting married. In 1907, Indiana was the first of more than thirty states to require compulsory sterilization of certain kinds of criminals and the mentally ill. The U.S. Supreme Court upheld the constitutionality of these laws in

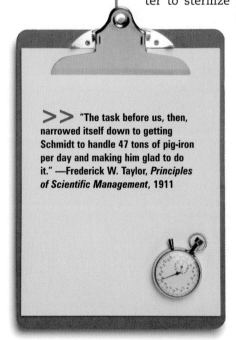

>> "The task before us, then, narrowed itself down to getting Schmidt to handle 47 tons of pig-iron per day and making him glad to do it." —Frederick W. Taylor, *Principles of Scientific Management*, 1911

1927, and they continued to be the law of the land in certain states until the 1970s. Prominent supporters of eugenics included Teddy Roosevelt, Woodrow Wilson, and Margaret Sanger.

# And in the end . . .

By the 1910s and into the 1920s, three sizeable challenges to the politics and society of the Industrial Age had arisen. All were in some way a reaction to the changes brought about by the Industrial Revolution. The establishment of the first labor unions created a system of industrial labor that has existed throughout much of the twentieth century. The agrarian interests associated with the Populists may have failed politically, but some of the principal tenets of their cause eventually came to fruition. Finally, the Progressives, who were the most influential of the three, enacted political, social, and educational reforms that are with us today.

By the 1910s, the word *progressive* had become almost synonymous with decency and cleanliness, and politicians of all kinds were careful to depict themselves as Progressives, even if their record showed them to be dyed-in-the-wool conservatives. The fact that such a wide array of political types claimed the Progressive label illustrates how powerful the Progressive impulse had become.

Many Progressives also sought to spread their ideals throughout the world, with the best of intentions. But promoting Progressive ideals abroad would generate a host of critics both at home and abroad. And it is to America's renewed interest in world affairs that we turn next.

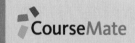

Visit the CourseMate website at www.cengagebrain.com for additional study tools and review materials for this chapter.

# Becoming *a* World Power

## Learning Outcomes

*After reading this chapter, you should be able to do the following:*

LO **1**  Explain the major reasons for the growing call in the late 1800s for the United States to develop an empire.

LO **2**  Describe the first moves Americans made toward empire.

LO **3**  Explain the major reasons for the Spanish-American War of 1898, and discuss the controversy over imperialism that developed after the war.

LO **4**  Describe the growth of imperialism in America during the Progressive era.

LO **5**  Discuss World War I, including reasons for the war, American experiences during the war, and effects of the treaty that ended the war.

> ## "Between 1867 and 1917, the United States became a true world power for the first time in its history."

Between 1867 and 1917, the United States became a true world power for the first time in its history. To a large degree, this was a result of the Industrial Revolution. The search for overseas markets and the ideology of manifest destiny (which Americans

had developed in conquering the West) spurred the United States to build up its navy in the 1880s and begin acquiring overseas territories. Many Americans also felt they had a duty to "civilize" the so-called "lesser" nations of the world, their superiority based in no small part on notions of racial superiority. Victory in the Spanish-American War in 1898 was a turning point, adding a string of island colonies in the Caribbean Sea and the Pacific Ocean to U.S. territory, and declaring to the world that the United States was a global power. During these years, American military might backed up American commercial interests, creating an "economic imperialism" that sometimes weighed on other countries almost as heavily as outright conquest. Many Americans vigorously protested their country's new imperialism, citing the U.S. government's violent atrocities, the racialist ideals that propelled America's imperial march, and the moral problem of allowing business interests to drive armed diplomacy. Nevertheless, these imperialist developments led the country into the First World War and then served as the basis for U.S. foreign policy for much of the twentieth century.

## LO¹ Why an American Empire?

While notions of racial superiority justified America's expansionist positions, America's creation of an overseas empire during the half-century following the Civil War was driven by four basic reasons: (1) the closing of the frontier, (2) economics, (3) religious and moral reasons, and (4) geopolitics.

### Manifest Destiny and the End of the Frontier

Global imperialism was simply an extension of the way America had "won the West." Historian Frederick Jackson Turner argued in an influential 1893 essay that America's frontier experience had played a key role in shaping America's national character, including its democratic political institutions and its free-spirited capitalism. In "The Significance of the Frontier in American History," Turner even suggested (with some trepidation) that the frontier was so integral to the nation's psyche that the nation required a new

**Treaty of Wanghsia** Agreement between China and the United States signed in 1844, opening several Chinese ports to American trade

Read Frederick Jackson Turner's frontier essay.

frontier to ensure the survival of its democracy. "American energy," Turner concluded prophetically, "will demand a wider field for its exercise." To Turner, the development of the idea of manifest destiny meant that many Americans felt it natural to continue to explore and conquer, even if that meant crossing seas and continents.

## Financial Reasons

Another—and in many cases more decisive—reason for the surge in American overseas imperialism was that American business leaders wanted access to overseas markets and materials. Like those who had first explored the American West, these business leaders usually received the assistance and protection of the federal government. They articulated a "glut thesis," which argued that the financial panics of the 1870s and the 1890s were the result of the overproduction of goods, as the industrialized economy endured painful fits and starts. One obvious resolution to overproduction is the creation of new markets, and this led business leaders and politicians to advocate American imperial adventures abroad. To a great extent, business interests drove American foreign policy very early on.

## Religious and Moral Reasons

Many Christian leaders believed that Christianity had made Western society the evolutionary pinnacle of civilization. American missionaries sought converts, believing they were bringing both progress and salvation to the "uncivilized" peoples of the world. The mood of Protestant imperialism was

captured in Reverend Josiah Strong's *Our Country* (1885), which argued that white Christian Americans stood at the top of civilization and therefore had a moral duty to bring less privileged peoples the benefits of progress and the fruit of the Christian Gospel.

Read an excerpt from Josiah Strong's *Our Country.*

The racialist tinge of this argument held that the United States should join the other nations of Europe in spreading the benefits of democracy and white civilization to the world. In his famous 1899 poem, *The White Man's Burden*, the British poet Rudyard Kipling urged the United States to embrace what he saw as its imperialist obligations.

Read Rudyard Kipling's *The White Man's Burden.*

## Geopolitical Reasons

Finally, beginning in the 1870s, several European powers raced to conquer vulnerable but resource-rich regions of Africa and Asia. Such conquests brought these countries substantial profits and a worldwide network of commercial and military bases. Many Americans feared that the United States, by remaining isolated from the land grabbing, would lose access to world markets and geopolitical power.

# LO² Beginnings

Dollars propelled the initial drive overseas, first throughout the Pacific, then to Latin America.

## Pacific Acquisitions

American businessmen and diplomats had long been attempting to gain access to markets in the Pacific, seeking, first, access to China and Japan, then permanent settlements in various islands in the Pacific. Their goal was to sell American goods to the nations of Asia.

### Asia

Ever since the Mexican-American War in the 1840s, the U.S. government had sought to increase commercial ties with China and Japan in hope of selling them more U.S. goods. Treaties with China, notably the **Treaty of Wanghsia** in 1844, had opened several Chinese ports to

>> "American energy will demand a wider field for its exercise." —Frederick Jackson Turner

American trade. In 1853, the U.S. Navy appeared in Tokyo Bay and ultimately forced Japan to open to the West. As the European powers continued to scramble for power in the Pacific, the United States risked losing access to Asian trade unless it created more links to the region.

## Samoa

Seeking its first permanent footholds in the Pacific, in 1856 the United States claimed a number of small, uninhabited islands strewn across the Pacific, and the tiny Midway Islands were annexed formally in 1867. In 1872, island chieftains in Samoa granted the United States a naval base at Pago Pago, but instability in the nation during the 1880s prompted Britain, Germany, and the United States to sign a treaty jointly occupying the islands. In 1899, the treaty was revised to grant the United States a protectorate over the eastern islands, which became today's territory of American Samoa.

## Alaska

Further Pacific expansion occurred in 1867, when the United States purchased the huge territory of Alaska from Russia. Secretary of State William Seward orchestrated the purchase, claiming that (1) Russia, which had been a Union ally during the American Civil War, needed the money; (2) the United States needed more land for expansion; and (3) Britain, which controlled today's Canada, needed to be warned off the continent; possession of Alaska, he pointed out, would surround Canada from both the north and the south. Alaska was so isolated and barren, though, that the purchase was lambasted in the newspapers and was commonly called "Seward's Folly."

## Hawai'i

But the major object of American expansion in the Pacific was Hawai'i. Since the 1850s the independent kingdom of Hawai'i had looked to the United States for protection against other colonial powers.

>> "Preparing for the heated term; King Andy and his man Billy lay in a great stock of Russian ice in order to cool down the Congressional majority." —Caricature of President Andrew Johnson and Secretary of State Seward carrying huge iceberg of "Russian America" in a wheelbarrow "treaty"

>> Queen Lili'uokalani.

It signed a trade agreement with the United States in 1875, and in 1887 it granted the United States the right to construct a naval base at Pearl Harbor, on the island of Oahu. By the 1880s, American businessmen had acquired a majority of the island's wealth through heavy investment in Hawai'ian sugar plantations. And in 1887, American settlers staged a nonviolent coup to transfer power from the Hawai'ian monarchy to the legislature, which the settlers had elected and thus had some control over.

In 1890, after a change in U.S. tariff policy imposed heavy duties on exports from the islands to the mainland, the same group of settlers urged the United States to annex Hawai'i, thereby granting its products exemption from U.S. tariffs. The Hawai'ian leader, Queen Lili'uokalani, rejected this scheme. In 1893, American rebels, with some aid from troops from a U.S. navy ship at Pearl Harbor, seized the queen and declared a provisional government under Sanford B. Dole, an American lawyer (his cousin was the pineapple magnate James Dole). The rebels applied for annexation to the United States but were rejected by President Grover Cleveland's administration, which considered the coup illegitimate.

Using Texas as a model, Dole's rebels remained in control of what they now called the Republic of Hawai'i and continued to agitate for incorporation into the United States. The rebels succeeded in 1898, when America, embroiled in a Pacific war against Spain, rediscovered the strategic importance of Pearl Harbor. Congress approved the annexation of Hawai'i, and, in 1900, the islands' people became U.S. citizens.

## Latin America

Another region of American economic interest was resource-rich Latin America. European powers had centuries-old colonial presences there, and under the growing expansionist mood, the United States set about undercutting European control and opening up American business opportunities in Mexico, Colombia, and the Dominican Republic.

An influential showdown came in the **Venezuela Crisis** of 1895. Independent Venezuela had quarreled with Britain since the 1870s over its eastern border with British Guiana, a region rich in gold and with a river that served as a major commercial route. The British Empire's unrivaled naval power meant that it usually prevailed in conflicts with weaker nations, but in 1895 Venezuela gained the support of the U.S. president Grover Cleveland's secretary of state, Richard Olney, who declared that the situation was under the domain of the Monroe Doctrine,

meaning that the United States was the controlling power in the Western Hemisphere. Britain backed off, especially when Assistant Secretary of the Navy Theodore Roosevelt (the future president) called for war to back up U.S. policy. A British and American team of negotiators then settled the boundary issue peaceably, though scarcely bothering to consult the Venezuelans.

The world's governments took note that Britain had surrendered at least some of its claim rather than antagonize the United States. Thus emboldened, the United States began envisioning an ever-growing role on the world stage.

## The Naval Buildup

Spurred by these kinds of acquisitions in the name of American business interests, in 1883 Congress authorized the construction of powerful all-steel, steam-driven battleships, armed with the latest long-range artillery. The North's decisive use of naval power during the Civil War influenced this buildup. Using ironclad warships, the Union had successfully blockaded several key Confederate ports, all but crippling the South in the process.

### Mahan

Another influence on U.S. military leaders was the work of Alfred Thayer Mahan, a former Civil War naval commander. In 1890 Mahan published *The Influence of Sea Power on History, 1660–1783*, which argued that, in modern times, national greatness was always based on naval strength. Using eighteenth-century Britain as a model, Mahan argued that

© Naval Parade, held in honor of Commander George Dewey (1837–1917) 1898 (oil on canvas), Pansing, Fred (1854–1912)/© Museum of the City of New York, USA/The Bridgeman Art Library

America must have warships to protect its merchants and must also maintain overseas colonies for naval supply bases.

## Buildup

The Civil War experience and Mahan's arguments led the United States to build up its navy. Between 1889 and 1893, the U.S. Navy grew from fifteenth largest in the world to seventh. In addition, Mahan's arguments about the importance of naval warfare led American strategists and policymakers to call for a stronger U.S. territorial presence overseas.

Read an excerpt from Mahan's *The Influence of Sea Power on History.*

## LO³ The Spanish-American War

Using this naval might, the next major international dispute—the Spanish-American War of 1898—transformed the United States into a major overseas power. Ironically, the war was not motivated by imperial appetites. Instead, it was fought for a range of humanitarian, geopolitical, and commercial reasons that, once the war was won, prompted the United States to take a larger global role at the turn of the century.

The Spanish-American War was ignited by Spain's harsh treatment of the Cuban independence movement. Cuba was one of Spain's last colonial possessions in the Western Hemisphere, but the Cuban people, resentful of Spain's heavy-handed rule, had struggled for decades to win their independence. In 1895, their resentment burst into violence when Cuban resistance leader José Martí sparked an interracial rebellion that the Spanish government attempted to put down with brutal force. This made Martí a martyr to the Cuban people. As the war continued, the political instability devastated Cuba's economy, which was a blow to Americans who had invested in Cuba's sugar plantations. Having an unstable nation so close to U.S. borders concerned American politicians, especially when American business interests might be compromised. If the Cubans won, that would also put an interracial regime dangerously close to home.

Recognizing a good story when they saw one, newspaper editors (notably Joseph Pulitzer's *New York World* and William Randolph Hearst's *New York Journal*) published graphic descriptions of the atrocities committed by the Spanish. These sensationalistic stories fomented anti-Spanish feeling among the American public, who may or may not have known of the substantial American investment in Cuba's sugar and who probably were unaware of the interracial nature of Cuba's fighting forces.

The war between Spain and Cuba had been raging for three years, and Spain was virtually defeated, when two events in February 1898 finally pushed the United States into the fray: (1) American spies intercepted a letter from Spain's U.S. ambassador to his superiors back home. Published from coast to coast, the letter disparaged U.S. President William McKinley as a petty popularity seeker who was not strong enough to intervene in Cuba; and (2) less than a week later, the American battleship U.S.S. *Maine* (stationed in Havana's harbor, ostensibly to protect American citizens in Cuba from riots) suddenly blew up, killing 266 men. Historians now know that the *Maine* exploded due to a fire that started in its coal bunkers, but at the time, war provocateurs argued that Spanish saboteurs were responsible.

Cubans did not want Americans to enter the war, considering it an unnecessary and unwelcome imperialistic grab. However, anti-Spanish animosities in the United States were at a fever pitch, and pro-war agitators such as Theodore Roosevelt and Henry Cabot Lodge insisted on entering the war. The Spanish government, aware of its inferior forces, offered to capitulate to American demands and recognize Cuban autonomy. Nevertheless, President McKinley, fearful of a biracial republic so close to the Florida coast, sought war in order to prevent the Cubans from winning. Two days later he asked

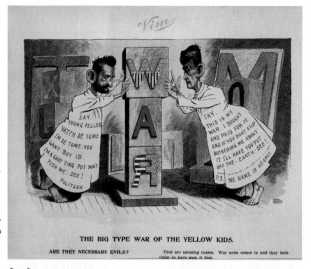

THE BIG TYPE WAR OF THE YELLOW KIDS.

ARE THEY NECESSARY EVILS?

>> Newspapermen Joseph Pulitzer and William Randolph Hearst published provocative, incendiary stories about Spanish atrocities in an effort to push the United States to war—and sell newspapers—a technique known as yellow journalism.

View a series of cartoons on the Spanish-American War.

Congress for the right to use the military to blockade Cuba.

Spain responded by declaring war on April 24, 1898. McKinley's war message to Congress proclaimed that the United States would fight Spain "[i]n the name of humanity, in the name of civilization, [and] in behalf of endangered American interests." McKinley thus presented the war, not as the beginning of an imperial conquest, but as a necessary humanitarian intervention, although he noted America's economic reasons behind the war as well. Congress tried to hold McKinley to this point by passing the **Teller Amendment**, which barred the United States from annexing Cuba, forcing the nation to leave it independent once the war was over.

## War on Two Fronts

American military strategists decided to fight Spain on two fronts: in Cuba and the Philippines.

### The Philippines

Like Cuba, the Philippines had long been a Spanish colonial possession, and Spain's fleet was stationed in Manila Bay. For months the U.S. fleet in the Pacific had been secretly preparing to invade the Philippines in the event of war, and, when war was finally declared, a squadron of American ships left its port in Hong Kong. In Manila Bay on May 1, the American squadron took advantage of its superior equipment to destroy or damage all Spanish ships, killing nearly four hundred Spanish sailors while suffering no American fatalities. American Commodore George Dewey became a hero in America for his leadership.

### Filipino Independence?

Lacking sufficient ground troops, Dewey was able to beat the Spanish fleet but was unable to occupy the islands. Filipino resistance leader Emilio Aguinaldo, who had been fighting the Spanish for years, declared the Philippines independent in June. In August, American reinforcements arrived, occupying Manila and barring Aguinaldo's forces from the city, a move that

Read two eyewitness accounts of the American naval attack in Manila Bay.

would have grave consequences. Filipino independence was not what Americans had in mind.

### Cuba

Meanwhile, back in Cuba, the United States mounted a rapid campaign to shatter the Spanish army and besiege the port city of Santiago, where Spain's Caribbean fleet was anchored. In June 1898, 17,000 U.S. troops invaded Cuba and quickly surrounded the city. The most colorful contingent of the American forces was the **Rough Riders**, led by the future president Theodore Roosevelt. An early and energetic supporter of the war, Roosevelt had long argued that American society needed to be more rugged and manly. It was in this spirit that he resigned his desk-bound naval post in order to lead a regiment of cavalry volunteers. Roosevelt and Leonard Wood, a veteran of the Indian Wars, gathered a mixture of Wall Street businessmen, Ivy League volunteers, western cowboys, and a few Native Americans to fight in Cuba.

### San Juan Hill

In early July 1898, the Rough Riders joined other American forces, including an African American squadron, in the attack on Santiago. Roosevelt's group successfully charged the hills overlooking the capital city, Kettle Hill and San Juan Hill (where he met up with the African American squadron, which had already claimed San Juan Hill). With these strategic positions now in hand, the American forces turned their attention to Santiago's harbor and proceeded to bombard the Spanish fleet, which was almost completely destroyed. Santiago surrendered on July 17.

Read an excerpt from Theodore Roosevelt's *The Rough Riders*.

### Spanish Surrender

American victories in the Philippines and Cuba prompted a full Spanish surrender. The war had lasted only four months, leading Secretary of State John Milton Hay to refer to it as "a splendid little war." In the peace treaty, signed in Paris, Spain granted independence to Cuba and ceded most of its overseas possessions to the United States, including Puerto Rico, the Philippines, and Guam, in exchange for $20 million. In addition, Congress had annexed Hawai'i during the war.

Within a matter of a few months, then, the United States had amassed an island empire in the Pacific and the Caribbean. It had not created a group of independent nations, but rather developed a string of subordinate nations, beholden to American business and military interests.

of the Teller Amendment. Now that the war was over and Cuba and the Philippines were clearly not independent, McKinley and other political leaders (including Roosevelt and Secretary of State Hay) pushed for annexation of the Philippines by declaring that the Filipinos (as well as inhabitants of Puerto Rico and Guam) were too weak to govern themselves.

### Annex the Philippines?

Many Americans were skeptical about further annexation. In early 1899, during congressional debates over ratification of the Paris treaty with Spain, Democrats and Populists declared that annexation violated America's anti-imperialist principles. William Jennings Bryan argued that the treaty should be accepted, but only as a stage in the liberation of all of Spain's former colonies. In the end, the Senate ratified the treaty with Spain, but just barely. The idea that America should persist in its colonial expansion was meeting rising opposition.

 Read Senator Albert Beveridge's speech in support of the war.

### The Anti-Imperialist League

In 1899, opponents of overseas expansion formed the Anti-Imperialist League, with leaders drawn from a number of disparate groups, including Andrew Carnegie, Samuel Gompers, Mark Twain, and Jane Addams. Labor leader Gompers opposed annexation from a racist and nativist point of view. He feared that Filipino immigrants (he called them "half breeds and semi-barbaric people") would flood the United States with cheap labor. It is important to recognize that, though they were on opposite sides of the debate over imperialism, supporters of expansion and anti-imperialists shared a rhetoric and logic about the superiority of American civilization and the white race.

### The Election of 1900

The showdown between pro- and anti-imperialist forces came in the election of 1900, a rematch of the 1896 contest that had pitted Bryan against McKinley. This time Bryan based his candidacy on condemning imperialism and the annexation of the Philippines. Thanks in part to the country's prospering economy, most Americans were uninterested in Bryan's arguments, and McKinley

© SuperStock Inc./SuperStock

>> Roosevelt gathered a mixture of Wall Street businessmen, Ivy League volunteers, western cowboys, and a few Native Americans to fight in Cuba.

## Why Become an Empire? Anti-Imperialism at Home

After the war—and even before—many Americans began to wonder whether the United States should become an imperial power. From the outset of the Spanish-American War, McKinley had assured the American public that the aim of the war was not to create an American empire but to protect the sovereignty of the Cuban people. That was the point

> **"** Is there anything grand or noble in any of these motives of war? Not a bit. **"**
> —*William Graham Sumner, in opposition to imperialism, 1881*

(now with Roosevelt as his running mate) once again emerged victorious. In subsequent years, anti-imperialism ceased to be a major issue in American politics. Detecting its lack of appeal at the ballot box, most American politicians became supporters of America's new imperial role.

## Anti-Americanism Abroad

If most Americans were supportive of a growing American Empire, Filipinos and Cubans were not. Both countries wanted independence, not American overlordship. Americans also frequently relied on violence and threats to preserve control in those countries. These two factors created deep veins of anti-American sentiment. Small nations were fearful that America would never allow them to be independent.

### Filipino Resistance

Enraged at the prospect of a permanent American presence, Filipino leader Aguinaldo launched the same type of guerilla war against the Americans that he had waged against the Spanish. In response, a large American force hastened to the islands and, between 1899 and 1902, fought a vicious anti-insurgency war. Both sides tortured and killed their prisoners, treating them as murderers rather than soldiers. American soldiers wrote home questioning the morality of their overseas experiences, citing atrocities like "the water cure," in which American soldiers would hold down a suspect, place a stick between his teeth, and force him to drink tremendous amounts of salt water. If the suspect did not divulge information, an American soldier would stomp on his stomach and begin the "cure" again. In 1901, American forces captured Aguinaldo, and future president William Howard Taft, sent by McKinley to create a government for the Philippines, persuaded Aguinaldo to call for peace.

The fighting subsided the following year: The war had claimed some 4,300 American lives, while

>> American imperialism was often imagined to be a civilizing experience, freeing the darker skinned people of the world from their various oppressions and turning them into happy Victorian businessmen.

one of every five Filipinos—more than 200,000—died either in combat or from disease or starvation. This was a major atrocity.

Read about torture in the Philippines.

Taft directed the establishment of a new government. The United States designated the Philippines an "unorganized territory" and made Filipinos U.S. citizens. Revolt smoldered there until 1906, and on some islands the fighting did not end until 1935. In 1946, the Philippines, whose people had fought valiantly alongside the United States in World War II, finally gained its independence.

### Cuban Resentment

Resentment of Americans also smoldered in Cuba. Although Cuba was declared independent on January 1, 1899, American occupation of the island continued for two more years while the U.S. government installed a Cuban regime that would be friendly to American commercial interests. The new relationship between the two countries was laid out in the **Platt Amendment** of 1901. Written to overrule the

> 66 We cannot retreat from any soil where Providence has unfurled our banner; it is ours to save that soil for liberty and civilization. 99
> —*Senator Albert J. Beveridge, in favor of the war, 1898*

 Read the Platt Amendment.

Teller Amendment and then added to the Cuban constitution, the Platt Amendment allowed the United States to militarily intervene on the island whenever revolution threatened. Many Cubans were infuriated when the United States invoked the amendment in 1906, 1912, and 1917. It clearly violated the vision of Cuban independence that the United States had articulated during the buildup to war.

## Humanitarian Assistance

At the same time that their government was guilty of violence and deceit, there were many Americans who genuinely sought to help the peoples of Cuba, the Philippines, Puerto Rico, and Guam. On these islands, American missionaries built churches and orphanages, educators built schools, and doctors built hospitals. One of those doctors, Walter Reed, in collaboration with William Gorgas and Carlos Juan Finlay, solved the mystery of yellow fever transmission. Still, the American-made regimes that had been established in these countries remained a source of anti-American sentiment throughout the twentieth century.

# LO⁴ Progressive-Era Imperialism

After 1900 the United States entered a period of heightened imperialistic activity. Under the energetic Progressive era presidencies of Roosevelt and Wilson, the United States took a bolder, more aggressive role in international affairs. Toward this end, Roosevelt, whose foreign policy credo was "speak softly and carry a big stick," supported Secretary of War Elihu Root's policy of increasing the U.S. armed forces. By 1906, only the navies of Britain and Germany were larger than that of the United States.

The United States used its new power to pursue three major goals: to (1) open trade with China, (2) build the Panama Canal, and (3) police Latin America to protect American interests.

## Trade with China

After winning the Spanish-American War, the United States sought to demonstrate its status as a major international power. American policymakers first turned to China to open trade. In 1899, U.S. Secretary of State John Hay called for an "Open Door" policy in China, which would allow all nations to trade with China on equal terms. This policy also aimed to prevent foreign powers from partitioning China as they had Africa.

## Forcing the Open Door

The Chinese **Boxer Rebellion** of 1900 helped Hay's plan. Angered by growing outside influence in their country, Chinese nationalists attacked embassies in Beijing in an attempt to oust foreigners. The United States joined a multinational military expedition to put the rebellion down and to rescue businessmen and diplomats who had sought refuge in the American embassy. After the multinational forces successfully suppressed the rebellion, most of the other powers agreed to  Read more about the Boxer Rebellion from Fei Ch'i-hao, a Chinese Christian.

Hay's Open Door policy in principle (although they did not always honor it in practice). The Boxer Rebellion, instead of ejecting outside influences, actually strengthened America's foothold in the Far East.

> **Boxer Rebellion**
> Conflict that erupted in China in 1900; Chinese nationalists attacked embassies in Beijing in an attempt to oust foreigners

## The Panama Canal

The United States next focused on Panama. Ever since the 1840s, American commercial and military planners had eyed Panama's narrow isthmus as a potential site for a canal. Such interest increased after 1898, when America's new empire required easier transit between the Atlantic and Pacific Oceans. Panama, however, belonged to Colombia, whose rights to the isthmus the United States had explicitly guaranteed in an 1848 treaty.

## Panamanian Revolt

In 1901, negotiations with Colombia broke down over the price of renting the right of way for a canal. Undeterred, Roosevelt, the American president, encouraged an independence movement among the Panamanian people. This would free them from Colombia and, presumably, lead them to grant the United States unobstructed access to build its canal. The Panamanians revolted successfully, thanks in part to an American naval blockade that prevented Colombian soldiers from getting to the scene of the rebellion. As a thank-you to the United States for its timely intervention, in 1903 the new Republic of Panama leased to it a 10-mile-wide Canal Zone. American companies immediately started construction.

## Building the Canal

Building the canal was no easy task. French engineer Ferdinand de Lesseps, who had built the Suez Canal in 1869, had already attempted to build a canal in Panama. He went bankrupt in 1887, after most of his work force died of yellow fever. By 1903, however, Walter Reed's work on the disease had made the threat of yellow fever a manageable concern. After cutting through mountains and dense jungle, and then constructing a series of innovative locks, workers completed the canal just before the First World War broke out in 1914. One of the world's modern mechanical marvels, the canal project used tons and tons of concrete and was the largest dam in the world at the time. It cut the sailing distance between America's Atlantic and Pacific Coasts from 15,615 miles to just 5,300.

Roosevelt's timely blockade bred a legacy of resentment in Colombia that damaged U.S.–Latin American relations for decades. Moreover, the presence of the Canal Zone eventually caused tensions between Americans and Panamanians until a treaty placed it under Panamanian control in 1999.

## Policing Latin America

Concurrent with the building of the Panama Canal, the United States assumed an interventionist role throughout Latin America. Much of this new activity was prompted by continued rivalry with other imperial powers. In 1902, for example, when the Venezuelan government was unable to pay its foreign creditors, British, German, and Italian naval forces threatened to bombard Venezuelan cities unless payments were resumed. Roosevelt regarded this action as a violation of the Monroe Doctrine; by a combination of threats and promises, he persuaded the European navies to withdraw.

### Instability as an American Problem

Roosevelt argued that instability in Latin America was likely to be a recurrent problem for American interests. He therefore announced, in 1904, his own amendment to the Monroe Doctrine (called the "Roosevelt Corollary"). The United States, he declared, would not only prevent European colonization of Latin American countries but would also intervene in the domestic affairs of any Latin American nation whose instability threatened the security of the Western Hemisphere. The policy allowed Roosevelt to intervene in the Dominican Republic, Nicaragua, Haiti, and Mexico, routinely resulting in American control of the contested lands for several decades (see Map 21.1).

Nicaragua's experience was typical. In 1909, an American mining company in Nicaragua became dissatisfied with the current regime and provoked a coup. President Taft sent troops in support of the coup and later helped American bankers finance the new regime. When this regime faced its own revolutionary discontent, Taft sent more soldiers to protect it. Thus Taft frequently used American troops to advance the interests of the American business community, a policy derided by critics as **dollar diplomacy**.

### Mexico

Taft and Wilson also intervened during the early stages of the Mexican Revolution, which began in 1910. A bewildering succession of soldiers, strongmen, and democratic idealists competed for power after the overthrow of the old dictator, Porfirio Diaz, whose policies had benefited American investors. Both Taft and Wilson tried to find a Mexican

**HELD UP THE WRONG MAN**

>> **"Held Up the Wrong Man."** President Theodore Roosevelt refusing to pay Colombia millions for Panama Canal rights.

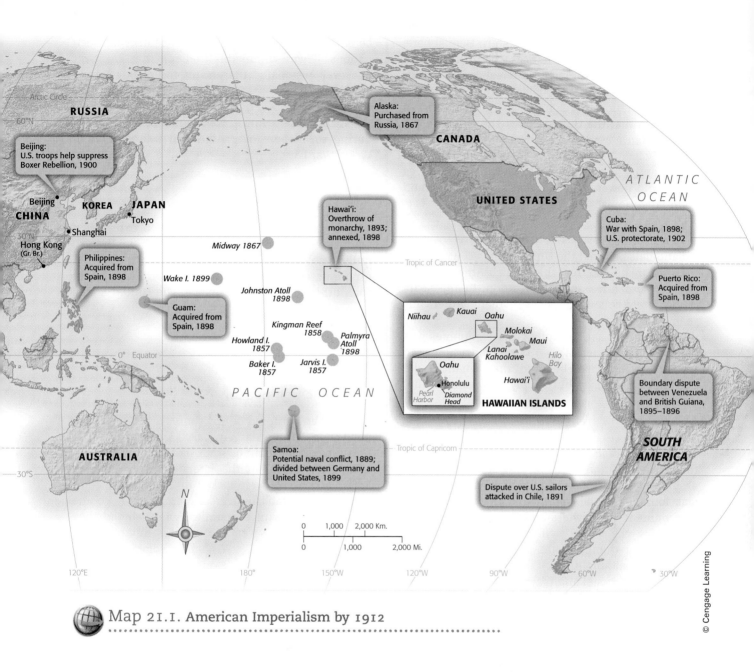

**Map 21.1. American Imperialism by 1912**

candidate who could take care of American businesses. One by one, these candidates proved either too ruthless or too ineffective, provoking political strife that often turned violent. In 1914 and again in 1916, Wilson sent troops to Mexico to restore order, first by capturing the port city of Veracruz, later by sending General John Pershing in pursuit of Pancho Villa, a Mexican general and kingmaker who had raided American towns in New Mexico. Neither of these expeditions solved Mexico's instability.

## America as a World Power

By the early twentieth century, the United States was committed to being a major player in Latin America and Asia. The belief that America's interests ended at its oceans had been shattered. Americans could no longer think of themselves as isolated from international affairs. Nor could they smugly see their nation as completely different from the European empires whose navies and armies had conquered much of the globe. But did American interests end at the nation's borders, at the Western Hemisphere, or never? What would America's role in the world be now that its commercial interests were worldwide? Should American business interests have a role in the nation's foreign policy? How salient was the notion that the United States should share the "white man's burden" to spread democracy and white civilization to the world? Americans fell into three camps when it came to viewing themselves as a world power: (1) isolationists, (2) realists, and (3) interventionists.

## Isolationists

Isolationists believed the United States could return to isolationism and treat the Spanish-American War and its corollaries as an aberration. In the years immediately following the war, many Americans seemed to favor this course of action, especially those who felt that controlling the Philippines was a betrayal of America's anti-imperialist roots. In general, isolationists believed that alliances did not improve security, but simply drew nations into costly wars.

## Realists

The so-called realists hoped the United States would follow the tradition of the leading states of Europe, assuming the role of a great world power. This belief was founded in the notion that the international environment was lawless and that all nations pursued only their own self-interests. Thus, power and military strength were the only meaningful factors in international affairs. Students of international relations use the term *realism* to describe this viewpoint.

## Idealists

Idealists believed that the United States could enter international politics not as a competitor but as a moral reformer, using its influence not to grab power for itself but to promote democracy and free trade around the world. Woodrow Wilson, elected president in 1912, was the most prominent proponent of this view. He

believed that the rules of international affairs could be changed to prevent or mitigate conflict between nations. It was within this tradition that President Roosevelt negotiated the end of the bloody Russo-Japanese War in 1905, an event that earned Roosevelt the first-ever Nobel Prize awarded to an American.

All of these points of view would be represented during the debate over American intervention in World War I.

# LO⁵ World War I

World War I, which lasted from 1914 to 1918, was a conflict of colossal proportions, killing more than 10 million soldiers and civilians, bringing down governments and empires, and pitting armies against each other all around the globe. The United States entered the war in 1917, just it time to allow it to try to manipulate the terms of surrender.

## The Reasons

### Economic Competition

World War I erupted out of conflicts between rival powers in Europe, largely based on the competition for colonial empires that had been building in the past decades. In the late nineteenth century, European nations were locked in a worldwide competition to establish overseas empires. At home they built powerful economies, while abroad they scrambled to turn weaker countries in Africa and Asia into colonial possessions that would serve as sources of raw materials. Britain and Germany were the two largest powers, and to many observers, a confrontation between the two expanding powers seemed inevitable.

© DeA Picture Library /Art Resource, NY

### Alliances

Anxiety about the impending clash between England and Germany led nearly all of Europe's most powerful nations to enter into alliances, each pledging to come to the other's defense in the event of a war. France and Russia joined England, calling themselves the

Allied Powers. Germany made treaties with the Austro-Hungarian Empire and Turkey. They were called the Central Powers. Forging these alliances set the stage for tragedy, because a conflict between any two nations was bound to trigger a wider war.

**U-boat**
Primitive but effective submarine invented by the Germans and used extensively in the First World War

who felt strong ties to their homelands. On the other hand, many of the nation's political and industrial leaders were Anglophiles, who instinctively favored the English.

## The Spark

The spark that ignited the war was the assassination of Austria's Archduke Franz Ferdinand, heir to the throne of the Austro-Hungarian Empire. He and his wife Sofia were shot on June 28, 1914, during a visit to Sarajevo, by Gavrilo Princip, a member of the Serbian nationalist group called the Black Hand, which was bent on driving the Austro-Hungarians out of Serbia. This event set off a chain reaction in Europe's military alliances. Austria declared war on Serbia, which

 Read a firsthand account of the archduke's assassination.

prompted Russia to help the Serbians, which led Germany to declare war on Russia and France, which triggered England to declare war on Germany. Over the next several weeks, many other nations joined the conflict, and fighting spread to the European colonies in Africa, Asia, and the Middle East (see Map 21.2).

## The European War

Hoping for a quick victory against its enemies to the west, Germany invaded France in August 1914. With British help, the French managed to hold off the German advance. A military stalemate resulted, and both sides dug into the fields of northern France. For the next four years, the Allied and Central Powers battled each other on what became called "the Western Front."

## American Neutrality, 1914–1917

Most Americans were baffled by the rivalries and alliances that had caused the war and horrified at the carnage in France. In the war's first years, Americans called it "the European War," distancing themselves from the conflict. Yet they could not ignore such a massive war, and their sympathies were mixed. Following the tremendous immigration that had resulted from the Industrial Revolution, many Americans were recent European emigrants

## Compromised Neutrality

Faced with divided loyalties, President Wilson urged his fellow citizens to remain "impartial in thought as well as action." Running for reelection in 1916, he turned the race into a referendum on neutrality. He won easily, campaigning on the slogan "He Kept Us Out of War."

Despite Wilson's best intentions, the United States was slowly being drawn in. With Allied and German armies stalemated in France, both sides realized that their best hope for victory was to starve their enemy into submission. With their economies in tatters, each side looked to the United States for supplies. By 1915, the economic incentive to trade with them proved irresistible. American farms and factories soon began to work overtime to meet the demands of the war-torn nations of Europe. But could this be done neutrally?

## Neutral Trading?

Both Allied and Central Powers believed it was essential to deprive their enemies of the benefits of trade with the Americans, and Wilson's call for all sides to respect American trade rights ran directly counter to the military strategies of both the English and the Germans. Britain and France, for instance, mined the North Sea, forcing American ships into British ports. There, the British detained supplies headed for Germany. When Wilson protested, the French and British agreed to pay for all materials seized in this way.

The Germans, meanwhile, realized that with Britain and France blocking their ports, it could not enjoy such advantageous trade. They concluded that their best hope was to prevent American goods from getting to Britain at all. To do so, they launched a new weapon that profoundly changed the nature of naval warfare and eventually brought the United States into war—the **U-boat**, a primitive

THE ROAD TO WAR,
SUMMER 1914

1 June 28
Assassination at Sarajevo

2 July 28
Austria-Hungary declares
war on Serbia

3 July 30
Russia begins mobilization

4 August 1
Germany declares war
on Russia

5 August 3
Germany declares war
on France

6 August 4
Great Britain declares war
on Germany

7 August 6
Russia and
Austria-Hungary at war

8 August 12
Great Britain declares war
on Austria-Hungary

Allied powers and
possessions, 1916        ♦♦♦♦♦♦ British naval blockade

Central powers and
Ottoman Empire, 1916     ———— Trench line, Western front, 1915

Neutral countries        ———— Eastern front, 1915

© Cengage Learning

Map 21.2 World War I

but effective submarine. On May 7, 1915, a U-boat sank England's *Lusitania*, a famed passenger liner that the Allies had used occasionally to transport war material. More than 1,000 civilians were killed, including 128 Americans. Provoked by anti-German newspaper editorials, mobs lashed out at innocent German-Americans.

Responding to Wilson's threats that the *Lusitania* disaster would likely force the United States into the war, Germany temporarily halted its use of the U-boat against passenger vessels. By 1917, however, Germany was nearly starved into submission and, in a last-ditch gamble, declared it would wage unrestricted submarine warfare against all shipping in

Library of Congress, Prints & Photographs Division, LC-USZC4-10986

Library of Congress, Prints & Photographs Division, LC-USZC4-10930

## Declaration of War

By the spring of 1917, the combination of German U-boat attacks and the Zimmerman Note left many Americans feeling that the time had come to admit they really were involved in the "European War." On April 2, 1917, Wilson asked Congress for a declaration of war. In his request, Wilson outlined the nation's grievances against the Central Powers and invested the war effort with a moral purpose. American soldiers would go to Europe, he insisted, not to punish Germany, but to help create a new international order. "The world must be made safe for democracy," he declared.

## A Mixed Reaction

Americans were not fully united in this decision. Six senators and fifty congressmen voted against the declaration. In addition, a substantial minority of the American public still favored neutrality. Unconvinced by Wilson's idealistic rhetoric, they insisted that sending American troops to settle a distant European war was a misguided departure from traditional American diplomacy.

## Forming Public Opinion

The government responded to these criticisms by taking unprecedented steps to mobilize public opinion. It formed the Committee on Public Information (CPI), a group led by journalist George Creel that recruited some of the nation's finest artists to create and distribute millions of pieces of war propaganda. On street corners and in theaters, "Four-Minute Men" delivered stirring pro-war speeches. Newspapers printed government-written stories detailing questionable tales of German war atrocities. Ubiquitous posters urged Americans to buy Liberty Bonds, conserve food and coal, and otherwise do everything possible to "Beat Back the Hun."

 Read a sample of a war propaganda pamphlet.

## Hyphenated Americans

In addition to worrying about popular support, government officials were particularly anxious about the loyalties of the nation's recent immigrants, many of whom maintained strong ties with their European homelands. These newcomers were branded "hyphenated Americans" (German-Americans, Irish-Americans), the hyphen suggesting that these recent arrivals might not have left their Old World allegiances behind to fully embrace their new American

the Atlantic. When Russia negotiated peace after the successful Bolshevik revolution of February 1917, Germany hoped it could handle a one-front war, even if the United States entered the war on the Western Front.

 View a graph comparing American trade with the Allies and Germany.

## Declaring War

### The Zimmerman Note

After the declaration of unrestricted warfare in the Atlantic, German-American relations deteriorated. Not only had Germany initiated a threatening campaign, but Americans discovered that Germany was also encouraging Mexico to attack the United States. On January 16, 1917, the German foreign minister, Count von Zimmerman, sent a note to Mexico in which he promised German support for a Mexican invasion, the goal of which was to reconquer New Mexico, Arizona, and Texas for Mexico. Unluckily for the Germans, the note was intercepted by the British, who eagerly turned it over to the United States. The so-called Zimmerman Note proved a powerful tool in rallying American public support for a war against Germany.

Read the Zimmerman Note.

identities. Creel's committee tried to apply its powers of persuasion to turn these newcomers into "100 percent Americans." The CPI included a "Division for Work with the Foreign Born" that encouraged recent immigrants to show their loyalty by purchasing **war bonds** and staging patriotic demonstrations.

## Wartime Repression

The government also took steps to silence critics. In 1917, Congress passed the **Espionage Act**, which meted out large fines and twenty-year jail terms to anyone who protested the draft or said anything that might impede the war effort. A year later the act was broad-

ened, making it illegal to say anything "disloyal" about the American form of government or the armed forces. The U.S. Postmaster General Albert S. Burleson was authorized to seize and destroy any publication he deemed treasonous—a power he exercised freely. School boards banned the teaching of German language and history. Universities fired professors who spoke out against the war. Towns changed street signs to erase German names. German-named foods were renamed: sauerkraut, for example, became "liberty cabbage." "Patriotic" mobs attacked German-language and socialist newspaper offices, beat innocent German immigrants, and, in at least one case, lynched a man wrongly suspected of being a German spy. Government-stimulated war fervor ran hot.

Several prominent Americans spoke out against these forms of repression. Eugene V. Debs was imprisoned for speaking out against the war effort. Hull House's Jane Addams was another outspoken opponent. Watching such dignified opponents be punished for their antiwar efforts led many Americans to question what freedom meant, and if it meant the same thing in wartime as in peace.

> *German-named foods were renamed: sauerkraut became "liberty cabbage."*

 Read the Espionage Act.

## American Involvement in the War Effort, 1917–1918

When Congress declared war in 1917, the United States was unprepared to recruit, train, equip, or transport a modern army across the Atlantic. It entered the war with no army and no stockpiles of military supplies. And, with the American economy booming, shifting to war production was a slow process. In fact, by the end of the war, the United States managed to mobilize little more than a small fraction of its economy and raised only a modest military force; fewer than 5 million men entered the armed services, and only 2.5 million of them went overseas.

### The American Army in Battle

In the end, Americans were slow to join the battle, as American political leaders refused to send troops that would fight under the control of French or English Allied commanders. President Wilson sought

U·S·A BONDS

Third Liberty Loan Campaign BOY SCOUTS OF AMERICA

WEAPONS FOR LIBERTY

Library of Congress, Prints & Photographs Division, LC-USZC4-1127 to maintain American independence, and only when the complete army was ready to fight did American soldiers fight. They fought in two major battles before Germany capitulated and ended the war.

Historians have debated the impact American forces had on the outcome of World War I. Some assert that, even after committing themselves, Americans made only a minimal contribution. Proponents of this view stress that, after such a long delay, American soldiers had little impact in either of the two military battles they fought. Other historians contend that this interpretation downplays the American impact. They argue that the U.S. declaration of war dashed Germany's hope for a quick victory on the Western Front after Russia had sued for peace. Food shortages were widespread on the German home front, and demoralized soldiers threatened mutiny. According to this interpretation, the entrance of the resource-rich Americans dealt a powerful psychological and military blow to the Germans and greatly hastened their capitulation.

## The Fourteen Points

Regardless of how large an impression the American military made on the battling nations, this did not inhibit President Wilson from attempting to determine the conditions for peace. On January 8, 1918, while the war still raged, Wilson issued a proclamation, called the **Fourteen Points**, outlining the principles he believed should shape the postwar peace settlement.

The statement came as a great surprise to the Allies. That an American president, who had brought his country into the war only a few months earlier, was attempting to dictate a sweeping peace program was certainly a shock. But Wilson's independent course was consistent with his actions and statements. To Wilson, the United States could lead the world to a more enlightened way of conducting international affairs. Some of his Fourteen Points involved proposals for resolving specific border disputes, but the rest of Wilson's ideas amounted to a blueprint for what he called "a world made fit and safe to live in." Among the major tenets were free trade, disarmament, and a "general association of nations" that would provide a forum for nations to resolve differences peacefully. Wilson advocated national self-determination, which would break up multiethnic empires and allow new national boundaries to be drawn along "clearly recognizable lines of nationality."

 Read the Fourteen Points.

## Making Peace

### Armistice

In October 1918, Germany made peace overtures to Wilson, agreeing to end the war on the basis of his declaration that there could be "peace without victory." The Allied powers wanted to fight on, believing they finally had a decisive advantage on the battlefield. The war had been viciously fought in Europe, especially after the introduction of new technologies such as planes, tanks, and chemical weapons like deadly "mustard gas." The Allied Powers wanted to punish German wartime atrocities. But they yielded when Wilson threatened to pull American troops out of the war if the Allies were unwilling to accept overtures for peace. On November 11, 1918, both sides signed an armistice ending the war.

### Debating Peace

After the armistice, Wilson made an unusual decision to travel to Europe himself to represent the United States at the peace talks. Crowds in Paris greeted him as a hero and applauded his vision for a better world. Despite this popular support, however, Wilson ran into difficulties at the bargaining table, as the victorious Allies pursued very different ideas about how to shape the postwar world. After four years of brutal war and suffering, the Allies had little interest in "peace without victory," and they were eager to punish their enemies and divide the spoils of Germany's overseas colonies. As a result, Wilson had only limited success in incorporating his vision for a new world order into the final peace treaty, which was signed in the French palace at Versailles on June 28, 1919.

### The Treaty of Versailles

The treaty included three major provisions: (1) reparations that forced Germany to accept full responsibility for the war and pay heavy fines to the Allies; (2) self-determination for nationalities; and (3) Wilson's "general association of nations," which the treaty called the League of Nations. Each of these provisions would have unforeseen consequences. Forcing Germany to pay steep financial reparations meant that the German economy could not recover from the war, leading to political instability that encouraged the rise of Adolf Hitler. The concept of national self-determination has led to a century of struggle in the Baltic and other areas, where

the United States never joined the League of Nations. The president stubbornly refused to compromise and was crippled by a stroke while waging his campaign. Woodrow Wilson died a broken man, in 1924.

### A Weakened League

In 1920, the League of Nations met for the first time, but it was diminished from the start by the absence of the United States. By the mid-1930s, the League was irrelevant, incapable of changing the course of events that would soon draw Europe into World War II. But the idea of a worldwide association of nations had been articulated and would surface again.

>> Crowds in Paris greeted Wilson as a hero, but he had limited success incorporating his vision for a new world order.

groups of people, seeing themselves as distinct nations, resist the rule of others. And the League of Nations would be toothless from the beginning, because the United States, of all countries, refused to participate.

### Wilson's Folly

Although Wilson had arrived in Europe as a conquering hero, when he returned to Washington he faced a desperate political fight to save his cherished League of Nations. Many Americans, he discovered, were already disillusioned about the nation's decision to get involved in European affairs. The champion of this brand of isolationism was Republican senator Henry Cabot Lodge of Massachusetts, who worked to block American participation in the new League of Nations because he believed it would draw the United States into future European conflicts. In particular, he objected to Article X of the League's charter, which would have committed the United States to defending the territory of other League members. Wilson considered this "the heart of the League," a provision that would require nations to join together to protect each other from attacks by international aggressors.

Wilson fought hard for the League, touring the country in a direct appeal to the public. But the Senate refused to ratify the Treaty of Versailles, and

# And in the end . . .

World War I underscored America's role as a significant power in the world. After the war, America for the first time replaced Great Britain as the world's greatest creditor nation, further enhancing American power.

But Americans' willingness to intervene in world affairs was not a foregone conclusion. After being

| What else was happening . . . | |
|---|---|
| 1899 | The Second Boer War in southern Africa between Great Britain and a handful of small African nations leads to the conversion of several small African republics into parts of the British Empire. |
| 1904 | Russo-Japanese War breaks out because of each nation's imperial ambitions over Manchuria and Korea. |
| April 15, 1912 | The *Titanic* sinks. |
| 1914 | First passenger meal is served on an airplane in flight. |
| 1923 | Frank Epperson invents the popsicle when he leaves his lemonade mix on a windowsill overnight. |

somewhat grudgingly brought into world affairs by a series of expansionist leaders, Americans continued to debate the importance of playing a role in world affairs. Between 1867 and 1918, the ethos of expansion was strong, and during the four decades following 1880, the United States had flexed its military muscle throughout Latin America, Asia, and Europe. It had done so to support American economic development, to establish the United States as a world power worth reckoning with, and because many Americans believed the United States was destined to share the benefits of democracy and white civilization with the rest of the world. In doing so, it confronted new problems, such as how colonial powers are supposed to manage relations with their subjected peoples. Was the United States to be a great liberating force for democracy in the wider world, or was it to serve the interests of the business classes who advocated dollar diplomacy? These debates would continue throughout the twentieth century.

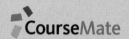 **Course**Mate

Visit the CourseMate website at www.cengagebrain.com for additional study tools and review materials for this chapter.

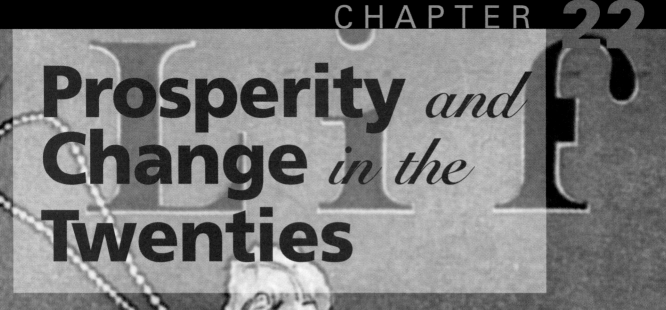

# CHAPTER 22

# Prosperity *and* Change *in the* Twenties

## Learning Outcomes

*After reading this chapter, you should be able to do the following:*

LO **1**  Describe the consumerism that developed in America during the early twentieth century, especially after World War I.

LO **2**  Explain the experiences of the nation that effectively put an end to the Progressive movement in America during the 1920s.

LO **3**  Describe the various kinds of leisure activities that became popular in America during the 1920s.

LO **4**  Discuss the strong reactions among various groups in America to the changing cultural mores of the 1920s.

**"America had begun its transition into what one historian has called 'the first years of our time.'"**

During the decade after the First World War, America became the richest society in the history of the world. It had entered what many observers believed was a "new era" of unending prosperity. As always, economic changes prompted social and cultural changes. Exhausted by constant efforts, postwar politicians from both parties largely gave up on the idea of "progressive" reform, which had dominated national politics since Teddy Roosevelt. They were tired of moral crusades. Instead, voters elected a series of Republican presidents who promised to facilitate business expansion rather than impose Progressive regulations. Corporations responded by accelerating production and advertising their goods from one end of America to the other, with unbounded boosterism and pep that masked potential troubles within an unregulated economic system. As a result, America witnessed an intensification of the mass consumer culture that had been growing since the start of the Industrial Revolution.

With this backdrop of "good times," new ideas that questioned the established order, such as pluralism, psychoanalysis, and relativity, entered the American vocabulary. A series of American writers picked up these themes and made American literature respected throughout the world for the first time, mostly by critiquing America's developing consumer culture. Also in 1920, for the first time, a majority of Americans were living in cities, creating a clash of values between those who lived in cities and those who remained in rural parts of the country. African Americans were attempting to refashion mainstream perceptions of their group. Women were looking to establish a new place in society. And the culture seemed to be liberalizing, a development that led to a widespread series of backlashes and America's first culture war between religious conservatives and progressives from all backgrounds.

In all this turmoil, the 1920s have been depicted by historians as many things: a "new era," a "return to normalcy," the "Roaring Twenties," a period of isolation. This variety of descriptions suggests that the period was characterized by many simultaneous changes. Most of the changes can be described as major shifts inward, toward private consumption, privatized business practices, an inwardly facing foreign policy, a widespread dislike and fear of "outsiders" (variously defined), and an end to the calls for broad social justice that had characterized the Progressive era. Ultimately, this swirl of cultural newness came to a halt with the 1929 stock market crash and the Great Depression that followed. But, before then, America had begun its transition into what one historian has called "the first years of our time."

## What do you think?

In the 1920s, immigration restriction was necessary to prevent the millions of immigrants from changing the culture of the United States.

| Strongly Disagree | | | | | Strongly Agree | |
|---|---|---|---|---|---|---|
| 1 | 2 | 3 | 4 | 5 | 6 | 7 |

# LO¹ The Consumer Economy

During the 1920s, the United States became the wealthiest nation in the world. It took several years for the American economy to recover from its conversion to wartime production during World War I, when goods like guns and naval ships were produced in lieu of consumer items. But by 1921, the American economy was on an upward surge. American per capita incomes grew by more than 30 percent during the decade, industrial output increased by 60 percent, and unemployment in most parts of the country stayed below 5 percent. Immense corporations dominated the economy, making their mark on national culture. And most people enjoyed rising wages and rising standards of living. In 1929, five out of every six privately owned cars in the world belonged to Americans.

The improved economy was both uneven and unstable, however, with only a few people really benefiting from the expansive economy. Many Americans, especially farmers in the South and the West, still lived in poverty, and the recession of 1921 hit farmers particularly hard. Overall, the percentage of national wealth that went to the poorest 60 percent fell by almost 13 percent during the 1920s, meaning that the wealthy were increasing their wealth at the expense of the poor. This poverty particularly affected many of the new immigrants, as well as Native Americans and Latinos living in the American Southwest. The wealth of the "Roaring Twenties" was stratified.

## 1920s Work

### Good Times

The economy was healthy for several reasons. For one, the industrial production of Europe had been destroyed by the war, making American goods the dominant products available in Europe. New techniques of production and pay were another significant factor in the booming American economy. Henry Ford was a leader in developing both. First, he revolutionized the automobile industry with his development of the **assembly line**, a mechanized belt that moved a car chassis down a line where each man performed a single small task, over and over again. Although this innovation dramatically sped up production, it alienated workers from the final product they were making because they worked on only one small aspect of a larger product. Ford had a wonderful solution to this problem: He realized that, in order to keep selling cars by the thousands, he would have to pay his workers enough for them to become *customers* too. His 1914 innovation, the "**five-dollar day**" (when a salary of $1.50 per day was standard), shocked other businessmen at first, but by the 1920s, other business owners were coming to understand that they could mass-produce consumer goods only if they also created a supply of consumers. In the 1920s, the economy began to transition from being driven by large industries (such as railroads and steel) to being driven by consumer dollars.

© Hulton Archive/Getty Images

>> In 1929, five out of every six privately owned cars in the world belonged to Americans.

>> Ford assembly line in 1920.

### Welfare Capitalism

Along with recognizing the need to pay higher wages, many manufacturers began to think of their factories not just as places of work but also as social settings, where men and women spent a large part of their waking hours. A handful of pioneers in "**welfare capitalism**," such as the Heinz Company (producer of soup, ketchup, and baked beans), reasoned that happy workers would be more productive than resentful workers. Heinz and other companies improved lighting and ventilation and also provided company health plans, recreation centers, and even psychologists to tend to their employees. Many companies shortened the workweek. And in some firms, **company unions** replaced the AFL in representing workers' grievances to management.

### Decline of Union Membership

The combination of company unions, high wages, and the hunger to own a car and other luxury goods spelled hard times for traditional unions, as did a growing suspicion of communism (described below). The decade witnessed a decline in the number of workers attached to unions in the AFL, from 4 million in 1920 to 2.5 million by 1929.

Employers kept iron fists inside their new velvet gloves, though. They **blacklisted** men who were known union organizers, spied on union activities, and pressured employees to sign anti-union pledges. Along similar lines, a group of manufacturers came together in the National Association of Manufacturers to promote what it called the "American Plan," which forced the maintenance of an "open shop" labor environment, meaning that labor unions could not force all employees in a specific company to join their union in order to work there. In addition, probusiness courts in the 1920s struck down a series of Progressive-era laws against child labor. Abusive forms of child labor persisted, particularly in the textile mills of the South. Working conditions in steel mills and coal mines remained atrocious as well.

### 1920s Consumerism

Despite these obstacles, ordinary working-class people enthusiastically entered the consumer society of the 1920s, buying a wide assortment of laborsaving devices. Speeding this process, domestic electrification spread rapidly throughout the United States, giving most urban families electric lighting and power for the first time. People could now aspire to own new inventions like cars, refrigerators, toasters, radios, telephones, washing machines, vacuums, and phonographs, as well as nationally marketed foods, clothes, and cosmetics.

### Advertisements

These new consumer products spawned advertisements, which were everywhere in the 1920s: on the radio and on billboards, in magazines and newspapers, even painted on rocks and trees. With nationwide marketing came nationwide advertising campaigns by giant companies like Kellogg's, Gillette, Palmolive, and Nabisco. Most of the money that consumers paid when they bought goods like toothpaste was used to pay for advertising rather than for the actual product. Supermarkets were another 1920s invention, replacing the old over-the-counter stores. Now the customer, instead of asking a clerk for items one by one, chose items from open shelves, put them into a basket, and paid for them all at once.

Albert Lasker, Alfred Sloan, and Bruce Barton were all pioneers of the field of marketing and advertising, heightening the American public's interest in orange juice (through a 1910s advertising campaign to increase consumption of oranges), tampons (by going into schools to explain to schoolgirls the process of menstruation—and how to manage it by using tampons), and baked goods (by inventing the maternal icon Betty Crocker). Bruce Barton's noteworthy 1925 book, *The Man Nobody Knows*, depicted Jesus Christ as the world's most successful businessman, who formulated a resonating message (as revealed in the New Testament) and

**welfare capitalism**
Industry's strategy of improving working conditions and providing health insurance for workers

**company unions**
Organizations of workers from a single company who represent workers' grievances to management

**blacklisted**
Denied employment to known union organizers

Read advertisements from the 1920s.

an institutional infrastructure (the Apostles) to spread the Gospel. According to Barton, Jesus was the businessman all Americans should emulate.

## Buying on Credit

Equally striking was a decline in the historic American emphasis on thrift. Instead of saving money every month, buying on credit with installment payments became a socially acceptable way to acquire goods. For industrialists, it was necessary to stimulate demand by encouraging people to spend money they hadn't yet earned. Car companies experimented with different forms of financing car purchases. The result was fantastic for car sellers, as more and more Americans bought cars on installment plans.

Issuing credit expanded throughout the 1920s. One leading historian of installment buying estimates that, by the end of the 1920s, Americans relied on credit to purchase nearly 90 percent of their major durable goods. Correspondingly, Americans saved a smaller percentage of their monthly income.

## Early Car Culture

In part because of installment buying, cars became very popular as well. By the late 1920s, there was

> *By the end of the 1920s, Americans relied on credit to purchase nearly 90 percent of their major durable goods.*

one car for every five people in the country. A car was the key object of desire for anyone who could scrape together enough money to purchase one. A group of sociologists studying a small midwestern town in the late 1920s found dozens of car-owning families still living in houses without bathtubs or indoor plumbing. Young people especially longed for cars; after all, cars bestowed freedom from watchful, restrictive parents.

## Adventures in Real Estate

The economic boom boosted real estate as well as consumer products, nowhere more so than in Florida. Florida was a remote backwater of America until the discovery of effective cures for yellow fever and malaria around 1900. By the 1920s, road and rail connections down to Miami made the area attractive for winter holidays, and between 1920 and 1925, parcels of land, or lots, began to change hands at rapidly escalating prices. In 1926, the weather intervened, as a pair of devastating hurricanes killed four hundred people, destroyed hundreds of housing projects, threw boats into the streets, and wiped out an entire town. After that, land in Florida appeared less attractive as an investment. Prices began to fall

>> Supermarkets like Piggly Wiggly (top) were another 1920s invention, replacing the old over-the-counter stores shown in this advertisement for Heinz ketchup.

COLUMBIA PICTURES *presents*

# WALL STREET

### A POWERFUL ALL-TALKING DRAMA
*with* RALPH INCE · AILEEN PRINGLE

*Directed by R. William Neill*

A "NAPOLEON OF FINANCE" forces himself to the top by ruthless selfishness and vindictive actions — only to be ruined, humbled and then regenerated by a woman who had ideals . . .

*a* COLUMBIA
*Production*

>> The glamour of Wall Street at the end of the decade is captured in publicity for the 1929 movie *Wall Street,* the second of its name, about a "Napoleon of Finance" and a woman with ideals.

© Lordprice Collection/Alamy

as steeply as they had risen, and thirty-one local banks failed. Much of the area was left a ghostly ruin and did not recover until after World War II.

## Stocks and Shares

If speculating on real estate seemed too risky, buying stocks had broader appeal. The managers, lawyers, accountants, advertisers, brokers, and other "white-collar" professional workers whose ranks increased through the 1920s invested in the stock market in great numbers. This meant that they bought shares, or small percentages, of a company, hoping that the value of the company would increase, which would therefore lead to a rise in the price of a share. This would give the owners of these shares a tidy profit when they sold the shares that they owned. Throughout most of the 1920s, the price of stocks and shares rose steadily, deceiving growing numbers of investors into thinking that the trend was destined to continue indefinitely.

At the same time, bankers in the 1920s devised the mutual fund, a professionally managed fund whose shares people could buy. The fund owned several stocks at one time, thus limiting the amount of risk involved for the individual investor. Because of this pretense of security and shared risk, mutual funds were a popular form of investment throughout the 1920s. Tens of millions of dollars poured into

Wall Street from all over the world, inflating stock prices far above their realistic value.

# LO² The End of the Progressive Era

## National Politics

These perilous but generally good economic times had an effect on politics. After the unprecedented challenges of the Progressive era, when politicians sought to rein in the most egregious effects of the Industrial Revolution, the 1920s saw the rise of a dominant Republican Party that embraced a "business-first" philosophy. These Republicans presided over national politics throughout the decade, holding the presidency from 1920 until 1933.

## Red Scare

Before the economic "good times" took hold, however, America confronted a **Red Scare**, or fear that the United States was vulnerable to a communist takeover. Why a Red Scare? In 1917, Vladimir Lenin and his Russian Bolshevik Party seized power in Russia, declaring the advent of world communism and the end of all private property. According to the plan spelled out by Karl Marx, Lenin believed that his communist revolution would spread to all the major industrial nations, and he called for workers' uprisings everywhere. This prompted a number of American politicians and businessmen to fear for the safety of the American capitalist system. (During the Russian Civil War, the Bolsheviks were called the "Reds" while the Mensheviks, who were moderate socialists, were called "Whites.")

On top of this, the pieces of a revolutionary puzzle seemed to be moving into place in the United States. American socialism had been growing with the labor movement. The Socialist Party presidential candidate, Eugene V. Debs, won almost 1 million votes in the election of 1920—from his prison cell. He had been jailed for making speeches against U.S.

participation in World War I, which he denounced as a capitalist endeavor. Many towns elected socialist mayors and council members, especially in the industrialized Northeast and along the northern stretches of the Mississippi River. And during World War I a variety of anarchists had bombed courthouses, police stations, churches, and even people's homes.

Politicians and businessmen reacted to these developments by initiating a hunt for potential revolutionaries. President Wilson's attorney general, A. Mitchell Palmer, set up a federal bureau to seek out communists and anarchists, and the years 1918–1920 witnessed the arrest and deportation of several hundred union members and foreign-born radicals who had usually committed no crimes but were suspected of favoring a Russian-style coup. To be American, the Palmer raids suggested, was not to be communist.

## Sacco and Vanzetti

Fears of political radicals surrounded the court case of **Sacco and Vanzetti**. Nicola Sacco and Bartolomeo Vanzetti were Italian immigrants living in Massachusetts. They became suspects in a 1920 payroll heist, and they were arrested, tried, and convicted of robbery and murder despite a flimsy trail of evidence. Under sentence of death, both proclaimed their anarchist beliefs but maintained their innocence in the heist. A long series of appeals followed, with civil libertarians and friends of the political left taking up the convicted men's cause, claiming that it was the men's ethnicity and political beliefs that had convicted them, not the evidence in the trial. Nevertheless, a final committee of inquiry concluded that Sacco and Vanzetti were indeed guilty, and both were executed in the electric chair in 1927. Scholars continue to dispute the defendants' guilt (most believe Sacco was guilty while Vanzetti's guilt is less certain). Nevertheless, the case encapsulated the American public's fears about communists and foreigners in the early 1920s.

Despite the paranoia of the Red Scare, it is obvious today that a "red" revolution was never a real possibility during these years. The economy was too good. Although some anarchists were willing to use violent methods to achieve their ends, and

although a small American Communist Party did follow instructions from Moscow, many American socialists were Christian pacifists rather than atheist revolutionaries. Eugene V. Debs himself had written a biography of Jesus, whom he depicted as a socialist carpenter.

## Race Riots

Fears of change also prompted a series of violent race riots in the years following the First World War. Even before the war was over, in 1917, white workers in East St. Louis, who had kept African Americans out of their unions, were appalled when African Americans agreed to work for lower wages than white workers would accept. Tempers flared when African Americans then agreed to work as strikebreakers. Fears of white women and black men fraternizing together at a labor meeting erupted quickly into a full-fledged riot. Three thousand men surrounded the labor meeting and, in the end, roughly 100 people died because of the ensuing violence.

The East St. Louis riot was only the beginning. In the summer of 1919 race riots broke out in more than two dozen cities across the United States. Chicago's were perhaps the worst, with dozens dying and hundreds more injured. But riots also broke out in Connecticut, Maryland, Arizona, Texas, Mississippi, and other states, demonstrating that racial tensions affected the nation as a whole, not just the South. They also put on vivid display the fact that many African Americans had begun to leave the South's system of Jim Crow segregation, heading to the supposedly more racially progressive parts of the country in the North, a broad movement called the **Great Migration**. African Americans were not always welcome in the new locales, and in the heated atmosphere of industrial conflict combined with post–World War I fears of radicalism, they suffered the most.

Even after race relations quieted down throughout much of the rest of the 1920s, they always remained potentially violent. In 1921, the most destructive of all the race riots took place in Tulsa, Oklahoma, where the one-day riot led to 800 injuries and 10,000 people becoming homeless as the racially segregated Tulsa neighborhood of Greenwood was essentially burned to the ground.

## Warren G. Harding

Once the economy settled down after two years of peacetime conversion, politics mellowed as well. Warren G. Harding won the presidential election of

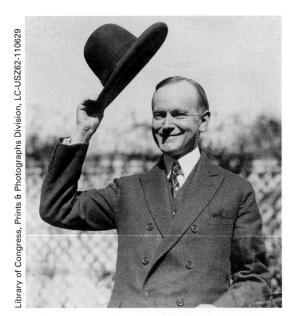

Library of Congress, Prints & Photographs Division, LC-USZ62-110629

>> Coolidge's presidency was notable for its paucity of action.

Volstead Act
Legislation passed in 1919 that laid down strict punishments for violating the Eighteenth Amendment

Dome came to symbolize the closeness between big business and government that characterized the 1920s. Other scandals plagued the Harding administration, including one in which Attorney General Harry M. Daugherty resigned for taking bribes.

### "Silent Cal"

In August 1923, President Harding died suddenly in San Francisco during a tour of the West Coast (just before the Teapot Dome Scandal came to light). Harding's flinty vice president, Calvin Coolidge, heard the news in his hometown of Plymouth, Vermont, while visiting his elderly father. A notary public, Coolidge Sr. administered the oath of office to his son late that night, and "Silent Cal," as he was known, became president.

Known for his ability to solve political problems with a minimum of words and minimal effort, Coolidge won reelection in 1924, easily beating Democrat John W. Davis (who carried only southern states) and the new Progressive Party's Robert F. La Follette, whose loss signaled the end of the Progressive era in national politics. Coolidge continued Harding's policy of minimizing the federal government's role in American life. He also restored his party's reputation for scrupulous honesty and integrity, which had been damaged by Teapot Dome, by creating a bipartisan commission to investigate the improprieties of the Harding administration. Coolidge also avoided using the federal government to crusade for a cause, something that had ultimately damaged Wilson's presidency and reputation. Coolidge's presidency was notable for its paucity of action.

## Prohibition

There was, however, one volatile issue that came to the forefront of American politics in the 1920s: Prohibition, or the outlawing of alcohol. After extensive political lobbying extending back before the Civil War, and empowered by the anti-German sentiment of the First World War (Germans being known for their extensive brewing tradition), Prohibition became the law of the land in 1919. The Eighteenth Amendment to the Constitution prohibited the "manufacture, sale, or transportation of intoxicating liquors" in the United States.

Prohibition was difficult to enforce. Congress passed the **Volstead Act** (1919), which laid down strict punishments for violating the amendment.

1920 by campaigning largely from the front porch of his house in Marion, Ohio. Harding openly declared his intention to abandon President Wilson's progressive ideals, including Wilson's idealistic international program, which had transformed American politics during World War I by expanding U.S. involvement in world affairs. Harding also signaled an end to Progressive politics by using the slogan of "a return to normalcy," and by "normalcy" (a newly coined word) he meant the pre-Progressive, probusiness politics of the late 1800s.

With the First World War over, Harding dismantled the National War Labor Board and other agencies designed to regulate private industry. Instead, he advocated independent control for corporations. After a two-year recession while the economy transitioned to peacetime production levels, the Republican ascendancy meant that politics in the 1920s would be predictably conservative.

Starting with Harding, three successive Republican administrations pursued limited government via conservative policies on tariffs, taxes, immigration restriction, labor rights, and business administration. For better or worse, these policies created a robust economy—one healthy enough to allow Americans to make light of a major scandal during Harding's administration, the Teapot Dome Scandal of 1923. Teapot Dome implicated Harding's secretary of the interior, Albert B. Fall, and Fall's willingness to lease government land to prominent American oil men in exchange for bribes. The scandal was exposed in the late 1920s, and Teapot

**moonshine**
Homemade corn whiskey

**speakeasy**
Clandestine bar serving alcohol during Prohibition

But from the start there were problems, not the least of which was the fact that enforcement required a high degree of citizen cooperation. This was simply lacking in many parts of the country. Rural Baptists and Methodists were usually strong supporters of Prohibition, and Prohibition was most effective in small towns of the South and Midwest. But even there, farmers with long traditions of taking a surreptitious drink were reluctant to stop doing so. Stills making "**moonshine**" whiskey proliferated in mountain and country districts. The most prominent journalist of the day, H. L. Mencken, joked that Prohibition was the work of "ignorant bumpkins of the cow states who resented the fact that they had to swill raw corn liquor while city slickers got good wine and whiskey."

Read a 1931 report on the difficulties of enforcing Prohibition.

Meanwhile, immigrants from societies with strong drinking traditions, such as Germany, Ireland, and Italy, hated Prohibition. They were demographically strong in cities and formed ethnic gangs (the most notorious of which was the Sicilian Mafia) that made and sold their own supplies of alcohol. Former saloonkeepers, who had been forced by Prohibition to close down, set up clandestine bars known as "**speakeasies**" and received their supplies from these gangs.

Police, customs officials, and Treasury agents pursued distillers and bootleggers, with little success. Gang leaders like Al Capone in Chicago bribed police and politicians to look the other way when alcohol shipments were coming into town. But bribery didn't always persuade public officials, and those who resisted bribes were often victims of intimidation and even murder.

A large part of the urban middle class found that, despite the problems associated with alcohol, the idea of *never* having a drink was generally unbearable. Novelist Sinclair Lewis described in his satiric novel *Babbitt* (1922) how a generally law-abiding real estate salesman went about preparing for a dinner party at his home. First he enters "a place curiously like the saloons of ante-prohibition days."

Admitted to a back room, he persuades the owner to sell him a quart of gin, then mixes cocktails at home before his guests arrive. They are all longing for a drink and are delighted when he asks, "Well, folks, do you think you could stand breaking the law a little?" After a couple of drinks each, the men declare that they favor Prohibition as "a mighty good thing for the working class" because it "keeps 'em from wasting their money and lowering their productiveness." But they add that Congress has interfered with "the rights—the personal liberty—of fellows like ourselves," for whom a drink could do no harm.

After fifteen contentious and tumultuous years, Prohibition was repealed in 1933, with the Twenty-first Amendment.

> **❝Well, folks, do you think you could stand breaking the law a little?❞**
> —*George F. Babbitt, in Sinclair Lewis's* Babbitt

# LO³ A New Culture: The Roaring Twenties

With the economy seemingly good, radical politics largely on the run, and national politics not terribly interesting, many Americans turned to a vast array of leisure activities. New technology, including moviemaking equipment, phonographic records, and expanded commercial radio, enhanced a vibrant social atmosphere, especially in the nation's cities. The "Roaring Twenties," as they were sometimes called, witnessed a dramatic expansion of popular culture. However, this interest in lighter fare led some to political and intellectual disillusionment, based on the sense that Americans were leaving behind the ideals of the Progressive era in favor of less socially engaged interests. Others were more interested in using culture to break stifling bonds of long-standing restrictions. African Americans, women, and leftist intellectuals were some of the groups pushing against the old social limitations.

## 1920s Popular Culture

In the 1920s breakthroughs in several media allowed the public to enjoy new diversions.

### Movies

Thomas Edison and other inventors had developed moving films at the turn of the century. After a slow

John W. Considine, Jr. presents
RUDOLPH VALENTINO in "The Son of the Sheik"
a Sequel to The Sheik
with VILMA BANKY
from the novel by E. M. HULL · Adapted to the Screen by FRANCES MARION
A GEORGE FITZMAURICE PRODUCTION
· UNITED ARTISTS PICTURE ·

B. DeMille and D. W. Griffith, replaced the melodramas of the 1910s. Urban movie houses were built and decorated like oriental palaces, far more lavish than they needed to be to show movies. This gave patrons, who regularly arrived in their best clothes, a sense of glamour and enchantment on their night out. Moviegoing was wildly popular, and stars such as Rudolph Valentino, Clara Bow, Mary Pickford, and Douglas Fairbanks Sr. enjoyed worldwide fame.

**jazz**
Rhythmic music derived as part of African American culture and popularized by both white and black musicians during the 1920s

**phonograph**
Invention that played recorded music; pioneered by Edison in the 1870s

 Read a classic, contemporary account of the impact of movies on viewers.

## Music

Along with the movies, **jazz** music came into vogue during the 1920s. Originally derived as part of African American culture, jazz followed ragtime music by "crossing over" to white audiences during the 1920s. Most jazz stars of the 1920s were black men such as pianist Duke Ellington and trumpeter Louis Armstrong, some of the first African Americans to have enthusiastic white fans. Before the 1920s, Americans who wanted to listen to jazz (or any other kind of music) had had to create their own sounds or attend a concert. The invention of the **phonograph**, pioneered by Edison in the 1870s and popularized in the first years of the 1900s, birthed the record industry. This enabled fans to listen to their favorite artists on their gramophones as many times as they wanted.

Furthermore, commercial radio began broadcasting in 1922, allowing people everywhere to hear concerts being played hundreds of miles away. That same year, Warren Harding became the first president to make a radio broadcast. Among the earliest groups to make use of the new medium were evangelical preachers. While they insisted on old, established virtues, they had no objection to using newfangled methods such as radio to help them spread the Gospel.

## Professional Sports

Radio promoted an interest in professional and college sports in the

couple of years, films caught on in the 1910s, and by 1920 a film industry had developed in Hollywood, California, where there was plenty of open space, three hundred sunny days a year for outdoor filming, and 3,000 miles between it and Edison's patents. Far away in California, ignoring the patents, which had made most of the top-quality moviemaking equipment very expensive, was relatively easy.

Once established in Hollywood, the movie industry made a series of artistic and technical breakthroughs that popularized the art form throughout the nation. Most exciting was the invention of talking pictures, which first appeared in 1927 with *The Jazz Singer*. At the same time, longer feature films with sophisticated plotting, by directors such as Cecil

> " Go to a motion picture . . . and let yourself go. . . . Out of the cage of everyday existence! If only for an afternoon or an evening— escape! "
> —*Saturday Evening Post, 1923*

1920s, especially baseball, boxing, and college football. Listeners could get real-time play-by-play, hearing the actions of their favorite local team or boxer. The increased popularity of sports during the 1920s made celebrities out of the best players, the biggest of whom was the New York Yankees' slugger Babe Ruth.

## Fads, Triumphs, and Sex Scandals

Games such as bridge and mah-jongg became popular during these years, and a national craze for crossword puzzles began. The nation took pleasure in reading about the first flight over the North Pole by Admiral Byrd in 1926 and the first trans-Atlantic flight by Charles Lindbergh in 1927.

Lindbergh became an international celebrity because of his aviation triumphs.

Americans enjoyed a steady stream of celebrity sex scandals too, like the one surrounding the disappearance of radio evangelist Aimee Semple McPherson in 1926. A theatrical preacher who had built up a radio audience and constructed an auditorium called the "Angelus Temple" in Hollywood, she disappeared while bathing in the sea in 1926. Disciples, finding her clothes on the beach, feared that "Sister Aimee" had drowned. She reappeared a few weeks later, claiming that she had been abducted and imprisoned in Mexico, had broken free, crossed the desert on foot, and daringly evaded her kidnappers. Investigators knocked holes in the story almost at once, especially when evidence from Carmel, farther up the California coast, showed that she had been enjoying herself in a love nest with an engineer from her own radio station. The widespread interest in this type of gossip-column fare was typical of a carefree, apolitical era.

## The "New Negro"

African American jazz musicians blossomed as the musical facet of a larger ferment among African Americans in the 1920s, known collectively as the **Harlem Renaissance**. Following the First World War and the race riots that followed, many African Americans had grown frustrated with America's entrenched racism and became motivated to challenge the prevailing order. They sought to establish themselves as different from their parents' generation, which they saw as unnecessarily kowtowing to white interests in an effort to advance through accommodation. Instead, the younger generation of African Americans declared it would rather "die fighting" than be further subjugated in American society. This new generation epitomized what one Harlem Renaissance leader, the philosopher Alain Locke, called "the new Negro."

Despite its seemingly political goals, the Harlem Renaissance was mostly a literary celebration, as prominent authors like Langston Hughes and Zora Neale Hurston emerged under its auspices. As African Americans moved north to escape sharecropping and the social segregation of the South, many headed to the large northern cities. No neighborhood grew more than Harlem, which was by real estate code the only large neighborhood in New York City where black people could live as a group.

Copyright © The Granger Collection, New York/The Granger Collection

>> Aaron Douglass was one of the most prominent visual artists of the Harlem Renaissance, creating images full of life and energy, and that often harkened back to Africa, giving pride and a foundation to a people often thought to be rootless.

Several intellectuals, such as W. E. B. Du Bois and James Weldon Johnson, sought to politicize the growing number of urban black people, although few leaders had much luck organizing politically. The NAACP, meanwhile, pursued a legal strategy to end forced segregation in America's cities. Throughout much of the twentieth century, the NAACP brought these challenges to America's courts, forcing the court system to evaluate the segregation that persisted in the United States. Whether the courts were willing to confront and overturn segregation was another matter altogether.

## Marcus Garvey

The Harlem Renaissance was not a political movement, though, and the legal strategies of the NAACP were unlikely to provoke a social movement. Marcus Garvey occupied this vacuum. The first black nationalist leader to foment a broad movement in the United States, Garvey founded the **Universal Negro Improvement Association** in 1914 and moved its headquarters to Harlem in 1916. Through parades, brightly colored uniforms, and a flamboyant style of leadership, Garvey advocated a celebration of blackness, the creation of black-owned and operated businesses, and the dream of a return of all black people to Africa. Indeed, he created his own line of steamships, the "Black Star Line," with the intention of tying together black-owned businesses in Africa, the Caribbean, and the United States. His organization won over more than 1 million members worldwide, although most mainstream American politicians ignored him. More damningly, the antipathy he suffered from other African American civil rights workers curtailed his power further. He suffered a harsh decline in the early 1920s, indicted for mail fraud while selling stock in the Black Star Line, and, in 1927, he was deported back to Jamaica, his birthplace.

On a variety of fronts, black urbanites were struggling to locate their political and cultural voice. These members of the Great Migration became vividly aware that racism did not stop north of the Mason-Dixon line.

## Changing Roles for Women

Women won the right to vote with the Nineteenth Amendment in 1920, one of the final great reforms of the Progressive era. The first election in which they voted put Harding into office. Many people expected the amendment to have dramatic consequences in national politics, but the female vote was actually split evenly between the candidates. Rather than swaying the balance in any one direction, unmarried women generally voted the same as their fathers, and married women generally voted the same as their husbands.

Winning the vote marked the triumphant end of a long and frequently bitter campaign. Suffragists had hoped to transform politics for the better. They imagined national politics as a locale where deals were brokered by unscrupulous groups of men in smoke-filled back rooms, and they intended to bring politics into the light of day and bring morality to bear on politics. In light of the corruption scandals of the Harding administration (namely, Teapot Dome), winning the vote had not achieved this, so now what were activists to do?

## ERA

Many activists turned their attention to economics and the job market. At the urging of Alice Paul, a former suffragist and now head of the **National Women's Party** (a political lobbying coalition founded in 1913), a group of congressmen proposed an **Equal Rights Amendment** to the Constitution in 1923. It read: "Men and women shall have equal rights throughout the United States and every place subject to its jurisdiction." The amendment's objective was to eliminate all legal distinctions between the sexes, such as those that permitted different pay scales for men and women doing the same job. Some women, especially trade unionists, opposed the amendment because it would have nullified laws that protected mothers and working women from harsh working conditions and excessively long hours. Congress did not approve the amendment until 1972, and then the necessary three-quarters of the states did not ratify it. In the years since, however, its equal-pay provision has become law.

## The "New" Woman

If the political successes largely stopped in 1920, the rest of the 1920s witnessed the development

**Universal Negro Improvement Association** Marcus Garvey's black nationalist fraternal organization that advocated a celebration of blackness, the creation of black-owned and –operated businesses, and the dream of a return of all black people to Africa

**National Women's Party** Political lobbying coalition founded in 1913 that promoted women's right to vote and to share political and economic equality

**Equal Rights Amendment** Proposed amendment to the Constitution meant to eliminate all legal distinctions between the sexes, such as those that permitted different pay scales for men and women doing the same job

> > "Flappers" were the decade's outspoken, independent women.

© Burke/Triolo/Brand X Pictures/Jupiterimages

of a distinct youth culture, especially among young single women. New fashions, notably short "bobbed" hair, knee-length dresses that seemed daringly short, public smoking, and dance crazes such as the Charleston all generated controversy. "Flappers" were the decade's outspoken, independent women, who scorned the "Victorian" inhibitions of their parents' generation. F. Scott Fitzgerald's *This Side of Paradise* (1920) and *The Beautiful and the Damned* (1922) evoked the cosmopolitanism of the era, especially its changing attitudes toward unchaperoned courtship and "petting." Margaret Sanger promoted the liberalizing culture of the 1920s as the leading advocate for birth control (a phrase she coined) and planned parenthood. Sanger became a touchstone for women's rights in the period, lecturing all over the United States and Europe. There are several reasons why the Protestant morality that had dominated American mores throughout the second half of the nineteenth century came under assault in the early twentieth century (see "The reasons why . . ." box).

## Disillusioned Writers, Liberalizing Mores

The 1920s also saw the coming of age of American literature. An influential group of writers, including poets T. S. Eliot and Ezra Pound and novelists John Dos Passos, Ernest Hemingway, and Gertrude Stein, found commercial America vulgar—so distasteful

## {*The reasons why . . .*}

There were at least four reasons why Protestant morality came under assault in the first decades of the twentieth century:

*Loss of biblical authority.* Charles Darwin's theory of evolution, which questioned the authenticity of the biblical story of creation, and therefore the Bible as a whole, was widely accepted in the second half of the nineteenth century. At the same time, European historians and intellectuals were developing a school of biblical criticism that examined the Bible as a historical artifact worthy of investigation rather than a book of revealed divine truth. The loss of biblical authority unmoored many people's beliefs in Christian morality, and in Christianity in general.

*Decline of universal morality.* At the same time, anthropologists and sociologists like Franz Boas and Robert Park began arguing that other cultures were not any less valuable or moral than white Protestant culture, just different from it. There were, these thinkers argued, no hierarchies of races or hierarchies of moral authority. If the value of a particular cultural was relative based on one's perception, this meant that any notion of universal morals was highly questionable as well.

*Psychology.* Meanwhile, psychologists like Sigmund Freud placed sexual desires at the heart of human urges, making sex a legitimate topic of discussion, indeed, a necessary one if someone wanted to learn the various drives that make one human. Sex was no longer an act to be held under wraps, but one worthy of exploration and even trial and error.

*Consumerism.* Nothing sells better than sex, a fact not missed by the new generation of advertising agents and marketers. At the same time, greater freedoms promoted by inventions like automobiles made it easier to escape the watchful gaze of parents. Meanwhile, movies promoted scintillating images of love and lust as well as valor and honor, at the same time providing a darkened environment for viewers, perhaps hand-in-hand, to enjoy these new images.

that they declined to participate altogether. They went to Europe, usually to London and Paris, where they formed intellectual expatriate communities. But in their self-exile they remained preoccupied by their American roots and wrote some of the most effective American literature of their age. Together, the writers of the 1920s are referred to as "the Lost Generation," mainly because of their disillusionment with the Progressive ideals that had been exposed as fraudulent during the First World War.

Other fine writers felt no desire to flee. Sinclair Lewis produced a long stream of satirical novels about 1920s America that won him a Nobel Prize for literature in 1930, America's first. Literary critic Malcolm Cowley, himself a Paris expatriate in the 1920s, observed that American literature was maturing rapidly and that "by 1930 it had come to be valued for itself and studied like Spanish or German or Russian literature. There were now professors of American literature at the great European universities. American plays, lowbrow and highbrow, were being applauded in the European capitals." It is, of course, ironic that most of the American writers of this formative period made their mark by deriding mainstream America for its jocularity. Their own erudition contradicted their claims that America was anti-intellectual.

# LO⁴ Reactions

With all these changes swirling around, many Americans felt uncomfortable with what they saw as the liberal mores of the youth culture and the diminishing of community life prompted by the Industrial Revolution. Some of these dissenters found a home in Protestant fundamentalism. Others rejected what they viewed as an increasing acceptance of cosmopolitanism and moral relativity. If the 1920s were an age of social and intellectual liberation, they also gave birth to new forms of reaction that created a clash of values.

## Religious Divisions

Protestants have always been denominationally divided, but in the 1920s, a split between modernists and fundamentalists became readily apparent, leading to a landmark court case.

## Modernists

On the one hand, a group of Protestants calling themselves **modernists** consciously sought to adapt their Protestant faith to the findings of scientific theories such as evolution and evidence that called into question the literalness of the Bible, something called Biblical criticism. As these twin impulses became increasingly accepted by scholars, some liberal Protestants stopped thinking of the Bible as God's infallible word. Instead, they regarded it as a collection of ancient writings, some of them historical, some prophetic, and some mythological. In the modernists' view, represented in the writings of the notable preacher Harry Emerson Fosdick, God did not *literally* make the world in six days, Adam and Eve weren't *actual* people, and there was no *real* flood covering the whole Earth. Men like Fosdick contended that these events were mythic explanations of human origins. Jesus was as central as ever, the divine figure standing at the center of history and transforming it, but Jesus would surely encourage his people to learn modern science and comparative religion, and to focus on other studies that enriched their knowledge of God's world and spread peace and tolerance far and wide. Not to do so was to be intolerant, and this was no way to act in a pluralistic world.

## Fundamentalists

On the other hand, the group of Protestants who have come to be known as **fundamentalists** (after the publication in the 1910s of a series of pamphlets labeled "the Fundamentals") insisted that the Bible should be understood as God's revealed word, absolutely true down to the last detail. In their view, the main points of traditional Christian doctrine, including biblical inerrancy, the reality of miracles, and the Virgin birth, must be asserted and upheld. Most fundamentalists were troubled by evolution, not only because it denied the literal truth of Genesis but also because it implied that humans, evolving from lower species, were the outcome of random mutations, rather than a creation of God in His own image. Traveling evangelists such as Billy Sunday, an ex–major league baseball player, and Aimee Semple McPherson denounced evolution and all other deviations from the Gospel as the Devil's work. They also attacked the ethos of the social gospel (for more on the social gospel, see Chapter 20).

**modernists**
Protestants who consciously sought to adapt their Protestant faith to the findings of scientific theories, such as evolution and evidence that questioned the literalness of the Bible

**fundamentalists**
Protestants who insisted that the Bible should be understood as God's revealed word, absolutely true down to the last detail; they asserted and upheld the main points of traditional Christian doctrine, including biblical inerrancy, the reality of miracles, and the Virgin birth

Read transcripts from the Scopes trial.

 Read H. L. Mencken's account of the Scopes trial.

## Scopes Monkey Trial

In 1925, the conflict between modernists and fundamentalists came to a head in Dayton, Tennessee, in the **Scopes Monkey Trial**. The case revolved around a state law that prohibited the teaching of evolution in Tennessee schools. John Scopes, a young teacher, offered to deliberately break the law to test its constitutionality (in order to obtain publicity for this struggling "New South" town) with the understanding that the **American Civil Liberties Union (ACLU)** would pay the costs to defend him. The trial drew journalists from all over America and was one of the first great media circuses of the century.

At the trial, the nation's most prominent defense lawyer, Clarence Darrow, volunteered to help Scopes. William Jennings Bryan, the three-time Democratic presidential candidate and former secretary of state, volunteered to assist the prosecution. Darrow, an agnostic, actually called Bryan as a witness for the defense and questioned him about the origins of the Earth. Did not the geological evidence prove the immense age of its rocks? asked Darrow. "I'm not interested in the age of rocks but in the Rock of Ages!" countered Bryan, who believed the Earth was about 6,000 years old. Scopes was convicted (the conviction was later overturned on a technicality) and fined $100, and the law against teaching evolution remained in effect. Press coverage, by urbane journalists such as H. L. Mencken and Joseph Wood Krutch, ridiculed the anti-evolutionists, but fundamentalism continued to dominate rural Protestantism, especially in the South and Midwest.

## Immigration Restriction and Quotas

If modern mores were one cause of fear, another was the transformation provoked by immigration.

>> Clarence Darrow and William Jennings Bryan provided the spectacle of the season in 1925's "Scopes Monkey Trial."

As we have seen in chapters past, millions of immigrants entered the United States between 1880 and 1920, and in the early 1920s many congressmen and social observers articulated a fear that the "Anglo-Saxon" heritage of the United States was being "mongrelized" by "swarthy" Europeans. These Europeans (Italians, Russians, or Greeks or other people from southern and eastern Europe) would be considered white by today's standards, but they were viewed as "others" during the 1920s because they were Catholics or Jews from countries in eastern and southern Europe, and they spoke foreign languages and cooked odd-smelling foods.

## Immigration Restrictions

The ideology undergirding the fears of American politicians was the idea of **Americanization**. This was defined as the notion that all American immigrant groups should leave behind their old ways and melt into the Anglo-Saxon mainstream. Some intellectuals were challenging this idea through concepts like the **melting pot** (in which all the nation's people contributed their cultural traits to a single mix, creating something altogether new) and **cultural pluralism** (the idea that each cultural group should retain its uniqueness and not be forced to change by a restrictive state or culture).

Despite the power of these countervailing ideas, acts of Congress in 1921 (the Quota Act) and

View the quotas established for all countries.

 Read a congressman's denunciation of quotas.

1924 (the **National Origins Act**) restricted the number of immigrants permitted to enter the United States, creating a series of quotas. These limits were based on immigration figures from the end of the nineteenth century, when most immigrants were from England, Ireland, or northern Europe. These actions appeased the widespread fear of the alien during these years, at a time when antisemitism, anti-Catholicism, nativism, and racism meaningfully influenced the ideas and positions of serious politicians and public figures.

One major result of the new immigration policy was that Italian, Polish, Hungarian, and Jewish communities no longer received a steady flow of "greenhorns" to keep them in touch with the old country. Instead, these communities gradually dissolved as their members learned English in public schools and followed work and housing opportunities into non–ethnically defined neighborhoods. This process of dissolution was mostly completed by the 1950s.

## Quotas

Reflecting Congress's implementation of quotas, many colleges and universities, especially in the Northeast, began instituting quotas to limit the number of Jews who could attend. Social fraternities and housing developments limited membership by racial and religious restrictions, and most attempts to circumvent these restrictions were met with violence. The boosterism and "pep" of the 1920s extended only so far. For many Americans, the national narrative only concerned the advancement of white, Anglo-Saxon Protestants.

## Social Intolerance

Perhaps unsurprisingly, along with immigration restriction a new nativism emerged in response to all the economic and social changes taking place. Immigration restriction was one arm of this nativism, and other aspects emerged as well.

### The Resurgence of the Klan

The **Ku Klux Klan**, an organization formed to "redeem" the South after Reconstruction, enjoyed a revival in the 1920s after being reborn in a ceremony on Georgia's Stone Mountain in 1915. Attesting to the power of movies during this era, the Klan's resurgence was in part inspired by the positive portrayal it received in D. W. Griffith's three-hour film *Birth of a Nation*. This movie is often considered the most influential in American film history for its innovative techniques and sweeping dramatic arc—despite the fact that it was overtly racist and lionized the Klan. The Klan of the 1920s saw itself as the embodiment of old Protestant and southern virtues. In this new era, the Klan enlisted members in the North as well, especially in cities, thus reemerging in response to the new urban culture of the 1920s, which it blamed on immigrants. Hiram Wesley Evans, a Texas dentist, was the Klan's Imperial Wizard during these years. He declared he was pledged to defend decency and Americanism from numerous threats: race-mixing, Jews, Catholics, and the immoralities of urban sophistication.

The Klan was mainly anti-Catholic in northern and western states. For instance, Klan members won election to the legislature in Oregon and then outlawed private schools for all children ages eight to

**National Origins Act**
Legislation that restricted the number of immigrants permitted to enter the United States, creating a series of quotas in 1924

**Ku Klux Klan**
A paramilitary organization formed to "redeem" the South after Reconstruction by intimidating newly freed blacks; after a temporary decline, the group reformed in 1915

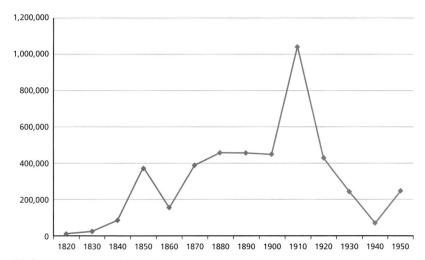

**Number of immigrants entering the United States, 1820–1950**

>> After peaking during the first two decades of the twentieth century, the immigration restriction laws of the 1920s led to a precipitous decline in the number of foreigners coming to the United States.

sixteen. This was meant to attack the Catholic parochial school system that had been established in response to the overt Protestantism taught in public schools in the 1800s. Oregon's Catholics fought back, eventually battling to the U.S. Supreme Court, which, in the case of *Pierce v. Society of Sisters* (1925), upheld the Catholic Church's right to run its own school system.

This second wave of Klan activity came to a highly publicized end when one of the organization's leaders, David (D. C.) Stephenson, was convicted of the abduction, rape, and second-degree murder of a woman who ran a literacy program in Indiana. When Indiana governor Ed Jackson refused to commute his sentence in 1927, Stephenson released the names of several politicians who had been on the Klan's payroll, leading to the indictments of many politicians, including the governor, for accepting bribes. Both the Klan and several Indiana politicians were shamed in the debacle.

## The Election of 1928

The multitude of changes during the 1920s and the variety of reactions against them were symbolized by the candidates in the presidential election of 1928. The election pitted the Democrat Al Smith against Republican Herbert Hoover. Hoover was idealized as a nonpolitical problem solver and an advocate of big business. He represented the freewheeling Republican values of the 1920s and also epitomized America's Anglo-Saxon Protestant heritage. Smith, meanwhile, was the Democratic governor of New York and the first Catholic to be nominated for president by one of the major parties. He represented the surging tide of social change. Although no radical, he was known to be a friend of the immigrant and a supporter of civil liberties and Progressive-era social welfare.

During the election, the major issue dividing the two men was Prohibition. That issue also symbolized the clash of values that had surfaced in American life in the 1920s: Hoover represented the rural and Protestant population that advocated and understood the reasons for Prohibition, while Smith represented the ethnic and urban groups who viewed it as restrictive and racist. Although Smith had a surprisingly strong showing in every large city, Hoover won in a landslide (see Map 22.1).

# And in the end . . .

The Democrats, with their hodgepodge of supporters, were on the rise, but as yet they lacked an issue that would propel them to power. That issue

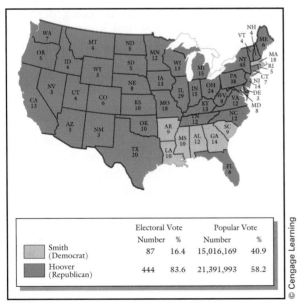

|  | Electoral Vote | | Popular Vote | |
|---|---|---|---|---|
|  | Number | % | Number | % |
| Smith (Democrat) | 87 | 16.4 | 15,016,169 | 40.9 |
| Hoover (Republican) | 444 | 83.6 | 21,391,993 | 58.2 |

© Cengage Learning

Map 22.1. The Election of 1928

## What else was happening . . .

| 1920 | Harry Burt, a Youngstown, Ohio, candy maker, sells first ice cream on a stick, the Good Humor bar. |
|---|---|
| 1922 | The Union of Soviet Socialist Republics is formed after communists take power in the Russian Revolution of 1917. |
| 1925 | Yale students invent the Frisbee while tossing empty pie plates from the Frisbie Baking Company. |
| 1927 | The first words are heard in a motion picture: "Wait a minute! You ain't heard nothing yet!" (*The Jazz Singer*) |
| 1929 | Color television pictures are transmitted in New York. |
| 1929 | Museum of Modern Art opens in New York City, celebrating the birth of modern art that developed alongside the Industrial Revolution. |

emerged quickly. In October 1929, the stock market, rising steadily from 1925 to mid-1929, began a steep drop. On October 29, later known as "Black Tuesday," 16 million shares changed hands and countless stocks lost almost all of their value. During the next three years, the supply of capital flowing into the economy contracted sharply, dozens of businesses went bankrupt, factories with inventory closed down, and growing numbers of men and women lost their jobs. Complex problems in the American and international economy meant that the crash wasn't just one of the periodic "adjustments" the market always experiences, but something much more

serious: an economic depression that would affect the entire world for a decade. The Great Depression would cause Democratic landslides throughout the 1930s, which saw the rise of Franklin D. Roosevelt as president and his New Deal plan of social action. It is to the Great Depression that we turn next.

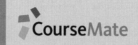

Visit the CourseMate website at www.cengagebrain.com for additional study tools and review materials for this chapter.

# The Great Depression and the New Deal

## Learning Outcomes

*After reading this chapter, you should be able to do the following:*

LO **1** Explain the underlying causes of the depression, and evaluate President Hoover's attempts to help the economy.

LO **2** Describe the experiences of both urban and rural Americans during the depression, and explain ways in which the depression affected American politics.

LO **3** Evaluate FDR's actions designed to alleviate the effects of the depression, and discuss the opposition he faced.

LO **4** Discuss the most significant long-term effects of the New Deal.

> **"***In the 1920s, many things seemed possible. Now the hurdles seemed insurmountable. Fear overcame hope.***"**

In 1928, when Herbert Hoover defeated Al Smith for the presidency, Hoover had every reason to believe that the future of the country was bright. In his Inaugural Address, he expressed his belief that the United States was "rich in resources; stimulating in its glorious beauty; filled with millions of happy homes; blessed with comfort and opportunity." He later said, "We in America today are nearer to the final triumph over poverty than ever before in any land in history. The poorhouse is vanishing from among us." Just eight months after his inauguration, Hoover was facing a very different situation. The stock market had crashed, the bottom had fallen out of an already weakened housing market, the markets for agricultural goods stalled, demand for consumer goods fell precipitously leading factories to slow production, and the United States entered into the Great Depression.

The Great Depression caused massive unemployment and declining wages. People lost their homes, their savings, their aspirations, and their dreams. The poorest faced the literal threat of starvation. Breadlines became common. Nearly one in four working Americans was out of work, and in some cities it was nearly every other person.

The Great Depression affected people's everyday lives in ways that are hard to describe. Americans were terrified of succumbing to a disaster they did not understand. In the 1920s, many things seemed possible. You were sure that if you worked hard you would have a job, and maybe even prosper. Now the hurdles seemed insurmountable. Colleges and universities produced year after year of graduates with little to no prospects for jobs. The birth rate declined. In an effort to increase the prices by limiting the amount of goods that reached markets, farmers in Iowa, Indiana, and elsewhere destroyed livestock and let milk rot, all while many urban dwellers teetered on the edge of starvation. Even Babe Ruth took a significant pay cut. Fear overcame hope. In the end, hope was revived before the economy was. The election of Franklin D. Roosevelt in 1932 inaugurated a new era of social and economic experimentation. Under Roosevelt's guidance, a "New Deal" of government intervention into the economy and everyday lives of Americans attempted to rein in the economic collapse. This chapter examines the causes and effects of the Great Depression before turning to Franklin D. Roosevelt's attempts to control them.

## What do you think?

**The New Deal did not end the Great Depression.**

| Strongly Disagree | | | | | | Strongly Agree |
|---|---|---|---|---|---|---|
| 1 | 2 | 3 | 4 | 5 | 6 | 7 |

# LO¹ The Economics and Politics of Depression

 Work with an interactive stock market module. There was no single cause of the Great Depression. Instead, a series of events combined to cause the economic crisis (see "The reasons why . . ." box).

## Statistics

The stock market crash and the collapsing world economy pushed the United States into the deepest economic decline in its history. The simplest of statistics explain the disaster: Between 1929 and 1933, about 9,000 banks closed. Business investments in industrial construction declined from $23.3 billion in 1929 to $10.1 billion in 1932. The automobile industry's earnings dropped 40 percent between 1929 and 1930. Between 1929 and 1932, the United States's gross national product declined from $103.1

## { The reasons why . . . }

### Three events were of paramount importance in causing the Great Depression:

**The stock market crash.**
Throughout the 1920s, the stock market seemed to reflect the strength of the U.S. economy, and stock investments increased dramatically. In part, this growth reflected the expansion of business profits during the 1920s. In addition, the federal government reduced taxes during the 1920s (especially for the wealthy), putting more money in the pockets of investors. But the most important factor affecting the rise of the stock market was credit. The most common form of credit for stock purchases was the **call loan**, which allowed a stock buyer to put down anywhere from 10 to 50 percent of a stock's price and borrow the rest of the money in order to make the full payment. The lender could then "call back" the loan and demand repayment when a stock fell below a certain price. By the end of 1928, there was nearly $8 billion in outstanding call loans.

When, in September 1929, the Federal Reserve Board raised interest rates, a move they hoped would prevent overspeculation in the stock market, banks cut back on lending because costs had increased. With less money available for loans, fewer people were buying stock, so stock prices began to fall. After a slight recovery of prices in late September, the market collapsed. Journalists and social watchers had begun to spread the word that the economic bubble was about to burst, prompting a selling frenzy. By early November, stock values had decreased an unimaginable $26 billion, more than a third of what the stock market's value had been in August. It would only get worse during the next two years. When the stock market finally stabilized in 1932, stocks had lost nearly 90 percent of their value.

**Internal weaknesses in the American economy.**
The stock market crash compounded existing problems within the American economy. The agricultural sector had been in a severe depression since the early 1920s. The industrial sector, including the

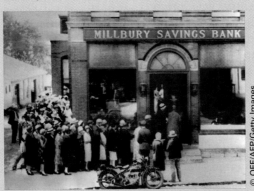
>> **Run on a bank, 1929.**

© OFF/AFP/Getty Images

vital home construction and automobile industries, was beginning to slow down from its amazing growth in the previous decade. If these markets had been strong, the nation's economy would not have been as vulnerable to the decline of the stock market. Instead, because so much of the 1920s boom was attributable to consumption, when people stopped buying goods the economy ground to a halt.

**The European economy.** The third reason had to do with problems in Europe. The economies of Britain, France, and Germany experienced problems similar to the United States's in the late 1920s: declining industrial production, low prices in agriculture, and overspeculation in the stock market. But the biggest problem stemmed from the end of World War I, when the Treaty of Versailles forced Germany to pay back the costs of the war. These reparations were difficult for Germany to pay back because the war had destroyed its industrial infrastructure.

The solution came from U.S. banks. In order to pay the reparations, Germany borrowed from American banks. Britain and France, in turn, used that money to repay the debts they had incurred during the war, most often to the U.S. government. The United States was sending money to Germany, which was giving it to France and Britain, which were sending it back to the United States. This cycle of debt, though very unstable, was supported by U.S. businesses because the borrowed funds also allowed European countries to buy U.S. products.

When the stock market crashed, this system fell apart. U.S. businesses that had lost money in the crash cut back on production and stopped buying products from European countries. In addition, after the crash U.S. banks wanted their debts repaid. This was impossible. When European countries couldn't pay back those loans and U.S. banks began to fail, the economic decline of both the United States and other countries became worse.

billion to $58 billion. The national unemployment rate skyrocketed from 3.2 percent in 1929 to nearly 25 percent in 1933. In some areas, the rate was even higher: In Detroit, for example, unemployment was more than 50 percent in the early 1930s. When people lost money, they could not buy products, forcing industries to slow production and lay off workers, which left even fewer consumers.

## Hoover

Naturally, most Americans looked to the president to solve the national crisis. But Hoover had a difficult time. One of his first efforts to help American businesses proved to be the most ruinous. In June 1930, Hoover signed the **Hawley-Smoot Tariff** (named for the congressmen who helped write the legislation). The bill raised American tariffs on foreign agricultural and manufactured goods by as much as 50 percent.

Hoover believed that raising prices on foreign products would protect American products from competition. But the effect was disastrous. European governments, already saddled with debts, were further damaged because the bill hurt their ability to earn money to pay back World War I debts. Furthermore, these nations retaliated with very high tariffs of their own, making it difficult for American businesses to sell their products overseas.

Despite the disastrous consequences of the Hawley-Smoot Tariff, Hoover was still hesitant to use the federal government to help Americans directly. He believed that citizens, businesses, and the government should work together voluntarily to overcome the

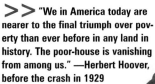

>> "We in America today are nearer to the final triumph over poverty than ever before in any land in history. The poor-house is vanishing from among us." —Herbert Hoover, before the crash in 1929

Library of Congress, Prints & Photographs Division, National Photo Company Collection, LC-DIG-npcc-03577

depression, instead of being rescued through government-mandated programs. He thus formulated policies based on his idea of voluntary cooperation, which held that business leaders would make sacrifices for the benefit of the nation. But in both farming and banking, the idea of voluntary cooperation failed to stabilize the troubled industries. Simply asking industry leaders and laborers to sacrifice for the good of the country was not going to be enough.

Hoover had better luck providing some relief to the unemployed. But again, he relied most heavily on voluntary organizations. Unemployed workers, the Red Cross, and church groups came together to offer surplus food to those in need. The Unemployed Citizen's League in Seattle, for instance, created a system whereby people could exchange work for food, clothing, and other goods.

Responding to perpetual public pressure, Hoover pledged some federal funds to assist the problem. He nearly doubled the budget for public works expenditures, which funded the Hoover Dam, one of the largest government construction projects ever undertaken. He also established the President's Organization on Unemployment Relief (POUR), which persuaded local organizations across the country to raise money and to form voluntary groups that would sponsor soup kitchens and clothing exchanges.

But Hoover's belief that the federal government should not come to the aid of its citizens elicited a stern rebuke from the population. In the depths of the Great Depression, relying on volunteerism was not enough.

### Hoover the Candidate for Reelection

Running for reelection, Hoover realized that he needed to do more to ease people's financial woes. In January 1932, he established the Reconstruction Finance Corporation (RFC). The RFC was a federally funded agency that loaned money to businesses with the hope that they would hire more workers. The RFC also

> **call loan**
> Most common form of credit for stock purchases; allowed a stock buyer to put down from 10 to 50 percent of a stock's price and borrow the rest of the money in order to make the full payment; the lender could then "call back" the loan and demand repayment when a stock fell below a certain price

> **Hawley-Smoot Tariff**
> Bill passed in 1930 that raised American tariffs on foreign agricultural and manufactured goods by as much as 50 percent; triggered European retaliation

>> Shantytowns like this one in New York appeared in parks in cities throughout the nation, earning the derisive nickname "Hoovervilles."

>> The Hoover Dam.

**Hooverville**
Popular name for a shantytown built by homeless Americans during the Great Depression

provided loans to states to undertake public projects such as buildings and roads.

But Hoover's plan, ambitious as it was, still didn't help the average American quickly enough. The RFC's cautious approach defeated its purpose of helping as many companies as possible. No matter what Hoover did, the Great Depression seemed hopeless to most Americans.

# LO² The Depression Experience in America

Numbers tell only part of the story of the Great Depression. The experiences of millions of Americans suffering in terrible conditions between the late 1920s and the early 1930s tell the rest. As hundreds of thousands of people in the nation's urban areas grappled with homelessness, rural America was pounded by a series of environmental catastrophes that made the situation even worse and exposed the fact that the government seemed powerless.

## Urban America

City life during the depression was a stark contrast to the carefree 1920s. In many places, homeless Americans built makeshift towns on the outskirts of cities and in abandoned lots and parks. They derisively nicknamed these towns "**Hoovervilles**" after the president. These people built homes from abandoned cardboard boxes, scrap lumber and metal, and anything else they could find to devise shelter. In some places, Hoovervilles grew enormous. For many it was the only alternative to living on the street.

Hoovervilles existed in virtually all of the nation's cities, but homelessness was a problem much larger than a few shantytowns. By 1932, there were an estimated 250,000 homeless children in the country. The homeless problem was far greater than even these numbers indicate, because people living in Hoovervilles were usually not counted as "homeless."

### African American Neighborhoods

In these hard times, African Americans suffered more than urban white people. African American neighborhoods were often already in a depressed state before the stock market crash, as business slowdowns and other signs of a weak economy in the 1920s hurt black communities first. In many communities, African Americans were routinely the "last hired and first fired" for jobs. Thus, even before the depression hit Chicago's South Side, home to

236,000 African Americans, all the banks and businesses in the neighborhood had already closed.

Many African American communities turned to self-help as the best way to survive. In Harlem, Father Divine led his Divine Peace Mission and created a network of businesses, church groups, and self-help organizations, enabling him to serve over 3,000 meals a day to the destitute and homeless in the neighborhood. Community members in Harlem began a campaign against white shop owners and building owners who charged too much for consumer goods and rent. The agitation led to the establishment of the Consolidated Tenants League (which organized strikes against landlords who charged too much rent) and the Harlem Boycott of 1934 (which discouraged consumers from purchasing products at white-owned stores).

 Read a brief contemporary history of depression-era Harlem.

## Hunger

In the cities, many suffered from hunger. Although the country's farms produced plenty of food, the lack of funds to support commercial transportation prevented most food from reaching urban marketplaces. **Breadlines** formed in all of America's cities. Hunger triggered a number of problems in the nation's cities, ranging from malnourishment to riots and looting.

The problem of hunger triggered major political activity, especially among women, who actively participated in a number of riots all over the country. In 1930, women in Minneapolis, Minnesota, marched on a local food store and raided its shelves. Food riots expanded to other parts of the country in 1931 and 1932; nearly every city in the country had some kind of protest movement driven by the lack of food.

 Read a story about Detroit in the Great Depression.

## Rural America

Rural dwellers suffered as well. For the most part, the depression simply exacerbated a decade-long prob-

lem of overproduction and lowered revenues. But rural poverty was intensified by a massive drought and a series of severe dust storms in the South and Midwest during the early 1930s. Southern states like Arkansas, Alabama, and Mississippi received less than half their normal rainfall during the early 1930s. Crop failures became commonplace. From the early 1930s to the early 1940s, parts of Kansas, Oklahoma, Nebraska, and Texas were called the "**Dust Bowl**" because the dust storms and drought were so punishing.

Crop losses plunged farmers even deeper into the debts they had acquired early in the Industrial Revolution. Foreclosures on farms became commonplace, and the dust storms and drought prompted an exodus from the rural regions of the country to the Far West. John Steinbeck's novel *The Grapes of Wrath* (1939) traced the story of Dust Bowl migrants making their way to California, where they hoped for a better life. The Okies (as the Midwest migrants were called) were not always welcome in California, however, and they suffered discrimination, just as African Americans did.

> **breadline**
> A line of people waiting to receive free food handed out by a charitable organization or public agency

> **Dust Bowl**
> Parts of Kansas, Oklahoma, Nebraska, and Texas that suffered punishing dust storms and drought from the early 1930s to the early 1940s

 Experience "Surviving the Great Depression: An Interactive Module."

> 66 The depression brought everybody down a peg or two. And the Negroes had but few pegs to fall. 99
> —*Langston Hughes, poet*

## Cultural Politics

While many businesses dried up during the depression, people still found time for leisure activities like attending movies or reading fiction. The films and novels of the period responded to the psychological needs of the people by offering either dreamy escapism or a leftist political message that criticized the current capitalist order. Cultural outlets grew so popular during the depression that one historian has argued that this "Cultural Front" helped move American politics as a whole to the left during the 1930s.

*In 1930, women in Minneapolis, Minnesota, marched on a local food store and raided its shelves.*

>> Huge dust storms like that to the right conspired with the economy against many farmers, forcing refugees to flee with all their belongings to California in search of a new life.

## Movies

During the Great Depression, nearly 60 percent of the nation attended at least one film a week. Hollywood studios responded by churning out more than 5,000 movies during the 1930s. This prodigious output came courtesy of the "studio system." Just as Henry Ford had pioneered the assembly line to mass-produce his automobiles, studios learned to streamline their production process to make many more movies. Both sound and color techniques were mastered in this era; they were employed with increasing frequency throughout the 1930s.

Responding to the psychological needs of depression-era audiences, Hollywood films served up seductive dreamscapes, most notably with stories of wealthy and carefree people. The "rags-to-riches" theme was immensely popular, as were musicals and gangster films. Hollywood films many times took gentle jabs at the upper classes, while reassuring the audience that the old rags-to-riches dream was still alive.

The films of Frank Capra are the most renowned of the era, and they often dramatized the fight to rise from poverty to success. At a time when many individuals felt powerless, Capra's films, such as perennial favorites *Mr. Deeds Goes to Town* (1936) and *Mr. Smith Goes to Washington* (1939), called for a return to the virtues of small-town communities, placing hope in the power of one man to stand up against the iniquities of big business, corrupt government, and a cynical media.

The struggle to realize the American dream was a popular theme in slapstick comedian Charlie Chaplin's films as well, most notably in his *Modern Times* (1936). Chaplin's character in the film, the Little Tramp, is rendered helpless in the face of daunting machines as the gears of business literally swallow him up. The Tramp is then thrown out of work and mistakenly jailed for being a dangerous radical. *Modern Times* captured the plight of American workers who were buffeted by the impersonal forces of modern industrial society.

Another performer buoyed everyone's spirits with her carefree antics and her attempts to always remain on the sunny side of the street:

Shirley Temple. Like many other performers, her work provided an escape from the harsh realities of the depression, but she also came to symbolize the fact that Hollywood was not accurately portraying the real woes that most Americans faced in the 1930s.

## Writers

In the 1930s a growing number of writers shared Chaplin's critique. During the prosperous 1920s, writers felt ignored in a society dominated by business concerns. When the stock market crashed and the depression hit, many intellectuals felt energized. "One couldn't help being exhilarated at the sudden collapse of that stupid gigantic fraud," said the leftist social critic Edmund Wilson.

Intellectuals basically agreed on the cause of the depression: for too long, they said, America had been devoted to unbridled competition, sacrificing the good of society for individual wealth. Many intellectuals subsequently called for government control and greater centralized planning. This position was most skillfully articulated by philosopher John Dewey in many articles and his books *A Common Faith* (1934) and *Liberalism and Social Action* (1935), and by writer Alfred Bingham in his journal *Common Sense*.

More radical critics were drawn to the Communist Party. During the 1930s, communism seemed an attractive alternative to capitalism, mainly because the Soviet Union seemed to be thriving. There were certainly problems with this contention—namely, that the Soviet Union was not doing as well as it seemed (its successes were mostly a product of its international propaganda) and that what advances it did have were coming at a brutal human cost under the harsh regime of Josef Stalin. Nevertheless, many intellectuals drifted dramatically leftward during these years.

Fiction writers moved left as well. Chief among them was John Steinbeck, who aimed to create a proletarian literature that sympathetically portrayed the struggles of the working classes. African American authors such as Richard Wright used their writing to examine the political activities of the Communist Party and the struggles for African American civil rights. The Southern Agrarians, notably John Crowe Ransom and Allan Tate, wrote

of their hopes for the nation to return to its rural roots in order to address the problems caused by modern industrial society.

## Radio

Radio was wildly popular during the 1930s, as technological developments during the depression extended its reach into American homes. By 1926, the National Broadcasting Company (NBC) had hooked up stations around the country, creating the first nationwide radio network. The Columbia Broadcasting System (CBS) followed a year later.

The same songs were now popular nationwide, and a handful of them dealt with depression themes (most notably, Bing Crosby's rendition of "Brother, Can You Spare a Dime?"). The songs of Woody Guthrie were about farmers affected by the depression. His song "This Land Is Your Land," although today regarded as a celebration of the country, is actually about the nation's suffering during the depression. The most popular music of the day, however, usually avoided economics and advised listeners to, as songwriters Dorothy Fields and Jimmy McHugh put it, stay "on the sunny side of the street." The upbeat grandeur of large swing orchestras dominated popular music, led by such masters as Duke Ellington, Count Basie, Glenn Miller, and Tommy Dorsey.

Radio also featured sitcoms, the most popular of which was *Amos 'n' Andy*, which captured an amazing 60 percent of the American radio audience. Beginning in 1929, millions of Americans listened to the comical misadventures of two black friends (played by two white actors who mocked black speech) trying to make their way in Harlem. Most episodes focused on "getting ahead," a topic on the minds of depression-era audiences. Amos was hardworking and hopeful, while his friend Andy was a lazy schemer, always looking to make a quick buck. Their elaborate plans inevitably failed for a variety of humorous reasons, but by the end of the show, offering a note of reassurance to their listeners, they always managed to salvage some self-respect.

In addition to its entertainment value, the radio also served as a key source of news. Over the

Sample a collection of popular culture from the 1930s.

course of the decade, a growing number of Americans, who had previously relied on newspapers to learn of daily events, preferred to get their news from radio commentators. Colorful personalities like Walter Winchell attracted listeners by freely combining the daily headlines with personal editorial opinions.

In sum, American popular culture in the 1930s was deeply influenced by the Great Depression. All forms of popular culture, from movies to fiction to radio, helped Americans deal with the nation's economic crisis. They also helped push American politics leftward, something made evident by the radicalizing politics of the era.

>> **What better time than the depression for a superhero to be born to save the day? Superman first appeared in Action Comics in 1938.**

## Radicalizing Politics

Predictably, political events were especially contentious. The political climate of the early 1930s created the impression of a nation out of control.

### Communist Party

In the United States, the party leading most of the organized protest was the Communist Party of the United States, which, under the direction of Earl Browder and William Z. Foster, sought to eliminate all private property and make the state responsible for the good of the people. With capitalism experiencing violent turbulence, communism seemed to many to be a plausible alternative. The party had led hunger marches in the early 1930s and continued its activities into the presidential election year of 1932. Its actions gained it considerable attention from the American public, making communism a greater force in American politics than ever before.

The Communist Party intended to use its strength during the depression to highlight racist dimensions of American society (which would show the worldwide communist effort to be the true egalitarian force in the world). Notably, the party funded the legal defense of nine African American boys who had been accused of raping a white woman in Scottsboro, Alabama, in 1931. The convictions of the **Scottsboro Boys**, as the nine

 Read more on the Scottsboro Trial, including several primary sources.

came to be called, served notice to the world that the United States retained its racist ways despite its efforts to promote an egalitarian rhetoric. The boys were tried separately, and four were released in 1937, after six years in jail. The other five languished in prison, their guilt never established conclusively, and remained imprisoned until the 1940s.

### The Bonus Army

But it was the protest of the **Bonus Army** that became one of the most influential protests in American history. The Bonus Army consisted of World War I veterans who demanded the immediate payment of their military bonuses (which were scheduled to be paid in the 1940s). In the spring and summer of 1932, about 15,000 veterans converged on Washington, D.C., to push Congress and the president to pass a bill authorizing early payment of the bonuses. Some illegally hopped on trains, and some came from as far away as California. When police attempted to evict the marchers, violence broke out and one police officer was killed. President Hoover then ordered the removal of all the protesters. On the

The Art Archive/Culver Pictures

**Hoover and Roosevelt, Inauguration Day, 1933.**

night of July 28, troops burned the veterans' encampment to the ground. Two protesters were killed and hundreds were injured. Hoover became a vilified figure, increasingly unlikely to win reelection.

## The Election of 1932

Lose he did. Franklin D. Roosevelt, governor of New York and a protégé of Al Smith, won the Democratic nomination in July 1932. Little known outside New York, Roosevelt had served under President Wilson and had been influenced by his cousin Theodore Roosevelt. After an unsuccessful run for vice president in 1920, Roosevelt was stricken by poliomyelitis, a disease that at times confined him to a wheelchair, which Roosevelt loathed and concealed from the public. Despite his polio, Roosevelt had responded to the Great Depression with vibrancy and cheer. His demeanor—jovial, flexible, perhaps unprincipled—sparked divergent opinions: Was he

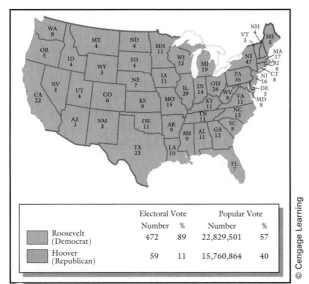

© Cengage Learning

| | Electoral Vote | | Popular Vote | |
|---|---|---|---|---|
| | Number | % | Number | % |
| Roosevelt (Democrat) | 472 | 89 | 22,829,501 | 57 |
| Hoover (Republican) | 59 | 11 | 15,760,864 | 40 |

Map 23.1. The Election of 1932

a humanitarian pragmatist or an arrogant politician? Regardless of one's perception of the man, Roosevelt's charm contrasted starkly with the somber Hoover, and Roosevelt's victory was assured. He received 22.8 million votes to Hoover's 15.7 million. The Electoral College was even more lopsided, as Roosevelt took 472 electoral votes to Hoover's 59 (Map 23.1).

In the months between Roosevelt's election in November and his inauguration on March 4, 1933, the Great Depression worsened. The Republicans blamed Roosevelt for the downturn because the president-elect would not comment on what he would do once in office. Hoover, meanwhile, was a lame duck president with little power. In February 1933, banks closed across the nation. Vagrants wandered the streets, and vigilantes had begun to incite riots.

> **bank holiday**
> Business day when banks are closed; used strategically by Roosevelt immediately after assuming the presidency
>
> **Brain Trust**
> Group of leading intellectuals charged with formulating policy with Roosevelt

# LO³ The New Deal

In his inaugural speech, in which he eloquently declared, "The only thing we have to fear is fear itself," Roosevelt tried to reassure the country about its future. Should the crisis continue, he would ask for power "to wage a war against the emergency, as great as the power that would be given to me if we were in fact invaded by a foreign foe." The very next day, March 5, 1933, Roosevelt declared a four-day national **bank holiday** and summoned Congress into special session to deal with the worsening situation.

These two actions signaled the beginning of a series of laws and programs intended to end the depression. Collectively called the "New Deal," these measures were designed to regulate the economy, provide for national recovery, and create a social safety net for all Americans. The New Deal was a collection of initiatives, each aiming to address political, economic, and social demands all at once. Once enacted, the programs of the New Deal expanded the role of the federal government into the economic lives of ordinary Americans to an unprecedented degree.

Read Roosevelt's inaugural speech.

## The First New Deal

Over the course of his first hundred days in office, Roosevelt dramatically boosted the nation's mood. With the help of what he called his **Brain Trust** (a

**Emergency Banking Relief Act**
Act passed on March 9, 1933, that established federal control over banks and, if necessary, rescued them with government loans

**Federal Emergency Relief Administration (FERA)**
Federally funded department creating economic programs to employ the unemployed

**Civilian Conservation Corps (CCC)**
New Deal program that enlisted unemployed young men ages eighteen to twenty-five in building and repairing highways, forest service sites, flood control projects, and national park buildings

**National Industrial Recovery Act (NIRA)**
New Deal act that instituted programs to regulate industry, establish labor rights, and improve working conditions

group of leading intellectuals charged with formulating policy), Roosevelt proposed a series of dramatic measures meant to reorganize the country's financial system and raise the living standards of all Americans, especially working Americans. He offered, he said, "relief, recovery, and reform," and that is the best way to characterize what historians call the First New Deal.

## Relief

First, FDR tried to provide relief to suffering people and the industries whose weaknesses compounded that suffering. Congress's first act was to address the banking crisis. Many Americans, afraid that banks would collapse, refused to place their money in them. The **Emergency Banking Relief Act**, passed on March 9, 1933, established federal control over banks and, if necessary, rescued them from disaster with government loans. Roosevelt then took the United States off the gold standard, meaning that the government would no longer redeem paper money in gold. With the end of the gold standard, the price of silver, stocks, and commodities rose, encouraging investment in these areas and putting money back into the economy.

Roosevelt next turned to helping people directly. Congress increased the federal contribution to city and state relief agencies by creating the **Federal Emergency Relief Administration (FERA)**, with funding of $500 million. FERA's chief administrator, Harry Hopkins, preferred public works projects to direct payments to people, believing that the former were more considerate of the recipients' pride. Thus FERA

set about creating economic programs that would employ the unemployed.

Reflecting this belief, one of FERA's most successful programs was the **Civilian Conservation Corps (CCC)**, established in March 1933. The CCC enlisted unemployed young men ages eighteen to twenty-five in building and repairing highways, forest service sites, flood control projects, and national park buildings. By 1941, 2.5 million young men had worked in military-style CCC camps. Enlistees received $30 a month, part of which they had to send home. Other projects started in 1933 included the Public Works Administration (PWA), which built roads and buildings, and the Civil Works Administration (CWA), which provided seasonal employment.

In addition to financial relief, Roosevelt supported a proposal that he felt would bring psychological relief to millions of Americans: the end of Prohibition. In February 1933, the Democratic majority in Congress submitted a constitutional amendment to the states that repealed Prohibition, and in December it was ratified as the Twenty-first Amendment.

## Recovery

FDR then turned to recovery. FDR's signature recovery act (and arguably the First New Deal's most meaningful piece of legislation) was the **National Industrial Recovery Act (NIRA)**. Under the steward-

>> Men of the Civilian Conservation Corps, or CCC.

Copyright © The Granger Collection, New York/The Granger Collection

ship of Secretary of Labor Frances Perkins (the first-ever female cabinet member), the NIRA instituted programs to regulate industry, establish labor rights, and improve working conditions. Section 7a of the NIRA guaranteed the right of labor unions to organize. As a result, labor representatives sat down with business and government officials in committees to set working standards and wage levels. The codes drawn up by these committees in every American industry established a forty-hour workweek, banned child labor, and implemented a minimum weekly wage.

The NIRA's most important creation was the **National Recovery Administration (NRA)**. Led by General Hugh Johnson, the NRA focused on the issue of "cutthroat" competition. In the early years of the depression, competing companies and small businesses had fought for survival by slashing prices, thus destroying profit margins, lowering workers' wages, and preventing national economic recovery. The NRA responded by enforcing fair-trade rules set by industry associations during the 1920s. More importantly, it encouraged companies and workers to meet and agree on prices and wages. Additionally, the NRA launched a public relations campaign in mid-1933, encouraging participants to stamp their products with a blue eagle and the NRA's slogan, "We do our part." The blue eagle became a symbol of the progressive optimism spurred by Roosevelt and his New Deal.

## Reform

Besides securing the rights of laborers, FDR's most dramatic gestures came through several reforms. In hindsight, we can see that these reforms changed the nature of American government for the rest of the twentieth century. These changes inserted the federal government into the American economy more forcefully than ever before by managing it, directing it, or controlling parts of it outright.

The first big program FDR passed was a farm reform proposal called the Agricultural Adjustment Act (AAA). The AAA attempted to address the great problem of agriculture, which was excess supply. The Agricultural Adjustment Administration offered farmers cash subsidies to *not* grow crops. With the drop in supply, the theory went, the cost of farm products would rise. Congress created the Emergency Farm Mortgage Act, which helped refinance farm loans and prevented a number of farms from being repossessed.

Second, an emphasis on cooperative planning found its broadest expression in the **Tennessee Valley Authority (TVA)**, created by Congress in May 1933. The TVA gave the federal government the power to build a series of dams on the Tennessee River in order to improve river navigation and, significantly, create electricity for the area's rural residents, the achievement for which the TVA is best remembered. The TVA brought electricity to poor and isolated populations in seven states.

A third group of reforms governed banking. In May 1933, Congress passed the Federal Securities Act, which regulated the stock market and prosecuted individuals who took advantage of "insider" knowledge to enrich themselves in stocks and bonds. In June 1933, Congress passed the Glass-Steagall Banking Act, which regulated the size of banks and created the Federal Deposit Insurance Corporation (FDIC), a program that guaranteed individual deposits of up to $5,000. These steps reassured millions of Americans that it was safe to put their money in banks again.

**National Recovery Administration (NRA)** Department that enforced fair-trade rules set by industry associations during the 1920s, encouraged companies and workers to meet and agree on prices and wages, and established a public relations campaign to mobilize support of the New Deal

**Tennessee Valley Authority (TVA)** Department created in May 1933 to build a series of dams on the Tennessee River in order to improve river navigation and create electricity for the area's rural residents

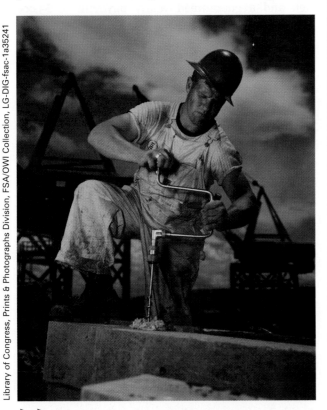

>> **Carpenter at work on Douglas Dam, Tennessee, under the auspices of the Tennessee Valley Authority.**

## The Hundred Days

Congress adjourned on June 16, 1933. Although it would enact many laws during the subsequent eighteen months, few would have the dramatic impact of these acts, all of which were passed within Roosevelt's first hundred days in office.

## Critics of the First New Deal

Despite his enormous popularity, Roosevelt never lacked for critics, many of whom looked on the New Deal with horror.

### Criticism from the Republicans

Republicans argued that periodic downturns were an inevitable part of the business cycle. In their view, the best cure for the depression was to let market forces take their course, knowing that, in time, there would be a new era of growth and recovery.

### Criticism from Conservative Democrats

Equally dismayed were conservative Democrats, who deplored Roosevelt's tampering with the gold standard and feared that his programs were increasing the power of the federal government at the states' expense. In 1934, Al Smith, the unsuccessful Democratic presidential candidate of 1928, and John W. Davis, the unsuccessful Democratic presidential candidate of 1924, joined a group of conservative politicians and business leaders in the Liberty League, an anti–New Deal organization. The League argued that many of Roosevelt's measures were leading America toward socialism. Citizens' lives, those in the League believed, ought not to be too much in the hands of the federal government. They saw it as immoral that farm products and livestock were being stored away or killed while a great number of Americans were suffering from hunger.

Southern Democrats also had their complaints. They were concerned that the new federal mandates might threaten Jim Crow segregation in the South. Because of their seniority in Congress, they were successful in exempting farm workers and domestic servants (who in the South likely would have been black) from receiving certain New Deal benefits.

### Criticism from the Left

If conservative Democrats saw the New Deal as an overextension of federal power, other voices on the Left saw it as a timid set of reforms that merely reinforced the American status quo. America's small Socialist Party, led by Norman Thomas, believed that the depression was evidence that capitalism was a failure. The New Deal, in the Socialists' view, had made the mistake of shoring up capitalism rather than getting rid of it once and for all. The even smaller Communist Party, which favored the abolition of all forms of private property, used the Soviet Union as an example of an economic system that (in theory) had no unemployment at all. During these years, the Communist Party attracted support from numerous sources, notably from African American sharecroppers in the South, mainly because of the party's opposition to racial segregation. Nevertheless, at its peak in 1938, Communist Party membership numbered just 75,000.

Another plan to redistribute wealth was proposed by novelist and Progressive crusader Upton Sinclair in his 1934 bid for governor of California. A former socialist, Sinclair championed a program called End Poverty in California (EPIC), which aimed to turn over idle factories and farms to workers' cooperatives. A powerful coalition of conservative business interests banded together to defeat Sinclair in the November election.

Another dramatic plan for reform emerged in 1934, when Senator Huey Long of Louisiana announced his "Share Our Wealth" plan. A former governor, Long proposed punitive taxation of the rich and a guaranteed yearly payment of $5,000 to every American family. He wanted to go even further than the New Deal in making the national government every citizen's guardian. The colorful Long had a history of flamboyance and corruption, and his national stature was on the rise when he was assassinated in September 1935.

 Hear Huey Long discuss his Share Our Wealth plan.

A more extreme rival of the New Deal was Charles Coughlin, a Catholic priest from Detroit. Coughlin was a spellbinding speaker, as talented a public performer as Roosevelt, and his weekly radio show had a largely Catholic audience of more than 30 million. Coughlin went from being an early supporter of the New Deal to being one of its harshest critics, accusing Roosevelt of being in league with communists and Jewish bankers. In 1934, Coughlin founded the Union for Social Justice, which argued for radical redistribution of incomes and a nation free of bankers. Coughlin's conspiratorial antisemitism eventually prompted his censure by the Catholic Church.

### Criticism from the Courts

Amid these voices of dissent, Roosevelt faced a new challenge in the Supreme Court. In its May 1935 decision in *Schechter Poultry Corp. v. U.S.*, the Court invalidated the NIRA on the grounds that it gave unconstitutionally broad powers to the federal government. The logic of the Court's decision, written by conservative Chief Justice Charles Evans Hughes, suggested that the other parts of the New Deal's legislation would be overturned when they came up for review.

## The Second New Deal

Despite the Supreme Court's challenge, Roosevelt believed that, without a national plan for economic reform, the country would succumb to demagogues like Long and Coughlin. Emboldened by the Democratic victories in the 1934 elections, Roosevelt laid out a new set of proposals in January 1935 that would push the New Deal even further in assisting the working and lower classes. Ultimately enacted by Congress in July and August of 1935, these new reform measures are known collectively as the "Second New Deal." Despite their passage, Roosevelt was aware that a judicial showdown about the constitutionality of his New Deal was on the horizon.

The Second New Deal can best be understood as Roosevelt's attempt to gain support from the working and lower-middle classes. Even if it cost him the support of the wealthy (whom he called "economic royalists"), Roosevelt decided to co-opt the ideas of some of his leftist critics by (1) pressing for more jobs, (2) strengthening the position of labor, and (3) providing a greater social safety net.

### More Jobs

One of the most notable programs of the Second New Deal was the **Works Progress Administration (WPA)**, which employed over 8.5 million Americans before it closed in 1943. WPA workers built roads,

 Read several of the WPA slave narratives.

dams, schools, subways, housing projects, and other federal projects. The WPA also sponsored cultural programs for unemployed artists and writers, who worked on original plays and artworks, compiled historical records, wrote a series of guidebooks for tourists, and gave classes and performances to the general public. In one of the most far-reaching WPA projects, the federal government hired historians and folklorists to interview former slaves about their journeys from slavery to freedom.

Roosevelt established other agencies designed to help Americans cope with the continuing depres-

sion. In May 1935, the administration created the Resettlement Administration (RA), which provided assistance in relocating workers away from economically weak areas and funded flood control and reforestation projects. The National Youth Administration (NYA), founded in June 1935, provided work relief programs, job training, and part-time work for men and women ages sixteen to twenty-five, including high school and college students.

### Labor Support

Perhaps more significant than the creation of these jobs was Congress's strengthening, in July 1935, the legal position of trade unions with the National Labor Relations Act (NLRA), also known as the **Wagner Act**. Even with the guarantees established under the NRA, unions had been vulnerable to court injunctions that prevented strikes. Plus, management had often refused to negotiate with them. The Wagner Act established a National Labor Relations Board to oversee industrial compliance and resolve employee grievances against management. In subsequent years, union membership grew dramatically (despite the unemployment rate), even among unskilled workers in the mining, steel, and automobile industries.

### The Social Safety Net

The third aspect of the Second New Deal (in addition to creating jobs and supporting unionization efforts) was the **Social Security Act**, passed in August 1935. This was probably the most far-reaching element of all 1930s legislation. Social Security was intended to provide a "safety net" for citizens who could not financially support themselves.

Different elements of the Social Security plan served different social needs. Social Security provided pensions to Americans age sixty-five and over. Unemployed people received assistance through a fund created by a payroll tax. Federal grants provided help for the disabled. Children of unwed mothers were covered under the Aid to Dependent Children Act (ADC), or "welfare." A federal program for national health insurance would have widened the social

**Works Progress Administration (WPA)** New Deal agency whose workers built roads, dams, schools, subways, housing projects, and other federal projects; the WPA also sponsored cultural programs for unemployed artists and writers

**Wagner Act** Legislation passed in July 1935, also known as the National Labor Relations Act (NLRA); strengthened the legal position of trade unions

**Social Security Act** Most far-reaching element of all 1930s legislation, passed in August 1935; intended to provide a "safety net" for citizens who could not financially support themselves

safety net even more, but Congress shelved the idea after complaints from the medical profession.

As a plan for social welfare, Social Security was cautious and limited in comparison to models in other nations. Germany, for example, had been putting many social safety net programs in place since the 1880s. In this country, Social Security, particularly its old-age pension elements, proved to be the most popular and enduring of New Deal measures. Indeed, Roosevelt said many times that the Social Security Act was the greatest legacy of his presidency.

## Attacks on the Wealthy and Large Corporations

As he pushed these programs through Congress, Roosevelt had observed the popularity of Huey Long's denunciations of big business and the rich.

>> Although retirement plans had existed in the industrialized countries of Europe for decades, they were new to the United States in the mid 1930s. This poster encourages the use of the new public benefit.

© Bettmann/CORBIS

Hence, Roosevelt usurped Long's rhetoric and created a "soak the rich" tax reform plan (passed as the Revenue Act of 1935), which imposed steep income taxes (up to nearly 80 percent) on wealthy Americans and large corporations. The Public Utility Holding Company Act, passed the same year, placed rigorous political controls on utility companies and warned that if they did not offer good service at low cost to customers, they would be broken up.

### The New Deal's Peak: 1935–1936

Congress passed a number of other New Deal measures as well, regulating specific industries, providing for further rural electrification, and carrying out additional farm reforms. This burst of political activity consolidated Roosevelt's reputation as a friend of the workingman and an opponent of special privilege. All together, the passage of so many transformative laws was a testament to the growing expectation that the government would take responsibility for the social welfare of its citizens.

By mid-1936, Roosevelt's political successes had bestowed him with tremendous popularity with the public, even though the American economy had yet to substantially revive and some 80 percent of American newspapers (generally owned by Republicans) went on record as opposing his reelection. During that fall's presidential campaign, the Republicans nominated Alfred Landon of Kansas, who was considerably more liberal than his party. Meanwhile, Charles Coughlin attempted to get his followers to join up with Huey Long's, to coalesce behind the new Union Party and its nominee, William Lemke.

Roosevelt easily won the election, by 11 million votes, carrying every state except Maine and Vermont, which went to Landon. Lemke won fewer than a million votes, while the Socialist candidate, Norman Thomas, and the Communist candidate, Earl Browder, attracted barely a quarter of a million votes between them. Farmers and workers, who were pleased with the relief acts and the union protection, joined middle-class homeowners, who were bailed out by the mortgage protection laws, to support Roosevelt. The Democratic Party had more than three-quarters of the seats in both houses of Congress. In 1936, the New Deal appeared invincible.

## Decline and Consolidation

After the election, the New Deal appeared to be at its height. But Roosevelt soon committed a series of political and economic errors that scuttled the most far-reaching elements of the New Deal. Rather than disappearing altogether, the New Deal entered a period of consolidation, when its changes in culture, labor relations, and politics took firm root in American life.

## Court Packing

The Democratic landslide of 1936 energized Roosevelt. In his second inaugural speech, he declared an attack on standards of living that left "one-third of a nation . . . ill-housed, ill-clad, [and] ill-nourished." Soon after, in February 1937, Roosevelt made what was for him an unusual blunder. Vexed by the Supreme Court's decision against the NRA in the *Schechter* case, its overturning of the AAA in 1936, and its unfavorable decision in five of seven other cases testing New Deal laws, Roosevelt resolved to change the Court's ideological makeup.

 Listen to one of Roosevelt's "fireside chats" regarding restructuring the judiciary.

The Constitution does not specify how many justices can sit on the Court, but by long-standing convention the number had been nine. Roosevelt now proposed laws that would allow him to appoint up to six new justices and would force judges to retire at age seventy. Given that the Court's opinions reflected the Republican attitudes of the 1920s, Roosevelt felt the Court's actions threatened American democracy in the 1930s. He felt he needed to fill the Court with supporters of the New Deal.

Congressional Democrats, arguing that Roosevelt had overreached, delayed considering this plan to "pack the court." Yet the need for the legislation seemed to diminish after March of 1937, when Justice Owen Roberts changed from his previous position and unexpectedly began voting to uphold New Deal laws, creating a 5-to-4 pro–New Deal majority on the Court. Some observers speculated that Roberts had changed his mind to protect the principle of a nine-judge court. In any event, during the next four years, Roosevelt had the chance to appoint seven new justices, allowing him to change the political tilt of the Court.

But the court-packing episode cost Roosevelt some popular support from Americans who were cautiously monitoring the rise of authoritarian dictators in Europe. New economic problems compounded the damage. In early 1937, satisfied that the nation was well on its way to recovery, Roosevelt slashed enrollment in the WPA, and the Federal Reserve Bank raised interest rates to fight inflation. As a result, production slowed, unemployment shot up, and critics declared a "Roosevelt recession." That fall, when Roosevelt called Congress into special ses-

sion to pass emergency relief legislation, Congress failed to act on his proposals. The Democratic Party suffered losses in the 1938 election, and congressional conservatives of both parties joined to block future New Deal measures.

## Consolidation

But all was not lost for FDR. The Supreme Court's newfound support of New Deal programs actually strengthened the New Deal and ensured that its reforms would last several decades. Also, the expenditures that were passed in reaction to the "Roosevelt recession" of 1937, although not as dramatic as Roosevelt had hoped, greatly eased the economic decline. They also lent new legitimacy to the idea that government spending could help induce economic recovery. This demonstrated a growing acceptance of the ideas of the British economist John Maynard Keynes, who had long advocated that governments should engage in deficit spending in order to stimulate a depressed economy.

# LO⁴ The Effects of the New Deal

Although the major political accomplishments of the New Deal had ended by the late 1930s, the programs that had already become law continued to influence American politics, society, and culture for the remainder of the twentieth century. The New Deal thus effected changes in the American landscape more far-reaching than just economics or legislation. Most especially, they affected culture, crime, labor, politics, race relations, and minorities.

## Culture

The New Deal included a number of programs that examined social realities that Hollywood and other cultural outlets often ignored. Problems such as poverty, crime, prostitution, and suicide had always existed in America, but New Deal cultural programs focused on their effects and placed them in the center of American social consciousness. For example, the Resettlement Administration hired photographers such as Dorothea Lange and Ben Shahn (whose photographs are represented in this chapter) to record the lives of Americans struggling through the depression. By documenting the breadlines, migrant camps, and withered farms of the era, these photographers made a powerful indictment of economic inequality. At the same time, the WPA hired artists to create murals, sculptures, and other artworks in post offices, airports, and schools. The

**Congress of Industrial Organizations (CIO)**
Broadly based trade union that recruited unskilled men and women on a large scale, particularly in the mining and clothing industries

**sit-down strike**
Action in which workers stop working and lock themselves in the factory so that strikebreakers cannot take their places

 Learn more about the cultural projects of the New Deal.

best known of these works depicted American farmers and workers and celebrated the working classes. The federal government also provided funds for actors in the Federal Theatre Project, musicians in the Federal Music Project, and writers in the Federal Writers' Project.

Other writers contributed to the aesthetic of these government cultural programs. Magazines ran stories about depression refugees. For instance, *Fortune* sent the journalist James Agee to the rural Deep South to write about poverty there. He wrote a book that has become a classic: *Let Us Now Praise Famous Men*, made even more powerful by the stark photographs of Walker Evans. Rural poverty became a way to symbolize the experience of the depression as a whole, as in John Steinbeck's *The Grapes of Wrath*. This novel showed a newly responsive federal government sheltering migrants in a work camp and providing the poorest of Americans with decent living conditions.

Library of Congress, Prints & Photographs Division, Work Projects Administration Poster Collection, LC-USZC2-5684

>> A production of the Federal Theatre Project.

## Crime

The New Deal also initiated a war on crime in an effort to snuff out the gangster-ridden crime syndicates of the 1920s. Spearheaded by U.S. Attorney General Homer Cummings and Director of the Federal Bureau of Investigation (FBI) J. Edgar Hoover, this initiative strengthened the FBI and led to the arrest and/or execution of notable American criminals Bonnie and Clyde (in 1934, for armed robbery), Charles Arthur "Pretty Boy" Floyd (in 1934, for armed robbery and murder), and John Dillinger (in 1934, alleged leader of the violent Dillinger gang). These criminals had become something like folk heroes in the 1930s, for both their seeming invincibility and their rebuke of the established system that had brought on the Great Depression. Removing them from the scene assured Americans that the law would dictate right and wrong in America.

## Labor

The New Deal benefited the American labor movement. Previous economic downturns had usually increased union rolls, but they had also made union members vulnerable to layoffs and replacement by strikebreakers. But after the New Deal, the NLRA guaranteed unions the right to organize and negotiate with their employers. In 1935, a new, broadly based trade union, eventually to be called the **Congress of Industrial Organizations (CIO)**, began recruiting unskilled men and women on a large scale, particularly in the mining and clothing industries. Under the able leadership of John L. Lewis and advocating a "culture of unity" to bring workers together despite differences in ethnic or racial background, the CIO rapidly became the nation's most powerful labor union.

Greater size engendered greater militancy. On December 31, 1936, for example, workers at General Motors (GM), led by Walter Reuther, went on strike in Flint, Michigan, demanding better pay, better working conditions, and recognition of their union, the United Auto Workers. Rather than simply not show up to work, as previous generations of strikers had done, GM workers staged a **sit-down strike**, locking themselves in the factory so that strikebreakers could not take their places. Although Roosevelt was openly critical of the strike, he refused to use federal troops to stop the strike. Roosevelt believed that industrial peace could be achieved only by integrating

 See a film about the San Francisco General Strike of 1934.

 Read an account of the 1937 violence at the Republic Steel plant.

> > Portrait of American bank robbers Clyde Barrow (1909–1934) and Bonnie Parker (1911–1934), popularly known as Bonnie and Clyde, circa 1933.

unions into the economy. Ultimately, GM gave in and negotiated with the union.

Not all strikes concluded so peacefully. For example, on Memorial Day 1937, strikebreaking police fired on a line of picketers in front of the Republic Steel plant in Chicago, killing ten workers. Roosevelt stepped in and helped convince the steel factory and mine owners to come to terms with unions. Such successes led to a rapid rise in unionization. By the 1950s, more than 20 percent of all American workers belonged to unions.

## Politics

The New Deal also dramatically altered American politics. Many workers revered Roosevelt, and his photograph was a ubiquitous fixture in urban households and small businesses.

The result was a fundamental realignment of American politics. "New immigrant" Catholic and Jewish voters, many of whom had been alienated by the Democratic Party's tilt toward southern conservatives, now flocked to the party. Democratic southern whites, who could not countenance joining the Republican Party, which was, after all, the party of Lincoln, joined them. So did a large majority

of African Americans, whose gratitude for New Deal relief programs led them to abandon the Republican Party in favor of the Democrats. The Democrats thus made a national majority by fashioning the alliance of the "producing" classes (farmers and laborers) they had dreamed of since the Populist movement.

## Continued Segregation

The successes of this New Deal coalition set in motion fundamental changes in the Democratic Party itself. The support of African Americans reflected the fact that some New Deal programs seemed to combat discrimination. The CCC, for example, briefly housed both black and white workers together. In addition, a number of black officials appointed to government posts assembled as an informal **Black Cabinet** to discuss African American issues, although FDR did not appoint a single black person to a cabinet position. Roosevelt relied especially heavily on his powerful wife, Eleanor Roosevelt, to serve as a conduit to the African American community.

Nevertheless, opposition to ending desegregation came from many quarters: labor unions, for example, consistently excluded African Americans

> > Although Roosevelt had an aristocratic background, the warmth of his conversational radio addresses, or "fireside chats," made many Americans feel they had a personal connection with the man.

from their ranks and prevented the inclusion of nondiscrimination clauses in the Wagner Act. At the same time, the Roosevelt administration often gave in to segregationist demands in the 1930s, meaning that many of the key benefits of the New Deal were denied to America's black population. The doling out of benefits primarily to America's white population has led one historian to label the New Deal as a time "when affirmative action was white."

## The Indian New Deal

At the same time, Roosevelt sought to address the concerns of other minorities. Shortly after his election in 1932, Roosevelt appointed John Collier as commissioner of the Bureau of Indian Affairs. In 1924, Congress had granted American citizenship to all Indians, an event that was thought to be the culmination in the perpetual attempt to incorporate Indians into American society. Collier took a different perspective. He sought to restore Indian culture and heritage and to regenerate tribal autonomy. He used a variety of New Deal agencies to create an Indian Civil Conservation Corps and Works Progress Administration. He also lobbied for the Indian Reorganization Act of 1934, which authorized the acquisition of land for reservations and provided special federal appropriations for schools and other forms of Indian self-government. Collier faced stern critics, including assimilated Indians who tried to discredit his ideas as communist plots against America. But for the most part, his ideas began a new chapter in American Indian history, redirecting the federal government's efforts from forcing assimilation to respecting self-reliance.

## Women

Women were also of course greatly affected by the New Deal. During the depression, increasing numbers of women went to work. While economically valuable, these efforts to support their families provoked hostility from many Americans who thought women workers were taking jobs away from men. Indeed, some scholars have seen within the Great Depression a "crisis of manhood," where men were unable to feed and clothe their families and where women had to come in to shoulder these responsibilities. In this critical mold, many New Deal policies addressed women as mothers rather than as work-ers, creating jobs programs for men, for instance, while providing support for women primarily in their domestic roles. In the Aid to Families With Dependent Children program, for instance, single mothers were eligible for aid only after they endured means and morals testing, testifying that they were not engaging in and benefiting from immoral behavior. Similarly, many of the programs targeting women became derided as temporary relief efforts (such as welfare) rather than full-scale entitlements earned by workers (such as Social Security and unemployment insurance). In the words of one historian, women were "pitied but not entitled" to New Deal benefits.

# And in the end . . .

The New Deal did not end the Great Depression. Throughout the 1930s, nearly 10 million men remained unemployed. What the New Deal did was bring the federal government closer to the lives of ordinary citizens than ever before, reshaping national politics and culture with a host of relief, recovery, and reform initiatives. In so doing, it transformed the way Americans thought about their government, leading them to assume that the government was there to prevent them from going without food or shelter, to assure them that they would not be helpless during times of unemployment, and to provide financial security when they

| What else was happening . . . | |
| --- | --- |
| 1930 | Vannevar Bush at MIT invents the "differential analyzer," or analog computer. |
| 1931 | Japan, seeking raw materials for its own industrial growth, invades Manchuria, bringing Japan and China into conflict that would erupt into war in 1937. |
| 1933 | Ruth Wakefield bakes the first chocolate chip cookie. |
| 1934 | The first laundromat, the "washeteria," opens in Texas. |
| 1934 | Amid its own economic depression, Hitler becomes dictator of Germany. |
| 1937 | Hormel introduces its canned pink mystery meat, Spam. |

got old. This change also inspired a movement to oppose the New Deal initiatives, although this "small-government" coalition would not mature until later in the twentieth century.

Emboldened by his successes, in 1940 Roosevelt decided to run for an unprecedented third term as president. Just as he had been willing to override tradition in his Supreme Court packing plan, so now he overrode the tradition established by George Washington of holding the presidency for no more than two terms. Running against Republican nominee Wendell Willkie, FDR urged voters not to "switch horses in mid-stream." Americans overwhelmingly responded, voting him to a third term as president. With the 1940 election, the nation left the problems of the 1930s behind and attempted to gain strength to meet the challenges posed by a world at war. It is to that world conflict that we now turn.

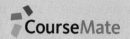

Visit the CourseMate website at www.cengagebrain.com for additional study tools and review materials for this chapter.

# CHAPTER 24

# World War II

## Learning Outcomes

*After reading this chapter, you should be able to do the following:*

LO **1**  Explain the various causes of World War II.

LO **2**  Explain America's foreign policy that developed after World War I and that was in place at the beginning of World War II, and describe how that policy changed as the war progressed.

LO **3**  Describe the events of World War II, both in Europe and in the Pacific, and explain why the United States acted as it did throughout the conflict.

LO **4**  Describe and discuss the American home front during World War II, paying special attention to long-term societal changes.

LO **5**  Explain how World War II was brought to an end, both in Europe and in the Pacific, and discuss the immediate aftermath of the war both in America and around the world.

> ## **"***Just as World War II transformed the world, it also transformed the United States's role in world affairs.***"**

If the New Deal could not end the Great Depression, a world war would. Beginning in the late 1930s, talk of war became more insistent and urgent in Europe. The financial uncertainty of the worldwide depression had created political vulnerabilities that assisted the rise of militant, expansion-minded dictators in Italy and Germany. Americans watched the continent nervously, uncertain how European affairs might affect them. Little did they know that, in the end, the Second World War would transform America even more than the New Deal.

The war prompted a tremendous mobilization of American resources, at a level unseen since the Civil War. Long-quiet industries were revitalized, the agricultural sector started to grow again, and the American economy ramped up from that of the low-production Great Depression years to the most powerful economy in the world. The demands of war created opportunities for women, who filled jobs left open by the men who enlisted in the service, and African Americans and other minorities, who did not hesitate to use the facts of Hitler's racism and antisemitism to demonstrate the flaws of the American promise. The ethnic enclaves formed during the massive immigration between 1880 and 1924 lost some of their unique character as well, dwindling due to 1920s immigration restrictions and calls for unity put forward by the federal government. Sometimes the concept of American unity excluded racial minorities, as it did in the internment of thousands of Japanese Americans, whose sole supposedly un-American characteristic was their country of descent. For the most part, however, Americans embraced the call for greater tolerance, a tolerance that prompted the civil rights movement and other liberation movements that were to come.

In the end, the war created a world dominated and heavily influenced by two major powers, the Soviet Union and the United States. Their attempts to remake the world torn apart by the Second World War are the subject of the next chapter. But first, to the war and the dramatic transformations it set in motion.

## LO¹ Causes of War

There were multiple causes of the Second World War, but the Great Depression was perhaps the most significant.

© AP Images

## Provocations

The stock market collapse between 1929 and 1932 ended American investment in Europe and caused economic slowdowns there. Without American dollars, European countries faced industrial decline, unemployment, and widespread homelessness for workers. The depression had spread around the world.

These problems increased political tensions. In France and Spain, fighting broke out between Communists and Nationalists over which group had the best plan to manage the disrupted economy. But the crash had a devastating effect on Germany, whose reparation payments for World War I were largely financed by American lenders. The crash forced American businesses to withdraw investments in Germany, causing their production to fall by half between 1929 and 1933. In 1933, with the economy in a shambles, Adolf Hitler's National Socialist (Nazi) Party ascended to power in Germany and ruthlessly consolidated its control of the state. Hitler then began a massive armament campaign that put millions of Germans to work on public works projects and in factories. In some ways, it was a militant and extreme version of the New Deal. The depression there was over by 1936, providing dramatic proof that the deficit spending advocated by John Maynard Keynes would work. A similar program for reform emerged in Italy under the dictatorship of Benito Mussolini.

But Hitler and Mussolini did not stop at economic reform. Driven by delusions of grandeur and by racist and antisemitic ideologies, and seeking to remake Europe (and, after that, the world) to match his nationalistic vision, Hitler defied World War I's Treaty of Versailles by occupying the industrialized Rhineland in 1936 and annexing German-speaking Austria in 1938. He was intent on expanding further, too. He roused the German public with promises of German power and antisemitic screeds that blamed Germany's plight on the Jews. Encouraged by Germany's example, Mussolini invaded and conquered Ethiopia in 1935 and Albania in 1939.

Meanwhile, on the other side of the globe, Emperor Hirohito of Japan was attempting to bring all of Asia under Japanese control. In 1931, Japanese forces occupied the Chinese territory of Manchuria. In 1937, Japan launched a full-scale invasion of China, occupying most of the large cities along the Chinese coast. By 1940, the two nations were stuck in a military stalemate: Japan was unable to defeat its much larger neighbor, while China's military suffered from internal political divisions. Japan had the upper hand, but it had not yet finished the military takeover.

## Reactions

Many Americans hoped the United States would avoid armed conflict. Congress passed a series of neutrality acts between 1935 and 1937 that placed

>> Benito Mussolini (left) and Adolf Hitler (right) both came to power promising to end the ravages of the worldwide economic depression.

> > The attempts of Japanese Emperor Hirohito to consolidate all of Asia under Japanese rule led to war with China in 1937.

Read Roosevelt's 1937 "Quarantine" speech. arms embargoes on all belligerent powers. Roosevelt signed these measures, but he was leery of the offensive actions of Germany, Italy, and Japan, calling in 1937 for the world community to "quarantine" these states.

France and Britain also seemed reluctant to oppose these aggressive nations. Britain and France had suffered greatly during the First World War and wanted to avoid further bloodshed. Their leaders hoped to appease Mussolini and especially Hitler by giving them some of what they wanted so as not to enrage them. In what has come to be called the **Munich Agreement** (1938), for example, the leading powers of western Europe allowed Hitler to annex strategic areas of Czechoslovakia in order to satisfy his territorial aspirations, and hoping he would go no further. Hitler had also begun denouncing and terrorizing Jews, communists, gays, and other groups he deemed undesirable. Many in France, England, and the United States did not agree with or condone Hitler's brutal actions (although some did), but they all failed to confront him.

The British claimed that appeasement promised to bring "peace for our time," but it was not to be so. Hitler continued his relentless expansion into neighboring countries. In March 1939, Hitler broke his various promises and moved into Czechoslovakia. He also demanded control over the German-speaking areas of Poland. British and French diplomats urgently solicited an alliance with Soviet leader Josef Stalin. But Stalin distrusted the West, which was, after all, the capitalist rival of his communist nation.

**Munich Agreement**
**1938 treaty in which the leading powers of western Europe allowed Hitler to annex strategic areas of Czechoslovakia in order to satisfy his territorial aspirations (strategy of appeasement)**

**nonaggression pact**
**1939 agreement between Stalin and Hitler that divided Poland between Germany and the Soviet Union and said the two nations would not attack each other**

British Prime Minister Neville Chamberlain, promising to bring "peace for our time," in 1938.

In August 1939, Stalin agreed to a secret **nonaggression pact** with Hitler that divided Poland between Germany and the Soviet Union. Unafraid of France and Britain, Hitler invaded Poland on September 1, 1939. Now understanding that appeasing Hitler would not work, Britain and France declared war on Germany. Europe was once again at war.

# LO² American Foreign Policy before the War

Americans at first tried to stay out of the war, but this became less feasible as Hitler's aggression continued.

## 1930s Isolation

In the United States, the Great Depression had provoked a strong drift toward isolationism. The trend was already manifested in the American rejection

**"good neighbor" policy**
American strategy of renouncing military intervention in Latin American affairs

**blitzkriegs**
"Lightning wars"; fast and brutal attacks staged by Germany on its neighbors starting in 1940

of the League of Nations following World War I, but during the depression many Americans remained preoccupied by domestic affairs. For more on the reasons why many Americans resisted involvement in European affairs, see "The reasons why . . ." box below.

## Latin America

Concerning foreign policy, FDR was initially of the same mindset as his predecessor, Herbert Hoover. He was not a strict isolationist, but he was not eager to engage too deeply in foreign affairs. Indeed, rather than help the troubled European economy in the 1930s, American policymakers focused their efforts on improving relations with nations closer to home, particularly in Central and South America. At his 1933 inauguration, FDR announced that the United States would pursue a **"good neighbor" policy** toward Latin America, thus renouncing military intervention in Latin American affairs and, during the next few years, signing treaties with various Central and South American nations. Their goal was to maintain political stability without using military means.

## The World's Arsenal

Despite this diplomatic activity in Latin America, isolationism remained the key feature of American foreign policy. But unrest in Asia and Europe was simmering, and, as a major world power, the United States could not look away for long. For one thing, the warring nations needed American guns and armor. From 1937 to 1941, then, Britain, France, China, and the Soviet Union all began rapid armament, boosting the American economy. At the same time, Roosevelt realized that the world was on the brink of a major war. He requested and received congressional authorization to build 50,000 warplanes per year, just in case. America was beginning to build its own defenses.

Through the late 1930s, the United States watched as Hitler and Stalin conquered Poland. Roosevelt pledged official U.S. neutrality, backed by polls showing that more than 90 percent of the American public did not want to go to war. But the overwhelming German victories slowly changed American public opinion. In 1939, American outrage over the invasion of Poland translated into a new neutrality act that allowed belligerent powers, particularly Britain and France, to buy arms from the United States. Roosevelt believed that France and England could win a European war on their own if the United States provided material assistance.

## *Blitzkrieg* and Doubt

This belief was negated when, in the spring of 1940, Germany launched a series of **blitzkriegs** (or "lightning wars") that succeeded in defeating most of its neighbors. In April and May 1940, the Germans

## {*The reasons why . . .*}

There were several reasons why so many Americans favored isolationism before the Second World War:

**World War I.** Their memories of the First World War made many Americans leery to get involved in European affairs. In 1914, Americans watched as a dizzying series of alliances led one nation into battle with another, without any apparent justification. The brutality of the First World War further made Americans shy away from any involvement in European affairs. Why risk American lives to protect European freedoms?

**The Great Depression.** The Great Depression deepened this isolationism. Most Americans were simply too focused on improving life in the United States to advocate getting involved in diplomatic disputes abroad.

**Respect for Hitler.** At the same time, some Americans had profound respect for Adolf Hitler, who had, after all, plucked Germany from its own economic depression in record time. By the late 1930s, American icons like the aviator Charles Lindbergh argued that the Nazis were unstoppable under the leadership of Hitler and that the United States should negotiate with them.

**Antisemitism.** Lindbergh, like Hitler, was also an antisemite. Although the worst abuses of the Holocaust would only begin to occur in 1941, by the late 1930s many American Jews were asking President Roosevelt to take a stronger stance against Hitler. Roosevelt, aware that a large majority of Americans would not want to get involved in war in order to save Europe's Jews, opted to wait until he could rally greater public opinion. That only occurred in December of 1941, with the bombing of Pearl Harbor.

>> During the 1940 Battle of Britain, German planes bombed London incessantly, destroying much of the city.

ripped through Denmark and Norway. Other German forces swept through Belgium and the Netherlands. On June 5, German armies attacked France and captured Paris after only six weeks of battle. Germany forced the French to sign a treaty creating a pro-German French regime, headquartered in **Vichy** and known by the name "Vichy France." By the summer of 1940, Germany controlled most of western Europe, and had conquered it with astonishing ease.

>> During the buildup to World War II, a strong bond grew between Franklin D. Roosevelt and Winston Churchill, and between the United States and Britain.

In the process, Hitler imprisoned the continent's Jews, gypsies, and other societal scapegoats in a web of concentration camps. Thus, since his rise to power, Hitler had intimidated, isolated, and concentrated European Jewry. By late 1940, the soldiers guarding these camps began killing the Jews. By 1941, Hitler began using death squads to kill entire villages of Jews in eastern Europe. By 1942, he had set up his infamous death camps. These horrific killings were later known as the **Holocaust**. Until 1940, however, few outside Europe knew about Hitler's processes of intimidation and murder (and even when they learned of them, few were spurred into action until much later in the war).

In Europe, only the British stood against the Germans. In the summer and autumn of 1940, the two nations fought in the **Battle of Britain**, in which Hitler attempted to break Britain's air power through heavy bombardment of British cities and by deliberately targeting British civilians, hoping to

**Vichy**
City in central France, head-quarters of the pro-German French regime installed in 1940

**Holocaust**
Systematic killing of 11 million Jews, gypsies, and other societal scapegoats in Nazi concentration camps all over Europe

**Battle of Britain**
Fierce battle fought in the summer and autumn of 1940; Hitler attempted to break Britain's air power through heavy bombardment of British cities

sap their will to fight. Many Americans sympathized with the British people suffering through the bomb attacks, the horrors of which were relayed nightly from London by radio correspondents.

## Partial Involvement

The devastation of Britain set the stage for American involvement. In May 1940, Roosevelt asked Congress to increase spending on American national defense and to authorize sending surplus arms to Britain. That same month, Winston Churchill was appointed Britain's prime minister. An inspiring speaker who had long warned of Hitler's growing power, Churchill pledged to fight the Germans in the streets of Britain, if necessary. Churchill also believed that an alliance with the United States was the key to Britain's survival. Determined to win Roosevelt's friendship and support, Churchill frequently wrote Roosevelt and later visited the White House for long stays.

## From Isolation to Intervention

American public sentiment favoring some form of aid, short of direct intervention, had been growing since Germany's invasion of Poland. Many Americans foresaw dangers for the United States should Germany conquer Britain. With control of Europe, Germany might become unbeatable. American Jews were especially active in advocating war, but in an America controlled by a white, Anglo-Saxon elite, and with American antisemitism still socially acceptable and growing, the urgings of American Jews did not carry enough weight to power a full-scale intervention.

In late 1940, Roosevelt approved the first peacetime draft in U.S. history. He also announced that the United States was giving the British fifty renovated naval destroyers, referring to the United States as "the arsenal of democracy." Roosevelt's

moves prompted criticism from the left and the right, but it was conservatives like William Randolph Hearst and Montana senator Burton Wheeler who formed an opposing organization, called the **"America First Committee."** Aviator Charles Lindbergh was the group's most notable spokesman (for more on Lindbergh, see "The reasons why . . ." box on page 410).

Opinion polls found that most Americans supported providing aid to Britain. American politicians responded. In the fall of 1940, Roosevelt, running for an unprecedented third term of office, repeatedly declared that the United

Read a 1941 Lindbergh address to the America First Committee.

States would not enter the war, but he warned that dangerous waters lay ahead. What he proposed instead was "aid short of war."

## Aid Short of War

Roosevelt handily won the election of 1940 and soon began articulating a plan for American involvement in the war.

### The Four Freedoms

America had to take a stand, Roosevelt declared, in order to create a world based on what he dubbed the **Four Freedoms**: freedom of speech, freedom of worship, freedom from want, and freedom from fear. This was Roosevelt's clearest statement yet that the United States would take a powerful role in creating a new order in world affairs. In almost every way, these four freedoms were directly opposed to what the Nazis were doing in conquering Europe. If Roosevelt had his way, the war would be fought on ideological grounds.

Roosevelt then pressured Congress, in March 1941, to pass the **Lend-Lease Act**, empowering the president to lend weapons and supplies to nations fighting the Germans or the Japanese. These measures became

Listen to the Four Freedoms speech.

even more urgent with a series of victories in late 1940 and early 1941 for the German, Italian, and Japanese powers (now in a formal alliance, known as "the Axis Powers").

In August 1941, Roosevelt met with Churchill in a secret conference off the coast of Newfoundland.

> *By the middle of 1941, the United States was in an undeclared shooting war with Germany.*

Roosevelt told Churchill he would give assistance but not declare war. The two leaders issued a set of aims known as the **Atlantic Charter**, which stated that the war was being waged in the name of national self-determination and was not a war of conquest. With the charter, the United States had committed itself to the defeat of Germany and the victory of Britain. But it was not yet at war.

Roosevelt ordered his navy to escort ships across the Atlantic, which was being heavily patrolled by German U-boats. The Germans sank U.S. ships in the fall of 1941, after which Roosevelt ordered the navy to fire on German and Italian submarines. By the middle of 1941, the United States was in an undeclared shooting war with Germany.

 Read the Atlantic Charter.

## Conflict in the Pacific

Events in Asia would tilt the nation toward formally declaring war. The Japanese conquest of China violated the American belief that China should be kept free from foreign domination and thus open to American trade. Japan did not stop there. In July 1941, Japanese forces occupied the French colony of Indochina, which included Cambodia, Laos, and Vietnam. Alarmed by the aggressive nature of these invasions, the United States perceived a Japanese plan to control all of Asia. It retaliated by cutting off all trade with Japan.

This was a grave threat to the Japanese. Without raw materials from the United States, the Japanese economy would slow down. The United States had therefore given Japan a difficult choice: either withdraw from Indochina and China or seek resources elsewhere. Japanese planners chose to look elsewhere: They invaded British and Dutch possessions in the East Indies. But they felt that the U.S. presence in the Far East was limiting their capacity to expand into other territories. In their view, the United States had to be forcibly expelled from Asia.

In September 1941, the Japanese imperial command decided to stage an attack on the main U.S. fleet in the Pacific, anchored at Pearl Harbor, Hawai'i. If they succeeded in handicapping the American fleet, they might be able to finish their desired conquests before the United States could rebuild. American intelligence officials had cracked Japanese codes in 1940 but were unable to discern where or when an attack might come.

 Hear Roosevelt's war message to Congress, December 8, 1941.

On the morning of December 7, 1941, Japanese bombers appeared in the skies above Pearl Harbor. The bombers sank or damaged eight U.S. battleships and killed 2,403 Americans before returning to aircraft carriers, some 220 miles away. At the same time, Japan launched offensives against American positions in the Philippines, Guam, and Midway Island, as well as British-held Hong Kong and Malaysia, in order to augment the resource-rich empire its planners had envisioned. Shocked and furious, Roosevelt announced that December 7 would become "a date which will live in infamy." He then asked Congress for a declaration of war. On December 8, both houses of Congress declared war with only one dissenting vote (Congresswoman Jeanette Rankin of Montana, a pacifist). Honoring

>> "AIR RAID PEARL HARBOR . . . This is no drill." —Navy Lieutenant Commander Logan Ramsey's first broadcast alert on December 7, 1941

**Atlantic Charter**
Set of aims issued by Roosevelt and Churchill stating that the war was being waged in the name of national self-determination and was not a war of conquest

**Grand Alliance**
Group of three countries allied to fight Hitler: the United States, Britain, and the Soviet Union

**four policemen**
Four major allies: the United States, the Soviet Union, Britain, and China; Roosevelt suggested that after the war, these countries exert their military power to ensure international peace

his alliance with Japan, Hitler declared war on the United States on December 11, making the war a world war.

# LO³ The War

In December 1941, the German-Japanese Axis seemed all-powerful. On all fronts, the Allies were losing. In the Pacific, the Japanese had mauled the Americans at Pearl Harbor and scored rapid victories in the Dutch East Indies and the Philippines. By mid-1942, Japan's quest for control of a unified Asia was almost complete. Meanwhile, German and Italian forces occupied much of North Africa and most of Europe except Britain. Despite his nonaggression pact with the Soviet Union, Hitler's armies were nearing Moscow as well. They had also begun the process of murdering all of Europe's Jews and political radicals in an effort to remake Europe in Germany's Aryan image; the Holocaust was under way.

These frightening developments brought the United States, Britain, and the Soviet Union together in a **Grand Alliance** that would eventually turn the

"AND HOW ARE WE FEELING TO-DAY?"

>> Britain's Winston Churchill, the U.S.'s Franklin Roosevelt, and the Soviet Union's Joseph Stalin imagined themselves, and were imagined, as doctors fixing an ailing world.

Copyright © The Granger Collection, New York/The Granger Collection

tide of the war. But it was a long journey from those initial defeats to eventual victory.

## The Alliance

Although most Americans viewed Japan as the main aggressor, Roosevelt and Churchill agreed that Germany posed the greater threat. For the time being, however, neither the United States nor Britain was strong enough to mount an attack. For many months, the Soviet Union was the only force battling the Axis on the European continent.

To help the Soviets, the United States and Britain sent $11 billion in trucks, food, and other supplies. The Soviets were grateful, but Stalin wanted a permanent alliance. The question was, on what terms? Stalin would not accept the Atlantic Charter because of its insistence on democratic elections, which might threaten his creation of a communist empire. Stalin also wanted to reclaim Poland from Germany, which was forbidden by the charter's commitment to national determination. Stalin had decided he would never agree to any European settlement that would let armies sweep eastward, unimpeded, toward Moscow. He wanted to ensure Soviet security from western Europe.

In May 1942, the Soviet Red Army struggled alone against Germany. Roosevelt, fearing the Soviets might make a separate peace with Germany, suggested that, after the war, the four major allies (the United States, the Soviet Union, Britain, and China) exert their military power to ensure international peace. Stalin enthusiastically agreed to this **four policemen** approach, believing it was Roosevelt's way of promising that governments friendly to Soviet interests would be installed in central Europe. Roosevelt probably envisioned only a general Soviet role in guaranteeing security. Thus, even as the United States entered the war, Roosevelt's vision of the postwar world was on a collision course with that of the Soviet leader, a course that would lead to the Cold War. For the time being, though, a remarkable alliance had been forged, one that brought together the largest capitalist nation in the world (the United States), the largest communist nation, which was still committed to the goal of world revolution (the Soviet Union), and the largest colonial power that was struggling to keep its vast global empire closed to American trade (Great Britain).

## The Pacific Theater, 1941–1942

Although the Allies agreed to make Germany rather than Japan their first goal, the United States had a larger presence in the Pacific than in Europe. Thus, American troops fought their first battles of the war in the Pacific. American forces suffered many defeats in those early months. In the Philippines, the Wake Islands, and near Australia, Allied troops lost repeatedly. Sensing an opportunity to eject the American presence from the Pacific once and for all, the Japanese now sought possession of Hawai'i. By taking Hawai'i, they hoped to end the American threat in the Pacific before the United States had fully mobilized for war.

Good news came in May 1942, when Americans finally slowed the Japanese advance at the Battle of the Coral Sea. Then in June, a Japanese plan to deal a knockout punch to American forces backfired at Midway Island, when the Japanese suffered a decisive defeat. After Midway, Japan had reached the limit of its expansion in the Pacific. It was no longer an offensive threat pushing toward the American West Coast. But what would it take to beat it back entirely? As it turned out, quite a lot.

## The European Theater, 1942–1943

In the early months of 1942, the Axis Powers reached the limit of their expansion in Europe. In the west, German U-boats had sunk more than four hundred American ships in the Atlantic and were handily in control of almost all of western Europe. In the south, German troops moved from Libya to Egypt, African land that they sought in order to shut down the Allies' last unfettered supply routes and win sole access to Middle Eastern oil. In the east, the Germans launched a summer counteroffensive in southern Russia and the Caucasus Mountains, tak-

ing Stalingrad on September 13. By the middle of 1942, the Germans had buttressed their hold on western Europe on all sides. Only Britain remained unoccupied.

For the Allies, better news came in late 1942, four months after Japan had been slowed in the Pacific. In October, British troops checked the Axis advance in Africa at the battle of El Alamein. Shortly thereafter, American troops arrived in North Africa, bottling up the Germans in Tunisia. The south was increasingly secure; Axis advances were repelled, and an avenue appeared through which the Allies could enter Europe. In the east, meanwhile, the Soviets stopped the German advance in the titanic Battle of Stalingrad. The Soviet Union slowly began to reconquer the lands it had just lost. After years of deadly war, the Axis advances were blocked on all fronts.

## Turning Points: 1943

In 1943, Allied leaders faced the question of how to translate these initial successes into a strategy for winning the war. Roosevelt and Churchill, avoiding a direct assault on France or Germany, agreed to invade Sicily and Italy, which the Allies succeeded in doing rather quickly. They were making progress on other fronts too. The United States had launched its first offensive in the Pacific at **Guadalcanal**, finally winning a foothold there. It also began a strategy of "island-hopping," in which it flew over heavily defended outer islands and attacked less defended islands, isolating Japanese strongholds. In Africa, by May 1943, all German and Italian forces had been defeated. The grip was loosening. American war power and materiel (equipment), together with the British and the other Allied forces, seemed to be strong enough.

 Watch a video of the war in Italy.

## The Tehran Conference

The first meeting between Churchill, Roosevelt, and Stalin took place in November 1943, in Tehran, Iran. Their main topic was the opening of the second front against Vichy France, which would bolster the Soviet forces fighting on the eastern front. At the meeting, the three powers set a launch date in mid-1944. In exchange for this attempt to surround Germany in Europe, Stalin agreed to open a front against Japan once Germany had been defeated.

© Rue des Archives/The Granger Collection, New York

>> The 1943 landing at Guadalcanal was a major turning point in the Pacific theater, giving the Allies a foothold to fight the Japanese.

## 1944: Victory in View

In early 1944, with the spirit of cooperation between the major Allies stronger than ever, Allied forces attacked German and Japanese troops on a number of fronts. But all eyes were on the planned Allied landing in northern France, which Hitler was anticipating.

### Normandy

Hitler didn't know where the attack was going to come from, though, and if the Allies failed to secure a foothold in France, Hitler would be able to rush troops back to Russia and possibly hold off the advancing Soviets, securing his empire. But on June 6, 1944, an amphibious American, Canadian, and

 See a video of news coverage of D-Day.

British assault on a 60-mile stretch of Normandy, France, supervised by American general Dwight Eisenhower, established a landing zone. After D-Day (short for "designation day," also known as Operation Overlord), 1 million Allied troops poured into France and struck eastward, taking Caen and St. Lô en route to securing Paris on August 25.

Moving swiftly, more than 2 million American, British, and other Allied troops entered France by September 5, and German defenses crumbled. By September 11, 1944, all of France, Belgium, and Luxembourg had been liberated, and the next day Allied troops entered Germany (see Map 24.1). On the eastern front, Soviet troops invaded the Baltic states and East Prussia in the north and the Balkans

and Hungary in the south. In the Pacific, American troops landed on Mindoro Island in the Philippines on December 15, and in a series of naval battles, destroyed most of Japan's remaining sea power (see Map 24.2). By late 1944, with Allied troops moving on all fronts toward Berlin and Tokyo, the defeat of the Axis was assured.

# LO⁴ The American Home Front

World War II was a remarkably destructive war, laying waste to much of Europe. Indeed, one would be hard pressed to overstate its destruction. The war killed off almost an entire generation—more than 23 million Soviets alone and about 62 million total. The war displaced millions more. Buildings—churches, castles, monasteries—that had stood for a thousand years or more were obliterated. Hitler's soldiers had annihilated nearly all of European Jewry—roughly 6 million Jews died in Nazi concentration camps. About half of the Jews killed were from Poland; the rest came from almost every other European nation, including France, Germany, the Ukraine, the Baltic states, Greece, and Italy.

The United States suffered too, but on a very different scale. Roughly 400,000 Americans died, and millions were injured. However, as unsettling and uncomfortable as it might seem to do so, the Second World War can be seen as an energizing event in American history rather than a destructive one. Very little American land or property was destroyed; the economy recovered from the Great Depression; and groups that were long excluded from full participation in American life slowly gained a measure of

© Roger-Viollet/The Image Works

>> The 1944 D-Day landing at Normandy, France was a major turning point in the European theater, allowing Allied troops to enter Europe easily.

© Hans Wild/Time Life Pictures/Getty Images

>> Coventry Cathedral in England was only one example of the devastation wrought by the war.

**GERMAN OCCUPATION ZONES AT WAR'S END**

BRITISH ZONE
Berlin
SOVIET ZONE
FRENCH ZONE
AMERICAN ZONE

ICELAND

NORWAY
Oslo
SWEDEN
Stockholm
FINLAND
Helsinki

NORTH SEA

DENMARK
See Inset
Copenhagen

Dublin
IRELAND
UNITED KINGDOM

⑬ German surrender, Reims, May 7, 1945
London

NETH.
Amsterdam
GERMANY
Berlin

⑫ Berlin falls, May 2, 1945

Russian front, February 1945 ⑪

Leningrad
Tallinn
Riga
Moscow ① Russian front, December 1941
Smolensk
Kaunas
Minsk
Tula

UNION OF SOVIET SOCIALIST REPUBLICS

③ Battle of Stalingrad, August 1942–January 1943

BELGIUM
Brussels
⑦ Invasion of Normandy, June 6, 1944
Reims
Paris
FRANCE
LUX.

Dresden
Prague
BOHEMIA-MOR.

Warsaw
Pinsk
GOV'T. GEN. OF POLAND
Kiev

Russian front, Spring 1944 ⑥

Stalingrad

② Russian front, November 1942

ATLANTIC OCEAN

Western front, June 1944 ⑧

⑨ Battle of the Bulge, Dec. 1944 – Jan. 1945

Berne
SWITZ.

Vienna
SLOVAKIA

Budapest
HUNGARY

Yalta

BLACK SEA

VICHY FRANCE

Western front, February 1945 ⑩

ITALY

Marseilles
Nice
Corsica (Vichy Fr.)

CROATIA
SERBIA
MONT.
ROMANIA
Bucharest

BULGARIA
Sofia

TURKEY
Ankara

Lisbon
SPAIN
Madrid

PORTUGAL

Italian front, February 1945 ⑤

Rome

ADRIATIC SEA

ALBANIA
Tirana
Salerno
Naples

GREECE
Athens
AEGEAN SEA

Damascus
SYRIA
LEBANON
Beirut

GIBRALTAR (U.K.)

Sardinia

Sicily

Rhodes (It.)

Cyprus (U.K.)

Crete (Gr.)

PALESTINE (BR. MANDATE)
Jerusalem
Amman
TRANS-JORDAN (BR. MANDATE)

SP. MOROCCO
Oran
Algiers

Port Lyautey
ALGERIA
Tunis

④ Surrender in Tunisia of Axis armies in northern Africa, May 13, 1943

Malta (U.K.)

MEDITERRANEAN SEA

Suez Canal

Cairo

FR. MOROCCO
TUNISIA

FRENCH NORTH AFRICA (Vichy France) Joined Allies November 1942

Tripoli

LIBYA (It.)

EGYPT

RED SEA

**Legend:**
- Axis Powers and satellites
- Farthest extent of Axis control
- Allied and Allied-controlled nations
- Neutral nations
- Advancing Western fronts
- Advancing Eastern fronts
- ✷ Major battles

© Cengage Learning

Map 24.1. Allied Advances and Collapse of German Power

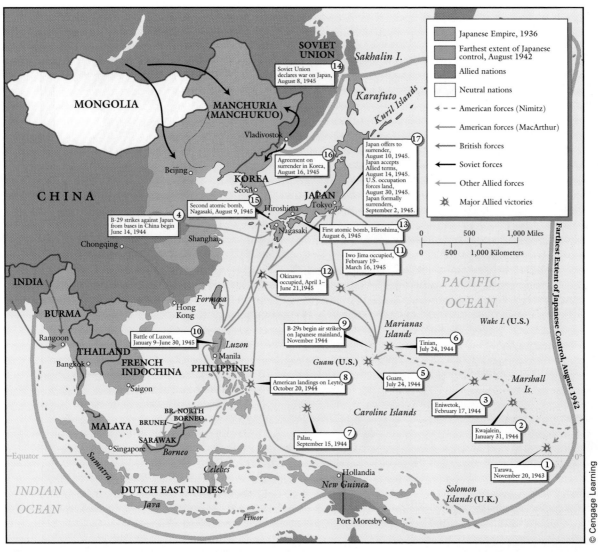

**Legend:**
- Japanese Empire, 1936
- Farthest extent of Japanese control, August 1942
- Allied nations
- Neutral nations
- American forces (Nimitz)
- American forces (MacArthur)
- British forces
- Soviet forces
- Other Allied forces
- Major Allied victories

Soviet Union declares war on Japan, August 8, 1945 — ⑭

Japan offers to surrender, August 10, 1945. Japan accepts Allied terms, August 14, 1945. U.S. occupation forces land, August 30, 1945. Japan formally surrenders, September 2, 1945. — ⑰

Agreement on surrender in Korea, August 16, 1945 — ⑯

Second atomic bomb, Nagasaki, August 9, 1945 — ⑮

B-29 strikes against Japan from bases in China begin June 14, 1944 — ④

First atomic bomb, Hiroshima, August 6, 1945 — ⑬

Iwo Jima occupied, February 19–March 16, 1945 — ⑪

Okinawa occupied, April 1–June 21, 1945 — ⑫

Battle of Luzon, January 9–June 30, 1945 — ⑩

B-29s begin air strikes on Japanese mainland, November 1944 — ⑨

Tinian, July 24, 1944 — ⑥

Guam, July 24, 1944 — ⑤

American landings on Leyte, October 20, 1944 — ⑧

Eniwetok, February 17, 1944 — ③

Kwajalein, January 31, 1944 — ②

Palau, September 15, 1944 — ⑦

Tarawa, November 20, 1943 — ①

*Farthest Extent of Japanese Control, August 1942*

© Cengage Learning

**Map 24.2.** The Final Assault against Japan

---

inclusion. This is not to say that World War II was a "good war": soldiers died, many suffered, and discrimination persisted. But it is true that the war had a transformative effect on the American home front.

## The War Economy

The economy showed the most remarkable improvement. Wartime mobilization boosted production, increased demand for labor, and rescued the national economy from the depression. And it did all this without the extreme measures advocated by some experts. For instance, there was no draft for labor, which would have ensured that all industries operated at maximum capacity.

## Manufacturing for War

But despite this, World War II initiated the most significant federal management of the economy in American history. When the war began, President Roosevelt implemented the War Production Board (WPB) to steer the economy into manufacturing weapons rather than consumer goods. Under WPB contracts, Ford, Chrysler, and General Motors shifted from making cars to producing tanks and airplanes. Firestone, Goodyear, and B.F. Goodrich ceased production of civilian car tires and made tires for jeeps, trucks, and airplanes.

In 1943, Roosevelt instituted the Office of War Mobilization (OWM) to oversee the distribution of

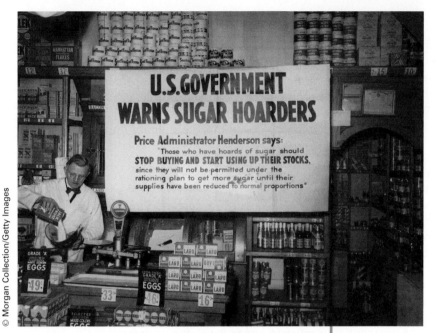

© Morgan Collection/Getty Images

## Paying for War

It was expensive to pay for all these war supplies. In total, the government spent $321 billion on the war effort. To pay for the war, Roosevelt did three things. First, he pushed for increased taxation, particularly on the wealthy and big business. Inheritance and corporate taxes were also assessed. Taxes paid for 45 percent of the war's cost. Second, the government issued U.S. Savings Bonds, which people bought in expectation of repayment, with interest, later. These bonds increased the national debt from $40 billion in 1940 to $260 billion in 1945, but they provided a lot of money up front to the government. Savings bonds were particularly attractive to Americans because government rationing already limited consumer spending. With nowhere else to spend their bigger paychecks, many people bought bonds.

Finally, the federal government rationed goods. For example, in order to redirect food to soldiers, the government sponsored the "Victory Garden" movement, which encouraged people to grow their own vegetables. More extensive rationing and price controls were also instituted. Early in 1942, Congress opened the Office of Price Administration (OPA), which had the authority to impose rationing and control wages, prices, and rents. Among their many sacrifices, Americans sporadically lived without sugar, butter, coffee, meat, or gasoline. Doing without certain luxuries brought the war closer to home for many Americans, creating an environment where civilians far from the battlefields felt that they were contributing to the war effort.

essential materials such as steel, rubber, and aluminum. Meanwhile, to conserve resources, the WPB banned production of nonessential items and prioritized war-related industries. Farmers produced crops in record amounts as well. Through careful direction, the government worked with industry to handle the explosion in war-related manufacturing.

## Labor

The expansion of the economy increased the size of the labor force. On one hand, 12 million Americans joined the armed forces, subtracting them from the domestic labor pool. On the other hand, formerly depressed industries were now replete with contracts, hiring men and women at unprecedented levels. Roosevelt established the National War Labor Board (NWLB) in 1942 to minimize labor disputes and set wages, working conditions, and hours. The government did not want strikes slowing down the production of war-related goods, but it also did not want workers to be squeezed or mistreated because of the more intense wartime production levels either.

This need for workers was a boon to unions. Union membership grew from 9 million in 1940 to nearly 15 million in 1945. Although some strikes did break out during the war, most laborers felt it unpatriotic to leave work while their compatriots were fighting. They were aided in this pledge by the Smith-Connally Act of 1943, which formally prohibited strikes. In return for working longer hours, workers received heftier paychecks.

## Opportunities

The sudden demand for labor, fueled by the notion that the United States was fighting a cadre of brutal racist dictators, led to increased opportunities for women and minorities. These groups were now offered high-paying jobs that had never before been available to them. At the same time, certain forms of discrimination continued. The record is mixed, but the changes provoked by the war prompted social changes that resonated long after 1945.

## Women

As millions of men enlisted in the armed services, U.S. industries needed more workers to replace them. American women filled this vacuum. By 1945, female employment outside the home had increased by more than 50 percent, to 20 million. In the process, women entered into fields that were not typically thought of as women's work, including industrial jobs in defense factories.

To promote American women's involvement in the effort, a government campaign featured the character of Rosie the Riveter, a robust, cheerful woman in overalls who labored on the assembly lines (see chapter opener). This campaign, coupled with the acute labor shortage, helped change employers' attitudes. Though they sometimes had to cope with the hostility of their male coworkers, women workers demonstrated diligence and skill. Women comprised more than a third of workers at shipyards and aircraft plants.

Women also served in military units during the Second World War. In 1942, the U.S. Army created the Women's Army Corps, and a few months later, the U.S. Navy created the WAVES (Women Accepted for Voluntary Emergency Service). During the course of the war, more than 86,000 women volunteered for the WAVES, serving in hospitals, defense jobs, wartime communications, and intelligence operations. These organizations anticipated the Women's Armed Services Integration Act in 1948, which formally allowed women to serve in the military during both peacetime and war.

Read about eight women who came to the front.

## African Americans

Just as the wartime demand for labor created opportunities for women, it opened doors for African Americans. The movement to challenge racial bias in employment began in the early 1940s. Months before Pearl Harbor, A. Philip Randolph, leader of the Brotherhood of Sleeping Car Porters (an African American union), started the March on Washington Movement. Its goal was twofold: (1) to pressure the government to develop and enforce antidiscrimination measures in the industries that had lucrative defense contracts and (2) to end segregation in the military. President Roosevelt feared that Randolph's threat to bring more than 100,000 African Americans to march on the capital might provoke a race war. In response, the president issued Executive Order 8802, which gave Randolph half of what he demanded. Executive Order 8802 established the **Fair Employment Practices Committee (FEPC)**, which required companies with federal contracts to make jobs available without regard to "race, creed, color, or national origin." Coupled with the demand for labor, the FEPC had some effect. In total, the percentage of African Americans in war production work rose from 3 percent to 9 percent during the war. Between 1942 and 1945, the number of African Americans in labor unions (traditionally the province of higher-skilled workers) doubled to more than 1 million. The average annual wage for African Americans quadrupled in the war years, from $457 to $1,976. Randolph's second demand, to integrate the armed services, would have to wait until after the war.

Despite the formal segregation enforced in the mili-

>> By 1945, female employment outside the home had increased by more than 50 percent, to 20 million.

| What else was happening . . . | |
|---|---|
| 1940 | Bugs Bunny debuts in "A Wild Hare." |
| 1940 | M&Ms® are launched in military ration packs. |
| 1944 | During the great Barnum & Bailey circus fire, the band begins to play "The Stars and Stripes Forever," the circus disaster march, to alert the performers that the situation is serious and not part of the show. |
| 1944 | British-born war evacuee Elizabeth Taylor stars in *National Velvet,* filmed in California. |

Just as World War II transformed the world, it also transformed the United States's role in world affairs. Between 1939 and 1945, the United States moved from being a neutral party to being a world superpower. Diplomatic successes played as important a role as military triumphs in this development: Roosevelt's ability to take the lead role in the Grand Alliance ensured that American power would endure. But these same forces propelled the Soviet Union to superpower status as well, and as the last shots of World War II were fired, the Cold War between the world's two superpowers was just beginning, with each power soon to have nuclear weapons to fight it.

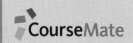 CourseMate

Visit the CourseMate website at www.cengagebrain.com for additional study tools and review materials for this chapter.

# Cold War America

## Learning Outcomes

*After reading this chapter, you should be able to do the following:*

LO **1**    Explain the causes of the Cold War that developed between the United States and the Soviet Union after World War II, and discuss some of the more serious incidents between the two countries.

LO **2**    Describe American life as it developed during the 1950s, including social, economic, and political issues, and evaluate the significance of the Cold War in these changes.

LO **3**    Explain the rise and effects of McCarthyism in American life.

LO **4**    Describe the breakthroughs forged by African Americans in the 1950s and the movement that came to be called "massive resistance."

© Image courtesy of The Advertising Archives

> **"Affluence and consumerism promoted a new style of life in America, as people moved to the suburbs, drove automobiles in massive numbers, and stayed home to watch television."**

Two impulses ran through the America that emerged from the Second World War. The first was the distrust, suspicion, and hostility engendered by the Cold War. The Cold War began when the United States, without question the most powerful country in the world following World War II, tried to use its power to proclaim a new global order based on democracy and capitalism. Meanwhile, the Soviet Union, which undeniably bore the brunt of the fighting during the war, with an astounding 23 million dead, rejected the American world order, favoring instead communism and a world revolution in the name of the worker. To protect itself from the American world order, the Soviet Union aimed to create a buffer of countries friendly to its communist system, regardless of whether those countries had democratically chosen communism. The Soviets' fear is understandable: After all, Germany had invaded the Soviet Union twice in thirty years. But where the Soviets saw a protective buffer of undemocratic states, the United States saw communism on the march. The result was an ideological, economic, and military contest known as the **Cold War**.

The second impulse running through postwar America was a far-reaching optimism that the world could be made a better, safer place and that the quality of life for most people in the world could fulfill Roosevelt's Four Freedoms, which had promised material and spiritual freedom after a decade and a half of struggle. In this spirit, the United States and its Allied Powers created the **United Nations (UN)** in 1945, an international organization that would foster discussions among the world's nations and monitor the well-being of almost all individuals in the world. The first meeting of the UN took place in San Francisco on April 25, 1945. In 1948, the UN adopted its Universal Declaration of Human Rights, which outlines the UN's view of inalienable rights reserved for all people, including life, liberty, security of person, and equal protection of the law. It also outlaws slavery, servitude, and torture.

On the home front, such optimism appeared less ideological and more material. Stoked by the rapid conversion to a peacetime economy and American consumers' eagerness to devour more and more goods after fifteen years of depression and war, the American economy grew stronger in the 1950s. Affluence and consumerism promoted a new style of life in America, as people moved to the suburbs, drove automobiles

**Cold War**
The postwar ideological, economic, and military contest between the United States and the Soviet Union

**United Nations (UN)**
International organization that fosters discussions among the world's nations and monitors the well-being of almost all individuals in the world

**containment**
U.S. strategy for dealing with the Soviet Union, with the intent of containing communism and not letting it advance any farther than it already had

in massive numbers, and stayed home to watch television. The conformity of this culture fueled a host of critics, including intellectuals, the youth, women, and numerous minorities. This chapter describes, first, the contours of the international Cold War, then how the Cold War influenced American life from 1945 to 1960.

# LO¹ The Cold War

## Background

The Cold War was decades in the making. American politicians had long been suspicious of a communist ideology that called for the destruction of international capitalism via worldwide revolution. In 1918, the United States had even landed 5,000 troops in Russia in an unsuccessful bid to aid anticommunist forces there (in the notable Polar Bear Expedition). The Americans were afraid that Karl Marx's prediction that communism might one day overthrow cap-

italism was perhaps coming true. More to the point, they were nervous when they saw "communism on the march," as the Soviet Union sought to expand its communist regime. After World War II, two issues mushroomed distrust and suspicion into a hostile Cold War: (1) atomic power and (2) the Soviet Union's intent to create buffer states between it and western Europe (see "The reasons why . . ." below).

## The Policy of Containment

Was communism advancing? The United States thought so. In a "long telegram" drafted in 1946 by George F. Kennan, the senior American diplomat stationed in Moscow, the Americans developed a plan of action that came to be called **containment**.

### The Policy

In his "long telegram," Kennan suggested that communism was on a collision course with capital-

Read a contemporary account by George Orwell on the UN impasse.

Read Churchill's iron curtain speech.

---

$\Big\{$*The reasons why . . .*$\Big\}$

In addition to historic fears about the threat of communism, there were at least two issues that pushed a basic mistrust into a volatile Cold War:

**Atomic fears.** Less than three months after Hiroshima, President Truman called for international arrangements to stop "the use and development of the atomic bomb." To do this, the United States called for international controls over the technology, saying that it would give up its atomic weapons after the controls were in place. The Soviets, however, did not believe Truman's promise that the United States would disarm. They insisted the Americans disarm first or the Soviets would be forced to create a bomb of their own. The Americans, in turn, feared that the Soviets needed to be forced to accept the nuclear controls by the threat of U.S. attack. A stalemate was in the works, and, in the following months, negotiations ground to a halt. The international wartime order would not segue gracefully into a peaceful postwar order. Hopes for postwar cooperation were dashed just

three months after the war, despite international efforts to create a peacemaking venue with the United Nations.

**Communism "on the march."** As talks over atomic disarmament collapsed, a debate about what to do with dilapidated central Europe produced even more tensions. The enormous Soviet losses in World War II convinced Stalin that the security of the Soviet Union depended on controlling its neighbors. In early 1945, the Soviets imposed communist-dominated regimes in several central European states. But where the Soviets saw a buffer, the United States saw aggressive invasions of sovereign countries. Another showdown loomed. Neither side responded to the overtures of the other. In March 1946, Winston Churchill publicly declared, "From Stettin in the Baltic to Trieste in the Adriatic, an iron curtain has descended across the continent." East of the "curtain" lay a Soviet-controlled sphere; west of it lay an American- and British-controlled one.

© iStockphoto.com/Andrzej Mielcarek

ism and that the Soviets would do four things: (1) perpetually seek to expand their territory unless checked by economic, political, and military pressure; (2) undermine Western colonial development in Africa and the Middle East; (3) develop their own economic bloc closed off to the rest of the world; and (4) attempt to penetrate Western civil society to promote Soviet interests. Kennan proposed that Western governments fight back. They should educate their publics about the Soviet threat, promote democracy abroad, and work to solve their own social problems in order to prevent exploitation by communists. What the West needed to do was contain communism and not let it advance any farther than it already had. President Eisenhower later referred to the policy of containment when he

 Read George F. Kennan's "Long Telegram." referred to unstable nations as dominoes, and said the United States was obligated to prevent the dominoes from "falling," which would begin a process of communist world domination. The idea of containing the dominoes (called the **Domino Theory**) propelled American foreign policy for the next five decades.

### Institutions of Containment

As Kennan was formulating the intellectual rationale for the Cold War, Congress passed the National Security Act of 1947, which created a unified Department of Defense, the U.S. Air Force, the Central Intelligence Agency (CIA), and the National Security Council (NSC). The passage of this act showed that, in the two years since the war, American leaders had given up on guaranteeing peace through the United Nations and were preparing for a long confrontation with the Soviet Union.

### The Truman Doctrine and the Marshall Plan

In addition to the stick of military containment, Americans also offered a carrot to the contested states of Europe. In 1947, Truman appealed to Congress to aid nations that might be susceptible to communist infiltration, an idea that came to be called the **Truman Doctrine**. In Europe, the plan was promoted by General George Marshall, and the

 Read the Truman Doctrine. specifics of the plan came to be called the **Marshall Plan**. The Marshall Plan sent

$13 billion to governments that promised to become or remain democracies, primarily Britain, France, and the Western occupied zones of Germany. There were some contingencies on how this money was spent, but the primary one was allegiance to the United States.

### Hardened Lines

Shortly after the Marshall Plan was unveiled, Moscow declared that Soviet-occupied countries would not be permitted to take American funds. Stalin was afraid that capitalism and democracy might stimulate anti-Soviet governments to form along its border, threatening Soviet security. In 1948, Stalin consolidated his control of eastern Europe by ousting the last eastern European government not dominated by communists, in Czechoslovakia. In 1955, the members of this union formalized their organization with the Warsaw Pact. The sides were beginning to harden.

*If the Soviets were creating a union of like-minded states, Truman felt the need to organize one too.*

### The Berlin Crisis

The first significant confrontation of the Cold War developed in Germany. The Allies had agreed to divide postwar Germany into four occupation zones (one for the United States, one for the Soviet Union, one for Great Britain, and one for France). The capital city of Berlin (which sat directly in the center of the Soviet zone) was similarly divided into four zones. In February 1948, the Americans, British, and French met in London to plan the economic reconstruction of their zones, and, on June 23, 1948, they announced the extension of the West German currency, the *Deutschmark*, into West Berlin. Fearing too much Western influence, Stalin was not prepared to allow this currency into the heart of the Soviet zone, so on June 24, the Soviets blockaded West Berlin, preventing food and supplies from entering the non-Soviet sections of the city. This was the first "battle" of the Cold War.

## Breaking the Blockade

The two sides were now directly opposed. But Truman had no desire to initiate actual fighting. He opted instead for a massive, peaceful air operation, authorizing an airlift of food and supplies for eleven months. The conflict over Berlin allowed the United States and the Soviet Union to face off without actually going to war. Truman knew that the Soviet Union had a massive military advantage in any European conflict (the United States had largely demobilized its army). On the other hand, at the time of the blockade, the United States was still the only nation with the atomic bomb. Meanwhile, an embargo placed on eastern European goods by Western nations convinced the Soviets to back down. The Soviet Union ended the blockade of West Berlin in May 1949. Truman's Berlin airlift had been successful.

© Iain Masterson/Alamy

>> This mural on the wall of Tempelhof Airport in Berlin depicts a German girl handing flowers of gratitude to an American soldier, in commemoration of the Berlin Airlift, the first "battle" of the Cold War.

## NATO

The events of the Berlin Crisis pushed American allies to formalize their commitment to one another in order to counter the growing power of the Soviets. They did so through a pact called the **North Atlantic Treaty Organization** (NATO) in 1949. Its key provision, Article V, declared that an attack against one or more treaty partners "shall be considered an attack against them all." NATO cemented an alliance of Western nations, a project that grew more urgent after Truman announced that the Soviet Union had successfully tested an atomic bomb of its own, in 1949. Churchill's "iron curtain" had fallen into place, and both sides were armed with nuclear weapons.

## Conflicts in Asia

By 1949, the two sides had consolidated their positions on either side of the iron curtain. But after the Berlin Crisis, the Cold War stalled in Europe and shifted its focus elsewhere. Asia was the first stop. Britain and France had huge colonial possessions in Asia and Africa, but after World War II they no longer had the money to maintain those empires. Moreover, the Atlantic Charter had plotted the Allied Powers at least rhetorically against colonialism. This allowed an opening for Soviet-backed revolutionary movements.

### "Losing" China

As nationalist battles in Vietnam, Laos, and Cambodia threatened Western colonial power (and would later lead to the Vietnam War), more immediate issues loomed in China. After a temporary alliance during World War II, a battle between Chinese Communists (under Mao Zedong) and Chinese Nationalists emerged in 1945. The United States funneled billions of dollars to the Nationalists even though America's diplomats warned that a communist takeover was inevitable. In October 1949, Mao completed his conquest; China was now controlled by a communist ruler. Mao soon signed a treaty with Stalin, while the Chinese Nationalists were forced to withdraw to the island of Taiwan.

The situation in China sent shock waves through the United States. Truman was accused of having "lost" China to communism, and some people even hinted that there were communist agents within the State Department. Mao's victory raised the stakes of containment. It looked like the United States was losing.

Read Mao Zedong's account of the Chinese Communist Party.

## American Rearmament

American leaders were determined to prevent other states from "falling." In a classified paper known as **NSC-68**, American diplomats portrayed an uncontrollably aggressive Soviet Union whose program for "world domination" required the "ultimate elimination" of any opposition. NSC-68's sweeping recommendations to stop the threat included a massive military buildup, the creation of hydrogen bombs, and the rooting out of all communists on American soil.

 Read excerpts from NSC-68.

To critics, NSC-68 seemed out of proportion to the threat. But on June 25, 1950, communist powers in North Korea invaded South Korea, thus beginning the Korean War. Afraid of what this meant for the march of communism, the National Security Council adopted NSC-68 as official policy. To prepare to impede communist progress, it embarked on a vast rearmament plan, increasing the 1951 defense budget from $13.5 billion to $48.2 billion. The Korean invasion had made the incredible—a worldwide communist takeover—suddenly seem plausible.

## The Korean War

Korea seemed an unlikely place for World War III to break out. It was remote, and it did not possess vital natural resources. But "losing" China had taken its psychological toll on American leaders. Thus when the North Korean forces (aided by Soviet planners) had easily taken the South Korean capital of Seoul, Americans felt the need to respond (see Map 25.1).

### The American Response

Truman immediately ordered troops into Asia. He also ordered the development of the hydrogen bomb and secretly dispersed atomic bombs and short-range missiles to American air and naval bases all over the world. At home, leaders drew up plans of what to do in case of nuclear war.

Despite these preparations, by late September 1950, things looked bad for the South Korean and American forces (who were led by the United Nations). Then a surprise attack led by the American general and UN commander-in-chief for Korea, Douglas MacArthur, at Inchon, a port near Seoul, helped turn the tide. Taking the enemy by surprise, UN troops cut the North Korean supply lines. The North Korean war machine collapsed, and UN forces recaptured Seoul. UN troops pursued the North Korean remnants all the way up the Korean peninsula, and by November, they were positioned close to the Chinese border, along the Yalu River. Would they now invade China, sparking World War III?

NSC-68

**Classified paper written by American diplomats that portrayed an uncontrollably aggressive Soviet Union and recommended stopping the threat through a massive military buildup, the creation of hydrogen bombs, and the rooting out of all communists on American soil**

### China Intervenes

As the UN troops approached the Chinese frontier, Mao grew concerned. Truman had decided against invading China, but Mao did not know this. On November 27, 1950, Chinese forces, officially called "volunteers," crossed the Korean border and attacked UN forces. Caught by surprise, UN forces reeled southward, and on January 4, 1951, communist troops recaptured Seoul. As the situation worsened, Truman wondered aloud about using the atomic bomb. But as winter gave way to spring, the UN troops again took the offensive, retaking Seoul in March 1951.

### Stalemate

Once UN forces reached the original dividing line between North and South (the 38th parallel), Truman halted the offensive. He was intent on avoiding an open conflict with China and the Soviet Union. General MacArthur, however, determined to carry the fight to China for a final showdown, publicly raged against the president, writing to congressional Republicans, "There is no substitute for victory." In April 1951, Truman relieved MacArthur of command for his insubordination. Addressing the American people, Truman said, "We are trying to prevent a third world war." A long stalemate settled along the 38th parallel, and many frustrated Americans treated MacArthur as a hero.

### Armistice

At this point, the American public wanted a president who would end the fighting without appearing to back down. Retired general Dwight D. Eisenhower, the Republican nominee for president, swept into office on a pledge to do just that. In late July 1953, North Korea, exhausted by the high casualties associated with the stalemate, agreed to an armistice. The armistice brought the Korean War to an end almost exactly where it had begun—but only after 35,000 American deaths, 114,000 Chinese deaths, and roughly 300,000 Korean fatalities (including both North Korean and South Korean casualties).

## A Cold War, Not a Hot One

In the wake of the Korean War, Eisenhower concluded that the United States could not afford

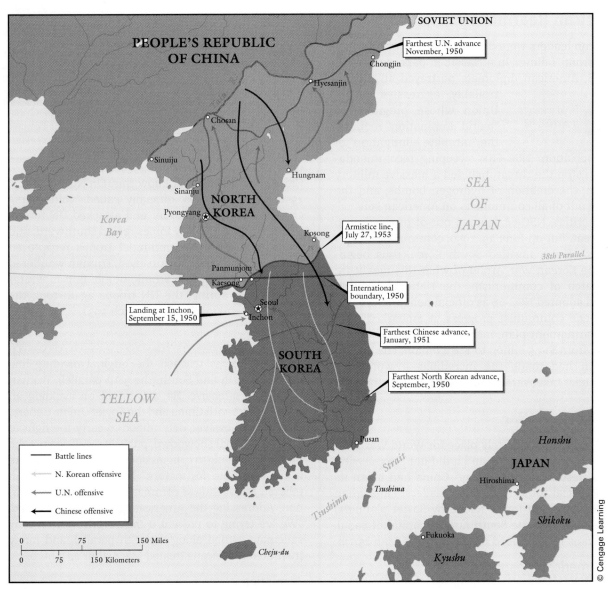

**Map 25.1. The Korean War**

another land war against the Soviet Union and its allies. While still committed to containment, Eisenhower relied less on open warfare and instead emphasized (1) covert operations, (2) formal alliances, and (3) the presence of nuclear weapons.

## Covert Operations

In this environment, one approach that maximized the effectiveness of American foreign policy was overthrowing uncooperative foreign governments through agencies like the CIA. The pattern was set in 1953, in Iran, and in 1954, in Guatemala. In both countries, the CIA and its functionaries acted on the U.S. federal government's belief that left-wing governments might be susceptible to communist influence, even if these governments had been democratically elected. The governments of Iran and Guatemala were both overturned covertly, and Eisenhower repeatedly resisted getting involved in situations that would have to be made public. The political instability that the CIA forced on these countries led to a forty-year civil war in Guatemala and a twenty-five-year dictatorship in Iran that was so authoritarian during the period of American sponsorship that it generated the

Read the National Security Administration's briefing book on the Iranian coup.

conditions of its own downfall. In 1979 these conditions would lead to a civil war that empowered the Islamic revolutionary Ayatollah Ruhollah Khomeini.

## Alliances

Another approach Eisenhower employed was the use of treaties. In Indochina, Eisenhower increased military aid to the new anticommunist state of South Vietnam and helped create the Southeast Asia Treaty Organization (SEATO). In this way, Eisenhower hoped to prevent a chain of "falling dominoes," or neighboring countries inexorably succumbing to communism one at a time.

## Nuclear Weaponry

The third approach was more frightening: hydrogen bombs. In January 1954 the United States articulated a strategy of "massive retaliation," by which it meant a substantial buildup of hydrogen bombs, each a thousand times more powerful than an atomic bomb. This strategy had its strengths. For instance, when the Chinese Communists in mainland China threatened the Chinese Nationalists on Taiwan in 1954 and 1958, American threats of massive retaliation helped hold the Communists at bay. But this experience also prompted the Chinese to seek Soviet aid in developing their own nuclear arsenal.

 Read John Foster Dulles's "Massive Retaliation" speech.

## The Arms Race Begins

Because of the fear of being outgunned and because of the occasional usefulness of the idea of "massive retaliation," an arms race began between the United States and the Soviet Union. America's first hydrogen bomb was tested on November 1, 1952. Within a year, the Soviet Union matched this achievement with a test of its own. American decision makers concluded that, if the United States was to continue to derive some advantage from the hydrogen bomb, it must stay ahead of the Soviets in numbers of bombs, destructive power, and the ability to deliver them swiftly. The Soviets responded in kind, with each side forcing the other to go higher and higher, accelerating the potential for an ever more devastating conflict. Eventually this policy came to be called "mutually assured destruction," or MAD, because the policy behind the arms race suggested that an attack by one side would almost necessarily mean a destruction of both sides in the conflict. Some Americans, notably the scientists who worked on the first nuclear bombs, protested the arms race. But the escalation continued.

## From Arms Race to Space Race

With time, hydrogen bombs were getting smaller and less complicated, meaning that smaller nations without bomber technology, such as Britain, France, and Israel, could develop atomic weapons systems. In August 1957, the Soviets tested the first intercontinental ballistic missile (ICBM), which could travel from one continent to another. Two months later, they launched the world's first artificial satellite, *Sputnik I*, into orbit.

These events inspired a wave of dread across America. The idea that the enemy had actually placed a device in space that was passing over the United States frightened the American public and ended confidence in American technological superiority. American war planners were alarmed as well, because the launch implied that the Soviets

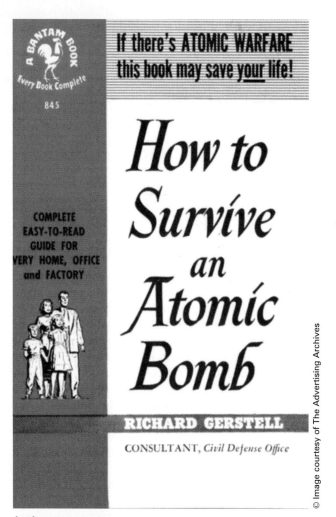

© Image courtesy of The Advertising Archives

>> During the unsettling arms race, the American public turned to booklets like this one, offering such unlikely cure-alls as covering one's head or ducking under furniture in the event of an atomic bomb blast.

>> When the USSR launched the world's first two artificial satellites in 1957 (*Sputnik I* and *II*, as represented in this Soviet postcard), many Americans were petrified that the Soviet Union was now literally hovering over the United States, and that the state of American science was inferior to that of its Cold War adversary.

could now deliver nuclear warheads to U.S. territory in about half an hour. The United States matched the feat of *Sputnik* three months later, in January 1958, by placing *Explorer I* into orbit. Over the course of the following year, the Eisenhower administration formulated major new science and education initiatives and established the National Aeronautics and Space Administration (NASA) as a central body for space research. The Soviet challenge inspired American government leaders to attain a new level of technological mastery, one that would ultimately lead to a moon landing. But in the short term, it merely heightened the mistrust that characterized the Cold War.

# LO² The Cold War Home Front

The Cold War shaped American domestic life in many ways. For one thing, it helped keep the economy hot despite the demobilization after World War II. Fear of nuclear war also inspired both a second Red Scare (usually called McCarthyism, as explained later in this chapter) and a religious revival. The Cold War contributed to a tide of conservatism, as many politicians warned that communists had gained a foothold in American political and cultural life. And this conservatism diminished some of the momentum of postwar liberals, who believed the rhetoric of World War II had given them leverage to pass their pro-union, antidiscrimination agenda. (Despite this, the fight against fascism remained a point of rhetoric for most civil rights liberals.)

Amid these uncertainties, many Americans adjusted somewhat comfortably to life in a Cold War, taking advantage of good wages and the new luxury items that appeared by the truckload. These values were unaffected by the anxieties provoked by the Cold War. Historians have for good reason called the period from 1945 to 1960 the Age of Affluence, even if that affluence was tempered by knowledge that, at any given moment, the Cold War might flash hot.

## Truman and the Postwar Economy

### The Fair Deal

At the end of World War II, Truman saw all the returning soldiers and feared that job shortages were imminent. With this in mind, in late 1945 he submitted a twenty-one-point plan, later called the **Fair Deal**, that sought to expand the welfare state initiated during the New Deal. The Fair Deal included  Read excerpts from Truman's message to Congress. increases to the minimum wage, federal assistance in building homes, federal support for education and health care, and an attempt to reach full employment through public works. Showing Truman's commitment to civil rights, the Fair Deal also renewed the Fair Employment Practices Commission (FEPC), which Roosevelt had established to end racial job discrimination in federal jobs.

Despite the Fair Deal's breadth, Truman faced many obstacles. For one, he was not terribly popular as president. His reserved demeanor made him seem small compared to the charismatic Roosevelt.

Moreover, Truman faced a hostile Congress: Although controlled by Democrats, Congress was led by an informal coalition of conservatives from both parties. As a result, Truman had few domestic successes.

## The Conversion Economy and Labor Unrest

Truman's problems were compounded by the truly tempestuous postwar economy. In the months after the war, the return of GIs pushed wages down, while inflation rose 25 percent during the first year. Labor organizers demanded increased wages to compensate, but because there were more workers available than ever before, employers felt little pressure to capitulate. The result of this impasse was a remarkable series of strikes. By the end of 1946, about 5 million workers had walked off the job in more than 5,000 strikes across the country. Workers were shifting jobs rapidly, and security seemed a faraway promise.

Truman, generally a friend of labor but worried about the economy, soon grew intolerant of the strikes. When two railroad unions went on strike in May 1946, Truman requested that Congress draft the strikers into the military, which would then force them to work. Although the strike was soon settled and the authority to draft strikers was never made law, union workers were angry at Truman for his threats. Meanwhile, conservatives complained that Truman had not taken stronger anti-union steps. That fall, a Republican slogan asked Americans if they had "Had Enough?" In November 1946, the public answered by sending a Republican majority to both houses of Congress for the first time since 1928.

## Taft-Hartley

With their new power, probusiness Republicans attempted to scale back the role of the federal government, particularly with regard to labor disputes. Led by Senator Robert Taft, Congress passed the Labor-Management Act (better known as the **Taft-Hartley Act**) in June 1947. Taft-Hartley banned the closed shop, meaning that jobs could not be exclusively limited to union members only. It also outlawed collective bargaining within industries and authorized the president to delay strikes by declaring a "cooling-off" period. Predictably, Truman vetoed Taft-Hartley, but Congress overrode his veto. Truman's presidency seemed destined for oblivion. And the rights of labor, which unions had fought for so ardently since the 1930s, were dramatically curbed—and would remain so for the rest of the century.

> **Taft-Hartley Act**
> Labor-Management Act of 1947 that banned the closed shop, outlawed collective bargaining within industries, and authorized the president to delay strikes by declaring a "cooling-off" period

## Economic Growth

After these initial flurries of uncertainty, however, the postwar economy picked up. Indeed, it grew red hot. From 1947 to 1960, the gross national product doubled. Wages went up, inflation stayed low, and leisure activities became accessible to more and more Americans. So did comforts like electricity, air conditioning, and indoor plumbing. Well more than half of all Americans were now considered "middle class." Fears about a distressed economic picture melted away as the American nation successfully converted to a peacetime economy.

## Consumerism

How did this happen so quickly? The change occurred because Americans were spending more due to higher wages, veterans' benefits, and demand that had been restrained during wartime. American industries were meeting people's desires by producing new products. Things like dishwashers, washing machines, and televisions rapidly moved from luxuries to necessities. *Automation* became a key word in the vocabulary of the American consumer. Fewer concerns about carrying debt helped as well, as credit cards became more popular in the 1950s.

Out of the emerging strong economy, business leaders greatly curbed the postwar wave of strikes by offering benefits like health insurance and pensions to workers. Labor leaders like Walter Reuther, however, were only marginally pleased with these offers. Reuther and others felt that the burdens of health care and retirement should not be borne by an individual company because that made retirement

>> **In 1947, Truman's presidency seemed destined for oblivion.**

plans dependent on the health of that particular company. Nevertheless, because they could not make much headway in crafting national health or retirement plans, Reuther and other labor leaders accepted the system whereby a single company provides a worker with health care and retirement—the system on which most Americans depend today. This model seems to be faltering in the present day as large corporations like General Motors and Bethlehem Steel suffer economic declines.

## Television and the Automobile

Out of this expanded economy, two products transformed American life more than any other: (1) television and (2) the automobile. In the 1950s, the technology behind the television was perfected, and it immediately became immensely popular. Nine out of ten American families owned at least one set by the end of the decade. Television changed the way Americans relaxed and recreated. Rather than attend social forms of entertainment like movies or sporting events, television allowed Americans to be entertained while staying home. Initially, neighborhood social and political clubs emerged to replace more casual social gatherings, but by the end of the 1950s, memberships in social clubs were beginning to decline as well. Furthermore, television produced

strong, indelible images that were disseminated widely, cutting through regional differences and creating a genuine national experience.

The automobile also transformed American life, and the 1950s were the years when cars were made accessible to many in the middle and lower classes. By the end of the decade, eight in ten Americans owned at least one car. Motels, drive-ins, and fast-food restaurants sprang up throughout the country, reflecting the dominance of this form of transportation. The suburbs expanded as well, in no small part because now nearly everyone could afford to drive to a job in the city. But Americans' love of cars came at a cost: Plans for extensive public transportation systems were put on hold. Rather than build train tracks or subway systems, the federal and state governments expanded the roads.

## Suburban Nation

A quirk in the GI Bill combined with the new interest in cars to change the nation as much as cars and television. The GI Bill made loans available for new homes, but it did not finance the renovation of old homes. For this and for other reasons, more and more Americans moved out of the cities to the green ring around them: the suburbs.

>> Rather than attend social forms of entertainment like movies or sporting events, television allowed Americans to be entertained while staying home.

>> The booming automobile culture of 1950s suburbia also led to a boom in that unique roadside accommodation: the motorists' hotel, or motel.

had fought for the Four Freedoms wanted to begin families. A baby boom resulted. After World War II, 76 million children were born in less than twenty years. In 1940, women were having, on average, 2.1 children; in 1960, they were having 3.5 children.

In the 1950s, the domestic ideal of the nuclear family became a dominant cultural image. Childcare experts, television, magazines, and politicians all propagated the notion that women should leave the work world and return home. For instance, according to many psychiatrists, caring for children was not simply a task, but was meant to be the central focus of women's lives. The concept of the child-centered family was popularized by Dr. Benjamin Spock, a pediatrician and expert on child development whose enormously popular manual, *Baby and Child Care* (1946), sold more than 50 million copies. Meanwhile, *Ebony*, a magazine for African Americans, celebrated the prosperity that allowed some black women to become primarily wives and mothers and no longer domestic servants. Black or white, domesticity was the presumed feminine ideal.

American politicians promoted women's roles as mothers and homemakers as well. In 1959, Vice President Richard Nixon proudly told Soviet premier Nikita Khrushchev that American women prided themselves on stocking their kitchens with the latest appliances. Debating the relative merits of capitalism versus communism, Nixon reasoned that American women were fueling the economy by spending, rather than by marching off to industrial

Suburbs had been growing since the 1890s and especially since the 1920s, but they expanded even farther in the 1950s. By 1960, suburbs claimed a larger portion of the nation's population than did the city, small town, or countryside. Most of this expansion was due to the work of developers like William Levitt, who transformed orange groves and empty fields on the outskirts of cities into large towns made of prefabricated homes. The rapid growth of the suburbs and the conformity that seemed to set in there had at least five important results: (1) the sudden end to the experimental gender roles created by World War II; (2) an increase in racial segregation; (3) a postwar religious revival; (4) a chorus of critics of conformity; and (5) a lasting environmental footprint outside America's major metropolises.

## Gendered Spheres

While women entered industrial and white-collar jobs during the war, the ethos of 1950s America suggested that women should stay home. Besides enforcing age-old stereotypes, there was a social reason too: following the war, the twenty-somethings who

>> Childcare experts, television, magazines, and politicians all propagated the notion that women should leave the work world and return home.

Read a transcript of the Kitchen Debate.

jobs as Soviet women did. The exchange between the two leaders became known as the **Kitchen Debate**.

Though suburban domesticity was promoted throughout American life as a desirable ideal, the reality was somewhat harsher than portrayed. Because many mothers had two or three children, their days were demanding. New suburban homes required a great deal of upkeep as well. Even with new household inventions, many of which were advertised as "time-saving," the amount of time women spent on housework actually increased during the 1950s. If women did have free time, they were encouraged to channel it into caring for their families.

For the women who did remain in the employment sector, there was an increase in occupational segregation between the sexes. With men returning from military service, working women were forced into an employment niche in the service sector. For the most part, they worked as secretaries, teachers, nurses, and waitresses. Most women's jobs offered few possibilities for career advancement.

During the 1950s, African American women made some gains, moving out of primarily domestic service and agricultural work and into clerical work, nursing, and teaching. In 1960, 58 percent of all African American women worked outside the home. Many Japanese American and Hispanic women also worked outside the home to support their families.

## Racial Segregation

The physical distance of suburbia hardened racial segregation. As millions of white Americans left the cities for the suburbs, millions of black Americans were moving from the South to the cities of the North or West. In New York City, about half a million Puerto Ricans moved into what had been the Italian American neighborhoods of East Harlem. As a symbol of what was happening elsewhere, during the 1950s, a majority of Italian Americans moved out of East Harlem, favoring New York's suburbs instead. These types of migrations created many racially defined urban ghettos. White realtors and politicians frequently made matters worse by excluding black people from certain neighborhoods or making home loans impossible for African Americans to obtain. Even when they could afford it, black people were routinely barred by covenant or custom from many neighborhoods. The federal government refused to insert protections against such practices in federal housing bills. As a result, the new suburbs were overwhelmingly white, and the cities housed higher populations of racial minorities.

## Religious Revival

If segregation was the rule concerning racial minorities, religious minorities—Catholics and Jews—developed a new kind of pluralism in these years. Previously denied access to many social arenas in American life, these minority groups took advantage of a 1950s religious revival to move more fully into the mainstream. Fears awakened during the Cold War, the baby boom, and the move to the suburbs all led to a dramatic religious revival in the 1950s. This was when "Under God" was added to the U.S. Pledge of Allegiance and "In God We Trust" was added to U.S. currency. What distinguished this religious revival from all previous ones was that Catholics and Jews were included; it was not solely a Protestant revival. As Catholics and Jews earned allowances for their public displays of religion, they expanded the scope of American religious life, moving beyond the Protestantism of yesteryear. This transition to acceptable pluralism led to many debates about the place of religion in American life, especially when Catholics sought federal funds for parochial schools and Jews sought to ensure protection by emphasizing the separation of church and state.

## Critics of Conformity

Life in the suburbs, with its stereotype of two cars, husband at work, wife at home, and children in the yard, seemed, to many, to be both refreshing after the uncertain depression years and boring because of its homogeneity. Focusing on this conformity, critics derided what they saw as *The Lonely Crowd* (1950), to use sociologist David Reisman's title, which described a society in which people were aware of the world around them, but the substance of the individual was never acknowledged or explored. Films such as *Invasion of the Body Snatchers* (1956) and *Rebel Without a Cause* (1955), novels like J. D. Salinger's *The Catcher in the Rye* (1951), the poetry of a youthful group of poets called the Beats, and sociological tracts like *The Lonely Crowd* and William H. Whyte's *The Organization Man* (1956) all focused on the supposed blandness of American suburban life at mid-century. Historians have noted how these critics understated the continued diversity of American life and the very real psychological problems of living in a world shrinking because of mass communications and unimpeded transportation. Furthermore, these critics overlooked other, perhaps more serious problems such as poverty, environmental destruction, and persistent racism. But they tapped into a psychological sentiment that was shared by many Americans who, supposedly living the American Dream, found themselves bored by it or excluded from it.

## The Large Environmental Footprint

Postwar suburban living, with its large detached houses, unwieldy yards, dependence on the automobile, and incursion into wild lands and wetlands, greatly enlarged the size of the average American's environmental footprint. As Americans left dense cities behind, they encroached on lands that had lain undisturbed for years. In doing so, they were also relying on goods and services that were not easily reclaimable by the earth, like petroleum for automobiles.

# Postwar Domestic Politics

As American social life changed in the 1950s, so did national politics, drifting toward conservatism and propelled by persistent fears of Soviet influence in the United States.

## Truman's Decline

Viewing Truman as a spent force after his labor troubles in 1947, the Republicans eagerly anticipated the presidential election of 1948. Their chances seemed dramatically improved by internal dissension among Democrats. First, Truman's support for civil rights (for example, his 1948 order to end segregation in the armed forces) antagonized southerners, who had been vital members of Roosevelt's New Deal coalition and loyal Democrats for nearly eighty years. Truman also put a civil rights plank in the 1948 party platform. In protest, southern delegates literally walked out of the Democratic National Convention and formed their own party, the States' Rights Democratic Party, then selected their own candidate for president. These so-called "Dixiecrats" threatened to disrupt the Democratic hold on the South that dated back to Reconstruction.

Second, Truman had alienated many liberals when he fired Henry Wallace from his cabinet. Former vice president Wallace had openly criticized Truman's Cold War policies and advocated greater cooperation with the Soviets. Wallace's followers formed the Progressive Party and nominated Wallace as their candidate. Truman was under assault from the right and the left, and this was just within his own party.

## Truman's Resurgence

For their part, Republicans nominated Thomas E. Dewey, indicating that they had made peace with some elements of the New Deal legacy. Dewey advocated several liberal policies, hoping to appeal to the middle of the political spectrum. In July 1948, however, Truman cleverly called Congress back into session and demanded that the Republicans pass an agenda based on their own party platform. When congressional Republicans refused to act, Truman attacked the "do-nothing Republican Congress." This made it appear as if they were making election-year promises that they did not intend to keep. Many union workers also returned to the Democratic fold, encouraged by Truman's veto of Taft-Hartley and by his calls for the nation to strengthen the New Deal (although he still lost union-heavy Michigan, New York, and Pennsylvania). Farmers came out particularly strong for Truman as well, giving him all but six states west of the Mississippi. In November 1948, Truman pulled off a stunning upset, defeating Dewey and helping recapture both houses of Congress for the Democratic Party.

## Democratic Eclipse

Truman viewed his election as a mandate for the Fair Deal. He was wrong. Upon starting his second term, Truman resubmitted the proposals in his platform, but, once again, a watertight coalition of conservative southern Democrats and northern Republicans meant that few of Truman's proposals became law. Southern Democrats continued to reject civil rights laws, and, in 1950, interest in Truman's domestic agenda was overshadowed by the Korean War. Frustrated and becoming increasingly unpopular, Truman decided not to seek reelection in 1952.

## Republicans Return

In the fall of 1952, Republican candidate Dwight D. Eisenhower won the presidential election, easily outdistancing the Democratic nominee, Illinois governor Adlai Stevenson. Republicans gained majorities in the House and Senate as well. The New Deal, the Fair Deal, and twenty years of Democratic power in Washington seemed to have run its course. But, like Dewey, Eisenhower, while favoring smaller government, did not fundamentally oppose the New Deal. And Cold War concerns would, in the long run, provide a new impetus for expanding the government. Eisenhower was a folksy conservative who was friendly to big business, but he was not averse to pouring money into the economy, especially for national defense. He defined national defense broadly, employing it as a pretext to fund the giant interstate project that built most of the nation's highways, as well as several housing projects.

By the end of his presidency, Eisenhower expressed reservations about these expenses. In his 1961 farewell address, he sounded the alarm against the "military-industrial complex" that tied the military too close to the economy and jeopardized American democracy. But during his presidency, Eisenhower had not been shy about expanding the federal government.

# LO³ The Second Red Scare

All this politicking took place with dramatic background music: the second Red Scare. For those caught in its sweep, it was more than just background music. The Red Scare was a crusade against communist influence within the United States. Its scope was wide and deep, curtailing civil liberties and quelling political dissent.

## Loyalty Oaths

This Red Scare began almost as soon as World War II ended; its prominence paralleled the progress of the Cold War. Fearful of allegations that there were communists working in his government, in 1947 Truman established the Federal Loyalty-Security Program, which investigated the backgrounds of all federal employees and barred hiring anyone who was deemed a security risk. Meanwhile, Truman's attorney general, Tom C. Clark, compiled a list of hundreds of organizations that were considered potentially subversive. The organizations were then subjected to investigations. Many state and city governments and private companies emulated the loyalty program and required employees to sign loyalty oaths. Between 1947 and 1965, roughly 20 percent of all working people in the United States were required to take an oath.

 Read Truman's 1947 loyalty oath.

## Nixon, Hoover, and McCarthy

With fingers pointing everywhere, leading Americans grew worried about an insidious conspiracy to overthrow the government. Congressman Richard Nixon, FBI director J. Edgar Hoover, and Senator Joseph McCarthy of Wisconsin were at the center of this storm. For his part, Nixon propelled himself to fame in 1948 by charging former State Department official

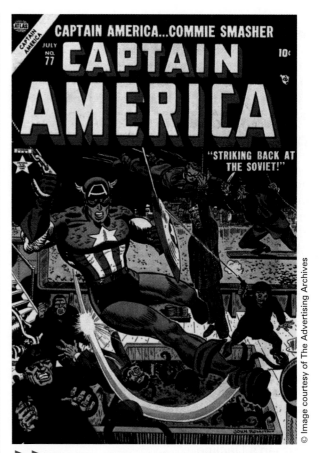

>> Even Marvel Comics' Captain America, now billed as "Captain America . . . Commie Smasher!" became a crusader against communism.

Alger Hiss with espionage. Although the evidence of his association with communists was shoddy and weak, Hiss was convicted of lying about his Soviet contacts in 1950. Decades later, his guilt is still debated by historians. Meanwhile, Hoover insisted that communists were everywhere, "even at your front door," and he instructed the FBI to keep tabs on people who might be associated with communism. In general, his investigations extended to any group that challenged conformity, including liberals, labor activists, civil rights workers, and especially homosexuals.

But it was Senator McCarthy who best leveraged the supposed threat to launch himself into prominence. His speeches were shrill and bombastic as he publicized his communist purges. In an infamous 1950 speech, the senator declared that the State Department was "thoroughly infested with communists." He claimed to have a list of more than two hundred communists, but he did not allow the press to confirm his evidence. In the end, McCarthy's demagoguery, which destroyed

>> "Today we are engaged in a final, all-out battle between communistic atheism and Christianity. The modern champions of communism have selected this as the time. And, ladies and gentlemen, the chips are down—they are truly down." —Senator Joseph McCarthy, 1950

lives, was based on false accusations. His influence reached deeply into American culture, so much so that the aggressive tactics of the Red Scare became known as "McCarthyism."

*Read McCarthy's speech warning of the communist threat.*

With Truman, Hoover, and McCarthy all asserting the presence of communists in the United States, Americans began pointing fingers at each other. Regardless of the evidence against them, once someone was labeled as a subversive, his or her life was often dramatically altered. These individuals found it difficult to find work, became socially isolated, and had a hard time recovering their reputation. This was most dramatically illustrated by accusations against Hollywood actors. The congressional House Un-American Activities Committee (HUAC) focused on Hollywood beginning in 1947. HUAC members believed that the movie industry was teeming with communists; they also knew that a formal investigation of Hollywood would generate considerable publicity. As part of the anticommunist purge, writers, directors, actors, and film executives were called to testify about their political beliefs and also those of their family, friends, and colleagues.

In 1947, a group of screenwriters and directors known as the **Hollywood Ten** appeared before HUAC and refused to answer any questions, citing their right to freedom of speech. The Supreme Court, however, denied them protection under the First Amendment. The members of the group, many of whom were or had been members of the Communist Party in the 1930s, were each charged with contempt, fined $1,000, and sentenced to a year in jail. More damningly, they were also put on a **blacklist**, which contained names of people deemed "subversive" and whom Hollywood executives agreed not to hire. The blacklist expanded to include hundreds of Hollywood professionals between 1947 and 1965.

**Hollywood Ten**
Group of screenwriters and directors accused of being members of the Communist Party

**blacklist**
Collection of names of hundreds of people deemed "subversive" whom Hollywood executives agreed not to hire

# LO⁴ Civil Rights Breakthroughs

Despite the tendency toward McCarthy-inspired conservatism during these years, minorities achieved significant breakthroughs. European immigrant groups, which had faced discrimination before the war, were generally assimilated into American culture during the war. They became accepted in social groups and the workplace in ways that would have been unthinkable just two decades prior. And African American groups began to mobilize their forces for what would become the civil rights movement.

## Desegregation in the Military

President Truman displayed an early example of this new consideration for minorities. Truman was the first president to address the NAACP at its national convention. More importantly, in 1946, Truman formed the first Committee on Civil Rights to assess the state of citizenship rights across the country. The Committee issued a report, *To Secure These Rights*, that recommended "the elimination of segregation, based on race, color, creed, or national origin, from American life." Based on these recommendations, Truman ordered the desegregation of the U.S. armed forces in 1948. The process was slow and laborious, and not complete until 1954. But it was a monumental accomplishment that brought black and white Americans together in the close confines of the U.S. military.

Desegregating the armed forces also sent a clear signal that the federal government was willing to challenge segregation in its own ranks. The armed forces became a model example that interracial desegregation could work, something that was not generally accepted before the 1940s (and, for many Americans, not until much later than that). That same year, Truman endorsed a plank in his party's platform at the Democratic National Convention that supported civil rights for all Americans, regardless of race, creed, or color. Though many Democrats expressed outrage, civil rights had entered the national dialogue.

## Desegregation in Sports

Professional baseball featured another popular example of civil rights liberalism. In April 1947, Jackie Robinson, a World War II veteran, made his major league baseball debut with the Brooklyn Dodgers. Aware that his presence would generate hostility, Robinson vowed not to retaliate against racist taunts. As expected, fans threw debris at him, rival players attacked him, and he was often barred

> 66 Mob rule cannot be allowed to override the decisions of our courts. 99
>
> —*President Dwight D. Eisenhower, September 24, 1957*

from eating with his teammates on the road. Despite these stressful hardships, Robinson flourished. He won the National League Rookie of the Year award in 1947 and the league's Most Valuable Player award in 1949, and later he became the first African American inducted into the Baseball Hall of Fame. Within a few years, a number of other stars of the Negro Leagues entered the historically white major leagues, successfully integrating a highly visible aspect of American cultural life.

## Brown v. Board

Legal challenges to segregation were meeting with some success as well, especially those led by the NAACP's legal team. The landmark case is *Brown v. Board of Education* (1954), in which the Supreme Court ruled that separate educational facilities for black and white people were "inherently unequal." This was a major breakthrough, overturning more than sixty years of legal segregation that began with *Plessy v. Ferguson* (1896). But it was slow to trigger changes. For one thing, President Eisenhower believed that states rather than the federal government should deal with civil rights, and he refused to endorse the decision. For another, the Court decreed in 1955 that desegregation of southern schools should proceed "with all deliberate speed," which was vague enough to allow southern states leniency in enforcing the new law.

Another near breakthrough came with Eisenhower's assistance. In September 1957, nine black students were selected to integrate Central High School in Little Rock, Arkansas. When classes began, the students were met by angry, racist mobs threatening violence, as well as by the Arkansas National Guard, which had been ordered by Governor Orval Faubus to prevent integration. Believing he had little choice but to uphold the Supreme Court's order in *Brown*, Eisenhower sent a thousand troops from the U.S. Army's 101st Airborne Division to Little Rock to protect the black students. They stayed for a month be-

>> Elizabeth Eckford endures the taunts of classmates as troops ensure blacks' entry into Little Rock's Central High School.

The Library of Congress via Newscom

Read the decision in *Brown v. Board of Education.*

 Read Eisenhower's response to the Little Rock crisis.

fore being replaced by the Arkansas National Guard, which looked on as white students taunted and tortured the African American students for the remainder of the school year. The following year, Faubus chose to close all of Little Rock's public schools in order to prevent further integration.

## Massive Resistance and the Black Response

Faubus was not alone. In the South, black advances were almost always met by **massive resistance** from the dominant white population. Certainly some white southerners supported racial integration, but the loudest and most agitated did not. African American activists and their white sympathizers were beaten, picketed, and generally maltreated, sometimes even killed. The *Brown* decision itself had led to the creation of several **White Citizens' Councils**, which were organized to defend segregation. The Ku Klux Klan also experienced a revival in the middle 1950s, especially in the South. And parts of the South, such as Prince Edward County, Virginia, chose to close their public school system and their public pools rather than be forced to integrate.

### Emmett Till

One of the most-discussed acts of racist violence occurred in 1955, when a fourteen-year-old Chicago-born African American boy named Emmett Till was beaten and murdered for supposedly whistling at a white woman who worked at a grocery store in Money, Mississippi. The woman's husband and his half-brother were arrested for kidnapping and murder, and the American public closely followed their trial in newspapers and on television, especially after Till's mother allowed reporters to photograph Till's badly beaten body. Although several African Americans testified that they had seen and heard the beating, the jury found the two men innocent. The world press also followed the story closely, leading one German newspaper to report, "The Life of a Negro Isn't Worth a Whistle." The communist presses also picked up the Till case and other civil rights abuses in order to make a statement about the hypocrisy of the United States's claims to be fighting for freedom in the Cold War. Although lynching was still, evidently, permissible in the Deep

South, the case of Emmett Till provoked outrage, leading many northerners who had been cool on civil rights to see the depth of segregation still extant in the South and making white southerners aware that the world was watching their actions; the two men acquitted of Till's murder were later ostracized by their local white society. Many later civil rights activists saw the murder of Till as a turning point in their lives, demonstrating that the legal system in the South was not going to protect them and that they needed activism to create change.

## Montgomery Bus Boycott and SCLC

Indeed, white resistance did not prevent African Americans from continuing to push for equal treatment and access to public services. In fact, civil rights activism increased in the late 1950s. Following a successful 1953 **bus boycott** in Baton Rouge and the public outcry over Emmett Till's murder, in 1955 Rosa Parks refused to give up her seat in the "whites only" section of a Montgomery, Alabama, bus. After her arrest, the African American community in Birmingham, which had been planning for such an event for more than a year, boycotted the city's bus system. Despite significant loss of revenue, the white owners of the bus lines refused to integrate their seating policy. They held out until 1956, when the Supreme Court declared that segregation in public transportation was unconstitutional.

The Montgomery Bus Boycott, a remarkable success, led directly to the formation of the Southern Christian Leadership Conference (SCLC), founded in January 1957 to challenge Jim Crow laws in a direct way. Several veteran civil rights activists were present at the inception, including Bayard Rustin, Ella Baker, Stanley Levison, Ralph Abernathy, and Martin Luther King Jr. King was selected as the group's leader. The SCLC initiated and organized massive revolts in the Deep South against racial oppression, and it embraced a philosophy of peaceful integration and **nonviolence**. But it would take increased grassroots protests to push the movement forward, protests that would start in 1960.

**massive resistance**
A campaign and policy begun by politicians in Virginia to craft laws and do whatever possible to resist racial integration; spread throughout the South

**White Citizens' Councils**
Committees organized in the 1950s and 1960s to defend segregation in the South

**bus boycott**
A campaign to boycott an area's buses until change is instituted; used frequently during the civil rights movement

**nonviolence**
Strategy for social changes that rejects the use of violence

# And in the end . . .

The conflicts over race in 1950s America would turn out to be dress rehearsals for the massive social changes that would come in the 1960s. But more than just civil rights were affected by the changes in postwar America. The political spectrum was colored by the Cold War for the next half-century. Americans were to have access to greater luxuries than in any other society in the history of the world. Jobs were mostly plentiful, and churches were generally full. But these changes came with some costs. Women were socially proscribed to remain in the home if the family could afford it. Racial disparities were made worse by restrictions in suburban housing. And the consumerist impulse of American life led many Americans to critique their society as hollow and bland. Whatever else it might be, the coming decade, when these complaints would have ramifications, would not be described as bland, conformist, or dull.

## What else was happening . . .

| | |
|---|---|
| **1947** | AT&T invents the cellular phone, which becomes commercially available only in 1983. |
| **1950** | Danish doctor Christian Hamburger performs the first sex change operation on New Yorker George Jorgensen, who becomes Christine Jorgensen. |
| **1954** | Ray Kroc buys the small-scale franchise McDonald's Restaurant and begins to turn it into the most successful fast-food chain in the world. |
| **1959** | The Beatles form. |

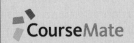CourseMate

Visit the CourseMate website at www.cengagebrain.com for additional study tools and review materials for this chapter.

# The Sixties

## Learning Outcomes

*After reading this chapter, you should be able to do the following:*

**LO 1** Describe John F. Kennedy's experiences as president that led some to label him the "ultimate cold warrior."

**LO 2** Discuss attempts made both by African Americans and by the legal system to provide voting and other rights to those citizens.

**LO 3** Discuss Lyndon Johnson's desire to build a "Great Society," and evaluate the relative success of his programs.

**LO 4** Explain the situation in Vietnam that President Johnson inherited from his predecessor, and evaluate the decisions he made over the next few years concerning the war there.

**LO 5** Discuss the growth of the "counterculture" in American society during the 1960s, and describe the various movements that began to gather strength as Americans with an agenda sought to have their voices heard.

> **"The transition to the excitement and disenchantments that we associate with the sixties took place slowly, beginning about 1963 or 1964."**

From today's perspective, the years 1960, 1961, and 1962 look a lot more like the fifties than what we have come to think of as "the sixties." The economy remained strong, those advocating for dramatic social change remained largely on the margins, and the child-focused world of the postwar years retained its grip in the ever-expanding suburbs. The transition to the excitement and disenchantments that we associate with the sixties took place slowly, beginning about 1963 or 1964. It culminated in 1968, as liberalism—America's dominant political system at the time, which stressed individual rights, democratic capitalism, and a generous system of social entitlements—seemed under attack from all sides. Nonviolent political stances—against racial discrimination and the Vietnam War—so infuriated resisters that they turned to violence, violence that included the assassinations of leaders like John F. Kennedy, Malcolm X, Martin Luther King Jr., and Robert Kennedy. Furthermore, sexual and social mores seemed to be changing and loosening, as a widespread drug culture emerged and as women pushed against society's long-held restrictions. African Americans and other repressed minorities also began to demand greater recognition and access to power. In the end, the agents for change provoked a conservative reaction that began mounting in 1968 and persisted for the next several decades.

## What do you think?

It is acceptable for the federal government to purposely deceive the American public in order to promote what the federal government defines as a national objective.

| Strongly Disagree | | | | | | Strongly Agree |
|---|---|---|---|---|---|---|
| 1 | 2 | 3 | 4 | 5 | 6 | 7 |

## LO¹ Kennedy and the Cold War

The sixties started conventionally enough. After eight years in the White House, Eisenhower was still beloved by much of America. But the Twenty-second Amendment, ratified in 1951 in reaction to FDR's four terms as president, did not permit Eisenhower, or anyone else, to run for more than two terms in office. Eisenhower tepidly endorsed his vice president, Richard Nixon, who had risen to fame through the anticommunist witch hunts of the 1950s Red Scare.

For their part, the Democrats nominated a young (forty-three-year-old) Massachusetts senator named John F. Kennedy. The scion of a prosperous Boston Irish family, Kennedy seemed to have been bred for the job. He was a World War II hero with an easy demeanor and a good sense of humor. He had been a middle-of-the-road congressman and senator, removing himself from debates about the tactics of the McCarthy supporters, although both he and Nixon promised to execute the Cold War more aggressively than had Eisenhower. Kennedy was also Catholic, and at a time when Catholics and Jews were just

© M&N/Alamy

beginning to feel part of the national mainstream, many Americans still believed he would be unable to lead the country without consulting the pope.

In a masterful performance in front of a group of Protestant ministers in Houston, Kennedy claimed that he felt it was inappropriate for any church to demand specific actions from a government leader. He hoped that both Catholics and Protestants would not vote for a candidate based on the candidate's religion alone. His Catholicism may have helped develop his character, but it did not dictate his moral life. In one stroke he made the anti-Catholic diatribes of his detractors irrelevant. More importantly, Kennedy rightly viewed his election as a generational transition and surrounded himself with young advisors, few of whom were older than fifty. In the end, Kennedy won an extremely narrow victory over Nixon, and though his Catholicism may have cost him some votes, he prevailed to become the first Catholic president in American history (see Map 26.1).

## President Kennedy

During the 1960 campaign, Kennedy often spoke of a "new frontier," although once he was in office, his agenda rarely diverged from that of standard-issue Democrats like Truman. Like Truman, he lacked a congressional majority to enact major new programs. As a result, Kennedy's calls for increased

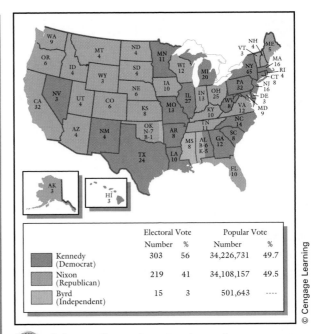

Map 26.1. The Election of 1960

| | Electoral Vote | | Popular Vote | |
| --- | --- | --- | --- | --- |
| | Number | % | Number | % |
| Kennedy (Democrat) | 303 | 56 | 34,226,731 | 49.7 |
| Nixon (Republican) | 219 | 41 | 34,108,157 | 49.5 |
| Byrd (Independent) | 15 | 3 | 501,643 | ---- |

© Cengage Learning

federal aid for education, medical care, mass transit, the unemployed, and a cabinet-level urban affairs department generally went nowhere.

 See a video of Kennedy's inauguration speech.

## Kennedy the Cold Warrior

But Kennedy did become an avid Cold Warrior. During the election, he vowed to take a more aggressive approach to the Cold War than Eisenhower had, by challenging communism all over the world.

### Nation Building

To do this, Kennedy sought the support of developing nations, which he intended to win by facilitating their economic and political maturation—a process known as **nation building**. Kennedy believed wholeheartedly in the doctrine of containment and announced his willingness to wage preemptive strikes to prevent the march of communism. The Kennedy administration pursued this policy all over the globe, specifically with his Alliance of Progress program, which provided $25 billion in aid to countries in Latin America. One response to the United States's promoting wealth for its allies was the construction, in 1961, of the **Berlin Wall**, built by the communist government to separate impoverished, Soviet-controlled East Berlin from the more prosperous West Berlin.

## Kennedy and Cuba

After the election, however, Cuba and Vietnam rapidly developed as the president's two biggest areas of concern, and nowhere did Kennedy's hard-line approach to the Cold War manifest itself more dramatically than in dealing with Cuba. Located ninety miles off the coast of Florida, Cuba had been a main concern of U.S. foreign policy since the Spanish-American War, for two reasons: (1) the United States feared political turmoil so close to its border, and (2) many Americans had invested in the country. These concerns were compounded with more serious ones when Fidel Castro took power in 1959 and established a communist regime. This new regime distressed Kennedy not only because it meant one more communist country in the world, but also because the Soviet Union now had an ally close to U.S. shores. Kennedy soon dedicated himself to removing Castro from power.

## Bay of Pigs Invasion

Under Eisenhower, the CIA had designed a plan to overthrow Castro. Kennedy implemented the plan in April 1961, when the CIA sent American-trained Cuban exiles back to their homeland to spark a rebellion. This seemingly simple scheme quickly went awry. Inadequate air cover, treacherous reefs, and swampy terrain meant that the 1,400 commandos had a tough landing. In addition, the plan was hardly a secret to Castro; there had been a lot of talk about the invasion in the Cuban immigrant community in the United States, and the news got back to him. When the commandos arrived on Cuban shores, Castro's forces were waiting to capture them as they landed.

Kennedy, wanting to conceal U.S. aims to overthrow or even assassinate another nation's leader, waffled as to how to salvage the operation. His options were to do nothing and allow the operation to fail, or send U.S. military forces into Cuba. He chose to do nothing, meaning that more than 1,200 exiles were captured and went on trial; some were executed, and most were sentenced to thirty years' imprisonment.

 Explore documents related to the Bay of Pigs invasion.

Those imprisoned were released in twenty months, in exchange for $53 million in food and medicine. It was Kennedy's greatest humiliation as president.

## Cuban Missile Crisis

After the Bay of Pigs incident, the president launched a multifaceted assault on the Castro regime, including radio broadcasts, assassination plots, and sabotage raids. Castro knew that another invasion of Cuba was imminent. Determined to protect his communist revolution, in April 1962 Castro agreed to allow the Soviet Union to base a few of its nuclear missiles in Cuba. These missiles were capable of reaching U.S. targets and therefore of triggering a nuclear war between the United States and the Soviet Union. The Soviet premier, Nikita Khrushchev, also knew the United States had missiles close to the Soviet Union, in American ally Turkey, and he wanted to have at least some semblance of balance in the arms race.

In October 1962, a U.S. reconnaissance plane photographed the storage site of the missiles. This shocking discovery set off a thirteen-day confrontation known as the **Cuban Missile Crisis**. Kennedy hastily convened a committee of top advisors to

> **Cuban Missile Crisis** Thirteen-day confrontation between the Kennedy administration and the Cuban communist regime in October 1962; Castro had agreed to allow the Soviet Union to base a few of its nuclear missiles in Cuba, thus potentially triggering a nuclear war between the United States and the Soviet Union

>> **The Berlin Wall, designed to prevent East Berliners from defecting to the West, became a powerful symbol of the Cold War throughout the remainder of the twentieth century.**

© Paul Schutzer/Time Life Pictures/Getty Images

discuss how to handle the situation. Options ranged from invading Cuba to negotiating, although most of Kennedy's advisors favored some form of direct standoff. Kennedy ultimately decided to establish a naval "quarantine" or blockade of Cuba to prevent the Soviet shipments of nuclear weapons. The tension heightened on October 27 when a U.S. pilot flying over Cuba was shot down and killed. The frightening standoff subsided only when the Soviets agreed to remove their missiles from Cuba in exchange for a promise that the United States would not invade Cuba. The Kennedy administration also privately pledged to dismantle U.S. nuclear missiles that were placed in Turkey. Successful negotiations meant that both sides had averted nuclear war, and the secrecy of the agreement about removing missiles in Turkey made it appear that Kennedy had won the standoff. The two sides also took steps to avoid getting that close to a nuclear standoff again, including putting a direct telephone line between the White House and the Kremlin.

## Kennedy and Vietnam

While Kennedy was dealing with Cuba, he was also supporting an anticommunist government in South Vietnam. U.S. forces had first entered Vietnam in the 1950s, after France removed itself as colonial overlord of the Southeast Asian country. With France gone, the country was partitioned in two halves. The south was led by the U.S.-supported leader Ngo Dinh Diem, the north by communist leaders like Ho Chi Minh. When Ho Chi Minh threatened to unify the nation under communist rule, the United States increased its involvement. First, it cancelled Vietnam's 1956 elections (which had been mandated by the Geneva Convention) because it feared the communists would win. Then it devoted resources to propping up the South Vietnamese government. By 1961, it was spending more than $40 million on improving the South Vietnamese police system and on establishing a number of programs to help the South Vietnamese battle communist-backed guerrilla forces in the south, called the Viet Cong.

The Viet Cong often fought with the assistance of the North Vietnamese military but were an independent unit. To prevent the Viet Cong from becoming too powerful in the south, Kennedy increased the U.S. military presence in South Vietnam from 5,000 to 16,700. The United States was slowly drawing itself in, all in an attempt to prevent another domino from falling.

But when an internal battle in South Vietnam between Catholic leaders like Ngo Dinh Diem and the Buddhist majority led to protests (several Buddhists publicly burned themselves to death to protest the repression of the Buddhist majority), the United States felt it was necessary to intervene in order to maintain stability. Diem was not doing the job and was making South Vietnam susceptible to a communist takeover. In August 1963 the U.S. ambassador to Vietnam, Henry Cabot Lodge, gave U.S. support (and $40,000) to a group of South Vietnamese generals who launched a coup against Diem. Within a few days, the U.S.-backed officers executed the old leaders and took charge. Nevertheless, political instability persisted, only increasing the apparent need for U.S. intervention. By 1963, Vietnam was a small but volatile front in the Cold War.

# LO$^2$ The Freedom Movement

As Kennedy navigated the difficult terrain of a multifaceted worldwide Cold War, a movement at home was emerging just as dramatically. After the

>> In one of the most horrific images of the decade, a Buddhist monk in Saigon makes the ultimate protest against the repression of the Buddhist majority by setting himself on fire.

civil rights victories of the 1950s, African Americans stepped up their activism in the early 1960s, using Cold War rhetoric to demonstrate that America itself was not living up to its claim of being a beacon of freedom.

## Expanded Nonviolence

Civil rights protests had been ongoing since the Second World War, but they increased in intensity and number in the early 1960s, beginning with the actions of a collection of university students.

### The Sit-Ins and SNCC

In one of the most influential protests in American history, on February 1, 1960, four black college freshmen from the North Carolina Agricultural and Technical College began a sit-in at a local Woolworth's lunch counter in Greensboro. The young men would not leave until they were served a cup of coffee, a practice regularly refused in a segregated society. The students sat quietly until the store closed. The next day, twenty-seven students sat in. Within a few days there were more students than seats at Woolworth's, which prompted the students to spread their protest to other white-only restaurants in the city. Within three days, there were more than three hundred students participating in the sit-in.

By the end of February, students in other southern cities began similar protests, and by late spring, almost seventy thousand students had participated in sit-ins all over the country. The students staged the sit-ins almost entirely in the Upper South, while the hardened system of Jim Crow intimidation prevented civil rights protests in the Deep South states of Mississippi, Alabama, South Carolina, and Georgia. And even in the Upper South, the students confronted humiliations and violence: Food was thrown at them, cigarettes were put out on their arms, and many were forcibly removed from their seats. But the students stayed true to nonviolent principles and refused to retaliate. In many cities (including Greensboro), southern business owners agreed to desegregate because sales had dipped so low.

> **"**Some way through, an old white lady, who must have been seventy-five or eighty-five, came over and put her hands on my shoulders and said, 'Boys I am so proud of you. You should have done this ten years ago.'**"**
> —*Franklin McCain, one of the original four sit-in protesters at Greensboro*

In May 1960, the students organized the Student Nonviolent Coordinating Committee (SNCC, pronounced "snick") and selected Marion Berry, a student activist from Fisk University in Nashville, as chairman. SNCC had the youngest and most energetic membership of the major civil rights organizations, spreading the student-led sit-in movement throughout the Upper South. A group mostly made up of college students, they practiced nonviolence and put forward a vision of a racially integrated America, which they called "the Beloved Community." Young people were particularly active in the growing civil rights movement because they didn't face the same kind of economic retaliation adults faced, like losing their job or having their loans called in.

### Freedom Rides

Rejuvenated by the sit-ins, civil rights organizations grew increasingly active. In 1961, the Congress of Racial Equality (CORE), which had been founded during the Second World War, renewed its efforts to test segregation in interstate transportation facilities by organizing Freedom Rides into the South. After notifying President Kennedy, the FBI, and the Justice Department, CORE volunteers of many races began their journey through the South.

On May 14, 1961, a Greyhound bus carrying Freedom Riders arrived in Anniston, Alabama. It was met by white supremacists who attacked the bus, slashed its tires, and threw a bomb on board. The terrified passengers exited the bus through flames and smoke. Once outside the bus they were beaten with bats, iron bars, iron chains, and bricks. The local hospital refused to help the wounded. Alabama governor John Patterson and Birmingham public safety commissioner Eugene "Bull" Connor did not prosecute the perpetrators.

CORE was forced to abandon its efforts. A week later, however, SNCC continued the Freedom Rides, and a bus left from Birmingham to Montgomery on a two-hour ride. At the bus station in Montgomery, the passengers were savagely attacked by hundreds of racist southerners.

## Results

The event generated national and international publicity. Predictably, communist propaganda eagerly reported stories of American repression, and newly independent African and Asian countries paid close attention to white supremacy struggles in the United States. On September 22, 1962, the Interstate Commerce Commission issued a new policy that required all interstate carriers and terminals to display signs indicating that seating "is without regard to race, color, creed or national origin." The efforts of the Freedom Rides were a legal success. They demonstrated the power of interracial activism, the philosophy of nonviolence, and skillful use of the media, all of which would become standards in the civil rights movement.

 Read oral histories and see pictures from the Freedom Riders' campaign.

## National Successes

While SNCC and CORE were orchestrating the Freedom Rides, other groups were attempting to dismantle social aspects of segregation.

### James Meredith, Project "C," and the Children's Crusade

In 1962, James Meredith sought to enroll as the first African American student in the history of the University of Mississippi. His attempt was met with strong segregationist resistance, prompting Kennedy to go on live television arguing against the inhumanity of persistent segregation. Kennedy also sent in federal troops to quell riots and ensure that Meredith be allowed to attend the university.

Building on the successes of non-violent protest, in 1963 the Southern Christian Leadership Conference (SCLC) under Martin Luther King Jr. launched a campaign in what was called "the most segregated city in America," Birmingham, Alabama. They called their campaign Project C, which stood for "confrontation." King and others organized marches—often bringing along children dressed in their Sunday best—protesting segregation even after Birmingham's mayor outlawed such protests. They marched anyway, and more than 20,000 black people were arrested, including thousands of children. Eugene "Bull" Connor, the notoriously brutal commissioner of public safety in Birmingham, directed his men to attack the protesters with police dogs, electric cattle prods, and high-powered water hoses. National media captured the action, sending images of children being arrested and women being beaten across the globe.

The campaign ended in bitter victory for the civil rights protesters, but only after white supremacists bombed the 16th Street Baptist Church in Birmingham during a church service, injuring several African Americans and killing four African American girls. Millions of Americans were outraged by the violence and demanded federal action. As pressure mounted, the Kennedy administration implored local white leaders to end the violence. Birmingham's white leaders agreed to meet with black leadership and adopted a desegregation plan. As a result, not only were parks and various public spaces desegregated, but black people also had access to city jobs previously denied them.

## March on Washington

In 1963, in an effort to push for federal civil rights laws, SCLC cosponsored the historic March on Washington for Jobs and Freedom. At the August 28 gathering, leaders from every major civil rights organization spoke. No other orator was as powerful as Martin Luther King Jr., who delivered his "I Have a Dream" speech from the steps of the Lincoln

>> The leaders of the civil rights movement made sure the media was present when southern racism was on full display, as in this 1963 demonstration in Birmingham, Alabama. President Kennedy said images like these made him "sick."

Hear Martin Luther King's "I Have a Dream" speech.

Memorial. King's ability to tap into both Christian and American symbolism was tremendously effective. He extolled the belief "that my four little children will one day live in a nation where they will not be judged by the color of their skin but by the content of their character." The simple, forceful demand for America to live up to its national creed was difficult to reject or dismiss.

## A Rift Appears

SNCC workers also helped organize the March. John Lewis, the new chairman of SNCC, had written a militant speech that demanded an immediate end to civil rights violations. Organizers, however, edited his speech, deleting Lewis's desire to march through the South "the way [Civil War General] Sherman did." SNCC activists became increasingly disaffected

>> Martin Luther King Jr. waves to supporters from the steps of the Lincoln Memorial during the 1963 March on Washington for Jobs and Freedom.

© AP Images

with what they considered the more cautious politics of other organizations. This disaffection and frustration would lead to dissent later on.

## Freedom Summer

After these early, hard-won successes, civil rights organizers led an effort to dismantle the discriminatory southern voting system, which denied most black people the right to vote. The work was tough: As volunteers went into the rural South and tried to convince black people to register to vote, they were under constant watch by white southerners and nearly always under threat. The most concerted effort emerged in the summer of 1964, when thousands of black and white volunteers headed south to establish "Freedom Schools" and register southern black people to vote in the upcoming election. The Freedom Summer was not without its share of violence, however. In Mississippi, Ku Klux Klan members, who were being supplied information by the state government, killed three young CORE members who were trying to register southern black

 Read an oral history from Estell Harvey, who experienced Freedom Summer firsthand.

voters. Of the three, two were white middle-class Jewish men from New York whose deaths created images of an interracial struggle against southern barbarity.

## Laws and Rifts

In the atmosphere of the popular March on Washington, activists pushed the federal government for new civil rights laws (indeed, support of these kinds of laws was one purpose of the march). Kennedy agreed, announcing his intention in the summer of 1963 to put forward a bill. The anticipation ended when the president was assassinated in Dallas, Texas, on November 22, 1963, in one of the iconic moments of the twentieth century (discussed next).

## The Twenty-Fourth Amendment and the Civil Rights Act

Within days after being sworn in, Kennedy's successor, Lyndon Baines Johnson, a tall Texan with a southern drawl, surprised everyone when he insisted that he would fight on behalf of Kennedy's legislative plan for civil rights. Johnson worked with several civil rights organizations and appealed to the public in press conferences. Johnson was driven

❝I remember the very first time that my dad, when they went to the courthouse, and they stood in the line so long, and, you know, they said the white people just looked at them, and asked them, 'Well, niggers, what are you doing here? You know you have no business here.' And they didn't even allow them to even register that very first day.❞

—*Estell Harvey, recalling her father's attempt to register to vote in the summer of 1964*

and focused about passing several laws. With his shepherding, in January 1964 the states ratified the Twenty-fourth Amendment to the United States Constitution, which outlawed the use of the poll tax in federal elections (it was extended to cover state elections in 1966).

Then, a major civil rights bill passed the House on February 10, 1964. After a failed filibuster by South Carolina senator Strom Thurmond, it won Senate approval late in June. On July 2, 1964, Johnson signed into law the **Civil Rights Act of 1964**. The act outlawed all discrimination in public facilities based on color, religion, sex, and national origin and established the Equal Employment Opportunity Commission to investigate violations of the law in employment—something that had never been done before. Discrimination remained permissible in some aspects of the private sphere, but the Civil Rights Act was of paramount importance in outlawing discrimination within the mechanisms of the state.

## Violence Continues

Despite the victories, or perhaps because of them, violence against civil rights activists continued, especially for the Freedom Summer workers. Even after dozens of their homes and churches had been bombed, FBI director J. Edgar Hoover refused to extend protection to civil rights activists. Fearing for their lives, some activists began carrying guns, and by the end of 1964, some organizations acknowledged their members' right to arm themselves, moving away from the nonviolent creed of Dr. King. Frustration was simmering. Successes were coming, but actually changing the nature of American life was a slow-moving process. It appeared as though there were two civil rights movements: one to end

legal segregation in the South, another to generate true economic, political, and social equality for African Americans. Civil rights activists were successful in addressing the first, but less successful when it came to the second. Despite the marches and the protests, equality still seemed to be a distant dream for many African Americans.

## Mississippi Freedom Democratic Party (MFDP)

In 1964, Fannie Lou Hamer and a collection of civil rights workers founded the Mississippi Freedom Democratic Party (MFDP). The MFDP was open to all citizens, regardless of race, unlike the Democratic Party for the state of Mississippi, which was restricted to white people. MFDP members traveled to the 1964 Democratic National Convention in Atlantic City in an attempt to be seated as the genuine Mississippi representatives of the national party. White southern delegates threatened to splinter the Democratic Party if the MFDP was seated. In order to avoid a complete collapse of the party, President Johnson (the party's nominee for the 1964 election) convinced the delegates to allow the MFDP to be seated

 Hear Fannie Lou Hamer's address to the rules committee of the DNC.

at the convention "at large," while still allowing the all-white Mississippi delegation to be seated. Some civil rights leaders felt betrayed. Some became disaffected with traditional, incremental civil rights activism.

By 1965, many SNCC workers eagerly listened to the fiery black nationalist rhetoric of Malcolm X, who advocated armed self-defense, a celebration and perpetuation of African American life, and a rejection of white assistance in the civil rights movement. The rift in the movement was growing.

## Voting Rights Act

But the legal victories were continuing. Although the Twenty-fourth Amendment had outlawed the use of the poll tax, other laws prohibiting black people from voting remained in place. But, through boycotts, marches, and sit-ins, SCLC and SNCC had galvanized many poor southern black people to participate in the movement. Through these organizations, a tremendous groundswell of activism had emerged. From January through March 1965, SCLC and SNCC led large marches in Selma, Alabama, to advocate dismantling laws that prevented black suffrage. State troopers met the Selma march with a bloody attack. On March 25, 1965, Klansmen murdered Viola Liuzzo, a white mother of five from Detroit who had volunteered for the voting registration effort. Hours after Liuzzo's murder, as the litany of abuses continued to mount, President Johnson demanded that Congress enact voting legislation.

On March 15, 1965, in a televised speech, the president introduced a comprehensive voting rights bill to Congress. "Their cause must be our cause, too," Johnson said. The president ended his speech with the words of the movement's anthem: "And we *shall* overcome." Over the objections of southern senators like Jesse Helms and Strom Thurmond, Congress overwhelmingly passed the **Voting Rights Act of 1965**. The new law outlawed attempts to deny suffrage to African Americans through literacy tests, poll taxes, or any other attempt to disfranchise citizens. From 1964 to 1968, the number of registered black people in Alabama jumped from 22 to 57 percent. In Mississippi the percentage of black registered voters leapt from a mere 7 percent to 59 percent.

 Hear LBJ's "We Shall Overcome" speech.

## Success and Rifts

By the mid-1960s, the civil rights movement had achieved substantial success. The Twenty-fourth Amendment, the Civil Rights Act, and the Voting Rights Act, as well as the local protests against segregation, were major milestones. Perhaps more important, the progress these activists made produced a major shift in the national consciousness regarding race, equality, and the meaning of democracy.

But there was discontent within the movement over the movement's tactics and goals, as many black Americans thought civil rights workers had ignored the poverty of American black people. Furthermore, as Vietnam began to escalate, many young black men were recruited into the armed forces and away from the civil rights movement. In the late 1960s, these issues— and the rift they created— would grow more apparent, and more violent. For six

 Hear King discuss Vietnam.

days in 1965, for example, riots engulfed the predominantly black neighborhood of Watts, in Los Angeles (discussed below), demonstrating that the United States's problem with race extended far beyond desegregating the South.

# LO³ The Great Society

## The Kennedy Assassination

While John Kennedy came into office promising a "new frontier" of liberal policies, his day-to-day agenda was made up largely of issues related to the Cold War and the civil rights movement. Tragedy struck before he could move beyond those objectives.

On November 22, 1963, Kennedy was gunned down while riding in an open limousine in Dallas. For four days, the nation collectively mourned its fallen leader. In death, the image of the brash Cold Warrior and the tepid civil rights supporter underwent a transformation to that of a liberal legend, the king of Camelot.

## Lyndon Johnson

Kennedy's replacement was a big Texan named Lyndon Johnson, who did not have Kennedy's charisma. What he did possess was political skill, and it was through him that the nation made its most significant attempt to expand the American welfare state.

Viewing poverty as more divisive than race, President Johnson sought to transform American liberalism through a series of programs intended to end poverty and expand education. In 1964, Johnson called for America to become a "Great Society," where "no child will go unfed and no youngster will go unschooled; where every child has a good teacher and every teacher has good pay, and both have good classrooms; where every human being has dignity and every worker has a job." Running on this platform, Johnson won a mandate for change in a resounding landslide election victory over Barry Goldwater in November 1964.

## Johnson's Great Society

Johnson took office with a degree of public support and sympathy that his two Democratic predecessors had lacked. Just five days after taking office in

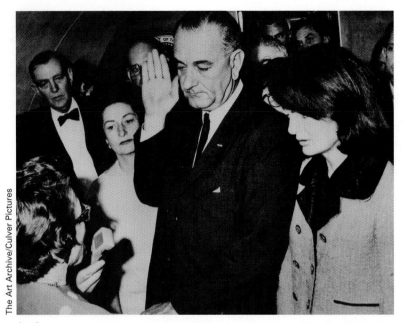

>> **Lyndon Baines Johnson being sworn in on Air Force One, with Jackie Kennedy, the slain president's wife, by his side.**

November 1963, Johnson asked Congress to honor the memory of President Kennedy by passing his civil rights bill. It did. After that, Johnson became interested more in addressing issues of poverty and education than in addressing issues of race.

## Declaring War on Poverty

In his State of the Union address of January 1964, Johnson called for the nation to undertake a comprehensive "war on poverty." Interest in the issue had been growing since the publication of Michael Harrington's *The Other America* (1962), a sweeping survey of the 40 to 50 million Americans who remained mired in poverty despite the fact that America in the 1960s continued to enjoy the post–World War II economic boom. Harrington argued that a poor "underclass," trapped in central cities and rural areas, was hidden from the consciences of affluent Americans. A report of the Council of Economic Advisers in January 1964 estimated that 22 percent of the nation's population lived in poverty, lacking adequate food, shelter, and clothing. Johnson wanted to defeat this scourge in the wealthiest nation in the world.

In August 1964, Johnson persuaded Congress to pass the Economic Opportunity Act (EOA), designed to attack poverty. The EOA comprised a number of agencies and programs, including (1) Head Start (a child-development program for disadvantaged preschoolers), (2) Volunteers in Service to America (or VISTA, to recruit volunteers for antipoverty pro-

grams), (3) work-training programs, (4) Job Corps (for inner-city youth), and more. Congress provided $3 billion for these programs in 1965 and 1966.

## The Great Society

Johnson wasn't done. After handily defeating the unabashedly conservative Barry Goldwater in the 1964 election, Johnson believed he had a mandate to expand the liberal state, one that would use the power of the federal government to ensure rights and opportunities to all. With a much stronger base in Congress, Johnson laid out a series of ambitious goals. In addition to massive new funding for education, health care, and welfare, Johnson called for stronger civil rights laws, the reform of immigration laws, the creation of cultural programs, and an expansion of Social Security. A flurry of new laws passed between 1965 and 1968 constructed the American system of social welfare that existed through the Clinton administration.

## Education

The first "Great Society" measure, passed into law in April 1965, was the Elementary and Secondary School Act, which granted $1.3 billion to school districts on the basis of how many students in that district lived in poverty; the money went to educational equipment, textbooks, and learning programs. In October 1965, Congress enacted the Higher Education Act, creating new funding for college education and enhancing existing programs. The Educational Opportunity Act of 1968 granted young people from impoverished backgrounds new access to higher education, particularly through the Upward Bound program and various scholarships.

## Health Care

In the early 1960s, millions of elderly and poor Americans lacked adequate health care. Johnson insisted that the government remedy this situation. Congress responded by creating Medicare (1965), which provided medical insurance for the elderly, and Medicaid (1968), which helped finance medical treatment for the poor. To combat other deficiencies of the nation's health-care system, Congress signed into law the Child Health and Improvement Act (1968), which provided prenatal and postnatal care for pregnant women and new mothers.

## Social Welfare and Other Programs

Johnson also undertook measures to address social welfare issues. He increased funding to programs such as Aid to Families with Dependent Children (popularly called **welfare**), while also increasing public eligibility for such programs. Congress continued to raise the minimum wage and to extend it to workers in sectors such as retail, restaurants, hotels, and agriculture. Another $1.1 billion went to economic programs in remote rural regions, in the Appalachian Regional Development Act of 1966. A large housing bill passed in 1965 to fund low- and middle-income housing. To direct federal housing policy, Congress approved the creation of a new cabinet position, Secretary of Housing and Urban Development (HUD), in 1966. Robert Weaver, the former president of the NAACP, was appointed the first head of HUD. Weaver was also the first African American member of any presidential cabinet.

Other Great Society acts similarly expanded the purview of the federal government in the areas of health, safety, and culture, including the Water and Air Quality Acts, the National Foundation of the Arts and Humanities, the Public Broadcasting Corporation (PBS), and several consumer safety standards.

## Race and Immigration

Johnson also bolstered his liberal credentials by appointing civil rights attorney Thurgood Marshall to be solicitor general in 1965 and then, in 1967, to serve as the first African American Supreme Court justice. Johnson's commitment to civil rights also prompted him to call for a liberalization of immigration laws; in 1965 he signed the **Hart-Cellar Act**, curtailing the quota system of the 1920s and permitting larger numbers of non-Europeans to settle in the United States. The unintended consequence was a dramatic rise in the number of Asian and Latin American immigrants. Of all the laws passed in the 1960s, the Hart-Cellar Act was one of the most influential in changing the nature, and appearance, of American society.

## Conclusion

The Great Society undeniably expanded the power and reach of the federal government during the 1960s. It helped reduce poverty levels and created a vast social welfare system that has lasted ever since. It was not without its failures, however. Public housing and racial segregation remained persistent problems, and many argue that the solutions proposed by Johnson's Great Society have made these problems worse, not better.

The pendulum, however, was about to swing the other way. Portended by Barry Goldwater's conservative 1964 candidacy for the presidency, and fueled in part by the perception that the federal government had grown too large, a conservative backlash was on the horizon. One issue would spur this reaction along: the Vietnam War.

**welfare**
Umbrella term referring to many government assistance programs, especially Aid to Families with Dependent Children

**Hart-Cellar Act**
Legislation passed in 1965 curtailing the quota system of the 1920s and permitting larger numbers of non-Europeans to settle in the United States

# LO$^4$ Johnson's Vietnam

Johnson inherited the same Cold War problems that Truman, Eisenhower, and Kennedy had faced. But over time, Vietnam was the Cold War flashpoint that flared most persistently. By 1964, U.S. troops stationed in South Vietnam had become mired in a complex civil war that would keep them there for nearly a decade.

## Initial Decisions

When Johnson took office in November 1963, he agonized over whether the United States should make a significant commitment to prevent South Vietnam from becoming a communist nation. He knew America might become embroiled in a lengthy war that would drain resources from his envisioned Great Society. But he also knew the United States had to retain credibility as a fighter of communism. Johnson's policy advisors were equally conflicted, offering a variety of recommendations about what to do, ranging from air strikes against the communist Viet Cong to complete withdrawal because victory seemed so unlikely. (Most, however, favored escalating the amount of American involvement in order to ensure communist defeat.) In the end, Johnson decided that fighting communism outweighed the risks involved. He sent more troops.

## Tonkin Gulf Incident

On August 2, 1964, the U.S. destroyer *Maddox*, a spy ship, was cruising in Vietnam's Tonkin Gulf to support South Vietnamese coastal raids on the north. The weather was poor, and in the fog, North Vietnamese patrol boats fired torpedoes at the *Maddox*. The

**Tonkin Gulf Resolution**
Legislation allowing the president to "take all necessary measures to repel armed attack against the forces of the United States and to prevent further aggression," which was used to justify U.S. involvement in Vietnam

**Ho Chi Minh Trail**
Winding path through North Vietnam, Laos, and Cambodia that the North Vietnamese used to supply the Viet Cong

**search-and-destroy operations**
Strategy used during wartime in which the U.S. Army would locate enemy forces, retreat, and call in airpower

*Maddox* destroyed the torpedoes and suffered no damage. The spy ship returned two days later to continue collecting intelligence. That night, sonar readings aboard the *Maddox* and a second U.S. ship, the *Turner Joy*, again indicated that North Vietnamese torpedoes were being launched at them. The U.S. warships opened fire and called for air support. This second "attack" proved unfounded—neither of the ships had been attacked. The indications that they were under fire were either the actions of an overeager sonar man or the deliberate misreading of information by those higher up the chain of command (see Map 26.2).

Despite the sketchy evidence of a second attack, President Johnson argued that this encounter was a blatant act of aggression by the North Vietnamese. By a vote of 416 to 0 in the House and 88 to 2 in the Senate, Congress passed the **Tonkin Gulf Resolution**, which allowed the president to "take all necessary measures to repel armed attack against the forces of the United States and to prevent further aggression." This legislation supplied Johnson with the "blank check" to increase U.S. support for South Vietnam.

## Expanding U.S. Commitment

The blank check provided by Congress allowed Johnson to expand the U.S. commitment to South Vietnam and to attack the Viet Cong full force without technically declaring war. By March 1965, Johnson had authorized heavy bombing and a U.S. troop commitment of 80,000. The U.S. military pursued a variety of war strategies, all of which were designed to crush the Viet Cong and North Vietnamese forces but cause minimum aggravation to China, which shared a border with Vietnam, and to the Soviet Union, which provided North Vietnam with military support. Like Korea and Cuba, Vietnam began as yet another attempt by the Cold War powers to attack each other through proxies—another attempt to stop a domino from falling.

## Battle

The Vietnam War was an attempt to fight both a counterinsurgency within South Vietnam and a civil war between North Vietnam and South Vietnam. Thus there were no clear boundaries or military victories.

### Tactics

The war was instead mostly a war of attrition, trying to inflict as much pain to the opposing forces as they were willing to take. Progress was determined by body count, not by territory gained. Beginning in March 1965, the United States began bombing North Vietnam, targeting the **Ho Chi Minh Trail**, a winding path through North Vietnam, Laos, and Cambodia that the North Vietnamese used to supply the Viet Cong. American bombers never completely blocked the path; supplies kept coming. The United States also began **search-and-destroy operations**, during which the U.S. Army would locate enemy forces, retreat, and call in airpower. Because Johnson did not want to provoke the Soviet Union or China, he never called for a full-scale ground war. Critics complained that this "war from afar" was simply pointless meandering through the jungle.

### The Soldiers

From the ground soldier's perspective, it was a difficult war to fight. Vietnam lacked any discernible front line, so one might just as easily die from a Viet Cong explosive left in a city bar as on patrol in the jungle. U.S. soldiers seldom met their enemy face to face, experiencing battle instead through unexpected snipers, land mines, and booby traps. Because the Viet Cong recruited from among all ages and sexes, any man, woman, or child could be the enemy. Army morale and discipline eroded over time, and, given the increased availability of illicit drugs in Vietnam, drug use among U.S. servicemen skyrocketed.

### The Tet Offensive

Despite these difficulties, by late 1967 many U.S. authorities told Johnson that the Viet Cong were on the verge of defeat: South Vietnam would be safe from communism. But on January 30, 1968, during the celebration of the Lunar New Year of Tet, the Viet Cong and the North Vietnamese army launched a surprise attack southward, occupying more than one hundred communities and military targets throughout South Vietnam. In the ensuing battle, terrible

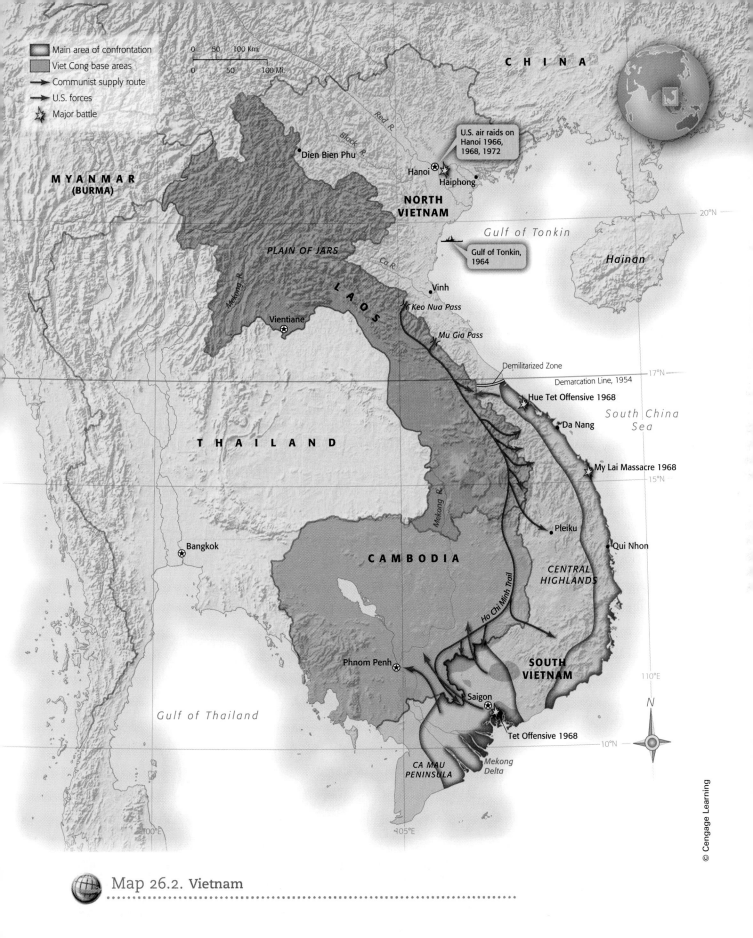

**Legend:**
- Main area of confrontation
- Viet Cong base areas
- → Communist supply route
- → U.S. forces
- ✦ Major battle

0   50   100 Km.
0   50   100 Mi.

CHINA

MYANMAR (BURMA)

Red R.

Black

Dien Bien Phu

PLAIN OF JARS

Mekong R.

LAOS

Vientiane

THAILAND

Bangkok

Gulf of Thailand

Mekong R.

CAMBODIA

Phnom Penh

CA MAU PENINSULA

Mekong Delta

Saigon

Tet Offensive 1968

SOUTH VIETNAM

Ho Chi Minh Trail

CENTRAL HIGHLANDS

Pleiku

Qui Nhon

My Lai Massacre 1968

Da Nang

Hue Tet Offensive 1968

Demilitarized Zone

Demarcation Line, 1954

South China Sea

Hainan

Gulf of Tonkin

Gulf of Tonkin, 1964

U.S. air raids on Hanoi 1966, 1968, 1972

Hanoi

Haiphong

NORTH VIETNAM

Vinh

Keo Nua Pass

Mu Gia Pass

Ca R.

20°N

17°N

15°N

110°E

10°N

100°E

105°E

N

© Cengage Learning

🌐 Map 26.2. **Vietnam**

damage was inflicted on South Vietnamese cities, and hundreds of villagers were killed. During the offensive, Viet Cong soldiers temporarily bombarded and entered the U.S. embassy in Saigon, the ultimate symbol of U.S. power in the region. After six hours of fighting, all the insurgents were dead.

Although stunned by the boldness of the Tet Offensive, U.S. forces eventually drove the Viet Cong out of South Vietnamese cities, after which the U.S. military command declared victory. The Viet Cong  would never fully recoup from the loss. But from a political perspective, the Tet Offensive constituted a major setback for Johnson, because the belief only deepened back home that the United States could never win the war, no matter how long it fought.

Read an account of the Tet Offensive.

## Domestic Criticism

The Tet Offensive, dispiriting reports from the front, and reports from questioning journalists all prompted many Americans to criticize the war. Indeed, the media initially had been generally supportive of the war effort, but as the army got bogged down, as the sunny reports from the administration were countered by gloomier reports from the front, the media became some of the war's harshest critics. Television coverage grew increasingly negative, and most reporters said the war could not be won on terms acceptable to the United States.

With domestic criticism of the war increasing and the U.S. government spending enormous amounts of money to manage the conflict, President Johnson reached his breaking point. On March 31, 1968, the president addressed the nation with a call for peace negotiations—which began in Paris later that year—and a dramatic reduction in bombing runs over North Vietnam. Johnson also withdrew from the presidential campaign to punctuate his desire to conclude the war. Despite Johnson's dramatic reversal, however, years of fighting in Southeast Asia lay ahead before U.S. leaders fully accepted defeat.

# LO⁵ Liberalism Adrift

By the middle of the 1960s, significant changes had taken place in American life. The civil rights movement had questioned America's commitment to equality and brought the issue of social justice more forthrightly to the table of public consideration. The Great Society had expanded the welfare state and redefined the role of government in American life. The Vietnam War provoked large-scale protests about what critics saw as a meaningless war. These protests swirled together, sometimes in concert, sometimes in conflict. The result was to make the late 1960s a contentious time, one in which most forms of authority were brought under scrutiny.

## Protests on Campus

Besides the civil rights movement, the first large-scale protests emerged from the youth culture of the 1950s.

>> Because the Viet Cong recruited from among all ages and sexes, any man, woman, or child—like these prisoners of war—could be the enemy.

© MPI/Stringer/Hulton Archive/Getty Images

## The New Left

Inspired by the civil rights movement, radical student activism began to spread across America's college campuses in the early 1960s. The seminal group was **Students for a Democratic Society (SDS)**, founded in 1959. SDS garnered public notice for declaring that young people were tired of older political movements, even older radical ones. The members of SDS formed the core of a self-conscious "New Left" movement, which rejected the Old Left's ideologies of economic justice in favor of an ideology of social justice.

Read the Port Huron Statement.

The SDS manifesto was the "Port Huron Statement" of 1962, which owed much of its rhetoric to the civil rights movement. It argued that the American idealism bred by the Cold War had been contradicted by the reality of segregation and the threat of nuclear war. The statement advocated "participatory democracy," which meant reconnecting average Americans with their communities and with society at large. While vague as a plan of action, the Port Huron Statement's language signaled that tempers were flaring and that protests were coming.

## Free Speech Movement

SDS fostered an atmosphere of restlessness on college campuses, as students nationwide challenged the limits of expression. In fall 1964, the University of California at Berkeley enforced a ban on public protests and on the distribution of political reading materials in an effort to rein in student political activity. When a member of CORE, Jack Weinberg, was arrested for passing out political literature, graduate student Mario Savio led a spontaneous demonstration in protest. The demonstrators surrounded a police car and prevented the police from taking Weinberg to jail. The standoff between students and the police lasted thirty-two hours; police eventually arrested the protesters. Savio and others argued that colleges should be domains of free political discussion.

News of the Berkeley event was reported nationally, and the Free Speech Movement, as it became known, spread to campuses such as Columbia, the University of Michigan, and Yale. Student activists across the country ultimately demanded further changes to academia, including student representation in university decisions and the modification of college curricula to include Black Studies, Chicano or Puerto Rican Studies, and Women's Studies programs. The university protests smoothly transformed into political rallies in support of the civil rights movement and in opposition to the Vietnam War, the two movements that sparked the most protest and outrage in the 1960s.

## Black Power, Chicano Power

At about the same time—the middle years of the 1960s—a new militancy was brewing in the African American community.

### Malcolm X and the Nation of Islam

As the civil rights movement fought its major battles in the South during the early 1960s, a new black nationalist movement was rising in the North. The **Nation of Islam** and its charismatic spokesman, Malcolm X, attained prominence for criticizing the timidity of mainstream civil rights protesters. The Nation of Islam's leaders rejected the integrationist perspective of these leaders, calling instead for an independent black nation-state. They demanded that black Americans patronize only black-owned stores. They declared that nonviolence was fruitless. As some white people ratcheted up their rejection of the civil rights movement, the Nation of Islam seemed for many black people to be a more realistic solution than nonviolent resistance.

Hear Malcolm X speak on black nationalist demands.

### Urban Riots, SNCC, and Black Power

Despite the political gains of the 1960s, black nationalist militancy continued to gather strength, as social and economic discrimination persisted. Beginning in the summer of 1965, following riots in the Watts section of Los Angeles, urban unrest became endemic to many northern black communities. The Watts riot exploded when a seemingly routine traffic stop erupted into violence. The riot lasted six days and left thirty-four dead and more than one thousand injured. Persistent racism was certainly one cause of the riots, but so was the civil rights movement's strategic decision not to address urban poverty.

SNCC hoped to tap into the urban rage by establishing chapters in the North and developing

**Students for a Democratic Society (SDS)** Organization founded in 1959 declaring that young people were tired of older political movements, even older radical ones; formed the core of a self-conscious "New Left" movement, which rejected the Old Left's ideologies of economic justice in favor of an ideology of social justice

**Nation of Islam** Black nationalist organization whose leaders rejected the integrationist perspective of mainstream civil rights protesters, calling instead for an independent black nation-state

Read a selection from Carmichael's and Charles V. Hamilton's 1967 *Black Power*.

programs to channel energy into constructive activities. Yet the increasing anger soon changed SNCC itself. In 1966, after being attacked by police during a peaceful march in Mississippi, SNCC chairman Stokely Carmichael rallied a crowd by calling for "black power," and the crowd began chanting the phrase. White people were purged from SNCC and instructed to go fight racism in white communities. This development alarmed many of both races: Roy Wilkins, the head of the NAACP, called it "a reverse Ku Klux Klan."

By the late 1960s, **Black Power** emerged as a movement bridging the gap between black nationalism and the civil rights struggle. Leaders in the Black Power movement argued that black people should have control over the social, educational, and religious institutions in their communities. Black Power advocated black pride at a time when blackness was stigmatized.

>> **Malcolm X in 1964.**

© Robert Parent/Time Life Pictures/Getty Images

## Black Panther Party

Perhaps no Black Power organization captured the attention of America more than the Black Panther Party, founded in 1966 in Oakland, California. The Black Panthers believed that providing goods and services to the most downtrodden people of the black community would be essential to a black revolution, and they developed free clothing and medical programs, as well as a free breakfast program that fed thousands of poor children each week. They began patrolling the streets in armed groups in an attempt to end police brutality. The Black Panthers were also frequently associated with the urban unrest that swept through many black communities in the late 1960s, particularly the riots in more than one hundred cities following the assassination of Martin Luther King Jr. on April 4, 1968. But Stokely Carmichael argued that the "white power structure" was the ultimate cause of such spontaneous upheavals.

## White Reaction

The racial violence of these years, as well as the angry separatism of Black Power leaders, prompted many white Americans to fear and condemn the Black Power movement. Referred to as the "white backlash," this sentiment gave a wider audience to conservative political leaders, such as Richard Nixon, who emphasized the restoration of "law and order" in the nation's cities. Angry white Americans began efforts to reclaim their past "outsider" ethnicities, prompting an ethnic revival that lasted into the 1970s. They also asserted that, with the civil rights laws, the country had already done all that it needed to do to dismantle the legal apparatus of segregation.

## The Chicano Movement

Following in the wake of the Black Power movement came several other movements to earn respect for their particular group. Hispanics powered one influential movement. Throughout the 1960s, most Mexican Americans were farm laborers in California and the Southwest. Many lived in dire poverty and faced discrimination. Between 1965 and 1970, labor leaders César Chávez and Dolores Huerta organized many farm laborers in a series of strikes. Their initial targets were grape growers, who were known for treating their employees badly. Chávez and Huerta drew national attention when they called

Read a speech given by César Chávez during one of his protests.

for a national boycott of grapes. In the highly charged atmosphere of the decade's social activism, the boycott was successful, and Chávez and Huerta won their demands for higher wages and better living conditions.

## The Women's Movement

As before, a movement to increase the voice of women in American life grew alongside activism for African Americans. The inception of the revived women's movement is usually identified as Betty Friedan's 1963 book, *The Feminine Mystique*. Friedan described "the problem that has no name," which she defined as the pervasive dissatisfaction of middle- and upper-class women who had confined their lives to raising children and keeping a home. Friedan's book sparked a long consideration of the social norms that defined a woman's role in American society.

In addition to the critique of middle-class gender roles, Friedan and a group of politically engaged women had grown frustrated by the federal government's refusal to enforce a provision in the Civil Rights Act that outlawed discrimination against women. To fight against this, the women sought to create an organization modeled on the NAACP that would fight for equality for women. In 1966, they created the National Organization of Women (NOW), a still-potent organization fighting for women's rights.

A second strand of the women's movement emerged more directly from the civil rights and students movements. These women were less interested in the pursuit of fulfilling jobs and in critiquing middle-class domesticity. Instead, they sought a broader cultural change to the way in which women were valued and viewed in society. They rejected the gendered aspects of standard social norms, more pointedly discussed the deeply entrenched social oppression faced by American women, and sought to revolutionize things such as the conception of female beauty and the legitimacy of marriage. Many members of this second strand were racial minorities, many of whom were already in the workplace and did not desire to fight for access to the workplace.

## The Vietnam War at Home

These contentious issues—the frustration of youth searching for a more authentic status quo, the rise of Black Power, women seeking to change American society's perceptions of gender roles—fused together with protests against the war in Vietnam. From 1965 to 1970, opposition to the war increased in proportion to the American military commitment, and by 1968 there were more than half a million American troops in Vietnam. Opposition grew from a small-scale protest movement to a mainstream force. By the early 1970s, it had had a major impact on American society.

### Teach-Ins

Opposition to the war crystallized on college campuses. There, the Free Speech Movement had politicized students, who were also of draft age (although, as students, they could defer). In March 1965, faculty and students at the University of Michigan held special night lectures and classes to speak out against the war. Such "teach-ins" spread to other universities in the following months.

### Escalating Antiwar Protest

In 1967, protests calling for an end to the war dramatically increased, and the antiwar movement became a mainstream phenomenon, as a number of leading politicians grew critical of the war. In 1966, Senator J. William Fulbright of Arkansas, the powerful chairman of the Senate Foreign Relations Committee, openly criticized the war. In 1967, Martin Luther King Jr. publicly criticized the war too. Many other religious leaders joined King in protesting what seemed to be an unjust war.

These streams of dissent converged by mid-1967 in massive protests. Campuses grew increasingly restive. In October 1967, the National Mobilization to End the War in Vietnam (MOBE) led a march of more than 100,000 people from the Mall in Washington, D.C., to the Pentagon. In addition, throughout the conflict more than half a million men committed draft violations, sometimes burning their draft cards. Thousands moved to other countries, primarily Canada and Mexico, to avoid the conflict.

### Counterculture

For many of their contemporaries, the radical antiwar protesters' attacks implied broader challenges to American culture. As a result, 1966 and 1967 saw the dramatic growth of a **counterculture** of young people consciously rejecting traditional politics, social values, and corporate consumerism. Counterculture adherents, sometimes called **hippies**, who rejected

**counterculture**
Social movement of the sixties that consciously rejected traditional politics, social values, and corporate consumerism

**hippies**
Counterculture adherents who embraced new attitudes toward drugs, sex, popular culture, and politics

Examine the "psychedelic '60s" through documents.

attempts to change American society and chose instead to "check out" of society, formed communities throughout the United States, such as the Haight-Ashbury section of San Francisco. Some formed communes, relying less on consumerism and more on sharing their possessions and responsibilities. Members of the counterculture often demonstrated their change in lifestyle by embracing new attitudes toward drugs, sex, popular culture, and politics.

Drugs and music often came together with politics in the counterculture. Throughout popular music, artists' work reflected the political currents at large. Bob Dylan and other folk singers wrote songs about civil rights and social justice, and spoke out against the Vietnam War. This musical output culminated in the Woodstock Music Festival, held in the summer of 1969 in upstate New York. Woodstock attracted 400,000 people to celebrate "peace, love, and freedom," symbolizing the ability of popular culture to be explicitly political and successfully promote an agenda of social justice.

## Social Divisions and Popular Unrest

### The Anti-Antiwar Movement

A considerable number of Americans were shocked by the antiwar protests and by the rise of the coun-

terculture. Although one poll in 1967 showed that 46 percent of the public thought the war was a "mistake," most Americans believed that the United States should attempt to win now that it was involved. As the antiwar movement spread, it provoked anger from conservatives, who saw it as treasonous. In 1970, construction workers (known as "hard hats") violently attacked antiwar demonstrators in New York City. The hard hats viewed their attacks as their patriotic duty against treasonous kids. It was true, however, that many of the war's protesters were students who had deferrals from the military, while most of the soldiers were from working-class families who did not have the money to go to college and thus had no way to avoid the draft.

### 1968

In 1968, such tensions began to split the Democratic Party, which had succeeded in the past as a coalition of union workers, racial and religious minorities, and New Leftists. In the aftermath of the Tet Offensive, an increasing number of Americans came to believe that the war could not be won. Discredited, President Johnson suffered a humiliating near-defeat in the New Hampshire Democratic primary in March against a peace candidate. Johnson subsequently withdrew from the race and backed his vice president, Hubert Humphrey. Robert Kennedy, the brother of John F. Kennedy, entered the race and attracted substantial public support. But, like his brother, he was killed by an assassin. With strong support among "establishment" Democrats, Humphrey won the party nomination, committing the Democrats to a continuation of Johnson's Vietnam policies.

Before he won the nomination, though, members of the New Left organized a protest against the war in August 1968 at the Democratic National Convention in Chicago. While Humphrey supporters defeated antiwar planks to the party platform inside the convention, between 10,000 and 15,000 demonstrators were protesting outside it. On the third night of the convention, police attempted to disperse the protesters. Fighting broke out, and hundreds were injured as police attacked demonstrators and passersby who were caught in the melee. Some protesters responded violently. Police then waded into the

>> Woodstock attracted 400,000 people to celebrate "peace, love, and freedom."

© BILL EPPRIDGE/Time & Life Pictures/Getty Images

crowd to beat the protesters who refused to follow their orders to disband. The violence, which played out on national television, was later described as a "police riot" in an official inquiry. Many people were appalled by the level of violence used against the demonstrators. Others viewed the police action as appropriate against the actions of the defiant youth.

Fears of becoming irrelevant and some legitimate concerns about the curtailment of free speech led some members of the New Left to become more militant. By 1969, SDS had dissolved because its members could not agree on tactics. One of SDS's offshoots, the "Weathermen" (or the "Weather Underground"), committed bombings and arson on various college campuses where technical aid for the Vietnam War was being developed. In 1970, three members of the Weather Underground died when a bomb they were preparing exploded in a Greenwich Village brownstone in New York. In the following years, much of the New Left movement dissipated as its former organizations collapsed while debating the issue of violence in political protest. The New Left was becoming more violent, and as such, it was becoming a polemical voice in American politics, rather than the unifying one it had hoped to become in the early 1960s.

## Nixon

Amid the turbulence, the Republican presidential nominee Richard Nixon argued for a restoration of "law and order" and "traditional values." He claimed there was a "silent majority" of Americans who still supported the Vietnam War and who hadn't joined the counterculture. Nixon also vaguely promised to end the war in Vietnam by achieving "peace with honor." The fall election featured three pro-war candidates (Nixon, Humphrey, and segregationist George Wallace, a Democrat who rejected the Democrats' civil rights plank), and ended in a Nixon victory.

## Nixon and Vietnam

After Richard Nixon took office in 1969, he began to withdraw American troops from Vietnam. This decreased the strength of antiwar protests. Nixon's solution (known as **Vietnamization**) attempted to replace U.S. troops with South Vietnamese forces and keep Vietnam from falling to the communists. While Vietnamization proceeded, Nixon continued bombing raids on Vietnam's neighbors, Cambodia and Laos, in an attempt to destroy communist posts.

And in April 1970, American forces invaded Cambodia to wipe out North Vietnamese staging areas. Nixon was trying to have it both ways: remain in the war, yet look as if he was pulling out.

The invasion of Cambodia reinvigorated antiwar protests, which erupted on a massive scale in 1970. The protests shut down more than four hundred college campuses, and more than 100,000 demonstrators converged on Washington, D.C., surrounding the White House. On May 4, 1970, Ohio National Guardsmen shot and killed four Kent State University students during antiwar demonstrations on campus. Days later, police killed two more students at Jackson State University in Mississippi during demonstrations. In both episodes, the use of deadly force by government troops against unarmed protesters shocked the country.

## Vietnam as a Mistake

The campus unrest eventually dissipated, and protests declined in 1970 and 1971. Nixon was also actively reducing the American troop presence in Vietnam from its 1969 peak of 540,000 to only 60,000 in 1972. But the widespread conviction that Vietnam had been a mistake deepened in American society and originated a trend of public suspicion of and cynicism about its political leaders. News of American troops' abuses of Vietnamese civilians shocked the public, most notably after reports surfaced in 1970 of a massacre of more than three hundred women, children, and old men in the

© John Filo/Getty Images

>> **A young woman reacts to the shooting of Kent State University student Jeffrey Miller by Ohio National Guardsmen. Miller was killed while protesting Nixon's expansion of the Vietnam War in 1970.**

village of My Lai. The June 1971 publication of a secret Defense Department study known as the **Pentagon Papers** was another disillusionment. It revealed that the government had lied to the American public over major events in the Vietnam War in an attempt to manipulate public opinion. More basically, many Americans questioned whether the threat of communism existing in Southeast Asia was really a threat worth spilling American blood for. This was just one of the reasons why the Vietnam War was so divisive in American society in the late 1960s and early 1970s. For more, see "The reasons why . . ." box below.

## And in the end . . .

In January 1973, the United States signed a treaty with North Vietnam to end the war. In 1975, the Viet Cong unified Vietnam under communist control. Yet the announcement did little to heal the

# { *The reasons why . . .* }

There are several reasons why the Vietnam War was so divisive in the United States:

*A questionable rationale.* After the Cuban Missile Crisis of 1962, many Americans were skeptical about the very rationale of the Cold War. Was communism really a threat to American well-being? Was fighting the Cold War worth potentially destroying all of humankind? Stanley Kubrick's 1964 film *Dr. Strangelove, or: How I Learned to Stop Worrying and Love the Bomb* made exactly this critique. Thus, while most Americans initially approved of American involvement in Vietnam (especially after the articulation of the Domino Theory and the Gulf of Tonkin incident), many Americans by the mid-1960s did not think fighting the Cold War was worth the potential costs. Plus, many Americans realized that the Vietnamese people simply wanted independence after centuries of colonial rule. Antiwar protests based on these critiques began in 1964 and gathered strength when President Johnson committed ground troops in 1965, which greatly increased the number of men who were drafted. At the same time, and despite the protests, many Americans still firmly believed the United States had to fight communism wherever it might be budding. To the war's supporters, the protesters seemed to be cowards unwilling to fight a dangerous enemy. From the beginning, it was a contentious war.

*Class conflicts.* These divisions developed class distinctions throughout the 1960s. The initial protests against the Vietnam War swirled together with the other protests of the era, particularly the civil rights movement and the student protests. These other movements were, at root, questioning the United States's commitment to extending liberty to all and, indeed, its very integrity as a nation. To those fighting the war, or to their families, this seemed unpatriotic or even treasonous. Furthermore, most of the initial protesters were university students with student deferrals from the draft, while many working-class young men did not have access to such deferrals. Thus, many of those protesting the war did so in front of parents whose children were fighting in it.

*Economic costs.* These arguments took a political turn when it became evident that the financial cost of the war was infringing on

the benefits proposed by Johnson's Great Society. In the end, the war cost $140 billion. To those who felt their tax dollars were better spent on improving education, eliminating poverty, and other social services, the Vietnam War seemed like a misappropriation of funds. For those who felt that fighting communism was the most important issue of the day, this money was well spent.

*Government deceit.* From these roots, the antiwar movement picked up steam once it became clear, well before the end of the conflict, that the federal government had deliberately deceived the American population about what was happening in Vietnam. This deception was confirmed with the 1971 publication of the Pentagon Papers, a secret history of the Vietnam War leaked to the *New York Times*. The study revealed that four presidents, from Truman to Johnson, had deceived Americans about American involvement in Southeast Asia, that the conflict would have been avoided had the United States honored the 1954 Geneva Convention, which mandated democratic elections in Vietnam, that Nixon had ordered carpet-bombing of large swaths of Vietnam, Cambodia, and Laos, and that the most important reason the federal government maintained troops in Vietnam was to avoid a humiliating defeat, not to improve the lives of the South Vietnamese or win a strategic battle in the Cold War. War protesters argued that the leaders of a democratic nation should not deliberately lie to their constituents in order to wage war. Many of the war's supporters argued that it was acceptable for the federal government to maintain secrets in the name of national defense.

*Anger.* These divisive reasons created anger and resentment on both sides. Some Americans spit on and harassed returning American soldiers, even though many of these veterans were simply eighteen-year-old kids who had been drafted into the army. Others declared that all protesters were spineless weaklings. These kinds of actions further polarized the sides, and the nation as well.

"There's Money Enough To Support Both Of You —
Now, Doesn't That Make You Feel Better?"

A 1967 Herblock Cartoon, copyright © by The Herb Block Foundation

---from The Herblock Gallery (Simon & Schuster, 1968)

wounds raised by years of internal argument over the war's merits. The war had led to the death of more than 58,000 American soldiers and some 3 million Vietnamese. But it also exposed deep rifts in American society. Perhaps the second tragedy of Vietnam, beyond the death toll, was that

## What else was happening . . .

| 1960 | Two hackers from MIT create the first computer video game, Spacewar. |
|---|---|
| 1963 | Harvey Ball, a Worcester, Massachusetts, commercial artist, devises the yellow smiley face for an insurance firm that wants to improve employee morale after a bitter corporate takeover. |
| 1964 | The G.I. Joe doll—dubbed "America's movable fighting man" by Hasbro—makes his debut. |
| 1965 | Biggest power failure in history causes nine-hour blackout in eastern Canada and the United States, leading to a surge in the national birthrate nine months later. |

it drained resources from programs that attempted to rectify social wrongs, such as poverty, hunger, and unequal education. It was the Vietnam War as much as anything else that derailed Johnson's Great Society. The Vietnam War also provoked a shift in American culture, both to the left, in the form of expanded women's rights and multicultural education, and to the right, in prompting a resurgence of social conservatism in the political sphere and a white ethnic revival that often scorned the advances African Americans had won. It is to these transitions that we will turn next.

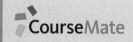

# CHAPTER 27

# *The* Limits *of* Liberalism: *The* 1970s

## Learning Outcomes

*After reading this chapter, you should be able to do the following:*

LO **1**  Evaluate Richard Nixon as president, focusing on his policies in the United States and abroad.

LO **2**  Describe the events of Watergate and its ramifications for the country.

LO **3**  Describe the economic conditions of the 1970s, including stagflation and the end of the post–World War II economic boom, and describe how Presidents Ford and Carter attempted to confront the problem.

LO **4**  Describe the perpetuation of 1960s-style activism and how it transformed into a politics of identity in the 1970s.

LO **5**  Evaluate the reaction to the 1960s social movements and describe the rise of the New Right.

© Allan Tannenbaum/Time & Life Pictures/Getty Images

# "Without a magnetic social vision to unify the populace, the 1970s came to be characterized as a time of turning inward."

The social activism of the late 1960s continued into the 1970s, but during the 1970s that activism ran into roadblocks. A variety of minority movements seemed poised to fracture any national unity that had been created in the struggle for African American civil rights, and the postwar economic boom came to a startling end in 1973, raising poverty and unemployment as contentious and serious issues. American politicians learned the limits of politics' ability to create change, and they simultaneously learned that they could not publicly discuss these limits and expect to be reelected.

This awareness of limits had many sources. The war in Vietnam ended in 1975, but only after it had increased friction and schisms between Americans and diminished American expectations of imperial power. In addition, the countless fabrications that Johnson and Nixon had fed the public about the progress of the war made many Americans suspicious of their country's leaders. Meanwhile, the civil rights movement had succeeded in winning political rights for African Americans, but it then faced social and economic limits that tested the reality of America's commitment to racial equality. And a series of new social movements—by women, Chicanos, American Indians, and others—that followed in the wake of the civil rights movement seemed to cast African Americans as just another minority group vying for institutional recognition. Interest in other causes, such as environmentalism, exploded during the 1970s as well. All this turmoil and diverse social action provoked a backlash from voters, who, by 1980, were willing to overlook one Republican president's shady dealings in order to elect another conservative to the nation's highest office. Many Americans had tired of calls for social justice, and this sheer exhaustion led many to turn inward, contributing to what one writer called the "me generation."

At the same time, while the economy had remained healthy during the 1960s, it soured badly during the 1970s, officially ending the long post–World War II boom. The economic decline lasted the entire decade, casting a pall over the other events of the era. While the causes of the downturn are complex, a significant part was played by the demise of American manufacturing. Companies moved out of the Northeast and Midwest, heading to the South or the West in order to find better weather, cheaper labor, and fewer unions. This demographic and economic shift created "the Sunbelt," a region stretching from Florida to California. As more companies moved to the Sunbelt, American politics and culture took on the traditionally southern cast of anti-elitism and antigovernment individualism. "Get government off our backs" became a staple slogan of the late 1970s—one that epitomized a tax revolt that opened the door for a rightward shift in American politics that Americans still live with today.

# LO¹ President Nixon

Richard Nixon, who had made his political name as a rabid anticommunist during the McCarthy years, who had served dutifully as Eisenhower's vice president throughout most of the 1950s, and who had nearly beaten Kennedy in the presidential race of 1960, finally won the office he so ardently sought in 1968. Some historians cite that year as the beginning of "the seventies."

As president, Nixon capitalized on divisions within the Democratic Party over the Vietnam War to beat the Democratic nominee, Hubert Humphrey. This son of a California grocer is considered one of our most complex presidents, reviled by liberals but not necessarily beloved by conservatives either. He was brilliant but unprincipled. Nixon responded to problems with a creativity and drive that stemmed not from concern for social justice, but from a persistent fear of how history would judge him. He was driven by a long-smoldering resentment against what he saw as "the Eastern Establishment," which he defined as the bankers, politicians, and businessmen who had controlled American social, cultural, and political life for years. More than anything else, Nixon hated the Democratic establishment, which he thought was perpetually out to get him. His

mistrust and suspicion would score him significant political gains in matters of foreign policy and the environment. But it would also lead to his historic downfall.

## Nixon's Foreign Policy

Nixon's greatest triumphs as president were in foreign policy. As explained in the last chapter, his Vietnamization plan simultaneously pulled American troops out of Vietnam and increased the American military presence in other nations of Southeast Asia. Nevertheless, by 1972, Vietnamization was in fact removing American troops from the country. The last of them left Vietnam in 1973. Most Americans were relieved to be removed from a situation that was perceived as a stalemated "quagmire," where American soldiers were dying while fighting a war that could not be won.

### Ping-Pong Diplomacy

As Vietnam simmered down as a national issue, Nixon saw that relations between China and the Soviet Union were beginning to break down. The two communist superpowers were still at odds, and, attempting to push the two further apart, Nixon began talks with China. His first step was to accept an invitation to send the American table tennis team to compete in a friendly international event in China. This gave his foreign policy toward China its name: Ping-Pong Diplomacy. The players were the first Americans invited into China since its founding as a communist country in 1949. In 1972, Nixon him-

>> In efforts to redirect the Cold War, Nixon became the first president to visit China, meeting with Mao Zedong and Zhou Enlai in 1972. With regard to Chinese-Soviet relations, Nixon confided to Zhou that if Moscow marched either east or west, he was ready to "turn like a cobra on the Russians."

© AFP/Getty Images

self went to China, and the two nations increased trade and cultural exchanges. They also agreed that the Soviet Union should not be allowed to expand farther into Asia.

## SALT and the Cold War

Increasingly worried about the cost of the arms race, Nixon also made overtures to the Soviet Union. Just months after going to China, Nixon went to Moscow to meet with Soviet premier Leonid Brezhnev. In this meeting he agreed to sell excess American wheat to the Soviets. The fact that their country needed wheat was an early sign that Soviet-style communism was not performing well economically, even though the Soviets attempted to hide this fact. Under the auspices of the **Strategic Arms Limitation Talks (SALT)**, the two leaders also agreed to freeze the number of long-range missile launchers and build certain new missiles only after they had destroyed the same number of older missiles. This did not signify an end to the Cold War, but it did demonstrate that the nations' leaders were beginning to recognize the problems inherent in an unchecked arms race.

Thus, within four years, Nixon, perceived as a hard-nosed anticommunist Republican, had removed the American presence in Vietnam, ceding it to communists, and made overtures to both China and the Soviet Union. This softened approach toward America's supposed enemies was executed largely by Nixon's assistant for national security affairs and, later, his secretary of state, Henry Kissinger. These more relaxed relations are labeled *détente* (a French term meaning "a relaxing" or "an easing").

## Latin America and Africa

As the Cold War cooled with China and the Soviet Union, it heated up in Latin America and Africa. Each time a nation in one of these regions elected a leftist—potentially communist—regime, the United States actively supported coups and the installation of new governments that would support U.S. interests. These new right-wing regimes routinely punished political opponents. For instance, the United States supported the ousting of Chile's Salvador Allende in 1973, opting instead to provide assistance to the authoritarian regime of General Augusto Pinochet. In Africa, the United States tolerated the racist regime of South Africa and sided with anticommunists in the Angolan civil war. But, taking a lesson from Vietnam, Nixon was leery of using American troops in these situations.

Read a State Department briefing on the status of Chile, 1970.

# Nixon the Accidental Liberal

While Nixon's foreign policies often represented significant breakthroughs, his domestic policies were even more transformative, although not always in the way Nixon's supporters had hoped. Upon entering office, Nixon claimed to be a typical small-government Republican. In reality, Nixon's relentless preoccupation with and fear of being defeated for reelection led him to advocate many goals of the left and of the Democratic Party. Cagily, however, while Nixon sought to increase budgets for liberal causes, he made these increases contingent upon greater local control. This put Democrats in a tough political position, because they could not reject funds for causes they had long advocated, but they could not control how those funds were spent locally. In this way, Nixon became an advocate of many liberal causes, but he did so while weakening the supposed Eastern Establishment he despised.

## Increasing the Size of Government

For instance, Nixon signed into law the National Environmental Policy Act (1970), which established the Environmental Protection Agency (EPA). He endorsed the Occupational Safety and Health Administration (OSHA), which sought to make workplaces safer. He doubled the budgets of the National Endowment for the Humanities (NEH) and the National Endowment for the Arts (NEA). Nixon also became the first president to embrace affirmative action, as discussed later in the chapter.

But each of these progressive developments came at a cost to the liberals who had long advocated them. For instance, Nixon's increases to the National Endowment for the Humanities were earmarked for popular artists in Middle America or for local museums, instead of the large museums in New York and Boston, which championed abstract art that was appreciated mostly by the well educated and affluent. Politically, Democrats could not reject his proposal to increase funding for the arts. It was a stroke of political genius: Nixon got credit for being a proponent of the arts, at the same time draining support from his nemesis, the eastern liberal elite.

**Strategic Arms Limitation Talks (SALT)**
Sessions held between President Nixon and Soviet premier Leonid Brezhnev, in which the two leaders agreed to freeze the number of long-range missile launchers and build certain new missiles only after they had destroyed the same number of older missiles

*détente*
French term meaning "a relaxing" or "an easing"; refers to more relaxed relations with America's supposed enemies, China and the Soviet Union

## LO² Watergate

Before Nixon could do more, he became mired in scandal. During his successful reelection bid in 1972, five men were arrested breaking into the Democratic National Committee offices at the Watergate Hotel in Washington, D.C. One of the burglars worked directly for Nixon's Committee to Re-Elect the President (CREEP), a fact that did not impede Nixon's landslide victory in the election. But print journalists, spurred by the investigative reporting of the *Washington Post*'s Bob Woodward and Carl Bernstein, continued to follow the story and discovered that orders for the break-in had been issued from high up in the Nixon White House. The Senate convened hearings, which were televised nationally.

While the testimony never revealed whether or not Nixon had ordered the break-in, what did emerge

> **❝I have never been a quitter. To leave office before my term is completed is abhorrent to every instinct in my body. But as President, I must put the interest of America first.❞**
>
> —*Richard M. Nixon, resignation speech 1974*

were Nixon's suspicious nature and illegal spying on Americans. Watergate became an investigation about much more than a simple break-in. The Senate learned that the president had taped nearly every conversation that had happened in the White House. When the Senate demanded to see the tapes, Nixon fired the special prosecutor leading the Senate's investigation, prompting a series of sympathy resignations within his own administration.

As the scandal mushroomed, Nixon's vice president, Spiro Agnew, admitted to tax evasion and bribery. He resigned and was replaced by Gerald Ford. The credibility of the entire administration was under attack. Americans watched the scandal with alarm. It seemed to confirm many people's beliefs that American leaders were untrustworthy. After the Supreme Court ordered Nixon to turn over the

 Hear Nixon's resignation speech.

 View a collection of Bob Woodward and Carl Bernstein's papers.

 Learn more about Watergate.

White House tapes, it was evident that he was going to be impeached. Nixon instead chose to resign from office, which he did after a speech to the nation on August 9, 1974. His new vice president, Gerald Ford, became president. To understand the reasons why Watergate was so pivotal to the 1970s political culture, see "The reasons why . . ." box on the facing page.

## LO³ The Troubled Economy and Politics Adrift

The backdrop for all this commotion was an economic recession that officially ended the great post–World War II economic boom. The two presidents that succeeded Nixon, Gerald Ford and Jimmy Carter, had little success in solving this problem.

### Economic Woes

In the late 1960s, Vietnam, the Great Society, and the costs of the arms race had diverted a lot of money from federal coffers, and Johnson had refused to

>> **President Nixon resigning, August 9, 1974. A scandal surrounding a break-in of the Democratic party headquarters in the Watergate Hotel during the 1972 presidential election led to numerous revelations of presidential abuse. Before Nixon was indicted, he resigned, and was pardoned by President Gerald Ford a month later.**

© AP Images

There were at least four reasons why the Watergate scandal was so pivotal in American life:

***The death of political idealism.*** The disclosures of Watergate put the nail in the coffin of the political idealism of the early 1960s. During that earlier period, social movements like the civil rights movement turned to the federal government and the American system of law to advocate change. After the decade of lies about the Vietnam War, the Watergate scandal validated many Americans' darkest suspicions that a politician's first priority was not to serve the public, but simply to get reelected.

***Americans turn inward.*** These suspicions led many Americans to turn away from politics, often choosing to search for answers to large social problems through the individual groups that gave them their identity. This, in turn, helped lead to the rise of identity politics, an effort to create social change not through politics but instead by changing American culture and society. America's politics seemed corrupt.

***The irony.*** One major irony of the Watergate scandal was that it served Republican ends. Since at least the New Deal, Republicans had been advocating a smaller role for government. The disaffection toward politics inspired by Nixon, a Republican, was a long-term boon to the Republican Party. After Watergate, many people began to see government as part of the problem rather than part of the solution, and thus they too began advocating for smaller government.

***New political scrutiny.*** Meanwhile, before Watergate, presidents were usually given a wide berth by the media and forgiven their personal flaws, which frequently went unreported. After Watergate, every dimension of a politician's life was deemed newsworthy. President Ford, who became president after Nixon resigned, was a talented athlete and former college football star at the University of Michigan, but he was widely portrayed as a goof and a bumbling klutz. Where there once had been deference and respect, now there was cynicism and ire.

raise taxes to pay for these expensive ventures. Furthermore, by the early 1970s, America's industrial sector was weakening due to the rise of foreign competition and decreasing demand for American goods. The economy was cooling after its long period of post–World War II growth. With the United States borrowing tremendous amounts of money, the value of the dollar decreased, meaning that it took more dollars to pay for the same goods. This condition is called inflation. Nixon did not really know what to do to control the problem. First, he made it more difficult to borrow money, which, he hoped, would lower the amount of investments and keep dollars spare. However, all this did was constrict the economy, leading to an economic recession.

In 1971, facing reelection, Nixon initiated the first-ever peacetime wage and price freeze. He also accepted large federal deficits. These initiatives reversed the economy long enough for him to win reelection in 1972, but his economic plan was erratic and short term, confidence remained low, and the American industrial sector was beginning to decline in the face of cheaper prices on imported foreign goods.

## Oil Embargo

The whole problem was compounded after the Yom Kippur War of 1973, which provoked the oil-rich nations of the Middle East to punish the United States for supporting Israel, a nation with friendly ties to the United States since its founding, in 1948. Oil prices quadrupled. Gas became hard to find, and long lines of drivers were seen waiting at filling stations. Other sources of energy were not immediately available. Beyond the daily frustrations of expensive gas at the pump, the oil embargo raised the cost of making goods and moving them from one place to another. Prices of all consumer goods went up. Thus, the American economy entered a complicated cycle in which prices kept going up (inflation) but the economy began losing jobs (or stagnating). Economists called this unique condition **stagflation**.

Stagflation is notoriously difficult to fight, because most of the tools the government has to control the economy—such as regulating the interest it charges banks to borrow money from the Federal Reserve banks—are primarily designed to either slow growth and end inflation, or increase growth and boost inflation. Tools to lower inflation while growing the economy do not exist. The economy would continue to perform badly throughout the 1970s, bringing to an abrupt halt the consistent economic growth the country had enjoyed since 1946.

**stagflation**
Economic cycle in which prices keep going up (inflation) while the economy is losing jobs (or stagnating)

## The Decline of Cities

Another force compounded these economic pressures. Since the Second World War, Americans had been leaving cities at alarming rates, heading to the suburbs, where good schools, bigger homes, and larger spaces beckoned. Stagflation slowed the American economy down, especially the manufacturing sector that was overwhelmingly based in large northeastern and midwestern cities like Chicago and Philadelphia. As these sectors declined in productivity, many Americans lost their jobs and left the industrial cities of the North in search of work in the South or Southwest. As businesses left, the tax base left with them, making the 1970s the roughest time in the history of most American cities. During the 1970s, more than 1 million residents left New York City; it took the city nearly two decades to make up that population loss.

## President Ford

After Watergate and the Vietnam War had discredited the role that government might play in solving deep social problems, the two presidents who followed Nixon appeared to be rudderless and without confidence that the American people would listen to, much less enact, their attempts to solve the country's problems. For his part, President Ford was the first president never subjected to a national election. A good-natured, well-liked man who self-effacingly admitted that he was "a Ford, not a Lincoln," Gerald Ford weathered the wrath of the American public in the aftermath of Watergate. And one of his first acts as president did not generate widespread goodwill: Ford offered Nixon a full presidential pardon. This action ended the possibility of criminal proceedings and, perhaps, of finding out whether or not Nixon had ordered the Watergate break-in. But the pardon did allow the nation to move beyond political scandal in order to focus on the dire problems of the economy and the Cold War. Unfortunately, Ford was unable to take complete control of either.

### Domestic Policy

Ford's chief domestic problem was stagflation, but, like Nixon, Ford had little luck tackling it. At first, he encouraged Americans to save rather than spend their money. Then he offered a large tax cut. Neither measure worked to improve the sagging economy.

Read an *SNL* transcript of Chevy Chase's impression of Gerald Ford.

With little national support, Ford regularly vetoed congressional bills, only to have his vetoes overridden.

## Foreign Policy

Ford had better luck overseas. He laid the basis of another arms agreement with the Soviets, which was finalized as SALT II a few years later, under President Carter. Ford's secretary of state Henry Kissinger negotiated between Israel and Egypt, leading to a short-term break in hostilities in the Middle East.

## President Carter

In 1976, Ford stood little chance of reelection. Affable and open as he was, even within his party he faced a strong challenge from California's former governor, Ronald Reagan, a symbol of the new Sunbelt conservatism that would dominate the 1980s and 1990s.

### The Election of 1976

The Democrats, for their part, took a chance and won. They nominated a little-known, one-term Georgia governor named Jimmy Carter. Carter struck a note with the electorate because he appeared to be honest, was a "born again" Christian, was progressive on issues of poverty and treatment of minorities, and was a southerner capable of talking to the demographically growing southern half of the nation (Map 27.1). Carter won the election, in which he competed against the ghost of Nixon as much as against Ford.

### Domestic Policy

Domestically, Carter faced the same economic conditions that Nixon and Ford had: stagflation. Carter could not manage it either, and when he proposed to increase government spending to create jobs (à la the New Deal), inflation skyrocketed. He then made the ultimate political blunder when he asked the nation to sacrifice on behalf of the "common purpose" and offered a list of small and specific proposals as to how that might be done. These modest proposals did not capture the public's imagination, and his political inexperience in Washington, D.C., contributed to his making several gaffes, which repeatedly made him look weak and ineffectual.

Carter was further burdened by the nationwide energy crisis, which had surged after the Yom Kippur War of 1973 and had not subsided since. By 1977, elementary and high schools were forced to close because there was not enough energy to heat them. Carter's ambitious plan to remedy the crisis combined higher taxes and a vigorous search for alternative fuels. This plan was met with general disapproval by Congress and did not pass. Making mat-

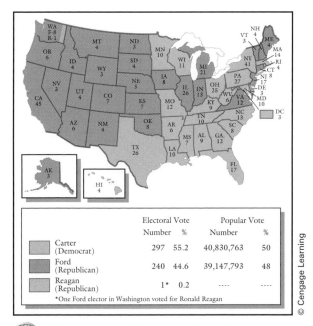

>> President Jimmy Carter, wearing the kind of sweater he urged all Americans to wear, in order to reduce their consumption of energy.

| | Electoral Vote | | Popular Vote | |
|---|---|---|---|---|
| | Number | % | Number | % |
| Carter (Democrat) | 297 | 55.2 | 40,830,763 | 50 |
| Ford (Republican) | 240 | 44.6 | 39,147,793 | 48 |
| Reagan (Republican) | 1* | 0.2 | ---- | ---- |
| *One Ford elector in Washington voted for Ronald Reagan | | | | |

Map 27.1. Election of 1976

ters worse, the meltdown of a nuclear reactor at **Three Mile Island**, Pennsylvania, in 1979 discredited nuclear power, a potentially viable alternative to oil. With an economy this troubled, Carter could not advocate any of the plans he had for expanding American social justice.

## Foreign Policy

Carter made more progress abroad. His longest-lasting achievement in foreign policy was in establishing human rights as an element of American policy. Doing so energized him to (1) call for the end of apartheid in South Africa, (2) give up control of the Panama Canal, and (3) cite human rights considerations as a factor in the granting of American aid. In the Middle East, Carter oversaw a peace agreement between Israel and Egypt, called the **Camp David Accord**, in late 1978. But this accomplishment was overshadowed just six months later when Islamic militants took fifty-two hostages from the

 Watch Carter's "crisis of confidence" speech.

American Embassy in Tehran, the capital of Iran. The militants were part of a coup in which fundamentalist Islamists seized power from the American-supported dictatorship, in place since 1953. The terrorists held the American hostages for more than a year. Each day that went by, Carter seemed more and more unable to handle the problem. But the inability to bring together the nation was not Carter's doing alone.

# LO⁴ The Rise of Identity Politics

One historian has described the social movements of the 1960s as a "coming together" of sorts, when large gestures—the civil rights movement, the War on Poverty—were intended to create a more unified and inclusive nation. The 1970s, however, served as a spin cycle, scattering the social energy of the sixties in a thousand different directions. Without a magnetic social vision to unify the populace, the 1970s came to be characterized as a time of turning inward or, to use a term from the era, a celebration of the culture of narcissism. People's interest in pet causes flourished, as did a variety of new faiths, most of which prioritized personal renewal or an individual relationship with God. Many of these themes were manifested in the southern tilt of American culture that began in the 1970s, and many of these melded seamlessly into the political New Right, which prioritized, above all, individual rights.

## Identifying with a Group

One of the most contentious and transformative sociopolitical events of the decade was the codification of identity politics. In other words, there was a resurgence of people's practicing politics and voting based on their identification with a particular group, rather than with the entire nation as a whole. Identity politics had been made acceptable by Catholics and Jews in the postwar era and had been made both politically potent and divisive by African Americans, Mexican Americans, Native Americans, and others following the civil rights movement, especially in the militancy that emerged in the late 1960s.

### African American Activism

America's black population was the first to embrace this brand of politics, which intended to change the culture as well as public policy. Despite the federal laws passed in the 1960s, racism against America's black people persisted. For the most part, racism was no longer legally codified or socially acceptable at the broad institutional level, but it remained entrenched in the personal-level institutions of society and culture. Thus, many African American activists broadened their focus from just politics to politics *and culture*, hoping to change the way Americans thought about their nation. Cultural acceptance was different from political acceptance. Political acceptance concerned the enforcement of color-blind laws, while social acceptance depended on an awareness of differences and a conscious decision to ignore them.

In response to this heightened awareness, "Black is beautiful" became a widespread call in the black community. Africa became a destination for many Americans seeking to understand their cultural past, a sentiment epitomized in and popularized by Alex Haley's 1976 bestseller, *Roots*. Attending historically black colleges acquired cultural cachet. Black Studies writers and professors established this field as an accepted academic discipline within America's colleges. The cultural politics of the Black Freedom Movement surpassed attempts to create protective legal structures to ensure equal access.

**Kama mama, kama binti**
(Like mother, like daughter)

>> In the 1970s, products like Afro-Sheen built their ad campaigns on heightened awareness and acceptance of African roots among black people.

Social and economic acceptance required different methods.

### Affirmative Action

Amid this transition toward greater interest in changing American culture, federal and state governments attempted to rectify the continuing effects of racism. Because many white Americans were afraid of dropping property values if their neighborhoods became racially integrated, and because of deeply entrenched fears of interracial mingling, schools generally remained segregated. To remedy this persistent problem, cities such as Boston and Los Angeles began busing students from one school district to another in order to desegregate schools. This action provoked much ire from parents, black and white, who had their children bused far from home. Riots erupted in Boston, and the level of suspicion increased between the groups on either side of the color line.

 See a slide show about the award-winning photo from the Boston busing crisis.

Meanwhile, the federal government developed programs of **affirmative action**, in which employers were supposed to ensure that a certain percentage of employees were minorities, or that a certain percentage of government contracts were given to minority-owned businesses. In another example of Nixon's ruthless politics, affirmative action's federal origins can be traced to his proclaimed free-market administration. He did this to cause political rifts between white and black laborers, which would, and did, break up a Democratic political coalition that was first formed by President Roosevelt in the 1930s.

Affirmative action also became policy in many of the nation's universities. In 1978, the Supreme Court upheld the legality of some elements of affirmative action, but disallowed the use of exact quotas, in a case that emerged when a white student claimed he was denied entrance to medical school because of the color of his skin. The case, *Regents of the University of California v. Bakke*, not only codified affirmative action in American education but also dramatically displayed the overwhelming backlash against affirmative action brought forward by many white Americans. Some members of this furious group

 Read the *Bakke* decision.

were the children of turn-of-the-century immigrants who, ignoring the centuries of racism and favoritism inherent in America's institutions, claimed to have never wronged America's racial minority groups during the time of slavery and conquest. They claimed that they were not responsible for paying the debt for America's offenses during the precolonial and colonial eras.

## The Chicano Movement

After the variety of successes won by labor leaders César Chávez and Dolores Huerta in the late 1960s, in 1970 a more radical aspect of the Chicano movement emerged and was embodied by the organization *La Raza*. This term literally means "the Race," although colloquially it is synonymous with "the People." *La Raza* explicitly focused on electing Mexican American politicians to office in the West and Southwest. Demonstrating their frustration with the persistent racism that they had confronted throughout their history, members of *La Raza* rejected the name "Mexican American" in favor of the more particular "Chicano," a term derived from barrio slang.

## Red Power

Heartened by African American and Chicano efforts toward social, cultural, and economic equality, many American Indians sought political redress as well. Many Indians lived at the poverty level, and most Indian reservations had no industry of any kind. The crushing poverty inspired protests.

© Bettmann/CORBIS

>> In 1969, a group of activists called "Indians of All Tribes" occupied Alcatraz Island, demanding the land be returned to the tribes that had once occupied it.

Holding several sit-ins of their own, in 1969 a group of activists called "Indians of All Tribes" occupied Alcatraz Island in San Francisco Bay. Demanding the land be returned to the tribes that had once occupied it, they intended to make an Indian cultural center out of the former prison.

The protest recalled the pan-Indian resistance of the early 1800s, although in 1970s language. Indeed, the activists boldly declared "Red Power!" echoing Stokely Carmichael's Black Power campaign of the late 1960s. In 1968, a group of Native Americans coordinated the American Indian Movement and began a series of audacious political protests, including occupying the federal Bureau of Indian Affairs building, Mount Rushmore, and Wounded Knee, South Dakota. The protests provoked headlines and benefited several moderate groups helping to craft laws in Washington, D.C. They wrote a dozen new laws and steered more than $100 million to educational and health programs on Indian reservations. Furthermore, the number of Americans who identified as Indians more than doubled between 1970 and 1990.

## The Women's Movement

The politics of identity moved beyond racial groups too. Throughout the 1970s, American women continued to press for increased political and economic rights.

### ERA and Equal Rights

Throughout the 1970s, women fought against sexual harassment in the workplace and for greater awareness of women's health issues. They also secured congressional approval of the Equal Rights Amendment to the U.S. Constitution, which would have made it illegal to discriminate based on sex. Furthermore, in 1972, Congress passed Title IX of the Higher Education Act, which obligated universities to spend the same amount of money on women's athletics that they spent on men's athletics.

### Roe v. Wade

The most controversial milestone of the women's movement was a landmark legal case. In 1973, the Supreme Court handed down a decision in **Roe v. Wade** that struck down laws in forty-six states that limited a woman's access to a safe, legal abortion. The decision, which referenced a woman's right to privacy, extending that right to her reproductive system, stunned the opposition, who generally felt abortion was morally equivalent to murder. The debate about abortion has increased the polarization between the left and the right ever since.

 Read the text of *Roe* v. *Wade.*

## Social and Economic Participation

In a change perhaps more profound than the debates about laws that delineated women's place in American society, in the 1970s women began to play a more active role in the economy and in forming the parameters of American social life. Like other minority groups, they fomented a social movement that existed outside of normal politics. For instance, consistently struggling against a "glass ceiling" that limited their ability to rise beyond a certain corporate level, in the 1970s women fought for and sometimes won the right to earn pay equal to that of men. Some companies opened day-care centers and job-training programs specifically for working mothers. Beyond economics, the 1970s saw a rise in the use of gender-neutral terms (for instance, using the terms *firefighter* and *flight attendant* in place of *fireman* and *stewardess*).

© Image courtesy of The Advertising Archives

**>>** The image of the ideal man transitioned from the masculine if inarticulate swashbuckler of the 1940s to the man who was more "in touch with his feelings."

## The Sexual Revolution

Some women also embraced their own sexuality in what was called the sexual revolution. There was a new cultural atmosphere in which women more openly discussed their sexual needs and desires, while sometimes flouting conventional arrangements, such as maintaining a single partner in a traditionally identifiable relationship. Divorce became more common. Breaking such long-standing taboos began a fundamental transformation in American gender relations. The image of the ideal man transitioned from the masculine if inarticulate swashbuckler of the 1940s to the man who was more "in touch with his feelings." Women forthrightly demanded equality in their private as well as their public lives, although in the 1970s, women were not always in agreement as to what exactly that meant.

## The Gay Liberation Movement

Also in the 1970s, gay men and lesbians began to demand equality as people living outside what had been perceived as the heterosexual norm. As barriers against racial and religious minorities collapsed, as women advocated and sometimes won equality, gay men and women still faced considerable legal discrimination. For example, consensual sex between two people of the same sex was illegal in nearly every state. In 1969, a police raid on the bar at the **Stonewall Inn** in New York City sparked the gay liberation movement. Gay men fought back against the police raid, proclaiming "Gay Power." The riot propelled many gay men and lesbians into politics and political activism, advocating for legal equality such as marriage rights. In 1977, Harvey Milk, on

>> In 1977, Harvey Milk became the first openly gay politician elected to public office in the United States. His sign, "I'm from Woodmere, NY," suggests that anyone from anywhere can be gay, challenging the notion that only freaks from radical locales are homosexuals.

being elected to the Board of Supervisors in San Francisco, became the first openly gay person to win a major political campaign. He was assassinated shortly thereafter and is an iconic martyr of the gay rights movement, which continues today.

**Stonewall Inn**
Site in New York City of the riots that ignited the Gay Liberation Movement in the late 1960s and 1970s; at the time of the riots, all fifty states had antisodomy laws, and police busts of gay bars were routine

## High Tide of Environmentalism

Demanding respect for the environment was another facet of 1970s social activism. Launched in 1962 by Rachel Carson's book *Silent Spring*, the environmental movement grew through the 1960s. In 1970, the United States celebrated the first "Earth Day," which stimulated greater awareness of humans' treatment of the land, sea, and air. Vital to 1970s environmentalism was advocacy of preserving unspoiled lands and promoting ecologically sound practices in industry, manufacturing, and automobile use.

Beyond creating valuable awareness, the political record of the environmental movement is mixed. Environmentalists cheered when Richard Nixon established the Environmental Protection Agency in 1970 and when Congress passed eighteen environmental laws throughout the decade. They rued the construction of the Trans-Alaska Pipeline in 1973, however. Other defeats loomed as well. Most damning was the sense that, in an era when Americans were searching for belonging, the cause of environmentalism asserted a species-wide identity, something too diffuse and broad to command much allegiance.

## Popular Culture

American popular culture also reflected the broader, inward-focused trend of the 1970s, often in increasingly flashy ways that demonstrated a more complicated morality, where one might feel like cheering for the traditional bad guy. The music of the 1960s icons Sly and the Family Stone, for example, transitioned from celebrating American unity and possibility in the 1960s to being more introspective and aware of the limits of broad social change in the 1970s. In one poignant instance, Sly changed the lyrics of one of his most popular 1960s songs from "Thank You (Falettinme Be Mice Elf Agin)" to, in 1971, "Thank You for Talkin' to Me Africa." In addition to demonstrating the decline of hope for broad social change, the changed lyrics also capture the rise of identity politics, with Sly looking for his roots in Africa rather than the United States.

x

>> John Travolta in *Saturday Night Fever* (1979) does most of his dancing by himself.

In the later 1970s, disco music throbbed in America's cities, articulating an individual desire to dance on one's own and pursue individual rather than societal goals. The 1979 film *Saturday Night Fever* enshrined disco music as a typical "seventies" cultural form, but the film also displayed as its depressing backdrop the decline and plight of American cities of the Northeast. In other landmark films of the era, such as *The Godfather*, *The Godfather, Part II*, and *Bonnie and Clyde*, viewers feel compelled to root for the success and freedom of violent criminals who defy traditional American morals. Thus the moral complexity of the period, with its dramatically changing social and economic background, inspired many vibrant contributions to the popular culture that also reflected the era's malaise.

# LO⁵ The Rise of the New Right

All these calls for change led to a combative conservative reaction. This movement, collectively dubbed the "New Right" by the press, scrubbed all potential intellectual elitism from conservatism, an elitism symbolized by William F. Buckley's *National Review* magazine, founded in the 1950s. Instead, through a variety of grassroots movements, social conservatives opposed abortion and what they saw as the moral decline of society, while economic conservatives urged tax cuts to limit the size and reach of government. Both types of conservatives continued to urge an aggressive stance against the Soviet Union. Both also strove to diminish government intervention in people's lives. The expansion of the federal state during the 1960s and what conservatives saw as the loosening of laws regarding morality spurred this new coalition, which would continue to grow for the remainder of the century.

## Economic and Political Conservatism

A key dimension of 1970s conservatism arose in opposition to what were viewed as excessive tax policies in an era of inflation. If government was deemed corrupt, went the refrain, why should a significant percentage of our income go to taxes? This sentiment was most evident in California, where skyrocketing house prices meant dramatic increases in property taxes. When homeowners could not pay these higher property taxes, they revolted and passed Proposition 13, which limited all further increases on property taxes to 2 percent a year. Within months, nearly three-quarters of other states passed similar laws.

The Republican Party capitalized on this populist anger, positioning itself as the antigovernment party. The state of California had a large economic surplus, so the decline in property taxes there did not limit services. In many other places, however, states could not afford to pay for public schools, road maintenance, or effective fire and police departments. In a familiar theme of the 1970s and 1980s, Americans would have to turn inward—to their communities—to solve these institutional problems. Those cities and towns that could afford a good level of local control thrived; those that could not faced dire straits.

## The Religious Right

Some of the shock troops of the New Right were evangelical Christians, a growing force in the 1970s. These Protestant evangelicals poured their efforts into three things: (1) forming an intense personal relationship with Jesus; (2) gathering converts, usually former mainline or liberal Protestants; and (3) advancing a political agenda that stressed traditional "family values" that countered the women's rights movement and the gay liberation movement. This new crop of evangelicals especially targeted feminism and was visibly enraged by the Supreme Court's *Roe* v. *Wade* decision, which has since served as a rallying cry for the entrance of the fundamentalist movement into American politics.

Institutionally, conservative Christians led by Rev. Jerry Falwell founded the **Moral Majority** political lobbying group in 1979, which, alongside tax-revolting economic conservatives, formed the other arm of the Republican party and helped elect Ronald Reagan to the presidency in 1980. Culturally, evangelicals became increasingly visible in popular music and fiction. Diminished were the paramount religious divisions between mainline Protestants, Catholics, and Jews, which had defined American religious life in the 1950s; surging were new divisions between conservatives and liberals of all faiths, but especially Protestants. Not only did the appearance of a more public aspect of faith reflect the "southernization" of American culture, but it also demonstrated the inward turn that took place in the 1970s, as religion became a realm of division and exclusion rather than one of inclusion and community building.

### "Family Values"

Predictably, the women's movement served as a touchstone for strong opposition. While many women sought to take advantage of the new opportunities open to them, a substantial percentage wanted to preserve the traditional roles of American womanhood. If securing the right to low-wage work was what the women's movement was about, some of these women thought the cost of equality too high. Others cited biblical passages about a woman's obligation to submit to her husband. Still others saw the women's movement and the sexual revolution as putting traditional families in jeopardy, by encouraging women to focus on themselves rather than their children. Phyllis Schlafly, a conservative activist, headed up the opposition. She founded STOP-ERA, claiming that the women in NOW were using politics to remedy their personal problems. She also asserted that the women in the women's movement were all lesbians, a mischaracterization intended to capitalize on America's homophobia. But Schlafly's tactics were effective. When Schlafly began STOP-ERA in 1972, thirty of the necessary thirty-eight states had approved the amendment. After she began her organization, the amendment languished, finally expiring without passage in 1982.

**Moral Majority**
Conservative political organizations begun by Rev. Jerry Falwell in 1979 and consisting of evangelical Christians who overwhelmingly supported the Republican Party

## And in the end . . .

At the end of the 1970s, the dominant news story was the Iranian hostage crisis that emerged during the final year of Carter's presidency. The crisis would help propel into office a president who projected a more positive image of the United States and who promised to return America to a perceived greatness of old. But rather than serving as a definitive transition, the election of Ronald Reagan solidified the changes that had taken place during the 1970s.

Reagan emblematized the return to political conservatism that had gathered strength in the 1970s, and he projected the Sunbelt image of a tough leader, unwilling to grant any ground to anti-establishment forces. He also saw government as more of a problem than a solution to many of society's problems, and favored low taxes. Reagan also paid homage (if usually only that) to minorities whose concerns had come to the forefront of 1970s identity politics. For instance, he appointed Sandra Day O'Connor as the first female associate justice to the U.S. Supreme Court. Many Americans were delighted to leave the 1970s behind, but the decade's legacy influenced developments for the remainder of the twentieth century.

| What else was happening . . . | |
|---|---|
| 1970 | The Beatles split up. |
| 1971 | London Bridge is purchased by an American and shipped to Lake Havasu City, Arizona, to be displayed as a tourist attraction. |
| 1974 | Art Fry invents Post-it® Notes by using a colleague's "failed" adhesive while working at 3M. |
| 1975 | *Popular Electronics* announces Altair, the first "personal computer." |

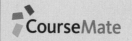

Visit the CourseMate website at www.cengagebrain.com for additional study tools and review materials for this chapter.

# CHAPTER 28

# Reagan's America

## Learning Outcomes

*After reading this chapter, you should be able to do the following:*

LO **1** Evaluate the domestic policies of Ronald Reagan as president, including the economic challenges the country faced in the 1980s.

LO **2** Describe the divisions and "culture wars" that plagued the nation during the 1980s.

LO **3** Discuss the problems Reagan's successor faced in paying for the "Reagan revolution."

LO **4** Describe the conditions for and aftermath of the end of the Cold War.

© David Paul Morris/Getty Images

## 66*Reagan defined the confident America of the 1980s—a stark contrast to the uneasy malaise of 1970s America.*99

The public figure who most successfully articulated many of the beliefs of the growing conservative movement was Ronald Reagan. Reagan combined conservative beliefs with the ability to bring those ideas to the public in a non-threatening way, so he was able to take advantage of his broad appeal to put conservative theories into practice. By advocating tax and budget cuts, he wooed economic conservatives, while his Supreme Court appointees usually made decisions that favored social conservatives. In foreign policy, he adopted strong anticommunist rhetoric and dramatically increased the military budget, even as changes in the Soviet Union diminished the communist threat. More than anybody else, Reagan defined the confident America of the 1980s—a stark contrast to the uneasy malaise of 1970s America.

Reagan's policies came with a cost: he ignored growing disparities in wealth throughout the decade, as the rich got richer and the poor got poorer. An equally contentious divide grew between social conservatives and social liberals. During the 1980s, the Democrats aligned more with social liberalism, while the Republicans established themselves as advocates for social conservatism. The debates between the two parties became increasingly polarized, spurring what many scholars now label a culture war.

## What do you think?

**With the conclusion of the Cold War, the world became a more open, accessible place.**

*Strongly Disagree*     *Strongly Agree*

| 1 | 2 | 3 | 4 | 5 | 6 | 7 |

## LO¹ Reagan's Domestic Politics

Toward the end of his presidency, Jimmy Carter was beleaguered by the stagnating economy, what he called the country's "malaise," and the Iranian hostage crisis. As an advocate of several of the identity politics movements, Carter also suffered from the mounting white backlash against them. In the 1980 election, Carter struggled to secure his party's nomination, and he emerged from the Democratic Convention severely weakened. He was no match for the charismatic personality of the Republicans' nominee, Ronald Reagan. Reagan, a former movie actor, handily won the election, and Republican candidates riding his coattails established a Republican majority in the Senate as well.

### Comfortably Conservative

Reagan synthesized the central themes of the conservative movement. These were defined as an almost religious belief in the power of the free market and a commitment to "traditional values," all under the umbrella of free-market anticommunism. But Reagan expressed these values in a way that eliminated the "crackpot" image previously associated with them. He succeeded as a conservative because he presented his conservative beliefs in a manner that did not alienate the general public. His personal charisma made conservatism palatable.

As president, Reagan proposed and had passed three key economic policies, comprising the so-called Reagan Revolution. First, he cut taxes by 25 percent over a three-year period. Reagan argued that tax cuts would produce new investment, which would, in turn, generate an increase in federal revenues. Rather than have taxpayers send money to support the federal government, he argued, revenues would eventually "trickle down" to the lower classes in the form of more jobs. This argument is known as **supply-side economics**. Second, Reagan made sig-

>> Reagan's personal charisma made conservatism palatable.

© Diana Walker/Time & Life Pictures/Getty Images

>> **The supposed trickle-down of wealth did not trickle down.**

nificant cuts in social programs, particularly welfare, food stamps, and unemployment compensation. Strategically, the administration avoided cutting such politically popular programs as Social Security and Medicare. Finally, the administration proposed a massive increase in military spending, equaling $1.2 trillion over a five-year period.

Economically, the Reagan revolution failed at first, then succeeded, then failed again. In 1982, Reagan's cuts produced an economic recession; the supposed trickle-down of wealth did not trickle down. By 1984, however, some of the policies, especially the large defense expenditures, sparked an economic recovery, allowing Reagan to coast to an easy reelection in 1984 against Democrats Walter Mondale and his running mate Geraldine Ferraro, the first woman to run on a major party's ticket (and another symbol of the success of the women's movement). By the late 1980s, however, Reagan's policies had produced the largest peacetime budget deficit in American history, which even conservatives agreed was bad for the economy.

© iStockphoto.com/Andrew Dernie

## Deregulation

Reagan also advocated limiting government involvement in business. Following this policy, he deregulated several industries from government control, including airlines (which led to strikes by air-traffic controllers) and savings and loan institutions (which led to a mammoth scandal, discussed later in this chapter). He also loosened regulations on air pollution and motor vehicles, actions that allowed corporations to continue polluting and delay installing air bags in cars for several years.

## Judicial and Administrative Appointments

While Reagan's fiscal policies reflected free-market conservatism, his judicial and administrative appointments appealed to social conservatives. He encouraged conservative positions on issues like abortion, school busing, affirmative action, and

 Read or listen to a collection of interviews with Reagan's closest advisors.

prayer in schools. Reagan appointed three conservatives to the Supreme Court, Sandra Day O'Connor (1981), Antonin Scalia (1986), and Anthony Kennedy (1988); he also named William Rehnquist (a Nixon appointee) as chief justice. These appointments did not ensure a conservative victory in every case, as some justices supported more liberal positions than others (especially, it turned out, O'Connor), but they were valuable bricks in the conservative fortress.

# LO² America in the 1980s: Polarization of the American Public

The American public has always been divided by wealth, politics, and religion. But in the 1980s these divisions figured more prominently in American society and in American politics. There were logical reasons for this. Throughout the decade the wealthier amassed increased wealth, and the poor slipped further into trouble. Also during the decade, the New Right emerged as an organized right-wing lobbying group. Their stress on moral issues and popular culture challenged those who had supported the new direction of social justice advocated in the 1960s and 1970s. Many cite the rise of the New Right as a reaction to the social liberalization and the identity politics of the previous decades.

## Divisions in Wealth

Reagan's tax cuts and his cuts to social welfare programs affected different groups of Americans differently. The policies clearly favored the wealthy. Their taxes dropped, and they benefited the most from

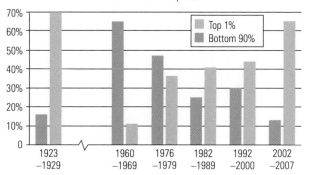

**Decline of The Middle Class**
Share of income captured

Source: CBPP calculations based on data from Piketty and Saez

Reagan's business-friendly policies, including deregulation of big industries. The number of American billionaires grew from just one in 1978 to forty-nine in 1987. The number of Americans earning more than $500,000 increased by a factor of ten.

On the other side of the scale, the poor were becoming poorer. The percentage of Americans living below the poverty line increased dramatically during Reagan's first term. Reagan's social welfare cuts took their toll.

It became increasingly apparent that this inequality was afflicting different racial groups differently. While the black middle class was in fact growing, and while the majority of impoverished Americans were white, the proportion of poor people *as a percentage of their race* indicated that people of color were vastly overrepresented below the poverty line. The African Americans, Puerto Ricans, and Chicanos who had moved to the northern cities after World War II had been hurt by the departure of large manufacturers. These manufacturers had moved either to the South or the West, where labor unions were less powerful or, increasingly, abroad, where businesses could find cheap labor and pay fewer taxes. While 1950s America was characterized by a robust

 Read an article discussing income disparities.

and growing population of middle-class Americans, the 1980s highlighted a reemergence of economic disparities that had been absent since the 1920s.

## The Rise of Japan and the American Trade Deficit

These economic problems were compounded by the rise of Japan as an economic power. Partly as a result of a deliberate American policy to build up a major East Asian ally after China became a communist country in 1949, Japan became the world's first fully modernized non-Western country. Japan's "arrival" became evident during a period of economic weakness in the United States in the early 1980s. A growing **trade deficit** with Japan meant that Japan was now successfully exporting products such as cars, steel, and consumer electronics to the United States, causing American congressmen to press for an increase in import tariffs on Japanese goods. Just as the economic muscle of oil-exporting countries had humbled the United States in the 1970s, the rise of Japan led many Americans to wonder if their nation's days as a superpower were numbered.

> **trade deficit**
> Inequality in trade whereby one country's exports to another outweigh the second country's exports to the first country

The economic rise of Japan in the 1980s led many Americans to wonder if their nation's days as a superpower were numbered. Hollywood picked up this theme in the 1986 film, "Gung Ho," which portrayed the Japanese takeover of a failed American auto plant.

## Continued Crisis in the Cities

These economic crises led to the continued breakdown of many American cities. While cities had always been portrayed as dangerous places, by the 1980s the growth of the suburbs, the departure of social organizations and industries, and the subsequent decline in tax revenues had solidified that image. Many major cities became symbols of decay, poverty, and racial disparity. Accelerating the decay, a cheaper form of cocaine called "crack" appeared in the mid-1980s. This drug was highly addictive, and its use spread rapidly throughout many inner cities. Meanwhile, inner-city youth seeking identity and security increasingly turned to gangs. Gang violence escalated throughout the decade, leading in some cities to an average of one gang murder per day.

Read Reagan's address on the campaign against drug abuse.

Perhaps due to racism, perhaps due to fear, lawmakers instituted harsh penalties for crimes committed in the inner cities. Possession of small amounts of crack cocaine, for instance, merited a punishment equal to that for owning much larger amounts of cocaine, the more expensive version of the same drug. As these penalties increased, so did the American prison system, which was disproportionately populated by racial minorities from cities. In addition to building prisons, the Reagan administration addressed the growing drug problem with a public relations campaign entitled "Just Say No." Nancy Reagan, the First Lady, spearheaded the campaign, and she got many celebrities to join in. Critics claimed that the campaign was nothing more than hollow rhetoric that missed the underlying provocations that drove drug use.

## Culture Wars

Beyond the alarming surge in drug abuse, a division of equal significance also confronted the nation. As the New Right had developed at the grassroots throughout the 1950s, 1960s, and 1970s, the movement increased its political leverage. With leaders like Pat Robertson, James Dobson, and Jerry Falwell, evangelical Christians made up the bulk of the shock troops of the New Right movement. Conservative radio personalities like Rush Limbaugh fueled the movement. With some success, they protested what they saw as the sexual licentiousness on television, the general permissiveness of American secular society, the emphasis on relativism and pluralism in America's educational system, and the liberties with which the courts had interpreted the privacy clause of the Constitution, especially regarding a woman's right to have an abor-

"I was making close to $2,000 a week selling weed when I decided to join the Unknown Vice Lords. Doing so allowed me to expand my drug-selling territory. Life seemed great." —Jeremiah, teen gang member

tion. Although Reagan only tacitly endorsed the New Right, he did make appearances with its leaders, giving the movement some mainstream leverage.

The rise of the New Right stimulated the formation of a left-wing opposition. Political liberals founded organizations like People for the American Way (1981) and older groups like the American Civil Liberties Union revamped and actively lobbied against the policies of the New Right. They presented a full agenda based on separation of church and state, individual privacy laws, and expanded systems of social welfare. Because the ensuing battle between the two sides has often taken place in the cultural realm, in areas such as education and popular entertainment (television, movies, music, and video games), it has come to be called "the culture wars." They continue today.

## AIDS

A third social crisis emerged in the 1980s, this one deadly. Autoimmune deficiency syndrome (AIDS) is a deadly disease that attacks a person's immune

## YOU CAN'T LIVE ON HOPE.

>> During the eighties, state departments of public health wielded the power of advertising in a massive effort to educate the public and prevent the spread of AIDS.

system, the system that powers a person's body to fight other diseases. AIDS is spread through transmission of bodily fluids, most especially by blood or semen. Because it compromises the immune system, it leaves the body vulnerable to other diseases. When undiagnosed or untreated, AIDS is deadly.

AIDS was first detected in the United States in 1981, and by 1988 more than 57,000 cases had been diagnosed. It was initially detected in American homosexual men, making politicians slow to respond to the epidemic because it affected people they could safely ignore. Reagan himself ordered his surgeon general, the leading spokesperson of matters of public health in the federal government, to refrain from discussing the AIDS crisis, dismissing it as only a gay disease. But AIDS rapidly spread beyond the gay community and has since become a disease that affects all Americans who practice unsafe sex or share unclean, blood-tainted intravenous needles (like the ones used to inject illicit drugs). Safe-sex education and heightened awareness have curbed the runaway epidemic of AIDS in the United States, but it is still a key concern of American society, and it roiled the veneer of confidence and prosperity in Reagan's America.

## LO³ Paying for the Reagan Revolution

Despite Reagon's upbeat image, his "revolution" had immense costs that were borne by his successors.

>> Jerry Falwell founded the Moral Majority in 1979, using it to lobby for conservative social change and provoking what has come to be called "a culture war."

## The 1988 Election

Reagan's vice president, George H. W. Bush, emphasized Reagan-style conservatism as he campaigned for president in 1988. In the campaign, he portrayed Democratic candidate Massachusetts Governor Michael Dukakis as a big-government liberal who supported high taxes and who was too soft on crime. Bush ran ads describing an African American Massachusetts prison inmate named Willie Horton who, released by Dukakis on a temporary furlough, kidnapped a Maryland couple and raped the woman. Whereas liberals in the 1960s had been able to scare the public with ads playing on fears of nuclear war, Bush turned *liberal* into a derogatory term that implied a connection between Democratic policies and social disorder.

Elected by a comfortable margin, Bush continued many of Reagan's social and economic policies. In appointing a very conservative justice, Clarence Thomas, to the Supreme Court, Bush increased the conservative majority on the Court. But his economic policies were not as successful. Indeed, in both domestic and international affairs, Bush struggled to manage several of the long-term problems that Reagan's policies had created. He was stuck paying for the Reagan revolution.

### Bush's Domestic Policies

Bush's first hurdle was cleaning up a savings and loan scandal produced by Reagan's attempt to deregulate that industry.

### The S&L Crisis

Unbridled from government oversight, large numbers of savings and loans (S&Ls) emerged to compete with banks as depositories of people's money. But instead of securing that money, S&Ls invested people's deposits in shady real estate deals, junk bonds, and other high-risk investments. Some of these high-risk investments were successful: Large companies used the money to buy up weaker companies, using their debt as a tax write-off and downsizing the weaker compa-

 See a timeline of events about the S&L crisis.

nies to make them profitable or eliminating them altogether. In the business world, this forced companies to streamline production and remain competitive.

Some S&L investors, however, were less successful in their investments, leading to waves of layoffs, companies burdened with huge debt, and overly consolidated industries. When several of these high-risk deals went sour, millions of Americans lost their savings in the S&Ls. President Bush orchestrated a program to allow depositors to recoup their lost savings, but this plan came with a price tag of nearly $500 million for Americans. American taxpayers were paying the price of bank deregulation.

> **"Read my lips: no new taxes."**
> —*George H. W. Bush, 1988 Republican National Convention, uttering a sentence that would come back to haunt him during his 1992 bid for reelection*

### No New Taxes?

The combination of Reagan's increased military spending, his tax cuts, and the payouts to rectify his deregulation created a huge national debt. During his campaign, Bush tried to maintain Reagan's optimistic demeanor and promised the American people that he would not raise taxes. This became untenable by 1990. That year, Bush and Congress produced a budget that raised taxes and cut defense spending. Reneging on his word about raising taxes would, in 1992, cost Bush his bid for reelection; even worse, it did little to forestall a serious recession.

### Recession

By 1990, unemployment had risen to 7 percent, and companies were regularly downsizing. The number of impoverished Americans rose by 2 million, and the cost of operating with a huge national debt was becoming apparent. Incredibly, Bush failed to respond. He eventually proposed tax credits and a middle-class tax cut, but these proposals came much too late to stem a recession.

## LO⁴ Foreign Relations under Reagan-Bush

Meanwhile, both Reagan and Bush supported an active, interventionist foreign policy. This was disastrous for balancing America's budget, but it did help end the Cold War.

## The End of the Cold War Era

When he first entered office, Reagan took a hard line with the Soviet Union, provocatively portraying it as an "evil empire." His efforts, along with the increasingly obvious economic collapse of the Soviet Union, helped initiate the end of the Cold War.

### Star Wars

Among the many facets of this plan, the bluntest was to increase the number of American weapons, reigniting the arms race that had slowed through the 1970s. Reagan revived military programs that Carter had cut. He dismissed overtures from the Soviet leader, Yuri Andropov, to cut back Soviet SS-20 missiles if the United States would refrain from deploying intermediate-range missiles of its own in Europe. Reagan also proposed to build new defensive weapons capable of "rendering . . . nuclear weapons impotent" by zapping them from space. This "Strategic Defense Initiative" or SDI (denigrated by critics as "star wars") violated the 1972 ABM Treaty, which forbade defensive systems capable of covering either the entire United States or the Soviet Union. Andropov and other Soviet leaders saw SDI

© Mike SARGENT/AFP/Getty Images

>> Gorbachev and Reagan on the first day of their summit meeting in December 1987.

Hear Reagan's "Evil Empire" speech.

as a rejection of arms control overtures in favor of a new quest for global military supremacy.

Reagan may have been betting that the Soviet Union could not afford to keep up with a revamped arms race against the United States. After all, in August 1980, shipworkers in Poland staged a series of strikes that led to the formation of the first independent labor union, Solidarity, in a communist-controlled country. The union's launch sparked a wave of sympathy strikes and indicated that the Soviet Union was having problems maintaining its empire.

### Perestroika

Relations between Reagan and the Soviets softened during Reagan's second term. The chief impetus for change was the arrival of a new Soviet premier, Mikhail Gorbachev. Gorbachev was a reformer (the Russian word for reform is *perestroika*) who was keenly aware of the exceptional costs of Reagan's burgeoning arms race. Thus, he sought to rectify the Soviet Union's financial problems by slowing the nuclear buildup. In 1987, the two leaders—Reagan and Gorbachev—agreed to eliminate thousands of intermediate-range missiles in the Intermediate Nuclear Forces (INF) Treaty. Relations improved when Gorbachev removed troops from Afghanistan, signaling Russia's willingness (and financial need) to stop actively promoting the spread of communism. With the Soviet Union's removal from Afghanistan, the American-supported Mujahideen took control, and the Mujahideen's inability to control the war-ravaged nation led to the rise of the Taliban, something that would have deadly ramifications for the United States in 2001.

### The Middle East

While relations with the Soviet Union simmered down in the 1980s, America experienced complicated new foreign policy problems. Its most complex international relations involved the Middle East. There, an attack in Lebanon was the initial flashpoint. The country immediately north of Israel, Lebanon had been torn apart since 1975 by a civil war between Muslims and Christians, and the small country had been turned into a battlefield by the foreign armies of Syria, the Palestine Liberation Organization, and Israel. Fearing the presence of troops from Soviet-friendly Syria so close to Israel, the United States sent peacekeeping forces to Lebanon in August 1982. The Hezbollah terrorist organization viewed U.S. peacekeepers as targets and kidnapped a number of American educators and missionaries. The worst blow came in October 1983, when Hezbollah terrorists attacked the barracks of U.S. peacekeepers in Beirut; a single suicide bomber driving a truck filled with explosives killed 241 Marines.

Of course, much of the U.S. interest in the Middle East centered on oil. Americans had become increasingly dependent on the energy source during the second half of the twentieth century. When America's oil supplies were repeatedly threatened throughout the 1970s and 1980s, the United States took military or diplomatic action. In 1980, for instance, Iraq, a militarily powerful oil-producing Arab state at the head of the Persian Gulf, attacked its neighbor Iran in an attempt to secure control of local waterways. The United States, the Soviet Union, and other Arab states in the region supported Iraqi dictator Saddam Hussein in his fight against Iran's militant Islamic republic. When Iran struck back against Iraq and its allies by firing missiles at their oil tankers, the United States responded by reflagging Kuwaiti tankers with American colors, bringing them under the defensive umbrella of the U.S. Navy. The threat of direct American military force reinforced the idea that the free passage of oil traffic was a key national interest. It also signaled deeper American involvement in the Middle East.

## The Iran-Contra Affair

Reagan's focus on both keeping left-wing governments out of Latin America and guarding American interests in the Middle East converged in the Iran-Contra affair. In 1985, at the urging of Israel, the United States sold weapons to Iran for use in their war with Iraq. Israel viewed Iraq as its most dangerous enemy in the region. Reagan did this despite an embargo against Iran (imposed after the 1979 hostage crisis) and the fact that Iran was an avowed enemy; indeed, the United States was at the same time offering support to Iran's enemy, Iraq. It sold weapons to Iran because top officials in the Reagan administration hoped that selling arms to Iran would ease relations between the United States and Iran.

More damning, however, was the discovery that members of Reagan's administration took the profits from the sale of arms to Iran and sent the money to a right-wing guerrilla group in Nicaragua called the *contras*, who were battling the left-wing government. It was never proven that Reagan was aware that the Iran arms sale funds had been diverted to the contras, but the nationally televised testimony of Lieutenant Colonel Oliver North demonstrated that Reagan was probably not aware of the *contra* affair and that he had not, therefore, sufficiently controlled his administration. At Reagan's behest, Congress investigated the affair, chastised the president, and indicted several of his men. The aftermath included resignations, fines, and imprisonment for a handful of Reagan's functionaries, and public embarrassment for the president.

Oliver North testifying in 1987.

© FILE/AFP/Getty Images

© iStockphoto.com/Dane Wirtzfeld

>> Much of the U.S. interest in the Middle East centered on oil.

>> In November 1989, the Berlin Wall came down.

## The Collapse of the Soviet Union

By the late 1980s, the *perestroika* initiated by Soviet premier Gorbachev had begun to blossom. Inspired by their exposure to capitalism, Western popular culture, and the loosened Soviet controls allowed by Gorbachev, in 1989, Poland, Hungary, and Czechoslovakia, then followed by Bulgaria and Romania, all overthrew their communist regimes. In November 1989, the Berlin Wall came down. In 1990, Latvia, Lithuania, and Estonia all declared their independence. In 1991, the once-mighty Soviet Union petered out, collapsing into a number of independent states—Russia, Ukraine, and many others (see Map 28.1). The USSR was no longer.

This meant that the United States had won the Cold War. Or, more realistically, that the Soviet Union had lost it. The policy of containment, first articulated in 1946 and lasting through the presidency of George H. W. Bush, succeeded in keeping communism from conquering and dominating the world. Capitalism had clearly triumphed over Soviet-style communism. Over time, it became apparent that Gorbachev's motives for *perestroika* were financial: The Soviet Union simply could not afford to maintain the huge military presence needed to keep its buffer states under disciplined communist control. The end of the Cold War led to a reduction of nuclear weapons by both the United States and the former Soviet Union, although many weapons still exist. It also allowed the United States to station fewer troops in Europe. To understand why the Soviet Union collapsed, see "The reasons why ..." box below.

## { *The reasons why ...* }

### There were several reasons why the Soviet Union dissolved in 1991:

***Containment and the arms race.*** Since 1946, the policy of the United States had been to contain communism where it was and fight any efforts to spread it beyond the Soviet Union. This policy was incredibly divisive in the United States, leading to several wars (both declared and undeclared), violent protests, and vast expenditures on military supplies and nuclear weapons. But it had succeeded in checking the expansion of communism in various parts of the world, including Southeast Asia. More importantly, it also had forced the Soviet Union to spend vast amounts of money fighting wars around the world and maintaining a huge nuclear arsenal.

***Widespread poverty.*** By the 1970s and 1980s, the draconian leadership of the Soviet Union and its overly centralized economic planning had led the countries of the Eastern bloc to lag behind the countries of the West, some of which had enjoyed technological advances absent in Soviet-controlled nations. In Poland, for instance, more than 60 percent of the population lived in poverty throughout the 1980s, while the people of Western Germany were faring significantly better. This led to protests in many of the countries of the Soviet Union, protests that were expensive to contain and defeat.

***Gorbachev.*** By the middle 1980s, it became clear to many in the Soviet Union that it was nearing bankruptcy and could not afford to keep fighting the Cold War or to maintain strict controls over its subordinate nations. In 1985, the Soviet premier Mikhail Gorbachev began a series of initiatives, called "glasnost" (openness) and "perestroika" (reform), aimed at softening relations with the United States, and perhaps ending the Cold War. This, of course, would also keep down the cost of the arms race. He also later tacitly invited the nations of the Eastern bloc to secede, suggesting the Soviet Union would not punish them for doing so.

***1989.*** In 1989, several Eastern bloc nations simply declared their independence from the Soviet Union. Poland, Hungary, and Czechoslovakia departed first, then Bulgaria and Romania. Only in Romania was there any resistance. In the other countries, the Soviet-backed communists simply stepped down. The most dramatic moment occurred in November 1989, when the Berlin Wall was destroyed in a public protest against Soviet rule and the Cold War more generally. By 1991, there were only a handful of nations left in the Soviet Union, and the union formally dissolved. Not all communist countries fell, however. Protests in 1989 in China were rebuffed, and the communist government there still retains control.

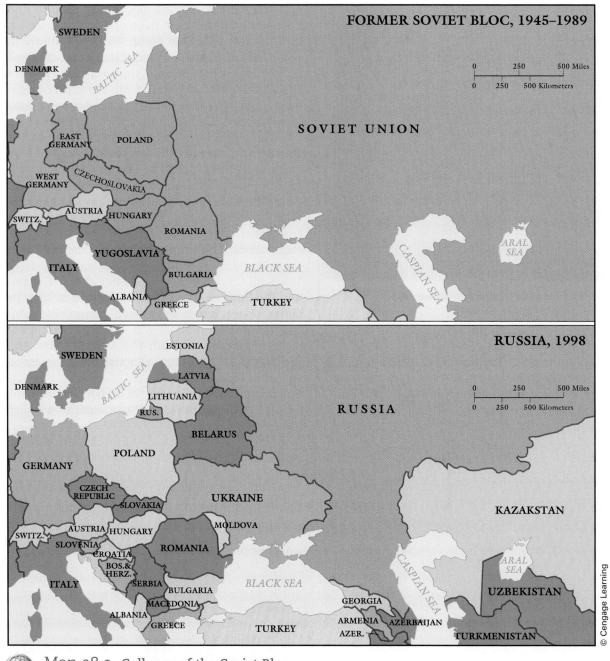

**FORMER SOVIET BLOC, 1945–1989**

SWEDEN
DENMARK
BALTIC SEA
SOVIET UNION
EAST GERMANY
POLAND
WEST GERMANY
CZECHOSLOVAKIA
SWITZ.
AUSTRIA
HUNGARY
ROMANIA
YUGOSLAVIA
ITALY
BULGARIA
BLACK SEA
CASPIAN SEA
ARAL SEA
ALBANIA
GREECE
TURKEY

0  250  500 Miles
0  250  500 Kilometers

**RUSSIA, 1998**

ESTONIA
SWEDEN
LATVIA
DENMARK
BALTIC SEA
LITHUANIA
RUS.
RUSSIA
BELARUS
POLAND
GERMANY
UKRAINE
KAZAKSTAN
CZECH REPUBLIC
SLOVAKIA
AUSTRIA
HUNGARY
MOLDOVA
SWITZ.
SLOVENIA
ROMANIA
CROATIA
BOS. & HERZ.
ITALY
SERBIA
BULGARIA
BLACK SEA
CASPIAN SEA
ARAL SEA
MACEDONIA
GEORGIA
UZBEKISTAN
ALBANIA
ARMENIA
AZERBAIJAN
GREECE
AZER.
TURKEY
TURKMENISTAN

0  250  500 Miles
0  250  500 Kilometers

© Cengage Learning

Map 28.1. Collapse of the Soviet Bloc

**ethnic cleansing**
Complete expulsion of an entire ethnic population from a particular area

## The Deadly Hangover

With the dissolution of the Soviet Union, several small, brutal wars emerged as people fought for control of their now-independent nations. Nowhere was this more troubling than in Bosnia-Herzegovina, a part of the former Yugoslavia. There the various factions engaged in **ethnic cleansing**, defined as the complete expulsion of an entire ethnic population from a particular area. With the Soviet Union no longer serving as watchful overlord, several nationalist movements clashed in civil wars throughout central and eastern Europe.

## Other Foreign Affairs

### Tiananmen Square

Meanwhile, in June 1989, several spontaneous prodemocracy rallies in China coalesced in Beijing's Tiananmen Square. The Communist Chinese government used force to end the rallies, killing at least several hundred of the student activists. This action strained U.S.-China relations and demonstrated that even as some governments were willing to liberalize their policies in certain arenas, such as economics, they would obstinately oppose any movement toward ceding political power.

 Read a U.S. briefing on events in China.

 Launch a news video about Tiananmen Square.

### The Persian Gulf War

The Middle East was another foreign policy crisis point. In 1988, the war between Iran and Iraq ended without a clear victor. The United States had actively supported Iraqi dictator Saddam Hussein throughout the struggle, despite selling arms to Iran in the Iran-Contra affair of 1985. In 1990, Hussein attempted to reestablish Iraq's control of the Middle East and ease some of his war debt by taking over the oil-rich tiny neighboring country of Kuwait. Bush feared that Hussein might threaten American oil supplies, and he responded by condemning the action and organizing a broad coalition of nations (including several Middle Eastern nations) in an embargo against Iraq. He set a deadline for Iraq to remove its troops from Kuwait and threatened to use the coalition to fight him if necessary.

In this game of brinksmanship, Hussein did not blink, and in January 1991, the Persian Gulf War began (see Map 28.2). It was more of a rout than a war: 40,000 Iraqis were killed, compared to 240 coalition troops. Hussein's attempt to attack Israel and break up the coalition against him failed after U.S. antiballistic missiles destroyed the bombs that were headed for Israel. Hussein had played his last card, and once the ground war began in earnest, in late February 1991, the war was over within days. Covered by satellite television and twenty-four-hour television news networks—both relatively new developments—Americans and the world watched from cameras in Baghdad hotels as missiles dropped and ground troops advanced. Vietnam was the first televised war, but the Gulf War was the first to be televised live.

In the end, Iraq quickly gave up Kuwait. Bush decided not to invade Iraq and remove Hussein because such an action would have destroyed the coalition he had amassed and also because he did not know who would succeed Hussein. This decision left certain factions in Iraq vulnerable to Hussein's harsh regime, including the Kurdish minority in northern Iraq and the Shia Muslims in the south, both of whom were hated by Hussein's Sunni Muslim base. But it also prevented the nation from erupting into civil war.

>> **Vietnam was the first televised war, but the Gulf War was the first to be televised live.**

©Danita Delimont/Alamy

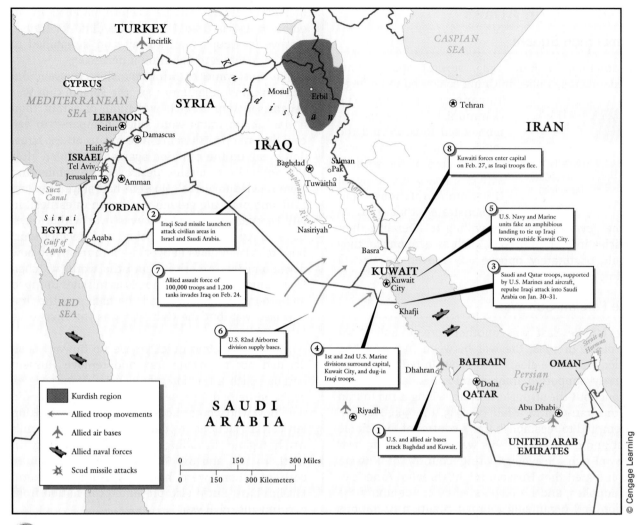

**Map 28.2. The Persian Gulf War**

- Kurdish region
- Allied troop movements
- Allied air bases
- Allied naval forces
- Scud missile attacks

1. U.S. and allied air bases attack Baghdad and Kuwait.

2. Iraqi Scud missile launchers attack civilian areas in Israel and Saudi Arabia.

3. Saudi and Qatar troops, supported by U.S. Marines and aircraft, repulse Iraqi attack into Saudi Arabia on Jan. 30–31.

4. 1st and 2nd U.S. Marine divisions surround capital, Kuwait City, and dug-in Iraqi troops.

5. U.S. Navy and Marine units fake an amphibious landing to tie up Iraqi troops outside Kuwait City.

6. U.S. 82nd Airborne division supply bases.

7. Allied assault force of 100,000 troops and 1,200 tanks invades Iraq on Feb. 24.

8. Kuwaiti forces enter capital on Feb. 27, as Iraqi troops flee.

© Cengage Learning

# And in the end . . .

When the war in the Persian Gulf ended in 1991, President Bush enjoyed strong support. His approval rating soared to a record-breaking 91 percent. But the weak American economy kept plaguing him. And it led to his losing the White House. A Democrat would assume the presidency in 1992.

Nevertheless, two historic transitions marked the years between 1980 and 1992. First was the American population's general shift rightward—politically, socially, and economically. Appeased by the friendly face of Ronald Reagan, large numbers of Americans lost interest in supporting the broad social welfare programs of the New Deal and the Great Society, favoring smaller government instead. And the second was the end of the Cold War, which terminated the fifty-year struggle between the United States and the Soviet Union. With the conclusion of the Cold War, the world became a more open, accessible place, and this development, sometimes called globalization, would be a key part of the world economy that would shape the 1990s.

| What else was happening . . . | |
|---|---|
| 1982 | PacMan is named *Time* magazine's Man of the Year. |
| 1986 | Tom Cruise stars in *Top Gun*. |
| 1990 | Children's classic *My Friend Flicka* is pulled from the optional reading lists for fifth- and sixth-graders in Clay County, Florida, because the book reportedly uses objectionable language. |
| 1991 | First used in 1979 in connection with the Iran hostage crisis, Tony Orlando and Dawn's 1970s hit "Tie a Yellow Ribbon 'Round the Old Oak Tree" has a resurgence in popularity as the anthem for American families with loved ones overseas during the Gulf War. As a result of the tremendous demand for yellow ribbon to tie around trees, one ribbon maker ships 30 million yards of it in a month. |

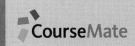

Visit the CourseMate website at www.cengagebrain.com for additional study tools and review materials for this chapter.

# America *in the* Information Age

## Learning Outcomes

*After reading this chapter, you should be able to do the following:*

LO **1**  Evaluate the presidency of Bill Clinton, discussing some of the major domestic and foreign issues the country faced during those years.

LO **2**  Discuss the technological revolution that took place during Bill Clinton's presidency, and describe the social and economic changes that took place as a result of this revolution.

LO **3**  Discuss the new focus on multiculturalism that grew during the latter part of the twentieth century.

LO **4**  Explain what makes the description of America as actually

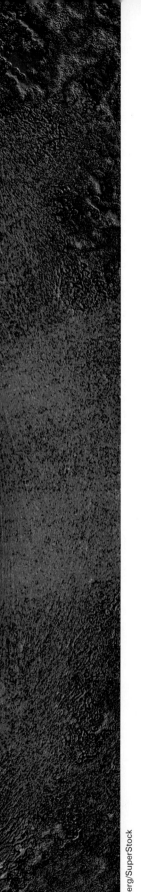

> ❝*Clinton's overriding commitment to conservative economic principles and liberal social principles set the agenda for American politics for the next eight years.*❞

America since 1992 has been shaped by four forces: (1) the rise of new information technologies, such as personal computers and the Internet, which have powered increased and inexpensive communications throughout America and the world; (2) a commitment to reducing trade restrictions between nations, which, aided by the rise of new information technologies, has made the world seem smaller and national boundaries seem less significant, a phenomenon labeled "globalization"; (3) a general acceptance of the idea that the United States is a multicultural nation and that racial and ethnic diversity, whether good or bad, is a permanent part of American life; and (4) the perpetuation of the culture wars, as battles over affirmative action, abortion, homosexuality, and gender roles have continued into the new century.

All of these developments have had their share of critics. Globalization has been criticized for limiting the capacity of American industry to recover since its decline in the 1970s and for exporting Western values to non-Western nations. Multiculturalism has been contested because of increased immigration from Latin America, especially Mexico, which has considerably changed the ethnic makeup of the United States. And the culture wars have provoked critics to complain that debates about cultural issues have gotten in the way of concern about important economic issues. And yet, these four changes, in various ways, helped bolster the American economy throughout the 1990s, as it adapted to a postindustrial, service- and information-based economy.

In addition to reducing trade barriers, America's international agenda during the 1990s focused on confronting and handling the end of the Cold War, as several states emerged to contest the extraordinary political and cultural influence of the United States, making the world a more complex, sometimes more dangerous, place. By the advent of the twenty-first century, global affairs had become central to Americans' conception of themselves and their nation. Politically, all of these elements would converge on the century's last president, William Jefferson (Bill) Clinton.

## What do you think?

Clinton's unabashed advocacy for opening up trade is a central legacy of his presidency.

| Strongly Disagree | | | | | | Strongly Agree |
|---|---|---|---|---|---|---|
| 1 | 2 | 3 | 4 | 5 | 6 | 7 |

## LO¹ The New Political Center

The 1992 presidential election illustrated many of the themes that would dominate American politics during the 1990s. Notably, the campaign saw the rise of Bill Clinton, a leader who combined rhetorical appeal with a political **centrism** that eclectically blended liberal and conservative philosophies and policies, sometimes called "the Third Way." The Third Way consciously sought to avoid the liberal social and economic politics of the New Left and the social and economic conservatism of the New Right. Indeed, Clinton's overriding commitment to conservative economic principles and liberal social principles set the agenda for American politics for the next eight years.

The 1992 contest also highlighted outsider candidates, such as Patrick Buchanan and H. Ross Perot, each of whom mobilized voters disaffected with the major parties.

## The Fall of Bush

But the initial frontrunner was the current president, George H. W. Bush. Saddled with a worsening economy, Bush's poll numbers declined throughout 1991. Compounding his problems was a sense of despair that took hold of the nation during 1991 and 1992. Stories of the poor economy and episodes illustrating deep divisions in America dominated the news media, including (1) the Clarence Thomas confirmation hearings, (2) the culture wars, and (3) the Los Angeles riots.

### Clarence Thomas

One such division emerged in October 1991, when law professor Anita Hill accused Bush's Supreme Court nominee Clarence Thomas of sexual harassment. Hill's testimony at Thomas's confirmation hearings split the country and the Senate. Those on the political right, who supported Thomas, considered Hill a symbol of aggressive feminism gone awry. Those on the left accused the right of ignoring women's claim to equal and civil treatment in the workplace. The controversy also invoked questions of race, because both Thomas and Hill were black, and both had worked at the Equal Employment Opportunity Commission. At one point, Thomas claimed that the Supreme Court confirmation hearings were nothing more than a "high tech lynching for uppity blacks." The Senate eventually confirmed Thomas by the narrow margin of 52 to 48.

### "Culture Wars"

At the same time, several books appeared alleging that multiculturalism on college campuses was undermining students' awareness of the Western intellectual tradition, which conservatives said contained the core of American values. This round of the culture wars saw commentators arguing over the role of multicultural education and affirmative action in universities and the workplace. Some saw the conservatives as xenophobic; others saw liberals as disrespectful of core American principles, although these were rarely defined. Issues like abortion, gay rights, and religion in the public sphere all seemed to be dividing the nation.

### L.A. Riots

Most troubling of all, however, was a deadly multi-ethnic riot that erupted in South Central Los Angeles in April 1992. An all-white jury acquitted four white police officers who had been videotaped beating a black man named Rodney King after King fled their pursuit, driving at speeds of more than 110 miles per hour to escape. The riots were broadcast live

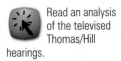
Read an analysis of the televised Thomas/Hill hearings.

© 1998 Ben Sakoguchi

>> Clarence Thomas claimed that the Supreme Court confirmation hearings were nothing more than a "high tech lynching for uppity blacks."

>> Video image of L.A. police beating black motorist Rodney King as he lies on the ground; taken by camcorder enthusiast George Holliday from a window overlooking the street.

to viewers around the nation, dramatizing long-standing tensions among many of the nation's ethnicities. South Central's problems had begun decades earlier, when in the 1950s white people abandoned the cities for suburbs and then again in the 1970s and 1980s, when companies moved out of the area, leaving many in the African American neighborhood without jobs. At the same time, new immigrants from Latin America and Asia moved into the area, as a result of the Immigration Act of 1965. The newcomers competed for the few jobs that remained. Korean Americans and African Americans were especially at odds. When the L.A. riots began, it was unclear who was on which side, or how many sides there were. In all, fifty-three people died, and nearly a billion dollars' worth of property was destroyed.

This level of violence, against the backdrop of the declining economy and other divisive political events, made Bush's America look like it was reeling out of control.

## The Rise of Bill Clinton

Despite these problems, Bush seemed a formidable enough candidate that few Democrats wanted to challenge him, especially after his popularity had risen so high in the aftermath of the first Gulf War. The field of Democrats had few nationally known figures, but, from the beginning, Arkansas governor Bill Clinton emerged as a party favorite. He polled well in the South, a region Democrats had lost since

1976. He defined himself as a political moderate; he was in favor of the death penalty and welfare reform, which were typically Republican positions. And he proved remarkably able to weather political scandal. During the New Hampshire primary, he obliquely admitted to accusations of adultery and apologized for his actions. The gamble worked, as voters seemed impressed by his honesty, and Clinton went on to win most Democratic primaries.

### Outside Challengers

Meanwhile, Bush was hampered by a challenge within his own party. Former Nixon, Ford, and Reagan advisor Patrick Buchanan launched a fierce right-wing campaign against Bush, capturing media attention and some primary votes. Later, Buchanan was given a prime speaking slot at the Republican National Convention, an opportunity he used to describe the nation as caught in a "religious war ... for the soul of America" between liberals and conservatives. The culture wars had gone prime time, and the speech struck many moderates as an indication that ideological extremists had taken control of the Republican Party.

Another political outsider played a pivotal role in impeding Bush's chances. In spring 1992, Texas billionaire H. Ross Perot launched an independent presidential campaign, calling for balancing the federal budget and attacking both parties as beholden to special interests. Perot's plainspoken style and outsider stance energized alienated voters, and, for a brief time in the summer of 1992, he topped the list of candidates in public-opinion polls. Perot drew supporters almost equally from Democrats and Republicans, but his attacks on establishment politicians, particularly in later campaign debates, were perceived as disproportionately harmful for Bush.

*The culture wars had gone prime time.*

At the Democratic National Convention, Clinton chose another youthful southerner, Senator Al Gore, as his running mate, and made the revival of America's moribund economy the centerpiece of his campaign. Taking as their campaign song Fleetwood Mac's "Don't Stop (Thinking About Tomorrow)," Clinton and Gore were the first presidential candidates to come from the post–World War II baby boomer generation, and they hailed themselves as the vanguard of a new style of leadership.

 Read Pat Buchanan's speech to the 1992 Republican National Convention.

**North American Free Trade Agreement (NAFTA)**
Legislation signed in 1993 that removed tariff barriers between the United States, Mexico, and Canada

**World Trade Organization (WTO)**
International agency designed to resolve disputes between trading partners and advocate free trade

## A Divided Electorate

Clinton's charisma carried him to victory, although the electorate was clearly divided. Clinton won a plurality of the popular vote, taking 43 percent to Bush's 38 percent, while 19 percent of voters backed Perot; many more Americans (45 percent of eligible voters) simply stayed home (Map 29.1). This fractured electorate gave Clinton a scant mandate for his programs.

## Bill Clinton, Free Trader

One of Clinton's chief messages, as candidate and president, was that America and the world were rapidly changing, making old ideological divisions obsolete.

### Clinton's "Third Way"

The key to Clinton's promise of innovation was what he called the "Third Way," a centrist and eclectic blend of policy ideas taken from both liberal and conservative perspectives. He supported programs that were popular with a majority of the voters regardless of who had first proposed the plan. He was a strong advocate of liberal proposals like Head Start, air and water quality regulation, and moderate gun control. But he also supported conservative programs, such as tough anticrime measures, welfare reform, and reducing the federal deficit.

### Free Trade

In the most substantial break with traditional Democratic policies, Clinton energetically advocated free-trade agreements that would open foreign markets to American companies and foreign companies to American markets. Many workers and the traditionally Democratic labor unions opposed trade deals,

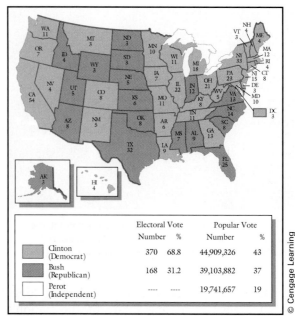

| | Electoral Vote | | Popular Vote | |
|---|---|---|---|---|
| | Number | % | Number | % |
| Clinton (Democrat) | 370 | 68.8 | 44,909,326 | 43 |
| Bush (Republican) | 168 | 31.2 | 39,103,882 | 37 |
| Perot (Independent) | ---- | ---- | 19,741,657 | 19 |

© Cengage Learning

## Map 29.1. The Election of 1992

fearing that American companies would move their manufacturing jobs overseas, which is exactly what happened. But Clinton argued that, by lowering costs to consumers, such agreements would aid technological change and result in a net economic plus for the United States—which is also what happened.

In 1993, Clinton worked hard to pass the **North American Free Trade Agreement (NAFTA)**, which removed tariff barriers between the United States, Mexico, and Canada. George H. W. Bush had begun negotiating the deal in the early 1990s, and Clinton supported and signed it in 1993. Two years later, Clinton secured American membership in the newly formed **World Trade Organization (WTO)**, an international agency designed to resolve disputes between trading partners and to advocate free trade. These were not uncontroversial issues in American life, but Clinton was convinced that the United States needed to work through the problems presented by modern information technologies and not fight against them.

>> Bill Clinton made the rounds of 1993 inauguration parties soloing and jamming on his saxophone.

© Brad Markel/Liaison/Getty Images

## Deficit Reduction

Clinton also made America's deficit reduction a priority, hoping to correct the imbalance created by Reagan's huge defense spending. Against bitter Republican opposition, Clinton passed a deficit reduction package that raised taxes on the wealthy and curtailed government spending. By 1998, the federal budget had gone from running a yearly deficit to showing a surplus, although there was still a tremendous debt to pay off.

## Post–Cold War Foreign Policy

In the post–Cold War world, international diplomacy was trickier than it might have at first appeared. While the demise of the Soviet Union had made the United States the only superpower in the world, it was unclear how Clinton should use American force. Should he walk softly and allow the nations of the world to work out their political problems themselves? If they engaged in civil wars, should he intervene? Or should he just use American power to force the nations of the world to adhere to American demands? He seemed to support UN peacekeeping missions, especially when they were acting on behalf of humanitarian efforts. But when in 1993 U.S. Marines in the East African nation of Somalia came under attack, Clinton withdrew American troops from the UN mission of which they were a part. In the wake of the Vietnam War, he was afraid to commit American troops to other nations' civil wars. This hesitancy prevented Clinton from intervening in Rwanda, where in 1994 the ethnic Hutu majority butchered 800,000 ethnic Tutsis.

Clinton was similarly hesitant to use American troops to create peace in the areas once controlled by the Soviet Union, especially in the Balkans, which had erupted in a series of ethnic wars between Bosnian Muslims, Serbs, and Croats. Through diplomacy, Clinton helped create the fragile state of Bosnia-Herzegovina. But the Serbian leader Slobodan Milosevic did not stop the ethnic violence, finally prompting Clinton, in 1999, to support a NATO aerial assault against the Serbs. He also committed the United States to support UN peacekeeping troops there.

## The Republican Surge

Clinton ran into further trouble when he tried to push for certain social policies that brought out the rancorous partisanship of the cultural wars.

### Policy Missteps

Upon taking office, Clinton fulfilled a campaign promise to end the U.S. government's ban on homosexuals' serving in the military. Civil rights groups applauded, but the measure was unpopular with military leaders and some members of Congress. Clinton quickly backtracked and offered a "Don't Ask, Don't Tell" policy preventing the armed forces from inquiring about the sexual orientation of their members, while restoring their right to remove known homosexuals from service. The strained compromise satisfied neither side.

Clinton suffered his most serious political defeat of the first years of his presidency with his ambitious proposals to change the nation's health care system. Clinton had made health care a central element of his campaign, responding to the fact that 37 million Americans lacked health insurance. Soon after taking office, the administration charged a task force, headed by First Lady Hillary Rodham Clinton, to develop a comprehensive health care plan.

As details of the proposals emerged (including a mandate that all employers offer insurance), small businesses and doctors began denouncing

>> Among the many compromises Bill Clinton stumbled into during the first years of his presidency, the "Don't Ask, Don't Tell" policy has provoked perpetual opposition from both the political right and the political left.

© Mark Peterson/CORBIS

the plan as big government run amok. In September 1993, opponents of the plan began running TV ads featuring "Harry and Louise," a fictitious couple appalled that the Clinton plan would prevent them from choosing their doctor. Republicans, who until this point had been unsure of how to treat the Clinton plan, launched an all-out opposition. By late August 1994, the Democratic leadership in Congress, divided by internal arguments over the plan, decided to abandon it. Genuine health care reform would have to wait.

## The "Contract with America"

The defeat of his health care plan and his waffling attitude about gays in the military eroded Clinton's popularity heading into the 1994 congressional elections. Conservatives were enraged by several of Clinton's social policies, while local issues (such as the nationwide push for **term limits** and a California ballot initiative to cut off illegal immigrants from social services) mobilized grassroots Republican voters.

The Republicans were remarkably united at this moment to take advantage of Clinton's weakness: House minority leader Newt Gingrich of Georgia pledged a "**Contract with America**," calling for significant tax and budget cuts, the return of many governmental responsibilities to the states, more defense spending, and a loosening of environmental regulations. The conservative coalition that was born in the 1950s and that matured in the 1970s and 1980s was coming of age in the 1990s.

The November 1994 congressional election results delivered a devastating blow to the Clinton presidency. Republicans gained a net total of fifty-two seats in the House of Representatives, recapturing control of the chamber for the first time since 1955. They also gained ten seats in the Senate. Clinton would have to govern with a hostile Congress for the remainder of his presidency.

## Clinton's Recovery

Gingrich began 1995 as Speaker of the House, championing his ambitious Contract with America. As promised, he did usher most of the proposals in Contract with America through the House. But the Senate rejected many of the proposals, and others passed the Senate only to be vetoed by the president. Clinton opposed the tax and spending cuts that were central to the conservative agenda, and he cleverly used his power to undercut popular support for Republicans. Notably, Clinton declared in his 1995 State of the Union Speech that "the era of big government is over." He thus seemed to agree with Republicans' antigovernment philosophy, while vetoing the biggest cuts, declaring certain government functions too vital to shut down.

## Closing Down the Government

As Clinton's popularity rose again, Gingrich overreached. In 1995, the president refused to approve the Republicans' budget, which would have forced cutbacks in federal spending on the environment, workplace safety, and consumer protection. In retaliation, Gingrich tried to pressure the president by refusing to pass any budget at all, forcing a shutdown of many federal offices around the country. National parks, museums, and federal agencies were closed, and many government employees were laid off. The shutdown proved to be a tremendous miscalculation on Gingrich's part: A majority of Americans agreed with the president that Gingrich had attempted to blackmail him. After three weeks, Republicans gave in and approved the funds needed to reopen the government. But the damage was done. Clinton enjoyed a resurgence of popularity, while the legislative initiatives of Gingrich's coalition slowed down.

## The 1996 Election

During 1996, an election year, Clinton again positioned himself as a centrist. Strategically, he agreed to sign a Republican-sponsored welfare act setting limits on the number of years that a person can receive welfare and giving the states more power to draft their own regulations. Although liberals denounced Clinton's approval of the bill, it deprived Republicans of a major campaign issue and solidified Clinton's high ratings.

As in 1992, Clinton also benefited from chaos affecting his rivals. Ross Perot mounted another third-party campaign, while the eventual Republican nominee, Kansas Senator Bob Dole, had to spend campaign funds battling other candidates. In contrast, Clinton ran unopposed. Furthermore, Dole, a World War II veteran, had amassed an impressive record of public service, but voters saw his age (seventy-three) as a liability. Tapping into these concerns, Clinton declared at the Democratic Convention that

Read Clinton's speech to the 1996 Democratic National Convention. his policies would better prepare Americans for the new challenges of the information age, building "a bridge to the twenty-first century." He coasted to an easy reelection, taking 49 percent of the vote to Dole's 41 percent. Clinton became the first Democrat since Franklin D. Roosevelt to be elected to two terms as president.

# LO$^2$ The Information Revolution

Throughout his two terms in office, Clinton was aided by a solid economic rebound, largely caused by a revolution in information technology.

## Economic Rebound

The American economy began to recover from its post-Reagan recession in 1992 and had shot upward by the late 1990s. In 1993, the United States' real annual growth rate in GDP was a healthy 2.7 percent; it ran more than 4 percent per year between 1997 and 1999, a level economists usually associate with high-growth economies in developing countries. Millions of new jobs were created during the 1990s, and the country enjoyed low rates of unemployment and slight inflation. The average price of stocks more than tripled during the decade, too; the composite index of the NASDAQ stock exchange, which listed many new technology company stocks, grew by almost 800 percent.

Clinton received some credit for this development, with many commentators pointing to his administration's deficit reduction plan as important groundwork for economic growth. A more common view, however, was that having a Democratic president and a Republican-controlled Congress prevented either from making new policies that might interfere with the economy's success. The news media saw Alan Greenspan, chairman of the Federal Reserve Board (the central bank of the United States, which tries to regulate the economy's ups and downs), as the wizard behind the economic growth. Greenspan succeeded in setting healthy interest rates and controlling the money supply to avoid both recession and inflation. The widespread praise for Greenspan subtly demonstrated a continuing public cynicism about the abilities of elected political leaders, a cynicism prevalent since Watergate.

## The Digital Age

### The Internet and Information Technologies

To explain this growth, many economists argued that an "information revolution" had taken place.

The rapid development of new information technologies (IT) such as cellular phones and personal computers led many analysts to explain the sudden economic rise as a result of the unforeseen savings brought on by expedited communications. Central to these gains was the Internet, a vast network of linked computers that allows information to be shared easily and instantly. Although universities and the federal government had developed much of the infrastructure behind the Internet in the 1970s and 1980s, it only emerged as a commercial tool in the mid-1990s, after inexpensive desktop computers became common fixtures in American homes and offices. As millions of Americans started going online, the Internet rapidly transformed into an electronic public square, a place to exchange ideas and sell wares, as well as to be educated and entertained.

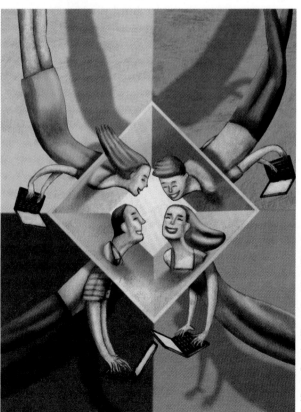

>> During the 1990s, the Internet rapidly transformed into an electronic public square.

## Other Communications

Digital technology fueled rapid economic growth in other areas of the economy, as computers streamlined manufacturing processes, helped American companies reach overseas markets, and revolutionized new areas of medical research, particularly in biotechnology. Underpinning the information revolution was the work of hundreds of new companies laying fiber-optic cable, building cell-phone towers, networking offices, digitizing libraries, streamlining computer chips, and designing websites. Expanding the lines of digital communication also helped usher in a broader network of cable television networks, including a number of 24-hour cable news channels, which was constantly on the lookout for up-to-the-minute news stories and which fractured the unity perceived when there were only a handful of national news outlets. It also ushered in a trend in which fewer Americans read newspapers.

## Costs

Even as productivity remained high and unemployment dropped, some saw a downside to this revved-up American prosperity. Many economists warned that the growth in the price of stocks was driven not by sound investment but by what Greenspan termed "irrational exuberance." Others warned of the widening disparity between rich and poor. Similarly, after NAFTA and other free-trade agreements lowered tariffs between the United States and other countries, it became more profitable for American companies to move their factories overseas to take advantage of lower labor costs. This left many American industrial workers unemployed and continued the decline of the American manufacturing sector.

## Benefits

Nevertheless, the economy of the late 1990s brought undeniable benefits. Earning power improved dramatically for the wealthiest Americans, work was plentiful, and unemployment was low generally. The healthy economy helped federal and state governments balance their budgets, while police across the nation reported a steady decline in the crime rate, a trend usually attributed to the "trickle down" of American prosperity.

## Consolidation and Globalization

The growth of the Internet and the information revolution had two other consequences beyond improving the economy: corporate mergers and increased globalization.

## Corporate Consolidation

First, the information revolution stimulated a round of large corporate mergers because business leaders were convinced they should try to integrate media content with its transmission. Thus, companies that produced television, films, or music made efforts to provide their material to consumers through all available media: phone, cable, or fiber-optic lines, over the airwaves, or on movie screens. This view was encouraged by Congress, which deregulated the industry in the Telecommunications Act of 1996.

Nowhere was this process more obvious than in the area of mass communication, as giant companies merged to create even bigger corporations, hoping to dominate aspects of the new information economy. The Disney Company bought the American Broadcasting Company; Time Warner bought Turner Broadcasting, only to then be taken over by Internet provider America Online. Each of these mega-corporations acquired a variety of media outlets, including television networks, cable channels, publishing houses, movie studios, home video stores, and Internet sites. This allowed them to both produce and distribute their news and entertainment programs. The result has been that much of the information received by most Americans now comes from a small number of multinational corporations. Ironically, in an age of choice symbolized by countless cable channels and infinite websites, Americans receive their news and entertainment from an ever-shrinking number of corporate sources. The market consolidations of the 1990s resemble those of the Industrial Revolution of the previous century.

## Globalization

The other dramatic result of the information revolution has been the speeding up of a process called globalization, defined as an interconnected web of contacts that extends across the globe. Globalization is easiest to understand in the business world, where companies from different nations have little difficulty working together because of the ease with which they can communicate and transport goods. Old-world parochialisms seemed to be dying off.

Viewing globalization as a positive force, the Clinton administration advocated it energetically. It was the reason Clinton cited when signing the NAFTA agreement. It was the source of Clinton's drive to expand fiber-optic cable lines throughout the globe. And it was the reason Clinton endorsed the founding of the WTO in 1995. Indeed, Clinton did not fight the creation of multinational corporations, defined as companies that have offices and production centers in more than one nation. Throughout the 1990s, these companies expanded busily, moving production centers to where the cheapest labor could be hired.

## Critics of Globalization

Not everyone was enamored with globalization. For their reasons why, see "The reasons why . . ." box below.

In 1999, protesters against globalization staged a large rally outside a WTO meeting in Seattle, effectively halting the meeting. In 2001, an equally large protest descended on Genoa, Italy, to protest a meeting of the World Bank and the International Monetary Fund. Individual activists targeted specific companies for unsavory business practices and for maintaining sweatshops. One popular T-shirt used the Nike shoe company's trademark swoosh as the *v* in the word *slavery*.

More daunting were militant critics of globalization who were furious about Western ideals' encroaching on their lands and cultures. The most prominent of these violent protesters was Osama bin Laden and his al Qaeda network in the Middle East. Throughout the late 1990s, bin Laden and his associates used pinpointed assaults on American installations in the Middle East to challenge, disrupt, and discourage the Western presence there. In 1998, bin Laden, the wealthy scion of a successful Westernized businessman, escaped an assassination attempt approved by President Clinton.

© Janine Wiedel Photolibrary/Alamy

>> Critics complained that 1990s "globalization" merely meant imposing Western ideals and products on everyone with disregard for native customs.

# LO³ Multiculturalism

By the 1980s, the transformations brought about by the Immigration Act of 1965 had become increasingly visible in American life, and the number of immigrants from Latin American and Asian nations mushroomed. There were only about half a million immigrants coming to the country each decade in the 1920s and 1930s. By the 1990s there were more than a million immigrants coming to the country *each year*. The census of 2000 revealed that, for the first time, Hispanics had become the country's largest minority group (at 13 percent of the total population), displacing African Americans (at about 11 percent), who had composed the largest racial minority group since the nation's founding.

## {*The reasons why . . .*}

There were several reasons why many people were disenchanted with the new globalization.

**Cultural imperialism.** Critics complained that globalization simply meant imposing Western ideals and products on everyone throughout the world with little regard for native or local customs.

**Job departures.** Labor unions argued that globalization was depriving working-class Americans of jobs, as reduced trading border made it easier for companies to build their products in one place and sell them in another.

**Environmental critiques.** Environmentalists argued that globalization was creating industries and pollution in countries that were not equipped to handle them. These countries often countered that it was unfair for the United States to engage in its Industrial Revolution before the advent of environmental laws while these late-comers now had to abide by a stricter set of rules.

Combined with the calls for political and social recognition from African Americans, Chicanos, and American Indians during the 1960s and 1970s, this widespread immigration made most attempts to prioritize the English origins of the American nation seem untenable and xenophobic. Even Nathan Glazer, a Harvard sociologist who had been a staunch critic of Black Nationalism and other forms of early multiculturalism, wrote a book in 1997 called *We Are All Multiculturalists Now*. Throughout the 1990s, corporations attempted to demonstrate their friendliness to minority groups (even if the realities of their hiring and promotion priorities did not always live up to the images they were trying to foster). And as this happened, racial and ethnic diversity became accepted as a positive good, something to be celebrated as a unique American achievement.

The heavily Hispanic and Asian post-1965 immigration was buttressed by huge numbers of illegal immigrants coming from Latin America, usually from Mexico. In search of better opportunities or searching for their families, illegal immigrants often came across the southern border of the United States, facing a treacherous crossing from Mexico. Although the number of illegal immigrants in the United States is unknown, the best estimates suggest that about 10 million illegal immigrants were living in the United States during the first years of the twenty-first century. Many of these illegal immigrants come from Mexico and other Latin American countries, but thousands more come from Europe and other parts of the world.

Critics complained that illegal immigrants were burdening America's social services, such as hospitals and schools, and were doing so without paying proper taxes. Illegal immigration became a political issue, especially in border states like California, Arizona, and Texas. Democrats often showed concern for the well-being of illegal immigrants, suggesting that amnesty for those already in the United States combined with an immigration policy more aligned with reality might be the best solution. Republicans seemed more concerned about the work that illegal immigrants were doing, arguing that those jobs would be better suited for those born in the United States or those who had come here legally. Both parties agreed that the current immigration laws were ineffective, and the stalemate continues.

# LO⁴ Two Americas

Although the economy remained good throughout the 1990s, several inexplicably violent events made Americans question the moral integrity of their nation. Was it really on the right track? Clinton made matters worse when he got caught in a highly politicized sex scandal. The result was the impression that, by the turn of the century, "two Americas" had formed, although it was hard to define either side beyond saying that one tended to vote Republican, the other Democratic.

## Discontent

With the economy humming along, few would have predicted that extreme instances of violence would flare up. But that is exactly what happened.

### Oklahoma City

In 1995, Gulf War veteran Timothy McVeigh protested the federal government's fiery intervention into violent antigovernment sects (those at Ruby Ridge, Idaho, and the Branch Davidians at Waco, Texas) by blowing up a federal building in Oklahoma

From TIME Magazine, 11/18/1993 © 1993 Time, Inc. Used under license.

>> In 1993, *Time* magazine used a computer composite of thousands of American faces to create what it called "the new face of America." That face was cocoa colored, with brown hair and hazel eyes. Its ambiguous ethnic and racial origin testified to the transitions that immigration had triggered in the United States since 1965.

>> In 1995, Timothy McVeigh, a Gulf War veteran, detonated a bomb outside the federal courthouse in Oklahoma City, claiming as a motive the federal government's attempts to shut down various American militias.

City. The blast killed 168 people, most of whom were children attending day care in the building. Authorities immediately captured McVeigh, and his actions provided a window into a widespread network of antigovernment militias that were scattered throughout the nation. These groups thought the federal government had become too big and was infringing too much on Americans' lives.

### James Byrd, Jr.

Three years later, in 1998, three white supremacists from Jasper, Texas, murdered a forty-nine-year-old black man named James Byrd, Jr. They then dragged him from the back of their truck for miles. Such a savage maiming had not been perpetrated for decades and was met with widespread horror by a nation that thought this kind of racial hatred was a thing of the past.

### Matthew Shepard

Later in 1998, two men attacked Matthew Shepard, a young gay man, for allegedly approaching them in a Laramie, Wyoming, bar. The men beat and robbed him, then tied him to a fence in rural Wyoming. Shepard died of brain damage shortly thereafter. Many Americans pointed to Byrd's and Shepard's deaths as a signal that, despite the acceptance of multiculturalism and America's pluralism, brutal racism and homophobia still existed in the United States.

### Columbine

In 1999, two high school students in Columbine, Colorado, went on a shooting rampage at their school. In a highly orchestrated attack, the two students brought weapons to campus and killed thirteen classmates and one teacher before killing themselves. No one has ever established a firm motive for their actions, but their violent actions and the number of copycats they inspired demonstrated discontent with some aspects of American society.

## Political Polarization

Americans viewed these tragedies with nearly universal disgust, and some interpreted this disgust as a sign that Americans were ready for strong hate-crime legislation. Others saw these events as the result of an overly permissive society that provoked, encouraged, and even glorified violence. These polarized perspectives gained further expression in a scandal concerning Bill Clinton's sexual liaisons.

### Lewinsky Episode

In 1998, a House of Representatives special investigator named Kenneth Starr determined that Clinton had inappropriate sexual contact with a White House intern named Monica Lewinsky. Clinton denied the claim, but when Starr found out that one of  Read excerpts from the Starr Report.

Lewinsky's friends had taped telephone conversations in which Lewinsky described the sexual conduct, Starr called Clinton's bluff. Starr overextended his reach, however, when he demanded that the House of Representatives impeach the president for committing perjury. Clinton's critics argued that his unethical behavior had degraded and sullied the office of the president. Others, without defending the

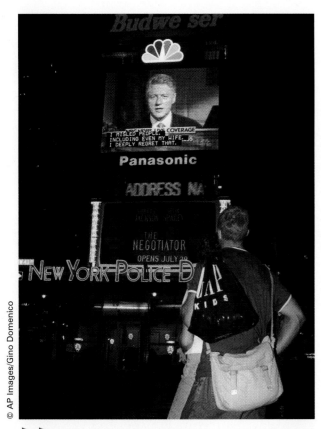

>> As the world watched, Bill Clinton's sexual improprieties further polarized an already polarized electorate, and led to the impeachment of an American president for only the second time in history.

president's actions, claimed that he was the victim of a new kind of information age political warfare, his private life exposed to public scrutiny in a way that few public figures could survive.

### Rebuking the Republicans

Polls showed that, although voters disapproved of Clinton's actions, they were also fed up with the partisan bickering associated with the Lewinsky case. Perhaps as a result, the congressional elections of 1998 delivered an unexpected rebuke to the Republicans. They lost six seats in the House of Representatives and held on to only a slim majority in the Senate. The unexpected losses prodded Newt Gingrich to resign. Despite the election results, Republicans pressed ahead with the impeachment of the president. In the Constitution, impeachment is defined as a formal accusation of "high crimes and misdemeanors." And on December 19, 1998, on votes of 228 to 206 and then 221 to 212, the House approved two articles of impeachment and sent the case for trial to the Senate. The vote in the House was divided almost entirely along party lines, with most Democrats opposing impeachment and virtually all

Republicans favoring it. These results foreshadowed the failure of the measure in the Senate, where Democrats had more than the 34 votes needed to block Clinton's removal from office. On February 12, 1999, the best prosecutors could secure was a 50-to-50 tie in the Senate over the issue of whether or not Clinton had obstructed justice and should therefore be removed from office. Clinton completed his term.

## The 2000 Election

While Clinton certainly bears responsibility for his actions, the assault against him was prosecuted with particular energy and vigor. As such, it was a symbol of a larger political divide, as Republicans attempted to position themselves as moralistic defenders of pre-1960s order and Democrats sought to portray themselves as capable of maintaining order while acknowledging the social liberalism of the 1960s and 1970s. Clinton's scandal did not bolster the Democrats' image, but Kenneth Starr's investigation, which much of the public considered trite and juvenile, had hurt Republicans.

### The Candidates

The divisions that had provoked all the controversy remained as fault lines in the 2000 presidential election. At first, the 2000 campaign promised to be dull, as most commentators regarded the respective party nominees as foregone conclusions. For Republicans, George W. Bush, governor of Texas and son of the former president, appealed to party regulars; a conservative, he had also compiled a record of working with Democrats to pass legislation. On the Democratic side, the favored candidate was Vice President Al Gore, who promised to continue the Clinton policies that had brought eight years of "peace and prosperity." Gore chose as his running mate Senator Joseph Lieberman of Connecticut, the first Jewish vice-presidential nominee. Gore faced a challenge from the political left, as the Green Party put forward the long-time consumer advocate Ralph Nader as its candidate. Nader argued that both Bush and Gore were beholden to big business and thus were not putting forward suitably different platforms, including ending corporate donations to political campaigns. Although Nader failed to win a single electoral vote, his candidacy may have sapped just enough votes from Gore to swing the election.

### The Vote

Neither major party candidate generated much enthusiasm. Gore was criticized as being stiff and

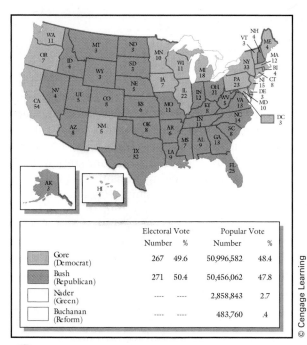

| | Electoral Vote | | Popular Vote | |
| | Number | % | Number | % |
| Gore (Democrat) | 267 | 49.6 | 50,996,582 | 48.4 |
| Bush (Republican) | 271 | 50.4 | 50,456,062 | 47.8 |
| Nader (Green) | ---- | ---- | 2,858,843 | 2.7 |
| Buchanan (Reform) | ---- | ---- | 483,760 | .4 |

 Map 29.2. The Election of 2000

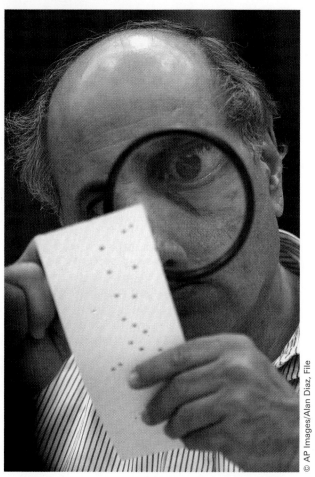

>> In the confusing aftermath of the 2000 election, millions of Americans learned what a "hanging chad" was, although knowing what it was didn't make the election's outcome any easier to discern.

wonkish; Bush was more affable, but many worried that he lacked experience and intellect. Uninspired and disillusioned with politics after eight years of scandal and partisanship, only 50 percent of eligible voters cast their ballots on Election Day. The lack of passion for either candidate was manifested in the extremely slim vote margins between the two. As millions of Americans tuned in to the major TV news networks to learn who their next president would be, they saw normally confident news anchors reduced to stuttering confusion. Projections switched back and forth on election night; neither candidate had captured the 270 votes necessary to win a majority of the Electoral College.

The results illuminated a peculiarity of the American electoral system not seen since 1888: a candidate with a minority of the popular vote was poised to win a majority of the votes in the Electoral College. Gore actually won the popular vote by more than half a million votes. Yet Bush emerged with a razor-thin lead of 1,784 votes in Florida, a tiny fraction of the 6 million cast in that state, but enough to gain the state's 25 electoral votes, which gave him a total of 271 electoral votes overall—the bare minimum needed to become president (Map 29.2).

## The Controversy

With this narrow margin, Florida law called for an automatic recount, a process made more complicated by claims of voting irregularities around the state. Gore's team pushed for recounts in counties carried by Gore, reasoning that disputed ballots from these areas might help their candidate if they were counted. Bush's staff resisted holding any recount in the hope of hanging on to their lead. In some locations, such as Miami-Dade County, recounts were abandoned after crowds of Bush supporters disrupted the proceedings. Gore went to court to ask for a recount of "undervotes," the thousands of ballots that the vote-counting machine could not read, and, on December 8, the Florida Supreme Court granted Gore's request.

Four days later, in the case of *Bush* v. *Gore* (2000), the U.S. Supreme Court voted 5 to 4 to halt the recount, allowing Florida governor Jeb Bush, brother of the candidate, to certify George W. Bush's 537-vote margin, thus making George W. Bush president. The conservative majority on the Court argued that Florida law made no provision for recounting undervotes and that the state had no fair way to evaluate partially marked ballots. Four justices dissented, insisting that the federal government had no right to interfere with Florida's attempt to determine the winner of its own electoral votes.

The confusing outcome provided more drama than had the year of political campaigning that preceded the election. It also revealed a sharply divided electorate.

| What else was happening . . . | |
| --- | --- |
| **1996** | As an April Fool's joke, Taco Bell runs a full-page ad in newspapers, including the *New York Times,* claiming that the fast-food chain has just bought the Liberty Bell for $1 million. The joke goes on to say that there are plans to rename it the "Taco Liberty Bell." For a full day, it is taken as a legitimate news event. |
| **1997** | Nevada becomes the first state to pass legislation categorizing Y2K data disasters as "acts of God," protecting the state from lawsuits that might be brought against it by residents in the year 2000. |
| **1997** | Scientists at Roslin Institute in Scotland clone a sheep, Dolly. |
| **1997** | Princess Di is killed in a car crash in Paris. |

# And in the end . . .

Bush's election seemed to signify the political doldrums of the 1990s. America had entered a new era of free trade, the economy had rebounded from recession due to the growth and expansion of new information technologies, and most Americans generally accepted America's increasing racial, ethnic, and religious diversity, although they remained uncertain about the country's immigration policies. Despite these exciting transitions, politicians seemed bound by Clinton's Third Way, and thus partisanship became contested within the boundaries of culture, not economic or social issues. Meanwhile, America's role in the world seemed limited to just economic and cultural imperialism, and most Americans were unaware that the effects of globalization were creating millions of potential enemies, some of whom were angry and dangerous enough to foment an attack on American soil. It is to globalization and its discontents that we turn now.

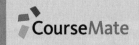 CourseMate

Visit the CourseMate website at www.cengagebrain.com for additional study tools and review materials for this chapter.

{ Speak Up! }

"I love the book and the online resources help a lot. The design makes reading much easier and everything is more inviting than a regular textbook. Thanks a lot!"
— Austin Jensen, Student at Western Illinois University

HIST was built on a simple principle: to create a new teaching and learning solution that reflects the way today's faculty teach and the way you learn.

Through conversations, focus groups, surveys, and interviews, we collected data that drove the creation of the version of HIST that you are using today. But it doesn't stop there—in order to make HIST an even better learning experience, we'd like you to SPEAK UP and tell us how HIST worked for you. What did you like about it? What would you change? Are there additional ideas you have that would help us build a better product for next semester's U.S. history students?

At **CengageBrain.com,** you'll find all of the resources you need to succeed in U.S. history—flash cards, interactive online quizzes, a robust eBook, primary source exercises, and more!

*Speak Up!* Go to **CengageBrain.com.**

# CHAPTER 30

# Globalization *and* Its Discontents

## Learning Outcomes

*After reading this chapter, you should be able to do the following:*

LO **1**  Describe the first term of George W. Bush, and explain how the events of his first year in office shaped his presidency.

LO **2**  Describe George W. Bush's plans for democracy in the Middle East, and assess the degree of success he had.

LO **3**  Discuss the domestic problems that America faced during George W. Bush's second term.

LO **4**  Explain some of the hopes and frustrations of Barack Obama's first years in office.

> ## “The advent of the information age spawned opportunities as well as challenges.”

The advent of the information age spawned opportunities as well as challenges. Cyberthieves capable of stealing information over the Internet used that information to apply for credit cards to make a quick profit. International markets became more challenging to predict and difficult to manage. Most deadly of all, many people in the world began to view America's predominant place in the global economy as a threat to their way of life. Several nebulous multinational groups, inspired by religious fanaticism and anti-Americanism and tied together by easy access to information and global communication, rose to challenge the United States, drawing the nation into what has come to be called the global war on terror.

President Bush initiated the policies and legislation in the war on terror, although this was never his intended goal. He had emerged from the troubled presidential election of 2000 somewhat weakened, but he nonetheless governed from the right, passing tax cuts and expanding America's military profile. And before his first year in office was over, vital Republicans had defected, and the humming economy of the 1990s seemed to be fading into a recession. Then, in September 2001, the focus of his presidency changed. Critics of America's international power struck a terrible blow against the United States by hijacking four airplanes and flying three of them into iconic American buildings, symbolizing an attack on America's trading prowess and military reach. The September 11 attacks propelled the nation into a global war on terror, which not only influenced America's international policies, but its domestic ones as well.

Bush's successor, Barack Obama, has confronted many of the same problems Bush did: a faltering economy, a complex morass of diplomatic issues, and a divided electorate. This chapter begins by looking at the presidency of George W. Bush and the challenges he faced, and then turns to the presidency of his successor, Barack Obama.

## What do you think?

The role of government is not only to keep its citizens safe from terrorist attacks but also to keep them safe from bizarre financial products and investment schemes.

| Strongly Disagree | | | | | | Strongly Agree |
|---|---|---|---|---|---|---|
| 1 | 2 | 3 | 4 | 5 | 6 | 7 |

## LO¹ George W. Bush

Winning only a minority of the popular vote, Bush came to office with no mandate. But he pressed ahead with his conservative agenda nonetheless. The centerpiece of this agenda was a large tax cut for wealthy Americans. And, despite critics' claims that the tax cut would wipe out the budget surplus created during the Clinton years, the Republican Congress passed Bush's $1.3 trillion tax cut. Some argued that Bush was simply continuing the Reagan Revolution of "starving the beast" of government regulations

© AP Images/Jim Collins

and entitlements that had developed since the rise of the Industrial Age at the end of the nineteenth century and was carried through the Progressive Era, the New Deal, and the Great Society. Bush similarly followed conservative strategy when it came to the environment, promising to search for oil reserves in the Arctic National Wildlife Refuge, which critics called America's last wilderness. He also pulled out of missile treaty agreements with Russia and refused to participate in an international agreement to control global warming.

But Bush faced a strong rebuke on May 24, 2001, when Senator Jim Jeffords, a Republican from Vermont, declared himself an independent, which shifted control of the Senate to the Democrats. Bush's policies seemed unlikely to pass, and his right-wing rhetoric had cost him necessary votes. In early September 2001 he was a president adrift.

## September 11

Bush's presidency was revived on September 11, 2001, when nineteen of Osama bin Laden's associ-

ates hijacked four U.S. airliners and attempted to fly them into various buildings across the country. Three of the four planes hit their targets. Two flew into each of New York City's World Trade Center towers, causing the 110-story towers to collapse. Another plane crashed into the side of the Pentagon, the government's central military office. On the fourth jet, passengers, aware of the unfolding tragedy through the use of their cellular phones, overtook the hijackers, and the jet crashed into a field in Pennsylvania. In total, more than 3,000 people died in the attacks.

The country was stunned by the tragedies, which were totally unanticipated by the public and which emerged from a source that was completely unknown to most Americans. Within hours of the attack, the Bush administration determined that bin Laden's al Qaeda network had masterminded the plan and that al Qaeda operated out of Afghanistan with the blessing of that country's ruling party, the Taliban, which had risen to power after it quelled an Afghan civil war in 1996. Its ideology of Islamic fundamentalism was combined with a severely repressive rule and also made it sympathetic to militant fundamentalist groups such as al Qaeda, who were willing to use violence to protest American involvement in the Middle East.

Throughout the 1990s, Osama bin Laden, the son of a wealthy Saudi developer whose allowance from his parents totaled $7 million a year, tried to rid the Middle East of any Western influence in order to return it to what he saw as its purer Islamic roots. To understand more about why al Qaeda was so angry at the United States, see "The reasons why . . ." box on the facing page. Bush, with the country's over-  Read a revealing biography of Osama bin Laden published by *The Observer* of London.

whelming blessing, decided to forge an international coalition and go to war against Afghanistan in order to oust al Qaeda.

## War in Afghanistan and War on Terror

The war in Afghanistan started in October 2001, and the Taliban were driven from power two months later. Unfortunately, U.S. and coalition troops found neither bin Laden nor many of his leading associates, who had likely fled to the mountains of Pakistan. Coalition forces and Afghanis have since had a difficult time establishing a stable government capable of holding the nation together.

The seemingly easy initial victory in Afghanistan and the stinging memory of the September 11 attacks prompted Bush to call for a larger war, which he called a "war on terror." While many said that a war of that magnitude could not be easily fought because there was no definable end, no specific battleground, and no specific enemy, most Americans went along with the president. He established military bases in Central Asia and the Philippines to combat militant Islamic insurgencies. He also sought to renew friendships with India and Pakistan in order to have well-positioned allies within the Middle East. He developed a new doctrine, called the **Bush doctrine**, which declared America's right to fight a "preemptive war" against any nation that, one day, might threaten the United States.

Bush also used the war on terror to reorganize the U.S. intelligence community. Shortly after September 11, he created the Department of Homeland Security as a cabinet-level position, the fifteenth cabinet department serving under the president. In 2005, Bush established the director of National Intelligence, which supplanted the CIA director as the principal intelligence officer in the nation, coordinating the efforts of the entire intelligence community.

Bush doctrine
Political principle articulated by President George W. Bush in which he declared America's right to fight a "preemptive war" against any nation that, one day, might threaten the United States.

## USA PATRIOT Act

September 11 also allowed Bush to push his conservative social agenda domestically. Defining his policies as useful in the war on terror, Bush passed

# {The reasons why . . .}

There were several reasons why Osama bin Laden and his al Qaeda network were so angry at the United States:

*Cold War blowback.* Throughout the 1980s, Afghanistan was the location of yet another Cold War proxy battle, with the Soviet Union attempting to exert control over Afghanistan and the United States supporting Afghan resistance fighters. (One American-supported organization was Osama bin Laden's Maktab al-Khadamat, which funneled weapons and guns to the Afghan fighters.) The war ended in 1988 when the Soviets departed, unable to control the country. Like the Soviet Union, the U.S. left in 1988, long before the country was politically stable. The subsequent instability led to several years of civil war and the rise of a radical Islamic government, the Taliban, that would later allow al Qaeda to use Afghanistan as its base of operations. The American and Soviet departure also allowed bin Laden to claim the role of the savior of the Middle East who had helped bring down the mighty Soviet Union.

*American involvement in the Middle East.* Osama bin Laden was radicalized during the Afghan civil war. Sensing that the Middle East had departed from its historic and godly ways, he laid the blame on outside influences, including American cultural and military involvement in the area. He was alarmed that, after the Gulf War of 1991, the American military had remained in the Middle East, and in 1996 he issued his first call for the United States to leave. Bin Laden and many others argued that the American military presence existed only to preserve American access to Middle Eastern oil. They did not want to be part of an American Empire. Bin Laden also did not want the Middle East to be exposed to what he perceived to be Western values, which to him included sexual licentiousness, tolerance of outsider faiths, and a revision of traditional gender roles.

*Israel.* Another flash point was American support for Israel. Since Israel's founding in 1948, the United States has supplied Israel with weapons and military support. Many, though certainly not all, Muslims believe Israel has no right to exist as a nation in the Middle East, on land that was largely populated by Muslim Palestinians before Israel came into existence. (Israel sits on land that is holy to Muslims, Christians, and Jews.) Several Middle Eastern nations came together in 1967 and 1973 to try to push Israel out of the Middle East, but the Israelis, with American support, resisted the attacks. American support for Israel has been a persistently contentious issue between the United States and many Middle Eastern nations. In a 1998 religious statement, called, in Islam, a fatwa, bin Laden formally objected to American foreign policy toward Israel and to the continued American military presence in Saudi Arabia. Seeing these as threats to the creation of the pure Islamic Middle East he envisioned, bin Laden also urged the use of violence against the United States until his demands were met.

*Islamic justifications.* While many people might criticize American involvement in the Middle East or its support for Israel, the vast majority do not resort to violence. To justify his violent diatribes, bin Laden embraced an Islamic schismatic movement that believed things could only be set right in the Middle East by restoring Islamic Sharia law (or, God's law) throughout the land. Bin Laden used Islam to justify the killing of innocent bystanders, arguing that, if they are right with God, they will enter Paradise for their sacrifice. The combination of legitimate complaint, wrong-headed scapegoating, advocacy of violence, and the promise of holy reward proved to be a deadly concoction.

George W. Bush **517**

Read about how the Justice Department strongly supports the USA PATRIOT Act.

Read about how the ACLU opposes many of the provisions in the USA PATRIOT Act.

another round of tax cuts, increased the size of the military, and cut back spending on social welfare programs. The war gave Bush the political capital to push for greater intrusions into privacy. In an effort to root out terrorism, the USA PATRIOT Act allowed the federal government to monitor—without judicial warrants—libraries, bookstores, banks, and even people's homes, although notable abuses of these policies have yet to emerge.

# LO² Remaking the Middle East?

With bin Laden still alive and plotting, Bush decided to use his recently declared right to "preemptive action" in the war on terror.

## Regime Change in Iraq

First on Bush's list was Iraq, the country his father had battled a decade before in the Gulf War, but which had been friendly toward the United States during the Cold War. Some of Bush's key advisors had been his father's advisors as well, and many of them were troubled by his father's 1991 decision not to invade Iraq in order to remove dictator Saddam Hussein. One of these was Bush's powerful vice president, Richard "Dick" Cheney.

The second Bush administration never quite clarified its rationale for deciding to invade Iraq, although it did argue that Iraq had a variety of

weapons of mass destruction (WMDs), including nuclear weapons, that it was planning to use against the United States. (This claim has since proved to be false, and CIA director George Tenet resigned for this failure of intelligence.) The administration also argued that there were traceable connections between bin Laden and Iraq (also, to date, unproven).

Critics and proponents alike disregarded most of this rhetoric and instead viewed the potential invasion as an attempt to remake the Middle East, which had been the breeding ground of much anti-American terrorism for three decades and which continued to be a crucially important region for the United States because of its large oil reserves. After several months of struggling for authorization, first from the U.S. Senate, then from the United Nations, Bush decided that their lukewarm approval was enough to merit an invasion. On March 19, 2003, 250,000 American and 45,000 British troops invaded Iraq, overtaking it and marching on the capital of Baghdad less than three weeks later. Six months later, U.S. forces rooted Hussein out of a dirt hole and handed him over to his Iraqi enemies, who hanged him after a speedy trial.

Read Secretary of State Colin Powell's speech to the UN advocating war with Iraq.

## A Democratic Middle East?

After the fall of Baghdad, Americans have attempted to create a democracy in Iraq. Violent attacks from insurgents have continued throughout the attempt to rebuild the nation (nearly ten times more Americans have died in Iraq since President Bush declared the war over), but some progress has been made. A hateful and hated dictator, Saddam Hussein was ejected. In early 2005, Iraqis voted for members of a constitutional convention, and in May 2005, the convention elected its first prime minister and cabinet. But the aggressively violent insurgency continues to kill American soldiers and Iraqis alike, leading many commentators, including some American military leaders, to suggest that creating a democratic state in Iraq might be impossible, with the more likely short- and perhaps long-term result being an enduring civil war between rival religious and ethnic factions.

## Abu Ghraib

In April 2004, at the same time U.S. forces were attempting to rebuild Iraq into what many hoped would be a stable democratic republic in the mold

>> A statue of Iraqi leader Saddam Hussein topples after being pulled down by a U.S. Marine vehicle in Baghdad's al-Fardous (Paradise) Square on April 9, 2003.

© GORAN TOMASEVIC/Reuters/Landov

of the United States, America's claims to be fighting to expand freedoms in the Middle East were undermined by reports from Iraq. These reports revealed that U.S. Army prison guards had tortured suspected terrorists in the Iraqi prison of Abu Ghraib. When pictures surfaced showing inmates strapped to electrical charges and stripped naked while being exposed to growling dogs, many Americans wondered how the U.S. government could claim to be advancing democracy while engaging in such behavior.

# LO³ Domestic Woes

As expenses for fighting terrorism mounted, the economy slowed considerably from the frenetic pace of the 1990s. One reason was that the information technology companies that had sustained much of the 1990s growth began to consolidate. The broad expansion associated with creating an entirely new industry began to slow down.

## Corporate Scandals

Concurrent with this slowdown, a number of corporate scandals erupted. The most shocking of these concerned the Enron Corporation, a large Houston energy company, which filed for bankruptcy in 2002. Badly overextending itself in its quest to consolidate different kinds of businesses and led by unscrupulous cheats, the company could not pay its bills, leading to a spiral of other business failures. Twenty thousand employees lost much of their pensions, while corrupt and mercenary executives, who saw the crash coming, cashed out before the company's decline and were well provided for. The scandal prompted a congressional investigation, especially because President Bush was a close friend of several of Enron's leaders, including its chairman, Kenneth Lay. Several other companies, including Arthur Andersen and Halliburton, also came under scrutiny, and many similarly fell into disrepute.

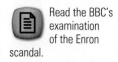

Read the BBC's examination of the Enron scandal.

## The Election of 2004

Bush came up for reelection with the newspapers filled with corporate scandals, continued insurgencies in Iraq, and a slowing economy. But his approval rating remained high, and many Americans praised his leadership following the September 11 attacks. In addition, the partisanship that had emerged during the Clinton years ensured that Bush would have a strong base of conservative supporters, no matter what his current political status.

### The Candidates

For their part, the Democrats nominated Massachusetts senator John Kerry, a Vietnam War hero who had alarmed many veterans when he came home from Vietnam and began publicly calling the war a mistake. During the election, Kerry argued that Bush had lost touch with middle-class Americans. He pointed to Bush's series of tax cuts for the wealthy and his overeagerness to intervene in Iraq despite the American population's tepid support. But Kerry was hurt by his lack of charisma and his uncertainty about what he would do in Iraq if he were elected president.

### The Election

Polls revealed that the election would be close. It was. In the end, Americans decided that Bush had done an acceptable job defending America's interests abroad. The president was also boosted by the continued development of Republican grassroots support in states vital to the election. In 2004, Florida was clearly a Bush state after the Republicans had spent millions of dollars there to develop and encourage voter turnout. In the 2004 election, no recount was necessary.

© AP Images/Pat Sullivan

>> In 2002, 20,000 Enron employees lost much of their pensions, while corrupt executives cashed out before the company's decline.

>> The destruction caused by Hurricane Katrina showcased the persistence of racialized poverty in America, as many of the poor neighborhoods that were destroyed when New Orleans' levees broke were overwhelming populated by black Americans.

## Hurricane Katrina

Seven months after Bush was sworn into his second term as president, a huge hurricane swept across the Caribbean, pummeling the Gulf Coast. It had been a mild, Category 1 hurricane as it crossed Florida from the Atlantic, but it picked up strength in the Gulf of Mexico, wreaking havoc on Gulf Coast cities in Florida, Mississippi, and Alabama. Then the storm took an unexpected northward turn, slamming into New Orleans. While many locals had fled the city, most of those who remained witnessed a harsh storm but, they thought, not one strong enough to destroy the city. They were wrong. After the hurricane had passed, it became clear that the storm had fatally weakened several already defective levees that protected the city from nearby waterways. Because much of the city sat below sea level, once the levees failed, the city filled with water. Entire districts drowned. People were told to go to the Louisiana Superdome for shelter, only to find the Superdome overcrowded, leaking, and generally unprepared to handle the crisis.

The federal government was slow to respond to the Katrina disaster, waiting several days to send in relief workers. The Federal Emergency Management Agency (FEMA), which was supposed to assist in these kinds of tragedies, was slow to coordinate the efforts and, in numerous instances, stopped or impeded state or local efforts to provide relief because of its insistence on being the principal relief coordinator. Meanwhile, news cameras televised the destruction for the world to see. People were stranded on roofs for days, holding signs that read, "Help us, please." The most badly affected were African Americans, who made up a disproportionate number of the city's poor people. In total, around 1,900 people lost their lives during the hurricane, and the catastrophe showcased the continued racial imbalance in America's impoverished class. It also demonstrated how political infighting among local, state, and federal authorities prevented vital help from arriving.

## The Credit Crunch

Domestic woes continued to mount throughout 2008, culminating toward the end of that year with the announcement that several of the nation's largest banks had overextended themselves and were filing for bankruptcy protection from the federal government. Most of these banks either had offered housing loans to unqualified buyers by enticing them through low, "teaser" rates or had purchased large numbers of these loans from other banks. When these buyers began defaulting on their loans, banks stopped receiving payments and went into a cash crisis. Unwilling to part with their cash resources, they made it more difficult for borrowers to obtain loans. Businesses stopped expanding, and people became increasingly unable to buy homes and goods. With the consumer market slowing down, the rest of the economy slowed down as well.

To address the need, the federal government passed a financial bailout in October 2008, offering as much as $750 billion of taxpayers' money to ease the credit crunch. The results of the bailout are

>> A trader outside the New York Stock Exchange following the end of trading on October 9, 2008. The Dow Jones Industrial Average dropped 678.91 points that day, to finish at 8579.19, closing below 9000 for the first time since 2003 and representing a crushing 40 percent loss in value for the year.

as yet unknown. What is known is that, with less money in the markets, a deep recession loomed, and worldwide stock markets reacted erratically. Some days showed record gains for many stocks; others showed deep losses. But the losses outweighed the gains, and the Dow Jones Industrial Average, the benchmark average of stock prices, declined by nearly 40 percent throughout 2008.

# LO⁴ President Obama

As Bush concluded his second term in office, the nation still appeared divided by culture wars, the economy seemed on the verge of collapse, and frightening foreign events continued to preoccupy Americans. American social and political divisions had infected nearly all debates.

In the atmosphere of Republican failure, Democrats sensed they could win back the White House and, perhaps, stop the conservative ascendancy that had been mounting since the 1970s. Democrats vowed to expand America's social programs, including nationalizing its health care system. They promised to take a less militant stance in world affairs, hoping to reach out diplomatically to potentially hostile countries. And they promised to rein in the war on terror.

## The Election of 2008

Within these debates, the Democratic Party witnessed the emergence of two historic candidates, Hillary Clinton, senator from New York State and former First Lady, and Barack Obama, a mixed-race senator from Illinois. Obama became, because of America's peculiar "one-drop rule," the first African American to win the nomination of a major political party. (The "one-drop rule" means that a person with even one drop of African blood is usually considered an African American.)

Obama, promising a change from the Third Way cultural politics ascendant since the 1980s, squared off against Vietnam War veteran John McCain, who, at seventy-two, would have become the oldest person to win the presidency. But McCain's candidacy was plagued by his ties to the increasingly unpopular George W. Bush and by a generally disorganized campaign. In addition, his vice-presidential candidate, Sarah Palin, the governor of Alaska, polarized the population with her folksy antigovernment rhetoric. Meanwhile, Obama's message of practical centrism and an end to the politics of division was greatly boosted by the economic turmoil taking place on the watch of a Republican president. On Election Day, the race was not a close one, with Obama handily winning the Electoral College and emerging with 52 percent of the popular vote to McCain's 46 percent—a difference of more than 7 million voters.

>> In 2008, Barack Obama became the United States' first African American president, but the job came with an unenviable mountain of economic, diplomatic, and domestic problems.

**>>** In 2009, Sonia Sotomayor became the U.S. Supreme Court's 111th justice, its third woman, and its first Hispanic. With Sotomayor's confirmation, the Court also for the first time did not have a single Protestant member, but six Catholics and three Jews. It was a measure of Catholic and Jewish acceptance in modern America that hardly anyone noticed.

# And in the end . . .

As president, Obama confronted a host of challenges. The expenses of waging a nebulous war on terror continue to mount. Instability in the Middle East has spurred a spike in gas prices, which has increased the cost of the basic necessities of American life, including food, travel, and energy. And the massive national debt, combined with the credit and housing crunches, has weakened the American economy so much that America's place as the single world power is now challenged by large developing nations such as China, Russia, and India.

Obama has, however, had some success in delivering on at least three of his major campaign promises. First, after a difficult year-long debate, in March 2010 Obama signed into law the nation's first comprehensive health care bill. The bill's aim was to ensure that all Americans had some form of health insurance, including the 40 million who, at the time of the bill's signing, did not have any. In fact, the bill made it a law that Americans have health insurance. The law also allowed parents to extend coverage to their children until they turn twenty-six years old. It also made it illegal for health insurance companies to deny insurance to people with preexisting conditions, a common occurrence before the bill passed. It gave small businesses tax breaks for offering health care for their employees. And it set a deadline to create a marketplace for affordable care.

In July 2010, Obama was also able to secure increasing banking regulation, attempting to prevent further financial crises in an industry that has quickly sped ahead of outdated laws and been hampered by thirty years of deregulation. And finally, in an effort to revitalize the economy, Obama also passed a large stimulus bill that initiated more than 75,000 projects across the nation.

But after watching Reagan, then Bill Clinton, then George W. Bush use the language of advocating small government (even if their actions did not live up to the rhetoric), it was predictable that a conservative backlash would emerge. Calling themselves the Tea Party Movement and embracing the folksy language of Sarah Palin, many conservative Americans protested what they saw as Obama's expansion of the federal government, a complaint made against Democrats since the New Deal. Indeed, in the 2010 congressional elections, Republicans won back control of the House of Representatives, although it wasn't entirely clear whether the results reflected a genuine sentiment against Obama's expansion of the welfare state or a broader discomfort with the stalled economy. (Republicans also made gains in the Senate, but it remained narrowly controlled by Democrats.) Facing a situation of divided government, Obama pledged to focus on jobs and the economy but also remained committed to the pursuit of other thorny issues like immigration reform, balancing the budget, and curbing the federal deficit.

## What else was happening . . .

| | |
|---|---|
| **2000** | Reality TV shows experience an explosion of popularity, beginning with *Big Brother* and *Survivor*. |
| **2001** | Apple launches the iPod, revolutionizing the music industry. |
| **2004** | A partially eaten, ten-year-old grilled cheese sandwich said to bear the image of the Virgin Mary sells on eBay for $28,000. |
| **2005** | Video-sharing website YouTube is launched by three former PayPal employees. |

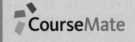

Visit the CourseMate website at www.cengagebrain.com for additional study tools and review materials for this chapter.

# Index

To help you take your reading outside the covers of *HIST*, each new text comes with access to the exciting learning environment of a robust eBook.

## Working with Your eBook

You can read *HIST* wherever and whenever you're online by paging through the eBook on your computer. But you can do more than just read. Your eBook also contains over 300 tested, live links to

 Primary source documents

 Historical simulations

 Maps

 Images

 Field trips

 Audio

 Video

 Interactive modules

 Websites

Each link gives you a brief introduction to the site, a direct connection to the site itself, and a set of multiple choice and reflection questions that you can answer online, print, and/or e-mail to your instructor.

Your eBook also features easy page navigation, different page views, highlighting, note taking, a search engine, a print function, and a complete user's manual (under Help).

# 1 THREE SOCIETIES ON THE VERGE OF CONTACT
# Prep Card

## What's Inside

Key topics in this chapter: America's Paleo-Indian Era; The Pre-Columbian Era; North America in 1492; African Politics and Society on the Eve of Contact; Europe in 1492; The Reformation and the Decline of Catholic Europe

## Learning Outcomes

**LO¹** Explain current beliefs about how the first peoples settled North America, and discuss the ways in which they became differentiated from one another over time.

**LO²** Describe the African societies that existed at the time the first Africans were brought to the New World as slaves.

**LO³** Describe Europe's experiences during the last centuries before Columbus made his first voyage to the New World in 1492.

## Chapter 1 Outline

## eBook Links

 9,000-year-old Kennewick Man
http://www.pbs.org/wgbh/nova/first/kennewick.html

 Article on the Paleo-Indians
http://www.desertusa.com/ind1/du_peo_paleo.html

 Simulation to Learn about the Aztecs
American History Resource Center

 The Decline of Chaco Canyon
http://www.learner.org/interactives/collapse/chacocanyon.html

 The Fall of the Mali and Songhay Kingdoms
http://www.learner.org/interactives/collapse/mali.html

 Interactive Study of European Feudalism
http://www.learner.org/exhibits/middleages/feudal.html

## Discussion Questions

1. Compare and contrast the tribes that were living in North America in 1492. What were some similarities? What were some differences?
2. Describe African society in Ghana and surrounding areas on the eve of contact with Europeans.
3. Describe life in Europe at the time the explorations of the New World began. Which experiences might have contributed to the willingness of Europeans to get involved in colonization?

## Group Activity

*Goal*
Find out more about what was happening in Africa and Europe at the same time.

*Task*
Divide students into groups of five to six. Either on large sheets of paper or on blackboards in the classroom, have each group prepare a **timeline** for events on the two continents. The line should be laid out horizontally on the paper or board. Groups should determine which events they think are most significant for each place. Place the events of one continent above the line; place the other continent's events below the line.

*Outcomes*
Students should acquire a greater appreciation for the complexities of both societies.

## Terms

## Assignments

1. Gather photos of structures typical of the various peoples of North America in the pre-Columbian era and create an exhibit to share with your classmates. Be ready to discuss your most interesting findings.
2. Whereas some North American pre-Columbian societies were matriarchal, most of Europe practiced patriarchy. Compare and contrast the two social organizations in a one-page table using the categories of family, politics, and economy.
3. Make a list of the most useful places to visit today to find out more about the following cultures: Mississippian, Pueblo, Anasazi, and Chinook.

## Beyond the Class

A selection of materials is in the Instructor's Manual and PowerLecture.

## What's Inside

Key topics in this chapter: Exploration and Discovery; Early Settlements and Colonization; England Founds the Southern Colonies; Founding the New England Colonies

## Learning Outcomes

**LO 1** Explain the reasons for Europeans' exploring lands outside Europe, and trace the routes they followed.

**LO 2** Describe the founding of European nations' first colonies in the New World.

**LO 3** Trace the expansion of England's holdings in the southern colonies.

**LO 4** Outline the reasons for and timing of England's founding of colonies in New England.

## Chapter 2 Outline

## eBook Links

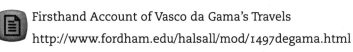

Firsthand Account of Vasco da Gama's Travels
http://www.fordham.edu/halsall/mod/1497degama.html

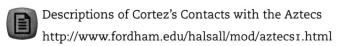

Columbus's 1493 Letter about His Findings
American History Resource Center

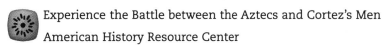

Descriptions of Cortez's Contacts with the Aztecs
http://www.fordham.edu/halsall/mod/aztecs1.html

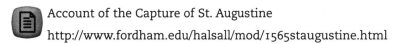

Experience the Battle between the Aztecs and Cortez's Men
American History Resource Center

Account of the Capture of St. Augustine
http://www.fordham.edu/halsall/mod/1565staugustine.html

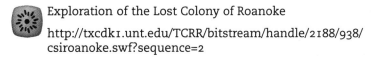

Description of the Founding of Santa Fe
http://www.common-place.org/vol-03/no-04/santa-fe/

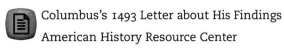

Exploration of the Lost Colony of Roanoke
http://txcdk1.unt.edu/TCRR/bitstream/handle/2188/938/csiroanoke.swf?sequence=2

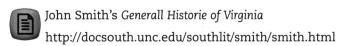

John Smith's *Generall Historie of Virginia*
http://docsouth.unc.edu/southlit/smith/smith.html

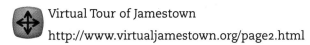

Virtual Tour of Jamestown
http://www.virtualjamestown.org/page2.html

John Rolfe's Account of Conditions at Jamestown after First Decade
American History Resource Center

The Economic Aspects of Colonial Tobacco Culture
http://www.tobacco.org/History/colonialtobacco.html

Contract of Indenture
http://www.virtualjamestown.org/wbind1.html

Maryland Colony's Toleration Act
http://odur.let.rug.nl/~usa/D/1601-1650/maryland/mta.htm

Participate in the Founding of a New Colony
http://www.pbs.org/wnet/colonialhouse/history/voyage.html

Plymouth Colony Archive Project
http://etext.virginia.edu/users/deetz/

 PBS Interactive History: Life in 1628 New England
http://www.pbs.org/wnet/colonialhouse/history/index.html

# Discussion Questions

1. Compare and contrast the interests of the French and the English in the New World, and describe how their respective attitudes influenced their patterns of settlement.
2. Compare the development of England's colonies in New England to those in the South. What were their similarities? What were their major differences?
3. Describe the early encounters between the Spanish and Portuguese explorers and the Indians of Central and South America, and explain how those confrontations led to European settlement there.

# Group Activity

*Goal*
Recreate the penning of a colonial agreement like the Mayflower Compact.

*Task*
Split the class into groups of five to six and have them draw up a compact under which they would like to live in a hypothetical colonial settlement. Then have students compare their own agreement with the Mayflower Compact.

*Outcomes*
Students will appreciate the modern as well as the traditionalist aspects of New England society.

# Assignments

1. Research the Columbian Exchange. Beginning with the most significant (in your opinion), list the top five items brought to the New World by the Europeans. Do the same for those things introduced into Europe from the New World.
2. Gather photos of three early Spanish missions in the American Southwest, and write a paragraph describing each one.
3. Explore online tourism sites for Maryland. What aspects of Maryland's colonial history have been neglected? Sketch out your own tourism website with the history you would emphasize to attract visitors.

# Beyond the Class

A selection of materials is in the Instructor's Manual and PowerLecture.

## What's Inside

Key topics in this chapter: English Holdings in North America Expand; Spain in North America to 1700; Growing Discord between English Colonists and Native Americans; Expansion of Slavery; European Wars for Empire Reach North America

## Learning Outcomes

**LO¹**   Describe the changes in European development of North America during the period from 1660 to 1700, and analyze the four distinct areas that began to emerge.

**LO²**   Discuss the English colonists' experiences up to 1700 with Native American tribes.

**LO³**   Discuss the English colonists' experiences up to 1700 with African slaves.

**LO⁴**   Discuss the European wars that had an impact on North America.

## Chapter 3 Outline

## eBook Links

 Virtual Tour of New Netherland
http://www.nnp.org/newvtour/index.html

 William Penn's Description of Pennsylvania
American History Resource Center

 The Story of James Oglethorpe and Savannah
http://www.georgiaencyclopedia.org/nge/Article.jsp?id=h-1058

 Letter by New Mexico's Governor about Pueblo Revolt
http://www.pbs.org/weta/thewest/resources/archives/one/pueblo.htm

 Explore the Origins of Florida
http://dhr.dos.state.fl.us/facts/history/summary

 Read about the "Middle Ground" at Chicago
http://www.encyclopedia.chicagohistory.org/pages/254.html

 Mary Rowlandson's Account of Her Capture
http://www.library.csi.cuny.edu/dept/history/lavender/rownarr.html

 Governor Berkeley on Bacon's Rebellion
http://odur.let.rug.nl/~usa/D/1651-1700/bacon_rebel/berke.htm

## Discussion Questions

1. Trace the growth of English proprietary colonies during and shortly after the Restoration in England, and discuss the reasons for their founding.
2. Describe and discuss the experiences of the English settlers with Native Americans during the Beaver Wars, Metacom's War, and Bacon's Rebellion.
3. Explain how and why American slavery developed as it did. Why were indentured servants not employed as they had been in the past?

## Terms

# Group Activity

*Goal*

Understand the degrees of forced labor in the colonial period and the significance of racial slavery.

*Task*

Have every student read the contract of indenture provided in the eBook link in Chapter 2. Divide the class in two, with one group preparing the argument that indentures are labor contracts and the other arguing that indentured labor is slavery. Have students debate each other in pairs, with each trying to convince the other.

*Outcomes*

Students will end up discussing the meaning of "free" labor and develop an appreciation for the meaning of racial slavery.

# Assignments

1. Prepare a poster about the "middle passage." Include illustrations and statistics, with detailed captions.
2. Find a website that provides tourist information on Pennsylvania, William Penn, and colonial times. What part of the state's history is most emphasized on this site, and what part seems to be neglected? Do you find the historical description accurate?
3. Essay: Choose the colony in which you think you would have felt most "comfortable," and write a one-page paper explaining why.

# Beyond the Class

A selection of materials is in the Instructor's Manual and PowerLecture.

## What's Inside

Key topics in this chapter: Expansion of Colonial Economy and Society, 1700–1763; The Chesapeake; Southern Colonies; The American Enlightenment; Great Awakening; African Slavery; Attempted Expansion of English Control

## Learning Outcomes

**LO 1** Describe the development of the English colonies during the 1700s, including a discussion of each group of colonies: New England, the Middle Colonies, the Chesapeake, and the Southern Colonies.

**LO 2** Discuss the impact of the Enlightenment and the Great Awakening on colonial society in America.

**LO 3** Chronicle the development of slavery in the American colonies, and analyze the reasons for changes in attitudes and in the legal system that helped the distinctively American slave system to flourish.

**LO 4** By 1763, American colonists had become used to making their own decisions and taking care of their own needs. Describe the events in England that contributed to this situation, and explain their effects on the colonists.

## Chapter 4 Outline

## eBook Links

 Cotton Mather Writes on Education
http://www.spurgeon.org/~phil/mather/edkids.htm

 Interactive Look at John Peter Zenger Trial
American History Resource Center

 Jonathan Edwards on the Great Awakening
http://www.nhinet.org/ccs/docs/awaken.htm

 A Doctor's Account of the Middle Passage
http://www.vgskole.net/prosjekt/slavrute/7.htm

 Various Resources on the Stono Rebellion
http://www.pbs.org/wgbh/aia/part1/1p284.html

 Images and Documents about Slavery
American History Resource Center

## Discussion Questions

1. Describe life in New England, the Middle Colonies, the Chesapeake, and the Southern Colonies as it existed in the first half of the eighteenth century. What made these colonial lives "American"?
2. Discuss the American Enlightenment and the Great Awakening of the 1740s. In what ways did they affect the lives of the colonists?
3. Explain the way the American slave trade operated, and describe life for a typical slave in America. Was this system of slavery modern or part of the Old World?

## Group Activity

*Goal*
Understand the Americanization of the Christian faith in the eighteenth century.

*Task*
Divide students into three groups: the laity, the clergy (Old Lights), and the revivalist preachers and evangelists (New Lights). Have clergy and evangelists prepare arguments that would draw laymen to their denomination. Have each member of the laity adopt a specific colonial persona. Match clergy, evangelists, and laymen in groups of three and let the preachers try to recruit the layperson who will explain his/her choice on the basis of his/her persona.

## Terms

*Outcomes*
Students will discuss the political, social, and economic factors that popularize particular churches and interpretations of faith.

## Assignments

1. Prepare a chart with pros and cons for living in each of the four colonial regions. Aim for "top five reasons" *for* living in the area you think was best, and "top five reasons" for *not* living in the other three.
2. Assume the persona of an elderly black man or woman on a plantation. As a slave who survived the "middle passage," you have been asked by your young grandchildren to tell them the story of how you were taken from Africa and enslaved. Write informally, as if you're actually telling the story.
3. Search online for information on the preaching of George Whitefield. Include information about his background: where he was born, how he was raised, and so on. Compile a list of the most interesting things that you find out about him.

## Beyond the Class

A selection of materials is in the Instructor's Manual and PowerLecture.

# 5 TOWARD REVOLUTION, 1763–1775
# Prep Card

## What's Inside

Key topics in this chapter: British Attempts to Maintain Control of the Colonies; Beginnings of American Resistance; Taxation without Representation, 1767–1773; The Shot Heard 'Round the World

## Learning Outcomes

**LO 1** What were Britain's main reasons for attempting to overturn salutary neglect?

**LO 2** Explain how the colonists responded to the new acts, and trace the evolutionary process that brought the colonies closer to true rebellion.

**LO 3** Trace the path to revolution in America from the Townshend Acts of 1767 to the meeting of the First Continental Congress.

**LO 4** Explain how the American Revolution began, and describe the first battles of the conflict.

## Chapter 5 Outline

## eBook Links

 Interactive Chance to Look at Life in America on the Eve of the Revolution
American History Resource Center

 More about the Stamp Act Congress Resolutions
http://odur.let.rug.nl/~usa/D/1751-1775/stampact/sa.htm

 Patrick Henry's Resolutions against the Stamp Act
American History Resource Center

 *Instructions of the Town of Braintree to Their Representative*
American History Resource Center

 Short Film on Benjamin Franklin's Life
http://earlyamerica.com/ben1.htm

 Dickinson's *Letters from a Farmer in Pennsylvania*
http://oll.libertyfund.org/?option=com_staticxt&staticfile=show.php%3Ftitle=690

 Eyewitness Account of Boston Massacre
http://www.law.umkc.edu/faculty/projects/ftrials/bostonmassacre/prestontrialexcerpts.html

 Eyewitness Account of Boston Tea Party
http://www.historyplace.com/unitedstates/revolution/teaparty.htm

 Text of the Coercive Acts
American History Resource Center

 Film on Lexington and Concord
http://earlyamerica.com/shot_heard.htm

## Terms

# Discussion Questions

1. List some of the major actions taken by the English Parliament during the 1760s and early 1770s that angered the colonists, and discuss specifically some of the acts that dealt with what the colonists viewed as unfair taxation.
2. The prerevolutionary period in America was one in which colonial writers "found" their voices. Discuss some of the most significant people and analyze their writings.
3. Discuss the significance to the colonists of the Tea Act and the Coercive Acts. Why did these particular acts seem so galling to the American colonists?

# Group Activity

*Goal*

Understand both sides of the issue on taxes in the American colonies.

*Task*

Locate an article that takes the stance that the British were correct in their treatment of the colonies, and one that defends the colonists' protests and then revolution. Give half the class copies of one article; give the second article to the other group. After one week to read the article and to research anything else they would like to discuss, the two groups will debate the issues.

*Outcomes*

By having to take a stand, students should become more aware that there were actually two equally valid schools of thought on the rights and duties of the colonists.

# Assignments

1. Go online and research political cartoons of the revolutionary period from 1763 to 1776. Create a poster that puts them in chronological and thematic order, thus building a "picture book" version of the political fight that led to the revolution.
2. Find the names of the individuals killed during the Boston Massacre. See if you can find information about their backgrounds. If so, share that information with your class.
3. Create a timeline for the most significant events of the 1760s and 1770s in the American colonies. (Perhaps your instructor will have a blank timeline that you can use.) Share these in class, discussing why you chose the events that you did.

# Beyond the Class

A selection of materials is in the Instructor's Manual and PowerLecture.

## 6 THE REVOLUTION
# Prep Card

**What's Inside** — Key topics in this chapter: From Rebellion to Revolution; The Declaration of Independence; War for Independence; Significance of the War; The War's Impact on the Following: Slavery, Native America, Women, and Religion

## Learning Outcomes

**LO¹** Describe the long-term causes and more immediate events that led the colonists into a true revolution against Britain.

**LO²** Discuss the various phases of the American Revolution, and analyze the circumstances that eventually helped the colonists win a conflict that Britain, by rights, should never have lost.

**LO³** Assess the significance of the American Revolution to the following groups: colonists, slaves, native populations, and women.

## Chapter 6 Outline

## eBook Links

 Lord Dunmore and His Proclamation to End Slavery
http://www.pbs.org/wgbh/aia/part2/2h42.html

 Interactive Module on Choosing Sides during the American Revolution
American History Resource Center

 Thomas Paine's *Common Sense*
http://www.ushistory.org/paine/

 Film about Drafting the Declaration of Independence
http://earlyamerica.com/independence.htm

 The Declaration of Independence
http://www.archives.gov/national-archives-experience/charters/declaration.html

 Film about the Life of George Washington
http://earlyamerica.com/gwlifemovie2.htm

 How the Revolutionaries Paid for the War
http://www.tax.org/Museum/1777-1815.htm

 "Spy" Letter from Howe to Burgoyne
http://www.si.umich.edu/spies/index-gallery.html

 A Continental Soldier's Account of His Experiences, 1780
American History Resource Center

 A Map of America after the Treaty of Paris
http://www.earlyamerica.com/earlyamerica/maps/peace/enlargement.html

 Interactive Module about Building a New Nation through Symbols
American History Resource Center

 A Quaker Attempts to Point Out Inconsistencies between American Freedom and American Slavery
http://www.rootsweb.ancestry.com/~quakers/petition.htm

 Primary Sources on the American Revolution and Religion
http://www.loc.gov/exhibits/religion/rel03.html

 The Virginia Statute of Religious Freedom
American History Resource Center

# Discussion Questions

1. How did the British colonists evolve from good citizens to revolutionaries who could compose and back something as special as the Declaration of Independence?
2. Consider the major battles of the Revolution. Which do you consider the most significant?
3. Describe the significance of the American Revolution to the development of the United States as well as to other countries of the world.

# Group Activity

*Goal*

Understand the divisions in colonial American society during the Revolutionary War.

*Task*

Divide students into groups of five to six. Have them make a list of the different theaters of the Revolutionary War (South, Middle Atlantic, New England, the Atlantic) and identify the different groups of Americans on the side of the Loyalists and the patriots. Based on the diverse alliances, let them discuss the odds of an American victory over Great Britain.

*Outcomes*

Students will understand that the Revolutionary War was not just a war against overwhelming imperial powers, but also amongst neighbors.

# Assignments

1. Search for details about the celebration of July 4 in the following years: 1876 and 1976. Write a brief essay detailing your findings.
2. Make a chart in which you list the strengths and weaknesses of both sides in the American Revolution. Write a paragraph detailing your findings.

# Beyond the Class

A selection of materials is in the Instructor's Manual and PowerLecture.

# 7 CONFEDERATION AND CONSTITUTION, 1783–1789
# Prep Card

## What's Inside

Key topics in this chapter: Early State Constitutions; The Articles of Confederation; Daily Operation of the Confederation; The Constitutional Convention; The Constitution; The Ratification Debate; The Bill of Rights

## Learning Outcomes

**LO¹** Describe the first state constitutions written and adopted after the United States declared its independence.

**LO²** Analyze the federal government as it existed under the Articles of Confederation.

**LO³** Describe the most significant issues that the United States had to deal with under the Articles of Confederation, and explain how the Articles failed to live up to the needs of the new country.

**LO⁴** Explain the need for the Constitutional Convention that met in Philadelphia in 1787, and describe the process of writing the Constitution.

**LO⁵** Describe and explain the major provisions of the Constitution created by the Philadelphia convention, especially concerning the separation of powers and the rights given to individual states.

**LO⁶** Explain the procedure established for ratification of the Constitution, describe the actions of its supporters and its opponents, and explain how and when ratification was eventually achieved.

## eBook Links

 Pennsylvania State Constitution of 1776
http://www.docheritage.state.pa.us/documents/constitution.asp

 The Articles of Confederation
http://avalon.law.yale.edu/18th_century/artconf.asp

 Text of the Northwest Ordinance
http://www.earlyamerica.com/earlyamerica/milestones/ordinance/

 Madison's Original Notes on the Constitutional Convention
http://teachingamericanhistory.org/convention/debates/0630.html

 Text of the U.S. Constitution
American History Resource Center

 The Federalist Papers
http://avalon.law.yale.edu/subject_menus/fed.asp

 Text of the Bill of Rights
http://odur.let.rug.nl/~usa/D/1776-1800/constitution/amends.htm

## Chapter 7 Outline

# Discussion Questions

1. What were the main problems with the Articles of Confederation?
2. Describe the Constitutional Convention that met in Philadelphia in the summer of 1787. What was its purpose? What did it actually accomplish?
3. Describe the process by which the Constitution was created in the summer of 1787, and explain how it became the law of the land.

# Group Activity

*Goal*
Gain a deeper understanding of the men who attended the Constitutional Convention in 1787.

*Task*
Obtain a complete list of the signers of the Constitution. Assign each student one or more people to research. Have students bring their information to class. Each person will tell about his or her signer, answering some specific questions, such as age, background, occupation, and so on. Assign two people who will record the information in a chart for each signer. Discuss the findings, looking for patterns.

*Outcomes*
Students should be able to discuss the characteristics the group had in common.

# Assignments

1. Locate a map of the United States in the 1780s and make a list of the different countries and territories it borders on.
2. Adopting the persona of a South Carolina slave, write a three-paragraph editorial on the U.S. Constitution and its compromises on slavery. Do you recommend ratification, or do you oppose it?
3. Analyze the Bill of Rights. Write a paragraph in which you assess how well you think your rights are protected under these amendments. If you were to compile a Bill of Rights for today, what would you include that isn't there? Would you leave out anything that is there?

# Beyond the Class

A selection of materials is in the Instructor's Manual and PowerLecture.

# 8

## SECURING THE NEW NATION, 1789–1800

# Prep Card

**What's Inside**

Key topics in this chapter: Creating a New Government: Many "Firsts"; Political Divisions Arise; The Rise of Two-Party Politics; Adams's Presidency: Dealing with Dissent; The Bloodless "Revolution of 1800"

## Learning Outcomes

LO ¹ Describe the creation of the federal government under the new Constitution.

LO ² Describe how disagreements over how the United States should be governed led to political divisions, and discuss some of the individuals who took strong stands on each side.

LO ³ Outline the country's development of a two-party political system.

LO ⁴ Discuss the issues of John Adams's presidency, and explain how he and the country dealt with them.

LO ⁵ Explain the convoluted political process that made Thomas Jefferson president in 1800, including the constitutional change designed to mend the problem.

## Chapter 8 Outline

## eBook Links

 The Naturalization Act of 1790
http://memory.loc.gov/cgi-bin/ampage?collId=llsl&fileName=001/llsl001.db&recNum=226

 A Virtual Tour of the Activities of the First Federal Congress
http://www.gwu.edu/~ffcp/exhibit/p1/

 Washington's First Inaugural Address
http://www.archives.gov/legislative/features/gw-inauguration/

 Interactive Modules on Washington's Life
American History Resource Center

 Documents Related to Gabriel's Conspiracy
http://www.pbs.org/wgbh/aia/part3/3p1576.html

 Washington's Farewell Address of 1796
American History Resource Center

## Discussion Questions

1. Discuss the creation of the new government under the Constitution of 1789. What challenges did the first constitutional government face?
2. Describe the formation of America's first two political parties, the Democratic-Republicans and the Federalists. What were their major differences, and who were the best-known members of each party?
3. What situations caused the most problems for President John Adams? Discuss matters both domestic and foreign.

## Group Activity

*Goal*
Gain a deeper understanding of the Bill of Rights.

*Task*
Divide the class into groups of from three to five students. Have each group discuss the ten amendments that make up the Bill of Rights, and then rank them from 1 to 10, according to which ones the group feels are most significant, important, threatened, needless, and so on, in today's world. Have a spokesperson for each group present its decision at the end of class, leaving enough time for discussion and/or disagreements.

*Outcomes*

The aim is to make students more aware of the significance of the Bill of Rights and to help them appreciate the work of America's first Congress in writing them and working for their ratification.

# Assignments

1. Research the Judiciary Act of 1790 and determine the location of the first courts established: the three circuit courts and the thirteen district courts. Plot their locations on a blank map. (Student Goal: To realize how compact the United States was when it first became a country.)
2. Study Alexander Hamilton's financial plan for the country. Write a one-page essay in which you either support or argue against his plan.
3. At the end of this chapter, three events are listed under the "What else was happening . . ." heading. Research those three events and locate an online source for each that provides you with more information. Answer questions on each in "newspaper style"—in other words: Who? What? When? Where? Why?

# Beyond the Class

A selection of materials is in the Instructor's Manual and PowerLecture.

**What's Inside**

Key topics in this chapter: Jefferson's Presidency and Jeffersonian Democracy; James Madison and the Election of 1808; Madison and the War of 1812; The Significance of the War of 1812

## Learning Outcomes

LO¹ Define Jeffersonian Democracy, and explain how Jefferson's presidency both defined and contradicted that political philosophy.

LO² Discuss the reasons for and the results of the War of 1812.

## Chapter 9 Outline

## eBook Links

 Interactive Journey with the Corps of Discovery
http://www.pbs.org/lewisandclark/into/index.html

 Lewis and Clark's journal
http://www.pbs.org/lewisandclark/into/index.html

 An Online Course on the Battle of Horseshoe Bend
http://www.cr.nps.gov/nr/twhp/wwwlps/lessons/54horseshoe/54horseshoe.htm

 Lyrics to "The Star-Spangled Banner"
American History Resource Center

 Satirical Cartoon about the Hartford Convention
http://loc.harpweek.com/LCPoliticalCartoons/DisplayCartoonMedium.asp?MaxID=16&UniqueID=12&Year=1814&YearMark=181

 Pictures of the Classical Revival Style in America
http://www.bc.edu/bc_org/avp/cas/fnart/fa267/neoclassic.html

## Discussion Questions

1. Discuss the various aspects of Jeffersonian Democracy. Why do you think this political tradition was named after the third president of the United States? How well do you think Jefferson practiced this tradition personally?
2. Explain how the Louisiana Purchase came about, and describe Jefferson's efforts to explore the region.
3. Give reasons why the United States went to war with Britain in 1812, and explain the real significance of the war to Americans.

## Group Activity

*Goal*
Understand the historical roots of national rituals like the singing of the anthem.

*Task*
Visit http://www.star-spangled-banner.info/, download the text and a variety of versions of the national anthem, and play them to students. Have students divide in groups of five to six and identify the historical references in the lyrics to the battle in Baltimore harbor. Also have students discuss the tune itself and how it may support the message of the song and serve the purpose of an anthem.

## Terms

*Outcomes*
Students will begin to think about national rituals in historical terms and think about the differences between history and myth.

# Assignments

1. Wikipedia is generally not considered a reliable source for college research, but this case is an exception. Check the site's entry for "Jeffersonian Democracy," where the concept is broken down into its major points. Print the page and write an informal one-paragraph essay in which you bring out what you see as the main elements of "Jeffersonian Democracy."
2. How do you feel about *judicial review,* the concept that the Supreme Court has the power to rule congressional changes to the Constitution unconstitutional? Be ready to argue your position in class.

# Beyond the Class

A selection of materials is in the Instructor's Manual and PowerLecture.

### What's Inside

Key topics in this chapter: Economic Nationalism; The Market Revolution; Social Changes during the Industrial Period; Reformers; The Creation of the Middle Class

## Learning Outcomes

**LO¹** Describe the economic system known as the American System.

**LO²** List the three specific parts of the Market Revolution in early-nineteenth-century America, and evaluate how America developed during this era.

**LO³** Describe the growth of America's middle class during the first half of the 1800s, and discuss some of the stronger movements toward reform during the era.

## Chapter 10 Outline

## eBook Links

 "On the Move": Roads, Canals, Steamboats, and Railroads
http://americanhistory.si.edu/onthemove/exhibition/exhibition_1_2.html

 Readings on Cotton Production in the South
http://eh.net/encyclopedia/article/phillips.cottongin

 A Firsthand Description of a Lowell Mill Job
http://www.fordham.edu/halsall/mod/robinson-lowell.html

 New York's Burned-Over District
http://history.sandiego.edu/gen/civilwar/01/burned.html

 Excerpts from Henry David Thoreau's *Walden*
http://thoreau.eserver.org/walden00.html

 A Narrated Slide Show about the Oneida Community
http://www.nytimes.com/slideshow/2007/08/03/travel/20070803

 Readings on Mormonism
http://www.nhc.rtp.nc.us/tserve/nineteen/nkeyinfo/nmormon.htm

 An Online Exhibition of the American Temperance Society
http://www.librarycompany.org/ArdentSpirits/

 Information on Horace Mann, Public School Educator
http://www.pbs.org/kcet/publicschool/innovators/mann.html

 A Selection from David Walker's *Appeal to the Coloured Citizens of the World*
http://www.duboislc.org/html/DavidWalkerAppeal.html

 Library of Congress Exhibit about the American Colonization Society
http://www.loc.gov/exhibits/african/afam002.html

 William Lloyd Garrison Speech and Biographical Information
http://www.spartacus.schoolnet.co.uk/USASgarrison.htm

 The 1848 Women's Rights Convention at Seneca Falls, New York
http://www.npg.si.edu/col/seneca/senfalls1.htm

## Terms

## Discussion Questions

1. Discuss America's transportation revolution in the first half of the 1800s. What role did government play in the development of roads, canals, railroads, and steamboats?
2. How did industrialization change America's urban areas during the early 1800s?
3. What various groups advocated what kind of reforms during the first half of the 1800s?

## Group Activity

*Goal*
Gain a deeper (or first-hand) understanding of social activism.

*Task*
Divide students into groups of five to six. Have them make a list of the social movements in the early nineteenth century and identify modern parallels to those movements. For a more ambitious class project, have students make posters and signs and operate a stand on campus to campaign for their different issues. Next, have students discuss their experience as social activists with political power, public debate, and the public sphere. Finally, return students to a discussion of social activists—especially women—in the early nineteenth century.

*Outcomes*
Students will form an understanding of the work of social activists and develop a respect for the long-standing tradition of reform movements in the United States.

## Assignments

1. Research the Oneida community, and write a brief paragraph describing how Oneida evolved over time.
2. Draw a map of the Erie Canal, identify at least three cities along its path, and research their origins online.
3. Research online the early designs for steamboats and explain their basic technology in a poster.

## Beyond the Class

A selection of materials is in the Instructor's Manual and PowerLecture.

# 11 POLITICS OF THE MARKET REVOLUTION
# Prep Card

## What's Inside

Key topics in this chapter: Politics in the Age of Jackson; Jackson's Presidency and the Development of Jacksonian Democracy; Jackson's Issues: National Bank, Panic of 1837, Indian Removal and Nullification; Democrats and Whigs

## Learning Outcomes

**LO¹** Describe the changes that took place in American politics during the first decades of the 1800s, and explain reasons for these changes.

**LO²** Explain how Jackson's approach to the "spoils system," the nullification process, the National Bank, Indian removal, and the Panic of 1837 reflect his vision of federal power.

**LO³** Explain the development of America's second two-party political system, the parties being the Democrats and the Whigs.

## Chapter 11 Outline

## eBook Links

 Historical Evidence on the "Corrupt Bargain" of 1824
http://edsitement.neh.gov/view_lesson_plan.asp?id=552

 An Andrew Jackson Campaign Song
http://www.contemplator.com/america/hunter.html

 Andrew Jackson's First Annual Message
American History Resource Center

 South Carolina's Ordinance of Nullification
http://avalon.law.yale.edu/19th_century/ordnull.asp

 Jackson's Proclamation Regarding Nullification
http://avalon.law.yale.edu/19th_century/jack01.asp

 An Interactive Account of Indian Removal
http://www.digitalhistory.uh.edu/learning_history/indian_removal/removal_policy.cfm

 The Seminole Revolt
http://www.johnhorse.com/

## Discussion Questions

1. Compare and contrast Andrew Jackson's campaign promises and his actions in the revocation of the national bank charter, the nullification crisis, and Indian removal. Did Jackson deliver as promised?
2. Describe the experiences of the Native American tribes involved in the Indian removal movement of the 1830s.
3. Compare and contrast the political style of John Quincy Adams with that of Andrew Jackson.

## Group Activity

*Goal*
Understand the debate over the monetary policy of the Market Revolution.

*Task*
Divide students into two sides—one opposed to, and one in favor of, the renewal of the charter of the second Bank of the United States. (You may want to assign a notetaker and a "chair" in each group.) Drawing on the reading of this and the previous chapter, have students gather as many possible different reasons for support of the

## Terms

national bank or opposition to it. In the next step, have students mix with the opposite group in one-on-one debates, and make this the basis of a larger group discussion over monetary policy in the Jacksonian era.

*Outcomes*
Instead of simply rejecting the bank opposition as "old-fashioned," students will get to appreciate monetary policy as a legitimate sphere of politics and public debate.

# Assignments

1. Compose a "Press Release" that might have been issued by Andrew Jackson's supporters during the presidential election of 1828. Compose another "Press Release" that might have been issued by the staff of John Quincy Adams.
2. Create a collage of drawings, poems, and other media that illustrates the experience of Native Americans who made the journey known as the Trail of Tears.
3. Write a two-paragraph essay on the reasons that South Carolinians opposed an increase in tariffs.

# Beyond the Class

A selection of materials is in the Instructor's Manual and PowerLecture.

# 12 A REGIONALIZED AMERICA, 1830–1860
# Prep Card

## What's Inside

Key topics in this chapter: Social Life in the Commercial North; Free Blacks in the North; Tenement Living; Social Life in the Cotton South; The White Defense of Slavery; Slave Society

## Learning Outcomes

**LO¹** Describe social life in the commercial North as it developed between 1830 and 1860.

**LO²** Describe social life as it developed in the South between 1830 and 1860 as a result of dependence on cotton.

## Chapter 12 Outline

## eBook Links

 Text of Song by a Recent Irish Immigrant Lamenting His Struggle to Find Work

http://tigger.uic.edu/~rjensen/song.htm

 Newspaper Account of an Anti-Catholic Riot in Philadelphia

http://www.yale.edu/glc/archive/953.htm

 Virtual Tour of a New York Tenement

http://www.tenement.org/Virtual_Tour/vt_hallruin.html

 Beechwood Mansion and the Astor Family

http://www.astorsbeechwood.com/history.shtml

 Reviews of *Uncle Tom's Cabin*

http://www.iath.virginia.edu/utc/sitemap.html

 Chapter 1 of *Uncle Tom's Cabin*

http://www.online-literature.com/stowe/uncletom/1/

 About *The Confessions of Nat Turner*

http://www.pbs.org/wgbh/aia/part3/3h500.html

 Harriet Ann Jacobs's Account of Life in the South after Nat Turner's Rebellion

http://www.pbs.org/wgbh/aia/part3/3h1519.html

 A Study of Slave Religion

http://www.gwu.edu/~folklife/bighouse/panel22.html

 Further Research in Slave Religion

http://www.nhc.rtp.nc.us/tserve/nineteen/nkeyinfo/aareligion.htm

 Excerpt from *Narrative of the Life of Frederick Douglass*
American History Resource Center

 American Slave Narratives: An Online Anthology

http://xroads.virginia.edu/%7EHYPER/wpa/wpahome.html

 An Interactive Journey on the Underground Railroad

http://www.nationalgeographic.com/railroad/index.html

## Terms

# Discussion Questions

1. Compare and contrast urban and rural life in the North during the mid-1800s.
2. Was *Gone with the Wind* an accurate portrayal of life in the South prior to the Civil War? Give examples to support your answer.
3. Describe the life of a typical slave in the plantation South.

# Group Activity

*Goal*

Understand the divisions slavery produced in the South.

*Task*

Divide students into two groups, and assign a notetaker and a chair to each group. Then, have one group think of all the ways in which one could aid fugitives as part of the Underground Railroad in the 1840s. Meanwhile, have the other group put itself in the position of white planters and slave catchers and think of all the clues a slave fugitive might provide and where the slave catchers would search. Then, have students share their collected escape and capture strategies in one-on-one encounters and see whether they can agree on who would have claimed victory in the contest.

*Outcomes*

Students will learn about slavery as a daily struggle deeply separating white and black southerners.

# Assignments

1. Research Ellis Island. Compile a list of the number of immigrants who entered the United States in each decade of the 1800s up to 1860.
2. Research slave marriages, and write a one-page paper in which you report your findings.
3. Find examples of Amish or Pennsylvania Dutch architecture and household furnishings. Place them in a folder, and include a caption describing specific elements in the illustration that represent that particular style.

# Beyond the Class

A selection of materials is in the Instructor's Manual and PowerLecture.

# 13 THE CONTINUED MOVE WEST
# Prep Card

**What's Inside**

Key topics in this chapter: Western Conquest and Development, 1820–1844; The Expansionist Spirit Rebounds; Manifest Destiny and American Dominance of the West; The Mexican War

## Learning Outcomes

**LO 1**  Describe the conquest and development of the West between 1820 and 1850 by white Americans.

**LO 2**  Explain how the expansionist spirit in the West led to political conflict at home as well as conflict with Mexico, even as it gave the United States its modern boundaries.

## Chapter 13 Outline

## eBook Links

 The Battle of the Alamo
http://www.thealamo.org/battle.html

 Letter from a Gold Miner in Placerville, California
http://memory.loc.gov/cgi-bin/query/r?ammem/calbk:@field(DOCID+@lit(calbk155div2)):

 A Map of the California Gold Country
http://malakoff.com/goldcountry/campmap.htm

 Text of the Fort Laramie Treaty
http://www.pbs.org/weta/thewest/resources/archives/four/ftlaram.htm

 Famous Mountain Men
http://xroads.virginia.edu/~hyper/HNS/Mtmen/home.html

 Antislavery Letter by a Member of the Liberty Party

 All about Texas Statehood
http://www.tsl.state.tx.us/treasures/earlystate/

 John L. O'Sullivan's "Annexation" Essay
American History Resource Center

 President Polk's "Message on War with Mexico"
American History Resource Center

 Whig Senator Thomas Corwin's Speech Opposing the Mexican War
American History Resource Center

 Democratic Senator Donald S. Dickinson's Speech Justifying the U.S. Acquisition of Territory
American History Resource Center

 The Mexican War
http://www.dmwv.org/mexwar/mexwar1.htm

## Terms

# Discussion Questions

1. How and when did Texas gain its independence, and how and when did it enter the Union?
2. How did President Polk go about ending the disagreement with the British over the Oregon Territory?
3. Why did the Mexican War of 1846 take place? Was the war necessary? Was it a good thing? Why or why not?

# Group Activity

*Goal*
Gain a deeper understanding of the pioneer world of the gold rush seekers.

*Task*
Have students split into groups of five to six and declare themselves "miners' camps." Have students try to organize the camps with the typical personas in the "diggings." Then, have students in each group write fictional letters home to their family and report on their lives in California. In the final step, bring the groups back together to discuss the difference between their fictional gold rush camp and their imagined life at home.

*Outcomes*
Student will appreciate the cultural tensions and diversities of the early American West.

# Assignments

1. Research the term "manifest destiny" in American political speeches and pick at least three examples to bring to class. Be ready to explain what caught your attention and interest.

# Beyond the Class

A selection of materials is in the Instructor's Manual and PowerLecture.

# 14 THE IMPENDING CRISIS
# Prep Card

**What's Inside**

Key topics in this chapter: Arguments over Slavery in the New Territories; The Compromise of 1850; The Kansas-Nebraska Act and New Political Parties; The Nation Catapults toward War; The 1860 Election, Secession, and Civil War

## Learning Outcomes

**LO 1** Describe the arguments that took place over whether slavery should be allowed to expand into the new territories, and explain how the Compromise of 1850 was supposed to settle the issue.

**LO 2** Explain how the Kansas-Nebraska Act affected the territories of Kansas and Nebraska, and describe the events that made "Bleeding Kansas" an accurate description for the region.

**LO 3** Discuss the events that propelled the United States into a civil war in 1861.

**LO 4** Explain why and how the southern states seceded from the Union, discuss President Lincoln's reaction, and describe the earliest physical conflict between the two sides.

## Chapter 14 Outline

## eBook Links

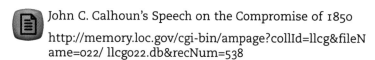 John C. Calhoun's Speech on the Compromise of 1850
http://memory.loc.gov/cgi-bin/ampage?collId=llcg&fileName=022/ llcg022.db&recNum=538

 Text of the Kansas-Nebraska Act
http://avalon.law.yale.edu/19th_century/kanneb.asp

 Contemporary Account: The "Sacking of Lawrence"
http://www.kancoll.org/books/gihon/g_chap13.htm

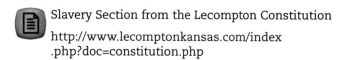 Slavery Section from the Lecompton Constitution
http://www.lecomptonkansas.com/index.php?doc=constitution.php

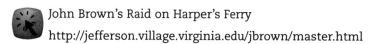 John Brown's Raid on Harper's Ferry
http://jefferson.village.virginia.edu/jbrown/master.html

 The First Lincoln-Douglas Debate on the Spread of Slavery
American History Resource Center

 Lincoln's "House Divided" Speech, 1858
http://www.historyplace.com/lincoln/divided.htm

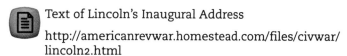 Text of Lincoln's Inaugural Address
http://americanrevwar.homestead.com/files/civwar/lincoln2.html

 "Declaration of the Immediate Causes Which Induce and Justify the Secession of South Carolina from the Federal Union," 1860
American History Resource Center

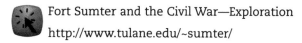 The Crittenden Compromise
http://avalon.law.yale.edu/19th_century/critten.asp

Fort Sumter and the Civil War—Exploration
http://www.tulane.edu/~sumter/

## Terms

# Discussion Questions

1. What was John C. Calhoun's reasoning in asserting the right of nullification for South Carolina and other states?
2. What were the major points of the Compromise of 1850?
3. What made Kansas so important that it became the first battleground of the Civil War—six years before Lincoln's election?

# Group Activity

*Goal*
Gain a deeper understanding of the actions of John Brown.

*Task*
Divide students into groups of five to six. Let half of the group argue that John Brown was a national hero fighting slavery, with the other side taking the position that John Brown was in fact a terrorist. After about fifteen minutes, see where students stand on the question and which position they found most convincing.

*Outcomes*
Students will get to think about political violence in one of the nation's most important inner conflicts.

# Assignments

1. Write a one-page editorial on the Dred Scott decision as either a Wisconsin or a Mississippi newspaper editor.
2. Locate lyrics to popular campaign songs for the elections of 1840 to 1860. Write a one-page paper describing what seems most unusual to you about the lyrics.
3. Write a first-person account of what you witnessed in the Senate during the Brooks-Sumner affair. Assume one of the following personae: (a) a senator from Pennsylvania; (b) a senator from Mississippi; (c) a female guest in the upstairs viewing gallery.

# Beyond the Class

A selection of materials is in the Instructor's Manual and PowerLecture.

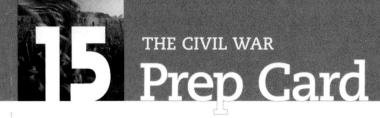

# 15 THE CIVIL WAR
# Prep Card

**What's Inside** Key topics in this chapter: Northern Advantages vs. Southern Advantages; The Fallacy of an "Easy War"; The Major Theaters of War; Full Mobilization and the Making of a Modern State; Growing Dissent; The Tide Turns; End of the War

## Learning Outcomes

**LO 1** Describe the areas of strength and advantage for each side at the beginning of the Civil War.

**LO 2** Explain why both sides in the Civil War believed the war would be brief, and describe the early conflicts that made that outcome unlikely.

**LO 3** Explain how preparing for and prosecuting the Civil War contributed to the transformation of the United States into a fully modern state.

**LO 4** Describe the actions of those who opposed the war in the North and of those who opposed the war in the South.

**LO 5** Discuss the events that occurred in 1863 and 1864 that demonstrated Lincoln's strong will and his eventual determination that the end of the war should bring a definite end to slavery.

**LO 6** Describe and discuss the events that finally led to the utter defeat of the South and the end of the war.

**LO 7** Assess the significance of the Civil War for the nation.

## eBook Links

 Results of the U.S. Census of 1860
http://www.civil-war.net/pages/1860_census.html

 A Southern Author's Justification for Southern Independence
American History Resource Center

 Battle of Manassas
http://www.nps.gov/mana/

 Stonewall Jackson's Official Report on the Battle of Manassas
http://www.civil-war.net/searchofficialrecords.asp?search
officialrecords=Jackson%201st%20Bull%20Run]

 Life in the Armies of the Civil War
http://www.civilwarhome.com/camplife.htm

 Lincoln's Proclamation Suspending *Habeas Corpus*
http://teachingamericanhistory.org/library/index
.asp?document=425

 Virtual Tour of the Draft Riots
http://www.vny.cuny.edu/draftriots/Intro/draft_riot_intro_set
.html

 Mary Boykin Chesnut's Wartime Diary from the Southern Home Front
American History Resource Center

 The Second Confiscation Act
http://www.history.umd.edu/Freedmen/conact2.htm

 A Study of the Emancipation Proclamation
http://memory.loc.gov/ammem/alhtml/almintr.html

## Chapter 15 Outline

Text of the Emancipation Proclamation

American History Resource Center

 Report from Congressional Committee Investigating the Fort Pillow Massacre

http://www.assumption.edu/users/mcclymer/His130/P-H/Pillow/default.html

 Text of Lincoln's Gettysburg Address

American History Resource Center

 General Carl Schurz's Impressions of the Gettysburg Battlefield after the Battle

http://query.nytimes.com/gst/abstract.html?res=9400E3DB123FE233A25757C0A9629C946496D6CF

 Lincoln's Second Inaugural Address

http://showcase.netins.net/web/creative/lincoln/speeches/inaug2.htm

## Discussion Questions

1. In the beginning, each side in the Civil War believed the war would be brief and that their side would win. What advantages did each side hold that made them feel this way?
2. How did Lincoln view the issue of slavery when the war began? How did this view begin to change as the war progressed?
3. Describe the two major battles of 1863 that did the most to demoralize the South.

## Assignments

1. Prepare a chart in which you list the major advantages for each side in the Civil War at the beginning of the war. Don't rely on your text only, but also do further research at reputable online sites.
2. Compile statistics on the losses in the Civil War. You will need casualty figures from the First Battle of Manassas, Shiloh, Antietam, Gettysburg, Spotsylvania, and the Wilderness Campaign. In addition, you should gather figures for each side for the entire war. Analyze your figures in two to three sentences.

## Beyond the Class

A selection of materials is in the Instructor's Manual and PowerLecture.

**What's Inside**

Key topics in this chapter: The Civil War Changes America; Hope and Reality for the Freed Slaves; Presidential vs. Congressional Reconstruction; Black Codes and the South during Reconstruction; Compromise of 1877 Ends Reconstruction

## Learning Outcomes

**LO¹** Describe the changed world of ex-slaves after the Civil War.

**LO²** Outline the different phases of Reconstruction, beginning with Lincoln's plan and moving through presidential Reconstruction to Radical Reconstruction.

**LO³** Explain how Reconstruction evolved at the individual states' level.

**LO⁴** Evaluate and understand the relative success of Reconstruction.

## Chapter 16 Outline

## eBook Links

Congressional Act Establishing the Freedmen's Bureau
http://www.sewanee.edu/faculty/Willis/Civil_War/documents/Freedmen'sBureau.html

Lincoln's Proclamation Vetoing the Wade-Davis Bill
http://odur.let.rug.nl/~usa/P/al16/writings/wdveto.htm

Library of Congress Picture Gallery of Lincoln's Assassination
http://memory.loc.gov/ammem/alhtml/alrgall.html

Andrew Johnson's Proclamation of Amnesty and Pardon
http://www.academicamerican.com/recongildedage/documents/AJohnsonProclamation.htm

Mississippi Legislature's Black Codes
http://chnm.gmu.edu/courses/122/recon/code.html

*Harper's Weekly* Editorial on Civil Rights Bill
http://www.impeach-andrewjohnson.com/05AJFirstVetoes/iiia-10.htm

Fourteenth Amendment to the U.S. Constitution
http://www.law.cornell.edu/constitution/constitution.amendmentxiv.html

Text of Military Reconstruction Act
http://itw.sewanee.edu/reconstruction/html/docs/recons_act_67.htm

Text of Second Reconstruction Act
http://www.historycentral.com/documents/secondreconstruction.html

Andrew Johnson Impeachment Trial
http://www.law.umkc.edu/faculty/projects/ftrials/impeach/impeachmt.htm

Fifteenth Amendment to the U.S. Constitution
http://memory.loc.gov/cgi-bin/ampage?collId=llsl&fileName=015/llsl015.db&recNum=379

Photo of Reconstruction Era South Carolina Legislature
http://www.loc.gov/exhibits/odyssey/archive/05/051100r.jpg

## Terms

 *Harper's Weekly* Cartoon on the Civil Rights Act of 1875

http://www.harpweek.com/09Cartoon/BrowseByDateCartoon .asp?Month=February&Date=27

 *Harper's Weekly* Cartoon on the Panic of 1873

http://www.harpweek.com/09Cartoon/BrowseByDateCartoon .asp?Month=October&Date=11

 Official Report on Success of the Mississippi Plan of 1875

http://itw.sewanee.edu/reconstruction/html/docs/mississippi_plan.htm

## Discussion Questions

1. Lincoln had one plan for bringing the rebel states back into the Union; Andrew Johnson another; and the Radical Republican Congress a third. Discuss the aims of each president, and explain why and in what ways Congress took control of Reconstruction.
2. Describe and discuss the major aims of the Freedmen's Bureau, and evaluate the degree of success its proponents achieved.
3. Some historians have described Reconstruction as a "splendid failure." Explain why they used this terminology, including examples of both successes and failures.

## Group Activity

*Goal*
Understand the successes and failures of Reconstruction.

*Task*
Separate the class into three groups and have a roundtable discussion of the Reconstruction years. Have one group argue for the good that came out of Reconstruction. Have a second group give reasons why Reconstruction was a failure. The third group should listen to the two sides debate the issue and select the group they believe presented the most persuasive arguments. Each student should then take 10 to 15 minutes to write an extemporaneous paper listing the major unresolved issues of Reconstruction.

*Outcomes*
Students should develop an awareness of why some programs fail or succeed.

## Assignments

1. Using the newspaper collections of your library, research the history of the reparations movement from the first calls for "40 acres and a mule" to the present, and write a 750-word editorial on the merit of reparations for slavery to African Americans.
2. Using a blank map (enlarged if necessary) and three different colors of ink, label each state that had slavery before the Civil War; the number of blacks in the state in 1890; and the number of whites in the state. You can find census figures for 1890 here: http://www2.census.gov/prod2/decennial/ documents/1890a_v1-01.pdf. From the General Tables in the Table of Contents, click on "Sex, General Nativity and Color" and go to Table 13, p. 400.
3. Choose a state that had slavery before the Civil War. Research the presidential elections of 1868, 1872, 1876, and 1880 in the state, and list the polling numbers for Democrats and Republicans in each of these elections. Write a paragraph in which you describe whether, and to what degree, the presidential voting patterns changed in your state during this period.

## Beyond the Class

A selection of materials is in the Instructor's Manual and PowerLecture.

# 17 THE INDUSTRIAL AGE
# Prep Card

## What's Inside

Key topics in this chapter: The Industrial Revolution; The Basic Industries; Harmful Business Practices; The Age of Innovation; The National Market: Creating Consumer Demand

## Learning Outcomes

**LO¹** Describe and discuss the development of the Industrial Revolution in America after the Civil War, concentrating on the major industries and their leaders.

**LO²** Explain why the late 1800s in America have sometimes been called the "Age of Innovation."

**LO³** Describe how America's regional and local markets merged into one truly national market, and how this influenced the consumer demand for products and services.

## Chapter 17 Outline

## eBook Links

 Andrew Carnegie and the Steel Industry
http://www.pbs.org/wgbh/amex/carnegie/sfeature/mf_flames .html

 Henry Demarest Lloyd's "The Lords of Industry"
http://www.fordham.edu/halsall/mod/1884hdlloyd.html

 An Overview of Rockefeller's Business Practices
American History Resource Center

## Discussion Questions

1. What were the basic industries of America's Industrial Revolution? What made the men who controlled them so successful?
2. Were the men who dominated business during these years "robber barons," as some suggested, or simply good businessmen? Explain your answer.
3. Explain how advertising and sales practices fed consumer demand during the late 1800s. What were the specific tactics used?

## Group Activity

*Goal*
Gain a deeper understanding of the long-term impact of the Industrial Revolution.

*Task*
Hand out slips of paper with the following question: "If we who are living in the twenty-first century could travel back in time to the late 1800s with our current knowledge and give advice to those who were making such significant industrial and business changes in America, what should we tell them?" Discuss the issue in class. If students don't get to these topics on their own, steer them toward discussing the environment, big business, labor needs, investing, new technology, and any other topics in which you are especially interested.

*Outcomes*
Students should learn to appreciate how those who are making changes sometimes do not grasp their long-term consequences.

## Assignments

1. Using the resources available at the website HistoryMatters (http://history matters.gmu.edu/mse/ads/online.html), search for examples from early mail order catalogs and compare them to today's catalogs. What has changed? What has stayed the same?
2. Research the life of Andrew Carnegie and write a 1- to 2-page paper in which you describe his very early life, his success in business, and his attitude toward the less fortunate at the end of his life.
3. Locate information on a railroad line that runs through the area where you live. Try to discover how significant the railroads were to the development of area cities, especially your hometown. Local historical societies will usually be very helpful with student projects.

## Beyond the Class

A selection of materials is in the Instructor's Manual and PowerLecture.

# 18
## CREATING AN INDUSTRIAL SOCIETY IN THE NORTH
# Prep Card

**What's Inside**
Key topics in this chapter: Urbanization; Immigration; Economic Disparity; The Politics of the Industrial Age; The Rise of Labor; Major Union Organizations; Strikes Spell Trouble for the Unions

## Learning Outcomes

**LO¹** Describe the evolution of urbanization in the United States in the last decades of the nineteenth century, and the disparities of wealth that emerged within those cities.

**LO²** Discuss immigration to the United States that took place in the last decades of the 1800s, including where most immigrants came from, why they came, and what their experiences were after they arrived.

**LO³** Discuss the ways in which politics in American cities functioned during the late 1800s.

**LO⁴** Describe early labor unions that were formed in the United States, including their goals, their activities, and their situations at the end of the nineteenth century.

## Chapter 18 Outline

## eBook Links

 Exhibit: Triangle Shirtwaist Company Fire
http://www.ilr.cornell.edu/trianglefire/

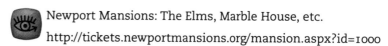 Newport Mansions: The Elms, Marble House, etc.
http://tickets.newportmansions.org/mansion.aspx?id=1000

 Andrew Carnegie's Essay "Wealth"
American History Resource Center

 Explore the Past of Ellis Island
http://www.historychannel.com/ellisisland/index2.html

 Virtual Tour of a Lower East Side Tenement
http://www.tenement.org/Virtual_Tour/index_virtual.html

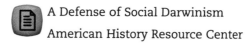 A Defense of Social Darwinism
American History Resource Center

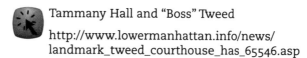 Tammany Hall and "Boss" Tweed
http://www.lowermanhattan.info/news/
landmark_tweed_courthouse_has_65546.asp

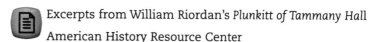 Excerpts from William Riordan's *Plunkitt of Tammany Hall*
American History Resource Center

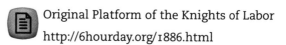 Original Platform of the Knights of Labor
http://6hourday.org/1886.html

 Terence Powderly's *Thirty Years of Labor*
American History Resource Center

 Excerpt from Andrew Carnegie's Autobiography
American History Resource Center

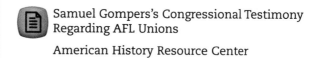 Samuel Gompers's Congressional Testimony Regarding AFL Unions
American History Resource Center

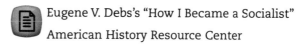 Eugene V. Debs's "How I Became a Socialist"
American History Resource Center

# Discussion Questions

1. What historical developments drove urbanization of the United States during the last decades of the 1800s, and what challenges and opportunities did this generate?
2. How did immigration affect America toward the end of the nineteenth and beginning of the twentieth centuries, especially in the cities, and how would you describe the typical immigrant experience?
3. How did city politics function in the late 1800s?
4. Explain the origins and growth of early unions in America. In which ways did they change the country?

# Group Activity

*Goal*

Gain a deeper appreciation for the diversity of Americans.

*Task*

Have each student find out as much as possible about where their ancestors originated. They should bring to class a list of every country mentioned by family members. As each student reads his or her list, write the country on the board, keeping a tally of how many times each country is mentioned.

Should they not gather much information, encourage students to research further on their own time. Should there not be much diversity, have students come up with plausible explanations for that as well. Be aware of the particular teaching moments that might occur when the difference between Euro-American ancestries and African American family trees emerges in your class.

*Outcomes*

By visually viewing just how diverse the background of one class is, students should gain a broader understanding of the true ethnic diversity that has made America what it is.

# Assignments

1. Choose a European country and research immigration from that country to America in the late 1800s. Things to look for: number of immigrants; reasons for coming; main places settled.
2. Check out unions in your local area and see how many you can list. Your local library, historical society, or Chamber of Commerce may be able to help you. Then look at the names of these unions and see whether you can determine what historical tradition in the labor movement (craft, industrial, socialist) they reflect.
3. Research the early rules of baseball at the time of the National League in 1876, then compare them to your research on the early rules of college football. Why do you think baseball had such broad working-class appeal, and why did colleges promote football instead?

# Beyond the Class

A selection of materials is in the Instructor's Manual and PowerLecture.

# 19 THE NEW SOUTH AND THE INDUSTRIALIZING WEST
# Prep Card

## What's Inside

Key topics in this chapter: The "New" South; Southern Society and Culture; The Industrializing West; The Populists; Problems of the Farmers

## Learning Outcomes

**LO¹** Evaluate the accuracy of the term *New South* in describing the post–Civil War South, and discuss ways in which the term was and was not appropriate.

**LO²** Describe the development of the American West that took place during the last half of the nineteenth century, addressing both the role that industrialization played and the final defeat of the native tribes on the plains.

**LO³** Discuss the problems that confronted America's farmers during the late 1800s, and describe how their attempts to solve those problems led to the formation of a new political party.

## Chapter 19 Outline

## eBook Links

Henry Grady's "New South" Speech
American History Resource Center

*Plessy v. Ferguson* Decision
American History Resource Center

Booker T. Washington's "Atlanta Exposition Address"
American History Resource Center

W. E. B. Du Bois's Thoughts on Booker T. Washington
American History Resource Center

Niagara Movement Statement of Principles
American History Resource Center

Sand Creek Massacre Editorials and Testimony
http://www.pbs.org/weta/thewest/resources/archives/four/sandcrk.htm

Chief Joseph's Retreat
American History Resource Center

The Dawes Act
American History Resource Center

The Populists' 1892 Election Platform
American History Resource Center

*The Wizard of Oz: A Populist Parable?*
American History Resource Center

## Discussion Questions

1. The post–Civil War South has been called the "New South." In what ways was this title appropriate? In what ways was it inappropriate? Just how "new" was the New South?
2. Describe the settlement of the American West after the Civil War. How important were railroads, mining, farming, and ranching in this process?
3. What major problems faced America's farmers during the latter decades of the nineteenth century, and what were some of the ways in which they tried to get help in solving those problems?

# Group Activity

*Goal*

Understand the approaches of Booker T. Washington and W. E. B. Du Bois on civil rights and black empowerment.

*Task*

Divide the class into two groups. Have one group read the Niagara Movement's statement of principles, the other Washington's Atlanta exposition address. Have the two groups oppose each other in the classroom as in a debate club. Each group should choose at least five speakers to convey their main arguments for their particular strategy on civil rights and black empowerment, as well as the main points critiquing the other group's position. Dissolve the groups and discuss the results of the debate. Which side would students take?

*Outcomes*

Students will develop a better appreciation of the dilemma that existed for African Americans in the Jim Crow South and will also appreciate that both Booker T. Washington and W. E. B. Du Bois had developed strategies that appealed to different parts of the African American community.

# Assignments

1. Provide a brief biographical sketch of Mary Elizabeth Lease, a prominent Populist speaker.
2. Make a collage of scenes from homesteads on America's Great Plains during the early farming years of the late 1800s and explain in a presentation to the class what we can deduct from these pictures about the opportunities and hardships of life on the prairie.
3. Create a PowerPoint slide that explains the Populist argument for the inclusion of silver in the national money supply and present this case to the class.
4. Write a one-page paper in which you describe how the system of sharecropping worked in the South.

# Beyond the Class

A selection of materials is in the Instructor's Manual and PowerLecture.

## What's Inside

Key topics in this chapter: The Reformers; State Political Reform; Women's Progressivism; Progressivism and National Politics; Progressive Influences on American Culture

## Learning Outcomes

**LO 1** Discuss the reform efforts of the Progressive era and the groups involved in those efforts.

**LO 2** Describe the methods used by the various states to bring about reforms in state governments during the Progressive era.

**LO 3** Discuss the involvement of women's groups in Progressive era reform movements.

**LO 4** Compare and contrast the progressivism of Theodore Roosevelt and Woodrow Wilson.

**LO 5** Describe ways in which American culture was influenced by the Progressive movement.

## Chapter 20 Outline

## eBook Links

 Jacob A. Riis's *How the Other Half Lives*
www.tenant.net/Community/riis/contents.html

 Hull House and Progressive Reform
American History Resource Center

 Margaret Sanger's Speech "The Morality of Birth Control"
http://www.americanrhetoric.com/speeches/margaretsangermoralityofbirthcontrol.htm

 Silent Film of Roosevelt Taking Oath of Office
http://www.youtube.com/watch?v=xDEHuPaFzSU&mode=related&search

 Text of "The New Freedom"
American History Resource Center

 Excerpts from *The Jungle*
http://www.online-literature.com/upton_sinclair/jungle/

 Frederick W. Taylor's *Principles of Scientific Management*
American History Resource Center

## Discussion Questions

1. What was life like for the working poor in America's cities in the early years of the twentieth century? Be as specific as possible.
2. Describe the major reform efforts of the Progressive era, both social and political.
3. How did the Progressive reformers influence national politics?

## Group Activity

*Goal*

Gain some insights about the intersection of politics and popular culture in American history.

*Task*

Have students prepare a brief outline of Roosevelt's biography prior to the class meeting. Then, share with them the famous cartoon and the story that triggered the phrase "Teddy's bear" (http://www.bearhollow.net/teddy_roosevelt.htm). In late 1902, Roosevelt was in Mississippi trying to settle a border dispute between Mississippi and Louisiana. An avid hunter, Roosevelt joined in a daylong bear hunt in Mississippi. At the end of the day, Roosevelt hadn't killed anything, whereas most of the hunters had. The apocryphal story is that some of the hunters cornered a bear, clubbed it, tied it to a tree, and invited the president to make the "kill shot." Disgusted, Roosevelt refused, but he ordered that some-one put the poor beast out of its misery. A cartoonist, Clifford Berryman, immor-talized the moment, and over the years the cartoon was redrawn several times. Eventually, the beast of a bear morphed into an innocent bear cub. A toymaker in Brooklyn, Morris Michton, requested and received permission to call the toy bears that his wife made "Teddy's bear." The toy bears became so popular that Michton's business grew rapidly, and within a year he formed the corporation known as the Ideal Novelty and Toy Company. You should point out to the class that Roosevelt hated being called "Teddy," and that he immediately left for a big game hunting safari in Africa after his second term in office.

Divide students into four groups and ask them to discuss the importance of manliness in Roosevelt's understanding of his presidency and his personality.

Bring the class back together and go over the results of the discussion.

*Outcomes*

Students might discuss how Roosevelt became the embodiment of a cultural shift around views of masculinity. Or, they may be more interested in discussing the ways in which the media of the early 1900s contributed to public perceptions of political leaders.

# Assignments

1. Write a one-page paper about Margaret Sanger and her efforts at trying to inform women about birth control.
2. Make a collage of photos of Theodore Roosevelt, including presidential photos and more personal ones that illustrate his personality.
3. Gather information on the Galveston hurricane of 1900, and write a paper explaining the new system of city government that was created there.
4. Write a 2- to 3-sentence paragraph about three of the most famous muckrakers.

# Beyond the Class

A selection of materials is in the Instructor's Manual and PowerLecture.

## What's Inside

Key topics in this chapter: Why an American Empire?; Beginnings of Empire; The Spanish-American War; Progressive-Era Imperialism; World War I Begins; America Joins the War Effort; America: From Neutrality to War; Making Peace

## Learning Outcomes

**LO 1** Explain the major reasons for the growing call in the late 1800s for the United States to develop an empire.

**LO 2** Describe the first moves Americans made toward empire.

**LO 3** Explain the major reasons for the Spanish-American War of 1898, and discuss the controversy over imperialism that developed after the war.

**LO 4** Describe the growth of imperialism in America during the Progressive era.

**LO 5** Discuss World War I, including reasons for the war, American experiences during the war, and effects of the treaty that ended the war.

## Chapter 21 Outline

## eBook Links

 Frederick Jackson Turner's Frontier Essay
American History Resource Center

 Josiah Strong's *Our Country*
American History Resource Center

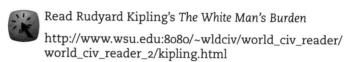 Read Rudyard Kipling's *The White Man's Burden*
http://www.wsu.edu:8080/~wldciv/world_civ_reader/world_civ_reader_2/kipling.html

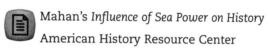 Mahan's *Influence of Sea Power on History*
American History Resource Center

 Series of 1898 Cartoons
http://www.digitalhistory.uh.edu/modules/worldpower/index.cfm

 American Attack on Spanish Fleet in Manila Bay
American History Resource Center

 Excerpt from Theodore Roosevelt's *The Rough Riders*
American History Resource Center

 Senator Beveridge's Speech "The March of the Flag"
http://www.historytools.org/sources/beveridge.html

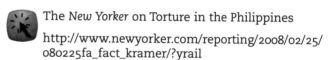 The *New Yorker* on Torture in the Philippines
http://www.newyorker.com/reporting/2008/02/25/080225fa_fact_kramer/?yrail

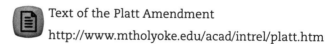 Text of the Platt Amendment
http://www.mtholyoke.edu/acad/intrel/platt.htm

 Account of the Boxer Rebellion
http://www.fordham.edu/halsall/mod/1900Fei-boxers.html

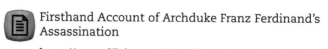 Firsthand Account of Archduke Franz Ferdinand's Assassination
http://www.lib.byu.edu/~rdh/wwi/1914/ferddead.html

 Graph Comparing American Trade with the Allies and with Germany
American History Resource Center

The Zimmerman Note

http://wwi.lib.byu.edu/index.php/The_Zimmerman_Note

 Sample of a War Propaganda Pamphlet

American History Resource Center

 Text of the Espionage Act

http://www.firstworldwar.com/source/espionageact.htm

 Text of Wilson's Fourteen Points

American History Resource Center

# Discussion Questions

1. How did World War I change the United States on the home front?
2. Discuss the events that drew the United States into World War I, and assess America's contribution to the war effort.
3. What were some reasons given by those who supported imperialism in the early twentieth century? What were some reasons given by those who opposed it?

# Group Activity

*Goal*
Discuss and understand the Alien and Sedition Act.

*Task*
Get a copy of the Alien and Sedition Act online and distribute it to the class. In groups of five or less, students should discuss whether the law was constitutional and in line with the principles of democracy and freedom. It may be difficult for them to answer this question, but you may trigger a similar thought process if you ask them to consider the kinds of antiwar protests we have seen more recently: whether these protests should be legal and whether they would have been a crime under this act. Next, ask students to list groups of Americans who would have most likely been opposed to involvement in World War I. Then, ask them to consider whether this list helps explain the naming of the Alien and Sedition Act. (Students will likely think of the many immigrants from Germany, Ireland, and southeastern Europe and identify an anti-immigrant bias in the law.)

Finally, you may want to bring the groups back together and discuss more broadly the extent to which the Constitutional democracy of the United States protects the practice of dissent.

*Outcomes*
Students will learn how fragile a constitutional democracy can be when under threat.

# Assignments

1. Through your local library, research the African American newspaper *The Chicago Defender* and its coverage of the war and the war industries from 1914 to 1919. Report your findings to the class in a 10-minute presentation. Why was this newspaper such coveted reading material in the South?
2. In an online research project, gather as much information as you can about the weaponry and technology first employed in World War I. Create a poster presentation of these new machines of war and explain how they might have changed the experience of soldiers in this conflict.

# Beyond the Class

A selection of materials is in the Instructor's Manual and PowerLecture.

**What's Inside** Key topics in this chapter: The Consumer Economy; The End of the Progressive Era; Prohibition; Cultural Change; Reactions to Modern Changes; Immigration Restrictions; The New Woman

## Learning Outcomes

**LO¹** Describe the consumerism that developed in America during the early twentieth century, especially after World War I.

**LO²** Explain the experiences of the nation that effectively put an end to the Progressive movement in America during the 1920s.

**LO³** Describe the various kinds of leisure activities that became popular in America during the 1920s.

**LO⁴** Discuss the strong reactions among various groups in America to the changing cultural mores of the 1920s.

## Chapter 22 Outline

## eBook Links

 1920s Advertisements

http://scriptorium.lib.duke.edu/dynaweb/adaccess/beauty/hairprep1917-1939/@Generic__BookTextView/518;nh=1?DwebQuery=1920+in+%3Cc01%3E#X

 1931 Report on Enforcing Prohibition

http://www.druglibrary.org/schaffer/Library/studies/wick/index.html

 Contemporary Account of the Impact of Movies on Viewers
American History Resource Center

 Transcripts of the Scopes Trial
American History Resource Center

 H. L. Mencken's Account of the Scopes Trial

http://www.law.umkc.edu/faculty/projects/ftrials/scopes/menk.htm

 Immigration Quotas by Country
http://historymatters.gmu.edu/d/5078/

 A Congressman's Denunciation of Quotas
http://historymatters.gmu.edu/d/5079/

## Discussion Questions

1. How was the Ku Klux Klan of the 1920s different from the KKK of the Reconstruction years? How was it similar?
2. Explain the significance of the Scopes Monkey Trial. How did this judicial spectacle come about?
3. Explain the ways in which the car changed the lives of Americans in the 1920s.

## Group Activity

*Goal*
Understand the phenomenon of the "flapper" and the "new woman" of the 1920s.

*Task*
In preparation for this exercise, students should research images of 1920s flappers online, look at video sequences of the Charleston and other dances, and listen to some performers of 1920s jazz music such as Duke Ellington. Then, in groups of five or less, have students

discuss these questions: What was different about the new woman of the 1920s? What was attractive about the fashion of the 1920s and the music? What may have made the decade liberating for young women in the city? Why would these practices appear threatening to some men? If students struggle with that question because their own sense of freedom of self-expression is so pronounced that they cannot imagine the 1920s as modern times, it may help to review women's issues before the 1920s, which focused more on family, social politics, and suffrage. You may want to display a cover page of the *Ladies Home Journal* (available online) prior to 1918 on your projector or PowerPoint to show the difference between Victorian womanhood and the image of the flapper. (Make sure to clarify with students that the flapper was a stylized and exaggerated media depiction of young urban women in the 1920s, and rarely a lived reality.)

*Outcomes*
Students will understand the relationship between gender identities, modernity, and consumption, as well as the reactions against the changes of the 1920s.

## Assignments

1. Through online research, look for magazine advertisements from the 1920s that market medicine, personal hygiene products, cameras, and radios. Create a poster presentation of these advertisements and explain how these new consumer products tell us something about the 1920s.
2. Prepare a list of famous black Americans who were a part of the Harlem Renaissance.
3. Research the details of the Dawes plan online and create a Microsoft PowerPoint slide that graphically explains the way American finance facilitated German reconstruction and reparations payments.

## Beyond the Class

A selection of materials is in the Instructor's Manual and PowerLecture.

### What's Inside

Key topics in this chapter: The Economics and Politics of Depression; The Depression Experience in America; The New Deal; Critics of the First New Deal; The Second New Deal; The Effects of the New Deal

## Learning Outcomes

**LO¹** Explain the underlying causes of the depression, and evaluate President Hoover's attempts to help the economy.

**LO²** Describe the experiences of both urban and rural Americans during the depression, and explain ways in which the depression affected American politics.

**LO³** Evaluate FDR's actions designed to alleviate the effects of the depression, and discuss the opposition he faced.

**LO⁴** Discuss the most significant long-term effects of the New Deal.

## Chapter 23 Outline

## eBook Links

 Interactive Stock Market Module
American History Resource Center

 Contemporary History of Depression-Era Harlem
http://memory.loc.gov/cgi-bin/query/r?ammem/wpa:@field(DOCID+@lit(wpa221011010))

 Story of Detroit in the Great Depression
apps.detnews.com/apps/history/index.php?id=49

 "Surviving the Great Depression: An Interactive Module"
American History Resource Center

 A Collection of Popular Culture from the 1930s
http://xroads.virginia.edu/~1930s/front.html

 Readings on the Scottsboro Trials
http://www.law.umkc.edu/faculty/projects/FTrials/scottsboro/scottsb.htm

 Franklin D. Roosevelt's Inaugural Speech
http://odur.let.rug.nl/~usa/P/fr32/speeches/fdr1.htm

 Huey Long's "Share Our Wealth" Plan
http://www.americanrhetoric.com/speeches/hueyplongshare.htm

 WPA Slave Narratives
http://xroads.virginia.edu/~hyper/wpa/wpahome.html

 Franklin D. Roosevelt "Fireside Chat" Text
http://www.hpol.org/fdr/chat/

 Cultural Projects of the New Deal
American History Resource Center

 Film of the San Francisco General Strike of 1934
http://www.archive.org/details/SanFranc1934

 An Account of the 1937 Violence at the Republic Steel Plant
American History Resource Center

# Discussion Questions

1. Compare the beliefs and actions of President Hoover and President Roosevelt in regard to the depression.
2. Who were FDR's most outspoken critics on the policies of the New Deal, and what plans did they propose that they believed would work better?
3. What were the underlying causes of the depression? Why did the Great Depression of the 1930s seem so much worse than any depression before or since?

# Group Activity

*Goal*

Reproduce the sequences of economic decline, unemployment, and deflation that marked the Great Depression.

*Task*

Divide class into groups of six. For each group, prepare labels with the following six roles: banker, manufacturer, worker/consumer [two], farmer, and savings account holder. Distribute these sets of tags to your groups and have them choose their roles. Then, deliver one of the following pieces of economic news to each group:

1. The farm foreclosed.
2. The bank lost its assets in the stock market crash.
3. The savings account holder decided to withdraw his money from the bank.
4. The manufacturer had to lay off half the workers.

Have each group determine the consequences in their respective microeconomies and produce a chart that outlines the chain reactions.

*Outcomes*

Students will develop some economic literacy and comprehend the connections between individual market decisions and the depression of the 1930s.

# Assignments

1. Through online research and the resources of the local library, find out as much as you can about the beginnings of the Superman comic. Create a poster with your findings and form a hypothesis as to why this comic became so popular in the depression.
2. Obtain a copy of the movie *It's a Wonderful Life* with Jimmy Stewart. Then write a one-page movie review that explains how this movie reflects the pains of the Great Depression and the endurance of the American people during this time.

# Beyond the Class

A selection of materials is in the Instructor's Manual and PowerLecture.

# 24 WORLD WAR II
# Prep Card

## What's Inside

Key topics in this chapter: Causes of World War II; American Foreign Policy before the War; War in Europe and the Pacific; The American Home Front; A World Remade, 1945

## Learning Outcomes

**LO¹** Explain the various causes of World War II.

**LO²** Explain America's foreign policy that developed after World War I and that was in place at the beginning of World War II, and describe how that policy changed as the war progressed.

**LO³** Describe the events of World War II, both in Europe and in the Pacific, and explain why the United States acted as it did throughout the conflict.

**LO⁴** Describe and discuss the American home front during World War II, paying special attention to long-term societal changes.

**LO⁵** Explain how World War II was brought to an end, both in Europe and in the Pacific, and discuss the immediate aftermath of the war both in America and around the world.

## Chapter 24 Outline

## eBook Links

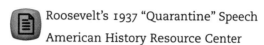 Roosevelt's 1937 "Quarantine" Speech
American History Resource Center

 1941 Lindbergh's Address to the America First Committee
American History Resource Center

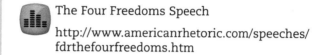 The Four Freedoms Speech
http://www.americanrhetoric.com/speeches/fdrthefourfreedoms.htm

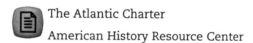 The Atlantic Charter
American History Resource Center

 Roosevelt's War Message to Congress, December 8, 1941
http://americanrhetoric.com/speeches/fdrpearlharbor.htm

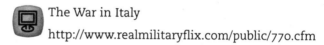 The War in Italy
http://www.realmilitaryflix.com/public/770.cfm

 News Coverage of D-Day
http://www.youtube.com/watch?v=YvYXGPEI03U&feature=related

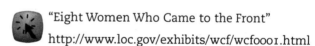 "Eight Women Who Came to the Front"
http://www.loc.gov/exhibits/wcf/wcf0001.html

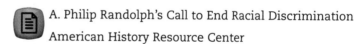 A. Philip Randolph's Call to End Racial Discrimination
American History Resource Center

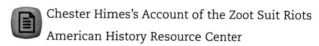 Chester Himes's Account of the Zoot Suit Riots
American History Resource Center

 Google Earth Map and Activity about Restored Topaz Internment Camp
American History Resource Center

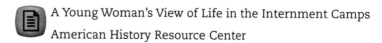 A Young Woman's View of Life in the Internment Camps
American History Resource Center

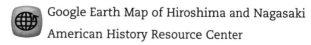 Google Earth Map of Hiroshima and Nagasaki
American History Resource Center

## Terms

# Discussion Questions

1. Discuss a current situation and/or attitude in America that shares some similarities with the treatment of Japanese Americans during World War II.
2. The WASPs and the WAVEs came closer to the battlefield than any American women until very recent times. Do women belong in battle? Is fighting for their country a right that women have gained, wanted or not?
3. Can you envision a time when Americans would unite in a common cause as strongly as they did during World War II?

# Group Activity

*Goal*
Gain an understanding of World War II as a personal experience.

*Task*
Divide the class into hypothetical families of four: mother, father, son, and daughter. With every student playing a specific role in the family, have the groups hold a dinner table discussion featuring the personal news they likely would share with the family. Let students discuss family news in three different years: 1940, 1943, and 1945. Ask them not only to think of the big events that certainly shaped family lives, such as relocation, the draft, a death in the family, but also the small things family members would have talked about with their loved ones at home and through letters from overseas.

You may also suggest that families can choose their ethnic and class background. What would change if the family lived in the deep South, was African American, was an immigrant working-class family in Milwaukee, and so on?

*Outcomes*
Students will understand the importance of the home front and the theaters of war and will appreciate history as a personal experience, not a development outside of personal life.

# Assignments

1. Make a timeline of the events chronicling Hitler's rise to power in Germany, from the time he joined the Nazi Party to the death of President Hindenburg. What things stand out most to you about his rise to power?
2. Study covers of the *Saturday Evening Post* during World War II that use the artwork of Norman Rockwell. Make copies of three covers that you feel are the most informative or inspirational for people living through the war. Write a brief informal paper explaining why you chose the covers you did. Caution: Do not use the Rosie the Riveter "We Can Do It" cover.

# Beyond the Class

A selection of materials is in the Instructor's Manual and PowerLecture.

## What's Inside

Key topics in this chapter: The Korean War; The Cold War; The Cold War Home Front; Suburban Nation; Postwar Domestic Politics; McCarthyism; Early Civil Rights Breakthroughs

## Learning Outcomes

**LO¹** Explain the causes of the Cold War that developed between the United States and the Soviet Union after World War II, and discuss some of the more serious incidents between the two countries.

**LO²** Describe American life as it developed during the 1950s, including social, economic, and political issues, and evaluate the significance of the Cold War in these changes.

**LO³** Explain the rise and effects of McCarthyism in American life.

**LO⁴** Describe the breakthroughs forged by African Americans in the 1950s and the movement that came to be called "massive resistance."

## Chapter 25 Outline

## eBook Links

 Account by George Orwell about the Impasse in the United Nations
American History Resource Center

 Churchill's Iron Curtain Speech
http://www.fordham.edu/halsall/mod/churchill-iron.html

 George F. Kennan's "Long Telegram"
American History Resource Center

 Text of the Truman Doctrine
American History Resource Center

 Mao Zedong's Account of the Chinese Communist Party
http://www.marxists.org/reference/archive/mao/ selected-works/volume-2/mswv2_23.htm

 Excerpts from NSC-68
American History Resource Center

 The NSA's Briefing Book on the Iranian Revolution
http://www.gwu.edu/~nsarchiv/NSAEBB/NSAEBB28/index.html

 John Foster Dulles's "Massive Retaliation" Speech
American History Resource Center

 Excerpts from Truman's 1945 Speech to Congress
American History Resource Center

 Transcript of the Kitchen Debate
http://www3.sympatico.ca/robsab/debate.html

 Truman's 1947 Loyalty Oath
American History Resource Center

 McCarthy's Speech Warning of the Communist Threat
American History Resource Center

 The Supreme Court Decision in Brown v. Board of Education
American History Resource Center

 Eisenhower's Response to the Little Rock Crisis
American History Resource Center

## Terms

# Discussion Questions

1. Describe the development of the era known as the "Cold War," explaining several of the major incidents that contributed to the tenseness of those decades.
2. Why did the American economy prosper so quickly after World War II?
3. Discuss the events that contributed to the growth of the new civil rights movement after World War II.

# Group Activity

*Goal*
Gain an understanding of the fears of a past generation.

*Task*
*Duck and Cover,* an Archer Productions film, shows how the government tried to ease the very valid fears of Americans about a nuclear World War III. Several years ago, the Library of Congress included this short film in its list of most significant American films ever. The film is 9:15 long, and it can be played directly from the following website: http://www.archive.org/details/DuckandC1951. Show the film in class; then discuss reasons why the government would have spent so much money and effort on propaganda of this sort. What purposes might it have served? How do the students feel about the film today?

*Outcomes*
Students will talk about what it must have felt like to be under the threat of nuclear war.

# Assignments

1. With the help of online research, create a timeline of the origins and consequences of the Berlin airlift. Create a poster to present in class, and explain how this event is crucial for our understanding of the new relationship between western Europe and the United States after World War II.
2. Gather information about the Central Intelligence Agency. Why was it created, and for what purposes? What kinds of activities did it pursue in its first fifteen years of existence?

# Beyond the Class

A selection of materials is in the Instructor's Manual and PowerLecture.

## What's Inside

Key topics in this chapter: Kennedy and the Cold War; The Freedom Movement; Lyndon Johnson's Great Society; Johnson's Vietnam; Liberalism Adrift; Social Divisions and Popular Unrest; Nixon and Vietnam

## Learning Outcomes

**LO¹** Describe John F. Kennedy's experiences as president that led some to label him the "ultimate cold warrior."

**LO²** Discuss attempts made both by African Americans and by the legal system to provide voting and other rights to those citizens.

**LO³** Discuss Lyndon Johnson's desire to build a "Great Society," and evaluate the relative success of his programs.

**LO⁴** Explain the situation in Vietnam that President Johnson inherited from his predecessor, and evaluate the decisions he made over the next few years concerning the war there.

**LO⁵** Discuss the growth of the "counterculture" in American society during the 1960s, and describe the various movements that began to gather strength as Americans with an agenda sought to have their voices heard.

## Chapter 26 Outline

## eBook Links

 Kennedy's Inauguration Speech

http://www.americanrhetoric.com/speeches/johnfkennedyinaugural.htm

 Documents Related to the Bay of Pigs Invasion

http://www.gwu.edu/~nsarchiv/NSAEBB/NSAEBB29/index.html

 Oral Histories and Pictures from Freedom Riders' Campaign

http://www.americanrhetoric.com/speeches/mlkihaveadream.htm

 Martin Luther King's "I Have a Dream" Speech

http://www.americanrhetoric.com/speeches/mlkihaveadream.htm

 Oral History from Estell Harvey

http://www.usm.edu/crdp/html/transcripts/manuscript-harvey_estell.shtml

 Fannie Lou Hamer's Address to the Rules Committee of the DNC

http://www.americanrhetoric.com/speeches/fannielouhamercredentialscommittee.htm

 LBJ's "We Shall Overcome" Speech

http://www.americanrhetoric.com/speeches/lbjweshallovercome.htm

 Martin Luther King Jr. Discusses Vietnam

http://americanrhetoric.com/speeches/mlkatimetobreaksilence.htm

 An Account of the Tet Offensive

American History Resource Center

 The Port Huron Statement

American History Resource Center

 Malcolm X Speaks on Black Nationalist Demands

http://www.edchange.org/multicultural/speeches/malcolm_x_ballot.html

 A Selection from Carmichael and Hamilton's 1967 *Black Power*

American History Resource Center

César Chávez Protest Speech

http://www.americanrhetoric.com/speeches/cesarchavezspeechmexicanamerican&church.htm

 Documents on the "Psychedelic '60s"

http://www.lib.virginia.edu/small/exhibits/sixties/index.html

 Vice President Spiro Agnew Denounces Antiwar Protesters

American History Resource Center

## Discussion Questions

1. Why has JFK sometimes been called the "ultimate cold warrior"?
2. Describe the experiences of African Americans who attempted to register and then vote in the South during the early 1960s. What legislation did the most to help them achieve this goal?
3. Discuss the motivations for the antiwar movement and its accomplishments. Do you think the movement was successful, or was it a failed movement?

## Group Activity

*Goal*

Understand pop culture in historical and political terms and experience a fun way of doing source analysis.

*Task*

(Tip: Prepare this activity one week early.) Ask students to each find one song that they believe defines the mood of the 1960s and bring a copy of the lyrics to class. Ask them to let you know their choice in advance so that you can bring a selection of their chosen titles to class to play. After an initial 15 or 20 minutes of listening to a few excerpts, split the class into groups of no more than five to discuss their songs. What makes the songs representative of the 1960s? How did the lyrics speak to the issues Americans wrestled with during that decade? How did rhythm, melody, and arrangement reflect the mood at the time? Finally, do students recognize elements of 1960s music in more recent and contemporary music?

*Outcomes*

Students will discuss the ways in which the music of the 1960s reflects the political culture of the decade.

## Assignments

1. Using online resources and your library, research riots in American urban centers between 1964 and 1969, create a timeline and/or map documenting the history of urban riots in the 1960s; present your findings to the class.

## Beyond the Class

A selection of materials is in the Instructor's Manual and PowerLecture.

## What's Inside

Key topics in this chapter: Nixon's Presidency; Watergate: Nixon to Ford; Carter's Presidency; America in the 1970s; Women, Gays, and Conservatives

## Learning Outcomes

**LO¹** Evaluate Richard Nixon as president, focusing on his policies in the United States and abroad.

**LO²** Describe the events of Watergate and its ramifications for the country.

**LO³** Describe the economic conditions of the 1970s, including stagflation and the end of the post–World War II economic boom, and describe how Presidents Ford and Carter attempted to confront the problem.

**LO⁴** Describe the perpetuation of 1960s-style activism and how it transformed into a politics of identity in the 1970s.

**LO⁵** Evaluate the reaction to the 1960s social movements and describe the rise of the New Right.

## Chapter 27 Outline

## eBook Links

 State Department Briefing on the Status of Chile, 1970
http://www.gwu.edu/~nsarchiv/NSAEBB/NSAEBB8/ch20-01.htm

 Nixon's Resignation "Speeches"
http://www.watergate.info/nixon/resignation-speech.shtml

 Collection of Woodward and Bernstein Papers
http://www.hrc.utexas.edu/exhibitions/online/woodstein/

 Watergate Information
http://www.watergate.info/

 *Saturday Night Live*'s Transcript of Chevy Chase's Impression of Gerald Ford
http://snltranscripts.jt.org/75/75dford.phtml

 Carter's "Crisis of Confidence" Speech
http://www.americanrhetoric.com/speeches/jimmycartercrisisofconfidence.htm

 Slide Show about Photo from Boston Busing Crisis
http://www.slate.com/id/2188648/

 The *Bakke* Decision on Affirmative Action
http://caselaw.lp.findlaw.com/cgi-bin/ getcase.pl?court=US&vol=438&invol=265

 Text of *Roe v. Wade*
American History Resource Center

## Discussion Questions

1. Explain the phenomenon of stagflation. Why did it emerge, and why was it so intractable?
2. Could the environmental protections that were put in place during the 1970s be made into law today? Why or why not?
3. Why is Nixon referred to in your text as the "accidental liberal"? Is that a good or a bad label?

## Terms

# Group Activity

*Goal*
Understand both sides of the ERA debate.

*Task*
Place an equal number of red and blue chips inside a container, and have each student draw one randomly. Assign those with one color to come up with arguments for the Equal Rights Amendment, and have those with the other color chip develop arguments against the ERA. Devote 30 minutes of the next class period to an informal debate on the issue. Encourage students to bring posters, signs, and, of course, serious reasons to support their positions. Do not allow them to swap sides with other students.

*Outcomes*
Students should develop a better understanding of the Equal Rights Amendment, not as a legal theoretical topic, but as an episode in the escalating culture war in late-twentieth-century America.

# Assignments

1. Locate the text of the proposed (and rejected) Equal Rights Amendment. Study the wording, and then write a position paper in which you try to identify what may have been so threatening about the ERA.
2. Conduct online research on the busing controversies of the 1970s. (You may want to limit yourself to one city.) Create a poster presentation for the class and summarize the positions of the parties involved.
3. Conduct online research, with the assistance of your library, on the cars produced in Detroit between 1972 and 1979, and then compare them to cars produced at the time by Nissan, Toyota, and Volkswagen.

# Beyond the Class

A selection of materials is in the Instructor's Manual and PowerLecture.

## What's Inside

Key topics in this chapter: Reagan's Politics; America in the 1980s: Polarization of the American Public; Reagan's Successor: George H. W. Bush; Foreign Relations under Reagan-Bush; The End of the Cold War

## Learning Outcomes

**LO¹** Evaluate the domestic policies of Ronald Reagan as president, including the economic challenges the country faced in the 1980s.

**LO²** Describe the divisions and "culture wars" that plagued the nation during the 1980s.

**LO³** Discuss the problems Reagan's successor faced in paying for the "Reagan Revolution."

**LO⁴** Describe the conditions for and aftermath of the end of the Cold War.

## Chapter 28 Outline

## eBook Links

 A Collection of Interviews with Reagan's Closest Advisors

http://www.pbs.org/wgbh/amex/reagan/filmmore/reference/interview/index.html

 An Article Discussing Income Disparities

http://www.leftbusinessobserver.com/Gini_supplement.html

 President Reagan's Address to the Nation on Drug Abuse

http://www.pbs.org/wgbh/amex/reagan/filmmore/reference/primary/abuse.html

 A Timeline of the S&L Crisis

http://www.fdic.gov/bank/historical/s&l/

 Reagan's "Evil Empire" Speech

http://www.americanrhetoric.com/speeches/ronaldreaganevilempire.htm

 U.S. Briefing on Events in China

http://www.gwu.edu/~nsarchiv/NSAEBB/NSAEBB16/

 News Story about Tiananmen Square

http://news.bbc.co.uk/onthisday/hi/dates/stories/june/4/newsid_2496000/2496277.stm

# Discussion Questions

1. Do you think Reagan was over- or underrated as president while he was in office? Explain.
2. Discuss the events of Tiananmen Square. How did Europe and the United States react to this massacre? Should they have responded differently? Explain.
3. Explain what happened in the Iran-Contra Affair. How dangerous was this scandal to Reagan's presidency?

# Group Activity

*Goal*

Understand the economic policy principles of the Reagan era.

*Task*

In preparation for this activity, ask students to study the timeline of the S&L loan scandal provided in the eBook links. Then, split the class in half and ask one side to form arguments in defense of deregulation and the other to argue for financial regulations. Have at least five students from each side deliver arguments in a debate club format. In the next step, have the entire class discuss how the changing attitude toward market regulations has shaped the American economy since the 1980s. Students may think of the recent subprime mortgage crisis.

*Outcomes*

Students will be able to identify the arguments for and against government regulation.

# Assignments

1. Conduct an online research project on the war on drugs and create a 10-minute presentation on its effect on foreign policy, the development of America's inner cities, police-community relations, and the nation's prison population.
2. With the assistance of your library, research newspaper headlines on the discovery of AIDS and write a one-page editorial in reaction to this media survey.
3. Conduct an online research project on the most popular movies and TV series of the 1980s. How did they reflect or contradict the social and economic trends of the decade?

# Beyond the Class

A selection of materials is in the Instructor's Manual and PowerLecture.

# 29

## AMERICA IN THE INFORMATION AGE
# Prep Card

**What's Inside**  Key topics in this chapter: The Twentieth Century's Last President; The Information Revolution; Multiculturalism; Two Americas

## Learning Outcomes

**LO¹** Evaluate the presidency of Bill Clinton, discussing some of the major domestic and foreign issues the country faced during those years.

**LO²** Discuss the technological revolution that took place during Bill Clinton's presidency, and describe the social and economic changes that took place as a result of this revolution.

**LO³** Discuss the new focus on multiculturalism that grew during the latter part of the twentieth century.

**LO⁴** Explain what makes the description of America as actually "two Americas" an accurate one.

## Chapter 29 Outline

## eBook Links

 Analysis of Televised Thomas/Hill Hearings
http://www.museum.tv/archives/etv/H/htmlH/hill-thomash/hill-thomas.htm

 Pat Buchanan Speech at 1992 Republican Convention
American History Resource Center

 Clinton Speech to 1996 Democratic Convention
American History Resource Center

 Excerpts from the Starr Report
American History Resource Center

## Discussion Questions

1. Do you agree with the outcome of the Thomas/Hill hearings? Why or why not?
2. Describe the personality traits of each of the major candidates who ran for president between 1992 and 2000. Do you think their personalities helped or hindered them in their campaigns?
3. What were the reasons for special prosecutor Kenneth Starr's investigation into Clinton's relationship with Monica Lewinsky?

## Group Activity

*Goal*
Understand the transformation of the information technology sector at century's end.

*Task*
In preparation for this activity, locate a copy of the movie *Office Space*, provide students with a brief synopsis of the story, and show them the opening scene of the film (stop-and-go commute to work with hip-hop on the car radio) as well as the climax of the story (the three protagonists abducting and beating up the fax machine in an empty field). Ask students to discuss, in groups of no more than five, these scenes: What made them funny? What do these scenes tell us about the lived experience of the information technology sector? What do they tell us about the reality of multiculturalism?

*Outcomes*
Using a piece of iconic comedy pop culture, students will learn to appreciate how economic, social, and cultural history come together in regular daily lives.

## Terms

# Assignments

1. In your home, time yourself on each of these two tasks. First, locate and list ten items that are marked "Made in China." Next, locate and list ten items that are marked as having been made somewhere other than China. Turn in your lists with the time it took for each. Add any comments you wish to make.

2. Prepare a timeline of the events that took place on the day of, and in the weeks following, the presidential election of 2000. In addition, write a brief informal essay presenting your opinion of the way the election was conducted. Be aware that your grade will come from your having prepared the timeline and completed the essay, and that you will not be graded on your opinion.

# Beyond the Class

A selection of materials is in the Instructor's Manual and PowerLecture.

## What's Inside

Key topics in this chapter: George W. Bush; Remaking the Middle East?; Domestic Woes; President Obama

## Learning Outcomes

**LO¹** Describe the first term of George W. Bush, and explain how the events of his first year in office shaped his presidency.

**LO²** Describe George W. Bush's plans for democracy in the Middle East and assess the degree of success he had.

**LO³** Discuss the domestic problems that America faced during George W. Bush's second term.

**LO⁴** Explain some of the hopes and frustrations of Barack Obama's first years in office.

## Chapter 30 Outline

## eBook Links

The *Observer's* Biography of Osama bin Laden
http://www.guardian.co.uk/news/2001/oct/28/world.terrorism

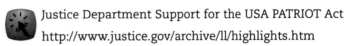
Justice Department Support for the USA PATRIOT Act
http://www.justice.gov/archive/ll/highlights.htm

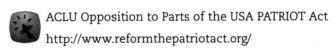
ACLU Opposition to Parts of the USA PATRIOT Act
http://www.reformthepatriotact.org/

Colin Powell's Speech to UN General Assembly Advocating War with Iraq
http://www.cnn.com/2003/US/02/05/sprj.irq.powell.transcript/

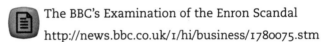
The BBC's Examination of the Enron Scandal
http://news.bbc.co.uk/1/hi/business/1780075.stm

## Discussion Questions

1. If you were choosing one action taken by the United States in the Middle East over the past decade, what would you consider to be the most significant, and why?
2. Explain the Bush doctrine, and compare this approach to foreign policy with the way presidents dealt with the threat of conflict during the Cold War.
3. Do you think the election of the nation's first African American president has finally put to rest any complaints about the continued existence of racism in this country? Why or why not?

## Group Activity

*Goal*
Understand the present as history.

*Task*
In groups of five or less, ask students to make a list of the five most important issues for Americans today. Then, ask them how historians will probably interpret the way Americans have dealt with these challenges.

*Outcomes*
Students will transition from a discussion of history to a discussion of current political affairs.

## Terms

## Assignments

1. Create a poster presentation of Hurricane Katrina with particular focus on the fate of New Orleans and its residents. What, do you think, were the most popular and influential images that shaped Americans' understanding of the disaster?
2. Do a follow-up on the Enron scandal. Find out the status of those most directly involved.
3. Write a paper about where you were and what you were doing when you found out about the events of September 11, 2001.

## Beyond the Class

A selection of materials is in the Instructor's Manual and PowerLecture.